SOCIOLOGY

Social Science and Social Concern

THIRD EDITION

D. C. HEATH AND COMPANY
Lexington, Massachusetts Toronto

RITCHIE P. LOWRY
Boston College

ROBERT P. RANKIN
California State University, Chico

SOCIOLOGY

Social Science and Social Concern

Published simultaneously in Canada.

Printed in the United States of America.

International Standard Book Number: 0-669-99648-3

Library of Congress Catalog Card Number: 76–8632

TO *Betty, Jim, Jo,*
Madge, Peter, and Robin

Preface

Perhaps the most difficult task that textbook writers face is to define their goals precisely. Too many of us are inclined to put disciplined planning aside and simply pour forth our accumulated knowledge. The result, quite often, is an overwhelming compilation of information, but with little organization or coherence.

Consequently, before beginning what has turned out to be a major rewriting and restructuring of this third edition, we carefully re-examined the basic instructional goals we wanted to pursue. The decisions we reached concerning our goals and the specific book features that would achieve them are described in the remainder of this preface.

1. *Guiding themes.* Good textbooks, like good novels, should communicate to readers some of the major intellectual themes that characterize the subject matter. Within this text, we have developed two themes that we feel are particularly important for the beginning student in sociology to understand.

Our primary theme is reflected in the title and deals with the dual nature of sociology, with its simultaneous use of rigorous *scientific prespectives and methods* and its *humanistic way of viewing society.* Each orientation leads to different kinds of information and understandings, which can then be applied to the processes and problems of human social life.

After introducing the theme in the title and discussing it in Chapter 1, we have systematically highlighted it within each chapter in two special ways. The awareness of sociology's scientific orientation and methodology is developed in each chapter by presenting an *Adapted Study,* which provides an ongoing model of social scientists at work. It also amplifies the discussion of a key topic within the chapter and introduces the student to classical and contemporary scholars in the field. Through the studies, we hope to emphasize the basic procedures of science and, at the same time, to develop an appreciation of the many techniques and scholarly styles that characterize different researchers.

Simultaneously, the humanitarian application of sociological knowledge is highlighted by the inclusion of a *So What?* box in each chapter.

These boxes, together with the conclusions to several of the studies, show that sociological research is not merely an academic exercise but is also a meaningful application of knowledge to important human problems. The *So What?* boxes give examples of the way in which sociological knowledge has been or might be utilized to answer value-oriented questions, such as "How can suicide best be prevented?"

Our second theme deals with the problem of *freedom versus conformity* in human society. Is behavior essentially spontaneous and unfettered, or is it primarily conforming and structured according to fixed norms? Under what conditions are people most and least free? This is one of the central scientific and humanistic issues facing sociologists.

This theme is introduced in Part 1 in the discussion of primary versus secondary relationships and it is reexamined in Part 2 in the discussion of George Mead's concept of the interacting "I" and "me" in the social self. The theme plays a major role in the organization of the chapters for Part 3. In that section, different types of group behavior are considered in sequence, ranging from more spontaneous to more structured forms.

Where Parts 1 through 3 deal essentially with apsects of social order and structure, Parts 4 and 5 deal with social dynamics, including changing institutional relationshiops, deviance, social and cultural change, and conflict. Since these processes can represent expressions of human spontaneity and freedom, each of the chapters raises the question of control. How can social processes be controlled or managed without inhibiting human freedom?

2. *Content coverage and organization.* Some of the basic content coverage and general organization of topics in this textbook are similar to the first two editions. However, *Parts 1 and 2 have been reorganized* to express more effectively the guiding themes. In particular, the special typology of human group behavior, utilized as a heuristic device in the earlier editions, has been more clearly linked to the issue of freedom versus conformity.

In addition, a major modification has been the addition of a *new Part 4,* which deals with social institutions. We have opted for an integrated rather than an isolated approach to six major social institutions. Instead of the usual analysis of the internal structure and functioning of isolated institutional areas such as politics or family life, we begin with a macro-level analysis of how and why all institutions come into being, are maintained, and eventually change over time.

Following this introduction to Part 4, we cluster together, in each of the following two chapters, three closely related social institutions and show how they interact with one another, sometimes competing and sometimes cooperating, in their attempt to fulfill one or more of society's basic needs. In an age when social institutions are becoming more plentiful and, in many cases, more specialized, we felt that any treatment of them would be incomplete without some attention to their interdependence and relatedness.

3. *Basic vocabulary.* We felt that another of our primary goals, as authors of an introductory text, was to do an effective job of *teaching the basic concepts* that represent the beginning of sociological literacy. In our view, an introductory course must be, in large part, a vocabulary course. To avoid teaching the "nuts and bolts" terminology is to neglect laying the foundation for effective communication and understanding. Therefore, we have concluded each of the five major parts of the text with a *Key Concept Review* that organizes key terms into convenient and logical conceptual networks that correspond to the major themes discussed in the preceding part.

We have tried to make the definitions and accompanying examples sufficiently detailed so that each entry is self-explanatory. Teachers can, therefore, have students review the terms in any order they wish. However, we have also attempted, where possible, to create logically sequenced clusters so that the initial term(s), usually rather broad ones, set the stage for later ones, which are generally more specific. Only the most important theoretical terms have been included in these clusters. Terms of lesser importance appear in an alphabetical, end-of-the-book glossary along with an abbreviated version of the key terms.

The rationale for these conceptual clusters stems from both cognitive and behaviorist learning theory. Cognitive psychologists, such as Piaget, tell us that the likelihood of new terms being assimilated into long-term memory depends, in large part, on the learner's ability to create *networks* that relate concepts to one another. The greater the number of cognitive associations formed, the more stable and familiar the entire cluster of concepts becomes. Furthermore, the critical role that *reinforcement* plays in concept learning is, we hope, adequately dealt with in this and the following features.

4. *Illustration program.* Our goal here has been to focus on and *visually reinforce* some of the major sociological concepts and theories. We felt that the traditional type of illustration program, composed of isolated pictures spread more or less uniformly throughout a text, was inadequate. Single pictures with limited captioning simply do not depict such complex ideas as (a) the functions and dysfunctions of deviance, (b) particularistic versus universalistic ways of viewing social situations, or (c) the various interrelated stages of development in social movements.

Consequently, the decision was made to build the illustration program around a series of self-contained *Photo Essays* capable of integrating the various aspects of such complex ideas. Altogether forty-six of these Photo Essays appear in this textbook, reinforcing and extending what we believe to be some of the critical concepts and theories in sociology. These Essays once again typify our orientation toward the integration of sociological knowledge, as reflected in the organization for Part 4 on institutions and in the Key Concept Reviews.

5. *Readability.* Nowhere have we struggled more diligently than with the problem of making this new edition as readable as possible. With the

assistance of a rewrite editor, each chapter has gone through at least two complete revisions in an attempt to match it to the literary capabilities of the average beginning student. This task has been accomplished, we think, without sacrificing any of the intellectual sophistication of the earlier editions. Considering the new features, we feel confident that we have actually *raised the book's intellectual level while lowering its level of literary difficulty.*

6. *Supplements.* Finally, in order to maximize the textbook's effectiveness, we have added a *Study Guide* to this edition and have expanded both the teaching aids and the number of test items in the *Instructor's Manual.*

RITCHIE P. LOWRY

ROBERT P. RANKIN

Contents

PART 3 Types of Group Behavior 165

7. Associations 256

8. Communities 300

9. Institutions 346

PART 4 Institutions and Their Interactions 399

11. Power Institutions: State, Military, and Technology 450

PART 5 Social Processes 509

12. The Dynamics of Deviance: Delinquency and Crime 512

13. The Dynamics of Change: Population and Demography 559

PART 1

The Discipline of Sociology

SOCIOLOGY is an academic discipline that struggles with fascinating questions about human beings:

- *Why do people conform most of the time in spite of occasional deviance?*
- *Why does the family persist in virtually all societies?*
- *To what extent are people really free?*
- *Why do reasonable people sometimes "lose their heads" in a crowd?*
- *What causes inequalities between rich and poor?*
- *Why are people still religious, even in today's rational society?*
- *Why do war and social conflict persist?*

The sociological approach to answering such questions is somewhat different than that of any other field of study. In Part 1 of this book, we will explore sociology's special perspective and show how this perspective opens up new ways of looking at life. Sociologists bring into consciousness truths about humans and their societies that would otherwise be hidden. Although this process is sometimes very painful and disturbing because it examines and confronts popular myths and beliefs, it is essential for a complete understanding of human behavior.

The uniqueness of the sociological perspective stems from the special way it combines the intellectual aspects of other fields. (1) It involves the use of a special method—*the tools and procedures of a science.* (2) In studying human behavior and societies, *sociologists attempt to bridge the gap* between a purely ethical concern for social issues and a study of social facts regardless of their value implications. (3) Sociology is a *generalizing rather than a particularizing discipline.* Journalists or historians, for example, often do thoughtful and useful analyses of social life, but they rarely have the occupational time or training to employ a rigorous scientific method. Philosophers and those trained in formal religion focus upon human values but frequently have difficulty distinguishing between social reality as it is and social reality as it ought to be. Leaders, activists, and planners are interested in what can be done about particular social problems and issues but have difficulty in producing generalized knowledge applicable to many different kinds of problems and issues in various social circumstances. As a discipline, therefore, sociology is somewhat of a hybrid, straddling the gap between scientific rigor and empathic understanding, between ethical commitment and detached neutrality, and between special human problems and a general interest in human behavior in all contexts, both normal and unusual.

Part 1 considers the unique methods and perspectives and the special problems of sociology as a science, as a humane and ethical study of human behavior, and as a generalizing discipline interested in social beings.

- Can human behavior really be studied scientifically?
- Can scientists be objective by using the scientific method?
- Does science dehumanize the study of society and human relationships?
- Do you think the following kind of suicide is justified?

Early in 1975, Dr. Henry P. Van Dusen, well-known Protestant theologian and former President of Union Theological Seminary, and his wife died. At first, it was believed that their deaths were from natural causes. Some months later, however, it became known that they had left a letter explaining their plan to take their own lives with an overdose of pills. Dr. and Mrs. Van Dusen explained that they had lived full lives, were ill and at an advanced age, and were afraid to die without dignity of some crippling disease. Furthermore, they were morally concerned about taking up space in a world with too many mouths and too little food, when the beauty and meaning of life had disappeared for them. As religious people, they were not afraid of death [Cousins, 1975, p. 4].

1

Sociology and the Scientific Method

SOCIOLOGISTS AT WORK

The kinds of questions raised above play an important part in any discussion of sociology as a social science. To people who would like sociology to be more a moral concern for social action to build a better society, it seems that sociology has tended too much toward a dispassionate scientism. To others, sociology seems to have become in recent years little more than a springboard for radical causes that encourage disruption in the normal processes of social life. Both of these views express a concern for the relationship between scientific knowledge about a society and the making of effective social policy. Specifically, is sociology an ivory-tower science about human behavior or is it a source of information that can lead to constructive social action?

Modern Sociology and Nineteenth-Century Roots

Interestingly enough, the question about the role of sociology has its roots in the 19th century origins of the discipline. Modern sociology was created during the revolutionary birth of modern Europe. More directly, it came out of the French Revolution and the scholarly concerns for the problems associated with industrialization and urbanization. August Comte (1798–1857), a Frenchman who lived through the aftermath of the Revolution, was one of many scholars who struggled with the question of what man can do to preserve social order and avoid anarchy. He is known as the father of sociology. Comte's answer to revolutionary chaos stressed the importance of science. He argued that, if biologists could discover laws governing the natural world, sociologists could do the same for society. There could be a science of society. Sociologists should work with the value-free objectivity and detachment of scientists as they studied how humans organized themselves into groups and how societies emerged and functioned. They should become men and women of analysis rather than men and women of action.

Comte was well-versed in biology himself and had observed how the natural sciences had moved through three stages of development: theological, metaphysical, and scientific. From supernatural explanations of events and from mere speculation about how the world functions, natural scientists had moved to rational and well-disciplined forms of analysis. Comte was certain that this also could be done with a social science and that the queen of all the sciences would eventually be sociology.

Many scholars subsequently took their cue from Comte and established one of the major branches of the discipline—academic sociology. Consequently, for most sociologists, especially in America, the rigorous search for knowledge through detached research and analysis has characterized the profession. Academic sociology [Gouldner, 1970] has so dominated the field that scholars of social and political commitment who increasingly claim another purpose for sociology have found difficulty in gaining acceptance. C. Wright Mills (1916–1962) is recognized as one of the precursors of today's crises within sociology. Mill's writings [1959] challenged the dispassionate stance of social scientists and insisted that there ought to be partisan commitment in the name of needed social change. Sociology as a science was too much allied with the status quo and the Establishment. It ought to go beyond traditional scholarship and play a role in bringing about significant, even radical, changes [Mills, 1959].

Long before Mills, however, Karl Marx (1818–1883) provided a basis for much of the current protest in modern sociology. The early writings of Marx hold great appeal for many students and young professors today, who seem to be demanding that sociology radically recapture something of the character of German Romanticism espoused by Marx. Lewis Feuer has argued that today's radicals are the children of affluent American life since World War II, whose affinity with Marx does not lie in the classical Marxist theme of exploitation, partly because they have not suffered injustices similar to those experienced in the first factory systems of England and America. Rather, they recognize and suffer from the alienation about which Marx wrote in his earlier years. Many have been reared in middle-class suburban homes and have come to resent the lack of human warmth and emotion in much of modern urban life. They are face-to-face with great impersonal institutions like the university and modern corporations. As students, they feel that they are merely IBM numbers and that their achievement is measured by academic grades of questionable validity as they prepare for jobs in bureaucratic organizations. According to some youthful rebels, nothing short of revolution, whether peaceful or violent, can change all this, and sociology ought to have a part in the struggle if it is to remain faithful to its heritage [Feuer, 1969; Keniston, 1968].

In short, contemporary sociology is a dynamic discipline that has emerged from a rich origin of 19th century scholarship with two main thrusts—scientific detachment and passionate involvement. It is struggling to find itself without surrendering its commitment to social science, on the one hand, or to social concern, on the other. We have entitled this book accordingly to reflect these competing commitments.

A new student in sociology thus has a dual challenge. The first is to try to comprehend a scientific discipline with its emphasis upon theory and research, since this will long remain a central responsibility for sociologists. The second is to wrestle with the question of how to make research relevant to the demands of social action and change. Sociology cannot use one approach at the expense of the other; it must fulfill both obligations and stand in creative tension between the two.

Throughout this book, we will deal with both themes. In later sections, we will discuss various aspects of today's action-oriented emphasis. However, we will begin in this chapter with an introduction to the scientific tradition in sociology. This will set the stage for an understanding of the adapted studies featured in every chapter, which illustrate how researchers go about their work.

Basically, sociologists are engaged in a scholarly study of human behavior in social context. In this endeavor, the primary purpose is to seek the truth about why individuals act as they do within various groups and societies. The discipline of sociology, especially in the academic tradition, seeks to establish a body of knowledge about human society that will be of use in explaining and predicting human behavior. This knowledge may be of value to decision makers and practitioners who must take action in daily human affairs. However, sociologists as scientists do not judge whether behavior patterns are right or wrong; they are concerned with why people do what they do. In searching for the answers, they identify, analyze, and scientifically manipulate social variables. To be sure, psychological differences between people are very important and individuals are unique in many respects. Nevertheless, there are regularities and patterns of behavior that emerge when we look at people who share the same social characteristics. These common characteristics are referred to as *social*

TABLE 1-1 Types and Examples of Social Variables

Social Variable	Descriptions or Examples
Sex	Male as compared with female behavior
Age	Contrasts between children, youth, young adults, and the aged
Race	Differences in behavior between blacks, whites, and others
Religion	Catholic, Jew, and Protestant, or folk religion versus modern religions
Ethnic group	Irish American as compared with Italian American
Social class	Blue-collar versus white-collar workers
Cultural perspectives	Contrasts in beliefs and values between Occidental and Oriental or between premodern and modern societies
Residential settings	Comparison of behavior in villages, communes, the suburbs, and large cities

variables; some examples of these appear in Table 1-1. Analysis of these variables provides sociologists with a way of making sense of human behavior that might otherwise appear to be merely random or accidental. Patterns of variations in social variables provide sociologists with clues to understanding why people in different settings consistently act as they do—for example, why delinquency and suicide rates are higher among some groups of people than others.

In addition, analysis of social variables enables sociologists to identify differences in behavior between different groups of people. For instance, we know that life for modern urban residents is vastly different from that of rural and/or premodern people. Analysis of the way social variables differ in these two groups reveals the different patterns of action in each context. Thus, the use of social variables helps sociologists as scientists to recognize important differences in human behavior easily and to define, describe, and interpret these differences.

It is not difficult to see why this sociological interest in identifying differences in human behavior first arose in 19th century Europe. Unanticipated problems and dramatically different life-styles emerged with the coming of modernization. With the growing emphasis upon individual freedom from kinship groups, the medieval church, and the closely knit community and neighborhood, a sense of rootlessness and impersonality developed. Urban life set people adrift from earlier traditions and their behavioral patterns changed appreciably. August Comte observed this in his own time and saw the possibilities of a scientific study of the consequences. Although he never realized this vision in actual research, others took the cue. Not long after Comte, Max Weber (1884–1920) in Germany conducted studies of modern bureaucracy, the rise of capitalism, and the role of religion that are still fundamental in sociology and are used throughout this book. On foundations laid by 19th century French and German scholars, sociology moved to the United States, where it developed rapidly through the 1900s.

The Scientific Method in Action: Emile Durkheim (1858–1917)

It is one thing to propose a scientific study of human society as Comte did. It is quite another to transform such a dream into reality. The key to this remarkable achievement was the *scientific method,* and one of the first scholars to utilize it was Emile Durkheim, a Frenchman. It was his classic study of suicide in 19th century Europe that helped establish a model for the use of the scientific method in the study of human behavior.

Durkheim lived in a century that was celebrating individuality. In premodern societies, individuals had been largely submerged in the group experiences of family, clan, and religious community. With the industrial revolution and the striking events of the French Revolution, the individual was being liberated economically (through capitalism), politically (through democracy), and religiously (through Protestantism). In this new era for Western societies, many scholars, Freud among them, were encouraging the liberation of individuals from the bonds of social groups.

Durkheim did not agree. As an individual who had largely broken away from his Jewish religious heritage and his strong family ties, he was a child of his time. He was politically allied with the radicals of his day who were insisting upon a balance of power and a pluralistic society. On the other hand, while others were welcoming this new day for individuality, Durkheim recognized that a stiff price was being paid for that freedom. People were rootless, lonely, and without clear-cut rules for living. It was Durkheim who developed most fully the concept of *anomie,* a state of existence where people suffer the dizziness of freedom and feel "a lack of rules."

Put another way, Durkheim tried to counterbalance the strong tendency of his contemporaries to overstate the case for individuality. He felt that individuals are fundamental, to be sure, but that they cannot be understood apart from society. Indeed, individualism is the result of society. In the following passage, Durkheim [1915, p. 347] speaks of the interplay between individual and society:

> On the one hand, the individual gets from society the best part of himself, all that gives him a distinct character and a special place among other beings, . . . his intellectual and moral culture. . . . But, on the other hand, society exists and lives only in and through individuals. . . . Society cannot do without individuals any more than these can do without society.

In doing battle with an oversimplified emphasis upon individuality, Durkheim has been criticized for *reification,* that is, for overemphasizing the importance of society. This was a risk worth taking, however, for he laid a foundation for the understanding of human beings that stands firm even today and upon which many scholars, such as Charles Cooley, George Herbert Mead, and John Dewey (discussed in Chapter 3), have been able to build. To be free as individuals is to be securely rooted in the social group, to practice its moral rules, to be disciplined according to its authority:

> Society, as Durkheim points out in *The Division of Labor* and in *The Rules of Sociological Method,* is manifest only in the diverse forms of constraint which rescue, as it were, the individual from the void. Authority and discipline form the very warp of personality; without authority man can have no sense of duty, nor any real freedom [Nisbet, 1965, p. 60].

In other words, sociology as a discipline is charged with a distinct and separate task from that of any other science, including psychology. The mental and emotional states of the individual are the subject matter of psychology. However, since these states cannot be fully understood without studying human society, which molds the individual, sociology has a mission of its own: the study of the social context of individual behavior. This opens the way for the use of the scientific method in sociology—that is, the rigorous and objective study of social facts in the real world. In his *The Rules of Sociological Method,* Durkheim insists upon a bold analysis of empirical data, facts from everyday life that can be counted, compared, and arranged in systematic order.

One such social fact is suicide, as measured by suicide rates. Suicide is a form of human behavior that occurs in every society, can be recorded in its vital statistics, and singled out for study. It was selected by Durkheim partly because it is such a good example of what seems to be an arbitrary act by individuals. Since most societies actively discourage suicide, they would seem, at first glance, to have nothing to do with causing suicidal behavior. So one way for Durkheim to show the fundamental importance of society was to show that even suicide is a reflection, not of individuality, but of the moral character of society itself. *Study 1* is an adaptation of his book.

▶ STUDY 1

The Social Origins of Suicide [1897][1]

Problem

Durkheim sensed that suicide, like crime, divorce, and economic maladjustment, was a symptom of a society in trouble. Suicide was not an isolated individualistic act that could be understood by studying individual personalities. Instead, it should be thought of as a reflection of *the moral condition of a social group or a society.* Every society has a certain aptitude for suicide;

[1]Adapted and abridged from Emile Durkheim, *Suicide,* J. A. Spaulding and G. Simpson, George Simpson, Transl.; George Simpson, Ed. (New York: The Free Press, 1951).

therefore, we should look for its roots in society rather than in individuals. Modern societies, like those in Europe and America, have set individuals too much adrift and made them too dependent on their own resources. Suicide appears to be one of the negative results. This is the problem: What happens to individuals when they lose their sense of group identity and support?

Hypothesis and Study Design

Durkheim had an educated hunch, a hypothesis, that suicide rates vary according to whether group solidarity is strong or weak. *Suicide varies inversely with the degree of social integration;* that is, higher rates occur where there is a low degree of group solidarity, where individuals are too loosely tied to society.

Though he began with this overall perspective, Durkheim soon began to refine his analysis of suicide into three distinct categories—egoistic, anomic, and altruistic. All three are to be understood in terms of the degree of social integration.

Actual cases of suicide from France and other modern societies provided Durkheim with data for testing his hypotheses. They were organized into *a study design* that made it possible to compare suicide rates from one time to another in Europe, one country to another, one religious group to another, one marital status to another, one occupation to another, and one economic and political situation to another. A systematic comparison of rates using this study design made it possible for him to test his hypotheses again and again. This was done openly and explicitly so that other scholars down to this very day could check his results and criticize his conclusions. This is the essence of scientific endeavor, ensuring that every step in the investigative process is open to replication by other scientists.

Method of Data Collection

Durkheim's study is an excellent example of *the use of documents or secondary sources of data.* This means that a researcher uses materials for a purpose that differs from the reason for their original collection. In this case, he turned to vital statistics. In his Preface, he acknowledges the help of the Chief of the Bureau of Legal Statistics in France and notes that his tables are drawn up from documents of the Ministry of Justice. Through these and other similar sources, he was able to study some 26,000 suicides and to classify them separately according to age, sex, marital status, presence or absence of children in the family, religion, location, calendar date, method of suicide, and so forth. This represents meticulous work on the part of the researcher in spite of the fact that the public agencies had already accumulated the data through years of record keeping. It is no easy task to work with a mass of information accumulated for other purposes and arrange the data creatively according to new and different hypotheses.

Findings and Interpretations

Throughout his book, Durkheim presents the pertinent data in tabular form, as is shown in Table 1-2.

In the light of his hypothesis, Durkheim expected to find higher suicide rates, which he called "social facts," in some countries than in others, in some historical periods than in others, among some categories of persons as compared with others. In some cases, he found suicide among people who were quite alone and isolated from any social group, and he called this type *egoistic suicide.*

TABLE 1-2 Rate of Suicides per Million Inhabitants for Three Periods Between 1866 and 1878 in Europe

				Numerical Position in the:		
Country	1866–1870	1871–1875	1874–1878	1st Period	2nd Period	3rd Period
Italy	30	35	38	1	1	1
Belgium	66	69	78	2	3	4
England	67	66	69	3	2	2
Norway	76	73	71	4	4	3
Austria	78	94	130	5	7	7
Sweden	85	81	91	6	5	5
Bavaria	90	91	100	7	6	6
France	135	150	160	8	9	9
Prussia	142	134	152	9	8	8
Denmark	277	258	255	10	10	10
Saxony	293	267	334	11	11	11

1. Among Protestant countries in Europe, suicide rates were relatively high, which Durkheim associated with a low degree of social integration. Protestants tend to stress individualism and free inquiry and to be loosely bound to the church. An underlying social condition of loneliness, and a commitment to personal rather than group values, can develop and can lead to egoistic suicide.
2. Among Protestants within each country, there were the same high rates and a tendency toward egoistic suicide. For example, in Austria from 1852 to 1859, suicides per million persons were 79.5 for Protestants, compared to 51.3 for Catholics and 20.7 for Jews.
3. Among single persons, there were high rates, which correlated with a low degree of family integration and loneliness.

Further analysis of the findings indicated, however, that egoistic suicide was by no means the only kind. Loneliness was not the only trouble with life in modern society; confusion and ambiguity were others. When individuals are too loosely committed to social groups, as many people are today, they are not quite sure of what is right and wrong, of the norms or rules for behavior. This usually comes with rapid social change and with shifts in moral values and moral guidelines. This was such a common condition of Durkheim's society in France and of similar societies that he referred to it as a state of anomie—that is, a lack of rules, a state of confusion and ambiguity. This led him to hypothesize that in this social situation the tendency was toward *anomic suicide:*

1. Among the divorced, suicide rates were high, which suggests a relationship with something more than loneliness, probably with a state of confusion or anomie. In Western societies, it is not entirely clear, for example, how divorced persons are to be treated and how they should feel about themselves. These societies have no clear-cut rules for divorce adjustment. In this regard, it is possible to characterize Western societies as anomic. The tendency in this context is toward anomic suicide.

2. Among the wealthy, especially those who have been suddenly thrust into affluence, the rates were high because of an inability to cope with the opportunities afforded and the lack of familiar restraints. A rapid change in the social and economic situation of these people created the risk of anomic suicide.

A third kind of suicide, *altruistic suicide,* emerged from Durkheim's interpretations of his findings in order to explain why it was that suicide rates were high in an occupational group like the military. He might have expected these rates to be low because a professional military person is tightly bound to the occupational group. There is less individualism and the rules for conduct are clear and firm; however, he found that in spite of this context suicide rates were relatively high. He was also aware of high rates among certain primitive peoples where there was strong social solidarity and little individualism. Such societies are often prone to ceremonial suicide, such as when the aged are left behind to die because they can no longer keep pace with a migrating group. Durkheim hypothesized that suicide rates were high in these cases because individuals become too tightly bound to the social group; the group becomes more important than the individual. Altruistic suicide results when military persons and members of primitive societies sacrifice themselves as individuals for the good of the group.

Durkheim's interpretations of his findings highlight one of the most critical stages in the research process, the need for more than a systematic series of tables describing raw data. Good research demands insight and creativity in terms of data explanation. When it came to the high rates of suicide among military personnel, Durkheim had to explain a seeming contradiction to his hypothesis. He was able to do so and still keep faith with the central theme that all three forms of suicide can be explained according to the degree of social integration, whether too low or too high.

Some researchers have questioned Durkheim's use of statistics. Categorizing whole countries as mostly Protestant or mostly Catholic may be too gross a measure for scientific accuracy. Furthermore, it is always possible that the differences between countries are due to social variables other than religion; that is, differences in suicide rates may be due not to religion as such but to differences in economic and political conditions.

Nevertheless, Durkheim's insightful analysis has led John Madge [1962] to call him "the early master of the indirect clue." Using Durkheim as a basis for a study of his own, Madge presents an advanced discussion of Durkheim's findings that includes the complexities of divorce and suicide. Madge argues that the impact of divorce varies according to whether it pertains to husbands rather than to wives and to whether it occurs in societies that approve or disapprove of divorce. He also notes that there is a difference between suicide rates in cases of divorce versus separation. Thus, another mark of provocative research is that it encourages future scholars to adapt and utilize its findings.

Conclusions and Implications

Durkheim focused upon suicide for several reasons.

1. Suicide is an indicator of the moral condition of society, the presence or absence of strong social bonds, the shifting character of norms for behavior.

2. It lends itself to empirical analysis through census data. Suicide rates can be treated as one form of social fact. By using the scientific method, hypotheses can thus be tested.
3. Findings from such a study can lead to practical implications, both academic and political.

Academically, the study has been of tremendous value. Contemporary sociologists refer to Durkheim's theoretical perspectives and research methodology as starting points for continued work, as the above illustration from John Madge's research indicates. Furthermore, the concept of anomie as developed by Durkheim is still helpful. Studies in crime and delinquency often make reference to Robert Merton's [1968] theoretical essay (discussed in Chapter 12), which in turn goes back to Durkheim's insights. These are but a few of the examples of the impact of Emile Durkheim upon modern scholarship.

In practical affairs, the relevance of Durkheim's final chapter on the "Practical Consequences" of his study of suicide cannot be easily overlooked. He sees suicide as a normal condition of social life; that is, it occurs with the kind of regularity that is also characteristic of births, deaths, marriages, and divorces. Even so, suicide is cause for alarm when its rates of increase reflect a menacing state of anomie. Durkheim was concerned about the loneliness and rootlessness that had been brought about by rapid social change. He did not have much hope that education, harsh penal response, or even stronger moral disapproval of suicide could get at the root cause of the problem. He did see promise, however, in the strengthening of social institutions. In today's modern society, there are few social groups that can cope with loneliness and anomie. The state is too far removed and impersonal; religion has lost much of its influence; the family has become small and fragile. According to Durkheim, the hope lies in the power of the work group. He envisioned associations made up of people who worked in common occupations, which would provide solid bases for belonging experiences for modern citizens. He referred to such groups as corporations and saw them not only as sources of a sense of community but as strong elements in the balance of power for a plural democratic society (discussed in Chapter 7). In short, the question of how to restore a sense of community in an impersonal society was Durkheim's deep personal concern. It is the same for us in the remaining years of the 20th century.

A special word of caution is necessary at this point. Durkheim's study is not offered here as the latest word on the problem of suicide. Rather it is given as a classic example of the use of the scientific method; furthermore, it was unique in its time for its focus upon the factors that break down social integration. For current knowledge about suicide, one must turn to more recent research [for example, Lester, 1972; Cornut, 1975]. Roger Cornut, Executive Director of San Francisco's Suicide Prevention Center, points out that his work is directed toward the individual and is heavily influenced by psychological definitions of alienation. Cornut's agency views the social integration of the individual, cultural factors notwith-

1-1 Suicide and Social Integration

Emile Durkheim's classic study in 1897 identified three major types of suicide. Each type, according to Durkheim, tells us something about the moral condition of societies and subgroups—that is, suicide is related to the degree of social integration people experience in different situations.

Anomic suicide results when individuals feel suddenly cut off from meaningful relationships with others and when rules governing acceptable behavior become confused and ambiguous. In 1972, police in Manhattan, New York, took three hours to persuade an unidentified man to leave the seventeenth-floor ledge of a building on Broadway. Anomic suicide is prevalent in modern urban environments and results from a lack of social integration.

United Press I

k Public Library Picture Collection

In contrast to anomic suicide, **altruistic suicide** results when individuals are tightly bound to social groups that require self-sacrifice for the good of group values. In traditional Japan, *hara-kiri* (ritual suicide) was common. Those who had been dishonored (for example, warriors who had lost battles) could bring honor upon themselves and their families by courageously taking their lives in an elaborate public ceremony.

'd Photos

Egoistic suicide results when individuals feel isolated and alone and, as a consequence, place emphasis upon individual freedom and the right to determine their own actions. In 1961, American author Ernest Hemingway died by a shotgun blast. Initially, his death was officially announced as an accident; but observers have since concluded that he probably took his own life when he realized, at the age of 62, that his creative and physical abilities were deteriorating. Egoistic suicide is prevalent among creative artists and intellectuals.

Therefore, a study of the different kinds of suicide indicates that human societies can sometimes provide too little social integration and, at other times, too much social integration. Humans can be either too free to act on their own or too compelled to conform to the wishes of others.

standing, as related mainly to personal educational background, family training, and life-development experiences. For example, data indicate that a large number of depressive and suicidal individuals suffer from some major loss in early childhood.

As Cornut points out, such data were not readily available or sought after in Durkheim's day. Furthermore, official statistics were unreliable. If Durkheim had had access to contemporary information, he might not have virtually ruled out psychological causes, and his public health approach may have become more of a *psychosociological* one. It is known today that most suicidal personalities have some common psychosocial characteristics. The main one is difficulty in relating satisfactorily with others on a sustained emotional basis. This seems to result from their frequent tendency to be overly sensitive to loss and rejection, to poor self-esteem, and, often, to excessive expectations for themselves and others. As a result, they can accumulate anger, and, in turn, become loners and alienate themselves from society. However, they generally remain ambivalent in their suicidal propensities, and, while many reject help by professionals, they still desperately wish they could make it, wish that someone would be accepting and nice to them. As a consequence, agencies like Cornut's act as last resorts for the suicidal and often make the difference between an impulsive suicidal gesture and a decision to live.

▶ SO WHAT?

One of the most consistently asked questions about sociological studies is "So what?" That is, do the research findings have any relevance to social action and public policy? This issue will be considered throughout this book when findings of research are presented. A box will appear in each chapter containing brief responses illustrating past and present uses of social scientific research to address major social problems. Though Durkheim's work was done a century ago, his findings have formally and informally become the basis for many programs dealing with the problem of suicide. For example, the work of Roger Cornut's Suicide Prevention Incorporated in San Francisco, founded in 1962 to deal with the highest suicide rate in the United States, is related to Durkheim's theories in the following ways:

1. Suicide and crisis intervention telephone lines are operated 24 hours a day, 7 days a week, by 160 volunteers. More than 1800 calls are received each month from people of all ages with all kinds of problems. Callers may remain anonymous if they wish. In this manner, they can talk out, rather than act out, their troubles with a sympathetic listener. Referrals are made to other community services, if needed. This provides at least momentary reintegration into society for those who feel anomic or alienated. In the last three to four years, there has

been a substantial reduction in the number of suicides in San Francisco (over 20 percent). This decrease has not been occurring in other California areas.

2. In addition to three suicide telephone lines, the Center operates two drug lines, a friendship line for the elderly, and has started a grief counseling service for the survivors of a suicide. This is recognition of the fact that social anomie and alienation may result from a variety of social factors throughout the life of an individual (for example, broken families, as in the case of Durkheim's interest in divorce).
3. Finally, the San Francisco Center has started a Minority Outreach Service. This offers free consultation, seminars, training, interviews, and the like, to minorities in the community who are not sufficiently reached by conventional mental health programs. This is recognition of the fact that different cultural groups may be influenced by different degrees and types of anomie and alienation (similar to Durkheim's interest in variations by religious categories). In recent years, the suicide rate among urban blacks, particularly the young, has increased substantially.

Durkheim's study sets the stage for much of the work presented throughout this book. It is a model of the scientific method of investigation, and *each subsequent study will follow essentially the same outline.* Durkheim's research defines and clarifies how to formulate hypotheses, manipulate social variables, and relate findings to an overall theory about human behavior. It points out clearly that acts that might seem to reflect individuality are to be understood, in large part, as determined or influenced by social patterns. Individuals commit suicide not as individuals alone. Rather, they act in a social context, as members of society and persons more or less integrated into social groups. We have begun to see, then, that sociology is the scientific study of human group life and its relationship to the behavior of individuals.

THE NATURE OF SCIENCE

What Is Science?

Science is not easy to define. One contemporary scholar, Earl Babbie [1973], suggests that it is best not to use an exact definition but rather to speak of specific studies as being more or less scientific, according to the quality of scholarly endeavor. The scientific rigor of the study is measured by the extent to which it is (1) logical; (2) deterministic (cause and effect); (3) general (beyond individual events or persons); (4) parsimonious (clearly defined topics); (5) specific (precise measures); (6) empirically verifiable (testing of theories in everyday life); (7) intersubjective (two scientists obtaining the same results from the same experiment); and (8) open to modification (relentless search for new insights). The more rigorously scientific the study, the closer it is likely to be to the truth about the world of the events being studied.

Natural and physical scientists have developed a high quality of scientific analysis, and their findings often lead to an improved life experience for humans. Can social scientists also move toward a more scientific understanding of society and human beings that will contribute to a better quality of life? The answer depends upon the continued efforts of the social sciences to develop reliable research methods. We turn now to this topic.

The Scientific Method

A scientific approach to a topic assumes that our common-sense notions about that topic need to be tested. Our hunches may not be quite correct. The testing process is known as research, and the major steps in a research procedure may be outlined as follows [Selltiz *et al.*, 1959; Miller, 1964]:

1. Statement of purpose and selection of an important problem.
2. Formulation of hypotheses and description of study design.
3. Selection of methods for data collection.
4. Research results obtained, analyzed, and presented.
5. Conclusions and interpretations specified in terms of implications for theory, further research, and/or solutions to problems.

This is the outline or model often used when a research report is prepared for one of the professional journals and thus becomes a part of the literature of social science. The model is oversimplified, however, for seldom does a project routinely follow such a neat procedure. Several of these steps normally go on at the same time and all of them are interrelated from the beginning to the end of a study. Furthermore, social research involves getting people to cooperate as subjects for study, finding qualified interviewers, coders, computer experts, and others to assist in the routine management of the project.

In fact, there is a critical contrast between the model and the actual practice of research. Earl Babbie [1973, pp. 5–10] points this out in dealing with survey research. He suggests that one reason for the tendency to debunk science is the growing awareness that day-to-day work on a project may be fraught with careless answering of questionnaires, inept interviewing, compromises in analysis, and even computer errors. And this is to say nothing of the fits and starts that may characterize the overall purpose and planning by the principal researchers. Scientists are human beings and are subject to the familiar faults and foibles of the species.

One of the most critical observers of social science research is Herbert Blumer [1969]. He insists that far too often today's researchers are more concerned about following the correct procedures and scientific protocol than they are in getting out in the real world of human affairs (the empirical world) and finding out what actually happens among human beings. Behind every worthwhile project, writes Blumer, there must be extensive exploration in the field to be studied and continuous inspection of what is observed through questioning and pondering on the part of the researcher. Only then can we "lift the veils" that obscure the real world we are trying to study.

Oversimplification is always a risk in any presentation of the steps in scientific research. Nevertheless, an ideal model can be extracted from the format used in Study 1, which reflects the five basic steps indicated above. This model will be used throughout this book.

STEP 1: Problem*—a large global concern reflected in a specific topic*

Durkheim's problem is one of the best examples. His was not a narrow insignificant matter that could be tested simply. He wanted to assess what was happening to the social bonds that give people a sense of belonging. Where were these bonds weak and where were they strong, and what could be done to give humans more sense of community? It took great ingenuity to deal with this global concern through an intensive study of suicide and its implications. This is the kind of ingenuity that Ph.D. candidates must show when selecting a problem for their dissertations. The sociological studies cited throughout this book began with a similar concern and creativity in the selection of the central problem. Some examples of a general concern reflected in a specific topic are the following:

The vital necessity for primary relationships, for love and recognition, and the problem of unwed mothers (Study 2).

The power of the human group in shaping individuals and their self-identity, and the problem of boys' gangs (Study 3).

The impact of an idea (work is holy) upon a major social revolution (the rise of capitalism), and the problem of Protestantism and modernization (Study 4).

STEP 2: Hypotheses and Study Design*—common-sense explanations that can be tested to see whether they are true or false*

There are many important questions that people can raise about human existence. Some of them are philosophical or religious and cannot be studied empirically through scientific methods. The question of a supernatural existence is an example since scientists cannot gather data from the natural world that will throw light upon such a question. On the other hand, many concerns can be formulated in terms of down-to-earth logical propositions that are called hypotheses. A *hypothesis* is a kind of educated guess or carefully constructed hunch that something is so. It is an *if–then statement: If* social ties are too weak or too strong, *then* there will be a greater possibility of suicide. Sometimes a hypothesis cannot be so simply stated; however, it must always be clear-cut and specific and subject to testing through a feasible study design. For example, Durkheim's hypothesis had to be *brought into focus* so that actual information about suicides could be arranged in tabular form to test the proposition. Is it true that there are more suicides among Protestants than Catholics? The data indicated that this is so. The explanations as to why this is so assume that Protestants have weaker ties to church and family. The findings, therefore, support the hypothesis, at least in part. This step in the research process takes a great deal of thought and creative trial and error. Studies presented in this book test hypotheses such as the following:

If all humans need primary bonds, *then* unwed mothers are more likely to be seeking love relationships than engaging in promiscuity (Study 2).

If Protestantism encourages devotion to thrift and saving for the future, *then* Protestants will be less consumer oriented and more likely to reject installment buying than Catholics (Study 4).

If the Printers' Union is democratic and experiences a turnover of leadership, *then* the "law of oligarchy," which refers to the concentration of power in the hands of a few people, should not be characteristic of this union (Study 7).

These are not the exact wordings from the studies. They are rephrased here in order to illustrate the meaning of a hypothesis. The *study design* refers to the way in which the data are collected and manipulated to throw light upon the hypothesis. The design is a result of the kinds of data needed to test the hypothesis. For example, in Study 2, in order to test the relationship between primary bonds and promiscuous sexual behavior, a sample of unwed mothers was interviewed. They were asked to categorize their contact with the unwed father according to whether it was a love, friendship, or casual relationship. The hypothesis required the use of data collected by interviews. Similarly, Study 4 used questionnaires with a sample of Detroit workers to determine the difference in attitudes toward work by religious identification. In contrast, in Study 7, the researchers used a variety of techniques. Observation of the daily social and political life of the printers indicated whether their union was democratic or oligarchic. Records of voting for positions of union leadership also disclosed these kinds of differences. In other words, a study design is determined by the kind of information necessary to test hypotheses and involves decisions about different research approaches, such as use of vital statistics (Durkheim), interviews (unwed mothers), questionnaires (Detroit Workers), or voting data and observation (Printers' Union). Once a design is selected, the special research methods needed to implement the design must be considered.

STEP 3: Methods of Data Collections*—the field work tools and techniques*

Reliable field work is essential if research is to be successful. It can sometimes be done by the scholar who initiates the study and is personally responsible for data collection. Most of the time, however, the author of the study, called the principal investigator, must rely upon other workers. The quality of the field work depends in large part upon the caliber of the workers and their training and supervision. It is not only important to pay workers adequately, but it is vital that they be suited for the tasks. Computer specialists must be good technicians. Those who administer the questionnaires or do the interviewing in the field must be able to listen intelligently and establish good rapport with the people being studied. Middle-age women make effective interviewers as a rule because they pose a minimum threat, in terms of role and status, to interviewees. When minority people are being contacted, workers from similar backgrounds are often the best suited. Always it is important for workers on a research project to be honest and committed to the tasks. In this way, the human errors that creep into the best of projects will be minimized.

Assuming that there are adequate funds and qualified workers, sound research may vary greatly in methodology; often more than one method is needed on the same project. John Madge [1962] suggests that most methods can be discussed under three headings: (1) The use of *documents;* (2) *observation*—personal and impersonal; and (3) *survey research* through questionnaires and interviews. All three types of research are illustrated by the studies included in this book. *Public documents* were skillfully used by Durkheim. *Personal documents* like diaries and letters are sometimes used by researchers, as in the study of Polish immigrants by Thomas and Znaniecki.

The use of *personal observation* is illustrated in Study 3. William Whyte moved into a slum and became virtually a member of a boys' gang. This is *participant observation.* It has the advantage of giving an insightful researcher an inside view of a human situation. First-hand knowledge unavailable by any other means can be obtained by becoming a part of a group or subculture. This is why it was helpful for Freeman to observe the Women's Liberation Movement as an active participant (Study 5), for Lowry to know his community as an involved citizen (Study 8), and Rankin to know the Methodist Church through participation as layman and minister for many years (Study 9).

Impersonal observation can also be a useful research method. This can take the form of watching group interaction through a one-way mirror or standing unobtrusively in an assembly room of a factory, as in the classic study of worker efficiency in the Chicago plant of Western Electric. Similarly, Becker and his colleagues, while not doctors themselves, observed young medical students (Study 9), and William Westley rode with and observed police without being a policeman (Study 12). Observation always poses problems even though it is a useful technique. The person observing may be biased and consequently may misinterpret what happens. In addition, an observer may influence how people behave just by being present. Researchers must make an effort to minimize such errors of bias or influence.

Data collection is often carried out by the use of *interviews and questionnaires.* The advantage of this technique is that the researcher can ask carefully planned questions that bear directly upon the purposes of

1-2 Methods of Data Collection

Social scientists use a variety of methods of data collection. Each has its own special strength and weakness.

Interviewing a carefully selected sample of a population, a scientist can identify important attitudes about political beliefs, sexual behavior, economic problems, and so on. However, interviewers can never be absolutely sure whether they are obtaining honest and unbiased answers to their questions, and extensive interviewing is costly in time and money.

Elsa Dorfman

In her many studies of nonmodern people, anthropologist Margaret Mead relied upon **participant observation**—living with and recording the behavior and attitudes of the people being studied. This method is popular in sociology, since intimate involvement in the life of a group can disclose knowledge not otherwise available. However, participant observers run the risk of influencing the actions and attitudes of those being observed by their very presence. Furthermore, scientists using this technique often find it difficult to maintain detachment and neutrality.

Theodore Schwartz, courtesy of Margaret Mead

Elsa Dorfman

Social scientist also utilize a variety of **public documents,** including newspapers, Congressional reports, statistical surveys, and the like. This readily available information provides a rich source of data for analysis. However, some public sources (for example, newspapers) are not always reliable.

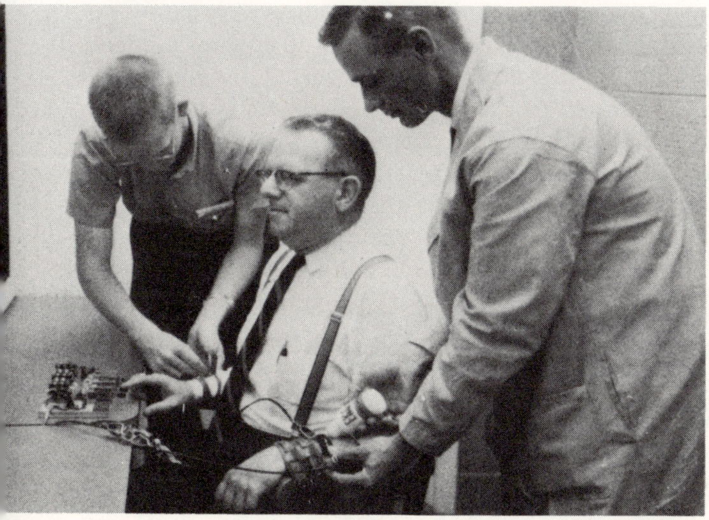

Copyright 1965 by Stanley Milgram. From the Film OBEDIENCE, distributed by the New York University Film Library.

Social scientists sometimes use **laboratory experiments** to simulate real-life situations. Stanley Milgram tested the extent to which volunteers were willing to inflict electrical shocks upon unknown subjects in response to orders from the scientist. Subjects were trained to fake pain. Milgram concluded that most people will follow the orders of authority figures even to the point of injuring others. Controversial experiments such as Milgram's raise the question of the extent to which people should be manipulated and misled during research. Some scholars have argued that studies of real-life situations (the willingness of Nazi concentration camp authorities to carry out orders without moral concern) can provide more reliable information.

the study. It is possible to reach a great many people this way, and there is value in getting information from large numbers of respondents. There are also disadvantages. Questionnaire construction is not a task for amateurs. It takes sophisticated scholars to know what questions to ask and how to ask them in a way that will ensure valid and accurate responses. Equally demanding is the task of assembling and interpreting the results and bringing them to bear upon the hypotheses. This is all a very costly process, beginning with the preparation and mailing of questionnaires, the training and dispatching of interviewers, and the coding and computer processing of the raw materials as they come in from the field.

At the same time, this can be a rewarding process. It can begin with informal and exploratory interviewing as in Whyte's study of street-corner gangs, Lowry's exploration of community leadership, and Rankin's study of clergymen and their wives. It can then proceed into more structured interviews, where the interviewer follows written questions from an interview schedule. This method was used by Vincent with unwed mothers and by Lenski in the Detroit field study on religion and economic behavior (Studies 2 and 4). Lenski's field workers followed a detailed questionnaire as they interviewed several hundred people. They asked questions similar to the following (Lenski, 1963, pp. 377–388):

> Some people tell us that they couldn't really be happy unless they were working at some job (or keeping house). But others say that they would be a lot happier if they didn't have to work and could take life easy. How do you feel about this? Why is that?
>
> Changing the subject a bit, do you think it's a good idea or a bad idea to buy things on the installment plan? Why do you feel that way?

This is an example of an open-ended questionnaire that permits the interviewer to probe for explanations and to obtain a depth of response. Obviously this calls for an expert interviewer and is so costly in time and money that such a project can cover only limited numbers of respondents. This is why most questionnaires are self-administered; that is, respondents can fill them out themselves, without any interviewers. This means that answers to a question are limited to the items listed. There is no way for the respondent to tell more about how he or she feels or why. Those writing the questions must try to think of every possible answer that might be significant. And almost always in the list of answers, there must be the "don't know" response. The following is an example of an item from a *self-administered questionnaire* (Ladd and Lipset, 1975, p. 4):

Do your interests lie primarily in research or in teaching? (Circle one choice.)

Very heavily in research.	(1)
In both, but leaning toward research.	(2)
In both, but leaning toward teaching.	(3)
Very heavily in teaching.	(4)

For whom did you vote in the presidential election of 1972? (Circle one choice.)

McGovern	(1)
Nixon	(2)
"Left" third-party candidate	(3)
Other candidate	(4)
Not eligible to vote	(5)
Did not vote	(6)

The advantage of a self-administered questionnaire is that it can be mailed out to many people inviting them to take part in the study. The large number of respondents makes it possible for the researcher to analyze results according to several variables: Male responses can be compared with female; Protestant with Catholic; white-collar worker with blue-collar worker; and so forth. The disadvantages of this type of questionnaire include the fact that anonymity of response makes it impossible for the researcher to judge the degree of honesty and sincerity of the response.

STEP 4: Findings and Interpretations—*systematic summaries of results as they pertain to the hypotheses*

This is one of the most crucial stages in a research project, for meaningful research is not simply a matter of putting down the total number of responses in each category. Even this descriptive summary demands very careful planning of tables and charts to highlight the findings. In addition, the totals must be presented in such a way as to test the hypotheses. Results must be depicted according to the relevant variables; raw figures must be transformed into percentages; and oftimes mathematical tests of significance must assess how important the differences are. Here is one example from the Lenski analysis of the data from the Detroit study (Study 4):

Hypothesis	Protestants are more likely to reflect the spirit of capitalism than Catholics.
The Spirit of Capitalism	The spirit of capitalism was measured using an index of 12 items, such as a positive attitude toward work, budgeting, saving money, and a negative attitude toward spending on the installment plan, and the like.
The Results	Of middle-class white Protestants, 53 percent were in step with the spirit of capitalism as noted above, compared to only 29 percent of working-class white Catholics.
The Interpretation	The hypothesis is supported by the empirical data; there is a difference between Protestants and Catholics on economic matters, which helps to confirm the global concern that an idea (work is holy) helped to spark the spirit of capitalism.
The Chart	(See also Study 4.)

Percentage in Step with the Spirit of Capitalism

	Middle Class	Working Class
Active White Protestants	53	40
Active White Catholics	38	29

STEP 5: Conclusions and Implications*—concise summary and what it means for theory and practice.*

The final step in the research process is more than a formal summary. It is a chance to sum up the major findings relative to the hypothesis and to point out the theoretical implications. Each study adds something to the body of knowledge, however modest the contribution. Even when a hypothesis is not supported by the data, this negative finding may be of value for future research.

In many cases, the conclusion will make it possible for the scholar to venture suggestions about new social policies that might be based on the findings. At this moment, he or she will become a partisan rather than an objective scientist. Along with Durkheim, the researcher will look toward some practical consequences. Throughout this book, there will be indications of how research relates to social policy and social action. These will often appear in the concluding section of the major studies. Other times they will appear in the "So What" boxes in each chapter.

LIMITATIONS OF SCIENCE

All science is subject to human bias. This is especially true for social scientists. Since human behavior is their area of study, they are actually part of the subject matter. Furthermore, human behavior patterns vary from one place to another and from one group to another. This is in contrast to the subject matter of the natural sciences. When a chemist studies hydrogen, he can assume that one hydrogen atom is very much like another, wherever it is found, and that the conditions surrounding it can be quite accurately controlled. The same is true when a physicist measures a metal bar; he can be quite sure that it will not stretch or shrink in length as long as natural conditions are the same. This is why Earl Babbie [1973, p. 50] quotes economist Daniel Suits, who calls the natural sciences the "easy sciences" because of the predictable nature of their subject matter.

The subject matter of sociology and the other social sciences is quite another story. These might well be called the "hard sciences" in that they deal with human beings whose behavior varies according to a variety of variables, such as sex, age, race, nationality, cultural setting, and historical period, to mention but a few. One cannot say that no two humans are alike. There is remarkable similarity and consistency in human behavior. If this were not so, it would be impossible for us to speak of human society as orderly and predictable. Still the matter of selecting a sample of individuals who are similar in all ways except for the one difference to be studied is no easy matter.

The scientific method helps to overcome the difficulties posed by human diversity. It is one way of striving to cope with the limitations of social science and the inevitable problems of bias. However, three additional problems also confront social scientists: (1) The question of whether humans are determined or free; (2) the question of whether scientists can always remain ethically neutral; and (3) the question of the extent to which scientific theories restrict the ability of scientists to discover reality. The remainder of this chapter considers each of these problems briefly.

Are Humans Determined or Free?

As scientists develop the tools and the know-how to control social variables and explain social behavior, the question arises: Are humans determined or free? This is not merely a philosophical question; rather, it engages today's sociologists in an active continuous dialogue. For example, Peter Berger argues that social science proceeds as if human behavior can be explained as completely as physical matter. This supposition leads to the notion that eventually all the variables that determine social behavior (for example, cultural context, family and child-rearing experiences, social class and occupation, level of education) will be discovered and investigated and, consequently, we will be able to explain how all human social behavior (religious behavior, for example) is determined. Berger criticizes sociology as a discipline when it tries to be so scientific that it studies humans as if they were mere prisoners and puppets of society.

> One chooses one's gods by choosing one's playmates. . . . Our bondage to society is not so much established by conquest as by collusion. . . . The walls of our imprisonment were there before we appeared on the scene, but they are ever rebuilt by ourselves. We are betrayed into captivity with our own cooperation [Berger, 1963, pp. 120–121].

The overly deterministic view of society loses sight of humans as free agents capable of nonconformity. Berger resents this and insists that human behavior is not completely determined; indeed, it is potentially creative and free. People are free to say "no" to the expectations of society and to perform as living actors rather than as prisoners or puppets. Thus we must think of "society as drama"—a perspective that sociology finds difficult in its struggle to be scientific.

Some sociologists welcome Berger's challenge to the discipline, while others, like Philip Selznick, call it a caricature of sociology and science:

> That men are living actors and not puppets is an essential premise of sociological inquiry, and no "dramatic" imagery is needed to undermine that truth. . . . The idea that sociology presents a rigidly deterministic image of man as a "prisoner" or "puppet" does no small disservice to the reputation of sociological theory and research. [Berger] has not fully absorbed the significance of studying *variation* as a decisive phase of inquiry [Selznick, 1964, p. 285].

Whereas Berger indicates that sociology cannot easily explain freedom in its analyses of behavior, Selznick insists that it is possible to study freedom in two ways: (1) We can identify the free person and the free group as phenomena, marked by autonomy, self-confidence, the capacity to use reason, and more that we do not yet fully understand; and (2) we can study the social conditions that make people and groups more or less free. It is an empirical fact that humans deliberate and decide between alternatives; they are free to do so. But it is also true that they decide within limits set by social conditions. How these conditions help to determine human choices can be studied scientifically. The problem, then, concerns not freedom versus determinism but rather freedom within what limits. More than this, Selznick challenges Berger's implication that "sociology properly speaks in the accents of alienation and that redemption is found when man is in society but not of it." At this point in the dialogue between these two scholars, Selznick makes a provocative reference to the risk of unrecognized bias:

> There is a religious conclusion latent here, and one that I respect. But I am sorry to see the study of man thus cruelly mocked in the interests of an unspoken theological premise. Sociology is indeed a humane discipline, above all because so large a part of what we do looks to the person as the touchstone of worth. On the other hand, it is wrong to seek in sociology a "personal" philosophy, whether of alienation or affirmation. For most of us, sociology pursued in a scientific spirit is its own humane justification. And that spirit commits us to a progressive erasure of special motifs and perspectives [Selznick, 1964, p. 286].

Can Science Be Ethically Neutral?

Sociologists confront the problem of ethics and moral responsibility as do all scientists. In striving to eliminate bias and achieve a value-free stance, there are at least two risks: (1) the risk of self-deception and (2) the risk of abdicating social responsibility. Both are related to ethical questions and scientists cannot escape them.

The first calls attention to the fact that scientists are never as objective and neutral as they may think they are. Scientists are first of all human beings with emotional commitment to the values of their own culture. They work not in a timeless vacuum but rather in the social context of their age and society. J. W. N. Sullivan [1949] has good grounds for suggesting that the founders of modern science, like Copernicus, Kepler, and Galileo, reflected a kind of "innate prejudice" of their times when they fastened upon mathematics as the key to the universe. They singled out from the total human experience those elements that could be measured quantitatively, and they exalted the mathematical method as science. Obviously, such a tendency does not imply complete neutrality but rather the influence of the prevailing philosophical perspective of the time and culture. Scientists have never been as value-free as they might think. New trends in modern science have corrected this early emphasis upon measurability as the essence of truth. Certain contemporary scientists are insisting that there are other avenues to the truth of existence and life experience. Sullivan [1949, p. 139] points to the humanistic elements that have crept into the writings of some scientists, who admit that science deals with but a partial aspect of reality. An element of free will in the universe is now admitted and determinism has been qualified in the following manner: "The new self-consciousness of science has resulted in the recognition that its initial claims were greatly exaggerated" [Sullivan, 1949, p. 148].

Those sociologists who recognize the validity of this new humility are likely to welcome the words of caution from Max C. Otto [1949]. Modern people have come to worship that which is called science. In fact, "they believe in Science and in what scientists tell them, very much as their ancestors believed in the Church and what they were told by the priests" [p. 90]. An aura of myth and legend has been built up around the "mystery" of modern science so that people approach it with awe and superstition and without question. It has become a kind of superhuman thing to be recognized with ritual and reverence.

This tendency to worship science can be counteracted when we realize that the quantitative method of study limits science to one type of subject matter only. We must also recognize that science is not a purely selfless pursuit of truth. As much as scientists try to discipline themselves with the rigorous method of investigation known as the scientific method, they are still human beings. That they are is most obvious in the humanistic sciences such as sociology, but subjective elements enter research even in physics and chemistry. One of the most subtle ways in which human values enter into scientific work is in the selection and formulation of a problem and in the presentation of the results. Problems tend to be approached according to whatever theoretical perspectives dominate the investigation. Without theoretical guidance, human observation tends to be random and unfocused; with it, our vision sharpens but our larger field of perception narrows. This process is illustrated in the next section.

Scientific Paradigms or Models: How the World Is Viewed

As important to science as the method of inquiry is the development of major paradigms. *Paradigm* has become a very meaningful term in the sciences. It refers to the fact that scientists assume a view of what the world is like and then work within that assumption. This tendency is also characteristic of everyday life, such as when people go shopping and expect to find the stores in their usual place, doing business at customary hours, and staffed by clerks playing customary roles. They have a view of the world—a model or paradigm—that permits them to act with confidence. An earthquake or a social upheaval such as a strike could change all this, but most of the time this model provides a framework for action.

Scientists proceed with similar assumptions when they do research. For a long time, physical scientists conducted studies of the earth according to the Ptolemaic paradigm—the sun goes around the earth. Much of what the Greeks discovered about the world was true even though they worked within a model of the universe that was later discovered to be false. There came a time when the Copernican view corrected the former one, and then scientific work was limited by new assumptions, by a new paradigm.

In a sense, paradigms are a kind of intellectual road map for practitioners to follow when doing their investigations. The map tells them what to look for, how to look, and what might be found. Thomas Kuhn [1970] points out that scientific paradigms exist to define the legitimate problems and techniques of study for succeeding generations of scientists. In the 18th century, the Newtonian paradigm conceived of light as material particles. Later, it was assumed that light was transverse wave motion. Today light is believed to consist of photons that exhibit some of the characteristics of both waves and particles. A scientist will look for different things, look in different ways with different tools, and find different results depending upon whether he or she believes light to be material particles, waves, or a combination of both.

In other words, scholars work within a school of thought. A common assumption of how things work aids scholarly work because it helps trained minds to focus upon problems with a concerted effort. Within the assumed view, all scholars can understand and learn from each other, which stimulates coordinated research and the accumulation of evidence. They all use the same language, operate from the same set of concepts and research tools, and share the explanation of their findings. In this respect, it is essential that scholars have models within which to work, to focus and coordinate their efforts, and to communicate their results.

At the same time, paradigms and models tend to narrow perspectives and to shut out certain information and insights that might have a bearing upon the search for truth. Paradigms, therefore, also restrict the vision of workers and bias the results of investigation. As a result, great leaps forward in the discovery of new knowledge must often await a new view of the world, a new paradigm. Physical scientists may find this to be true as they struggle with questions about the prediction and control of cancer and earthquakes. Social scientists at this moment appear to be searching for new or revised paradigms adequate for the effective understanding and control of poverty, deviance, and environmental devastation. Several of the major paradigm revolutions that have occurred in the field of sociology are discussed below.

MAJOR SOCIOLOGICAL PARADIGMS

Functionalism

For many decades, a sociological perspective known as *functionalism* has prevailed. Functionalism goes back to the beginnings of sociology. Finding inspiration in the perspectives of Comte and Durkheim, Herbert Spencer (1820–1903) developed a theory of social evolution based upon Charles Darwin's view of the survival of the fittest in nature and the evolutionary process. Spencer spoke of a natural development from simple societies to complex ones, culminating in modern industrial bureaucracies. An American clergyman, William Graham Sumner (1840–1910) proposed that social change was a natural organic process, largely beyond the control of human intervention. Societal rules and regulations, the mores and folkways (discussed in Chapter 4), emerged gradually as they were needed. Customs evolved to fulfill functions needed to maintain social order, and this process created inevitable but slow change.

The assumption of this view was that human society is essentially organic. Functionalists maintained that human society, much like the human body, consists of individual parts, each of which functions (that is, does some kind of work) to accomplish specific goals. At the same time, each part is intimately related to all other parts so that the whole organism develops in accordance with natural and predictable patterns.

Essential to any discussion of functionalism are the terms *functional* and *dysfunctional,* which appear frequently throughout this book. When something (a social variable, a pattern of behavior, a process of interaction, a belief) is designated as functional, the sociologist means that it is useful and serves specific purposes for the maintenance of the social system being analyzed. A dysfunctional phenomenon is a disadvantage or detriment to a social system and tends to cause social and cultural disorganization and disruption. For example, John Seeley [1959] suggests that slums are prevalent in modern urban centers because they are functional. To be sure, they are clearly dysfunctional insofar as they encourage school dropouts, vice and crime, poor health and living conditions, and the like. At the same time, however, slums serve useful goals by providing about the only environment within which marginal and outcast members of society may live without creating a continual strain and threat of disruption in the larger community. Drug addicts, alcoholics, indolents, prostitutes and pimps, fugitives, social missionaries, the poor, and unemployed migrants living together in the slum are not a severe daily threat to more middle- and upper-status residents in other areas of the city. The police find it easier to control a group of "deviants" concentrated in a slum than a population of them scattered throughout the city at large. Furthermore, the slum in the past has provided a social context that prepares some citizens for future roles in society (for example, the professional boxer and the ward politician).

The Deviance and Disorganization Perspectives

The functional perspective became so popular in sociology that it spawned a variety of theoretical models during the early years of the discipline. At the turn of the century, American sociologists conducted studies of social problems in the hopes of developing modest reforms to aid the poor and the deviant without disrupting the functioning of the larger society. The *deviance perspective* (discussed in Chapter 12), which developed from this interest, assumed that a certain amount of deviation from accepted norms (even extreme forms) was natural and unavoidable. For example, slums, and the human excesses that took place within them, would always be with us. However, studies might identify the causes of some deviation in the hopes of reforming some residents and of providing assistance to others. Causes of deviance were often analyzed more in terms of societal failure than individual failure—that is, deviance was attributed to social disorganization, or the inability of the existing social system to provide for the needs of its members. This accounts for the close relationship between the deviance and the disorganization perspectives.

In the 1920s, the Chicago School of Sociology concentrated upon studies of urban areas of disorganization (this view is discussed in Chapter 8). *Disorganization theory* assumed that problems arose when certain groups and areas in society began to break down in terms of their norms, rules, and social bonds; the slum was considered one example of this process. In other words, where deviance theory assumed that some problem behavior was unavoidable and natural, and where functionalism assumed that problem behavior could be a meaningful adaptation to special conditions, disorganization theory viewed problem behavior as essentially pathological. The drug use, marital dissolution, crime, and the like found in the slum were considered to be the result of individual or collective pathology. Therefore, scientific study focused upon the measures that might be taken to restore normal healthy functioning in those areas. Urban renewal, for example, was developed as an attempt to reorganize areas assumed to be inherently disorganized.

Symbolic Interactionism

Functionalism also stimulated the creation of other major models of the social system. Drawing upon the work of Austrian psychoanalyst Sigmund Freud (1856–1939), as well as on some of the basic assumptions of functionalism, American social psychologist George H. Mead (1863–1931) proposed the concept of the social self (discussed in Chapter 3) and contributed to the formation of another perspective—*symbolic interactionism.* This view focuses upon interacting individuals, rather than upon an abstract social group, and argues that research should show how people give meaning to concrete social situations. In other words, slums should be analyzed in terms of the different meanings given to life-styles in those contexts by residents and nonresidents.

The research of Carol Stack (discussed in Chapter 4) in an all-black slum in the Midwest provides an interesting illustration. The American white middle class sees slum life as disorganizing, dysfunctional, unnatural, and evil. Therefore, they judge the behavior of slum residents accordingly. For example, when the poor use food stamps for other than the official purpose (that is, to obtain food because one is officially defined as hungry), the middle class sees this behavior as an illustration of deceitfulness and cheating. As Stack indicates, however, survival in a slum context may depend upon an elaborate exchange system among residents of the community. Some families do need food, but others need transportation, baby sitting, furniture, and the like. Since the food stamp program is designed to assist only the hungry, slum residents with other needs have learned to use the stamps as a form of local money with which they buy and sell goods and services among themselves. Far from being cheating, this unauthorized use of the stamps represents a system of survival in a hostile and isolated environment.

Symbolic interactionists studying this situation would be interested in how the interacting residents of the slum interpreted their situation and, thereafter, managed to change or alter it. As a result of its focus, this perspective tends to develop more sympathy for the outcast or underdog than do the disorganization and deviance models. In the same manner, interactionists would focus upon the way in which straight middle-class residents of society define slums as isolated areas of control for the unwanted, uncared for, and different. This is the meaning of the slum for nonresidents.

From the 1930s to the 1960s, social events of such a serious nature occurred that sociologists could no longer explain them fully by use of the more traditional models and perspectives, especially the simple functionalist perspective. Two world wars, an international economic depression, deterioration of the social and physical environment, widespread narcotics use, revolutions of independence, urban strife, and other tumultuous events of the three decades made the notion that all things must somehow be functional and natural, the result of some deviant people, or merely the consequence of social disorganization seem less tenable as explanations.

At the same time, sociologists became aware of the ethical and moral risks in analyses like Seeley's work on the slum. Functional could be interpreted to mean desirable or good. Certainly the slum is good for neither the residents nor the society as a whole. The important question is whether there are alternative values, social practices, and institutions that can be designed to eliminate the slum while still meeting peoples' diverse needs. Can urban life be reorganized, progressive treatment centers constructed, repressive laws and police tactics redefined, employment for all citizens provided? Many sociologists felt that answers to these types of questions called for new theoretical perspectives, for new models and paradigms. As a consequence, the period from the 1960s has been marked by sociological debate, argumentation, and questioning.

Labeling, Social Change, and Conflict Theory

Howard Becker has proposed a *labeling theory* view (discussed in Chapters 3 and 12), which argues that deviants are deviant, not because of inherent and unavoidable forces, but because they are labeled that way by others and eventually come to see and accept themselves in terms of these often arbitrary categories. This perspective argues that a person's behavior is shaped by the expectations of others. When someone who commits a criminal act is labeled "criminal" and then perceives that others now "expect" criminal behavior of him or her, that person behaves accordingly.

This theory is indebted to the symbolic interactionists for many of its fundamental perspectives; that is, people see themselves as others see them. In this view, the way to solve the problem of deviance is by delabeling and relabeling. Modern proposals to decriminalize narcotics use and prostitution are based upon this new perspective.

Radical sociologists have called for an abandonment of traditional functionalism, and scholars like C. Wright Mills (1916–1962) have argued against traditional neutrality on the part of social scientists (discussed in the following section). From this challenge has come a resurgence of interest in scientific theories that view *change* and *conflict* (Chapters 13 and 14) as needed rather than as dysfunctional aspects of the social order. No sociologist denies the importance of change and conflict in human society. However, the more traditional and conservative argue that major changes should come about slowly through fundamental shifts in attitudes and beliefs, and they see conflict as usually being disruptive. Newer views deal with change and conflict as basic processes in and of themselves, with constant interplay between the two. As we will see in Chapters 8 and 13, when change brings about industrialization in rural communities, conflict between management and labor, unionization, and strikes may result.

In contrast to the traditional conservative view, new, more radical perspectives, stemming from Marxism, view the domination of some groups by others as the major fact of contemporary social life. For example, slums must be seen as existing only to benefit a few at the expense of many. Although they are costly to the straight middle class (higher taxes to support increased police protection) and they are harmful to the residents, slums serve the interests of small ruling elites. They become centers for financially profitable illicit activities (prostitution, pornography, drugs, alcohol). Furthermore, slums can be used to restrict the political activities of disadvantaged ethnic groups. By being confined to slum life, many American blacks must concentrate almost totally upon subsistence living rather than upon pressuring the social system for equal opportunity and justice. Radicals also argue that popular myths serve the interests of ruling elites. If residents of slums can be convinced to define themselves as inherently deviant and inferior, they will be less likely to think in terms of revolutionary change.

Therefore, the newer perspectives that concentrate upon social change and conflict maintain that, even if things momentarily look peaceful and unchanging, the potential for violent response is always present in society. The answer to human problems, then, is to make people aware of the nature of power and the positive role that conflict can play in bringing about needed changes in prevailing power structures. For example, the slum will disappear when prevailing economic elites are displaced by new economic relationships that are egalitarian rather than undemocratic.

The major paradigms, models, and theoretical perspectives, together with other important sociological views, are depicted in Table 1–3, which shows the historical development of sociology. This table depicts the com-

TABLE 1-3 Development of Sociology

1800 — 1850 — 1900 — 1950 — 1970s

Selected Contributions of Scientists and Theorists from Various Fields

- **Auguste Comte** (1798–1857) uses tools of natural science to study society.
- **Karl Marx** (1818–1883) writes economic and social critique of capitalism.
- **Alexis de Tocqueville** (1805–1859) analyzes American political system.
- **Ferdinand Tönnies** (1855–1936) studies social organization.
- **Herbert Spencer** (1820–1903) develops theory of social evolution influenced by Charles Darwin.
- **Emile Durkheim** (1858–1917) applies scientific method to study of human behavior.
- **Max Weber** (1864–1920) does classic studies in law history, economics and sociology.
- **Sigmund Freud** (1856–1939) develops psychoanalysis.
- **Robert E. Park** (1864–1944), **Louis Wirth** (1897–1952), and others study urban society in the Chicago School of Sociology.
- **George H. Mead** (1863–1931) develops theory of the social self.
- **C. Wright Mills** (1916–1962) proposes a radical sociology.
- **Herbert Blumer, Erving Goffman,** and others develop symbolic interaction theory.

Periods of Major Theories and Paradigms

- Evolutionism[a]
- Functionalism[a]
- Reformist approach to social problems and interest in disorganization and deviance[a]
- Symbolic interactionism[a]
- Survey research and quantitative methods[a]
- Interest in social conflict[a]

Important Historical Events

Industrial Revolution

American Civil War

World War I

Computer Revolution

Depression

World War II

Korean War

Vietnam War

a The arrows indicate the years of greatest influence for a given theory. For example, although Functionalism is still an important theory in sociology, it was predominant from the mid 1800s to the 1950s. Today it is being challenged by other developing theories.

1-3 Scientific Paradigms and Views of the Slum

Scientific paradigms (world views) are necessary in order to tell investigators what to look for and what might be found. However, paradigms also tend to narrow perspectives and shut out insights that might have a bearing upon reality. For example, scientists using different paradigms view the nature and causes of modern urban slums in distinct ways.

Hap Stewart/Black Star

Scientists using the **functionalist perspective** argue that the slum, with its "bright light" area of prostitution and X-rated movies, is a necessary social safety valve. It provides work for some citizens who might not otherwise be able to obtain employment, and it provides an "acceptable" outlet for the pent-up frustrations of middle-class citizens. Since slums meet some basic social needs, functionalists conclude that they should merely be contained through modest reforms.

Scientists using **conflict theory** argue that the slum exists because of inherent conflict between members of straight society and members of groups defined as deviant or undesirable (criminals, ethnic minorities, uncontrollable individuals, and so on). People defined as undesirable are forced to live in isolated communities where they cannot represent a threat to larger society. The role of the police is to enforce this compulsory isolation. Traditional theorists using this paradigm see conflict as dysfunctional and argue for more humane and compassionate attitudes towards groups defined as undesirable.

John Launois/Black Star

J. Albertson/Stock, Boston

In contrast to functionalists, scientists using a **disorganization perspective** argue that the slum is a result of a breakdown in norms, values, and social bonds. A general pathological condition develops, reflected in blight and environmental deterioration. Disorganization theorists conclude that new forms of social organization (for example, urban renewal programs) are the only way to solve the problems of the slum.

Louis Draper

Scientists using a **radical perspective** reject traditional functionalism and build upon conflict theory. They argue that the slum actually functions to enhance the advantages of the privileged (wealthy slum landlords) at the expense of the underprivileged (racial and ethnic minorities). Radical theorists, therefore, argue for a complete transformation of the existing social, economic, and political order.

petition between various perspectives. This continuing ferment in sociology—the clash of different models and theories—has led to a reexamination of the meaning of the scientific method, its appropriate use, and the proper role of theory in scientific work. It has also lent particular urgency to the question of whether scientists can avoid moral responsibility for the implications of their work.

Can Science Escape Moral Responsibility?

The problem of eliminating unwanted biases, then, is one of the concerns that confronts every scientific sociologist, conservatives and radicals alike. A growing concensus indicates that scientific objectivity in the laboratory does not excuse scientists as citizens and humans from taking part in the crucial discussions of social issues. As Max Otto [1949, p. 106] puts it:

> Ethical neutrality throughout the whole range of science was harmless in Francis Bacon's day because science was relatively powerless. It is not harmless in our day because science is powerful. The means now placed in man's hands by scientific discoveries, if employed without ethical supervision, threaten to make an end of everything worth striving for.

Though Otto is talking about the physical sciences, and especially about the potential of nuclear energy, the same conclusion is applicable to sociological research. Used incorrectly or unthinkingly, theories and findings about deviant behavior, social problems, or merely everyday behavior can be employed to repress and manipulate human behavior in undesirable and destructive ways.

A value-free science in terms of rigorous research, utilizing the scientific method, is one thing. It is quite another thing to engage the findings of science in morally responsible decisions and to recognize the moral implications of using different perspectives of the nature of human group life. Both challenges confront us today, especially in a discipline like sociology. This book focuses upon these challenges by considering sociology to be scientific and to be morally concerned.

CONCLUSION

Sociology and the scientific method have been the focus of this chapter. This consideration comes first in an introduction to sociology because it lays the groundwork for the remainder of this book. Sociology is far more than an interesting consideration of dramatic social events and social problems, although this too is a part of it. Sociology is a rigorous discipline for the study of human beings and human society. It is important to understand this at the outset.

Therefore, we have introduced several of the important sociologists both past and present. We have presented the first of a series of scientific studies in sociology, Durkheim's *Suicide*, as one example of the scientific method in research. Other kinds of research have been suggested in order to anticipate the material in subsequent chapters of the book.

Finally, there has been a good deal of attention given to the most basic of all issues in science, and especially in the social sciences, namely the problem of human bias. This has been done so that we will avoid an oversimplification of the sociological venture. To do research or to observe and analyze human beings meaningfully while remaining objective is not an easy task. This orientation calls for special training and a new way of looking at the human world. Therefore, this new perspective is discussed in depth in Chapter 2, "The Sociological Perspective."

REFERENCES

Babbie, Earl R. *Survey Research Methods.* Belmont, Calif.: Wadsworth Publishing Company, 1973.

Berger, Peter L. *Invitation to Sociology: A Humanistic Perspective.* Garden City: Doubleday and Company, 1963.

Blumer, Herbert. *Symbolic Interactionism: Perspective and Method.* Englewood Cliffs, N.J.: Prentice–Hall, 1969.

Cornut, Roger. Unpublished letter to Ritchie Lowry. 7 October 1975. Information sheets and bulletins contained in letter available from San Francisco Suicide Prevention Incorporated, 3940 Geary Blvd., San Francisco, Calif. 94118.

Cousins, Norman. "The Right to Die," *Saturday Review,* 2 (14 June 1975), p. 4.

Durkheim, Emile. *The Elementary Forms of Religious Life.* Joseph Ward Swain, Transl. London: George Allen & Unwin, 1915.

Feuer, Lewis S. *The Conflict of Generations.* New York: Basic Books, 1969.

Gouldner, Alvin W. *The Coming Crisis in Western Sociology.* New York: Basic Books, 1970.

Keniston, Kenneth. *Young Radicals.* New York: Harcourt, Brace and World, 1968.

Kuhn, Thomas S. *The Structure of Scientific Revolutions,* 2nd ed. Chicago: University of Chicago Press, 1970.

Ladd, Everctt C. and Seymour M. Lipset. *The 1975 Survey of the American Professorate.* A questionnaire mailed to professors nationwide (results to be analyzed and published).

Lenski, Gerhard. *The Religious Factor: A Sociological Study of Religion's Impact on Politics, Economics, and Family Life.* Garden City, N.Y.: Doubleday, 1963.

Lester, David. *Why People Kill Themselves: A Summary of Research Findings on Suicidal Behavior.* Springfield, Ill.: Charles Thomas, 1972.

Madge, John. *The Origins of Scientific Sociology.* New York: The Free Press, 1962.

Merton, Robert. "Social Structure and Anomie," *Social Theory and Social Structure.* New York: The Free Press, 1968.

Miller, Delbert. *Handbook of Research Design and Social Measurement.* New York: David McKay Company, 1964.

Mills, C. Wright. *The Sociological Imagination.* New York: Oxford University Press, 1959.

Nisbet, Robert A. *Emile Durkheim.* Englewood Cliffs, N.J.: Prentice-Hall, 1965.
Otto, Max C. *Science and the Moral Life.* New York: New American Library Mentor Book, 1949.
Seeley, John R. "The Slum: Its Nature, Use, and Users," *Journal of the American Institute of Planners, 25* (February 1959), pp. 7–14.
Selltiz, Claire, Marie Jahoda, Morton Deutsch, and Stuart W. Cook. *Research Methods in Social Relations,* rev. ed., 1 vol. New York: Holt, Rinehart and Winston, 1959.
Selznick, Philip. Review of *Invitation to Sociology* by Peter Berger, *American Sociological Review, 29* (April 1964), pp. 285–286.
Sullivan, J. W. N. *The Limitations of Science.* New York: New American Library Mentor Book, 1949.

- As new nations spring up in the world today, is each one unique? What would the sociologist say? The historian?
- Are unemployment, war, and divorce merely personal problems that require special treatment for the individuals involved? Or are they the result of basic societal problems that require public-policy solutions involving all citizens?
- What makes some groups personal and intimate, while others are impersonal and formal? Why is this difference important for human group life?
- In what way is the family a basic group in all human societies?
- Is illegitimacy primarily the result of sexually promiscuous behavior by young lower-class women?
- Is organized crime today a result of family controlled syndicates, status striving by marginal ethnic groups, a single centralized authority (the Mafia), or the corruption of legitimate bureaucratized businesses?

2

The Sociological Perspective

In the previous chapter, the emphasis was upon the manner in which sociology uses the scientific method. Although other social sciences also strive to be scientific, there are significant differences between sociology and these other disciplines. In this chapter, it is important to point out some of these differences, and then to introduce the discipline of sociology as the study of group life.

SOCIOLOGY AND THE OTHER SOCIAL SCIENCES

Sociology differs from other social sciences primarily in the purpose and scope of its treatment of human behavior. Its purpose is to search for the ways in which all humans are similar to one another and different from nonhuman creatures. Even though each human being has unique characteristics, it is nevertheless possible to *generalize* about certain aspects of human behavior that are universal and apparent everywhere. The best way to make this clear is to start with an illustration.

Sociology as a Generalizing Perspective

The First New Nation is the title of a book about the birth and development of one modern nation, the United States. The author is a sociologist, Seymour M. Lipset [1963]. The book deals with historical incidents and with individuals like George Washington. It is similar to a history book, but there is a major difference: its purpose is to point out how the American Revolution and the nation that emerged therefrom are similar to the new nations of today that have been springing up in Africa, Asia, and Latin America. By studying the United States, the first new nation to break away from the old colonial empires of Europe, we can better understand what is happening elsewhere.

Lipset *generalizes* from a study of America and finds that in the early stages of nationhood people are likely to turn to one strong leader who can pull together diverse factions into a new social order. Every new nation will tend, therefore, to have a "George Washington"—a leader with seemingly extraordinary talents or unusual spiritual appeal who symbolizes the need for social unity. For example, Kwame Nkrumah played this kind of role and became the first prime minister of the new nation of Ghana in 1957, and Ho Chi Minh has been called by many the George Washington of Southeast Asia because of the role he played before, during, and after the Vietnam War.

Lipset also examines other special characteristics of the American experience to determine what factors may encourage a new leader to become a democratic head of state or an authoritarian leader. He sees the level of literacy and the stage of economic development in the newly emerging nation as important (see also Chapter 11). When few people can read and write, and when there is a great gap between rich and poor, there is more need for authoritarian control at the top. Therefore, there is a tendency for many new nations today to begin with dictators. The United States was able to move quickly toward universal suffrage and the balance of power between president, legislature, and judiciary largely because many Americans could read and write and shared a common heritage of individual participation in governmental affairs. Even so, the early colonists in America went through stages of development that can, in general, be expected of all emerging nations.

Lipset's book is an example of the way a sociologist works: interested in historical events not as unique incidents that will never happen again, but as patterns of development in human society that will occur over and over. The sociologist seeks to *generalize and universalize.* Two scholars who spell this out more completely are Pitirim Sorokin and C. Wright Mills.

Sorokin [1947] not only speaks of how sociology differs from history, he also shows how it differs from disciplines like economics. The latter seeks to discover general laws of economic behavior, such as the law of supply and demand. This law states that, for example, when factories produce too many automobiles and flood the market, there is not enough demand for them and prices are expected to decline. Car manufacturers are then expected to limit supply in order to balance it with demand and thereby keep prices high. This is oversimplification to be sure. Nevertheless, it illustrates how economics is also a generalizing science searching for universal patterns of economic behavior, in this case, buying and selling behavior in a relatively unregulated market economy. Economists also assume that workers in such a society are motivated toward jobs that pay higher and higher wages, even if this means traveling to distant places. In other words, human beings are assumed to be "economic beings" or "homo economicus," moved by economic self-interest and utilitarian rationality regardless of religion, morality, family ties, and other noneconomic factors.

Sociology is both similar to and different from economics. Sociology tries to complement economics by looking beyond purely economic motivations to a consideration of the other dimensions of human life. In doing so, sociologists discover that the promise of jobs in large cities will not always lure coal miners away from their families and neighborhoods in the hills of West Virginia. The sense of family and familiar surroundings can be more important than jobs and wages. Sociologists find also that Catholics in Detroit are more reluctant than Protestants to leave their families for better jobs. The spirit of capitalism and individual striving for success regardless of family ties is stronger among Protestants (see Study 4 in Chapter 4). Sociology does not deny the strong influence of economic factors in an industrial society, but it insists upon studying humans as "homo socius" in addition to the more limited perspective of economics. *The sociological perspective, in other words, is more inclusive;* it generalizes from a broader base than the other social sciences. For this reason, it is a very important discipline that integrates the findings and fills in the gaps left by the other more specialized social sciences—economics, political science, human geography, and anthropology. Sociology frequently fills in these gaps in the study of human behavior through the special study of social institutions, morality (mores and folkways), family and neighborhood, peer groups and subcultures, and differences in social class.

Sociology's broad inclusive perspective has great practical value when it comes to devising public policies for complex social problems. Realistic social reform must always take into account the many factors that help to bring about inequalities and injustices. For example, poverty is not merely an economic problem resolvable by purely economic programs. As we will see in later chapters, being poor can be related to such factors as family structure, community life, racial identity, and even religious commitment. Furthermore, trying to relieve the suffering of individual victims of social disorder is but one aspect of social reform; more essential is to perceive the underlying social causes that brought about the suffering and then attempt to change these conditions. C. Wright Mills has made important contributions in this regard through his emphasis upon the universalistic perspective of sociology.

Sociology as a Universalistic Perspective

C. Wright Mills [1959] distinguished between a *personal-troubles* and a *public-issues approach* to the study of human social problems. Personal troubles occur within the individual as a result of unique and limited experiences. Troubles are private matters, colored by the character and uniqueness of the individual, whereas public issues transcend the individual and deal with major social values that affect all members of a society. Institutional arrangements built upon these values are seen as the cause of social problems, and institutional alterations are seen as the cure for the problems.

Mills argued that sociologists make a serious mistake when they study problems as personal troubles, since the real function of the discipline is to utilize a more general public-issues approach. A personal-troubles analysis leads one to conclude that alcoholism, poverty, suicide, crime, and so on are the result of laziness, lack of personal will or integrity, weak character, and the like. In contrast, a public-issues analysis leads one to conclude that these kinds of problems result from a hypocritical state-approved view of alcohol consumption, repressive economic structures, intolerable prison systems, and the like.

Utilizing Mills' concept, William Ryan [1971] has distinguished between exceptionalistic and universalistic views of social problems. The *exceptionalistic* viewpoint sees problems as occurring in particular categories of persons in unpredictable ways. For example, some people explain poverty among urban ethnic minorities as a consequence of inadequate education, illiteracy, and family dissolution *within these groups.* They assume that what results is an unrelated and confused variety of deviance, including crime, sexual promiscuity, drug use, and alcoholism. In contrast, the *universalistic* viewpoint sees problems as resulting from imperfect and inequitable social relationships *in the larger community and society.* Inadequate schools and a lack of adequate community services for urban ethnic areas results in an unbroken cycle of poverty. Furthermore, the universalistic view argues that problem behavior is both predictable and preventable by public action. We know under what conditions poverty might lead some people to drug use, some to alcoholism, and others to crime. In addition, an improved school system and the development of needed community services (employment assistance, transportation, reasonable economic loans) would break the cycle of poverty and make the problem behavior less likely.

Clearly, the exceptionalistic (personal-troubles) viewpoint and programs are easier to use and to devise. This, however, does not negate their validity in all instances. In fact, a dilemma exists in that both the exceptionalistic and the universalistic (public-issues) perspectives are sometimes useful in different contexts. For example, the medical care approach for individuals suffering from (or threatened by) smallpox is exceptionalistic. It is designed to aid and assist only those people afflicted or threatened by the illness, just as the exceptionalistic approach to natural disasters is designed to assist the injured. In the latter case, specially prepared teams of police, medical personnel, and government agents are sent to the town hit by a tornado, the community suffering from a flood, or the city struck by an earthquake. Although such responses will help individuals after a disaster has occurred, it does not show how we might prevent similar events in the future. A smallpox outbreak could be the result of unsanitary conditions that exist because of poverty, corporate irresponsibility, inadequate or ignored governmental regulations, or the like. Most urban flooding occurs because of inadequate utilization or misuse of natural resources, and some cities (like Los Angeles) experience earthquake damage because we insist upon locating them along major fault lines and constructing them in inadequate ways. These latter conclusions require a universalistic viewpoint.

Mills gives further examples of a universalistic public-policy perspective using the problems of unemployment, warfare, and marital dissolution. If only one person is unemployed in a city of 100,000 population, that is his or her personal trouble, which can properly be understood and dealt with by looking at the individual's character, skills, or opportunities. However, when 15 million people are unemployed in a nation of 50 million employees, what is required is an analysis of the major economic and political institutions of the society. In his discussion of the problem of warfare, Mills points out that the personal problems of war involve how to survive it, how to die with honor, or how to contribute to its termination. In contrast, the larger policy issues of war involve its fundamental causes, the nature and characteristics of those who command the war, or the impact of war upon political, familial, and religious institutions. A final example is the problem of marital dissolution. In a marriage, a man and a woman may experience various personal troubles, but if the divorce rate for the society reaches 26 divorces for every thousand women who are between the ages of 14 and 44 (this was the U.S. rate in 1973), a fundamental societal issue is involved. One must then examine the institution of marriage and the relationship of the family to other important social institutions. This latter type of focus is what is meant by the universalistic perspective of sociology. In addition to its generalizing and universalistic focus, sociology is different from the other social sciences in one last and important way: It studies human relationships and group life.

2-1 Should Social Problems Be Resolved As Personal Troubles or As Public Issues?

Exceptionalistic views see social problems as being caused by the personal troubles of particular individuals and groups in society. As a result, programs or actions to resolve the problems are designed to assist the individuals who are suffering or to deter individuals from engaging in the problem behavior.

During the depression of the 1930s, public and private agencies established "soup kitchens" to feed unemployed men. Unemployment was often seen as resulting from a lack of adequate skills, knowledge, or training in certain groups (lower classes, ethnic minorities, newly arrived migrants).

United Press International

The police and other law enforcement agencies conduct raids to seize illegal drugs and arrest users and pushers. The problem of drugs is often seen as resulting from character weaknesses in users and evil motivations of pushers.

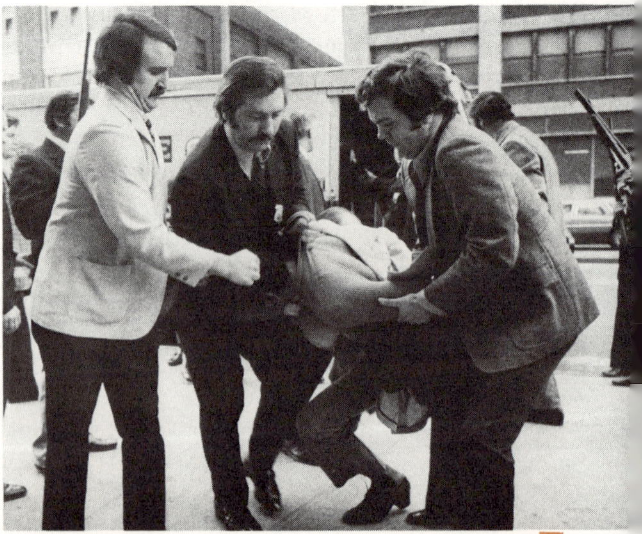

United Press International

Exceptionalistic programs to resolve problems can seem humane or practical, but they do not get at the real causes. A bowl of soup cannot solve unemployment, nor can a few arrests limit the availability of drugs for many citizens.

Universalistic views see problems as being related to major social issues that are a result of imperfect or inequitable social relationships. Universalistic programs or actions to resolve problems are designed to change the fundamental forms of behavior and norms of society in a lasting way.

State Historical Society of Wisconsin

Publicly sponsored work programs can provide the unemployed with jobs and the opportunity to use and develop skills. They can also provide society with important needs (for example, new highways) that, in turn, encourage further economic development (the automobile, gasoline service stations, and so on).

Donald Dietz, Dietz/Hamlin

Some studies indicate that commercial drugs are currently produced at a rate two to three times the expected requirements. Also, television advertising encourages the "accepted" use of "uppers," "downers," and other behavior-altering narcotics. Therefore, illicit drug use is but a small part of the modern drug problem. A universalistic approach would control the legal production and distribution of drugs.

The difficulty with universalistic programs to solve social problems is that they are often costly (work programs) or they cannot be implemented effectively because of special interests (drug manufacturers).

SO WHAT?

Many programs established to solve social problems are both costly and ineffective, partly because they tend to use a personal-troubles exceptionalistic viewpoint (influence the behavior of individuals) rather than a public-issues universalistic perspective (change the social context within which people act). As Amitai Etzioni [1972, p. 45] puts it. "What is becoming increasingly apparent is that to solve social problems by changing people is more expensive and usually less productive than approaches that accept people as they are and seek to mend not them but the circumstances around them." The following examples substantiate this view:

1. A Department of Health, Education, and Welfare study found that, if the total cost of America's driver education programs is compared to the approximately 60,000 annual deaths on the nation's highways, this approach to good driving "saves" lives at a cost of about $88,000 per life. Other studies have indicated that there is little correlation between whether a person has taken a driver education course and later safe driving behavior (as measured by arrests, involvement in accidents, and the like). The one variable that does seem most important is good or bad driving habits by members of a person's family (father, mother, husband, wife, sister, brother, and so on). In contrast to driver education, the introduction of seat belts costs about $87 per life, and studies show that they effectively save lives in automobile accidents. Furthermore, some studies suggest that 10,000 or more lives may be saved each year as a result of lowering the speed limit in order to conserve energy. The major cost involved is new speed limit signs. In summary, driver education courses are designed to change the habits of individual drivers, whereas seat belts and lower speed limits are designed to change the highway context for all motorists, including drivers and passengers alike.

2. American public and private agencies spend millions of dollars annually attempting to persuade citizens to drink alcohol only in "moderate" amounts or not at all, particularly when operating a motor vehicle. Studies indicate that this propaganda and advertising approach is almost totally ineffective. Alcohol consumption continues to rise nationally, and alcohol-related traffic deaths, especially for teenage drivers, have increased. In contrast to the American approach, Norway has severe, but meaningful, penalties for driving while drunk. These include periods of compulsory public work (picking up trash along highways), mandatory jail sentences that do not interfere with one's work (a person goes to jail for the night and is released during the day to go to work), and application of the law without exception (a member of the Norwegian royal family will be equally punished if guilty). As a result, many Norwegians use taxis, or the driver for the evening does not drink when spending a night on the town.

THE STUDY OF GROUP LIFE

The familiar quotation, "No man is an island," dramatizes the fact that one of the most important things about human beings is that they live in groups. They interact with one another and are dependent upon one another. To be human is to be in touch with others; to lose touch is to suffer some measure of dehumanization. Human beings are basically social beings. Thus the study of groups is fundamental to the understanding of human behavior. Sociology is, in large part, the study of human groups.

Groups are many and diverse—family, gang, club, crowd, school, church, job, audience, and so on. It is through the group structure of society that we are socialized; and it is through the group that society patterns human behavior in routinized and predictable ways. The individual and society could not possibly develop, as we know them, were it not for human groups. It is, therefore, important that we define what a group is and then delineate the various types of human groups.

A group is a number of individuals who take each other into account. Thus a group consists of more than an assembly of people who happen to be together on a street corner or on a bus. Some measure of social interaction between the gathered individuals is required. Sometimes the relationships are intimate and long lasting, as in a family. Sometimes they are fleeting and temporary, as in a crowd. Sometimes the members of a group are physically far removed from one another. Whatever the situation, though, there must be interplay before there is a group experience. Human relationships are fundamental if an aggregate of persons is to become a group.

Human Relationships and Group Life

We have seen that Durkheim rejected physiological, psychological, and cosmic explanations of suicide, since these approaches could not explain many of the observable variations in rates and patterns of suicide. Instead he examined various forms of social relationships (marital status, religious affiliation, national origins, occupational status) by drawing upon data from vital statistics and census reports. Such raw data that come from these reports represent categories or *aggregates* of individuals—that is, a certain number married, a given percentage Protestant, a particular ratio of employed to unemployed. Sociologists, then, utilize human aggregates as their basic materials for research.

Also apparent, however, is that Durkheim, in his interpretation of his findings, treated these aggregates as more than simple categories. He implied that being married, a Protestant, or unemployed let individuals enter into specific kinds of relationships with others, both in the same category and in other categories. Those with common attributes shared similar values, beliefs, and perspectives, and when they came into contact they related to one another in terms of these common elements. Population aggregates, then, were seen as the basis from which a complex system of relationships between similar and different individuals could arise.

2-2 Human Aggregates and Groups—The Focus of Sociology

Sociologists use statistical and census reports to obtain basic data for their research. These kinds of reports usually describe **human aggregates**—for example, the number, ages, and occupations of commuters who ride the subway during rush hour in certain cities.

D. Dietz/Stock, Boston

Aggregates consist of individuals who merely possess some common trait (commuting) but who do not have to interact or take one another into account in order to engage in their behavior (riding the subway to and from work). Aggregates, though, form the basis for human group behavior. If the subway were to stop unexpectedly, these passengers might begin to interact collectively in order to find out what had happened and to decide what to do about it.

Once humans begin to interact with one another, human aggregates become **human groups,** the basic focus of the sociologist. In addition, interacting individuals begin to pattern their behavior collectively in predictable and routine ways, though they still remain individuals with special identifying characteristics.

J. Berndt/Stock, Boston

Family or neighborhood groups consist of individuals of different ages and ethnic backgrounds (aggregate traits) who relate to one another in intimate ways (group traits).

J. Albertson/Stock, Boston

Patriotic or community service groups consist of people of different occupations and sexes (aggregate traits) who share common rituals and beliefs (group traits).

If interactionist qualities are not present in an aggregate or between aggregates, sociologists do not call them true social groups. For example, unless all blue-eyed people in the United States conceive of themselves as a distinct grouping, interrelating with one another and others on this basis, sociologists would not use this characteristic to explain variations in human behavior between blue-eyed and brown-eyed segments of a population. In the same manner, all persons who will reach the age of 21 next Monday constitute a statistical category. Sociologically speaking, however, this is not a group. Membership in the 21-next-Monday group will probably never influence anyone's social behavior. Other sorts of capricious and special-purpose categories, such as all American League baseball players with batting averages above .300, do not constitute social groups to the sociologist. Arbitrary classification of individuals into categories based upon some factor of identification is not enough.

When, however, population aggregates begin to interact systematically in predictable ways, they become the focus of sociology because they then are participating in human relationships, which constitute the primary interest of sociological research. The concept of social group implies interaction between two or more individuals. "Group" and "interaction," therefore, are inseparable concepts. As humans relate to one another, they build social systems, which consist of an enormous variety of social groups. These groups become the atoms, and interrelated groups become the molecules of society, thus forming a structure that can be used to explain variations in human behavior.

Social interaction, however, is quite different from the mechanical reaction of atomic particles or billiard balls colliding with one another. Social interaction is the result of consciously taking others into account and basing one's own actions upon this perception. Physicians interact with other physicians, with patients, nurses, hospital technicians, and the general public. Members of a sports audience respond to the cheering of those around them, to the actions of the competing teams, and to the directions of cheerleaders. Individuals in a family interact with one another as brother, sister, son, father, mother, uncle, aunt, and so on. They also interact with other people as representatives of their family. This process is such a basic part of our existence as humans that we cannot even think in other terms. Suppose, for example, you were asked, "Who are you?" Your response would have to be in terms of relationships and groups: "I am a student majoring in the social sciences," or "I am the youngest of three sisters in a professional family." You would conceive of yourself and your relationship to others in interactionist and group terms.

One last illustration of the importance of group life and social interaction highlights the significance of sociology as a discipline that focuses upon these aspects. Have you ever wondered why, when thinking through a difficult problem or when contemplating a future action, such as giving a speech, you often talk to yourself when alone? Though we are individuals, we imaginatively become a microcosmic society of several different interacting selves. Laboratory experiments have disclosed that, even when one's lips do not *visibly* move, the individual still covertly activates the appropriate nerve ends that would produce speech when attempting to solve difficult problems. Related experiments have indicated that deaf mutes who speak with their fingers covertly activate the nerve endings in their fingers during the same situation. Thinking or solving problems is communication or interaction with imaginary roles within one's mind. You imaginatively deliver a speech, listen to yourself delivering the speech, react as an audience might react, and judge your performance in terms of the imaginary reaction. (Chapter 3 will discuss why this happens.)

In studying human relationships and groups, sociologists face the problem of how to limit their horizons—that is, how should they decide what to examine and where to limit the scope of that examination. There are formal groups and informal groups, groups based upon sexual, political, cultural, and racial differences, small groups and large groups, and on and on. Therefore, the first requirement is to identify the basic and fundamentally important types of relationships and groups. Two of the most important are primary and secondary groups.

Primary Versus Secondary Groups

Charles Cooley [1937] first identified *primary relationships* as the form of interaction between individuals that is characterized by "intimate face-to-face association and co-operation." He called such relationships primary for several reasons. First, they are basic and universal to all human societies. For example, some form of intimate and cooperative familylike grouping is found in all societies. Second, the newborn infant's first exposure is to them, and consequently they play a primary role in the social development of the child. Third, and most important, these relationships lead to a "fusion of individualities," to a feeling of belonging whereby one's self becomes identified with the beliefs, values, and purposes of society. Cooley described this feeling as one based upon empathy and characterized by the expression "we."

Cooley felt that the most important primary groups, though by no means the only ones, were the family, the play group of children, and the neighborhood or community group of elders:

> These are practically universal, belonging to all times and all stages of development; and are accordingly a chief basis of what is universal in human nature and human ideals. . . . The religion or government of other civilizations may seem alien to us, but the children or the family group wear the common life, and with them we can always make ourselves at home. . . [Cooley, 1937, pp. 24, 27–30].

However, the notion of intimate and face-to-face association can be somewhat misleading. American sociologist Ellsworth Faris [1932] suggested that persons involved in primary relationships need not maintain an intimate face-to-face relationship in order to sustain a feeling of mutual identification and cooperation, nor is a sense of "we" to be found in all face-to-face situations. Family members communicating by letter over vast distances may be engaged in a primary relationship, though they do not physically confront one another. Interaction between a robber and a bank clerk, a prostitute and her client, or individuals involved in a debate is physically intimate, but it is often far from primary. A primary relationship is one in which persons are uniquely related to one another in personal, informal, and total ways.

Sociologists use the concept *secondary relationships* to refer to interaction that does not possess primary attributes. Primary and secondary relationships can be thought of as opposite ends of a continuum representing all kinds of human relationships. At the primary end, we find personal, informal, and total interaction; at the secondary end, we find impersonal, formal, and partial interaction. Most real world relationships are a combination of both; however, as is the case with all scientific concepts, these idealized types make analysis of the empirical world clearer.

The primary relationship is personal in that it meets the individual's deepest and most meaningful needs. It is an informal situation where one is accepted as a total person, not just for some special purpose. In primary situations, we feel free to discuss our fears, hates, loves, and antagonisms. We are not bound by rigid rules and specified forms of conduct, and we are relatively free to experiment with a full range of human emotions in our interactions with others. In primary situations, we are accepted by others for what we are as total personalities, and, we, in turn, accept and treat others on the same basis.

Secondary relationships are situations in which the individual's personal needs are of little consequence or concern. They are highly formalized patterns of interaction with specific duties and obligations rather rigidly prescribed. Free expression of human emotions is not permitted to play a significant part in the interaction between individuals. Since each individual in the secondary situation must follow prescribed rules for behavior, he or she is important only as a partial self, only for the particular contribution that the individual is expected to make to that situation. This notion of the contrast between primary and secondary relationships is illustrated in Table 2-1.

Table 2-1 highlights the fundamental importance of *both* primary and secondary relationships to the maintenance of social life. Neither is good nor bad, desirable nor undesirable. A judgment about the value of these relationships depends entirely upon the nature of the social situation. Secondary relationships during a game or in the classroom help the teacher, student, and team member to perform their special tasks more effectively. They help maintain a kind of democratic process for the good of the individuals involved. If team members and opponents were to respond to one another during a game in only primary ways, the resultant form of inti-

TABLE 2-1 Primary and Secondary Relationships in Social Situations

	Primary Relationship	Combination	Secondary Relationship
Characteristics	Personal Informal Total	Personal–impersonal Informal–formal Total–partial	Impersonal Formal Partial
Examples	Family	Peer group (team)	Classroom
Interaction	Child–parent	Member–teammate	Student–teacher
Nature	Involves feelings of love, anger, jealousy. Rules of conduct and behavior are broadly defined. Parent–child interaction is spontaneous and ever-changing. Child is accepted for its strengths and weaknesses. The family group, as a whole, is of primary importance. A "we" feeling develops.	During the game, each team member is expected to perform in prescribed fashion, without personal feelings entering in. Each has a specific job to do. After the game, members interact in personal and intimate ways. The team is of importance during the game. Individual members are important too. An "I–we" feeling develops.	Minimum of human sentiments. Student–teacher interaction is rigidly prescribed. Class attendance is taken; students must sit in same seats; teacher is expected to give lectures. Student is judged only on ability to perform on examinations. The classroom is no more important than what the individual student gets from the situation. An "I" feeling develops.

mate interaction could hinder the playing of the game. One might not throw a ball to another, knowing that the latter had a sore hand or was afraid to catch it. In the classroom, primary interaction would make it difficult, if not impossible, for the teacher to judge the academic capabilities of the students rationally. The teacher's grading would be affected by personal attachments, positive and negative, to particular students.

Depending upon the particular social context, both primary and secondary relationships may become crucial to the survival of individuals and the social system. For example, World War II studies of the performance of soldiers during combat indicated that a strong sense of attachment to one's buddies was an important factor in making an effective fighting man. The soldier felt committed to protecting the group, not just himself, in the face of seemingly insurmountable odds. In contrast, research on the Vietnam conflict suggests a highly individualized fighting man, who used solitary routine as an escape from the stresses of warfare [Moskos, 1971, pp. 74–75]. These conflicting findings undoubtedly relate to the different context of the two wars and demonstrate the necessity for both types of human relationships.

The Family as a Primary Group

One of the best examples of a primary group is the well-integrated family. It is not made up of persons equal in age and authority, since parents must take major responsibility. It is not entered into voluntarily on the part of children. Nevertheless, the family is a group that can make possible the most profound emotional ties and evoke the deepest feelings of both love and hate, both harmony and hostility. A brief summary of what sociologists know about the family as a primary group illustrates sociology's focus upon group life and social relationships (also see Chapter 10).

1. *Most people belong to two families—the family of orientation and the family of procreation.* The former is the group into which the individual is born and is reared. At a certain time in life, the individual is launched from his or her first family and, in most cases, moves very soon into a new marriage and parenthood, a new family of procreation.

2. *Family structure differs from one society to another.* In some societies, all blood relatives are closely bound in the large family or kinship group, while in other societies, the individual leaves the first family and establishes a new family in a different location, often quite removed from the kinfolk. We refer to the latter as the small family because each husband and wife leave the kinship unit to set up their own household and live within the nuclear unit. The small family is called the conjugal unit (husband–wife–children) and the large family is known as the consanguine unit (several nuclear units associated in the larger kinship group). The small family is most likely to be found in modern societies, where the individual leaves the family of orientation to seek a job or select a spouse.

3. *Primary ties vary, and there is ambivalence in every family.* Love relationships may or may not be strong in a premodern kinship group, and yet the family is usually held together permanently by social and economic expectations. Divorce may be rare because husband and wife are not free to pursue a job as individuals but are instead inextricably bound to the kinship group; they have nowhere to go apart from the family. In addition, divorce may be considered unethical and virtually unthinkable. By way of contrast, marriage in modern society is expected to culminate a period of courtship during which husband and wife freely select each other on the basis of love.

Not only are there variations in the character of family ties, but ambivalent feelings are likewise bound to occur in the intimacy of any primary group. Close friends or close family members have strong feelings of love and resentment or even hate. When these feelings occur at the same time in the same person, we refer to them as ambivalence. Husband and wife who love each other most of the time can enter into violent disputes. They feel so strongly about each other and have so much invested in each other that they experience strong emotions, both positive and negative. Similarly, parents and children are often ambivalent. Children are utterly dependent upon parents for a long period of time. Responsible parents meet their many needs and a bond of love emerges between them. Thus, there is mutual fulfillment of needs in the family group. At the same time, tensions develop in the best of families. Sigmund Freud hypothesized that some of the love–hate feelings result from rivalries between the sexes in the family. The son resents the father because both son and father are rivals for the mother's love. Freud called this rivalry the Oedipus complex and implied that it could be found in all human families.

His hypothesis has been modified, however, by anthropologist Bronislaw Malinowski [1927], whose studies revealed that hostility within the family appears to stem in large part from the necessity of child discipline. Freud was right when he found almost inevitable hostility between father and son in the Western family (Europe for the most part), but according to Malinowski, this hostility was due not to sex rivalry but to the fact that the father was disciplinarian and exercised authority over the child. To be disciplined and made to conform to group norms of what is right and wrong is painful for the child and resentments build up against the person who must say "No." Malinowski submitted as evidence for his counterhypothesis the fact that in other societies, where the father does not discipline his child, little father–son rivalry seems to exist. For example, among Australian aborigines, the uncle in the kinship group exercises authority over the child and he is the one who is resented. The father in this matriarchal family system works with his family of orientation and merely visits and enjoys his own wife and children. It follows that when families differ in structure from the father-centered family of Western societies to the mother-centered families in other parts of the world, love–hate relationships within the family differ also.

Bernard C. Rosen's research [1962, pp. 612–616, 618–624] on achievement motivation in the United States as compared with Brazil offers convincing evidence of how subtle and significant these deep emotional relationships in the family are. He found that Brazilian boys, on the average, score lower on achievement motivation than their American peers and that this difference can be traced to the contrasts in family interaction. In a Brazilian family, boys are not taught the skills that would help them "to reach the top of the ladder" or to become important nor are they given much chance to become independent. There are three reasons for this lack of motivation: (1) an authoritarian father-centered family; (2) excessive protectiveness, especially on the part of the mother; and (3) early indulgence. Most boys in Brazil do not revolt against the severe father figure but become submissive, and their mothers do not help them to become otherwise. Consequently boys do not learn to do things because their achievements might seem to compete with their fathers'. At the same time, mothers are constantly overprotective and overindulgent. It is common for them to expect much of their sons and to give their sons the im-

2-3 The Functions of Primary and Secondary Relationships

In order to meet the various needs of human individuals and societies, two different kinds of relationships arise. **Primary relationships** are intimate, informal, and total, while **secondary relationships** are impersonal, formal, and partial.

R. Lee/Anthro-Photo

In primary groups, members of all ages and sexes engage in face-to-face interaction in order to perform necessary community tasks cooperatively—for example, the preparation of food in a premodern society.

H. Armstrong Roberts/E. P. Jones

Secondary relationships enable individuals to perform complex work collectively, particularly in the large-scale organizations of modern society. Individuals perform isolated tasks and relate to one another in formal ways (through bureaucratic titles, prescribed seating arrangements, rules governing behavior, and so on). A sense of independence (an "I" feeling) develops in secondary groups.

United Press International

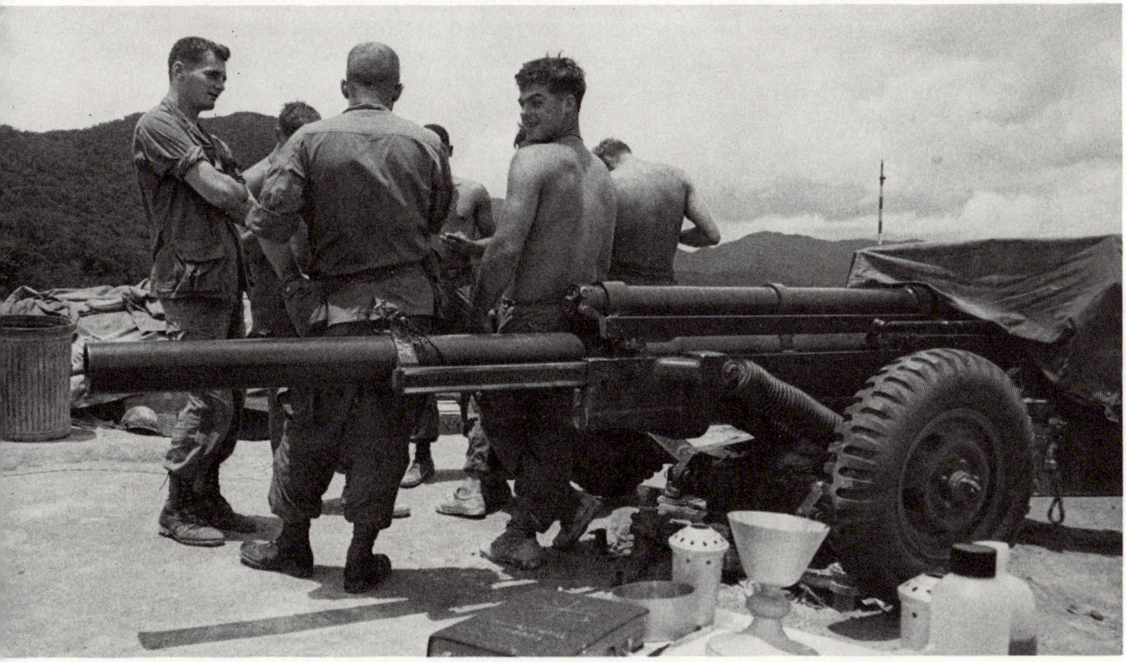

In other contexts, primary relationships provide individuals with a collective identity and emotional support in threatening and hostile situations—for example, in the military during warfare. A sense of dependence upon others (a "we" feeling) develops in primary groups.

pression they will attain greatness. All the while, the boys are not actually being prepared with necessary skills and encouraged to become independent. The result is that, when the boys come face to face with reality and find that they do not have the ability to step into positions of eminence, they soon become disillusioned with themselves and their world. This situation is a likely source of ambivalence, arising from *love* for parental protection and indulgence and *resentment* over parental deception and failure.

In contrast to the Brazilian boys, American boys studied scored higher in aspiration at all social class levels. It is hypothesized that a different family experience helps to account for this. In families in the United States, although the father is often the final authority, he is not so apt to exercise severe dominance, and he is likely to teach his boys basic skills and insist that they become autonomous and do things on their own. Mothers likewise are likely to stress independence training.

In the cross-cultural study of Brazilian and American boys, we have evidence that, although all families are primary groups, the degree and character of primary relationships vary. This difference can have a bearing upon what kinds of persons are prepared for the larger society, whether they are individuals striving for achievement or individuals limited in skills and aspirations.

As the preceding discussion indicates, primary relationships and groups can often be found in unexpected settings, operating in unusual ways. Just such a unique context was found by Clark Vincent in a 1954 study of illegitimacy, used as the second example of a scientific study in this book.

▶ STUDY 2

Unwed Mothers and Primary Relationships [1954][1]

Problem

From 1938 to 1958 in the United States, the estimated annual number of illicit births increased 42 percent (to over 200,000); the proportion of illicit births to all births increased 8 percent; and the proportion of illicit births for unmarried females in the childbearing ages increased 33 percent. By 1973, annual illegitimate births totalled about 407,300 [Bureau of Census, 1975]. Thus, by any measure, illegitimacy is becoming a problem of concern to many.

In his 1954 study, Vincent was interested in investigating the nature of the *relationship between the father and the mother* as an important social factor in *explaining the causes of illegitimacy.* Few previous studies had examined the

[1]Adapted and abridged from Clark E. Vincent's "Unwed Mothers and Their Partners in Illicit Sex," *Unmarried Mothers* (New York: The Free Press, 1961), Chap. 4.

role of the unmarried father. Furthermore, his study also questioned much of the popular mythology about illegitimacy. For example, contrary to general opinion, the increase in the illegitimacy rate was least among young women (15–19 years of age) and most among women between the ages of 25 and 29. This suggested that the popular view of illegitimacy as resulting from exploitation of a young inexperienced girl by an older sexually aggressive man should be critically examined.

Hypotheses and Study Design

As an explanation for illegitimacy, the notion of the father as a sexual exploiter tends to be an *ex posto facto* assumption. This theory is offered *after* illicit impregnation of the female and is, therefore, merely a guess as to the *causes* of illegitimacy. The explanation is a result of prevailing American customs and beliefs. Males are traditionally viewed as dominant. They are expected to protect females and provide for children while women bear the children and care for them. In addition, despite increasing freedoms in modern society, illicit pregnancy is still condemned, although illicit sexual union is often tolerated. The notion of the male sexual exploiter, then, does not explain the cause of illegitimacy. On the contrary, this notion becomes a way in which society can lessen the blame for the woman who must care for the child, strengthen the typical role of the male as dominant, and yet condemn the act as morally bad. The *ex post facto* explanation is a convenient rationalization. What might be an alternative explanation for illegitimacy?

Three working hypotheses can be formulated: (1) *A primary type of relationship is a prerequisite to illicit sexual relations* for those with a high degree of ego involvement in sexual relations; (2) *the development of such a relationship is facilitated by work associations* that provide socially acceptable opportunities for familiarity and privacy; and (3) *the probability of an illicit union* resulting from a primary relationship *increases when the potential male partner's socioeconomic status is higher than the woman's.*

To test these hypotheses, Vincent designed a study based upon interviews of unwed mothers. Information was sought concerning the nature of the relationship between the unwed mother and unwed father and the educational/occupational level of both. Unlike Durkheim, who utilized vital statistics, Vincent relied upon *questionnaire responses* and *interviews.*

Method of Data Collection

Information was obtained from three different sources:

1. A 1954 sample of 201 unwed mothers taken from Alameda County (California) private practice, maternity home, and county hospital care was analyzed to compare the educational level of the unwed mothers with the educational level of the unwed fathers.
2. Another sample of 850 unwed mothers in the Alameda County group were asked in interviews: "What was the relationship between you and the father of your baby?"
3. The occupation of a sample of 531 unwed mothers was compared to the occupation of the male sex partner. These occupational matchings were correlated with the type of relationship between the couple based upon three possible categories—love relationship (primary), friendship (both personal and impersonal), and casual relationship (secondary).

Findings and Interpretations

The three hypotheses tended to be supported. First, of the 850 unwed mothers interviewed, 41 percent responded that they had had "a love relationship of some duration" with the father of their baby; 29 percent indicated "a close friendship relationship"; and the remaining 30 percent suggested that they had had a

TABLE 2-2 How Occupations of Unwed Mothers and Their Sexual Partners Correspond to Type of Relationship Between Them

Unwed Mother's Occupation	Number	Type of Relationship	Occupation of Sex Partner (number)
Nurse	10	Love	Physician (5), salesman (2), serviceman (2), professor
Teacher	10	Love	Teacher (9), serviceman
Lab technician	2	Love	Chemist, writer
Medical receptionist	4	Love	Dentist (2), intern, lab technician
Office secretary	6	Friendship	Salesman (4), serviceman, lawyer
Bookkeeper or cashier	2	Friendship	Butcher, professional sports player
Office clerk, file clerk, typist	14	Love	Office clerk (4), accountant (2), college student (2), store manager (2), engineer (2), salesman, writer
Telephone operator	4	Love	Lineman (3), salesman
Telephone operator	6	Casual	Laborer (3), salesman, brakeman, welder
Waitress	11	Casual	Serviceman (5), waiter bartender, musician, salesman, bus driver, night watchman
College student	33	Love	College student (30), serviceman (3)
College student	9	Friendship	College student (6), mechanic (2), salesman
High school student	14	Love	High school student (8), college student (4), teacher, hospital attendant
High school student	4	Casual	Farmer (2), high school student (2)

Source: Adapted from a table in Vincent's original study, which contains data for 531 cases.

"casual relationship." Therefore, 70 percent of these unwed mothers indicated that some degree of primary relationship was involved. This implies that unwed mothers by and large are not women who have been merely exploited sexually by aggressive men. Rather they are women who have entered into sexual companionship willingly in search of love and meaningful interaction. In some cases, they are women who have been deprived of primary relationships so that they turn to illicit lovemaking to fulfill a basic need. There is, therefore, personal ego involvement in the sexual relationship.

Second, analysis of the sample of 201 unwed mothers showed that the educational differences between the illicit sex partners paralleled the differences between husband and wife pairs in the United States: 56 percent of these unwed mothers were within three years of the same age as the fathers, and 21 percent were four to six years younger. This age difference also approximates husband–wife pairs in the larger population. The oldest males were found to be the sex partners of the oldest, most educated mothers; the youngest males the partners of the youngest, least educated mothers.

Finally, as Table 2-2 shows, unwed mothers reporting a love or primary relationship had partners whose occupations were closely related to, but at a higher level than, their own. Those mothers reporting a friendship relationship had partners whose occupations were less closely related but more equal to their own. Those reporting a casual or secondary relationship had partners whose occupations were at lower levels and not directly related to their own.

Conclusions and Implications

This study points out *the misleading nature of popular mythology regarding illegitimacy,* especially the notion that "evil causes evil." Obviously, the occupational association between man and woman is an important variable in this problem. This does not mean that it causes illegitimacy but rather that it is one of the many complex factors. With the decline in the importance of the family in contemporary society and the rise of the prevalent ethic that considers those working together as "one big happy family," it is not surprising to find that, in many cases, the job has taken on intimate primary characteristics. Individuals are often thrown together in mutual situations of great personal involvement. They begin to act in more personal, less formal, and more total ways towards one another. When sex relations are experienced in this environment, they often tend to be an expression by the female of ego involvement. If it were possible to interview unwed fathers, we might state the same thing for males as well. Although there is no easy cure for illegitimacy, an effectual deterrent seems to be the development, from infancy through adolescence, of a positive self-identity in the female (and the male) through the traditional socializing agencies such as the family.

A special word of caution is necessary. The reader must guard against a tendency to overgeneralize from the scientific studies that appear in this book. Vincent's analysis does not explain all cases of unwed motherhood any more than Durkheim's study explained all cases of suicide for all places and times. In his continuing research, Vincent [1967] has found different patterns of illegitimacy by race and age for unwed mothers. Therefore, social variables other than the mere presence or absence of primary ties influence this form of behavior. Nevertheless, Vincent's 1954 study does show the fundamental importance of primary relationships, even when, according to the popular mythologies of the time, the presence of primary relationships is unexpected.

In summary, sociology is a distinct discipline, somewhat different from the other social sciences, insofar as it focuses upon human relationships and group life. However, although human groups are the fundamental interest of sociological analysis, sociologists have not yet developed a generally accepted system of classifying groups beyond the simple contrast between primary and secondary relationships. Every sociologist (and every textbook) tends to utilize a somewhat different approach, although certain kinds of group behavior, such as the behavior of crowds, gangs, families, institutions, associations, and communities, are recognized by all sociologists as being universally important. Yet these are not merely different types of groups. They have a special relationship to one another and occupy a particular place in the larger social structure in terms of their basic nature and purpose. The next section of this chapter develops a typology of human groups that suggests just what this relationship is and just what place these behaviors occupy in the social structure. Part 3 of this book is organized according to this typology.

TYPES OF HUMAN GROUPS

Rationality in Human Behavior

The basis of our typology of human groups is the concept of *rationality.* As used by sociologists, the concept *rational* does not mean what it implies in popular speech. We typically refer to a person as rational if his or her actions make sense in terms of certain goals, especially if we accept and admire these same goals. Thus, we say that an Adolf Hitler or an assassin is "irrational" or "not rational." Sociologically, the concept of rationality does not denote this evaluative element. Whether a series of human actions are rational or not is determined solely by the fact that the actions are organized by an actor into a planned sequence of interrelated behaviors in order to achieve some ultimate goal, as in this illustration:

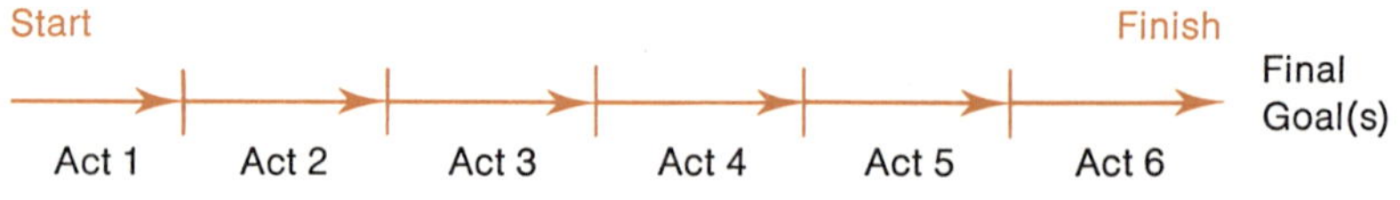

In other words, Act 2 naturally follows Act 1; Act 3 follows Act 2; and so on. After the six acts are completed, the final goal will be attained. For example, when John Smith gets out of bed in the morning, he first washes his face, then brushes his teeth, then gets dressed, then eats breakfast, and so on. All these individual acts are done in interrelated sequence so that John can awaken himself and get to work. In that sense, his early morning

Table 2-3 Types of Human Behavior Arranged by Degree of Rationality Present

	Irrational	Nonrational	Rational
Type of Individual Acts	Unrelated, random, haphazard	Related, but often often unthinkingly	Deliberately related
Goals	Absent	Present, but often unstated	Present and overtly recognized
Origin of Behavior	Spontaneous, unanticipated	Spontaneous, but structured and organized	Deliberately planned
Resulting Behavior	Loss of control	Unconsciously organized; therefore often emotional	Consciously organized, therefore usually unemotional
Examples	Extreme psychosis or collective hysteria	Action of a crowd at an athletic event	Scientist conducting an experiment using the scientific method

behavior is rational, whether or not going to his job is a sensible thing, and whether or not he is interrupted along the way by some other event.

By defining rationality in this way, it is possible to conceive of all human behavior as falling into three broad overlapping categories: irrational, nonrational, and rational. These types of behavior are compared in Table 2-3. Because irrational behavior is unordered and usually unpredictable, it cannot really be analyzed scientifically; however, luckily it is rare. Humans most often organize and pattern their behavior. Therefore, sociologists are fundamentally interested in nonrational and rational forms of group action.

The distinction between nonrational and rational behavior is largely one of degree. Humans may, through a series of adjustments to their environment, find themselves aligned in group action on a spontaneous, nonplanned basis. On the other hand, they may consciously and deliberately plan their group behavior. The German sociologist Ferdinand Tönnies (1855–1936) has employed this distinction in describing the differences between "natural will" (*Wesenwille*) and "rational will" (*Kurwille*). Natural will is associated with emotional and impulsive action, whereas rational will is associated with action in which means are arranged and deliberation becomes important. A host of other writers in sociology and psychology have employed somewhat similar notions. For example, we have considered Charles Cooley's distinction between informal emotional primary relationships and formal contractual secondary relationships. Primary relationships involve the spontaneous and emotional characteristics of nonrational behavior; secondary relationships are deliberately and unemotionally planned and organized in a rational way.

Human group behavior, therefore, may arise in a spontaneous, unplanned, and emotional way, or it may be the result of deliberate, planned, and structured actions. In both cases, however, the behavior has pattern and form, which makes analysis possible. For example, we can detect the difference between the spontaneous and emotional outbursts of a crowd at an athletic event with the deliberate and planned actions of speakers in a formal lecture presentation. However, *each type of behavior is predictable* because it follows general patterns and forms. We can describe with equal accuracy typical crowd responses at a professional football game to actions of the referees or teams and the behavior of speakers at a formal lecture.

To distinguish between these two basic categories of group behavior, we shall refer to the former as *more spontaneous* and the latter as *more structured.* In other words, some types of human groups are largely spontaneous in nature (mobs and crowds); others are more structured (large-scale organizations in political life and business, the military bureaucracy of the Pentagon); and some are *combinations* and mixtures of both elements (private clubs and pressure groups). Furthermore, some groups tend to retain their basic nature as more spontaneous and/or more structured through time and from one social setting to another. A crowd at a modern rock concert, political demonstration, or sporting event and an ancient Roman crowd in the Circus Maximus could be characterized as essentially spontaneous, and this quality would influence the behavior of the individual American or Roman in the same general manner. Standard Oil of New Jersey and the Pentagon are both large-scale organizations, highly structured in nature, and, therefore, the behavior of business or military bureaucrats within these organizations will show common patterns and characteristics.

Finally, there is one additional type of group, a variation of the combinations category, which also tends to fall between the extremes of largely spontaneous and mostly structured behavior. Groups of this type are often marked by varied and complex mixtures of spontaneous emotional and deliberate organized action; however, unlike combinations, their nature as mostly spontaneous or structured will vary over time and from one social setting to another. To distinguish this type of behavior, we shall use the term *changeable* groups. Examples of such groups can be found in the status systems (classes and castes) and the communities (villages, towns, and cities) of societies. Status groupings can vary from spontaneous class interaction in an emerging industrial nation, through the relatively informal but nevertheless quite effective practices of discrimination and segregation in some parts of the United States, to the highly organized and deliberate patterns of exclusion in the traditional caste system of India. Similarly, communities range from primary like villages to secondary, highly formalized megalopolitan clusters. Furthermore, large cities and complex caste systems include within their organization elements of many or all of the other kinds of group behavior—spontaneous, structured, and combination forms.

A Typology of Human Groups

We can now construct a typology of human groups that categorizes behavior according to whether it falls into one of two polar types, depending upon the degree of spontaneity or rationality present; whether it consists of combinations or mixtures of the two extremes; or whether it is changeable in nature. This categorization is represented thusly:

More Spontaneous Forms		Combinations		More Structured Forms
COLLECTIVITIES	←→	ASSOCIATIONS	←→	INSTITUTIONS

← (Changeable Forms: STATUS GROUPINGS, COMMUNITIES) →

Not all sociologists would agree completely with this typology. It is used in this book to make orderly discussion of human group life possible. In addition, although primary relationships are often associated with more spontaneous forms of group behavior, and secondary relationships with more structured forms, both primary and secondary relationships may be found at almost any point in the spectrum of human groups.

As this typology suggests, *collectivities, associations,* and *institutions* are three of the most fundamental and basic forms of human groups that sociologists study. *Status groupings* and *communities* represent the two additional forms that combine in complex and diverse ways attributes of the others. Much of the text that follows will be concerned with discussing in detail each of these types of groups and their impact upon human behavior in detail. These groups can be found in different societies in the forms listed in Table 2-4.

TABLE 2-4 Examples of Basic Types of Human Groups

Type of Group	Examples	Type of Group	Examples
Status groupings	Classes Castes Estates	Collectivities	Populations Mobs Crowds Audiences Publics Social movements
Associations	Clubs Small families Pressure groups Service organizations Sects and denominations	Communities	Villages Towns Cities Suburbs Metropolises
Institutions	Large kinship groupings Schools and universities Church establishments States and nations Large corporations		

Another caution is also worth noting at this point. Real world examples of groups do not always fit neatly within single categories. For example, audiences are often organized and planned within the framework of an institution, such as the university, and may gradually become purposeful and more structured. However, audiences bring together an aggregate of individuals, usually strangers, who interact with one another in emotional ways and for short periods of time. In most respects, then, all audiences are collectivities. Whenever we work with typologies in social science, we must expect to find exceptions and to make qualifications. Actually, we tend to talk in terms of what Max Weber called *ideal types*—that is, conceptions about the real world abstracted from empirical observation and idealized. In the real world, most human group life contains complex mixtures of all types of behavior. It is necessary, however, to distinguish the various types in order to detect order and pattern in the complexity.

To complete our typology, we shall delineate the criteria needed to describe the important differences between the various groups. Groups possess four basic distinguishing characteristics: (1) The manner in which they are formed; (2) their internal structure and organization; (3) their function or purpose; and (4) their typical life span or duration. Each of these characteristics tends to vary according to degree of spontaneity exhibited by group members. As we have already seen, groups may be impulsive or deliberate in their formation. In addition, they may be structured and organized in informal and personal ways or through highly formalized and rigidly prescribed patterns of interaction. Groups may serve purposes that are single and specific, or varied and general. These purposes or goals can also be private (serving the group's own interests) or public (transcending the personal interests of group members). Finally, the life span or duration of a group may range from hours or days to many years or generations.

There is, in addition, a relationship between these criteria. If a special issue confronts the citizens of a community, they may rapidly form a pressure group to deal politically with the problem. The purpose of this group, which arises out of a spontaneous and emotional reaction to the issue, are specific, private, and special. Thus, once the issue has been settled to the satisfaction of those interested in it, the group disbands. Compare this to a church that has a long history and tradition of generations. Its purposes are many and varied and may include a parochial school and recreational facilities. It may have a high degree of formal organization, which may include ties to a national and international institution. The church, as a group, outlives the lifetime of its individual members.

The various characteristics of the basic types of human groups and the relationships between them are depicted in Table 2-5.

Use of the Typology in Sociological Analysis

In addition to providing a way of discussing the work and research of sociologists, the typology will be employed throughout this book as an aid to

TABLE 2-5 Characteristics of Human Groups According to Basic Type of Group

Characteristic of the Group	More Spontaneous	Classification and Type of Group: Combinations and Changeable Forms			More Structured
	Collectivities	*Status Groups*	*Associations*	*Communities*	*Institutions*
Formation	Less rational; emotional response to stimuli in the environment	Often spontaneous, followed by conscious behavior that can become highly structured	Planned and deliberate, but involving emotion and intimacy	Planned and/ or spontaneous	Most planned and deliberate form of behavior; more rational
Structure and Organization	Elementary; informal and more unstructured; emotional involvement	Informal, but can become highly routinized and formal	Both informal and formal	Can be both formal and informal; often becomes highly formalized	Highly formal; development of bureaucracy
Function and Purpose	Single and extremely limited in scope	Purposes broaden but remain basically private	Can have single or multiple purposes but private in scope	Many purposes, which can become public in scope	Many public purposes
Life Span	Very short; minutes and hours, rarely days	Longer than that of collectivities, depending upon eventual form	As long as private purposes of group are served or redefined	Many generations	Duration of the group may be indefinite

analysis of human behavior. For example, particular forms of groups may vary in nature from one society to the next and from one period of time to the next. Families in modern America are basically associational in nature, whereas larger kinship groupings in traditional societies are institutional. This distinction can tell us much about the different functions of familial groups in various social contexts. The existence of differences in types of groups also tells us something about the rise and development of major social movements. The labor movement in the United States has been characterized as a transition in behavior from early collective action (informal gangs clashing with police), through associational action (private organizations competing for power with others), to a contemporary, more institutionalized nature (a part of the major American power structure).

Typologies of this kind have provided ways for sociologists to analyze major social problems in a provocative and creative manner. For example,

Daniel Bell [1953, pp. 131–154] and other scholars [Ianni, 1971, p. M25] have applied the same kind of concepts to studies of organized syndicated crime in America. Early immigrants to urban communities, particularly from Southern European countries, faced the problem of adapting to different social and cultural demands. For many of these new citizens, crime became functional. Marginal activities (numbers rackets, selling protection, prostitution) were among the few avenues open to them for status mobility. Some youths formed street-corner gangs (see Study 3 in Chapter 3) to gain a sense of identity and achievement. Some families became the basis for early involvement in criminal activities and, thus, the "myth" of an American Mafia was born.

Through the years, both the nature of crime and the position of the immigrants changed. Crime became institutionalized. Businesses and political organizations used prostitution as a fringe benefit for clients. Gambling became more respectable. Crime became a part of the American commercial and consumption ethic. At the same time, family syndicates were increasingly involved in legitimate enterprises. Organized crime today is thus a curious result of a variety of historical processes, beginning with the spontaneous collective response to a new environment, and followed by integration into a prevailing status system; involvement with strong community and family-based ties; patterning after American associational behavior; and the institutionalization of underworld pursuits. (Chapter 12 deals with crime in more detail.)

In the chapters that follow, we will be using this same type of analysis to trace patterns of social change for a variety of groups. We will see in what ways and under what conditions collective behavior gives rise to associations; how associations become institutionalized; how status systems change from spontaneous groupings to more formal occupational communities. The typology of human groups, then, not only permits analysis of social structure but also aids in analyzing social change.

CONCLUSION

In summary, individuals are starting points for society because, in their interactions with one another, they create a variety of groups to give meaning, structure, and direction to their behavior. Interacting individuals and the groups they form are the basic elements of social structure and the special focus of the discipline of sociology. They are what gives human society its form, content, and order.

To analyze the form and content of society, sociologists use general and universal perspectives. They search for universal social elements whose arrangements are predictable, given specific social contexts. They also focus upon a public-issues rather than a personal-problems approach to specific social problems.

Such broad perspectives have identified, among other things, two basic types of social relationships: primary and secondary. Both are fundamentally important and provide humans with the capacity to engage in spontaneous, emotionally expressive interaction, or formal, deliberately planned behavior. The resulting social order can be seen as consisting of five different types of group behavior that are interrelated to one another in complex and provocative ways. Finally, no part of this structure and order is static and unchanging. Therefore, social change and its underlying causes also constitute a particular interest of sociology.

The remainder of the book will utilize the orientation developed in this chapter as a basis for presentation of material. Part 2 discusses two basic elements of the social order that make group life possible: the social self and human culture. This section also dramatizes the generalizing and universal perspectives of sociology. Part 3 contains separate chapters on each of the five basic forms of group behavior. Their origin, nature, and importance are discussed in detail. As an example of the way in which types of groups can be interrelated in complex ways, Part 4 singles out institutions for special consideration. Chapters 10 and 11 in Part 4 discuss the way in which several basic types of institutions both support and conflict with one another in human society. Finally, Part 5 considers three basic types of social processes that account for the dynamic quality of human group life: deviance, change, and conflict.

In short, each major section of the book sets the stage for the discussion that follows. The basic elements of self and culture make various types of group behavior possible. The variety of groups combine and relate in complex ways to give human society its total structure and order. In addition, these types of groups can compliment or compete with one another. These interrelationships also give human society its dynamic and changing character.

REFERENCES

Bell, Daniel. "Crime as an American Way of Life," *Antioch Review, 13* (Summer, 1953), pp. 131–154.

Cooley, Charles H. *Social Organization.* Elsie Jones Cooley, Ed. New York: Charles Scribner's Sons, 1937.

Etzioni, Amatai. "Human Beings Are Not Very Easy To Change After All," *Saturday Review, 55* (3 June 1972), p. 45.

Faris, Ellsworth. "The Primary Group: Essence and Accident," *The American Journal of Sociology, 38* (July 1932), pp. 41–50.

Ianni, Francis A. J. "A Crime Family's 65-Year Journey Into 'Legitimacy,'" *The New York Times* (29 May 1971), p. M25.

Lipset, Seymour M. *The First New Nation.* New York: Basic Books, 1963.

Malinowski, Bronislaw. *Sex and Repression in Savage Society.* New York: Harcourt, Brace and World, 1927.

Mills, C. Wright. *The Sociological Imagination.* New York: Oxford University Press, 1959.

Moskos, Charles C., Jr. "Men Under the Gun," *Transaction* (now *Society*), *8* (July–August 1971), pp. 74–75.

Rosen, Bernard C. "Socialization and Achievement Motivation in Brazil," *American Sociological Review, 27* (October 1962), pp. 612–624.

Ryan, William. *Blaming the Victim.* New York: Pantheon Books, 1971.

Sorokin, Pitirim A. *Society, Culture and Personality.* New York: Harper & Row, Publishers, 1947.

U.S. Bureau of Census, *Statistical Abstract of the U.S., 1975.* Washington, D.C.: U.S. Government Printing Office, 1975.

Vincent, Clark E. "The Pregnant Single College Girl," *The Journal of the American College Health Association, 15* (May 1967), pp. 42–54.

▶ KEY CONCEPT REVIEW

To aid you in mastering the basic concepts of Part 1, we have organized key terms into convenient and logical conceptual networks.[1] The following study procedure is recommended:

1. Quickly scan each cluster of terms noting their organizing label. Try to get a sense of how they are related.
2. Try to define and give an example of each term. If you have a study partner, you can do this orally.
3. Check your definitions and examples against the review that follows. If you are still uncertain about a term, reread the appropriate section in the chapter. Concepts and terms defined in other chapters and reviews are italicized. Also consult the glossary at the end of the book.

CLUSTER 1
The Language of the Social Scientist

Science and the Scientific Method
Social Science
Sociology
Social Variable
Hypothesis
Study Design
Data Collection
Participant Observation
Personal Observation
Survey Research

CLUSTER 2
Organizing Perspectives of the Sociologist

Functionalism
Disorganization
Deviance
Labeling Theory
Conflict Theory
Symbolic Interactionism

1. The Language of the Social Scientist

	Definition	Example
Science and the Scientific Method	The unbiased systematic study of social and physical phenomena. Ideally, scientists are expected to work with an attitude of openness, cooperation, skepticism, objectivity, and amorality. They are also expected to employ a systematic problem-solving method involving: (1) defining a problem; (2) formulating testable hypotheses and a suitable study design; (3) selecting data collection techniques; (4) gathering, ordering, and analyzing data, and presenting empirical findings; and (5) drawing conclusions that have broad theoretical implications and can be retested by other scientists.	Social scientists, combining rigorous investigative techniques with an open-minded spirit of inquiry, have questioned scores of popular beliefs, many of them considered to be "self-evident" truths, concerning human social behavior. The research reviewed in this text, for example, was instrumental in qualifying such widely accepted myths as the following: (1) Illegitimacy is usually the result of evil older men who sexually dominate innocent young girls (Vincent, Study 2); (2) as organizations grow in size, the "iron law of oligarchy" causes power to concentrate among fewer and fewer leaders

[1]For a more complete discussion of this feature of the text, see the Preface.

	Definition	Example
		and mass apathy to prevail among the grass-roots members (criticism of Michels' theory, pp. 267–273); and (3) black slum families are characteristically lazy, apathetic, and lacking in personal initiative (Stack's study of The Flats, pp. 141–145).
Social Science	The branch of science that attempts to explain human behavior at both the individual and group levels. Social science is subdivided into several disciplines, each of which focuses upon particular aspects of human behavior.	The disciplines usually considered social sciences are anthropology, economics, human geography, political science, psychology, and sociology. Historians also often use social scientific methods.
Sociology	The scientific study of human social life. Sociologists study the social *self,* social *roles,* social *interaction, culture,* and forms of *group behavior.* Whereas the other social sciences tend to focus upon only one area of human behavior (economic, individual, political, and so on), sociology integrates findings from all of the social sciences in its attempt to be a universalistic view of human social life.	A sociologist studying inner-city ghetto life (as William Whyte did in Study 3), might conduct interviews with residents, observe daily life and interpersonal relationships, and study vital economic, political, and legal documents. In this way, the sociologist could describe the following: the self-conceptions of residents; important social roles in the ghetto; kinds of social relationships; the norms and values of ghetto life; and types of group behavior. This description would lead to an integrated and broad-ranging view, which could become the basis for generalizations about human life in other similar ghettos.
Social Variable	Any measurable characteristic that describes shared and regularized patterns of social behavior. Social scientists manipulate variables by observing how they change from one role to another, from group to group, from place to place, or over time.	Variables are characteristics such as sex, race, age, income, occupation, religious affiliation, place of residence, and so on. Durkheim studied differences in suicide rates (patterns of social behavior) by looking at the variables of nationality, marital status, religious affiliation, occupation, and education (Study 1).

	Definition	Example
Hypothesis	An unproven statement about a relationship between two or more variables, which can be empirically tested using the scientific method. A hypothesis is often referred to as an "if–then" statement. For example, if certain variables are present, then a specific social behavior will result.	An example of a hypothesis is the following: Students tend to become more distrustful of authority after taking a course in sociology. In other words, if the variable of having had a sociology course is present, skeptical attitudes will result. How would you design a scientific test of this hypothesis?
Study Design	A researcher's plan for collecting and analyzing data in order to test hypotheses.	To test whether taking a course in sociology makes students more distrustful of authority, a researcher might (1) interview a sample of students about their attitudes toward authority before and after taking a sociology course; or (2) observe the behavior of students towards authority figures (teacher, parents, and so on) before and after taking a course.
Data Collection	The methods used to collect information, as they relate to the hypotheses and the study design. In sociology, the most widely used data collection techniques tend to be documentary research, interviews, participant observation, personal observation, and survey research.	In the above example, the interviews with students could be either (1) structured or (2) open-ended. Public opinion polls regarding peoples' attitudes towards authority might provide pretested questions that could be used. Decisions about these aspects of the study would involve the question of the best method of data collection.
Participant Observation	A data collection technique in which the researcher actually becomes a participating part of the group life being studied. By being intimately involved, the researcher gains first-hand knowledge and insights that might not otherwise be observed. At the same time, by being a part of the study, a researcher might bias the results because of personal actions or feelings.	William Whyte (in Study 3) and Ritchie Lowry (in Study 8) studied the life of street gangs and small-town leaders by actually living among these groups and participating in their activities for several years. The question is: Can either Whyte or Lowry be completely unbiased about the attitudes and behavior of people who were their friends (and enemies)?

	Definition	Example
Personal Observation	A data collection technique in which the researcher observes behavior as inconspicuously as possible. In contrast to the participant observer, who seeks involvement with the subjects of the study, the personal observer avoids involvement in order to remain detached and not to influence the results of the study.	Child development laboratories frequently have special playrooms equipped with one-way mirrors, behind which researchers study the childrens' natural behavior. If researchers were in the same room with the children, the play patterns might be influenced by the presence of adults. Industrial efficiency experts sometimes disguise themselves when studying worker productivity, since workers tend to act differently in the presence of management personnel.
Survey Research	A data collection technique in which the researcher administers a set of questions (usually pretested) to a *sample* of a group or population, using highly structured questionnaires or personal interviews.	The National Census, taken every 10 years, is an example of extensive and continuing survey research. It involves the use of both door-to-door interviewers and mailed questionnaires. Public and political opinion polls (Gallup, Harris, and so on) are also examples of survey research.

2. Organizing Perspectives of the Sociologist

	Definition	Example
Functionalism	This perspective views society as an organic system, which, like the human body, is composed of many interrelated parts. Each part functions (1) to maintain itself and (2) to satisfy some basic need that is vital to the stability of the overall system. Functionalists, therefore, focus upon the positive contributions every part of a society makes to the whole.	In studying a city's red-light district, a functionalist might point to the fact that it serves as a necessary safety valve by providing (1) an outlet for pent-up sexual urges (prostitution and porno theatres); (2) a compact area within which society's threatening deviates (drunks, drug addicts, perverts, and so on) can be corralled and controlled; and (3) a meaningful home and haven for such people until some are able to remove themselves or become rehabilitated.

	Definition	Example
Disorganization	This perspective views social problems as resulting from the breakdown of the existing social order. Disorganization results when people reject existing *norms, values,* and *institutions.* Like functionalists, those using a disorganization perspective tend to see the normal social order in a positive light, since it represents order and control. Disorganization is seen as abnormal and a threat.	Someone with a disorganization perspective might view a city's red-light district as evidence that the family and church are failing as effective social institutions. Prostitution might be seen as reflecting the family's inability to control sexual behavior, and bars as evidence of ineffective religious training.
Deviance	This perspective assumes that a certain amount of deviation from accepted *norms* (even extreme forms) is natural and unavoidable. It assumes that human nature itself contains the seeds of deviance (for example, Mead's volatile aspect of the social *self,* pp. 86–90. It also assumes that some deviance is desirable or necessary and that some subcultures naturally encourage deviance.	Someone viewing the red-light district from a deviance perspective might study (1) personal sources of deviance in individual alcoholics, prostitutes, criminals, and so on; (2) the way in which prostitution is the only source of income for some women or alcoholism the only release for anxieties for some men; or (3) the red-light district as a subculture that encourages deviant behavior as a new norm.
Labeling Theory	Labeling theorists maintain that social labels or names (smart, stupid, bum, violent, and so on) have a powerful influence on individual behavior when the label is internalized into one's *self* concept. Once society labels an individual, and the label is internalized, that person begins to modify his or her behavior in order to fit the prescribed *role.*	A labeling theorist might look at the various deviates within the red-light district and hypothesize that society has driven many of them there by (1) defining their behavior as undesirable; (2) rejecting them, causing them to accept and internalize the deviant image; and (3) forcing them to seek out one another and form a deviant subculture to survive.
Conflict Theory	Conflict theorists view society as a collection of self-interest groups, each one consciously or unconsciously vying for power with all other groups. Conflict is seen as a natural and unavoidable outgrowth of human nature and the quest for *power* and control. All human interaction is considered to have a potential for conflict, which is seen as the way to bring about needed changes.	The conflict theorist might view the red-light district as an area where the disadvantaged are corralled and exploited by an unscrupulous self-seeking elite (slum landlords, vice kings, drug dealers, and so on). The only response of the residents is to engage in conflict (sometimes violent) with straight society, in order to change the existing power relationships.

	Definition	Example
Symbolic Interactionism	This perspective focuses upon interacting individuals rather than upon broad abstract groupings, social systems, or institutions. It studies how people perceive, interpret, react to, and alter their concrete social situations.	A symbolic interactionist would study life in the red-light district in terms of its meaning for the individual residents and participants. What meaning do the prostitute and her "John" attach to their brief encounter? What do they experience before, during, and after their relationship? How do prostitutes, pimps, and clients attempt to control and manipulate their daily encounters?

PART 2

Elements of the Social Order

IN PART 1, we saw that human society is made possible by interacting individuals who create a variety of groups. Sociology is a unique social science in that it focuses intently upon this group structure of society. Two central questions related to this focus arc:

1. What is it about human nature that allows individuals to interact in group terms?
2. What causes these various social groups to integrate into a stable and predictable social order?

In Part 2, we will consider two major elements of the social order that provide answers to these questions. Human group life is possible only in so far as individuals develop social selves that are reflections of the larger group nature of society. This creation of social selves is possible because humans can symbolically share values, beliefs, and general rules governing behavior. In other words, they can create a culture. Thus, in a human society, the existence of *social selves* and a *shared culture* make predictable and permanent patterns of interaction over long periods of time possible—in other words, they are essential for the creation of a social order.

As we will see, the absence of animal-like instincts and the capacity for symbolic language play a key role in creating selves and culture. Furthermore, all forms of human behavior are characterized by these two elements, even deviant, unusual, or different kinds of behavior (for example, groups of marihuana users or street-corner gangs).

We will also consider a number of special problems that all societies face. For example, what happens to individuals when the normal processes for creating social selves break down? What happens to societies when subgroups possessing different values and beliefs come into contact with one another? Chapter 3 considers in detail the concept of the social self and the relationship of the self to larger society. Chapter 4 considers the origin and nature of human culture and the relationship of culture to group life.

- ▶ What accounts for the differences between animal and human societies? Is it instincts, heredity, or environment?
- ▶ What are the causes of the generation gap? Is parent–youth conflict unavoidable?
- ▶ Could you guess what the following diverse groups have in common: marihuana users, military recruits, members of Alcoholics Anonymous?
- ▶ Are some people "born" leaders, or do the necessities of group life create leaders?
- ▶ Where would you stand on the following issue?

In 1976, the Methodists held their General Conference representing church members throughout the world. One issue was whether to ordain avowed homosexuals as clergy and approve of their appointments to positions of religious leadership. The issue pertained to men and women and their perceptions of themselves, as they relate to one another and to society.

3

Self and Society

DEVELOPMENT OF THE SELF

The notion of the development of a social self refers to the fact that individuals become "human" not through the biological process of birth but rather through a continual process of relating to other humans in the context of group life. This concept of the self can be summarized as follows: We cannot say that the self *is;* we can only say that it *becomes.* This process of becoming continues throughout life as the individual is successively socialized or readied for each new stage in the life experience. Only when we understand something of this lifelong process of becoming can we begin to comprehend the quality of human nature and the dimensions of human existence.

The Origin of the Self

People are group-related beings who become human through involvement in social life. Durkheim found that a sense of belonging is basic to human beings. Although the belonging experience takes place in many ways, it is most intimate in the primary group, beginning with the human family. Interaction between infant and mother begins almost at the moment of birth and sets the stage for other primary ties that develop within the family and, eventually, with peers.

When the infant is born, he or she comes into the world as an organism with certain biological needs and impulses. Like other animals, the human infant can not contend with the natural environment and must be fed, protected, and housed. However, unlike other animals, humans do not possess instincts that can act as automatic channels to guide infant actions. An instinct is a pattern of behavioral response that is physiologically lodged within the neuromuscular structure of the organism and is transmitted by heredity. Generation after generation of a particular species of bird will instinctively build the same kind of nest, in the same way, in response to the same environmental conditions. Humans build houses because of a basic need for protection but not as a result of any nest-building instinct. They build a variety of houses in all sorts of environments. Animals cannot voluntarily manipulate or subvert instinctual patterns of behavior such as sex. However, humans can control their sex life, even choosing to subvert or rechannel sex completely, as in the case of the priest or nun. Humans can even choose to starve themselves, as did Mahatma Gandhi in his passive resistance to British rule in India.

The newborn human infant is completely dependent upon the social and cultural environment into which he or she is born. This dependence is required not just for the fulfillment of their physical and biological wants but also for their full personal development as human beings. As American social psychologist George Herbert Mead pointed out, the impact of society upon the individual can be most dramatically observed in the first few years of life of the young child. To begin with, the infant has only vague feelings of comfort or discomfort—tissue feelings. In this discomfort, the infant cries and the social world responds. When a parent responds with a dry diaper, warm milk, or affection, there are physical consequences. There are also psychological consequences, especially when a parent responds to the child with love and pride. We sometimes refer to these as overt and covert consequences. The latter are more subtle and hidden, perhaps, but they refer to the parent's love and acceptance, which are just as necessary to the infant's survival as food and physical protection.

When parents respond to the baby's cries and satisfy its physical needs, it is as if they are reading the infant's mind and anticipating needs. Parents are empathizing with another human being and putting themselves into

3-1 Expressions of the Human Self

George H. Mead described the social self as consisting of two competing aspects.

Wide World Photos

Heavyweight boxing champion Muhammad Ali exemplifies the spontaneous, creative, and emotional **"I"** that accounts for human freedom. The "I" enables us to run risks by defying social conventions and, thereby, creates feelings of uniqueness and independence.

Wide World Photos

Public figures, like Marilyn Monroe, also often exemplify the objective and responsive **"me"** that accounts for human conformity. The "me" enables us to act as we believe others want us to behave and, thereby, creates feelings of relatedness to and dependence upon others.

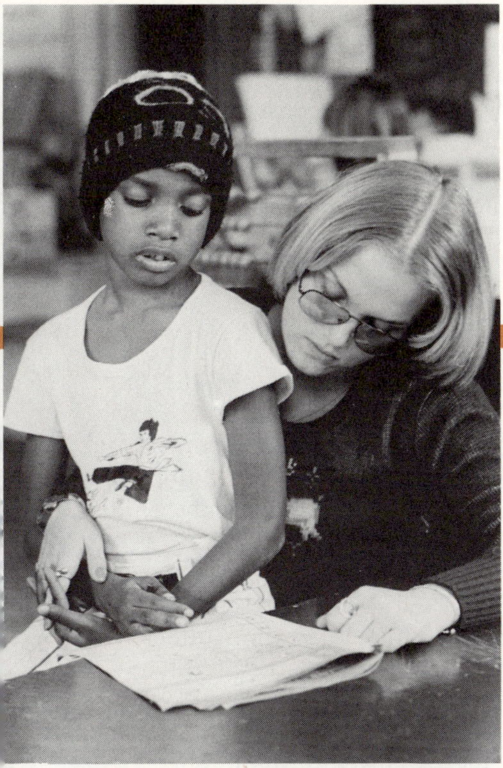

Elizabeth Hamlin, Dietz/Hamlin

Similar to Mead's concept of the "me", Charles H. Cooley described the social self as being the result of the way in which we think others perceive of us.

The **"looking-glass" self** develops when we detect approval or disapproval by others and we alter our behavior accordingly. Young children are particularly likely to be sensitive to what they believe teachers, parents, or friends think of them.

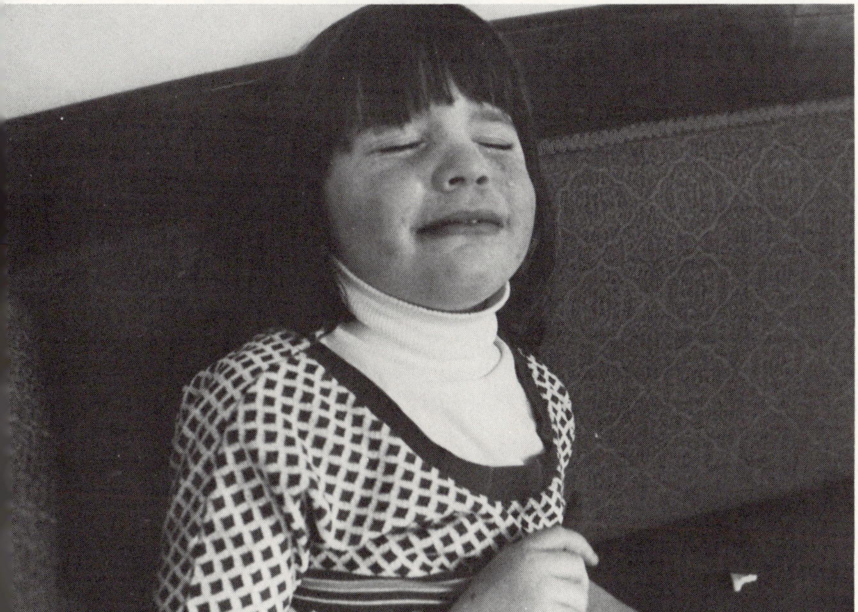

Elsa Dorfman

Anxiety, fear, and feelings of anomie may result when the self becomes **isolated** from human interaction, as in the case of autistic or feral children. In this case, uncontrollable behavior results from an inadequate social self.

that other role. Parents may also communicate delight to the infant by fondling and singing or engaging in baby talk. Before long, the baby begins to talk back and register happiness and contentedness. The baby begins to take part in this most primary of all human interactions and soon even anticipates responses of the parents. The child can begin to put himself or herself in the place of a parent in a very elementary way and to manipulate the parent with cries and gestures. The child is being prepared for the elaborate communication that later takes the form of complex language or symbolic interaction.

The "I" and the "Me"

Mead [1934] suggested that the self is made up of the "*I*" and the "*me*." The "I" represents that great reservoir of spontaneous expressive behavior that abides in every normal infant and child. It is at first unorganized and undisciplined. It stands ready to send the small child off in all directions regardless of risks and inconvenience. It is often reflected in the child's devilish expression when threatening to defy the world. The "I" is the actor, present in the self from the very beginning in unfettered form.

The "me" takes time to develop and is the part of the self that seeks to control the "I." Only gradually does the child learn from interaction with the surrounding world that there are some things the "I" must not do. Mother says "No, no," until the child knows what this means. Then the child's "me" stops the "I" before the child pulls the lamp off the table. In the traditional Western family, the "me" begins with the mother. Later it may become both parents and the entire community of persons who help to socialize the child: peers, teachers, friends, and the like. All are internalized and made a part of the child's own self-conception.

One thing that especially distinguishes the human self is the ability to learn how to control actions before they take place. There is, for example, an internal conversation between the "me" and the "I" within the child about whether it is wise to pull the lamp down, or to touch the hot stove, or to kick father. The "me" is the part of the self that cautions and controls the "I" according to what mother, father, brother, sister, and others expect. Mead assigned the term "minding" or thinking to this internal conversation. As is true of all human behavior, minding is learned in the process of social interaction.

Mead suggested that, ideally, there should be a kind of balance between the creative and daring "I" and the cautious and conforming "me." He felt that the social self would be most effective when it possessed both individual and group dimensions. If too controlled, a child might become too timid—a result of an overabundance of the "me." On the other hand, the child might be reared so as to possess a too fully developed and unrestrained "I." This lack of restraint could lead to a lack of self-control and, therefore, ineffectual relationships with others. The "I" and the "me," then, are natural, normal, and necessarily integrated aspects of the fully developed human self.

Stages of Learning

In what way do the "I" and the "me" develop into a fully balanced self? In the process of self-emergence, the child goes through three related stages: *a stage of imitation, a play stage,* and *a game stage.* After the first year or so of life, as the infant matures physically and begins to move about and observe the surrounding world, it begins to copy the actions of its parents. While father is in the living room reading the evening newspaper, the child will sit beside him and also "read." As the mother prepares dinner in the kitchen, the child will sit on the floor and play with pots and pans. Obviously, since the child cannot yet truly comprehend complex patterns of action, such as reading and cooking, such behavior remains basically imitative. Since lower-order animals can also be taught acts by simple imitation, the child at this first stage of development cannot yet be considered a full social being.

In the second, or play, stage of development, the first meaningful sense of personal self begins to emerge in the child. Mead pointed to the language of the young as an indication of the nature of this process. Why is it that, when children first learn to speak, they refer to themselves as "me" or by a given name? "*Me* do cooking" and "*Peter* read newspaper" precede "*I* do" and "*I* read." In this second stage, the child has, for the first time, started to become a social being. However, it cannot yet conceive of itself as an individualistic initiator of acts in a social context. The child is only playing at the roles of life, and these roles are determined by others, primarily mother and father. The child has been exposed to others in the social world only as an object of their attentions (for example, "Peter, don't do that!"). Thus, a human infant can only conceive of itself as a "me," an object of social actions.

The final stage of the child's self-development takes place as the infant increases its facility to handle language and communication and, thereby, to perceive the complexities of human interaction. The child now begins to appreciate his or her potential as a subjective initiator of social behavior, an "I" who has the power to influence the actions of others. This awareness forms the basis for the emergence of Mead's fully developed "I–me" self. The child no longer simply plays at particular social roles but begins to project itself imaginatively into a variety of roles, real and fanciful. The child *takes* roles in contrast to merely playing them. It begins to *empathize,* that is, to put itself into another's place and imagine what the other person feels. As far as we know, this ability to empathize is unique to human beings. Mead called this stage of development the game stage since he felt that, to participate effectively in a game, one must be able to assume or take a role.

The difference between *role playing* and *role taking* can be seen by contrasting the play of the very young with adult team sports. Nursery school children frequently play alongside each other with blocks or building cards but rarely with each other. Whether their actions do relate to one another is often accidental. This parallel play satisfies the children

3-2 Stages of Learning in the Socialization Progress

Socialization is the process whereby individuals learn the skills, roles, rules, and values of their society. Three stages characterize this learning process.

Very young children begin to learn adult behavior by imitating **isolated acts.** Young children may act lovingly toward dolls and stuffed animals, as their parents act lovingly toward them. At this earliest stage, children play by themselves and are not conscious of social roles or relationships with others.

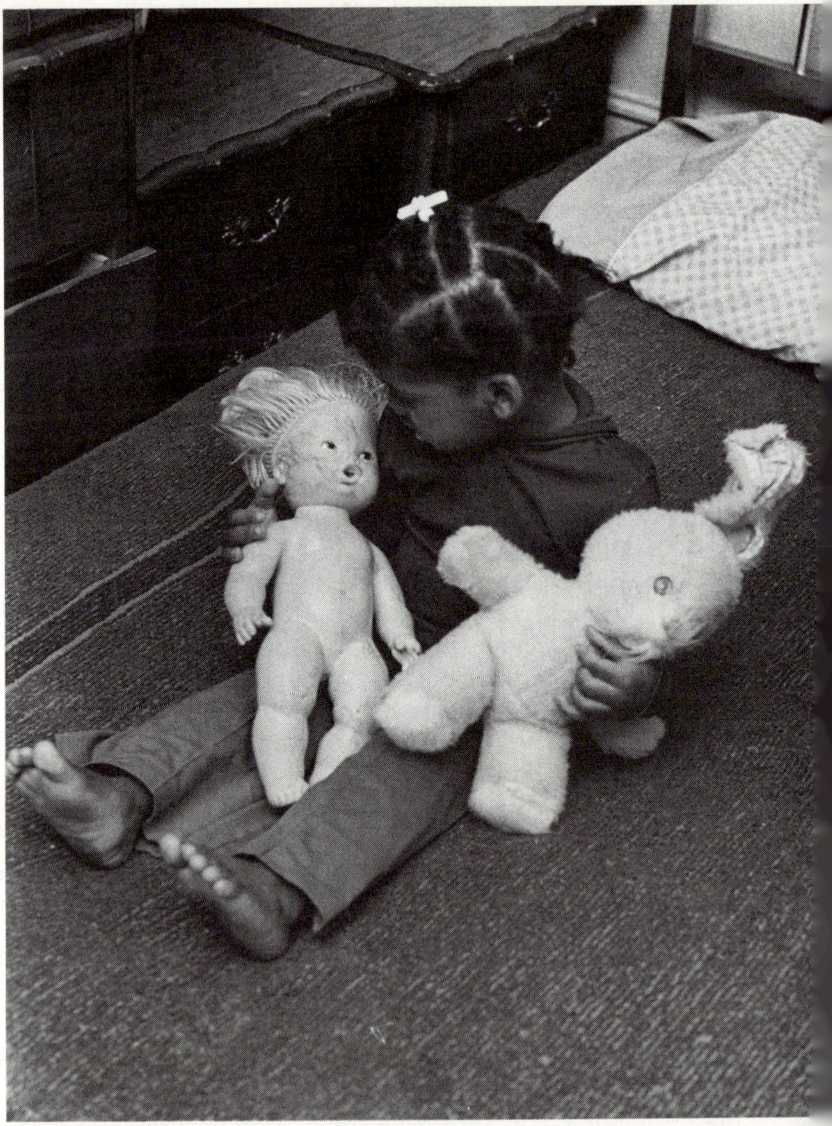

Dorothy Gloster

A. Kaufman Moon/Stock, Boston

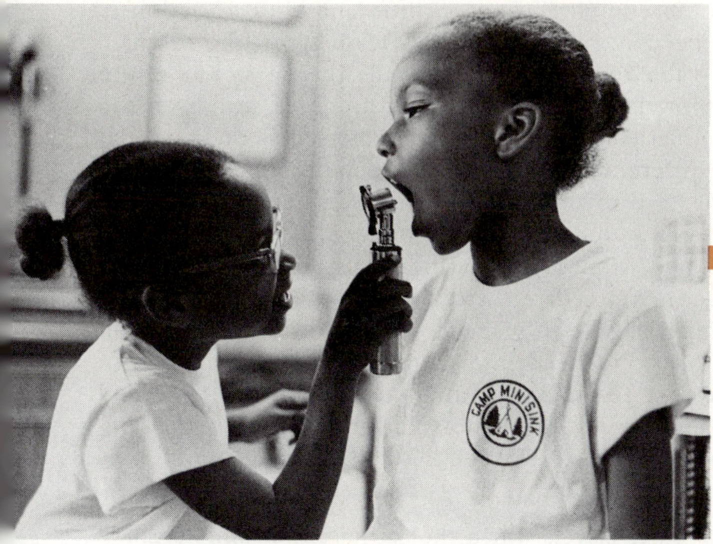

In the second stage, children begin to copy the sequence of **interrelated acts** associated with specific adult roles. They may play at being a doctor and a patient. Behavior, however, is still essentially imitative, and the children are not yet sure of what being a doctor or a patient really entails.

Elizabeth Hamlin, Dietz/Hamlin

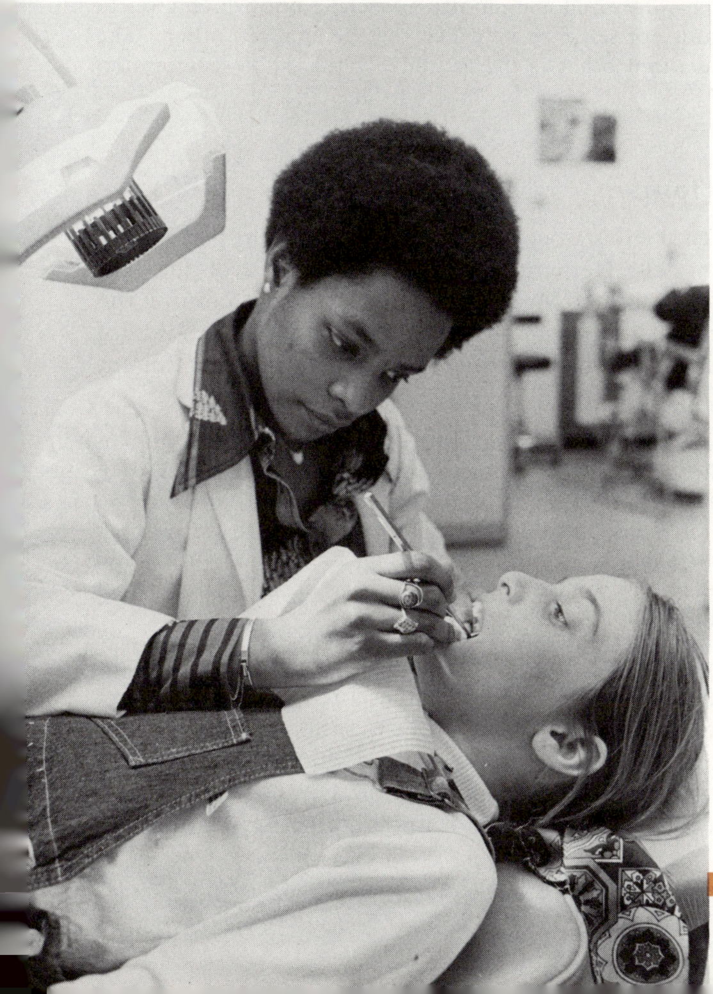

In the final stage of learning, older children begin to take, not merely play at, the **roles** of doctor and patient. They are conscious of the need for both participants to relate to one another in prescribed ways. They also can visualize themselves as actually becoming a doctor or a patient, and they can imagine what it is like to occupy the other role in the relationship.

until, as they learn more complex games, a different kind of action is necessary. In order to become fully skilled in a team sport like baseball, the participant must be able to assume empathically the roles of all of the teammates, the players of the opposing team, the umpires, and even the spectators. The player must conceive of himself or herself as the potential initiator of a variety of different acts. Through role playing alone, the player can learn, as a shortstop, to throw the ball to first base when it is hit in his or her direction. However, knowing where to throw the ball when there are baserunners present necessitates anticipating the baserunners' reactions by imaginatively projecting oneself into their roles. To be a fully capable baseball player, one must be able to visualize one's own role in relation to many others. This role taking leads the player to imagine a number of different actions that can be initiated—a putout at first, a throw to second for an attempted double play, or a throw home to protect against the winning run. In the game stage, children develop this ability, as Mead indicates in the following passage:

> The attitudes of the other players which the participant assumes organize into a sort of unit, and it is that organization which controls the response of the individual. . . . What he does is controlled by his being everyone else on the team. . . . The organized community or social group which gives to the individual his unity of self may be called the "generalized other." The attitude of the generalized other is the attitude of the whole community [Mead, 1934, p. 154].

THE SELF AND GROUP LIFE

Symbolic Interactionism

This view of the self continues in sociology as one of the respected perspectives and social models. Herbert Blumer [1969] is one of the best representatives of George Herbert Mead and is credited with coining the term *symbolic interactionism.* It is a distinctive approach to the study of human group life and human conduct that sees the self as the embodiment of a dynamic process of interaction:

> Nothing esoteric is meant by this expression. It means merely that a human being can be an object of his own action. Thus, he can recognize himself, for instance, as being a man, young in age, a student, in debt, trying to become a doctor, coming from an undistinguished family and so forth. In all such instances he is an object to himself; and he acts toward himself and guides himself in his actions toward others on the basis of the kind of object he is to himself [Blumer, 1969, p. 12].

Nonsymbolic reaction does sometimes take place in human contexts—for example, when one raises one's arms in fright as a reflex action without thought of what this gesture means to oneself or to others. Most behavior and interaction between humans, however, is *symbolic;* it means something, as when a boxer raises his arms to feint a blow in order to trap an opponent. Any gesture can become a part of human communication, but it must have the same meaning for all the actors involved. If an extended hand is interpreted as a hostile gesture instead of a friendly one, the symbolic nature of the action has been misinterpreted and communication has broken down.

The first premise of symbolic interactionism according to Blumer [1969, pp. 2, 6] is "that human beings act toward things (physical objects or other humans) on the basis of the meanings that the things have for them . . . and human groups are seen as consisting of human beings who are engaging in action." In short, humans must be able to interpret the world in order to interact with it. We sometimes say that people "live in different worlds" or that they are "worlds apart" in their understanding. What we mean is that their interpretations of things differ widely as a result of their rearing and socialization. In responding to their environments, humans act in terms of what meaning the environment has for them.

Closely related to this process is Mead's concept of the human being as an *organism having a self.* This means that humans become objects to themselves:

> In asserting that the human being has a self, Mead simply meant that the human being is an object to himself. The human being may perceive himself, have conceptions of himself, communicate with himself, and act toward himself [Blumer, 1969, p. 62].

In other words, we see ourselves as a distinct part of the environment. Our interaction with ourselves and others is colored by how we see ourselves. The self is not, therefore, a static and unchanging "ego"; it is instead a reflexive process of continual interpretation and reinterpretation as life goes on. It deserves further elaboration in the following section, especially with reference to the concept of *the looking-glass self.*

The Self and Social Interaction

All of us possess subjective "I" and objective "me" aspects of self. These aspects are developed in us as children as we perceive others acting toward us and ourselves acting toward them. What people think of us at church, in the office, at school, and at play determines what we think of ourselves and what kind of actors in the drama of social life we will become. Charles Cooley called this process the *looking-glass self.* As we use a mirror to visualize our physical appearance, so we use the actions of others towards us in our interpersonal relationships to visualize ourselves as human beings. We are quick to note how others react to us, and we symbolically interpret what their reactions mean. We conclude that they either approve or disapprove of us. Depending upon our estimation of what others think of us, we proceed to develop definite feelings about ourselves: feelings of pride and self-confidence or feelings of shame and chagrin. Self-feelings, therefore, are dependent in large part on the image we see reflected in the mirror of group life. This is partly what is meant by saying that we put ourselves in other people's places.

Of course, we can be oversensitive to the reactions of others and can read into them disapproval when it is not there. Or, on the other hand, it is possible to assume that others like us when they do not. However, whether we are accurate in interpreting people's actions toward us or not, our self-image still depends on the way in which we define their actions. For example, if you were to go home this evening to be greeted at the door by an irate husband or wife, furious parents, or children who proceeded to heap abuse upon you, your self-concept would rapidly begin to change. Moreover, this change would take place whether or not their actions were justified. Another illustration can be drawn from studies of mental illness. Certain forms of mental illness can result when individuals lose the ability to interpret the reactions of others correctly or effectively. What to others is a hand extended in friendship can become for the paranoiac a gesture of extreme hostility. Nevertheless, although interpretations of behavior can vary, the process of assessing ourselves and our particular place and role in life is the same for us all. We all look to the actions and reactions of others towards us for clues, and we interpret those in terms of our own self-conceptions and notions of the world.

This continuous process of self-development and self-interpretation is basic to all human social situations. Different people may use the process for various ends—for example, to train children to participate in the accepted games of their culture or to mobilize whole populations for totalitarian ends. Thus, whether baseball or totalitarianism is a desirable or undesirable form of human behavior, the same fundamental social processes are involved in both; in fact, these processes are related to every area of individual activity in society. A great work of literature could not be created without the author's ability to take roles imaginatively. As you read this book, you will try to take the sociologist's role, among others, in order to understand the subject more clearly. Individuals could not love or hate if they were unable to project themselves into the roles of others and, thereby, imagine what these others feel. As a matter of fact, all human emotions (hate, love, jealousy, compassion, sympathy, and anguish) are the result of the objective and subjective selves that all of us possess as products of our social environment.

In the above discussion, we have indicated that the infant gradually becomes human as it progresses through the stages of self-emergence. What happens, however, if this process is inadequate? How do we know that a baby must be cared for and loved by other humans in order to develop socially? Is there any empirical evidence? Sociologists have recognized the difficulty in answering these questions since human infants normally receive adult human care during child rearing. In addition, such care is usually considered adequate. At the same time, there are unusual cases, sometimes recorded, of children raised largely without human attention or of children raised by adults who did not provide adequate emotional care. These cases provide some answers for the above questions.

The Cases of Feral and Autistic Children

On 10 June 1962, *The San Francisco Chronicle* newspaper carried the following article:

The "Wolf Boy"

INDIA—Tarzan, the fictitious "apeman" created by Edgar Rice Burroughs, could well have sprung from Lucknow, a region surrounded by jungles in North Central India. . . . For many years, legends have spread throughout the area about "wolf boys" and other children reared by wolves, leopards, and bears . . . , all animals supposedly receptive toward lost human babies. It was a rare moment in January, 1954, when a railroad attendant stepped up to an empty freight car in a Lucknow siding, pushed open the door and found a carriage inside.

Who put the carriage there was never learned. But the naked, filthy nine-year-old boy in it became one of the most studied, controversial figures in medical history.

When the starving youth—later named Ramu—was brought to Balrampur Hospital, doctors were amazed to find his hands bent inward, unable to grip. Ramu ate only raw meat. He snarled at hospital attendants and struggled every time he was washed and dressed. In his hospital bed he was a pitiful sight, trying to bite doctors, lapping water with his tongue and cringing in fear when exposed to intense light.

After an initial examination, hospital superintendent D. N. Sharma concluded that Ramu did indeed have a jungle background and was a "wolf boy" brought up in an animal's lair. He had been convinced, he said, because of his double set of upper jaw incisors used to devour raw meat, his clawlike hands with ingrowing nails, and pressure scars on his knees—a sign that he had walked on all fours.

But there was another medical faction which blamed physical and mental damage at birth as the causes for the boy's abnormal condition. . . . As soon as the commotion over Ramu had died away, Dr. Sharma began treatments to restore the boy to normal conditions. At first, Ramu responded physically. . . . In 1960 he began to recognize his attendants and made gurgling sounds of delight when he saw visitors. Doctors even became hopeful of teaching him Hindi.

But eight days ago, after eight years of trying to humanize Ramu, Lucknow doctors admitted defeat, stating that the "wolf boy" would probably never be cured. For Ramu, despite his signs of improvement, had once again reverted to his old habits. He uttered weird cries as he did when first taken to the hospital and he took no further interest in what went on around him. . . . Now estimated to be 17 years old, he continued to sit idly in his wheelchair (he could no longer crawl or stand) or lie in his bed, seemingly unaware of what the doctors had done for him—and of the crowds of curious people who still came to see the "wolf boy." [Ramu died at Lucknow Hospital in April 1968.]

Myths of human children raised by animals have fascinated the public mind for centuries. Social scientists have also been interested in these stories since they illustrate what would happen to children raised without normal human relationships, especially after the publication, in 1940, of *Wolf Children and Feral Man* [Singh and Zingg, 1940], which contained a description of two alleged "wolf girls" discovered in India. References to this book became a part of many sociological discussions on the formation of the self in the infant [Gesell, 1940]. Scientists frequently referred also to examples of "attic children," children occasionally found after having been chained in attics for long periods of time [Davis, 1940a, pp. 554–564; 1947, pp. 432–437]. These children often exhibit the same nonhuman animal behavior as Ramu in the above article.

In 1959, articles appeared in *The American Journal of Sociology* by two professors who questioned the authenticity of these reports of children raised by animals. William Ogburn [1959, pp. 449–454] presented evidence based upon a lengthy investigation of one wolf-boy report, similar to Ramu's, which indicated that original claims were false. He pointed out that there was no reliable evidence to indicate that Parasram, the boy he studied, had been raised by wolves. Ogburn concluded that whereas this did not discount all stories of children raised by wolves, it did indicate that accounts of this sort are difficult to evaluate scientifically because myths are easily created and spread. The basic questions still remained, however. How can one explain the reported animalistic behavior of Ramu and the "wolf girls" of India? And how would a child deprived of a normal social environment develop? That is, what kind of impact would this social deprivation have on the child?

In addition to Ogburn's article, Bruno Bettelheim's [1959, pp. 455–567] research on autistic children sheds light upon these questions. *Autistic children* are those who suffer from a form of schizophrenia, a mental illness that results from extreme isolational deprivation. When this happens to an infant and young child for whatever reason, autistic behavior—a withdrawal into a world of fantasy that is seemingly nonhuman—may result. As Bettelheim observed and recorded the bizarre behavior of autistic children, he found their antics to be identical to those of the feral children. This led him to hypothesize that feral children appear to act like animals not because they were reared by animals but because they are autistic.

Autistic behavior is indeed animal-like, as Bettelheim discovered through many years of work with severely disturbed children. Such children are often mute or their speech is incomprehensible. Speech, he observes, perhaps more than any other characteristic, separates human behavior from animal behavior. Autistic children shun humans and generally seem to have an affinity for pets and animals. They have an acute sense of smell and touch. They have little perception of heat or cold, often tearing off their clothes and running outside in winter. They scream and howl, eat raw food like animals, using hands and mouth to attack it directly, and defecate without regard for time or place. They sometimes attack another person ferociously with "claws" and teeth. Many prowl about at night when the threatening and hostile world of humans is no longer present. And they exhibit a noticeable inability to laugh, another characteristic that distinguishes humans from animals.

Autistic behavior is so nonhuman and repulsive that parents are often unable to cope with it. They may either abandon autistic children, allow them to run away, or, as in America, place them in institutions. It is logical to assume, then, that the reports of feral children are actually reports of autistic children who have been abandoned. It lends credence to Bettelheim's reference to human narcissism. It is possible, he writes, that as humans we refuse to admit that such behavior can be engaged in by other humans. We are quick to blame animals and to believe that such children are feral, that is, reared by nonhumans.

If autism is not attributable to nonhuman rearing, how then can we account for it? According to scholars like Bettelheim, it can develop in homes where parents are intelligent and middle-class but fail to accept a child and to give the normal love and care that is so fundamental. In one case, Bettleheim records, Joe, the son of highly intelligent and ambitious American parents, was born while his father was in medical school, worried about money problems, and physically and mentally exhausted. His mother was frightened and fearful of the responsibilities of taking care of a new baby. The parents fought constantly. Joe became an unhappy baby, frequently restless and crying, and his parents' reaction was to ignore him for long periods of time. This pattern continued at a later age when Joe was turned out to play by himself.

At the age of four, he was placed by his parents in an institution where he remained until nine years of age. At that time, when he entered the Orthogenic School of the University of Chicago, he exhibited all the behavioral traits of the feral child, including extreme aloneness and withdrawal and an obsessive desire to maintain monotonous patterns of action. As an autistic child, he had virtually stopped existing as a human being. In such cases, treatment calls for a kind of retracing of all the early steps in the normal rearing process, a recreation of the early processes of symbolic interaction between human beings. Sometimes there is gradual emergence of the social self; sometimes there is failure.

Bettelheim's conclusion is that extreme isolation—emotional and sometimes physical—can cause the disturbed behavior of autistic individuals. It appears to arise not from the humanity of animals, especially wolves, towards human infants, but from the inhumanity of some people, especially parents, toward children. In other words, feral children seem to be produced, not when wolves behave like mothers and fathers, but when human parents behave like nonhumans. The tentative conclusion must be that, while there are no feral children, there are some very rare examples of feral parents, that is, of human beings who become feral to their children.

In tracing the development of the self thus far, we can see that the infant is born into society with the potential for becoming human. Unlike many other animals, human infants are totally dependent upon others for the fulfillment of all their social, as well as biological, needs. If these needs are not met satisfactorily, the results can be tragic for both the individual and society. The process whereby society carries out this task is called *socialization.*

Socialization as a Life Process

For the orderly maintenance of society and the individual, the infant must learn the essential elements—the skills, knowledge, and values—of the society into which it is born. It must first be taught the necessary skills required for living in society, such as walking, eating, and communicating. It must be taught to control organic functions through bladder and bowel training. These skills are fundamental if society is to maintain orderly and patterned processes of interaction and behavior. They are also fundamental to the child's developing a unique sense of self-awareness. The child can then conceive of itself as one who has control over its environment and itself through the possession of special social skills. These skills vary from one society to the next and from one group to the next. A lower-class urban child learns to play in the street and avoid the menace of traffic at the same time. A primitive child learns to track and kill game. An aristocratic child learns the niceties of appropriate speech and manner. Each develops a sense of self in the context of its particular society, and each is prepared for future life in that environment.

Socialization also transmits the basic knowledge of a society, which allows individuals to employ their skills intelligently in situations. Primitive people learn of the gods and spirits that rule their world and how to control them through appropriate rituals. The 20th century Western child attends school and studies courses in the basic sciences and humanities. The child of the aristocrat learns family genealogy and studies etiquette in private schools. Thus, through the accumulation of appropriate skills and knowledge, these different individuals become potentially productive members of their particular social systems.

Finally, socialization is the process whereby society orients the individual towards those values and beliefs it deems ultimately important. For example, our schooling consists of more than the acquisition of basic skills and knowledge. Many high schools require that all students take courses in state, local, and national government. In a democracy, we traditionally look upon the school as one of the most important socializing agents for transmitting the values of freedom, equality, and fraternity. In addition, the church in modern Western society serves the function of exposing individuals to the values of human brotherhood. As we shall see in our discussion of culture, values differ greatly from one society to another. The people of Dobu Island near New Guinea make a virtue of treachery and ill will. The Zuni Indians value sobriety and inoffensiveness above all other goals. One cannot become a fully social American, Dobuan, or Zuni until one has been exposed to the values of the corresponding society through the socialization process.

This concept implies, however, something more than mere routine or rote learning. Through socialization, individuals personalize or inculcate the skills, knowledge, and values of their society into their own self-conceptions. If you are an expert auto mechanic or cook, you have become so because you learned your skill from society—in the school, at home, through interpersonal contact with a friend, or by studying and reading the books available on these subjects. But you are not simply like a vase that has been filled with water. Your skill as a mechanic or a cook helps identify the unique "you." Your self becomes personally identified with the skill: "Jane is an excellent auto mechanic." Or "Tom cooks good pancakes."

The same is true for the learning of knowledge and values. Individuals become identified with special kinds of knowledge and with certain values: "She is the one who knows all about American history." Or "He is the nonconformist in the crowd." It is this interdependent relationship between society and the individual that makes the socialization process so fundamentally important. One could not exist without the other. You are an individual precisely because you are social, and society exists because of the roles individuals take and play. When something does go wrong with the socialization process, as in the case of the autistic child, the consequences are serious for society, for the individuals produced in these circumstances are not fully social. As has been shown, the autistic child lacks all three of the elements that make up a meaningful sense of self—skills, knowledge, and values.

When studying the process of socialization, sociologists can distinguish two different patterns: (1) *Differential socialization* takes place when socialization varies from one stage of an individual's life to another; (2) *resocialization* can occur when individuals must be prepared for new life experiences. Each of these variations of the socialization process has been the subject of provocative social research and theory.

Differential Socialization: The Example of Parent-Youth Conflict

Although Mead suggested that the fully developed self begins to emerge in the young child, we should not assume that socialization has, at that time, completed its task. The elements of society transmitted by the socialization process require constant reinforcement and sustenance throughout the life of the individual. Social learning, in this sense, is a lifelong process. Socialization, however, varies from one group context to another or from one age to another; furthermore, it differs in degree and form throughout one's life.

In contemporary America, for example, socialization tends to be formally concentrated in the years from birth to the age of about 21. During this period, the child and adolescent are exposed to family, school, and church as the prime agents of socialization. At the same time, the peer group—the play group, gang, or close friends—plays an important role informally in transmitting to the individual basic skills, knowledge, and values. In the later years of life, especially among the aged, the socialization process may all but disappear, both informally and formally. Persons in their 60s or 70s may be physically unable to attend church and other community affairs. A great many of the problems of old age in modern society are a direct result of this change in the socialization process, aggravated by physiological and psychic changes in the individual. Aged persons feel unwanted and useless, and their self-concepts suffer as a result. Society also pays a price by not utilizing the talent that can frequently be found in this age group.

Much parent–youth conflict is a result of what sociologists call the *differential rate of socialization.* Parents seem conservative and unyielding to children because of the differences between them in skills, knowledge, and values. The child is constantly exposed to the newest of rapidly changing knowledge, while the parent finds it increasingly difficult to apply ideas and values learned in another social context. The conflict is heightened since both the parents' and the children's self-conceptions are related to what they have learned from society. Neither will easily or willingly change their ideas, because human beings find it painful to abandon part of themselves. Basic disagreements in knowledge and values, then, often become internalized by parents and youth and, thus, become highly personal.

The novelist can often capture the significance of this parent–youth conflict with profound insight. For example, Claude Brown, in writing about his own life in the black ghetto of Harlem, senses the alarming gap between older blacks, who had been reared in the South, and their children, who are growing up in the urban world of New York City. The parents are trying to transmit the values and perspectives of the only cultural milieu they really know. For them, what is judged as good and correct differs from Harlem's larger view of good and bad behavior. In this context, parents find it difficult to understand even the slang of their children:

> Living in that house . . . must have been terribly hard. Everybody was far away, way back in the woods. If Mama heard that one of her friends had come home and found her husband in the bed with some other woman, she'd say, "She should've poured some lye on her." If somebody had poured some lye on her, she'd say, "Yeah, that was good for that old heifer, that old no-good whorish hussy."
>
> This was the way they felt about it. This was all the stuff that came from the backwoods. I suppose the Harlem tradition, the way of life in Harlem, had come from the backwoods. All that mixing up lye and throwing it in somebody's face, all that was just as backwoods as working roots. These people just seemed to believe in that, like cutting somebody's throat. They didn't seem to be ready for urban life.
>
> [My parents] were going to try to guide us and make us do right and be good, and they didn't even know what being good was. When I was a little boy, Mama and Dad would beat me and tell me, "You better be good," but I didn't know what being good was. To me, it meant that they just wanted me to sit down and fold my hands or something crazy like that. Stay in front of the house, don't go any place, don't get into trouble. I didn't know what it meant, and I don't think they knew what it meant, because they couldn't ever tell me what they really wanted. The way I saw it, everything I was doing

> was good. If I stole something and didn't get caught, I was good. If I got into a fight with somebody, I tried to be good enough to beat him. If I broke into a place, I tried to be quiet and steal as much as I could. I was always trying to be good. They just kept on beating me and talking about being good. And I just kept on doing what I was doing and kept on trying to do it good.
>
> They needed some help. The way I felt about it, I should have been their parents, because I had been out there on the streets and I wasn't as far back in the woods as they were. I could have told them a whole lot of stuff that would have helped them, Mama and Dad and Papa, everybody, if they had only listened to me. . . .
>
> I could sense that fear in Mama's voice when I told her once that I wanted to be a psychologist.
>
> She said, "Boy, you better stop that dreamin' and get all those crazy notions outta your head." She was scared. She had the idea that colored people were supposed to want to work in fields or be happy to be a janitor [Brown, 1965, pp. 278–281].

Kingsley Davis [1940b, pp. 523–535] deals with this same parent–youth conflict from the perspective of the sociologist. He suggests that in every society there is a difference between the generations. Older people find it impossible to put themselves in the adolescent's place. At the same time, most young people, with all of life before them, view the world differently than their parents do and think of them as overly cautious and outmoded. This gulf becomes exaggerated in a rapidly changing society like ours. When parents look back and try to remember what it was to be 16 or 17, they fail even more seriously because the recent teen-age culture has changed so radically that parents have never really been there. Therefore, parents seem terribly old-fashioned to the young and youth appears to be strange and frightening to the older generation.

This clash of perspectives is compounded, as Kingsley Davis points out, by two other factors, the physiological and the psychological. Physiologically, as parents get older, they lose their vigor and daring, and often their good health. Life slows them down; they do not have the youthful energy to expend and are frequently shocked at the risks their children may take. Psychologically, they are no longer as idealistic about what can be accomplished in life. They begin to experience the declining years and must face unrealized dreams. They have learned to live by compromise and accommodation, neither rejecting ideals nor expecting to realize them perfectly. They live by more pragmatic values and call themselves "more realistic."

Teen-agers, on the other hand, are going through perhaps the most zestful period of life when they are intellectually keen but without wide experience. They see ideal solutions to problems and assume that they can be brought to fulfillment. This is the time of life when a person may be very religious or very radical in crusades to save the world from injustices. Youthful idealism and zest helped to bring about the civil rights movement on behalf of American blacks and other deprived groups, including women. Parents of the youthful demonstrators in the 1960s and 1970s may have been sympathetic with the idealism of their children but in many cases thought it very unrealistic. The parents had long ago learned to live with the compromises of a segregated warlike society. Therefore, in the eyes of the teen-ager, the adult is far too conservative and gives lip service to ideals but settles for less than the best. Young people's lack of faith in this pragmatic and, according to them, deceitful adaptability of adults is reflected in the saying, "Never trust anyone over 30"—a familiar slogan among youth during the 1960s.

Thus, as a result of conflicts arising from their physiological and psychological differences, the younger and older generations become exceedingly critical of each other, and the gap between parents and children widens because of differential socialization. According to one theory [Tamney, 1967] feelings of conflict exist also because the child feels forever in debt to the parent regardless of age. The feeling of being subjected to the authority and power of another person does not encourage open and honest communication and interaction. Hence parents and children sometimes find it difficult to experience close intimate companionship. Youths find an easier relationship with peers who have no restrictive claims upon them. This is partly why peer groups are so important in the processes of both socialization and *resocialization*, another important concept related to the formation of the social self.

Resocialization: Military Recruits and Marihuana Users

As individuals move through life, they must learn new behavior patterns and take on new values with every major change in the life cycle—new school experiences and jobs, marriage, parenthood, the empty-nest stage of marriage, retirement and aging, and so forth. Much has been written about the resocialization process for the person who enters military service, as so many males did in our society from World War II to the time of the transition to an all-volunteer armed force. According to one study in 1969 [Moskos, 1970], "about one-half of all adult American males have been in the armed forces with close to 90 percent of them spending their entire military service in the enlisted ranks."

Boot camp takes a raw recruit for the military and conditions him or her into attitudes, skills, and commitments appropriate for a career, which, in many ways, contrasts with careers in civilian life. This resocialization process takes advantage of the following factors:

1. The military establishment recruits individuals when they are young for the most part. The young are not only more fit physically, but they are psychologically more flexible and capable of adjusting to new expectations.
2. The military begins the process by cutting many of the recruit's former ties with civilian life: new dress and hair cuts, a long initial period without leave to return to family and friends, and long days

of activity designed to build emotional ties to and dependency on the military.

3. New norms in keeping with military discipline are drilled into the recruits: strict hours for getting up and going to bed and for all the day's tasks, the military salute and special language, the new dress and bearing, the "spit and polish," and endless military courtesies.
4. Military sanctions or forms of punishment for disobedience are all part of the soldier-making process.
5. Finally, the new way of life is dramatized again and again through military ritual: parades, ceremonies of promotion and recognition, daily tributes to the flag, and so forth.

Perhaps next to the family, the American military establishment has the greatest advantages in the socialization process: early and exclusive access to human beings, continuous and long-range involvement with individuals, and the authorization to pass on traditional norms and values that underlie behavior patterns. The transmission of values is fulfilled by the human family largely through the primary face-to-face interactions that typify family life. A similar authorization in the military cannot succeed solely through the formal ceremonies and impersonal demands that characterize the armed forces. Here, too, there must be primary ties developed through face-to-face contacts within military life. Such ties emerge between buddies in small units within the formal large-scale organization. Moskos investigated the widespread discontent among enlisted men in the American military services during the Vietnam War and found that effective performance stemmed from a mutual survival desire within small primary units, rather than from any ideological commitment to the avowed patriotic purposes of the war.

The resocialization that takes place in the military takes full advantage of the primary ties that spring up within every large impersonal organization. In fact, without these ties, any commitment to a new way of life would indeed be superficial. Recognizing this, the military makes the most of buddy groups. It also enlists the aid of former agents of socialization when it encourages the soldiers' families, churches, and schools back home to honor and admire military personnel, life, and virtues.

Interestingly, like the military, groups of marihuana users in our society must also resocialize new recruits. In contrast to the military, however, they must do so without the conventional support of family, church, and school. The process of remaking an individual into an acceptable member of an unconventional group is much the same, nevertheless. Howard Becker studied the making of a marihuana user and concluded that it involves a learning process that goes on within a primarylike group. Trusted peers not only teach novices how to smoke the drug so as to enjoy it, but how to justify the experience even though it is considered immoral and illegal by a large part of conventional society.

3-3 Desocialization and Resocialization During the Life Cycle

The process of socialization does not end when the young adult has learned the roles and values of society. As individuals move through different periods of the life cycle, new experiences require a continuous process of "delearning" or "relearning." This desocialization–resocialization cycle is particularly characteristic of modern societies, where change is rapid and individuals are exposed to a variety of experiences. The process of delearning and relearning can be found in unusual and bizarre settings (the military and the Ku Klux Klan), as well as in normal group contexts (family, peer group, community).

The military must teach the recruit new roles (professional killer) and values (destroying an enemy is good) that are opposed to civilian roles and values. In order to do this, a period of desocialization (basic training) deliberately separates the recruit from former socialization experiences (no leave to visit family, new dress and short haircuts, specified hours to go to bed and to eat, and so on). In this context, the recruit becomes totally dependent upon the drill instructor for a new sense of self and identity. During bayonet practice, D.I.s frequently yell "Kill, kill, kill!"

N. Sapieha/Stock, Boston

United Press International

Antisocial secret societies, like the Ku Klux Klan, utilize both the appeal of former roles and values and the appeal of special uniforms and ritual which symbolize new roles and values. The recruit is taught that the Klan stands for white Christianity (the cross) and 100-percent Americanism (the flag). At the same time, hoods and robes, a burning cross, and special uniforms for leaders distinguish the group as separate and different from larger society (see Chapter 6). Klan members, therefore, are willing to use violence and other disapproved methods to achieve racial purity in the name of God and country.

The aged face the special problem of "natural" desocialization, as their families grow up and leave them in nursing homes, their failing physical powers make it difficult for them to maintain personal relationships, and so on. As a result, many homes for senior citizens have initiated programs that attempt to provide resocialization experiences by young adults who come to the home to talk and play games with the residents.

Elizabeth Hamlin, Dietz/Hamlin

> No one becomes a user without (1) learning to smoke the drug in a way which will produce real effects; (2) learning to recognize the effects and connect them with drug use (learning, in other words, to get high); and (3) learning to enjoy the sensations he perceives. . . . Learning to enjoy marihuana is a necessary but not a sufficient condition for a person to develop a stable pattern of drug use. He has still to contend with powerful forces of social control that make the act seem inexpedient, immoral, or both [Becker, 1963, pp. 58–59].

Becker began his research in the early 1950s, with a study that focused upon 50 marihuana users in Midwestern American cities. Half of them were professional musicians, many of whom he observed in the normal course of their work. Becker was himself a musician, and thus he lived and worked with colleagues in taverns and night clubs in Chicago, in a small university town (Champaign–Urbana, Illinois), and in Kansas City, Missouri. It was just after World War II, when many musicians, including Becker, were continuing their education under the G.I. Bill. His study is a good example of participant observation, for many of his insights and much of his information came from on-the-job association with musicians, many of whom were also marihuana users. He was not satisfied, however, to generalize from what he knew of his personal associates; he interviewed other types of musicians along with marihuana users in other occupations.

Becker was not willing to center his attention on the prevailing question: Why do they do it? This approach presupposes that marihuana use can be explained as a result of "some trait which predisposes or motivates [a person] to engage in that behavior. In the case of marihuana use, this trait is usually identified as psychological, as a need for fantasy and escape from psychological problems the individual cannot face." [Becker, 1963, p. 42]. Becker rejects this approach in favor of a developmental one: Users gradually enter into the experience and then acquire motivations, that is, justifications and explanations of why they take part in this deviant activity.

In interviewing marihuana users from several different occupations (musicians, laborers, machinists, people in the professions), he studied the history of the person's experience, noting carefully the subtle changes in attitude and the reasons for these changes as the subject moved from non-user to novice, to casual user, to regular user. He hypothesized that certain things had to happen to transform marihuana use into a pleasurable experience; if these did not happen or did not continue to happen, the experience would fail and be discontinued. His method of research, which he called "analytic induction," required that "every case collected in the research substantiate the hypothesis."

Becker found remarkable consistency in the stories of users as to how they progressed from one step to the next. The novice is invited to try marihuana by users in face-to-face interaction. He is not likely to get high the first time but must be instructed on how to draw the smoke in with a lot of air, unlike smoking a cigarette. He often learns the technique by watching others do it. When he gets high, it is frequently an ambiguous experience; it is not clear whether the sensations are pleasurable or not. For some, it may seem frightening and produce conventional thoughts about the terrible effects of drug use. The smoking takes places, however, among peers who are supportive and who reassure the novice that there is no real danger involved. More than this, the peers point out that the effects of being high (dizziness, thirst, distorted sense of time and distance) are indeed to be enjoyed.

The learning experience for the novice is not complete even so. He must become the object of his own observation, able to use the drug effectively, to enjoy its effects, and to recognize the drug as producing the effects. In short, the taste for marihuana is socially acquired, the product of the self interacting with peers and with itself. This is a symbolic interactionist perspective of human behavior, which comes primarily from George Herbert Mead, as Becker points out in his analysis. According to this perspective, behavior develops because of one's ability to interpret events, not as a result of predisposing traits.

Becker does not stop here. He goes on to explore the process through which the new user becomes comfortable and at ease with a deviant behavior pattern. Most smokers are secret deviants (see Chapter 12); that is, they try to find ways of hiding their experience from family, church, and occupational group. At first, this consideration is a major source of concern and may lead to non-use either temporarily or permanently. On the other hand, those who continue to smoke marihuana in a society where its use is considered wrong are able to make adjustments.

As a matter of fact, drug users often develop an ideology that enhances their self-respect in unconventional circles and even encourages them to participate in crusades to change laws and social attitudes. That they have been at least partly successful is evidenced by the modifications of previously repressive marihuana-use laws in some states. This social action to change prevailing attitudes and laws recalls our reference, in Chapter 1, to labeling theory, which is discussed in more detail in Chapter 12. Behavior that is labeled as wrong by conventional society at one time (like marihuana smoking) may gradually become accepted at a later time.

The central focus of our discussion of marihuana use in this chapter, however, is upon resocialization. As individuals enter into this new experience, they must be taught new definitions of the situation. This is possible through symbolic interaction within the social group. It is dramatized over and over in the quotations from the Becker study:

> Take in a lot of air, you know, and . . . I don't know how to describe it, you don't smoke it like a cigarette, you draw in a lot of air and get it deep down in your system and then keep it there. . . .
>
> I didn't take my eyes off him for a second, because I wanted to do everything just as he did it. I watched how he held it, how he smoked it, and everything. Then when he gave it to me I just came on cool, as though I knew

exactly what the score was. I held it like he did and took a poke just the way he did. . . .

I didn't get high the first time. . . . I don't think I held it in long enough. I probably let it out you know, you're a little afraid. The second time I wasn't sure, and he [smoking companion] told me like I asked him for some of the symptoms or something. . . .

I heard little remarks that were made by other people. Somebody said, "My legs are rubbery," and I can't remember all the remarks that were made because I was very attentively listening for all these cues for what I was supposed to feel like. . . .

It started taking effect, and I didn't know what was happening, you know, what it was, and I was very sick. I walked around the room, walking around the room trying to get off, you know; it just scared me at first, you know. . . .

The average person isn't ready for that, and it is a little frightening to them sometimes. . . . You have to reassure them, explain to them that they're not really flipping or anything, that they're gonna be all right. You have to just talk them out of being afraid [Becker, 1963, pp. 41–58].

The importance of Becker's study to sociological research is unrelated to the continuing debate about the medical effects of marihuana use. To assess this kind of issue, one must turn to different scientific sources [Duster, 1969; Fort, 1968; Kolanski and Moore, 1971; Smith, 1970]. Rather, Becker's findings are important because they illustrate the ways in which subgroups most often resocialize members into new life experiences. Lifelong processes of socialization and resocialization make the individual and society continually dependent upon one another.

THE INTERACTION OF SELF AND SOCIETY

We have seen that close personal relationships are essential both for the individual and for society. The social self emerges only through interaction that begins in the primary group. The whole socialization process takes place most effectively in such a setting. This interdependence, however, often creates tensions and anxieties for individuals. As a consequence, self-identity can become a problem in some settings.

Self-Identity in Mass Society

The human self is so dependent upon meaningful forms of group identity that when this condition is not available the consequences for both the individual and society may be serious. Psychoanalyst Erich Fromm [1955] goes so far as to say that there are two things that characterize humans everywhere and at all times: (1) They are hostility-prone; and (2) they are anxiety-prone. Both of these characteristics accompany primary ties and produce ambivalent feelings among the interacting persons. Group living has built-in frustrations that result from the necessary limiting of social action through rules and regulations. The bumptious energy of the individual must be curbed and held within boundaries for the good of the group. Behavior must be controlled, and control can be a painful and frustrating experience that produces hostilities even in the most ideal of groups.

The anxiety-prone character of humans is also universal according to Fromm. It exists because of the universal need for group life and the special human dependence upon primary groups. This does not mean that we have an instinct for anxiety, any more than we have an instinct for hostility. It does mean that, through the long period of infancy and childhood, the human being comes to depend upon group experiences with family, friends, and others to such an extent that the developing individual becomes lost without them. Take away a person's ties with other humans and he or she becomes anxious and, at times, even emotionally and physically ill. So desperately does a person need to belong that deviant forms of behavior will often be adopted to combat a feeling of being lost. When Fromm first developed this theme, he was trying to explain why Germans turned so unquestioningly to Hitler and the Nazis preceding World War II. In an urbanized Germany, there was a weakening of the primary ties with family, friends, and the church. "Mass man," suffering loss of primary ties, was vulnerable to demagogues who offered a quick way of belonging to a kind of pseudocommunity, the German tribe of "pure" Aryans. In Chapter 8, we will discuss in more detail the problem of feelings of a loss of community in contemporary society. For the moment, this reference to Fromm's theory serves to dramatize the anxiety-prone nature of human selves and offers a partial explanation of why people sometimes turn to fascism or totalitarianism.

Fromm's theory about the close interdependence of the self and society can also be applied to other contexts of human experience. Similar processes can be found in urban slums where youth suffer fragmented family life and turn to the streets. Peer groups may take the place of kin groups. Gangs may become family surrogates and important agents of socialization for the members. This was the focus of a classic sociological study by William Foote Whyte, the subject of the final section of this chapter.

The Example of Peer Groups and Gangs

The overall theme of this chapter has been the relationship between the self and society. The self emerges in social interaction and thrives in dynamic group settings. Similarly, society cannot exist apart from the individual human actors who make up social groups, both large and small. This perspective is examined in rich detail in William Whyte's analysis of a street-corner society. This study is a remarkable analysis of male juvenile gangs in an American city. It also offers an interesting contrast to the research approach of Emile Durkheim and Clark Vincent in the first two chapters.

▶ STUDY 3

Street-Corner Boys [1937][1]

Problem

When a creative young scholar is set loose to make a study of some aspect of human society with no strings attached, just what happens? This kind of opportunity came to William Whyte when he graduated from Swarthmore in 1936 with an A.B. degree in economics. He was awarded a three-year Junior Fellowship by the Society of Fellows at Harvard and was free to do whatever he wished in the way of scholarly work. His research topic was chosen for its own sake rather than as a fulfillment of the requirements for a Ph.D. degree.

As a consequence, one of sociology's most interesting and creative studies of a small local social system was created. Whyte decided to focus upon a slum district in Boston. He was not concerned with this small segment of American society because of its social problems. Rather, he wanted to find a way of analyzing the section of the city he called "Cornerville" to show *what actually goes on within small groups and societies.* Whyte was particularly interested in the *impact of small group structure upon the individual group members.*

Hypotheses and Study Design

The overall hypothesis of Whyte's study was that *intragroup social structure and activity are largely determined by the goals and values of group members,* both individually and collectively. More specifically, he hypothesized the following:

1. Human groups differ according to *diverse goals and values.*
2. Group leaders differ in terms of whether members need emotional support from a leader who expresses friendship and camaraderie or whether they need a "take-charge" leader who makes decisions about goals and business affairs. The former may be called *expressive* leaders; the latter, *instrumental* leaders.
3. Group members differ in status and role by virtue of *their skills and level of commitment* to the goals and values of the group.
4. Individual self-fulfillment emerges in accordance with the *interaction between self and society.*
5. *Social change* influences the rise or fall of small groups.

Whyte's study design involved what is called *the case study.* This method does not depend upon quantitative analysis (as in the case of Durkheim's study of suicide) but is rather a qualitative description of a day-by-day human interaction. Using this approach, it is possible to go beyond description to explanation involving comparisons between groups and changes over time. Both individual and collective social actions can be analyzed and compared.

[1]Adapted and abridged from William Foote Whyte, *Street-Corner Society* (Chicago: University of Chicago Press, 1943; 6th ed., 1961) and from the discussion in John Madge, "The Study of Subcultures," in *The Origins of Scientific Sociology* (New York: The Free Press, 1962), Chap. 7.

Method of Data Collection

This study is an excellent example of *participant observation.* There was a refreshing naiveté about Whyte's methodology, reflected in the fact that he set forth with little formal training in research techniques. After unsatisfactory attempts at door-to-door interviewing and barroom conversation, he finally went to a settlement house on Norton Street in the heart of Cornerville. There he was told to talk with "Doc," a native of the area who knew everybody, a man of 29 and the leader of the Norton Street Gang.

Early in 1937, Whyte met Doc and explained at length his desire to study Cornerville. From that day on, the researcher was introduced everywhere as Doc's friend and thus was immediately accepted in the innermost circles of the neighborhood. He got a room with an Italian family, who soon came to look after him like a son, and started to learn Italian and take part in many of the activities of the Italian subculture. By this time, he had decided that he would focus his attention on people, not communities. To do so, he became as involved with them as possible as a participant observer. He came to enjoy them and their way of life so much that they accepted him as part of the family. At one point, he quipped that he was turning from a participant observer to a nonobserving participant.

When he played on their bowling teams, he played to win, and yet he learned early that he was not to go too far in trying to be one of the boys. When he tried to swear like them or probe with too many questions, he was quickly corrected. He was to learn by listening and watching. This he did day and night for four years. During the project, Whyte was married and took his wife to live in an apartment in the area. The apartment was just across the street from a group of about 50 whose activities could be charted by a method that Whyte called positional mapping. He noted with care which members hung around together. Seldom were rival members found in the same subgroup. Almost always, those who grouped together agreed on issues and actions. One way of studying the social system was to observe the subgroupings within the system. It was important also to analyze the leaders and how they differed in various situations.

Participant observation as a method in research is time-consuming and costly. Seldom has it been used for a study as intensive as this one. Furthermore, risks of bias and impressionistic interpretations are ever-present. Nevertheless, as in this case, it can be productive and can result in provocative insights—insights that can easily be missed when the researcher does not get on the inside of the subgroups that make up the total system. Whyte's appraisal of his work is best reflected in his own words:

> Although I could not cover all of Cornerville, I was building up the structure and functioning of the community through intensive examination of some of its parts—*in action.* I was relating the parts together by observing events between groups and between group leaders and the members of the larger institutional structures (of politics and the rackets). I was seeking to build a sociology based upon observed interpersonal events. That, to me, is the chief methodological and theoretical meaning of *Street-Corner Society* [p. 358].

Findings and Interpretations

It is quite clear that Whyte did not have his hypotheses formulated before he went to Cornerville. They developed gradually as he observed the marked differences between two groups—"corner boys" (Doc's gang) and "college boys" (Chick's gang). Although all the boys grew up in the same neighborhood, there were at least three kinds of boys delineated according to social levels—the college boys at the top, the intermediaries, and the corner boys.

In a low status group, which prizes integration and social solidarity (the Norton Street Gang), *the expressive leader* (Doc) *emerges.* He keeps the action going in order to strengthen primary ties for single young adults whose home is the street corner and whose family is the gang. He is the spender who puts present pleasures above future gains. Gang rules and relationships are informal and democratic, and the leader keeps his position at the top by virtue of superior skills related to gang values: his adolescent prowess as fighter, his present contacts beyond the corner, his intelligence and concern for each member, his bowling abilities (bowling was a religion to the Nortons), and his way with girls.

In contrast to Doc's Gang, *in a group that aims to improve its status and get ahead* (the Italian Community Club, or Chick's Gang), *the instrumental leader emerges.* He (Chick) has contacts with higher status girls and influential people. His emphasis upon foregoing present pleasures in order to meet the costs of college and professional schools is in keeping with the needs of boys who value upward mobility. He insists upon formal rules and constitutional proceedings in the group. He is not the warm and popular leader but the one who symbolizes striving for success. His skills are those of the go-getter and the diplomat, and he uses situations and contacts to his own advantage.

The third type of boys, intermediaries, were few in number but belonged to both groups. They served as go-betweens and facilitated communication between the top and bottom social levels of Cornerville. For example, Whyte found that a college boy spoke to a corner boy through one of the intermediaries. This mediating role was necessary because of the keen rivalry between the two gangs in terms of different goals and values and different styles of leadership.

The rivalry appeared not only in bowling but also in competition for girls. Chick's college boys made deliberate plays for girls with some class and status. They would go outside of Cornerville to invite the superior girls of the Italian Junior League when girls were needed to make up the cast for a dramatic production. When the Aphrodite Club girls in Cornerville no longer served the status needs of Chick's Gang, they were no longer included in the social events of that group. In fact, Chick finally married a girl who was not from Cornerville at all but was more in keeping with his new position as a young lawyer after he graduated from an Ivy League law school.

Doc and his boys were interested in girls, too, but with quite a different perspective. They dated Aphrodite girls partly to draw them away from Chick's Gang. Doc first dated Helen on a dare and later continued to date this most attractive of the Aphrodite girls to reaffirm his leadership role. It was Doc who brought his Nortons and the Aphrodite girls together for a time. This interest in girls, however, threatened to split the gang, and members forced Doc to choose between them and the girls. Doc decided in favor of gang unity and the Nortons and Aphrodites soon drifted apart. Gang solidarity was one of the primary values for Doc and his boys. A member who got serious about a girl was lost to the gang. Thus marriage was considered desertion and was played down.

The Norton Street Gang's emphasis upon the importance of primary ties was a function of special member needs and goals. The boys had grown up together and had developed strong group loyalties over the years. They spent far more time on the corner with each other than at home with their families. At the time of the study, they were all single young adults. They were more apt to spend their small savings on each other than to save them toward a college education. Indeed, most of the corner boys were high school dropouts. The boys were either unemployed or casually employed and thus had no ties with an occupational group. This primariness did not mean, however, that within the Nortons there was equality.

Members of the group differed in status and role according to different skills and levels of commitment to the values of the group. The internal social structure clearly set Doc and his associates (Mike, Danny, and Long John) apart at the top of the status ladder. These were the boys who made the decisions and had the leadership ability. They were expected to score highest in bowling and achievement with girls. Figure 3-1 indicates the social structure of the Norton Street Gang. So important were group expectations that they had much to do with the superior

FIGURE 3-1 Sociogram of Doc's Gang: The Nortons

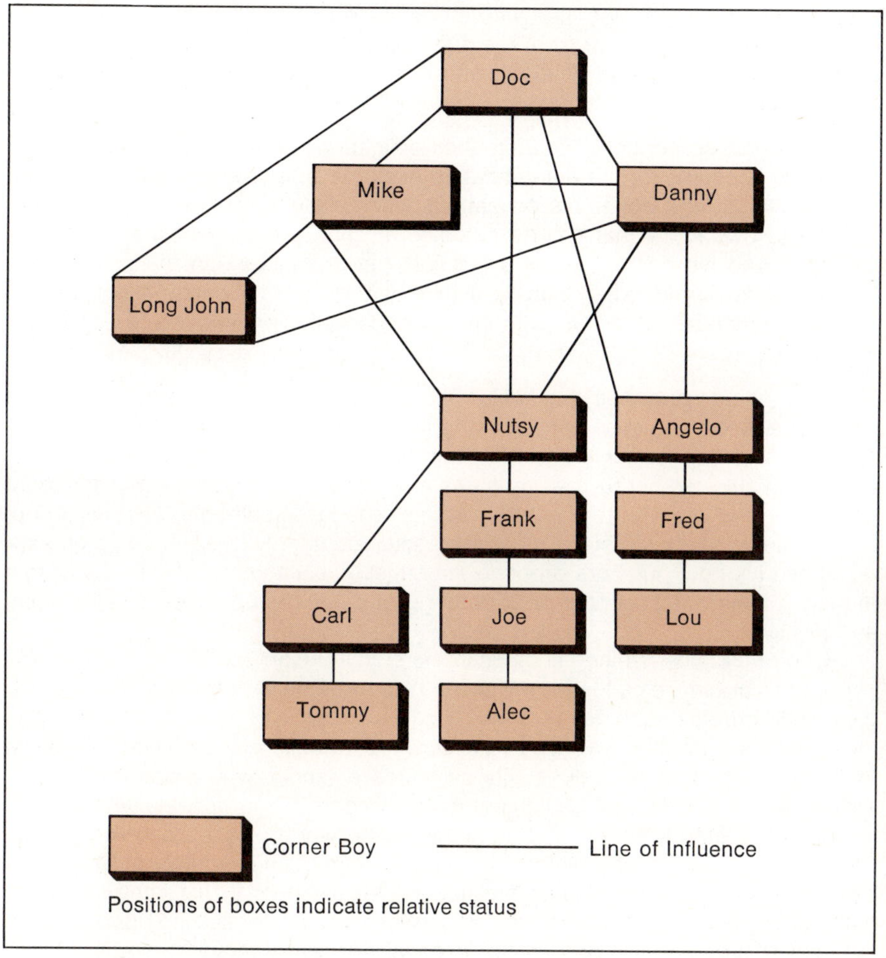

From William F. White, *Street Corner Society,* 2nd ed. (Chicago: University of Chicago Press, 1955), p. 13.

performance of leaders as compared to the performance of other gang members. The boys at the bottom of the structure, Tommy and Alec, were least apt to reflect the values of the gang. At one point, Alec would have left the group for marriage if his proposal had been accepted. And when Alec boasted of being able to beat any member in bowling, the group put sufficient pressure on him so that he lost his poise and collapsed completely in a crucial game. Nutsy had formerly been the leader of the Nortons but lost his position when he began going steady with a "no good" girl.

Finally, Whyte observed how social change, group expectations, and self-concepts were all interrelated in Cornerville society. He traced, for example, the rise and fall of Doc's popularity among his boys. When Doc suffered from unemployment and from failure in a political venture, he was bothered by dizzy spells and withdrew from his status position in the gang. His position in the structure depended upon his immediate ability to fulfill the functions of leadership. Leadership is a matter of group functions more than personality. Thus when Doc's situation changed from the man with money who can buy favors for his boys to the unemployed person, or from the success to the failure in the political campaign, his own self-image changed and likewise his place in the group. Whyte summarizes this point as follows:

> Not all the corner boys live up to their obligations equally well, and this factor partly accounts for the differentiation in status among them. The man with a low status may violate his obligations without much change in his position. His fellows know that he has failed to discharge certain obligations in the past, and his position reflects his past performances. On the other hand, the leader is depended upon by all members to meet his personal obligations. He cannot fail to do so without causing confusion and endangering his position [p. 257].

Just as individual positions within the group changed, so the Norton Street Gang as a whole changed over time and finally ceased to exist. When conditions changed, it no longer served the needs of the corner boys. With these changes, Long John suffered perhaps as much as any member. His status was dependent upon his friendship with Doc in the Nortons. When Doc shifted to another group, Long John was left without a place for social identity. He had nightmares as a result and his bowling score dropped appreciably. It was only after Doc saw to it that Long John was accepted into another group that he regained his self-esteem and position.

One of the most striking findings in the study of Cornerville was the contrast between Doc and Chick Morelli. Whyte was confronted with the fact that the two gangs had created such different leaders. His explanation for this is based upon the hypothesis that the boys who were upwardly mobile and ambitious to get on to college had different values. They needed a leader who responded to the middle-class teachers and settlement-house leaders of Cornerville, who aspired to behavior patterns that were acceptable in the world of achieving Americans. Chick proved to be such a leader. He was an immigrant from Italy at the age of eight and soon became one of the major breadwinners in his family after his father died. He worked hard and developed the capacity for seizing opportunities. His mother urged him to prepare for college, and every move he made pointed toward his aspiration to become a lawyer. When he organized the Italian Community Club, made up of the best students in his high school class, he insisted upon setting up formal rules and clearly stated purposes and programs. One stated purpose was that of community service. Yet it was clear that club membership was considered one way of gaining recognition and getting ahead as individuals.

The primary value in this group was not the gang and its long-term solidarity. In fact, group unity was somewhat weak in comparison to the Nortons partly because the inclusion of noncollege boys in the membership diluted the common value system. It was also partly because Chick was not the expressive leader who aimed to keep things going smoothly among the members. He was the executive type who insisted upon the rules and upon getting things done even at the expense of the approval and happiness of members. His leadership was challenged on occasion by dissatisfied members in the group, and at one point there was talk of impeachment. It is implied that Chick would not have emerged as the leader of the Nortons. He was head of the college boys chiefly because of his drive and success orientation. In short, Chick emerged as leader of the college boys because he came closest to realizing the norms that the group valued most highly. Later, after finishing law school, he ran for political office. He identified not with the Democratic party, which was strong in Cornerville, but with the higher status Republican party. He polled relatively few votes in his own neighborhood, a fact he attributed to jealousy among the people he had left behind.

Conclusions and Implications

A gang has a basic reason for existence as does every human group: It exists as long as it *fulfills expected functions or needs for those who belong, as well as for the larger society.* It is most stable when its functions are clear and a common value system is shared. It is least stable and may cease to exist when there are few shared values and the original functions no longer remain. In the course of group life, some members rise to the top of the social structure and become focal points for interaction. Leadership and status position are assigned on the basis of who most embodies the values and goals of the group. Individual needs must be met, at least in part, for all members to continue functioning in the group.

The interaction of self and society can thus be studied in sociology through observation of specific groups by a scholar who becomes an "insider." This method of research is time consuming and demanding, but it is an invaluable way of gaining first-hand insights that can be used to develop theory and encourage other kinds of research. As John Madge [1962, p. 210] comments: "This is a deceptively simple book presented with great charm and modesty, but it is also a book that provides the raw material for an important advance in sociological understanding."

Theoretically, Whyte's study is empirical verification of the sociological perspective with which we began this chapter: We are not born human; rather we are made human through the process of self-formation. Specifically, Whyte is arguing that leaders are not born so much as they emerge to meet the needs and expectations of group members within a given setting.

Whyte's study also contains practical implications, especially regarding the question of how to deal with juvenile delinquency (discussed in more detail in the work of Short and Strodtbeck in Chapter 12). Specifically, Whyte took a strong position opposing the kind of social work that was being conducted in Cornerville. As John Madge points out, Whyte opposed it for the following reasons:

> The social workers were completely unable and unwilling to deal with corner boys. Instead they bent their energies to stimulating social mobility, extending middle-class standards and middle-class rewards to lower-class natives who were maladjusted in terms of the local society. . . . Whyte himself abandons his customary detachment and comes out strongly against the settlements. He accuses them of increasing the friction between corner boys and college boys, of suppressing the natural leadership of Cornerville and attempting to substitute alien leaders, of forcing the individual to subordinate himself to people that he recognizes are different from his own [Madge, 1962, pp. 253–254].

Social workers saw their mission almost solely in terms of rescuing a few Cornerville boys from their Italian blue-collar setting and sending them on to college and middle-class "respectability." In Whyte's view, this approach was wrong. It ignored the significance of Cornerville values, which were shared by most of the citizens there, and overlooked the importance of native leadership among corner boys and others like them.

For his time, Whyte's argument was a progressive and universalistic perspective of the problems of slum life in American cities (see Chapter 2 and the discussion of C. Wright Mills and the need for a universalistic view of social problems). It is a view that speaks forcefully even today as we confront continued crises in the inner cities. It suggests that viable programs for urban reform must take into account the unique life-styles and value systems of minority peoples and the significant native leadership that they can provide. In these terms, Whyte's conclusions about Cornerville are still relevant and influential. Many programs in the 1960s and 1970s incorporated similar perspectives. The "war on poverty" during the administration of President L. B. Johnson included an emphasis upon the use of native leadership from within poverty groups. Low-income citizens in many counties were appointed to local Economic Opportunity Councils and had much to say about how money was to be spent in reform programs. Minority peoples have also been well-represented in many similar programs.

▶ SO WHAT?

Whyte's research is an example of dozens of studies that have shown the close interdependence of self and society. Those that have utilized the concepts of socialization and resocialization have gradually led to social action programs designed to help groups of individuals labeled as deviants by larger society. Arguing that society has played a part (has socialized) some people into seeing themselves as narcotics users, alcoholics, or sexual deviates, these groups utilize techniques of desocialization and resocialization. Three types of self-help groups have developed:

1. Organizations of those labeled as "deviates" may attempt to free themselves of this label through dramatic social action or persuasion. For example, the Gay Liberation movement argues that homosexuals are essentially like all other people (the straights), except in their private sexual preference—Gays hold jobs, pay taxes, sometimes marry and raise families, vote in elections, and so on.
2. Special environments may be created within which the labeled deviate can develop a new self-image. For example, half-way houses have provided a substitute for isolated prisons. In a half-way house, the individual can obtain a job, engage in dating and courtship, participate in community life, and otherwise become a visible part of normal everyday life.
3. Self-help organizations can encourage strict conformity to conventional norms and provide positive role models. For example, Alcoholics Anonymous insists that the member admit alcoholism as an unavoidable physical disease and adopt lifetime abstinence as the only alternative. A. A. also stresses upward mobility by retelling Horatio-Alger-like stories about members who "hit the bottom" on skid row while drunk but later achieved success in marriage and jobs through participation in the program.

CONCLUSION

In this chapter, we considered the most fundamental element of human society, the social self. A person is born, however, only with the potential for becoming a fully social being. This potential must be developed through the process of socialization, whereby society transmits the fundamental skills, knowledge, and values necessary for the survival of both the individual and the social system as a whole. Such a process is best carried out through primary relationships in intimate human associations like the family and peer groups.

This process of creating and sustaining social beings is difficult and complex. For one thing, it is a life-long endeavor. Since at different ages and stages in our maturation process, we are called upon to participate in a variety of experiences, society must continually provide channels of socialization for us. Such channels are normally concentrated in the early years of life, but later socialization for military service or for the world of business is also crucial. When socialization processes are not available, as in the case of the aged or certain isolated children, major social problems are created. In addition, differential rates of socialization, as in the case of parent–youth conflict, can constitute important problems for society.

Socialization is complicated by the fact that many groups normally compete for the allegiance of individuals. Such competition between the peer group and a weakened family in urban America can help us to explain certain problems like narcotics use and delinquency. Sometimes the family of one's birth competes with the family of one's marital choice. Even peer groups (school versus neighborhood) can compete with each other. The demands of friends and associates often compete with the values and beliefs generated by family or church.

Yet neither the social individual nor human society would be possible without the mutual interdependence of the one on the other. It is this interdependency, with its inherent conflicts, that gives to society its rich complexity and changing, dynamic character. We see this illustrated in Whyte's study of street-corner gangs. Having considered the self, we now turn our attention to the nature of *culture*, the second major element of the social order. More specifically, what kinds of values, beliefs, and norms shape the self-conceptions of humans. And what is the nature, purpose, and role of culture in the organization of human society?

REFERENCES

Becker, Howard S. *Outsiders: Studies in the Sociology of Deviance.* New York: The Free Press, 1963.

Bettleheim, Bruno. "Feral Children and Autistic Children," *The American Journal of Sociology, 64* (March 1959), pp. 455–467.

Blumer, Herbert. *Symbolic Interactionism: Perspective and Method.* Englewood Cliffs, N.J.: Prentice–Hall, 1969.

Brown, Claude. *Manchild in the Promised Land.* New York: The Macmillan Company, 1965.

Davis, Kingsley. "Extreme Social Isolation in a Child," *The American Journal of Sociology, 45* (January 1940) (a), pp. 554–564.

———— "The Sociology of Parent–Youth Conflict," *American Sociological Review, 5* (August 1940) (b), pp. 523–535.

———— "Final Note on a Case of Extreme Isolation," *The American Journal of Sociology, 50* (March 1947), pp. 432–437.

Duster, Troy. *The Legislation of Morality.* New York: The Macmillan Company, 1969.

Fort, Joel. "Social Problems of Drug Use and Drug Policies," *California Law Review, 56,* (1968).

Fromm, Erich. *The Sane Society.* New York: Holt, Rinehart and Winston, 1955.

Gessell, A. *Wolf Child and Human Child.* New York: Harper & Row, Publishers, 1940.

Kolanski, Harold, and William T. Moore. "Effects of Marihuana on the Young," *The Journal of the American Medical Association, 216* (April 1971), pp. 486–492.

Madge, John. *The Origins of Scientific Sociology.* New York: The Free Press, 1962.

Mead, George H. *Mind, Self and Society.* Chicago: The University of Chicago Press, 1934.

Moskos, Charles C., Jr. *The American Enlisted Man.* New York: Russell Sage Foundation, 1970.

Ogburn, William F. "The Wolf Boy of Agra," *The American Journal of Sociology,* 64 (March 1959), pp. 449–454.

Singh, J. A. L., and R. M. Zingg. *Wolf Children and Feral Man.* New York: Harper & Row, Publishers, 1940.

Smith, David E., Ed. *The New Social Drug: Cultural, Medical, and Legal Perspectives on Marihuana.* Englewood Cliffs, N.J.: Prentice-Hall, 1970.

Tamney, Joseph B. "Family Solidarity and Fertility," in *Family and Fertility.* W. T. Liu, Ed. Notre Dame: University of Notre Dame Press, 1967.

- Is there really much difference between animals and humans? Do both have language and culture?
- Incest calls forth strong feelings of disgust among humans for the most part. Why?
- What is the basis of morality among human beings? Are some things considered right behavior by all humans everywhere?
- Are American black families in low income ghettos unstable or are they understandably different from middle-class white families because of different environmental needs?
- What is your reaction to the idea that the Protestant religion helped in the rise of capitalism and the profit system?

4

Culture

As we have seen, socialization is the process through which the social self emerges and through which the social heritage is passed on from one generation to another. Social scientists use the concept of *culture* to refer to all aspects of this social heritage. However, they make special reference to culture as the sum total of meaning and life-style among persons who live with each other in a society. In other words, humans are social creatures who share a common culture; that is, they share a set of understandings about what is right and wrong, what is valuable, and what human existence is all about.

In the last chapter, we spoke of humans as beings who interact with each other symbolically. Every human gesture, sound, and word has meaning according to the cultural context. To be socialized is to grow up within a cultural context and to become familiar with all the subtle actions, innuendos, idioms, and jokes that outsiders cannot fathom. To say that people live in different worlds is to refer largely to the cultural differences that separate people. In this chapter, we will concentrate upon the significance of culture and the ways in which humans are cultural creatures.

THE NATURE OF CULTURE

Culture is not an easy concept to define. Scholars emphasize different aspects and continue to struggle for a precise focus and meaning. Thus, we can introduce only some of the basic considerations that must be understood with respect to so complex a notion.

One classic definition, that of E. B. Tylor, indicates the *inclusive* nature of culture. Tylor states [1871, p. 1] that "culture, or civilization, . . . is that complex whole which includes knowledge, belief, art, law, morals, customs, and any other capabilities and habits acquired by man as a member of society." Other definitions similarly stress the fact that culture is the *totality* of the human way of life as distinguished from animal existence. Leslie A. White [1947, pp. 686–698] refers to it as an organization of phenomena that is dependent upon symbols, phenomena that include *acts* (patterns of behavior); *objects* (tools and things made by tools); *ideas* (beliefs, knowledge); and *sentiments* (attitudes, values). Culture has also been defined to include human material as well as nonmaterial dimensions. Human artifacts tell a great deal about what people value and how they go about meeting their biological and cultural needs. Thus anthropologists can reconstruct the social and cultural life of a prehistoric people from the material objects unearthed at an archeological site.

The cultural elements of human existence, however, are primarily mental or ideational. The things that count are ideas, meanings, and purposes. A piece of chalk may be a material artifact, but the important thing about it is what it means within a given cultural setting. It may be used in a schoolroom to write symbols on the blackboard or it may hang as an amulet about a person's neck to ward off evil spirits. Scholars generally agree that the key to culture lies in the mind, and that these *mentifacts*, or ideas, are the foundation of culture. Culture is thus largely abstract; nonetheless, it is a fundamental part of human reality, both material and nonmaterial.

We will return to the notion of the ideational aspect of culture later in this chapter. For the moment, however, culture can be better understood by comparing it with the concepts of self and society.

Culture, Self, and Society

All too often we refer to culture without making it clear just how it relates to the self and society. One way of defining culture and distinguishing it from the self and society is to compare human and animal "societies." Nonhuman living creatures (like ants and bees) do form what some scholars have called humanlike social systems. Individual differences are limited, however, because the behavior patterns are largely built-in, that is, instinctive. In contrast, young humans combine social and genetic capabilities in learning the techniques and ideas of their elders, and this process creates the "personality." Through a long period of dependency, children take on the behavior patterns of their family, the habits that give regularity to the society and, at the same time, allow for the infinite variety of individual differences. "The habits that are acquired by youngsters are part of their culture. In one sense, the habits *are* the culture; if all the habits of all the people were changed, the culture would have changed" [Bohannan, 1963, p. 18].

Paul Bohannan speaks of culture as the *medium of personality.* When a baby is born, he leaves a biophysical relationship for a social relationship through which his personality emerges within a cultural context. He takes on a way of life with a style and a meaning.

> Culture, as it is acquired with the growth of personality, becomes the *medium* of that personality. You cannot swim without water, and water is the medium of swimming; you cannot paint a picture without paint, and the paint becomes the medium for expressing the message of the picture. The difference between the culture and personality is the same as the difference between the medium and the context of the picture. They are, at one level, the same thing. At another level, they are distinct because they have been viewed with completely different purposes and techniques [Bohannan, 1963, pp. 20–21].

Some things about the human personality, like the emotions of love and hate, are the same the world over. On the other hand, a personality reflects the culture within which it emerges; there is a "basic personality" shared by a large proportion of the people in a single society. Since a given society rewards certain personality types more than others, in accordance with its norms and values, most persons conform to expected behavior and strive for society's goals. After all, humans are reward-seeking animals, which accounts for the similarity of personality within a cultural context. At the same time, in every society, there are unique qualities of personality and individual differences depending upon differences in physical nature and social conditioning. It is no wonder that "every man is in certain respects like all other men, like some other men, and like no other man" [Kluckhohn and Murray, 1949, p. 35].

Therefore, humans are both like and unlike one another, whereas other "social" animals are basically like one another. George Murdock [1932, p. 213] suggests that this is because lower animals live in societies that do not possess culture. In ant societies, the interaction is instinctive; in human societies, it is cultural. In place of a mating instinct, there is the institution of marriage, a result of the cultural heritage. The human sexual impulse does not predispose people to a permanent union. Humans move through courtship and into marriage and family life because of learned norms and values of society. This conclusion leads Murdock to observe that "not society, but culture is the distinctly human phenomenon. . . . The proper study of sociology is culture."

The basic unit of human society is not the "individual" but the *social role* that is taken by the individual. All too often there is an implication that society is merely a collection of individuals. This gives the false impression that social order is simply the result of individuals grouping themselves into an organic whole, much as cells make up a biological organism. But society is a cultural achievement; that is, society has regularity and predictability because individuals learn to act out prescribed roles of mother, breadwinner, leader, priest, and so on. These social roles can be defined as clusterings of social expectations. For example, when one becomes a parent, specific kinds of patterned behaviors are expected. A parent is expected to provide the child with the love it needs, to be its primary agent of socialization, and to provide the discipline needed to keep the child from being socially disruptive. Parental interaction with children is in accordance with culturally determined social roles (expectations). At the same time, as unique personalities, mothers and fathers can play their roles in different ways. No two parents play the parental role exactly alike.

All humans act in accordance with a number of social roles, each of which is culturally defined. Together these roles become the building blocks of human society in the following ways.

1. *Roles are related to a social position* within a group or society. In a family, for example, the position of parent carries with it a certain *status*, which calls for behavior that is appropriate for that status. The status is the position; the role is the pattern of behavior that goes with the status. Both the status and role are determined according to cultural norms (cultural expectations). Parents are responsible for earning a living and making decisions about jobs, the family dwelling place, and the disciplining of the children. As a consequence, certain privileges of status accrue to parents.

2. *Roles are defined according to the value system of a culture.* For example, masculinity is culturally determined and reflects what males value and consider right or wrong for them. Traditionally, males in our culture have been expected to be tough, unemotional, aggressive, and daring. Fathers have been expected to project this kind of role model for their sons. When values change, however, roles and status are also effected. In Chapter 5, we discuss in detail the development of the women's movement, which is challenging these traditional beliefs about male versus female roles.

3. *Roles are interrelated and form role sets.* No one can play the role of father apart from everything else. Every man in traditional Western society must learn to play several roles simultaneously. He must be plumber, labor union member, churchman, citizen–voter, and husband, as well as father. He must be friend to his children, as well as disciplinarian. Often the roles seem to fit together harmoniously. A "good" father and husband is a playmate for his young children, a companion for his wife, and a success on his job. Frequently, however, there are inevitable *role conflicts.*

It may not be easy to be successful at work and still find time for one's family. It is difficult to be a pal one day and a disciplinarian the next.

The discussion could apply equally well to any family role, including that of mother. It is particularly illustrative when applied to fathers, however, because that role does not seem to be determined by biological factors. The father does not bear or nurse the child. Nevertheless, society needs someone to help care for the child and rear it. Fatherhood, therefore, is encouraged by strong cultural expectations; thus, culture, not biology, requires the father to play his role in relationship to the child. The mother is more obviously bound to her child through biological ties. Nevertheless, the manner in which a mother fulfills her responsibility is also culturally determined.

Society, then, is a network of social relationships made possible by interacting humans as social selves in accordance with cultural norms and expectations. People relate to one another as husband and wife, child and parent, employer and employee, and the like. Since roles are defined culturally, regularity and predictability in interaction are possible. Culture, self, and society are therefore integrally related, and "they are different ways of looking at the same thing" [Bohannan, 1963, p. 7]. All of these, however, would be impossible if interacting humans could not share the same expectations. Language—both spoken and silent—is fundamentally important in understanding the nature of culture.

Language: Spoken and Silent

Humans are not cultural beings just because they possess "intelligence." Many animals are intelligent and some live in societies. The critical difference between humans and animals, the difference that makes culture possible, is *symbolic language*. Symbolic language enables human beings to communicate knowledge that can be stored in the memory of a person, in a library, and in computers. Once stored, the knowledge can be retrieved for use over long periods of time. It can also be called upon whenever it is needed to transmit ideas from one generation to the next. Consequently, human society does not have to start anew with the birth of each individual. We begin by learning as much as we can about the rich heritage of the past; it is said that "we stand on the shoulders of giants."

At the outset, it is important to differentiate between symbolic language and sign language. Humans use both. A *sign* is a gesture or a sound that has immediate and direct significance; it is a signal with obvious intent. When a person has a sharp pain and writhes in agony, this is a sign or signal to all who can see that something is wrong. A *symbol* is quite different. It is a gesture or sound that has an agreed-upon meaning that is not obvious and must be learned. When a person has a sharp pain, writhes in agony, but also says, "My heart again; call the doctor," symbols have been added. These would mean nothing to an animal, but they have special meaning to human beings attending the sick person. The words "heart," "call," and "doctor" stand for specific actions, roles, and meanings.

An animal may react to a sign if it is obvious enough or, perhaps, if it is startling. In contrast, a human will react to both the sign and the symbol. A word like "halt" may be a sign to a dog who has been trained to respond. It can be more than that to a soldier. The latter learns to react almost automatically when he hears a sound, but he also knows that if he does not obey there will be a whole series of consequences. Similarly, when a mathematician says, "Let x equal speed and *y* equal distance," he uses these symbols to solve mathematical problems. A religionist says, "Let us pray," and religious behavior results. A child at play says, "You be the bad guy" and thereby initiates an elaborate game of cops and robbers.

The point is that humans are able to communicate in a language that is so flexible that almost any gesture or sound or written word can stand for whatever is agreed upon. The human vocabulary is rich in number of words and the complexity of their meaning, and it has enabled humans to build up a vast fund of knowledge through the ages. It is this kind of language that sets humans off from all other living creatures and leads an anthropologist to write:

> Without language, man would be little better off than the animals, as is proved by studies of deaf-mutes and other speechless persons. In a society without language, each individual would have to begin exactly where his parents began; he could possess only individual habits, not group habits; his behavior, in short, would be confined to the organic level [Murdock, 1932, p. 212. Reproduced by permission of the American Anthropological Association from *The American Anthropologist* 34(2), 1932.]

Some scientists have recently achieved success in teaching higher-order animals (apes, gibbons, monkeys) to use human symbols to communicate with themselves and with humans. One of the best examples is the story of Washoe, a female chimpanzee, who has learned to use the American sign language of deaf-mutes. Scholars at the University of Nevada in Reno [Gardner and Gardner, 1969] have worked for many years on this experiment, but they have been unable to demonstrate conclusively whether an animal like Washoe will transmit her knowledge effectively to her offspring. Other scholars are studying the ability of primates to use computers to communicate with themselves and with others [Fleming, 1974, pp. 31–46; Premack, 1971, pp. 808–822; Premack and Premack, 1972, pp. 92–99]. In addition, continuing research with porpoises has also revealed remarkable ability to communicate with members of their own species.

At the same time, some scientists suggest that humans are perhaps more dependent upon their biological origin and nature than was originally believed [Wilson, 1974]. Humans are citizens of two worlds—the biological and the cultural. Nevertheless, it is still true that cultural influences predominate among humans while biological factors determine the behavior of animals almost entirely. The following quotation from an American classic in sociology serves to emphasize the contrast between animals and humans:

4-1 Animal Versus Human Learning

Humans and some animals are both similar and dissimilar. They are similar in that some animals and all humans possess intelligence (the ability to learn from one another) and live in societies (groups where individual acts are taught by adults to the young).

In his studies of geese, Konrad Lorenz found that the young learn by imitating the actions of adults. In this way, they are taught how to protect themselves from danger, seek out food, and express affection and dependence (see Chapter 14).

Elizabeth Hamlin, Dietz/Hamlin

Jamyl Smith/Metamorphosis

In the same manner, human young often imitate the behavioral acts of human adults.

Elizabeth Hamlin, Dietz/Hamlin

Humans are dissimilar from animals in that they possess symbolic language—the ability to communicate stored knowledge from one generation to the next.

Therefore, most human learning involves the communication of knowledge by symbolic language (written or spoken) within group contexts.

Elizabeth Hamlin, Dietz/Hamlin

Symbolic language also makes it possible for humans to learn in isolation and without directly relating to or imitating adult behavior.

> As to structure, human nature is undoubtedly the most plastic part of the living world, the most adaptable, the most educable. Of all animals, it is man in whom heredity counts for least, and conscious building forces for most. . . . Other living creatures nature could largely finish: the human creature must finish himself [Park and Burgess, 1921, pp. 95–96].

In summary, human culture would not exist, as we know it, were it not for symbolic language. This kind of language is a systematic means of communication through the use of phonetic or written symbols. It creates, sustains, and alters consensus in a society; and it enables individuals to share common prespectives, attitudes, beliefs, and values. It is a unique human achievement.

Communication among humans also takes place through silent nonverbal means, such as the significant exchanges of meaning that come from the raising of an eyebrow (surprise or puzzlement); the wiping of the forehead (weariness or nervousness); the extending of a hand (friendliness or hostility); and other gestures. Such exchanges take on specific meaning according to cultural definition—a clenched fist can mean friendship or hostility, a sense of collective solidarity or a threat of violence.

Language can be both liberating and confining. It is *liberating* in that people can be socialized into a culture and thereby made human only after learning to communicate symbolically. Helen Keller, made blind and deaf by a brain fever before she was two years old, did not become a complete social self until one day, as a young girl, she perceived that her teacher was communicating with her through symbols. As her teacher, Ann Sullivan, wrote:

> We went to the pump, where I had Helen hold her cup under the opening while I pumped. As the cold water poured forth and filled the cup, I spelled out "water" by tapping on her free hand. The word, which followed so immediately upon the sensation of the cold water running over her hand, seemed to puzzle her. Then she let the cup fall and stood as if she were rooted there. A completely new expression lighted her features. She spelled out the word "water" again and again. She knelt down and touched the earth and wanted to know its name, and she did the same for the pump and the nearby trellis. Then she turned around and inquired about my name. I spelled out "teacher" in her hand . . . [Keller, 1904, p. 316].

Language can also be *confining* in that it restricts people's perceptions to their own cultural perspectives and symbols. As Paul Bohannan reminds us, those who speak English have a separate word for each distinct color in the spectrum. Other people develop languages that do not place the same value on color variations. For example, the Japanese have only one word, *aoi,* to describe both blue and green, which are lumped together as "nature colors." This does not mean that Japanese people do not see both blue and green but that their culture sees no need to make this distinction. In the same manner, the Eskimo people have a number of words that indicate small variations in weather and temperature, whereas those of us who live in more temperate climates tend to rely upon only two words: hot and cold. Little wonder that something is lost when translations are made from one language to another.

The work of anthropologist Edward T. Hall contains many examples of the way in which spoken and silent language are related to one another and the way in which both are related to cultural symbols and social behavior. For example, he indicates the different ways in which various cultures talk about space [Hall, 1973, pp. 172–173, 182–183]. The people who live on the atoll of Truk in the Pacific Ocean region speak about small spaces much differently than Americans. They treat open spaces as completely distinct, without dividing lines, as we know them. At the same time, they have not developed a nomenclature for the edges of objects as elaborately as Westerners have done. For example, the Westerner can talk about the rim of a cup as round or elliptical or square in cross section; as straight, flared, or curved inward; as plain or decorated; and as wavy or straight. In contrast, the Trukese separate parts that we think of as being built into the object.

> A certain decoration or carving at either end of a canoe-shaped food bowl is thought of as being separate or distinct from the rim in which it has been carved. It has an essence of its own. Along the keel of the canoe the carving, called the *chunefatch*, has characteristics with which it endows the canoe. The canoe is one thing, the chunefatch something else [Hall, 1973, p. 173].

At the same time, the peoples of Truk consider trees separate from the soil out of which they grow. Hall points out that this can make the settling of land claims unbelievably complicated, since one man can own the trees while another owns the soil below. To Westerners, an open space in a field consists of land, trees, rocks, streams, and any other natural objects within that larger context, and, when buying a piece of land, one purchases everything upon it (excluding legal easements, rights of way, and state and public natural resource rights).

Language, then, in whatever form, is fundamental to human personality and society. Symbolic language, however, gives humans the flexibility of meaning and the long-term information storage and retrieval capability that permits them to transmit their culture from generation to generation. As mentioned earlier, the essence of any culture is its knowledge, values, and beliefs—its ideational aspects.

The Ideational Quality of Culture

As sociologists have studied modern Western peoples, they have been especially interested in the impact of ideas, ideologies, and ideational elements upon behavior patterns and social organization. For example, they have made frequent use of attitude and opinion tests to examine the impact of prejudice and discrimination upon black–white relationships. In addition, sociologists have devised techniques of content analysis for analyzing literature and mass media presentations. Content analysis involves the

4-2 Signs and Symbols in Human Language

Humans communicate with one another by either **signs** or **symbols.** Signs are gestures that have a direct and immediate meaning. Symbols are gestures that have indirect meanings which must be learned in the context of specific cultures. Some human gestures—such as the clenched fist—can be both signs and symbols in the same situation, depending upon the meanings seen by different people.

For Sonny Liston, Muhammad Ali's fist became a sign in 1965, when the challenger was knocked down in his return bout with the heavyweight champion. Ali's fist was a weapon of physical force which enable him to retain the championship. When Ali gestured over Liston's prone body, he was symbolizing victory.

Wide World Photos

During the summer Olympic Games in Mexico City in 1968, when victorious black American athletes raised their fists during the playing of the national anthem, many white Americans considered the gesture an insult and a sign that blacks wanted to punch whites in the nose. To black Americans, the gesture symbolized unity and solidarity with their brothers.

United Press International

Robert Cohen/Black Star

When members of a crowd watching a political parade and demonstration raise clenched fists, observers frequently interpret the gesture as a sign of defiance or threat. For those using the gesture, the act can symbolize enthusiasm or support for collective ideals.

"From the Depths," by William Balfour Kerr

In this 1906 painting by William Balfour Ker, the fist is a sign of impending disaster for the upper classes. For the lower classes, the fist symbolizes needed revolutionary change and a cry for help.

systematic observation and recording of important symbols, social roles, and the like that appear in books, movies, and television programs. This technique can identify the major cultural values of a society.

Finally, public opinion polling procedures can also identify the attitudes, values, or beliefs of a people regarding different kinds of issues and problems. Furthermore, these cultural elements can then be matched with other social variables (age, sex, educational level, and so on) or previous attitudes and beliefs in order to detect cultural conflict and change. In the next section, "Elements of Culture," we will discuss norms and values in detail. For the moment, one brief example of content analysis will illustrate the *ideational nature of culture.*

Sociologists have long been interested in the types of heroes and villains with whom people identify in their literature. Using the results of content analysis, Orrin E. Klapp [1954, pp. 56–62] has distinguished three social types that can be found in popular culture—the hero, the villain, and the fool. Each of these types is depicted through a variety of labels:

Heroes: Underdog, champ, big shot, emancipator, he-man.

Villains: Bully, liar, traitor, Red, dictator.

Fools: Crackpot, fanatic, sissy, cheapskate, sap, sucker.

All three types are, of course, oversimplifications of real world personalities. The hero is one who is admired because of unusual merit or ability; the villain is an idealized figure of evil; and the fool is a caricature of defect and weakness. As such, public heroes, villians, and fools—whether fictional or associated with living individuals—tell us much about a people's basic beliefs and values, and what they consider good and bad behavior. Furthermore, Professor Klapp suggests that these idealized types operate within one's self-conception as norms of self-judgment and role models for emulation or avoidance. They provide convenient symbols around which groups can reaffirm their basic values and beliefs and organize their collective responses.

The most obvious place where the three social types serve these kinds of societal functions is in organizations, as in a military establishment. Heroic figures are important in perpetuating the tradition and discipline of the organization. The enemy as a villain becomes the exaggerated personification of evil. Fools constitute behavioral patterns that must be avoided in order to be a good military man. ("Don't be a gold brick"; "cowards will die first in combat"; "only fools are taken in by the apparent humanity of the enemy.") Studies of the infantry soldier—the "grunt"—in Vietnam disclosed, ironically, that in combat heroes are often as disliked as cowards. The hero can expose one to unnecessary dangers and risks [Moskos, 1970].

In addition, recent research in military sociology has disclosed that the newer social role of military manager creates conflicts for many officers who still are motivated by older conceptions of heroic military roles

[Janowitz, 1960]. The modern military leader is most frequently involved in matters such as recruitment and training of personnel, acquisition and distribution of equipment, or routine administration of bureaucratic procedures. Battles and wars may be won on the basis of how successfully these managerial tasks are accomplished. Yet this view conflicts with the traditional concept of the military hero as one who dramatically leads his men into combat or plans a grand strategy. This conflict creates problems in terms of recruiting and retraining capable men for managerial duties.

In Chapter 12, we will discuss a study that examines a similar problem, the use of violence by the police. To some extent, this problem also is a result of conflicts between managerial or routine roles and heroic roles. The heroic role of the "cop" is associated with the dramatic solution of a heinous crime, the "good pinch," and a blazing gun battle. The "cop on the beat," however, rarely gets the opportunity to participate in these kinds of events. Most police time is occupied by routine patrolling, issuing traffic tickets, or filing daily reports. It should not be surprising, therefore, that many police are tempted to use illegal violence when apprehending criminal suspects; they are, perhaps, simply trying to act out the traditional heroic role of law officer that continues to be perpetuated by the commercially motivated mass media. The cultural concepts of the hero, the villain, and the fool, therefore, can help explain such contemporary social problems as police violence and ineffective military performance.

In summary, the sociologist's concept of culture centers on those aspects of human ideational life that can be identified in social attitudes, aspirations, values, and beliefs. Based upon our present knowledge, human society, because of its cultural elements, seems to be unique in relation to that of other animals. Insects, for example, can exhibit a high degree of "group" interaction. Ants and bees organize into workers, fighters, breeders, and the like. Although insect behavior appears to be the result of different factors than human interaction—that is, instincts versus role taking—biologists sometimes talk about the "social insects." However, ants and bees do not create, transmit, and share ideas. Humans alone possess this potential, and the ability to communicate through the use of a complex symbolic language is the factor that accounts for this difference.

As sociologists, we are interested not in what certain ideas should or should not be, but in whether they are useful in a specific group context. For example, neither the heroic nor the managerial role in the police or military is inherently or universally desirable or undesirable. Although we may lament the gradual disappearance of the heroic role, there is a social reason for this disappearance. The glamorous and dynamic hero would be out of place and dangerous when operating electronic machinery or pounding the beat. Managerial roles have become more functional in modern society, while heroic roles are often dysfunctional. The sociological perspective thus examines the usefulness of ideas within a group context. As was indicated in Chapter 1, this allows the human ideational world to be studied in a value-free manner, while the study remains value-relevant. Such an approach is the special job of the sociologist.

ELEMENTS OF CULTURE

Norms and Values

Although sociology is interested in all ideational aspects of culture, special emphasis is placed upon norms and values and the way in which they relate to social structure. This section will deal with these two concepts in detail, and the final section of the chapter will critique a classic study of norms and values in Western societies.

Norms are the *rules and regulations governing behavior* in a society. They specify what must be done, as well as when, where, and how it can be done. In this sense, they are the blueprints or the designs for living. They prescribe the patterns of behavior that are necessary to maintain ordered relationships and interaction in any society. They are transmitted to each individual through the socialization process. When a scholar writes that every year hordes of "barbarians" in the form of newborn babies enter a society and must be transformed into cultured creatures, he means in part that they must learn to behave according to the norms of the society.

Values are the *purposes or goals* that a society pursues (power, wealth, justice, equality, love, and so on). In order to attain these goals, society must establish norms that order and direct the activity of its individual members. Since life is of value, there are norms that assure the preservation of life—the ethics of medicine, laws against killing, the expectation that soldiers will take enemy lives in order to preserve life in their own society. Since babies are of value and must be reared within the security of the family, there are norms that restrict sexual behavior and that uphold the principle of legitimacy and the responsibility of the father to his child. So deep-seated are American commitments to private property and the pursuit of monetary success that we take for granted the norms that guide our pursuit of these goals. In fact, such norms are hallowed by religion and made sacred, as will be seen in our discussion of the Protestant ethic later in this chapter.

One of the best statements depicting the fundamental significance of norms and values is that of William Graham Sumner (1840–1910), a professor in the Divinity School at Yale. Over the years, he collected information about the customs of people in many lands. He found that marked cultural contrasts were evident: What was right behavior in one setting was offensive in another. One of his central themes is that "the mores can make anything right." That is, the ways of doing things—the mores—within a given society come to be so much a part of the social habit pattern that they are accepted without reflection. In quoting a German scholar, Sumner [1906, pp. 60, 62, 76, 77] makes the point that conscious reflection is the worst enemy of the mores:

> The mores are social ritual in which we all participate unconsciously. The current habits as to hours of labor, meal hours, family life, the social intercourse of the sexes, propriety, amusements, travel, holidays, education, the use of periodicals and libraries, and innumerable other details of life fall under this ritual. Each does as everybody does. . . . The great mass of folk-

ways give us discipline and the support of routine and habit. . . . The mores have the authority of facts. The mores come down to us from the past. Each individual is born into them as he is born into the atmosphere, and he does not reflect on them or criticize them any more than a baby analyzes the atmosphere before he begins to breathe it. . . . It is only in so far as things have been transformed from the mores into laws and positive institutions that there is discussion about them or rationalizing upon them.

As implied in the quotation, Sumner distinguishes between three different kinds of norms: *mores, folkways,* and *laws.* Norms can vary according to (1) whether they deal with matters of greater or lesser importance; and (2) whether they are unwritten rules that have common agreement and usage or are written into law and thus become formalized. One example of how an unwritten agreement becomes written law comes from a problem in the early days of TV quiz programs in America. In the 1950s, quiz programs became very popular, and Americans assumed that producers and participants were living up to the unwritten law of honesty. This was taken for granted as part of the mores of the culture. Suddenly, in 1959, it was publically charged that those being questioned on some television quiz programs were receiving advance information about the questions to be asked during the program. The American public was outraged at being cheated and misled. At that time, there was no written law against such conduct. Soon thereafter, laws were passed that now make it illegal and a criminal offense to engage in such performances. These laws emerged from a normative consensus among Americans and marked a new attempt to ensure morality in the mass media of television.

Mores and folkways are both informal types of norms that seem to be similar. In fact, Sumner often refers to them as if they were the same. A distinction does exist, however. Mores are norms that relate to matters of great concern and urgency in a society, while folkways in general deal with less critical matters. Folkways are important matters of etiquette and custom that help to order human behavior and make it predictable. For example, when a person loses his temper and fires a gun wildly out the window he is violating a neighborhood more. When he swears in public, he is violating a folkway. The latter neighbor is a nuisance but not a menace. Shooting a gun, however, threatens the lives of innocent neighbors.

According to Sumner, mores are those norms that are justified by tradition, accepted in society because they have the authority of being social facts, and never questioned or widely debated by the majority of citizens. Mores, therefore, are fundamentally conservative; that is, they function to maintain the status quo and perpetuate unchanging patterns of behavior for long periods of time. Since mores are neither created on a strictly rational basis nor maintained by conscious deliberation, some are eventually regarded as *sacred.* They are revered and respected for assumed suprahuman or transcendental qualities and character. Religion, then, characteristically concerns itself with the mores of a society by inculcating them with the authority of God, gods, or mystical and suprahuman beings.

The tradition of ancestor worship in many Far Eastern societies is an illustration of this process. The mores that govern behavior in such societies carry with them dogmatic authority and severe sanction for deviants.

The conservative nature of mores, however, creates a problem for many societies, especially in the modern world. People do not question their mores until they come into contact with other societies possessing different ones. Within a society consisting of complex and heterogeneous subgroups, contact between differing mores is heightened. As a matter of fact, in such a society some individuals and groups, such as social critics, intellectuals, or expressive deviants, may take on the special job of questioning prevailing mores. Once scrutinized, the mores can lose their vitality and naturalness. Sacred writings proscribing norms from the past can become out of date, inappropriate, or, in sociological terms, dysfunctional in a rapidly changing social context.

In our own society, we find the use of certain foods in preference to others, abstinence from certain behavior at given times, and the repetition of special phrases in rituals. All of these norms may at one time have had particular and important meaning to people in a given social context. Change, however, has made them less meaningful and, therefore, less important. When such a situation occurs, we frequently see the development of new mores arising from the intimate daily interaction of individuals in the group context. For example, Roman Catholics have become freer to marry non-Catholics and to eat meat on Fridays. American couples no longer hide the fact that they are living together outside of wedlock. And state laws are becoming less severe with respect to the personal use of marihuana.

The distinctions among the different types of norms are summarized in Table 4-1.

TABLE 4-1 Types of Norms (Examples from Western Societies)

	More Spontaneous	More Structured
Less Important	*Folkways:* Styles of dress (with or without a bra); where and how people should walk on a sidewalk; proper eating habits (use knife and fork); acceptable styles and types of houses	*Laws* (Misdemeanors): Truancy, minor theft, illegal automobile parking, loitering
More Important	*Mores:* Incest and cannibalism taboos, sexual behavior in public	*Laws* (Felonies): Robbery, murder, embezzlement, bribery

As this table illustrates, one way to differentiate norms is to speak of them *as more or less important* and *more or less structured.* Folkways and minor laws, those referring to misdemeanors, are norms that help to establish social order but are somewhat less important. Such norms are subject to continual change according to prevailing attitudes and beliefs. For example, styles of dress (the size of lapels on men's coats or the length of the hemline on women's skirts) and speed limits (limits may be higher because of superhighway construction or lower because of fuel conservation needs) constantly change over fairly short periods of time. Furthermore, these changes are relatively easy to accomplish. New fads and fashions (discussed in Chapter 5) easily give rise to new folkways, and simple legislation and legal rulings quickly change the nature of less important laws.

In contrast, the more important laws and mores are difficult and slow to change since they are based upon tradition and tend to take on a sacred character. The controversy over the death penalty, as demonstrated by the continuing debate and the ever-shifting position of state legislatures on the issue, is a good example. Americans have been very reluctant to give up the death penalty, especially in cases where very important and highly structured norms (kidnapping, killing of police officers, and so forth) are violated. They have likewise been slow to accept changes relative to mores and laws relating to marriage; for example, many still disapprove of divorce. And, although there is growing tolerance of couples who live together without being legally married, Americans generally consider this behavior to be threatening to the ideal relationship of monogamous marriage. In fact, for people who are devoutly religious, such behavior is considered a violation of God's law as recorded in the Bible or other sacred scripture. Furthermore, there appear to be virtually no changes in American mores and laws relative to bigamy.

Taboos against incest and cannibalism in most societies also provide interesting examples of the strength of the mores. The majority of Westerners find the thought of these two acts physically and psychologically repulsive. These thoughts are transmitted from one generation to the next through the socialization process, thereby guaranteeing that few, if any, acts of incest or cannibalism will be committed. The revulsion is based upon the idea that the two acts are fundamentally "unnatural" or nonhuman. To have sexual intercourse with one's close relative or to eat another human is considered animal-like, or worse. Yet, such views really have little validity when viewed in the light of scientific research. Who are one's "close" relatives? Are they members of the nuclear family, members of the extended family, residents of a neighborhood, residents of a larger community, all blood relatives including distant cousins? In some societies, engaging in sex with members of the same larger tribe is considered incestuous; in others, incest is a matter of sexual contact between members of the same nuclear unit. Therefore, the unnaturalness of the act depends entirely upon various cultural definitions, which are sometimes reflected in laws.

Cannibalism is another example. Where survival is of fundamental concern, and only the bodies of the already dead are involved, even churches have sometimes accepted the necessity of consuming human flesh. The famous examples from history are the Donner Party in the 1800s and the Uruguayan plane crash in the Andes in December of 1972. In 1846, a party of emigrants to California, lead by George Donner, were trapped by winter snows in a pass in the Sierra Nevada Mountains. In order to survive, some members consumed the flesh of dead members of the party. In 1972, a plane carrying a rugby team from Montevideo to Santiago crashed in the Andes Mountains. Over a 10-week period, two young survivors managed to make their way out of the 18,000-foot-high wilderness to get help from Chilean authorities. Fourteen other survivors were found still alive, although weak from injuries and starvation. A sensation was created in the world press when some survivors disclosed that cannibalism was used for survival. Representatives of the Catholic Church in Latin America issued statements indicating that, despite violation of a fundamental norm, these acts seemed necessary in this case, particularly since only the flesh of the already dead (excluding children) was consumed [Read, 1974]. However, many people still felt that members of the Donner Party and survivors of the Andes plane crash should have chosen death rather than cannibalism. This is an excellent illustration of the strength of the mores in controlling and determining human behavior.

In addition, *norms may be distinguished according to whether they are spontaneous in origin or more structured and deliberately planned.* Folkways and mores arise spontaneously and are passed on through informal processes of socialization. Laws are written and formalized. Folkways and mores, therefore, are the fundamental province of primary-group contexts: family, peer group, church. In contrast, laws are devised, altered, and enforced by more secondary types of groups: law enforcement agencies, court systems, and the profession of law. As a consequence many persons believe that the most effective way to control behavior is with norms that operate through primary groups (particularly mores) rather than norms that operate through secondary groups (formal laws). This kind of reasoning lies behind the arguments of those who maintain that laws dealing with essentially moral matters (taking narcotics, drinking alcohol, prostitution) should be decriminalized; that is, the problem of control should be removed from the law and placed in the primary institutions of society.

Conflicting and Complementary Norms

Besides studying various types of norms, sociologists also study the manner in which norms complement or contradict one another. It is quite common to speak of patterns of culture and to suggest that various aspects cluster together to form a cultural constellation or cultural trait. In part, this means that norms tend to *complement* each other and reinforce the overall way of life. We find an example of such a cultural complex in Western societies, where family norms and work norms have clustered to form a patriarchal social system. The father has been the accepted authority figure in the family; marriage has been monogamous; the wife–mother has found her place "in the home." The father has taken on man's work and served as the breadwinner, while the mother has done the woman's work and served as homemaker. People have been free to select their own mates and the mating process has involved the fusion of sex and love. Romantic courtship is expected to culminate in faithful, monogamous marriage, especially for the woman. The normative pattern for love, marriage, family, and work life have thus established a "moral" system for guiding behavior.

Norms and values are very closely associated in all cultures. In our own pattern of culture, we value individuality and freedom in mate selection, marriage, and work life. We value the concept of marriage as a lifelong love relationship held together by internal bonds of faithfulness and mutual compatibility. We value the tradition of patriarchal authority and the division of labor between husband and wife. Realization of these values calls for behavior according to the norms of chastity and fidelity, free choice of mates, freedom to divorce when compatibility and love go unrealized, and the division of labor, which emphasizes father–breadwinner and mother–homemaker. These norms permeate most of our society's practical everyday life.

In other words, the pattern of culture that is most familiar to many Americans is a constellation of values, attitudes, and beliefs that forms a system of morality, a prescription for right or wrong behavior expressed as our norms. Many of our norms fit together and reenforce the total way of life. Therefore, just as cooperation is necessary for orderly group life, a system of complementary norms is necessary for a stable coherent ideational life.

In most societies, however, and especially in modern ones, *normative conflict* also is a prevalent and necessary part of daily life. For example, the modern single person is confronted with perplexing choices because of new-found freedoms in dating and courtship. The male in our society has always faced the peculiar dilemma of whether to heed the norm of chastity before marriage or the norm of sexual experience that characterizes the masculine peer group. Now the female also shares some of this same perplexity. The norm of chastity has relaxed for her. Many factors help account for this: cultural contacts with other societies where premarital sex is acceptable; the new place of modern women as equals with men in dating–marriage–working relationships; the weakening of Puritanical attitudes toward sex; the open discussion and availability of birth control techniques along with new ideas of "right and wrong" relationships between the sexes.

Some sociologists working in this field are beginning to suggest a new way of evaluating the sex relationship. Lester Kirkendahl indicates that perhaps we are coming to the time when we will not ask whether there

4-3 Normative Conflict: The Reverence for Life

It is obvious that individuals and groups frequently conflict over differing values in contemporary society. However, conflict can also arise when people accept the same value (goal) but disagree over the means (norms) for achieving that value. The "reverence for life" is an example.

United Press International

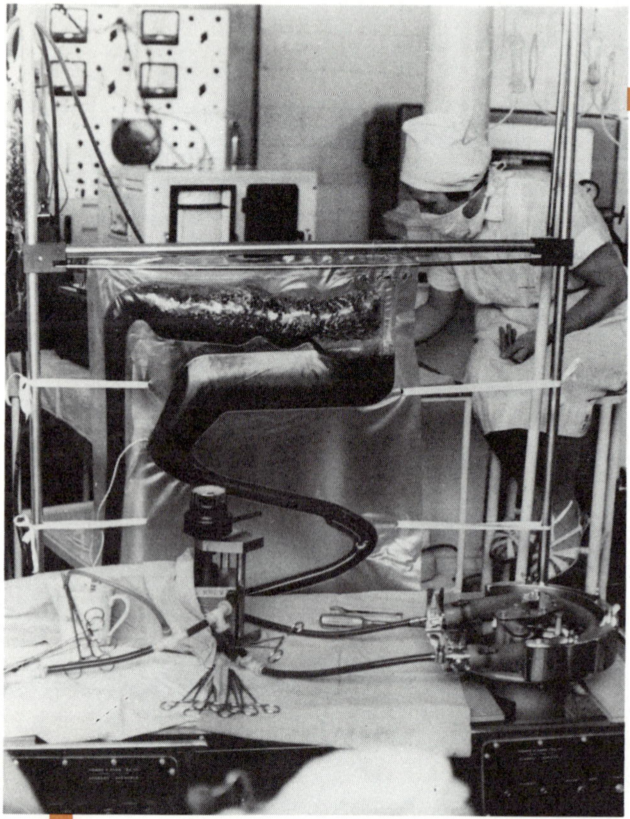

For some people, human life is so important that they believe every method should be used to sustain it in any form, including the most sophisticated and expensive medical technology. Refusal to use these methods is seen as an act of murder.

F. Siteman/Stock, Boston

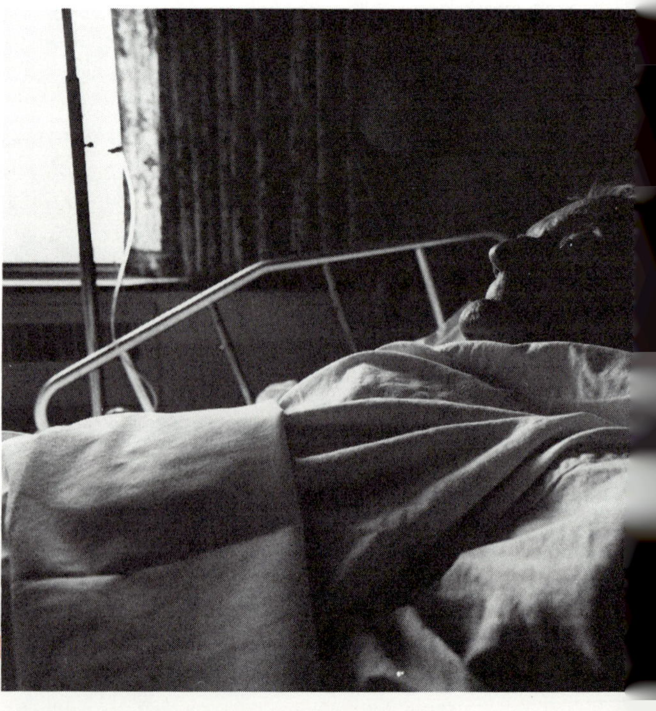

For other people, human life no longer exists when individuals cannot function physically, intellectually, or emotionally. In this state, people are seen as entering a state of living death. Permitting them to die normal deaths is considered to be the highest expression of a reverence for human life in its most meaningful form.

United Press International

United Press International

In 1975, 21-year-old Karen Ann Quinlan fell into a comatose vegetative state after apparently drinking alcohol and swallowing pills. For nearly seven months, doctors kept her emaciated body "alive" by the use of a respirator. With the emotional support of their parish priest, Karen's parents went to court seeking permission to remove her from the artificial life-support system and (as her mother put it) "let God determine her fate." In 1976, a Morris County, New Jersey, superior court judge turned down the Quinlan's request. On appeal, the New Jersey Supreme Court reversed the decision, ruling that, if doctors and a hospital ethics committee agree there is no reasonable possibility of Karen's ever emerging from her present condition, the life-support system might be withdrawn without any civil or criminal liabilities to anyone involved. This case does not resolve the continuing normative conflict over what constitutes appropriate medical care for patients who seem to be irreparably ill. Still to be decided are the following kinds of questions: What constitutes life? When does death occur? Should a patient's rights be protected by the state when they are unable to speak for themselves?

has been premarital sex but rather what the quality of the male–female relationship has been: Has there been mutual love and respect in all relationships, sexual and otherwise? Ira Reiss [1960 and 1971] makes a case for a new sex code—permissiveness with affection. He suggests that perhaps a measure of permissiveness in sex, if it is an expression of genuine respect for the other person, may be more "moral" and more in keeping with our democratic values than the old rigid requirement of chastity. This is not to say, however, that Reiss has scientific proof that the "new sexual morality" is more functional than the old. It is only to suggest that changes appear to be taking place in normative sex behavior.

Thus, the cultural context consists of many norms that complement one another. To heed one norm, such as chastity, is to encourage another norm, such as a monogamous marriage based upon love fused with sex. At the same time, it is also common to find norms in conflict, especially in rapidly changing societies. Old norms may conflict with new ones that emerge to meet new social conditions. The norms and values that make up a role such as mother–wife may be at odds with norms and values required of other roles such as wife–partner or married career woman. Conflict can also result when an individual has commitments to various groups. In a marriage where the wife and husband come from different religious backgrounds, conflict may develop because of competing commitments to church and to family. These conflicts can involve disagreements over whether to raise the children in one faith or the other; whether to use birth control techniques; and the like. Individuals are thus confronted by conflicting and competing norms; this situation gives rise to several cultural processes whereby groups of individuals can adapt to the situations of conflict.

Normative Adaptation: The Example of American Blacks

Two forms of normative adaptation, ethnocentrism and acculturation, are processes that tend to minimize conflict and, therefore, to maximize a high level of cultural cohesion. *Ethnocentrism* is the tendency for members of a group to think of their own cultural patterns as the best and most desirable. Indeed, we are all socialized to accept our own values as though they were the only worthy ones. For example, in American culture, is not monogamy based on enduring love regarded as the ultimate in marriage? In fact, some of us are reared with so little contact with other cultural patterns that we come to think of ours as the only ones. We take them for granted, and we never think of questioning them. This attitude has both advantages and disadvantages for us and for the larger society. It means that we are attuned to our own way of life and are happy with it by and large. We are committed to our own culture and society in such a way as to make for social solidarity. Furthermore, we enjoy the security of knowing how to behave and what to expect of our fellows. There is a kind of group egotism here, which helps to strengthen the social system within which we live. Ethnocentrism tends to minimize the tendency toward anomie and a feeling of rootlessness.

At the same time, however, ethnocentrism helps to encourage prejudice against those who differ from us. It can lead to hostilities between different racial and ethnic groups and can even foster major conflict between nations. It certainly makes it difficult to understand peoples whose norms and values differ from our own and to appreciate them as human beings. Even scientists find it difficult to eliminate cultural bias from their studies, for scientists are human too and are imbued with the norms and values of their own culture.

Acculturation is a process that takes place as we come into contact with peoples of differing backgrounds. When a Vietnamese girl and an American soldier are married, they tend to trade cultural perspectives. The American comes to understand and appreciate certain of the Asian ways. He may come to value contemplation in order to give balance to his Western activism. If he brings his wife to the United States, however, she will probably take on more of his ways than he will of hers. Her submissiveness as a wife may be attractive to him at first and yet, in America, she may become more aggressive. She may even take a job and become a working wife, as many wives in American marriages do, and go through a distinct resocialization process. There is some evidence from research on mixed marriages that tensions developed in the Japanese–American marriages that took place after World War II, partly because of this change in the wife's behavior. After acculturation, the wife was no longer the "sweet and submissive" partner whom the soldier had married in the foreign country.

Ethnocentrism, then, represents a form of cultural adaptation related to segregation and isolation in intergroup relationships. Members of a group ideationally separate themselves from those they judge to be foreign and strange. Acculturation, on the other hand, represents a process whereby individuals modify or alter their previous norms to conform partially with new standards and values; that is, they are "forced" to adopt new norms and values to guide their behavior. Finally, a third form of cultural adaptation to conflict—*cultural change*—can take place. Where acculturation results in new normative forms that may contain some characteristics of older forms, cultural change results in the emergence of completely new and different norms. In Chapter 13 we will discuss cultural change in detail, particularly the connection between technological innovation and changing norms. In this chapter we will conclude our discussion of cultural adaptation with a fascinating piece of research by Carol Stack [1974].

Stack's research is remarkable and important on several counts. First, as a young middle-class white woman, she was able to study black family life in an economically deprived ghetto by observing, participating in, and eventually becoming accepted into that life. Second, Stack's findings seriously question prevailing popular and scientific myths and stereotypes about blacks and the poor. For almost 50 years, scholars have helped perpetuate the belief that (1) the black family is essentially matriarchal and matrifocal (centered around the woman, particularly the mother) because black families are (2) fatherless or maleless; and (3) the black poor, like other poor groups, do not want to work or share the work ethic values of the larger society. Thus, many scholars have assumed that black families socialize their members, especially the young, differently than do white middle-class nuclear families, thereby producing deviance and disorganization in the form of antisocial behavior, ineffective education, and lower levels of occupational attainment. Some recent research has begun to criticize this prevailing view [Berger and Simon, 1974, pp. 145–161; Davidson and Gaitz, 1974, pp. 229–245].

In her participant-observation study, Stack wished to test the new findings in the context of on-going, daily family life in a black community. She selected an area she calls The Flats, the poorest secton of a black community in a Midwestern city she calls Jackson Harbor (population over 50,000). There is little industry in the city and in 1968, a year of record national economy, black unemployment in Jackson Harbor was 20 percent. Among working blacks, over 60 percent were service workers (maids, cooks, janitors, etc). In 1959, 80 percent of the white families made more than $4000 annually, while 60 percent of the nonwhite families made less. In The Flats, crowding is severe, and most homes are small wood-framed houses, bungalows, and shacks in need of major repairs.

> The streets and front yards are cluttered with broken glass, beer cans, and old cars. Old tires and bed springs fill back yards. Porch doors, screens, and broken windows go unfixed. During the winter snowstorms, the streets in The Flats, many of them unpaved, gravel streets, are the last in the city to be cleared. Although temperatures go below zero in Jackson Harbor without fail every winter, many houses have doors and windows that do not fit tightly. A common trick to seal cracks in the window casements is to fill them with water on a freezing day to provide a frigid seal until the first thaw. . . . I visited only a few houses that were not roach-infested. In one home roaches exceeded one per square foot on all of the walls inside the house [Stack, 1974, p. 3].

How do black families adapt to such severe conditions, when neither the economic resources nor the necessary public services are provided them?

Stack finds that the stereotypes of poor black families as fatherless, matrifocal, unstable, and disorganized are not the unique characteristics of those living substantially below the poverty level in urban America. Quite the contrary, residents of The Flats show remarkable resilience and resourcefulness in the face of perpetual poverty conditions. By means of a process of *cooperative domestic exchange,* the urban black family develops a tenacious active network of human relationships that often lasts a lifetime.

Stack's analysis of this network illustrates the processes of normative adaptation discussed above. Ethnocentrism is enforced in the use, by the residents of The Flats, of first names in one another's presence to refer to neighbors and friends. Surnames are used infrequently and may not even be known by long-time acquaintances, and the coining of nicknames is a creative and important pastime. Nicknames personalize, endear, and dramatically expose the unique qualities of an individual. They also distinguish ingroup members from the potentially hostile outgroup. Surnames are used in The Flats when residents deal with the whites who enter the community as social workers, landlords, teachers, and the like. As Carol Stack became accepted in the community as a member of one of the extended kin networks, she was informally called "white Caroline" to distinguish her from a niece of one of the families who was known as "black Caroline."

The unique adaptation pattern known as the cooperative exchange system operates to fulfill basic needs in the absence of adequate resources. Stack points out that alliances between individuals are constantly being formed as *kin and friends exchange objects and services, and thus establish obligations to one another.* For example, food stamps, rent money, television sets, hats, dice, cars, cigarettes, furniture, and other objects are shared. In addition, services such as babysitting, driving to stores, errands, caring for the aged, the serving of meals, and the like are shared. Few black families living on welfare could survive without this system, since they cannot accumulate the surplus of basic necessities needed to remove themselves from poverty. The web of intimate social relationships is greatly enlarged through habitual swapping, which provides a primary context of much needed personal support—a rare attribute in many white communities, with their emphasis upon isolated nuclear family units. The swapping–exchange system is also necessitated by the fact that residents of The Flats cannot keep their resources or needs a secret—privacy is a luxury only in middle-class America. Through gossip, the community immediately knows about a new car, clothes, money, or an unexpected hardship. In short, the larger cultural values of self-sacrifice, generosity, and a sense of community are modified and take on new meaning in The Flats because of the special needs of that environment.

▶ SO WHAT?

As we have seen in the previous "So What?" boxes, the results of sociological research can be used in public policy in two ways. First, concepts, theories, and/or scientific findings may be consciously employed. For example, we saw in Chapter 3 how labeling theory and the concepts of desocialization and resocialization have been used by self-help groups to organize rehabilitative programs for former alcoholics and drug users. Second, sociological knowledge may be used implicitly. A study can encourage additional research that leads to further insights about a problem. The resulting fund of accumulated knowledge eventually becomes the basis for programs. In Chapter 1, we saw how Durkheim's study of suicide was followed through the years by many other studies. This research finally led to programs like those of the San Francisco Suicide Prevention Center. In addition, there is a third way in which sociological studies are useful: Scientific findings can become the basis for assessing the effectiveness of existing programs. Carol Stack's study of The Flats can be put to this use.

During the early 1970s, the food stamp program for the poor was criticized by many politicians. Stack's investigation shows that some of these criticisms were justified. However, her findings also disclose aspects about which both the critics and defenders of the program were unaware. Critics charged that food stamps were frequently misused by the poor, that those who did not need them often obtained them, and that the program encouraged poor people to become dependent rather than to work in order to obtain money for food. Stack found that the poor did use the stamps in unintended ways to achieve unanticipated goals. Stamps in The Flats were not so much seen as a means to feed one's family as they were seen as a necessary currency in an elaborate system of exchange—a currency needed to obtain critical services not otherwise available. Furthermore, Stack found that the food stamp program was based upon middle-class values that were irrelevant to the poor. Personal accumulation of wealth (a reflection of the work ethic's emphasis upon saving) was not only impossible because of low incomes, but individual saving would also threaten the exchange system of The Flats, which depended upon community-wide cooperation and sharing. Therefore, the critics were partly right: The program didn't work the way it was supposed to. But their reasoning was wrong: Middle-class standards could not be used to judge the behavior of the poor.

What are the practical implications of such an assessment? Using Carol Stack's findings, a social planner might consider the following kinds of alternatives.

1. Although the program does not seem to be a success in terms of providing many needy families with food, it might be considered a success in other terms. It could be seen as a relatively inexpensive and easy way of providing the poor with a needed system of currency with which to "purchase" necessary services. Furthermore, food stamps assist the poor in building a strong interdependent community life based upon sharing.

2. If the program is discontinued, new programs will have to be designed to provide the poor with (a) a currency of exchange to substitute for the absence of money and/or (b) services that are unavailable in poor communities (child care, transportation, home repair, and so on).

In Chapter 6, the "So What?" box considers other programs designed to eliminate or ease the burden of poverty (low-cost housing, income maintenance, and so on). These are assessed in the same way, using the results of sociological theory and research.

Studies like that of Carol Stack also raise another important question that concerns sociologists. How is it that cultures can contain characteristics of both uniformity and variability? For example, the social networks found in The Flats are similar to those found in some white neighborhoods because they are based upon values (a sense of community and neighborliness) found in some white communities. At the same time, the black family networks with their nicknames and swapping are a unique and different adaptation to unusual kinds of problems. How can we explain this seeming paradox of culture, its simultaneous uniformity and variability? Answers to this question could lead to partial solutions for dangerous and threatening intergroup and intersocietal conflict.

Cultural Contrasts: Sources of Uniformity and Variability

Cultural uniformity results from the shared basic nature of humans, common characteristics of social structure, and relatively similar life demands. As we have seen in our discussion to this point, all people, no matter what their particular societal context, must be made human through the same socializing processes. They are all socialized as infants in primary groups and thus come to learn the skills, knowledge, and values their society deems important. Whatever language they learn is uniform in phonetic principles, general construction, and use. Furthermore, all humans have need of both formal and informal group contexts for ordering their group actions. Thus, a peer group or a bureaucracy looks much the same whatever the context. In this sense, human group life everywhere is a uniform attempt to satisfy universal needs, both biological and psychological.

At the same time, it is obvious that humans do not behave in the same manner everywhere and at all times. They act and speak differently in different cultural contexts. The norms and language of drug users vary in many respects from those of the straight community. Bureaucracies in feudal China were not completely like modern state bureaucracies; for example, in premodern China, excellence in humanistic skills (like writing poetry) was considered an important part of the "civil service examination."

Human behavior, in this sense, can be contrasted to animal behavior. Ants of the same species will build the same kind of hill in the same manner whether the species is found in China or in California, but the home of the Chinese villager differs greatly from the three-bedroom two-bath ranch house of the California suburbanite. These architectural differences reflect variations of values and norms between the Chinese peasant family and the contemporary American urban family. What are the social variables that account for these *cultural differences,* which are often reflected in the way humans manipulate the physical environment?

Differences in *the stage of sociocultural development* account for many cultural contrasts. In many Asian villages, even today, people are preurban and preindustrial in their technological development. They are still in the hoe-culture or plow-culture stage. Large families are needed to eke out a living with hand methods of farming and handcraft. High birth rates are also important to balance the high death rates in places where scientific medicine and sanitation are not yet established. Thus, an extended family system that values the family name, symbolized in the veneration of ancestors and aged persons, takes precedence over individual freedom. The norms forbid youth to select their own mates and assert themselves apart from the family. Their behavior differs from ours because their norms and values are based upon a premodern stage of socioeconomic development.

Geographical differences also play a part in bringing about cultural contrasts. Human beings adjust in the tropics with different housing, clothing, and foods than those in the arctic regions. In addition, we find interesting variations in family life as well as work life. It is risky, however, to imply that geographical contrasts explain most cultural contrasts. People have the ability to control their physical environment in remarkable ways. This is especially true for modern society. Our technological know-how makes it possible to transform either the tropic or the arctic regions to suit our needs and to support our urban culture patterns. Urban people behave much the same whether they are in one climate or another. Furthermore, groups of people living in the same type of geographical area often behave quite differently.

Cultural drift is a concept sometimes used by scholars to explain puzzling contrasts between people living in the same region and at a similar stage of socioeconomic development. What explanation is there for the case where one tribe of primitive peoples makes a cultural hero of the man of peace who never loses his temper and another tribe nearby encourages the man of war, who is admired for his tough-guy stance? It is often impossible to explain for sure why value systems vary so greatly. One hypothesis is that at some point in each tribe's history the leader who emerged to meet the social needs of the group was, in the one instance, a person of restraint (for example, the reasoning diplomat) and, in the other, a person of hostility (for example, the fearless warrior).

One need not look beyond one's own society to find curious or unusual norms. In 1956, Horace Miner published a brief article describing American culture as it might be seen by an anthropologist from another culture. The Nacirema, according to Miner, seem to have a fundamental belief that the human body is ugly and its natural tendency is toward debility and disease.

> Incarcerated in such a body, man's only hope is to avert these characteristics through the use of the powerful influences of ritual and ceremony. Every household has one or more shrines devoted to this purpose. The more powerful individuals in the society have several shrines in their houses, and, in fact, the opulence of a house is often referred to in terms of the number of such ritual centers it possesses [Miner, 1956, p. 503. Reproduced by permission of the American Anthropological Association from *The American Anthropologist* 58(3), 1956.]

Miner goes on to describe the curious norms that arise as a result. Each household shrine has a box or chest, built into the wall, which contains many charms and magical potions. These preparations are obtained from medicine men and herbalists who are the only ones who understand the contents and curative powers of the potions. Below the charm box is a font, where every day each member of the family, with head bowed, mingles different sorts of magical liquids in the font and engages in a brief rite of ablution. Particularly important in this daily, morning ritual is the mouth rite. A small bundle of hog hairs is inserted in the mouth together with magical powders or pastes and is moved in a formalized series of gestures. Miner suggests that the Nacirema have such a pathological horror and fascination with the mouth that they believe that, without the ritual, "their teeth would fall out, their gums bleed, their jaws shrink, their friends desert them, and their lovers reject them." We might add that many non-Westerners have often referred to America as a "bathroom culture."

We have seen so far that cultural variations can be interpreted as adaptations to situations of normative conflict and as ideational adjustments to certain conditions (such as the stage of societal development or conditions of extreme poverty). These variations seem to imply that cultural elements (norms, values, beliefs) are largely the result of social preconditions. Is such an assumption necessarily valid? Or is the possibility that cultural elements precede and influence social factors and events just as likely?

CULTURE AND THE SOCIAL ORDER

Although sociologists study patterns of culture and cultural relationships, they focus primarily on the relationship between culture and the social order. How does the group structure of a society reflect a people's basic values, beliefs, aspirations, and norms? How are particular norms related to different types of group behavior?

Culture: Cause or Consequence?

The question of whether culture causes the social order or vice versa is a complex one because there is such close interplay between these two dimensions of human life. What comes first, the idea (culture) or the interaction (social order)? Norms and values, as ideas or cultural elements, certainly influence the interaction of groups that make up the social order. On the other hand, group interaction sets the stage for the development of appropriate norms and values.

The latter point will be illustrated first: Modern technological society, with its potential for self-annihilation through atomic warfare, has virtually abandoned the idea of total warfare as a means of settling political disputes. Total warfare can no longer be considered a functional means of interaction for anyone. As yet, however, no stable set of norms and values stressing international peace and collaboration has emerged in our culture.

International interaction has changed, but compatible ideologies are still in the making.

The debate between those who recommend military preparedness and those who urge arms limitation and disarmament symbolizes today's attempt to create a new set of ideas for coping with such destructive capabilities. As these new ideas emerge and become accepted and formalized on a worldwide basis, we will be witnessing the development of culture as a product of changes in group life. Such development is very slow and difficult, as we have seen in the failure of the League of Nations after World War I and the struggles of the United Nations after World War II. International law and order is still an unachieved goal for the world and its realization will depend upon a new ideology, a changing cultural perspective. This is possible, however, because *culture does change in response to changes in the social order.*

By way of contrast, *cultures may sometimes influence or determine the social order.* For example, as we have seen, the monogamous family system in our society exists partly as a reflection of the importance we place on the values of freedom and individualism. Extended and polygynous systems in other societies reflect, in part, the values of duty, filial piety, and male superiority. Both sets of values are supported by both mores and laws. In the United States, single-spouse marriage is prescribed by both custom and law; property is typically shared; divorce generally is easy to obtain; and the rights of children are defined. The monogamous family, then, works to sustain an equal and companionable relationship between husband and wife and to protect the individual freedom of all family members. Conversely, polygynous family systems work to stress the duty and responsibility of the male, to emphasize the inferior role of the female, and to permit utilization of children in the basic labors of the family. In both cases, values and norms have become behavioral guides that proscribe particular forms of interaction.

These examples have been oversimplified to illustrate the basic relationships involved. In reality, *the relationship between culture and the social order is one of mutual influence.* Values may stimulate particular forms of group interaction, which, in turn, may conflict with existing norms; this conflict leads to new norms that cause further changes in the pattern of social interaction, and so on. For example, the existence of divorce reflects the importance attached to individual freedom in our society. At the same time, however, a high rate of divorce threatens another basic value, the idea of an enduring love relationship between man and wife. Labor laws protect the young child, but they create problems when teen-agers cannot obtain gainful employment. The practice of community property guarantees the freedom and independence of the wife, but, by abolishing male property control, it undermines the prestige and authority of the male. This change in the husband's status and role within the modern family can, as a result, give rise to social and psychological problems for all family members. Culture and the social order, therefore, are constantly interdependent.

The Sociological Orientation

Sociologists are more concerned with the interrelationship between social life and ideas than they are about their relative importance. Which element is of most importance depends upon the specific situation and context under analysis. In addition, ideas from one area of social behavior may be related to other areas of behavior. For example, religious beliefs affect not only religious behavior but also economic, political, and social behavior. In turn, economic and political behavior may also affect religious beliefs.

One scholar who has done much to strike a balance and to provoke study and discussion of the role of ideas is Max Weber, the German sociologist. Although it would be impossible to summarize adequately the profound and extensive contributions of Weber, it is important to sketch his central themes and point out the risks of oversimplifying and misinterpreting his work. In so doing, we will draw heavily upon the work of Reinhard Bendix [1960] and J. Milton Yinger [1970], who are perhaps the most valid and insightful sources.

Modern capitalism, which ushered in major changes in Western social structure, came into being about 400 years ago. Something happened in Western culture that nurtured what has been called the "spirit of capitalism" and set into motion a whole new notion of the meaning of work. What happened was the timely birth of a new idea, which has come to be known as the *Protestant ethic.* It was an idea about human salvation that led to an emphasis upon work as something people should not do because they had to but because it represented an ideal way of life. For a person not to work incessantly, whether they were rich or poor, was for the person to fail God, other people, and themselves. Thus, a religious idea produced a work ethic, which, in turn, spurred capitalism—a rational form of economic behavior that called for the deliberate getting, saving, and reinvesting of money. Capitalism did not emphasize "getting and spending" for comfort and pleasure; rather, it affirmed the ascetic denial of self in order to gain through capital investment. It became a way of life for all modern people but especially for the bourgeoisie, the middle-class merchant, the earliest urban residents, who found a spiritual home not in traditional Catholicism but in Protestantism.

Bendix [1960] has called *The Protestant Ethic and the Spirit of Capitalism* Max Weber's most famous, as well as his most controversial, book.

> In it he traced the influence of religious ideas upon the conduct of men and challenged the Marxist thesis that man's consciousness is determined by his social class. . . . *The Protestant Ethic* was destined to serve as an introduction to this major theme of Weber's life-work, a specification of the interrelation of religious ideas and economic behavior as the focus for further research. Weber's particular thesis—that Puritan ideas had influenced the development of capitalism—became the subject of a voluminous literature [Bendix, 1960, pp. 71–72].

The remainder of this chapter will consider Weber's study and modern reactions to it as an example of the sociological orientation that sees culture and the social order as mutually interdependent, that is, as both cause and consequence of social behavior.

Max Weber's Study of Capitalism

According to Weber [1930, 1958], the Protestant ethic means hard work, frugal living, and a benevolent but reserved manner, which has about it an air of impersonality even toward kin and friends. The Protestant ethic, however, did not develop as an intellectual support for the spirit of capitalism. It arose through the teaching of John Calvin, who maintained that according to divine Providence some are elected to be saved and some to be damned. Nothing humans can do makes any difference, for they are always too imperfect to be worthy. People are saved only through the grace of God. Nor can any person know whether he or she is among the chosen few to be saved. It appears that people can make one of three responses to this idea: (1) They can arrive at a *quietism* or acquiescence; (2) they can live with *abandon* since there is nothing to gain or lose; or (3) they can become *activists.* It was the latter course that most early modern people chose to take.

The terrible uncertainty of not knowing whether one was among the elect may well have led to the work ethic as a means of proving to oneself and to others that he or she must indeed be among the chosen. The work ethic led to economic success and prosperity, which seemed to be a mark of election. Thus to work as if all the world were a monastery was to work for the glory of God. And to work in this way was, incidentally, to advance business and industrial enterprises. Inadvertently but surely the Protestant ethic sparked the spirit of capitalism.

In contrast to the Western experience, Weber maintained that other peoples had the material preconditions for rational capitalism but lacked the strategic cultural setting. Their religions failed to produce the work ethic that appeared to be essential and that first came to life in the West with Protestantism. Weber's argument about Protestantism in the West was not without sound evidence even though he did not undertake research to compare the Protestant and Catholic predisposition to capitalism. He merely cited plausible evidence that Protestants appeared to make better capitalists than did Catholics. He left the research and empirical testing to other scientists (the Detroit study by Lenski that follows is an example.) Weber did, however, take great pains to show that the Protestant ethic was only one aspect of Western culture that contributed to modern economic life and that it was a factor that arose partly from the socioeconomic conditions of the time, that is, from the ethics of trade and the character of urban life.

Although Weber gave special attention to the relationship between Protestantism and capitalism as they were both emerging in the 15th and 16th centuries, he was also interested in the continuation of this phenomenon in contemporary society. Modern capitalism still includes traces of the Puritan spirit long after the original religious rationale has been modified by the rise of welfare and consumerism. Although the work ethic of the Puritan era has largely been transformed into a social ethic, the work-oriented norms and values of production capitalism are still in evidence. People still feel guilty if they are not working, and politicians still strike a responsive chord when they speak of individual initiative and striving for success as opposed to statism and collectivism. Contemporary scholars continue to take cues from Max Weber as they design research projects for the study of human behavior in current situations. One of the best examples of such projects was an attempt to compare Protestants and Catholics in Detroit to see whether there are significant differences in their economic, familial, and political behavior that might be attributed to the presence or absence of the Protestant ethic and to differences in religious heritage.

▶ STUDY 4

The Religious Factor: A Modern Test of Weber's Theory [1958][1]

Problem

There is a growing concern in America about the loss of individualism and the work ethic as *a problem of social change.* The American frontier nurtured a tradition that began with the rise of modern capitalism. It was a tradition that pictured the good person as one who works hard, often from dawn until dark, saves money and invests it for credit, and "makes good" without help from welfare. This tradition is reflected in Ben Franklin's advice in 1748 to a young tradesman:

> Remember, that *time* is money. He that can earn ten shillings a day by his labour, and goes abroad, or sits idle, one half of that day, though he spends but sixpence during his diversion or idleness, ought not to reckon *that* the only expense; he has really spent, or rather thrown away, five shillings besides. . . . The sound of your hammer at five in the morning, or eight at night, heard by a creditor, makes him easy six months longer; but if he sees you at a billiard-table, or hears your voice at a tavern, when you should be at work, he sends for his money the next day [Franklin, 1748, pp. 87 ff; and Weber, 1958, pp. 48 and 49].

This is, in part, what is meant by the spirit of capitalism. This spirit, however, is changing. Work is no longer so greatly idealized. Leisure time and recreation are more highly valued today. The trend toward a welfare state that provides all kinds of social security is becoming more acceptable to Americans.

[1]Adapted and abridged from Gerhard Lenski, *The Religious Factor: A Sociological Study of Religion's Impact on Politics, Economics, and Family Life* (Garden City, N.Y.: Doubleday and Company, 1963).

Within this changing social milieu, how much of the traditional work ethic still remains? Which Americans are most likely to embrace it still, and why? Do ideas and cultural prespectives play a part in this kind of social change? What aspect of culture plays the most important role?

Hypothesis and Study Design

Lenski hypothesized that *religion plays a significant part in determining how people behave* economically, politically, and in their family life. This hypothesis provided the basis for empirically testing Weber's thesis that Protestantism helped spark the spirit of capitalism. The following type of assumption, for example, could be tested:

> Protestants as compared with Catholics are more inclined to view work as important in and of itself. Therefore, they are more likely to have small families so that they will be freer to move about and take better jobs. They are more likely to avoid installment buying, to save money, to vote Republican, to question the national trend toward a welfare state, to emphasize individual achievement and intellectual autonomy, and the like.

In order to test this hypothesis, Lenski divided the Detroit community into *four major religious groups:*

1. White Protestants—41 percent of Detroit; 267 cases in the study.
2. White Catholics—35 percent of Detroit; 230 cases in the study.
3. Black Protestants—15 percent of Detroit; 100 cases in the study.
4. Jews—4 percent of Detroit; 27 cases in the study.

Method of Data Collection

During personal interviews, individuals in each of these groups were asked about personal background, religious beliefs, church attendance, economic behavior, political attitudes and behavior, and family life. The field work for this *survey research* was done in 1958 and was directed by the Detroit Area Study Program at the University of Michigan. Graduate students in sociology, closely supervised by a professor, conducted the interviews and participated in the analysis of the findings. This method of data collection, unlike most political opinion polls, was not merely an attempt to gather descriptive information. Instead, it is a good example of theoretically directed research that uses a hypothesis to determine the type of questions to be asked and the type of data to be collected. Furthermore, the sample must be representative of the larger population so that the responses to questions are reliable. Lenski and his colleagues were systematically testing Weber's theory four centuries after the emergence of capitalism.

Findings and Interpretations

Analysis of the data indicated that a white Protestant is more likely than a white Catholic to do the following:

1. Consider his *work important* and have a *small family.*
2. *Avoid installment buying* and *save money* for the future.
3. *Vote Republican* and *question the welfare state.*

4. Take a *liberal view of freedom of speech* but *hesitate to push for racial integration* in the schools.
5. *Migrate* and leave close family ties in order to obtain education, a better job, and a higher position in the class system.
6. Develop a commitment to the principles of *intellectual autonomy.*

Lenski's findings also indicate that white Protestants advance further in their jobs than do Catholics; they are more upwardly mobile. This is true even when social class is held constant. The findings show that Jews tend to be the most successful and black Protestants the least successful. White Protestants and Catholics fall between these extremes.

Lenski asked the Detroit respondents to rank the following in order of importance in a person's job:

1. High income.
2. No danger of being discharged.
3. Working hours short; lots of free time.
4. Chances for advancement.
5. The work is important and gives a feeling of accomplishment.

Closest to the Protestant ethic, as conceived by Weber, is the notion that a person's work is important and gives a feeling of accomplishment. Nearly half of those interviewed ranked this as the most important aspect of their job. This response shows what a strong hold the classical Protestant ethic has *on all segments of the American population.* It is especially evident among middle-class Americans and has impacted across racial and religious lines.

The opposites of the Protestant ethic are the attitudes toward work expressed in Items 2 (job security) and 3 (short hours). *Most of the respondents did not put these at the top of the list.* In fact, only 4 percent of all respondents ranked "short hours" first. These findings verify the generalization that the work–achievement attitude, which came into the modern world with the spirit of capitalism, and the Protestant ethic have gathered a momentum of their own and currently pervade all segments of our society.

At the same time, Lenski's findings also make it clear that modern people differ in their commitment to the spirit of capitalism according to religious activity and social-class origin. Lenski first distinguishes between white Catholics and white Protestants according to whether they are active or marginal in their church attendance. He next breaks each of these four groups into two other categories, according to whether they come from the middle or the working class. Lenski then measures the difference in degree of influence of the spirit of capitalism for each of the eight possible groups. The findings, given in Table 4-2, show the continuing influence of religion, the importance of religious involvement, and the role of social class:

In short, active middle-class Protestants were found to be most influenced by the spirit of capitalism; active working-class Catholics, least influenced. In addition, religiously active Protestants were more influenced than marginal Protestants; active Catholics were less influenced than marginal Catholics. Thus, *being active, Protestant, and middle class led one to accept the spirit of capitalism,* while being active, Catholic, and working class led one to reject the spirit.

TABLE 4-2 Degree of Influence of the Spirit of Capitalism for White Protestants and Catholics by Religious Involvement and Social-Class Origin

Degree of Influence	Rank Order	Religious Group	Religious Involvement	Social Class
Most	1	Protestants	Active	Middle
	2	Protestants	Marginal	Middle
Moderate	3	Protestants	Active	Working
	3	Catholics	Marginal	Middle
	4	Catholics	Active	Middle
	5	Protestants	Marginal	Working
Least	6	Catholics	Marginal	Working
	7	Catholics	Active	Working

Lenski's findings relative to politics and the family run in a similar direction: *White Protestants are more apt to be Republicans and to take more status quo attitudes toward social change.* One example is their attitude regarding desegregation in the public schools. White Protestants tend to resist this, as well as other direct-action programs in the realm of civil rights. This resistance is in keeping with the ethic of individual striving and a reluctance to have government interfere with a person's freedom to achieve through individual initiative. Family life reflects similar concerns. Lenski's data point up *differences in child rearing between Protestants and Catholics.* The former are apt to value programs that emphasize self-direction, perseverance, and intellectual autonomy over those that emphasize popularity and obedience.

Conclusions and Implications

Lenski concludes that, in view of the evidence from both his study and elsewhere, apparently the *strict environmental position,* which explains economic, political, and family behavior solely in terms of one's social situation, is untenable. This is not to deny that social conditions, especially those of an economic nature, are powerful forces influencing one's behavior. However, other factors (religion, for example) also exercise a significant influence. In short, it does make a difference whether a person is Protestant or Catholic, even in a modern city where secular trends have eroded religious involvement. *Religious rearing leads to beliefs and views, which in turn affect behavior.*

Although Lenski's study is an important contribution to contemporary knowledge about the relationship between economic and religious behavior and beliefs, five special research problems are worth particular comment. We list them in Table 4-3 as an example of the need for continual criticism of ongoing research in sociology and the necessity to consider alternative strategies.

Those scholars who have made these kinds of criticisms of Lenski's study also commend him for spelling out each step of the analysis so that his errors stand out clearly and can be assessed by other scientists. In addi-

TABLE 4-3 Problems in Lenski's Study and Alternative Research Strategies

Research Problem	Explanation	Alternative Research Strategy
1. Representativeness of the sample.	1. Too few blacks (100) and Jews (27) in contrast to Catholics and Protestants (497).	1. Eliminate blacks and Jews and concentrate upon comparing white Catholics and Protestants.
2. Possible bias by including special subgroups.	2. Black behavior in relation to the work ethic tends to take on a special character in American society, as Carol Stack showed.	2. Do a special study of blacks and do not include this in an analysis of other groups.
3. Subgroup differences not recognized.	3. All Protestants are lumped together, although there may be large differences by different denominations.	3. Other research has shown, for example, that Congregationalists and Southern Baptists differ on doctrinal matters and major social, political, and economic issues [Glock and Stark, 1966]. Separate studies needed.
4. Validity of measures of the Protestant ethic.	4. Measures like "attitudes toward work" and "more or less" successful adaptation to occupational careers tend to be simple and vague.	4. Design other studies that analyze in detail other possibly important variables and define the work ethic in a more detailed fashion.
5. Question of causality.	5. Is religion really the cause or consequence of other social behavior? Lenski's study never really resolves the problem of cause versus effect.	5. Whereas religion is one variable that might explain commitment to capitalism, other variables, including Marx's notion of purely economic factors, should be investigated.

tion, his field work is described in such detail that other competent researchers can replicate his work in the best scientific tradition.

Perhaps the most significant contribution of the study is that it may well encourage other research into the relationship between religion and human behavior. As Lenski indicates, social scientists have failed for too long to recognize the importance of religious associations and subcommunities in the life of the larger society. Religious orientation and involvement does have an impact upon secular institutions and the overall cultural climate of a society, as we shall see again in Chapter 10.

CONCLUSION

We have recognized culture as the totality of human social life. Culture distinguishes humans from other living creatures, and the basis of culture is symbolic language. Through the use of symbolic language humans can establish an ideational life, thereby giving meaning and purpose to their raw experience. Language also makes it possible for people to store and retrieve information so that a cultural heritage can be accumulated and passed on to succeeding generations. This capacity to manipulate symbolic language is what makes humans the only culture-bearing social animal. Finally, language makes possible the formulation of the norms and values through which human behavior patterns are learned.

Sociologists are interested in all aspects of culture, but they place special importance upon the ideational quality of norms and values. Human behavior is normative rather than instinctive. Norms are agreed-upon behavior patterns that give order to human society; they are the blueprints for behavior and are found in the form of mores, folkways, and laws. Through the socialization process, the individual learns to identify with the values and the normative behavior patterns of the larger culture. Culture becomes the medium of human personality and it is through culture that human life takes on style and meaning.

The normative order does not function perfectly even in the most stable of societies. There are normative conflicts that become especially significant in rapidly changing societies. By and large the father role and the breadwinner role complement each other as a Western man lives up to the expectations of his cultural setting. There are times, however, when society's norms conflict: The demands of a man's job, for example, may make it difficult for him to fulfill the responsibilities of fatherhood. In addition, cultural perspectives differ between one subculture and another within the same society. Thus, when white welfare workers attempt to serve black residents of an urban community, there are often problems of cultural contrast and misunderstanding.

The study of culture brings out the existence of cultural similarities and cultural differences. Human interaction does follow similar patterns as universal needs (biological and psychological) are pursued in family, religious, economic, and political contexts. On the other hand, cultural contrasts are marked from one people to another and, within our own society, between one subculture and another. What is correct behavior in one cultural context may seem very wrong in another. The study of the black family in our society is one good example of this contrast. In the light of such contrasts, it is often difficult to arrive at a cross-cultural understanding between peoples, especially when there is a tendency for all people to be ethnocentric and to feel that their own culture is the best.

Finally, we have examined the close relationship between culture and social structure by reviewing Weber's research, which ties religious thought to economic behavior. In Chapter 13 of this book, we will discuss the causes of change in greater detail. For the present, however, we can observe that cultural elements, as ideational phenomena, can be both causes and consequences of social phenomena. Weber not only sought scholarly evidence to support his argument that a religious idea contributed to the cultural ethos of the modern capitalistic era, but stimulated others to struggle with the problem, as well. One such attempt was presented in the Detroit study of 1958.

In summary, the social self and cultural norms and values constitute essential elements of the social order. Although these are certainly of interest to the sociologist, the major focus of the discipline is on group life. The following section of this book, therefore, contains separate chapters discussing in detail each of the five basic forms of group behavior described in the typology in Chapter 2.

REFERENCES

Bendix, Reinhard. *Max Weber: An Intellectual Portrait.* Garden City, N.Y.: Doubleday and Company, 1960.

Berger, Alan S., and William Simon. "Black Families and the Moynihan Report: A Research Evaluation," *Social Problems, 22* (December 1974), pp. 145–161.

Bohannan, Paul. *Social Anthropology.* New York: Holt, Rinehart and Winston, 1963.

Davidson, Chandler, and Charles M. Gaitz. "'Are The Poor Different?' A Comparison of Work Behavior and Attitudes Among the Urban Poor and Nonpoor," *Social Problems, 22* (December 1974), pp. 229–245.

Fleming, Joyce Dudley. "The State of the Apes," *Psychology Today, 7* (January 1974), pp. 31–46.

Franklin, Ben. *Advice to a Young Tradesman.* Sparks edition, II, 1748.

Gardner, R. Allan, and Beatrice T. Gardner. "Teaching Sign Language to Chimpanzees," *Science 165* (15 August 1969), pp. 664–672.

Glock, Charles Y., and Rodney Stark. *Christian Beliefs and Anti-Semitism.* New York: Harper & Row, Publishers, 1966.

Hall, Edward T. *The Silent Language.* New York: Anchor Press/Doubleday, 1973.

Janowitz, Morris. *The Professional Soldier: A Social and Political Portrait.* New York: The Free Press, 1960.

Keller, Helen. *The Story of My Life.* New York: Doubleday and Company, 1904.

Klapp, Orrin E. "Heroes, Villains and Fools, As Agents of Social Control," *American Sociological Review, 19* (February 1954), pp. 56–62.

Kluckhohn, Clyde, and Henry A. Murray. *Personality in Nature, Society and Culture.* New York: Alfred A. Knopf, 1949.

Miner, Horace. "Body Ritual Among the Nacirema," *The American Anthropologist, 58* (June 1956), pp. 503–507.

Moskos, Charles C., Jr. *The American Enlisted Man: The Rank and File in Today's Military.* New York: Russell Sage Foundation, 1970.

Murdock, George Peter. "The Science of Culture," *The American Anthropologist, 34* (1932), pp. 200–215.

Park, Robert E., and Ernest Burgess. *Introduction to the Science of Sociology.* Chicago: University of Chicago Press, 1921.

Premack, Ann James, and David Premack. "Teaching Language to an Ape," *Scientific American, 227* (October 1972), pp. 92–99.

Premack, David. "Language in Chimpanzee?," *Science, 172* (21 May 1971), pp. 808–822.

Read, Piers Paul. *Alive: The Story of the Andes Survivors.* Philadelphia: J. B. Lippincott Co., 1974.

Reiss, Ira L. *Premarital Sexual Standards in America.* New York: The Free Press, 1960.

__________. *The Family System.* New York: Holt, Rinehart and Winston, 1971.

Stack, Carol B. *All Our Kin: Strategies for Survival in a Black Community.* New York: Harper & Row, Publishers, 1974.

Sumner, William Graham. *Folkways.* Boston: Ginn & Company, 1906.

Tylor, E. B. *Primitive Culture.* London: John Murray, 1871.

Weber, Max. *The Protestant Ethic and the Spirit of Capitalism.* Translated by Talcott Parsons. London: George Allen & Unwin, 1930; New York; Charles Scribner's Sons, 1958.

White, Leslie A. "Cultural vs. Psychological Interpretations of Human Behavior," *American Sociological Review, 12* (December 1947), pp. 686–698.

Wilson, Edward O. *Sociobiology: The New Synthesis.* Cambridge, Mass.: Harvard University Press, 1974.

Yinger, J. Milton. *The Scientific Study of Religion.* New York: Macmillan, 1970. A portion of this material has been adapted from Yinger's *Religion, Society, and the Individual: An Introduction to the Sociology of Religion.* New York: Macmillan, 1957.

▶ KEY CONCEPT REVIEW

To aid you in mastering the basic concepts of Part 2, we have organized key terms into convenient and logical conceptual networks. Two terms are included here (role and status), though they are discussed in detail in Chapter 6, since they constitute an essential aspect of social structure. Refer to the study procedure recommended on page 73 and follow the same procedure here:

CLUSTER 3 The Social Self—Basis for the Social Structure	CLUSTER 4 Understanding Social Structure	CLUSTER 5 Culture
Self	Social Structure	Culture
"I" and "Me"	Social Role	Values
Looking-Glass Self	Social Status	Norms
Generalized Other	Achieved Status	Mores
Socialization	Ascribed Status	Folkways
	Role Set	Laws
	Role Conflict	Acculturation
		Assimilation
		Ethnocentrism

3. The Social Self—Basis for the Social Structure

	Definition	Example
Self	"Miniature societies" that humans possess in their views of themselves in relationship to others. Individuals become social beings, not by biological birth, but by continually relating to others, both in their daily lives and in their imaginations.	Hermits, isolated prisoners, and shipwreck victims (like Robinson Crusoe) are never socially alone. In their imaginations, they talk to themselves or to nonhuman creatures (dogs, spiders). They may look around when they accidentally stumble, even though they are physically alone.
"I" and "Me"	George Mead identified these two complementary aspects of the self. The "I" represents the spontaneous, unrestrained, creative, and often nonconforming aspect; the "me" represents the cautious, predictable, and conforming aspect. Mead pictured peoples' inner lives as the continuous interaction between the "I" and the "me."	The small child who climbs onto mother's elegantly set dinner table to reach the flowers in the center and creates chaos is behaving according to the dictates of the "I." At the next dinner party, remembering mother's punishment, the child's "me" suppresses the desire to climb, and the child instead asks mother for a flower.

	Definition	Example
Looking-Glass Self	The conscious self-image that people form of themselves as a result of how they perceive others reacting to them in social situations. Charles Cooley likened this to obtaining a physical self-conception by looking in a mirror. We obtain a social self-perception by looking in the mirror provided by the actions of others towards us.	Although everyone has a looking-glass self, people vary in terms of how sensitive they are to the reactions of others. Those who are highly sensitive and image conscious usually have unstable self-images (like Charlie Brown and Snoopy or like many entertainers—Marilyn Monroe, for example). These people are sometimes referred to as *other-directed,* in contrast to *inner-directed* persons who have relatively stable self-images not totally dependent upon the approving responses of others (Lucy, Christ, Mahatma Gandhi).
Generalized Other	A person's general impression of what others, as larger groupings or communities, expect of him or her. It is a composite overall impression formed through interacting with others and subsequently internalizing and unifying their attitudes and expectations.	By the time a child is skillful enough to participate in organized sports (for example, Little League Baseball), he or she has learned all the roles connected with the game (such as the roles of other players, coaches, umpires, parents, fans) and has a good sense of what is expected in terms of personal performance on and off the field.
Socialization	The process whereby an individual learns the skills, roles, rules, and values of a society and develops a social (self) identity. Socialization is a lifelong process that usually involves learning in different but related subgroups (family, peer group, occupation). When a new subgroup replaces an older one in the life of an individual, we then say that the person has been desocialized from the old subgroup and resocialized into the new one.	Parental discipline, formal schooling, and on-the-job occupational training are all familiar forms of socialization. Basic training in the military or the novitiate period in religious training are familiar examples of desocialization and resocialization. The story of Eliza Doolittle who was converted by Dr. Higgins from a lower-class flower girl into a social sophisticate is another example of desocialization and resocialization.

4. Understanding Social Structure

	Definition	Example
Social Structure	The stable patterns of interpersonal and *role* relationships that make social group behavior orderly and predictable. Shared *culture* (norms and values) also makes such patterned interaction possible.	Traditional Western family structure involves (1) a father–provider role (considered most valuable and, therefore, of highest status); (2) a mother–homemaker role (next most valuable; next highest status); (3) a child–learner role (least valued; therefore lowest status). *Power* and *authority* are distributed accordingly and control family interaction. The traditional roles are being challenged by those arguing for new relationships, for a newer, more democratic social structure.
Social Role	The expected pattern of behavior and the network of rights, privileges, and responsibilities that accompany each position (*status*) in the social structure. Role and status are the two fundamental aspects of social structure. They may be thought of as the two sides of the coin labeled "social structure."	Television viewers expect their weekly medical heroes (for example, Dr. Marcus Welby) to exhibit ideal behavior in the physician's role—that is, working long hard hours for altruistic motives; expertly blending patient involvement and compassion with detached scientific objectivity; resolving occasional conflicts between allegiances to both organized medicine and individual patients. They also expect to see medical heroes treated with respect and deference by their patients.
Social Status	The position assigned to various roles within the social structure based on their estimated social value. As used by sociologists, status is attached to roles on an impersonal basis and does not reflect the quality of a person's role performance. Entire segments of a society (for example, the working class), as well as individuals, may share a status.	To be a first stringer or a starter on an athletic team usually carries higher status than being a reserve, despite individual ability or contribution. Likewise, within large organizations, bad managers usually receive higher status and greater rewards than good workers at the production level.
Achieved Status	Social status that has been achieved through personal striving and accomplishment.	John D. Rockefeller rose from a poor immigrant background to the role of industrial giant, a position that carried great wealth, power, and responsibility.

	Definition	Example
Ascribed Status	Social status that is assigned to someone on the basis of inherited characteristics (sex, race, age, religious affiliation of family, and so on) without reference to individual striving and accomplishment.	Nelson Rockefeller was a white male baby, born into a powerful family with high status, strong religious affiliation, and great wealth. Unlike his grandfather, high status was assured him regardless of personal striving and accomplishment in later life.
Role Set	The many roles, some complementary and some conflicting, that cluster around a single social position (*status*).	Marcus Welby not only must act out a doctor–patient role but also doctor–nurse, doctor–doctor, doctor–administrator, and doctor–family roles, among others. Some of these role sets support others; some conflict with others.
Role Conflict	Situations where a person faces conflicting elements within a single role or conflicting roles within a *role set.*	With most patients, Dr. Welby can balance a personal relationship with scientific objectivity. However, he would find this difficult if his patient was his wife or child and he might have to ask another doctor to take charge because of the role conflict.

5. Culture

	Definition	Example
Culture	For most social scientists, all aspects of life (mental, physical, behavioral, emotional) that characterize a society. Sociologists focus upon the ideational elements of culture (values, norms, attitudes, beliefs) as *mentifacts,* and upon the physical elements (tools, houses, technology, and so on) as *artifacts.*	Any human group, no matter how heterogeneous its background, will develop a culture to meets its particular needs. For example, professional athletic teams (for example, in baseball) draw together players from all over the world. Nevertheless, a distinctive "jock" culture arises, characterized by (1) a unique language ("wheels" means legs; to "motor" means to run); (2) different norms (bench jockeying; arguing with umpires); (3) unusual values (being a "free" spirit; learning to play despite pain); (4) special beliefs (bad luck to step on the third base line).

	Definition	Example
Values	Anything (object, idea, behavior) that is perceived as intrinsically rewarding and therefore becomes an object of human pursuit (a social goal). Norms and values have a *means–ends relationship* within a culture. Norms are the means of regulating behavior so that socially desirable ends (goals that are valued) can be attained.	Values may be material (wealth), ideational (justice, freedom, equality), or behavioral (temperance, aggressiveness). Sociologists stress the ideational aspects of values (the idea of work as essential). For example, America has been studied as a culture of violence in which individual aggressiveness is valued.
Norms	Agreed upon and, therefore, expected patterns of behavior that accompany a particular social *role.* Norms can be thought of as a set of blueprints about what constitutes proper role behavior in given situations.	In American society, parents are expected to support and socialize their children, and children are expected to heed and obey their parents. In the Israeli Kibbutz (see pp. 414–417), other adults are expected to take over some parental roles. In the Soviet Union (see pp. 418–420), the state expects parents to indoctrinate their children politically.
Mores	The informal norms that are considered most essential to a society's survival. Mores are usually informally taught through primary groups and are accepted by most people without question, since individuals internalize the values involved as their own.	The incest taboo and prohibition of cold-blooded murder are examples of nearly universal mores, that is, they appear in almost all socieites. People internalize these norms so that the mere thought of committing incest or unemotional murder makes many of them physically ill.
Folkways	Informal norms that are not considered vital to a society's survival. They carry less severe sanctions than mores and are much more likely to be morally questioned.	Such matters as etiquette, fashion, and language usage involve folkways. Violations are met with sarcasm, frowns, kidding, and other forms of mild abuse. Fads in unusual styles of dress or language (topless swim suits or the use of four-letter swear words by youthful antiwar demonstrators in the 1960s) are common.
Laws	Deliberately planned norms that are formally enforced by specially authorized *secondary groups* (courts, police, and so on). Laws tend to flourish in formal and heterogeneous *Gesellschaft*-like (see page 303) societies, characterized by conflicting values and isolated primary relationships and groups.	America's highly legalistic culture is partly a result of a heterogeneous population and a pluralistic value structure. Our laws govern behavior all the way from language usage (swearing in public) through hitchhiking to mass murder (airplane sabotage).

	Definition	Example
Acculturation	When groups or individuals from different cultures interact with each other, each adopts elements of the other's culture. One group or individual may predominate over the other, although some degree of mutual modification usually occurs.	The U.S. military occupation of Japan following World War II produced considerable Westernizing of Japanese culture (political democratization, rapid industrialization, changes in family life and womens' rights, and so on) and some Easternizing of American culture (meditation cults, Japanese gardening, open-space architecture, and so on). However, Japan was more Westernized than the U.S. was Easternized.
Assimilation	The process whereby a group replaces its culture (language, customs, and so on) with another, often dominant, culture of a larger society. Assimilation causes a group to be absorbed into another culture.	The "myth of the American melting pot" maintains that Southern European immigrant groups have, for the most part, become assimilated into the larger white Anglo-Saxon Protestant culture. Recent research, focusing upon the development of ethnic pride, questions this belief.
Ethnocentrism	The tendency to see the customs and values of one's own culture as qualitatively superior—the only "right" way—in contrast to all other cultures. Ethnocentrism builds group integration and loyalty but results in distrust, suspicion, and avoidance of outsiders.	Groups such as the Ku Klux Klan (see p. 236), street-corner gangs (see pp. 108–113) and extremist religious cults (see pp. 248–252) are characterized by high degrees of ethnocentrism. During war, governments actively promote ethnocentric attitudes by using derogatory labels and names to characterize the enemy as inferior outsiders (vicious Japs, cruel Heines, commie Gooks, and so on).

PART 3

Types of Group Behavior

Contrasting Forms of Human Behavior and Group Life

	More Spontaneous Forms		More Structured Forms
The Social Self	I		Me
Interpersonal Relationships	Primary		Secondary
Culture As Norms	Folkways and mores		Laws
Human Groups	Collectivities	Associations	Institutions
	←	(Status groupings / Communities)	→

IN CHAPTER 1, we referred to the dialogue between Peter Berger and Philip Selznick concerning the question of whether humans are determined or free. Do social conditions primarily determine what we do, or are we free to innovate and deviate from group expectations? Is behavior essentially spontaneous and relatively unfettered, or is it conforming and structured according to fixed social norms? This is one of the central philosophical and scientific issues with which sociologists have had to deal. In our discussions thus far, it has been apparent that both kinds of behavior are to be found throughout human life; there is both freedom and conformity.

In Chapter 2, for example, the distinction was made between primary relationships (intimate and often quite spontaneous) and secondary relationships (formal and often quite structured). Also in Chapter 2, a typology of five basic types of human group behavior was proposed, using a similar comparison between less structured and more structured behavior. Somewhat related to the same dichotomy was the comparison between the "I" and the "me" in George Mead's concept of the social self, discussed in Chapter 3. According to this view, the fully developed self is a balance between creativity and conformity. Finally, in Chapter 4, the discussion of norms suggested that these guidelines for human behavior can range from informal expectations (folkways and mores) to formalized norms (laws enforced through highly structured institutional processes). This consistent contrast between spontaneity and formality is summarized in the accompanying diagram. However, care must be taken not to oversimplify the obvious complexity of human behavior.

Freedom and conformity can be found in both the spontaneous and the structured forms of social life. For example, the self, as a kind of "little society," involves a continuous interaction between creativity and conformity. The social self emerges in a primary group, usually the family, and carries over into secondary relationships where conformity to norms is more formalized. In primary contexts, the expressive "I" also is given opportunity for release and norms are sometimes spontaneous and flexible. At the same time, a primary group can be very confining, and individuals, especially those approaching young adulthood, may want to escape to secondary contexts (leave the small town for the city) in order to experience a new kind of freedom and individuality. As a matter of fact, the informal folkways and mores of a small town may seem more restricting than the formal laws of an urban center. Human interaction, therefore, is very complex and includes a never-ending interplay between the desire to be free and the necessity to conform to self-perceptions, interpersonal demands, and normative expectations. We have considered some aspects of this interplay in Chapters 1–4.

In Chapters 5–9, we will discuss another aspect of this issue. We will examine in detail each of the five basic forms of human group behavior, ranging from the more spontaneous through mixed to the more structured. In each case, the discussion considers major concepts and theories and central social problems upon which sociologists have focused. In addition, the issue of freedom versus conformity is an underlying theme.

In Chapter 5, for example, we will see how individual participation in collectivities—the most spontaneous form of group behavior—can provide outlets for the release of the emotional "I". People participating in fads and fashions often give free expression to individual attitudes and values. However, members of crowds, mobs, and social movements can also become caught up in collective passions that lead to a loss of behavioral control, to "blind" conformity to the actions of others, and to unthinking extremist actions.

In Chapter 7, we will discuss associations as types of human groups characterized by a mixture of both spontaneous and structured forms of behavior. The problem of bureaucracy will be a major focus. Modern bureaucracies tend to stress obedience to formal rules and regulations. As a result, members frequently engage in spontaneous behavior that strikes out against red tape and impersonality and reflects a striving for individual freedom. Yet, bureaucracy was designed as an impersonal system so that humans would be free from the personal demands of others. In the modern bureaucratized university, for example, all students should be free to study as they please, based upon their personal abilities and preference, not according to the special prejudices of teachers, other students, or the administration.

In Chapter 9, we will see how institutions—more formal and structured groups—require a high degree of membership commitment and conformity. At the same time, processes may develop within these contexts that provide for individual expression. Patients in a mental hospital can find ways of acting as individuals in spite of the rigid rules and regulations of the instituion. Professionals, like physicians and college teachers, resist coercion by bureaucratic restrictions and insist upon the necessity for creativity and altruism in rendering important human services.

In a similar manner, Chapters 6 (on status groupings) and 8 (on communities) consider groups that are variable and can be found in either spontaneous or structured forms. In both cases, freedom and conformity will vary. Residents of urban communities are freer than members of rural communities to pursue personal interests, as are people in modern classlike societies as compared to those in castelike societies. While the impersonality and uncertainties of life in cities or class societies can lead to feelings of alienation and anomie, citizens of small towns and castes know what others expect of them and what to expect of others—they have greater security but fewer chances for individuality.

We begin our discussion of these forms of human group behavior with the most spontaneous and unstructured—collectivities.

- When disaster strikes as in a flood or fire or earthquake, do humans stampede just like animals?
- How and why do new fads and fashions come about?
- Do people really "lose their heads" in a crowd?
- Can riots and revolts be predicted? Should they be prevented or controlled?
- Can social movements like women's liberation actually change society?
- Do you agree with sentiments expressed in the following exchange between Betty Friedan and Simone de Beauvoir [1975, pp. 12ff]:

Friedan: ". . . the Women's Movement, which we have both helped to influence by our books and through our thinking, has emerged as the largest and fastest-growing—perhaps the only vital movement for basic social change—in the Seventies. But it has reached in America and, to some extent, in the world, a kind of crest and now it is floundering a little on a plateau."

de Beauvoir: "Yes, I think that's true here in France."

5

Collective Behavior

WHAT IS COLLECTIVE BEHAVIOR?

As the typology of group behavior in Chapter 2 indicated, human groups differ along a continuum. Some are short-lived and have little structure; others have a long life and are highly organized. In this chapter, we will consider the most elementary and least structured forms of human groups, those known as *collectivities.* Collectivities are usually transient and temporary, although occasionally they do develop into long lasting groups. If they perpetuate themselves, they may become well-established associations or institutions. Whatever fate ensues, collective behavior involves individuals in emotional, often volatile, sometimes violent behavior. Collectivities can include panic, fads, and fashions, riots, audiencelike crowds, revivals, and social movements like women's liberation.

Collective behavior is often related to the process of social change. It may arise in defense of established norms and values threatened by change or in a struggle for new norms and a radical reordering of society. It may also be the way in which human beings react when a natural disaster destroys a community or when individuals are "carried away" with the excitement of a revival meeting or a football game.

Whatever the circumstance, people seem to take leave of their senses at times. They act so strangely that they appear to be abnormal or deviant. They are seemingly not themselves. As a result, scholars have found it difficult to arrive at sound explanations of what happens. The earliest perspectives assumed that collective behavior was not at all like normal behavior; they sought to explain what happened to individuals psychologically when they were caught up in a panic, a riot, or a social movement. Social psychology is one discipline that has dealt extensively with this phenomenon. This focus upon psychological dimensions—what happens to individuals—has prevailed in much of the work done by sociologists. Only recently, in the 1960s and 70s, have sociologists begun to turn their attention to collectivities as forms of group behavior rather than arenas for individuals to act out their emotional and interpersonal dramas. Now scholars are suggesting that, even in a panic or a crowd, humans act like humans; they behave according to norms and in keeping with the normal process of group decision making. In fact, the study of collective behavior is still in a state of flux and development, and, consequently, it offers a good example of how theory emerges in sociology.

THEORETICAL PERSPECTIVES

The French scholar, Gustave Le Bon [1917], was one of the first to analyze the psychological mechanisms at work when individuals are caught up in the excitement of a crowd. He pointed to the irrationality and unpredictability of behavior when people act in unison under the influence of collective emotion. Le Bon seems to imply that there is a kind of "collective mind," which exists over and above the sum total of individuals. This emphasis upon the collective mind is no longer accepted by sociologists today, nor is the concept of irrationality and unpredictability considered the central focus. Nevertheless, Le Bon's work is important as a pioneer study of crowds and collective behavior. It is a good example of the early stress upon individual psychology and the tendency to imply that crowds are the prototypes—that is, the best examples—of collective behavior.

The University of Chicago scholar, Robert E. Park, also helped set the stage for continued study of this form of human behavior. His Heidelberg University doctoral dissertation, *Masse und Publikum* [1904], has just recently been translated into English and published along with other essays by Park [Elsner, 1972]. He saw "crowd and public as groups without a past or future" and "without tradition." He heightened the contrast between normal behavior and collective behavior. He emphasized the importance of the latter in bringing about social change in established institutions. At the same time, Park pointed up the contrast between crowd and public: The crowd suppresses the differences between individuals and is "of one mind," whereas the public recognizes individuals with differing values engaging in rational discussion and debate over a public issue. The public arrives at consensus but does not impose unanimity upon its members as does a crowd [Elsner, 1972, pp. xi, xiv].

One of Park's students, Herbert Blumer, has become one of the most prominent contemporary scholars in the field of collective behavior. In 1939, Blumer wrote an essay in which he defined the field, described the mechanisms at work that account for how people behave in unstructured situations, and distinguished between *elementary collective groupings* and *social movements* [Blumer, 1939, pp. 221–228]. Elementary forms of collective behavior emerge from the restlessness that occurs when established ways are disturbed and changes come about in old institutions. Blumer speaks of four basic groupings: the acting crowd, the expressive crowd, the mass, and the public. These are not lasting forms of behavior and they soon give way to more organized ones, which can become the basis for social movements. A workers' strike can result in a labor movement, which in turn can lead to organized forms of union activity. In the early 20th century, an attack on the saloons by ardent women led to the prohibition movement and to organizations like the Anti-Saloon League and the Women's Christian Temperance Union [Odegard, 1928]. In Blumer's terms, a social movement is the transition between elementary collective behavior and established social organizations.

A contemporary contribution to the theory of collective behavior comes from the work of Neil Smelser [1963], who acknowledges his debt to Blumer. Professor Smelser argues that collective behavior is not as different from other forms of group behavior as most writers imply. Even though relatively unstructured, collective behavior need not be discussed in terms that imply mysterious or unusual forces at work. It is not set apart completely from normal behavior by virtue of some unusual setting (panic in a burning theater), or by a unique kind of communication or interaction (circular emotion that builds up hysteria), or by special psychological characteristics (loss of critical faculties and regression to a childlike state or even an animal-like state). Collective behavior, even in its most elementary forms of panic and crowd action, is not totally different from other forms of behavior. It can be understood and analyzed and predicted by the sociologist, as well as by the psychologist. The task of the sociologist is to ask: What are the social determinants of collective behavior? Smelser answers this question by making use of a concept from the discipline of economics. He refers to "the logic of value-added" and indicates that even panic, a seemingly unpredictable form of human behavior, can be traced through predictable stages to a logical outcome.

The Logic of a Value-Added Approach

In economics, the term *value-added* is a concept related to the stages in the process of production. Iron ore is converted into automobiles through the stages of mining, smelting, tempering, shaping, combining steel with other parts, painting, delivering to the retailer, and selling.

> Each stage "adds its value" to the final cost of the finished product. The key element in this example is that the earlier stage must combine according to a certain pattern before the next stage can contribute its particular value to the finished product. It is impossible to paint iron ore and hope that the painting will thereby contribute to the desired final product, an automobile. Painting, in order to be effective as a "determinant" in shaping the product, has to "wait" for the completion of earlier processes. Every stage in the value-added process, therefore, is a necessary condition for the appropriate and effective addition of value in the next stage. The sufficient condition for final production, moreover, is the combination of every necessary condition, according to a definite pattern [Smelser, 1963, pp. 13–14].

As the iron ore moves step by step toward the finished automobile, the vision of what it is going to become is increasingly certain or determined. Once it is shaped in the form of automobile parts and painted, one can predict that it is to become an automobile and not something else.

The economic concept of a value-added process can be adapted to an analysis of collective behavior. In sociology, it is possible to use the same logic in studying a social situation like panic. If we define panic as a "collective flight based on a hysterical belief," as Smelser does, the major social determinants that must be interrelated in a definite pattern to produce panic are as follows:

1. *Structural conduciveness* must exist. For example, panic requires a situation wherein strain may easily develop as in a flood or in a money market; where avenues for escape from apparent danger are limited; and where communication of panicky reactions takes place. A disaster situation is not conducive to panic when escape routes are completely open or completely closed and/or where individuals are isolated from one another and do not communicate hysteria. In other words, the structure of the situation must be appropriate as the first stage in the sequence of value-added events leading to panic.
2. *Strain* must be added as the second step. Panic participants must define the situation as holding an immediate threat, the exact dimensions of which are not known. There must be uncertainty as to the outcome, a sense of the uncontrollable, and a feeling of helplessness. To be sure, there are psychological and cultural differences between individuals and groups when it comes to defining situations as "dangerous." Some are more susceptible to danger and possible panic than others.
3. *Anxiety* in the form of general apprehension, which provides the atmosphere for hysterical belief, must be added as well.
4. *The precipitating factor* must be present to transform the vague anxiety into fear of a specific threat. This is the factor that "con-

firms" the suspicions and uneasiness of anxious people. For example, a sonic boom may conceivably precipitate panic in people who fear an atomic war. The boom itself may bring to mind latent anxiety that is already present. In a tense situation, precipitating incidents may be quite trivial. They are immediate signals announcing that the predicted threat (the enemy bombing, the bank failure, the broken dam) has come to pass.

5. *Mobilization for flight* is the final necessary condition for a panic. Here we refer to someone or some incident that triggers action. As Professor Smelser phrases it: "Usually a primitive form of leadership arises to touch off a panic. Someone (a 'flight model') starts running, and others join." He points to two phases of the actual route. The first is the original action in response to the triggering event. The second is contagious buildup of emotional reaction, which comes from seeing others panic. This is the fear that feeds upon itself. The result may be a series of subpanics that reach a climax sometime after the initial flight.
6. *Counterpanic forces* also exist and influence the outcome of panic situations. Smelser refers to these in his treatment of prevention and control of panic. At each stage of the above process that builds toward panic behavior, counterforces may be brought into operation. Such forces may include:
   a. *Facilities* that may be used to reduce the danger and risk of panic. A new dam or ditch may reduce flood possibility. An educational program may inform individuals in order to reduce strain and anxiety. The public may be warned of what to expect.
   b. *Organization* that may serve to channel behavior according to expected roles. When policemen and firemen play their roles faithfully even in times of disaster and when leaders in a situation stand firm in a crisis, panic is not so apt to occur.
   c. *Norms* for behavior can perform a basic part in the prevention of panic. Fire drills serve to establish regular behavior patterns appropriate for a crisis. More fundamental, however, are the deep-seated norms that call for protection of family and friends. Often these prove to be "natural aids" in preventing panic, as people in crisis turn to loved ones rather than to flight. Traditional norms, however, may create a different response. Sometimes panic turns out to be partly a "scramble to some loved one." As Killian points out in his study of disaster referred to elsewhere in this chapter (see pp. 183–184), this tendency to turn to family may help to paralyze a community in crisis. Thus, norms may have both functional and dysfunctional results in the context of panic.
   d. *Values* are likewise deep-seated and are not easily ignored by human actors even in severe crisis. Faith in a fundamental institution like the Bank of England may serve to avert panic in spite

of signs of financial fiasco. Soldiers on the battlefield may turn to prayer rather than panic, or they may rely upon their confidence in the fighting unit in the face of great odds [Smelser, 1963, pp. 12–21, 131–169].

In summary, Smelser seeks to cope with the complexity of collective behavior by showing how each social determinant contributes to the final "product" or outcome. Each is a necessary condition and stands in a particular relationship to the others. Each alone is not a sufficient condition for panic, but when each adds to a total sequence, the outcome is not mysterious or unpredictable but determined by factors that can be assessed and measured by social scientists. Behavior of persons in a panic, therefore, is subject to analysis like other forms of behavior and is determined by social as well as psychological conditions. Smelser assumes that there are psychological mechanisms at work: Structural strain excites feelings of anxiety, fantasy, hostility; some people are more likely to respond hysterically or to be more suggestible than others; collective outbursts and movements are more conducive to irrational action. His primary focus, however, is on the social determinants. Therefore, Smelser's perspective is solidly in the sociological perspective. Can this theory, then, be used to help understand contemporary incidents of violent collective action?

The Kent State Tragedy and Smelser's Theory

Is the value-added theoretical perspective helpful in understanding what happened in 1970 at Kent State University, when the National Guard fired on students, killing four and wounding several? One scholar [Lewis, 1972, pp. 87–96], who was present during the crisis, thinks it is; he has shown how virtually all the conditions outlined by Smelser were present at Kent State on 4 May 1970.

1. *Structural conduciveness.* Kent State students had for some time been among the leading anti-Vietnam War protestors. The central area of the campus known as The Commons had been a free speech area and the students' "turf." When President Nixon sent troops into Cambodia in the spring of 1970, the campus came alive with plans for protest. Rumors of extreme action led the mayor to call in the National Guard and the governor to order the Guard to stop all student assemblies anywhere on campus except in the classrooms. For three days, there were confrontations between the Guard, who represented the War and the invasion of students' rights, and the students, who formed acting crowds with the familiar structure: acting core, cheerleaders, and spectators.
2. *Strain.* The major source of strain was the presence of the Guard on the students' turf. Student hostility centered upon the soldiers who tried to restore order after the burning of the ROTC building

and sought to enforce the order against assemblying when a rally was called for Monday noon, May 4th. Communications between contending forces were largely in the form of hostile gestures. Therefore, the Guard became angry when students disobeyed the order against assembly, thinking they fully understood it. Students were confused about the order and resentful over the very presence of the Guard.

3. *Anxiety, ambivalence, and hostility.* Students who felt anxiety over the situation probably did not attend the rally. For the most part ambiguity prevailed according to Lewis. It was never quite clear to many students whether the rally was in violation of a new and resented norm. Nor was it clear whether the Guard would really enforce it. The majority of students were sure that the soldiers would not fire their guns. They felt relatively safe, therefore, in challenging members of the Guard who were seen as the "enemy."
4. *Precipitating factors.* Lewis cites two crucial events as key factors: (1) the action of the Guard in making a stand in front of the burning ROTC building and (2) the assemblying for the Monday noon rally. As hostile exchanges took place leading up to the rally (the Guard had been on campus about 40 hours by the time of the rally), the student crowds gained an increasing feeling of omnipotence. Students felt that they had the Guard on the run when the action shifted to the practice football field nearby. The Guard drove students onto the field but thus maneuvered itself into a kind of encirclement. Apparently, the soldiers realized that the students were aware of this situation. In any case, at this point, events moved quickly to the climax.
5. *Mobilization for action.* No formal leadership emerged among the Kent State students. "Events" served as models of leadership, as Smelser indicated might sometimes happen. The core members of the student group acted in provocative ways as their closest supporters cheered them on. The large surrounding group of spectators stood by as if in sympathy. The actors threatened soldiers with gestures, yells, and the throwing of missiles. Most of the exchange was relatively harmless until the soldiers threw tear gas and the students threw it back.
6. *Counteraction by law enforcement personnel.* One of Smelser's themes emphasizes the importance of the behavior of those responsible for keeping order in a social situation. If counteraction is appropriate, a collective outburst may never take place even if all other factors are present. Smelser suggests four principles for crowd control [Smelser, 1972]:
   a. Prevent communication between crowd members themselves so that hostile beliefs cannot be disseminated. At Kent State, the

Guard did not try to interrupt communication. Instead, it kept itself as the focal point for hostile reaction.

b. Prevent interaction between crowd leaders and followers. The Guard did not move in and arrest the leaders in the student crowds.
c. Never bluff action against a demonstrating crowd. Here again the Guard made the wrong moves when soldiers entered into the game of throwing tear gas cannisters back at students and when 16 Guardsmen knelt and pointed their M-1 rifles at students in the parking lot. So confident were students that this was a bluff that some shouted, "Shoot, shoot, shoot."
d. Avoid entering into controversies with the crowd. At Kent State, the Guard was the central focus for controversy and there were hostile feelings on both sides.

After the Guard drove a group of students onto the practice football field, it was only 5 or 10 minutes until the shooting and killings took place. Regardless of such factors as deliberate intent, ill-trained troops, political hatred, and the like, it is evident that the elements of collective behavior were present at Kent State in 1970. Knowledge of these elements and how they are interrelated could help to avoid similar tragedies in the future.

Functions of Collective Behavior

The application of Smelser's theory to Kent State raises the following questions: (1) Is collective action essentially unlike other behavior? That is, if both students and guardsmen had acted "normally" (rationally), many assume that the tragedy would not have taken place. Therefore, collective behavior seems unnatural. (2) Is collective action essentially bad, that is, dysfunctional? Kent State resulted in deaths and injuries, inflamed passions and hatreds, led to lengthy court battles, and the like. Weller and Quarantelli [1973, pp. 665–684] have developed a theory of the functions of collective behavior that attempts to address these kinds of questions.

They point out that not all collective behavior is the same. Sometimes it springs out of new relationships between people who perhaps have not known each other, as in a panic or lynching. Sometimes it occurs among people who may know each other and have old abiding relationships, as when policemen riot and when friends attend a revival together. Similarly, collective behavior may differ according to whether new norms must be agreed upon as in a panic or a police riot, or whether there are old established ways of behaving, as in a lynching or a revival. This suggests that collectivities are not always new experiences entirely; they may serve to reenforce tradition as well as to spark social change. Table 5-1 depicts at least four types of collectivities according to relationship, on the one hand, and norms, on the other.

Thus, collectivities can be either like or unlike other forms of human behavior. Similarly, they can be both functional and dysfunctional within the context of the prevailing norms of a society. Type A is the "purest," the most typical form of collective behavior. It brings together people who have not known one another previously and places them in a situation for which there are no prevailing rules for behavior. Therefore, the group must form quickly and develop new norms. In this sense, it is unlike normal behavior. However, the resulting action is not necessarily uncontrollably "wild," since the new norms specify agreed-upon rules that govern subsequent behavior.

TABLE 5-1 Type of Collectivities[a]

		Social Relationships: New Ones Without Precedent	Social Relationships: Old Ones With Tradition
Norms	New Ones Without Precedent	TYPE A: Riots, panics	TYPE B: Fads and fashions, rioting police
Norms	Old Ones With Tradition	TYPE C: Looting, lynching	TYPE D: Revivals, crowds at sporting events

[a]Adapted from Jack M. Weller and E. L. Quarantelli, "Neglected Characteristics of Collective Behavior," *The American Journal of Sociology, 79* (1973), p. 79. The presentation here differs from the original table.

In contrast, Type D is collective behavior that takes place within established institutional settings. Old friends and associates attend a revival meeting or a baseball game together and engage in emotional interaction according to prescribed and traditional norms. Yelling "Kill the umpire," drinking too much beer, or hearing the voice of God, though excessive forms of behavior in other contexts, have become accepted in these situations.

Types B and C represent combinations of the other two types. In Type B, new norms are generated, although the behavior takes place within established institutional settings. Rioting police know one another and are bound together by their relationships and traditions. The stress of the situation, however, causes them to redefine the situation, thereby leading to collective rather than rational behavior. New fashions emerging within old business firms would also be an example of this type of collective behavior. Type C is defined as a form of collectivity that follows old and established patterns but brings together relative strangers into a new situation. Lynch mobs are examples; they act as previous lynch mobs have acted although the people involved are not the same.

In summary, collective behavior is extremely complex and can consist of different types of group action. Such action is not abnormal or unnatural, although it does possess characteristics that distinguish it from more structured and rational forms. As tragic as some instances of collective behavior seem to be, collective action can perform important and needed functions within the social order. In some cases, it helps to *hasten social change* (for example, when striking school teachers alert society to the need for reforms in education). In other cases, it helps to *slow up social change* and preserve needed tradition (for example, when revival meetings keep alive religious involvement). This is not to say that collective action is always functional and advantageous; it can also be dysfunctional. Emotional outbursts often result in destruction of property and injury or death to human beings. This is why social scientists and civic leaders have long been interested in the question of control. Is it possible to predict the development of panics, riots, and major social and revolutionary movements? Is it desirable to attempt to prohibit or control these kinds of behavior? The rest of this chapter will deal with these questions by focusing upon the broadest classifications of collective behavior: elementary forms versus lasting forms.

ELEMENTARY FORMS OF COLLECTIVE BEHAVIOR

Panic

Panic is one of three familiar types of elementary collective behavior along with *crazes* and *crowds*. It is one of the most random forms, analogous to what happens to the regular pattern of ants when an ant hill is toppled over. Not all theorists agree with Smelser that the course of panic behavior can be predicted. Nevertheless, there is general agreement among scholars that panic is the most elementary form of human behavior and is often contagious. Individuals lose their heads when overcome with fear and become highly suggestible. The sight of one person fleeing or jumping overboard may incite others to do the same. In panic, individuals momentarily lose their critical faculties and their ability to act in a highly rational manner according to accepted norms.

Social scientists, by studying what happens to people in panic, have been able to dispel some popular misconceptions. One such misconception is that people in panic behave like animals in a stampede. The outward appearances of panic behavior, such as when frightened humans simultaneously rush toward an exit, often contribute to these misleading parallels. Similarly, it is frequently assumed that, when a crisis comes to a community, people will flee in wild pandemonium or they will be rendered helpless by indecision and thus become completely dependent. Another inaccurate assumption is that during a disaster the social order will be so destroyed or distorted that officials can effectively control movements of the population according to detailed plans.

So persistent are these popular misconceptions that some government officials and experts in disaster relief work base their training programs on them. For example, nurses have been told that the most common reaction to disaster is panic, characterized as ". . . blind, flight-reaction, manifested by wild running about . . . or otherwise disorganized hysterical behavior. Absence of judgment and logical thinking will be conspicuous" [American Psychiatric Association, 1955, p. 437]. Furthermore, there have been instances where public officials hesitated to give warning and take responsible action in crises for fear of triggering panic. In the face of such popular notions of panic behavior, what are the scientific findings?

Enrico L. Quarantelli [1960, pp. 68–79] has done research on collective behavior during disasters. One of his articles deals with an appraisal of the many accounts of what actually happens when a disaster takes place. He had access to data collected in England during World War II; in Port Jervis, New York, during a flood; and in Worcester, Massachusetts, when that city was hit by a tornado. He also refers to reliable observations of what has happened in times of disaster in Southern communities where black–white relations have been carefully patterned. In all, he uses 50 references.

In these diverse contexts of collective action, Quarantelli tests several hypotheses:

1. *The familiar impression of people fleeing without purpose or predictability from the scene of disaster is incorrect.* Some are reluctant to flee and resist evacuation and others are triggered into flight by the desire to find family or friends.
2. *The dependency image is also false.* After the initial shock of crisis, most citizens take the initiative in rescue and recovery without even waiting for direction from officials.
3. *Likewise the control image is false.* Civic and governmental authorities tend to imply that they alone know what ought to be done. Their feeling is that when people respond to crisis by themselves they only "make a mess out of things." For example, unplanned withdrawal and rescue are seen as unfortunate and disruptive, but evidence points to the contrary conclusion. The task is usually far too great for official agencies, so it is fortunate that spontaneous action reflecting normal cultural patterns often takes precedence. Rescue operations and evacuation do not always have to be controlled by authorities to be effective.

These hypotheses do not deny that there are situations in which the social order is threatened. There may be normative confusion and a breakdown of accepted forms of behavior. Humans do lose their bearings temporarily in crises. On the other hand, humans panic as cultural beings.

Their behavior even in disaster is understandable in terms of their values and commitments. They do things that are not as meaningless as they may appear at first glance [Quarantelli, 1960, pp. 68–79].

Evidence from the situations Quarantelli studied supports his hypotheses. This evidence can be summarized as follows:

1. In Bootle, England, a city of 55,000, people were bombed nightly for a week during World War II with only 10 percent of the houses escaping serious damage. Yet one fourth of the population remained asleep in their homes during the raids. Only 37 percent of the London mothers and children who were eligible for evacuation left the city during the war crisis. Furthermore, even during periods of heavy bombing in London, evacuees drifted back nearly as rapidly as they were being evacuated. Similar findings are on record for Germany and Japan during World War II. This should not be surprising. Human beings have a very strong tendency to continue with their established behavior patterns rather than initiating new courses of behavior.

Data from American scenes of disaster substantiate this finding. For example, in Port Jervis, New York, during a flood crisis in the 1950s, there was rumor of a broken dam and newspapers reported that most of the 9000 inhabitants had fled. Actually only an estimated one fourth fled. Analysis of those who did flee Port Jervis points up another misconception: It is often assumed that when people flee they do so in "flight-panic." Panic is flight where the individual ceases to play any social role whatsoever and merely flees. Withdrawal of this type is extremely rare. Most withdrawal behavior involves definite role playing, especially within primary group relationships. Thus in the so-called panic flight from Port Jervis, there was no solitary flight, and 23 percent of those escaping even made attempts to assist community members outside of their original fleeing group.

2. In general, disaster victims work out their own private withdrawal arrangements. For example, when a tornado hit Worcester, approximately 10,000 persons were made homeless. However, only about 50 individuals were housed by the public authorities. Displaced persons instead moved in with other family members, intimates, neighbors, and generally ignored the formal agencies. Such behavior also suggests that the belief that kinship and primary ties have been greatly weakened in modern mass societies and that the protective functions of the family have been transferred entirely to large-scale organizations is an exaggeration of fact. Other evidence is similarly convincing and leads to the conclusion that most people in crisis do not become "completely irresponsible and totally impotent." In fact, most do not even turn to public agencies for help.

3. Victims of disaster tend to act independently of official command and control. While this may prove awkward and disruptive at times, it can also function to relieve public agencies of an impossible burden and to engage formal social groups (family and friends) in crisis recovery. It is often assumed that cultural norms and values are so disturbed in a crisis

5-1 The Social Nature of Human Panic

Marlborough Gallery, New York

This oil painting by Juan Genoves (entitled ''Gente Corriendo'') typifies popular and official myths about human behavior in panic situations. Disasters (such as earthquakes, wars, and floods) are assumed to cause people to lose control of themselves, to become helpless by indecision, to flee like stampeding animals, to forget family and friends, and to become totally dependent upon formal authorities. In contrast to these myths, studies show that humans interact in crises much as they do in normal circumstances—that is, according to traditional roles, relationships, norms, and values.

Wide World Photos

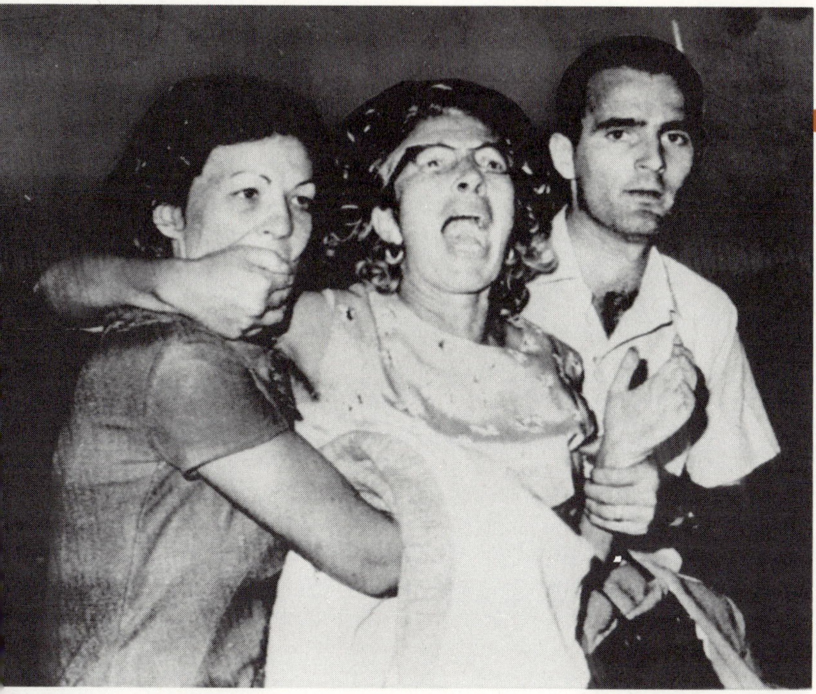

Some individuals may momentarily become hysterical, but groups of bystanders and neighbors are quick to give assistance. After a 1967 earthquake in Caracas, Venezuela, a terrified woman is helped from her home.

Wide World Photos

When authorities become involved, they are not needed to control irrational behavior; rather, they can supply needed equipment. In 1967, a woman is helped aboard an Army amphibious landing craft as she escapes the rising floodwater in Harlingen, Texas.

United Press International

Flight is often triggered by a desire to find and help family and friends to safety. In 1975, Vietnamese refugees help each other ashore from private boats, 60 miles southeast of Saigon, after abandoning embattled cities in the north.

Wide World Photos

People are quick to take the initiative in protective actions, with or without directions from officials. In 1965, volunteers form a human chain over a roof in order to pass sandbags for reinforcing a weak spot in a dike during a flood of the Red River in East Grand Forks, Minnesota.

that formal plans for disaster relief will take precedence. The empirical findings belie this assumption. There is, at best, only temporary and limited suspension of some norms. For example, after disasters in the South, black and white evacuees are sometimes housed together. A relaxation of the norms of segregation might thus be inferred. However, such a relaxation does not necessarily mean a suspension of traditional norms but merely a continuation of the custom that permits blacks to seek refuge at the homes of friendly whites. This is not the same phenomenon as integrated housing.

Quarantelli concludes that careful consideration of what people do in desperate situations leads us to modify, if not to refute completely, many of the popular notions about the character of collective behavior. Panic does occur among human beings. Nevertheless, it is not as widespread as believed, and it is not as random as it seems. Much of human behavior, even in cases of extreme community disruption, reflects conditioned patterns of behavior according to familiar roles. Flight behavior is rare, and even some of this is socially responsible behavior [Quarantelli, 1960, pp. 68–79].

Further explanation of Quarantelli's findings may be found by carefully observing the social structure during times of disaster. Lewis Killian did so by analyzing behavior in Texas City, where a disastrous explosion occurred, and in three Oklahoma towns struck by tornadoes [Killian, 1952, pp. 309–313]. He found that when catastrophe strikes, the social system is not destroyed; people do not completely lose their role patterns of behavior. Role conflict, which is ever-present in human society, is brought into bold relief and individuals are forced to choose between conflicting loyalties. The father role, for example, may conflict with the occupational role of public official, and an individual may face the question: Shall I stay at my post as policeman or rush to help my family? Nevertheless, people do not stampede like animals; they behave like human beings with norms and values. In the four communities that Killian studied following disasters, most of the persons interviewed admitted a critical conflict of loyalty between family and job or community responsibility. When asked—"What was the first thing you thought of after the disaster struck?"—most spoke of immediate thoughts of family or intimate friends.

> The great majority of persons interviewed who were involved in such dilemmas resolved them in favor of loyalty to family or, in some cases, to friendship groups. Much of the initial confusion, disorder, and seemingly complete disorganization reported in the disaster communities was the rush of individuals to find and rejoin their families [Killian, 1952, p. 311].

To sum up our discussion of panic, lifetime social conditioning is not reversed, even in a crisis, as easily as is sometimes supposed. Behavior will follow expected lines of action for the most part, and officials cannot readily manipulate movements. Quarantelli states:

> While it is evident that there is more social and community than personal or small group disruption, disasters do not create situations of total social anomie. Only some of the customary large-scale behavior patterns are rendered ineffectual, and this usually only in relatively extensive and devastating crises. And in such situations new social patterns quickly emerge after the impact to restore a social equilibrium [Quarantelli, 1960, p. 78].

We refer once again to the ant analogy: Even as ants scurry to restore familiar paths after the anthill has been toppled, so humans hasten to recover orderly processes of behavior after a crisis. The analogy is crude, indeed, especially when we realize that ant behavior is instinctive in contrast to the learned cultural patterning of human behavior. Yet it serves to stress the resiliency of human societies, even in the face of devastation.

Craze

Unusual or bizarre behavior is often called a craze. Smelser defines a craze as "mobilization for action based on a positive wish-fulfillment belief" [Smelser, 1963, p. 171]. If panic tends to be a headlong rush away from something, a craze is the opposite, "a rush with sound and fury toward something [they] believe to be gratifying—viz., in manias, booms, bandwagons, 'fashion races,' and fads" [p. 170].

Modern societies are especially conducive to craze behavior since they are characterized by rapid change. In traditional societies, the emphasis is upon security through identification with the familiar. In a changing situation, there is frequent loss of identity and security as the familiar either disappears or is altered. The future is open to new forms of identity and seemingly unlimited opportunities for success. It is possible to "get rich quick" and to gain sudden widespread recognition through the right stroke of luck. In politics, there is the unexpected sweep of events as delegates at a convention get on the bandwagon for a dark-horse candidate. In religion, there is the phenomenon of revivalism. Many are apt to be carried along with waves of fashion in the arts and in morals as well as in dress. Crazes, in whatever form, reflect the restlessness and changeability of people, especially in the modern world.

One of the most scholarly treatments of fashion as a form of behavior similar to the craze is that by Edward Sapir [1937]. In premodern societies, custom prevailed to determine the ongoing pattern of dress and behavior. The emphasis then was upon the group and the sanctity of tradition rather than on individual expression. The Renaissance awakened the desire for innovation, and the industrial revolution increased the technological ease with which fashions could be diffused. At the same time, the emerging idea of the "common man" greatly increased the number of those willing and able to be fashionable. Thus the "familiar merry-go-round of fashion" came into being in Western societies, and people in all social classes became engaged in "experimenting with custom."

However, fashion is both conforming and liberating, as Sapir suggests:

> Fashion is custom in the guise of departure from custom. Most normal individuals consciously or unconsciously have the itch to break away in some measure from a too literal loyalty to accepted custom. They are not fundamentally in revolt from custom but they wish somehow to legitimize their personal deviation without laying themselves open to the charge of insensitiveness to good taste and good manners. Fashion is the discreet solution of the subtle conflict [Sapir 1937, p. 140].

There is a crazelike character to fashion since many people feel a kind of compulsion to take part; they are swept along with the group by strong desires for approval. Some go too far and nullify the very purpose of fashion. For example, good-hearted women of middle age sometimes fail when they try to seem younger than they are, and older men ofttimes try too hard to be mod in their dress. Said former President Harry Truman, as he met with General Douglas MacArthur, the World War II military hero:

> He was wearing those damn sunglasses of his and a shirt that was unbuttoned and a cap that had a lot of hardware. I never did understand . . . an old man like that (MacArthur was about seventy) and a five-star general to boot, why he must go around dressed up like a nineteen-year-old second lieutenant [Miller, 1974, p. 294].

Sapir's analysis is of special significance in pointing up the social implications of fashion. In custom-bound societies, individuals are usually content to accept the customary dress and style of life appropriate to their respective social classes. There is little chance for upward mobility and thus little thought of trying to adopt the dress or life-style of others. In modern societies, fashion tends to be a symbol of membership in a social class also, but with this marked difference: Social mobility is possible in an open society. Thus it is very common for individuals to express their social-class aspirations by taking the fashions of those whom they admire. When the symbols of high status are gradually adopted by those of lower status, even if in a cheaper form, the privileged are nudged toward new symbols, thus starting a new round of fashion changes. Changes in bathing suits may be an illustration of this: As bikinis are mass produced, those in the avant-garde move on to string suits.

The anonymity of urban life also encourages people to express their individuality through fashion. Daring clothes that cast aside modesty and tradition in favor of self-assertion and freedom from the restraints of society have become commonplace. American youth in recent years have expressed this through their rejection of formal dress. Not only have many young women gone braless, but both men and women have made it the style to wear faded patched bluejeans and hiking boots, even to dress-up occasions like concerts, weddings, and funerals. This emphasis upon casual dress pervaded all levels of American society as witnessed by the fact that nearly all clothing shops in the 1970s featured mass-produced bluejeans for men and women of all ages. Fashion can be a kind of victory for the individual as he or she tries to escape the boredom and regularized existence of modern society. Fashion races in art, thought, and morals are also common among modern peoples and reflect much the same need for self-identification.

It is no mystery why fashion has become so widespread in modern society. Fashion has become institutionalized through heavy investment by big business, whose advertising reaches into every home, deliberately encouraging the compulsion to be chic and contemporary, and to be like others. In times of economic crisis, leaders invoke citizens to spend in order to get "the country moving again." In this sense, both fads and fashions have a crazelike compulsive quality and are frequently manipulated for special purposes. Furthermore, both panic and crazes can give rise to crowd behavior.

Crowds: Expressive and Acting

A crowd may be defined as a loosely organized aggregate of people. It is usually short-lived and spontaneous. It is most likely to form in a social setting where there is restlessness and anxiety and where norms are in a state of flux and change. In such a setting, individuals are prone to become highly emotional and irritable. They are easily triggered into action by suggestion and may begin to feel anonymous and not responsible for their actions. Individuals caught up in a crowd feel collectively powerful because of their commitment to a single purpose, which seems in that moment of action to have unqualified approval. According to Blumer [1939, pp. 221–282] and other scholars, the process of crowd behavior usually follows several stages:

1. *Milling* takes place during initial stages of a crisis when there are vague and poorly defined feelings that something has gone wrong. There are aimless groupings of anxious people highly sensitive to each other and obsessed with the crisis.
2. *Circular reaction* occurs as one excited person stimulates another and in turn builds up more emotion in himself. Restlessness becomes contagious.
3. *Collective excitement* spreads to more and more people and the crowd grows in size and intensity. Individuals lose their critical ability and are carried away with the surge of emotion.
4. *Social contagion* is the end result and the mood of approaching climax infects the collectivity.

Although a crowd is not highly structured, it does take on rudimentary form. Spontaneous leaders shout suggestions and help to trigger the vague restlessness into action. There is a nucleus of core members, who are quick to heed the suggestions, and a large group of bystanders, whose very presence lends strength and justification to the cause. Crowd leaders are often those individuals who are most hostility-prone or emotionally ready for extreme behavior that violates established norms and values. Core members likewise tend to differ from mere onlookers in age (more youthful), education and social status (more deprived), and emotional involvement (more attuned to the action).

Some crowds are by no means hostile or destructive. This may be true of curious crowds gathered at the scene of an accident or conventional crowds gathered to watch a football game. These groups are interested in expressing feelings rather than acting them out. An American revival meeting is a good example of an *expressive crowd.* The social setting is one of expectancy on the part of many individuals: There are feelings that "things are not right with the world" and divine forces are on the verge of miraculous action. The milling process goes on during preparation for the coming of a dramatic figure like Billy Graham. The evangelistic spirit is heightened among the faithful, and emotion is spread to others as the circular reaction takes place and collective excitement builds up. The mood must be established over a period of time in anticipation of the revival. The faithful are called into long periods of prayer for the success of the meetings.

This period of preparation is essential. In earlier periods of American history, apparently much of this preparation was spontaneous as unpaid and untrained Protestants spread the word to friends and neighbors. In more recent evangelistic enterprises, like those of Billy Graham, the process has become highly organized with a large paid staff that carries on the buildup and manages the meetings and the follow-up program. Whether a revival service is spontaneous or arranged, the secret of its success lies in its appeal to people who are lonely, deprived, frightened, or morally perplexed. In such a crowd experience, people are often malleable and they frequently enter into a sense of oneness through singing, clapping, and other rhythmic movements.

In an *acting crowd,* many of the same experiences prevail. The chief difference is that in an acting crowd, whether hostile or benevolent, in place of expressive singing, dancing, or similar forms of release, there is a fanatic focus upon some object (person, building, and so on). This most often takes the form of a hostile outburst, which releases a great reservoir of hatred, resentment, or greed. The object of blame is usually identified and fixed upon during the milling process. Suggestions for action are shouted by an emotional leader, and the crowd may swing into action as if it were one great streamroller, with the core members providing the uncontrollable force and the onlookers adding the sense of power and approval. In that moment, there appears to be no thought of norms and values and no respect for authority figures; there is only a single-minded obsession with the task at hand.

Social scientists, therefore, describe the acting crowd as a fanatic group that takes itself too seriously and will not tolerate being crossed. Rational individuals have been submerged into an engine of emotion that it is rigid and absolutist, cannot abide ridicule or criticism, and is fanatically com-

5-2 Methods of Crowd Control

The control of crowds, especially in heterogeneous mass societies, is a continuous problem for authorities charged with maintaining the peace. Two types of theories play a major role in the selection of the most appropriate and desirable methods. First, different methods must be used for **expressive crowds** versus **acting crowds.** Second, methods must relate to the basic processes of crowd formation and evolution.

Expressive crowds consist of members who convey their feelings by collectively chanting, cheering, clapping, singing, and so on, rather than by acting out their feelings (for example, at an athletic event). As a result, the behavior and attentions of members of an expressive crowd are relatively peaceful and multiple (some people cheer, some watch, some talk to each other). Control methods are generally designed to keep expressive crowds from becoming acting crowds.

E. Herwig/Stock, Boston

Alex Webb/Magnum

Since the members of the crowd are easily triggered into action by suggestion, it is desirable for authorities to remain impassive and neutral. Artificial barriers can separate expressive crowds from the object of attention (or from opposing expressive groups), thereby lessening the chance of an incident that would lead to an explosive response.

Boston Police Department

J. Albertson/Stock, Boston

When members of a crowd begin to feel anonymous and part of a mass, they lose a feeling of responsibility for their actions and are more likely to engage in violent behavior. Authorities can use megaphones to call out to crowd members ("Please clear the street." "Make way for the ambulance."), thereby personalizing the situation for many participants by making them feel responsible for individual actions.

When dealing with peaceful expressive crowds, authorities can often maintain order merely by expressing similar emotions. Waving at passing participants or gesturing a victory or peace sign can signify official approval of the peaceful actions and expressive behavior.

United Press International

In contrast to expressive crowds, acting crowds engage in directed collective behavior toward some specific object. For example, in Grant Park, Chicago, in 1968, antiwar demonstrators used benches as barricades against the police before a planned march on the Democratic National Convention.

P. Vandermark/Stock, Boston

Since acting crowds behave as one mass group, police mounted on horseback may attempt to break the crowd into smaller groups. This tactic redirects the single focus of the crowd and breaks down the process of collective excitement and social contagion.

Ken Ishii/Black Star

Acting crowds feel powerful because of the commitment to a single purpose. Japanese riot-control police, protected by helmets and shields, form a phalanx and march upon crowds to disperse them. These special units strikingly resemble traditional *samurai* soldiers, and, though unarmed, symbolize countervailing power and authority.

Charles Moore/Black Star

Some authorities utilize a variation of game theory, assuming that members of an acting crowd calculate the costs of participating against the goals to be achieved. Police may attempt to make the costs greater than the goals by threatening crowd members with force. The problem with this tactic (aside from the moral issue) is that extremely fanatic acting crowds may then turn upon authorities and precipitate a police riot. This happened during the antiwar demonstrations in Chicago in 1968 when police attacked crowd members with clubs after having been pelted by rocks and other missiles.

mitted to its "right" course of action. It is obsessed with its omnipotence and at the same time fearful of persecution; it is thus ruthless with the heretic, unbeliever, or seeming traitor. It projects its own fanatical spirit upon the enemy, assumes the enemy is motivated by the same emotions, and moves with rage to destroy any sign of opposition. Pent-up hostility is released, and people do things in crowds that they would never do alone. Both internal and external controls are momentarily suspended.

The novelist can often capture this character of the acting crowd more dramatically than the social scientist. For example, John Steinbeck's novel, *In Dubious Battle,* speaks of the hostility that builds up in a California farm town between the poorly paid migrant workers of the 1930s and the growers and townsmen, the outgroup against the ingroup. This is his story about the battle for workers' rights, which preceded his *Grapes of Wrath.* A medical doctor who serves the camp of migrant workers "thinks too much" to be fanatical about the "cause" as seen by the Communist party organizers. Doc observes what happens as if he were a social scientist and muses about collective behavior:

> ". . . Group-men are always getting some kind of infection. This seems to be a bad one [the strike]. I want to see, Mac, I want to watch these group-men, for they seem to me to be a new individual, not at all like single men. A man in a group isn't himself at all, he's a cell in an organism that isn't like him any more than the cells in your body are like you. I want to watch the group, and see what it's like. People have said, 'mobs are crazy, you can't tell what they'll do.' Why don't people look at mobs not as men, but as mobs? A mob nearly always seems to act reasonable, for a mob. . . ."
>
> "It might be like this, Mac: When a group-man wants to move, he makes a standard. 'God wills that we recapture the Holy Land'; or he says, 'We fight to make the world safe for democracy'; or he says, 'We will wipe out social injustice with communism.' But the group doesn't care about the Holy Land, or Democracy, or Communism. Maybe the group simply wants to love, to fight, and uses these words simply to reassure the brains of individual man. I say it might be like that, Mac" [Steinbeck, 1936, p. 104].

Mac, who is the labor organizer and Communist, resents the philosophic objectivity of Doc. He realizes, however, that crowd action can be unpredictable and uncontrollable in large part. Later in the narrative, Mac discusses crowd behavior with London, one of the leaders in the camp.

> "It's a damn funny thing about a bunch of men, how they act. You can't tell. I always thought if a guy watched close enough he might get to know what they're goin' to do. . . . Maybe London knows. He's been bossin' men all his life. How about it, London?"
>
> London shook his head. "No," he said, "I've saw a bunch of guys run like rabbits when a truck backfired. Other times, seems like nothin' can scare 'em. Y' can kind of feel what's goin' to happen before it starts though."
>
> "I know," said Mac. "The air gets full of it. I saw a nigger lynched one time. They took him about a quarter of a mile to a railroad overpass. On th' way out that crowd killed a little dog, stoned it to death. Ever'body just picked

> up rocks. The air was just full of killin'. Then they wasn't satisfied to hang the nigger. They had to burn 'im an' shoot 'im, too" [Steinbeck, 1936, p. 195].

Thus, we see Steinbeck describing through the eyes of his central characters the manner in which crowd behavior can climax collective excitement and social contagion. Even the organizer, Mac, is worried, for once these forces are released they are difficult to channel and control. He refers to the crowd as one big animal stronger than all the participants put together. However, is Mac right? Is it impossible to control crowds?

The Problem of Crowd Control: The Cases of Student Protest and Urban Disturbances

Collective outbursts like acting crowds and riots are considered by many to be threats to the established social order. Not only can they produce injury, death, and the destruction of property, but they also represent challenges to prevailing governmental authority and political leadership. It is not surprising, therefore, that politicians and community leaders have turned to researchers for help in the problem of crowd control. This was particularly true in the United States during the 1960s and early 1970s, a period marked by dozens of student demonstrations and urban "riots." Two studies of collective behavior are cited here to illustrate the way in which social science deals with the problem of crowd control.

The first study by Richard Berk uses a *gaming approach* to study a student–faculty crowd at Northwestern University on 9 May 1972 [Berk, 1974, pp. 355–373]. Where Steinbeck, as a novelist, used a contagion theory of collective behavior and echoed Le Bon's notion of a crowd mind, Berk concludes that crowd behavior follows relatively normal group decision-making processes based upon anticipated rewards and costs. He postulates that each member of the crowd is engaged in a game, with each participant's return on investment being dependent upon the actions of others involved in the game. For example, one person cannot undertake a lynching and one inmate cannot liberate a prison. In a crowd, the potential costs per person of playing the game decrease as the numbers of participants increase [Berk, 1974, p. 363]. Therefore, if factors like the size of a crowd, the costs of participation, and the goals to be achieved can be manipulated, the future actions of the crowd can be controlled.

In 1972, after attending a campus rally at which the university president delivered an unsatisfactory talk on a local housing issue and several speakers argued about what ought to be done about President Nixon's mining of Haiphong Harbor, the Northwestern campus crowd dispersed with a wide range of reactions. Some people were pleased and some were not at the final decision to hold a student referendum over whether to strike in protest to the war issue. In order to return to their dormitories, many students moved along Sheridan Road, a main city thoroughfare; instead of using the sidewalks, many chose to take to the middle of the street. This act was clearly defiant even though there was no organized march. Small groups of students simply strolled along about 20 feet apart talking about the events and issues. At first, there were about 250 jaywalkers with no organized plan of action.

Militants wanted to trash, that is, steal openly in large groups as a form of protest. This would have meant invading nearby stores and seizing merchandise. Moderates wanted to march but not hold up traffic, and others were ambivalent. These differences of opinion led to a general milling about until there was a precipitating incident—three students called for help in dragging a nearby fence into the street in order to block traffic (similar action had taken place here some two years earlier to dramatize a student strike). The three had "seized the time" and provided a symbolic call to action. There was still debate and difference of opinion as to whether to proceed with the barricade, which according to some would symbolize Nixon's blockade of the Harbor, or whether to turn to more or less drastic action. Some students merely left the scene, while others stayed and debated about how disruptive to be. Within minutes, however, it became clear that erection of the barricade would proceed and that others would not intervene. The fence was moved toward the main intersection by 50 students and another 50 followed in the street. In 10 minutes, the barricade was established and about 250 students milled about, many still arguing. By this time, however, Berk observed that there were no longer two crowds, the militants and the moderates; indeed, all were swept along by the emotional contagion. They were not all equally committed, but there was no clear separation between activists and spectators.

At this point, Berk theorizes that the crowd was engaged in collective decision making. Differences of opinion, based upon realistic estimates of the situation and the inherent risks involved, were being debated. The decision to barricade represented a meaningful compromise between militant proposals to trash and moderate proposals to march. It represented the best cost–reward scheme for attracting the largest number of participants, who could share some risks with the hope of some success.

> Later, when students were asked what they had been thinking at this critical time, their answers differed. Even those committed to the barricade (including persons later arrested trying to maintain it) were weighing many considerations. Should they make a "public antiwar statement," "bring the war home," generate a 1970-style strike, stimulate the militancy of 1970, embarrass the university president, and/or "train" political activists? Should they risk "turning off" the public, punishment from police or the University? . . . In the hours that followed, the divisions of opinion did not change. The street was blocked and used as a forum for many speakers. Police were called, but did not move against the students or their barricade. Seven students chose to be arrested the next morning rather than to disperse. Traffic was rerouted [Berk, 1974, p. 362].

Berk concludes his study with observations about the social-control implications of three characteristics of crowds:

1. *Environmental conditions* influence group decision making. Since large numbers of people produce a sense of mutual support, peaceful dispersal of developing crowds has become one aspect of modern crowd-control training. Dispersal also helps eliminate aggravating conditions; crowd members must be able to see the actions taking place (erecting the barricade), be relatively close to other acting members, and be able to interpret events and actions as appropriate to the situation.

2. The second characteristic is that crowds vary according to their *perception of the cost–reward balance of their action.* The milling process is required to determine the rewards and costs, to develop a sense of concerted action, and to come to a common realization that each person's payoffs depend upon the actions of others. As a consequence, community leaders have often attempted to control collective behavior by either heightening the costs of on-going action or offering rewards for discontinuing action. Most probably, the action of the police in rerouting traffic simply maximized the rewards and minimized the costs in this case. Also, leaders did not offer alternative forms of action whereby the crowd's goals could be achieved in other ways.

3. Finally, Berk suggests that crowds differ from other groups in that participants operate with *incomplete and unreliable information.* Communication is difficult and confused because of noise and unclear symbols, and rumor supplants rational discourse. Emotions run high, and crowd leaders usually try to produce quick rewards in order to sustain commitment and avoid dispersion. In order to counteract this process, many communities have established public and private rumor or information centers in times of crisis. Concerned citizens can telephone these centers for the latest information about what is actually happening, where to go for planned and controlled rallies, and what rational action may be taken. Such centers have been established in Boston, by both advocates and opponents of the busing of school children, with some degree of success.

While the gaming approach to crowd behavior raises basic questions about the contagion theory and its view of the irrationality of collective behavior, it tends to complement the *emergent-norm theory.* This theory implies that there are no fundamental changes in the capacity to reason. Not only are humans found to behave according to norms, but they are able to produce needed new norms in the heat of the moment, in problematic environments. They are capable of assessing probable rewards and costs and of making rational attempts to gain optimal outcomes. Crowd members are like members of other groups except that they must "get themselves together" and implement goal-directed action during their first and only meeting, as Berk points out. This leads him to make this telling observation:

> Even under the most favorable environments, this [agreed-upon action in the first meeting] would be extremely difficult; and crowds operate in problem-

atic environments. It is these difficulties rather than crippled mental capacities that may account for "irrational" crowd behavior [Berk, 1974, p. 370].

In other words, crowds are groups of human beings who must make up their collective minds quickly in strange situations where old norms and/or relationships fail to meet new needs [Weller and Quarantelli, 1973]. Crowd decision making, as described by Berk, is similar to that of other groups and involves rational attempts to gain optimal outcomes.

The insights generated by the research of Richard Berk are useful primarily in understanding situations involving single crowds and delimited issues. However, what mechanisms are involved when there is a large-scale breakdown in prevailing norms and social interaction, which leads to massive collective action? Analysis of the so-called urban "riots" of the 1960s provides some answers. One of the most studied of these incidents was the Watts area collective action, which took place in Los Angeles from August 11 to August 17 in 1965. The course of events in Watts parallels the value-added perspective of Smelser and has been used as a prime example of what happens in cases of large-scale urban disturbances [DeFleur *et al.*, 1972, pp. 363–348].

Several days of rioting were triggered by the arrest of a black man on a Los Angeles freeway by a white policeman. The setting was especially conducive to the crisis. Watts is a poverty area of the city with high rates of in-migration, a dense population of minority peoples, and a poor transportation system to link it with the community at large. While housing is relatively good in comparison with other urban ghettos, and while there are many parks and playgrounds, Watts is characterized as having a high rate of unemployment, many adults without adequate education or employment skills, inadequate schools for the children, a high percentage of families on welfare, and all the attendant problems of consumer exploitation, illegitimacy, crime, delinquency, and disease. Such a situation is tinder awaiting a precipitating event to spark a collective outburst.

As indicated in what became known as the McCone Report [1965], local police were quite ineffective in trying to maintain order during the rioting. There were too few law enforcement officers, and they became targets of resentment among the blacks and other minority peoples of the area. The problem of police–community relations was one of the most critical. It was only after more anonymous officers from the outside (County Sheriff's Department and National Guard) were called in that order was gradually restored. Although the Report criticized governmental authorities for not calling in the National Guard sooner, it was generally more sympathetic with the police and politicians than with the disadvantaged citizens involved. The Report did point up the need for improvement in conditions of employment, education, and police–community relations along with general social reform, but it failed to probe the depth of the problem according to one of the Commission's members, sociologist Robert Blauner.

Blauner wrote a rejoinder to the McCone Report in which he admitted that the Commission was given only 100 days in which to work [Blauner, 1966, p. 3]. Thus it is understandable that the Report is brief and sketchy. However, this urge for speed does not excuse superficiality. The report suggests nothing new about the conditions of the urban poor; it reiterates the fundamental importance of education for the future of the black citizen but fails to confront the immediate job crisis of the unskilled. Blauner says it whitewashes the police and implies that the cry of police brutality is more a misinterpretation of fact and a paranoid reaction of the blacks themselves than a legitimate grievance; it fails to admit clearly that the dominant community is responsible in large part for the plight of the poor; it blames a minority of agitators for the uprising against law and order and focuses upon the problem of riot control. The most glaring weakness of the Report according to Blauner is its complete failure to see the meaning of the outburst.

It is Blauner's opinion that the Watts riots did not represent "an explosion—a formless, quite senseless, all but hopeless violent protest—a spasm—an insensate rage of destruction." Collective action was not the irrational behavior of a few radicals, a view implied by the Report's emphasis upon the 2 percent who took part in contrast to the many "responsible" black citizens in the area who were not active participants. Rioters were ghetto peoples trying to say something like this to the dominant society: "We have abided indignity and frustration long enough. It is time we insist upon becoming citizens in our own right rather than natives dominated by colonial masters." Blauner submits evidence from interviews with black residents that shows a broad base of community support for the 2 percent who actively led the rioting. The actors in a collective outburst always represent only a few core members; this does not mean, however, that the many bystanders are unsupportive.

There is evidence that many Watts blacks felt a strange new pride in their own community for rising up against a kind of colonial rule over them, a pride verbalized by Stan Sounders, a Watts boy who attained All-American football honors at Whittier College and spent two years abroad as a Rhodes scholar.

> "It was a masterful performance," he said, the morning after one of the worst nights of rioting. "I sense a change there now, a buzz, and it tickles. For the first time people in Watts feel a pride in being black. I remember when I first went to Whittier, I worried that if I didn't make it there, if I was rejected, I wouldn't have a place to go back to. Now I can say 'I'm from Watts'" [*Life*, 1965, p. 18].

In contrast to the McCone Report, Blauner sees the riots as a demonstration of a spirit similar to that of anticolonial crowds revolting against their master. Members of the McCone Commission failed to catch this meaning because of their primary commitments to control, law and order, a white-dominated status quo, and a middle-class ethic. Blauner concludes:

> What is needed—in addition to jobs—is an experimental program for finding innovations that might link the values and social patterns of the Negro lower class with the social and productive needs of the greater society, thus reversing the trend toward alienation. Before the meaningful recommendations can be made that are in line with the enormity of the problem, the sociological and cultural character of the Negro low-income community must be understood [Blauner, 1966, p. 3].

Here, then, is a different approach to the problem of controlling collective behavior. Rather than focusing only upon the incident, it views the behavior (the riot, an acting crowd) as a symptom of something more fundamentally wrong within the social order. In this sense, Blauner's approach is a radical critique of the society and involves suggestions for major changes in the social, cultural, political, and economic structures. It argues that attempting to manipulate collective behavior after it has broken out is locking the barn door after the horse has escaped. What is needed, instead, is a preventive program, one that alters the larger social context that encourages collective behavior as the only outlet for justified grievances. In the type of research being done on collective behavior, therefore, we see a clear illustration of the conflict in sociology (discussed in Chapter 2) between traditional conservative views and more radical activist perspectives, between exceptionalistic and universalistic approaches to human behavior.

This conflict in perspectives has led to a number of other important studies. One such study was done by Caplan and Paige on behalf of the National Advisory Commission on Civil Disorders [Caplan and Paige, 1968, pp. 15–21]. Working through the Institute for Social Research at the University of Michigan, they selected a random sample of citizens in the ghetto areas of Detroit and Newark in 1967 and conducted interviews with rioters and nonrioters. They conclude that the *riffraff* theory and the *relative-deprivation* theory of rioting are both incorrect. The rioters who were studied were not always riffraff—that is, the poorest of the poor, the hard-core unemployed, the least educated, the unassimilated migrants and newcomers to the city, and the deviants and emotionally distrubed. Nor were they always found to be those who felt deprived relative to others, frustrated because conditions were not getting better fast enough or because whites were better off than blacks.

On the other hand, Caplan and Paige [1968, pp. 20–21] did find empirical support for a third theory—the *blocked-opportunity* theory—which emphasized environmental conditions rather than individual inclinations. Blacks who most resented the discrimination (loss of opportunity) in a white society were the ones most likely to riot. They were more bitter than nonrioters, more likely to blame discrimination as an obstacle to employment and to agree that "sometimes I hate white people." Fewer rioters felt the country is "worth fighting for in a major world war."

Rioters showed more distrust than nonrioters of blacks "who make a lot of money" [Caplan and Paige, 1968, pp. 20–21].

In attempting to give leaders and planners a more precise indication of how to address the problem of urban disturbances, other social scientists built upon the Caplan–Paige findings about blocked opportunities for black citizens. Seymour Spilerman [1970, pp. 627–649; 1971, pp. 427–442] studied the frequency of disorders in different American cities. He concluded that the larger the city's black population relative to the white population, the greater the likelihood of disorder. Furthermore, among cities with the same racial composition in population, no one city seemed more riot-prone than any other. This could imply that American blacks have developed a sense of racial solidarity nationwide through television, other mass media, and political action, and they are most likely to mobilize for collective action in places where they have numerical strength.

Morgan and Clark [1973, pp. 611–624] have suggested that it is more important to study the severity of riots than their frequency. The degree of severity is determined largely by the level of grievance and resentment harbored by the minority population. Grievance is related to feelings of *relative* deprivation about *housing inequality* and *job inequality*, for the most part. Over a 21-year period (1949–1969), Gallup polls showed that the proportion of American blacks satisfied with housing decreased 9 percent, while whites were increasingly more satisfied. In studying data from 42 cities, Morgan and Clark found that the greater the sense of housing inequality on the part of blacks, the greater the likelihood of urban disorders. They expected to find the same results relative to job inequality but found just the opposite. The greater the job inequality, the less the likelihood of disorders. They explained this by saying that perhaps high rates of job inequality for blacks reduced their expectations for upward mobility and produced a "what's the use" attitude. Another explanation can be found in the Gallup poll finding that the proportion of blacks satisfied with their jobs increased 21 percent during the 1949–1969 period. The feeling of relative deprivation is apparently not as great for jobs as it is for housing. In summary, according to Morgan and Clark, it behooves leadership in cities to give serious attention to housing if the recent tendency for blacks and other disadvantaged groups to explode in collective outbursts is to be controlled. We will return to the theory of relative deprivation in Chapter 14.

Continuing research shows that panic, crazes, and crowd behavior are all predictable forms of elementary collective behavior. Traditional analysts have identified methods of controlling such behavior, while radical analysts have identified ways of preventing it by altering social conditions. The lasting form of collective behavior—social movement—involves many of the issues already discussed but differs in some ways from the elementary forms.

5-3 Types of Riots: Myth and Reality

Popular myths about riots assume that this type of behavior always has the following characteristics:

1. Aggression is directed toward people and usually involves attacks by one ethnic group upon another (race riots).
2. Uncontrollable and violent "riffraff" participate, while "respectable" citizens do not.
3. Behavior is irrational and purposeless.
4. Mobs continuously roam the streets "looking for trouble."
5. Only the forces of law and order can quell riotous behavior and maintain the peace.

In contrast to these beliefs, studies have identified three different types of "riots," each with a different cause, character, and purpose.

Wide World Photos

Closest to the popular myths are people-oriented riots. In 1961, white and black youths advanced on each other, armed with boards and other weapons, after blacks attempted to buy tickets to an all-white theater in Chattanooga, Tennessee. Yet these forms of violent behavior are strikingly different from the popular beliefs in some ways. They are often triggered by peaceful incidents (attempt to integrate a theater). They usually involve organized groups (gangs of white and black youths), not uncontrollable individuals. Violence is sporadic and spontaneous (breaks out near a theater and then subsides), not continuous and unending.

United Press International

Some riots are property-oriented and can be more properly called "rebellions." In the 1960s, American blacks in urban ghettos rebelled and expressed their frustrations by looting stores and shops. Some respectable black citizens (adults, women as well as men) participated and others gave tacit emotional support to the behavior. Looters picked merchandise which symbolized their exclusion from many of the benefits of larger white society and they attacked stores owned by outside whites or businesses which represented white dominance. For example, ghetto grocery and liquor stores frequently charge higher prices than their counterparts in white suburban shopping centers.

United Press International

During the 1968 demonstrations in Chicago, it became evident that peace authorities can sometimes riot and attack expressive crowds of citizens. This results when police leaders lose control of their men who feel that their authority has been threatened by the crowd. Police use violence in an attempt to coerce respect (see Study 12). In Chicago, police attacked middle-class white youths, whom they saw as representatives of a disrespectful "hippie" subculture.

▶ SO WHAT?

In addition to the theories that identify fundamental social structural problems encouraging collective behavior (studies of the Watts rebellion), research findings are related to specific crowd-control tactics utilized by community leaders and the police.

1. As we have seen, people in a crowd are triggered into action by suggestion and may begin to feel anonymous and not responsible for their actions. Feeling impersonal, they do things that they would not do alone because both internal and external controls are momentarily suspended. Therefore, crowd-control agents can attempt to personalize the experience for selected participants, thereby encouraging feelings of responsibility and the necessity for the personal control of behavior. This tactic was used in the spring of 1956 when the campus of the University of California at Berkeley was subjected to several days of "panty raids"—mobs of male students invaded female residences in search of clothing, resulting in $12,000 of property damage [Kerr, 1956]. At some of the women's residences crowds were turned away because a few male student leaders helped dissuade the approaching group of raiders. Selected campus leaders (those generally well-known and recognizable) yelled at friends in the mob, using first names and asking what they were doing. This personalized the context for those participants, making them aware of their role in deviant and unacceptable behavior.

2. We have also seen that individuals in a crowd feel collectively powerful, almost omnipotent, because of a commitment to a specific goal. As a consequence, specially trained units of the Japanese police are provided with helmets and shields that cover them from head to toe. In a phalanx formation, they slowly march upon a crowd, forcing it to disperse without having to resort to violence. The phalanx symbolizes effective countervailing collective power. Furthermore, the riot-control unit positions itself between the specific goal and the crowd, thereby breaking down the focus of collective attention. American crowd-control units frequently use unarmed mounted (on horseback) police for the same purposes. To participants in a crowd they represent "higher" and more powerful authority.

3. In expressive crowds, people are highly malleable and enter into a sense of oneness by singing, clapping, or chanting. Therefore, the playing of the national anthem can be an effective way of redirecting the behavior of threatening crowds into controllable actions. This is particularly true when this tactic is used in a context that symbolizes societal unity (for example, at an athletic event).

LASTING FORMS OF COLLECTIVE BEHAVIOR

Social Movements: Channels for Social Change

In contrast to elementary forms of collective behavior, a *social movement* is a transition from the least structured types of human action to more highly organized and institutionalized forms. It may represent either a reform or a total replacement of the old social order. Social movements are characteristic of a changing society. They are ways of channeling the processes of social change and are, perhaps, the best examples of the origins of institutions.

> Social movements can be viewed as collective enterprises to establish a new order of life. They have their inception in a condition of unrest, and derive their motive power on the one hand from dissatisfaction with the current form of life and, on the other hand, from wishes and hopes for a new scheme or system of living. The career of a social movement depicts the emergencies of a new order of life. In its beginning, a social movement is amorphous, poorly organized, and without form; the collective behavior is on the primitive level that we have already discussed, and the mechanisms of interaction are the elementary, spontaneous mechanisms of which we have spoken. As a social movement develops, it takes on the character of a society. It acquires organization and form, a body of customs and traditions, established leadership, an enduring division of labor, social rules and social values—in short, a culture, a social organization, and a new scheme of life [Blumer, 1939, p. 255].

To be more specific, when we speak of social movements, we have in mind such collective enterprises as the labor movement, the women's liberation movement, the peace movement, and the civil rights movement. These all represent gradual and pervasive changes in the values of people. Blumer refers to them as cultural drifts that correspond with shifting values and beliefs within a society. Specific social movements may emerge within a general cultural trend and focus upon some definite goal in keeping with the new values. Thus, as the drift toward a new role for modern women occurred in Western societies, feminist movements worked for the woman's right to vote, to be employed outside the home, to be an equal companion in modern marriage, all of which culminated in new demands by women's liberation leaders and organizations in the late 1960s and early 1970s. We will return shortly to a study of the contemporary women's movement. First, however, we will consider various theories about the origin and nature of social movements.

Origin and Nature of Social Movements

One body of theory in social science conceives of social movements as spontaneous responses to larger processes of *cultural change.* This view sees movements as being nonrational, determined by societal forces unconsciously at work upon individuals. The difficulty with such a view—similar

5-4 The Evolution of Lasting Social Movements

Social movements pass through three distinct stages of development from spontaneous to more structured forms, unlike elementary collective behavior which tends to die out in its earliest stages. This process of evolution enables movements—like civil rights and women's liberation—to become forces for lasting social change.

United Press International

In the earliest stage, emotionally-oriented leaders express vague feelings of dissatisfaction by engaging in spontaneous and provocative public acts. A black woman refuses to sit in the back of the bus, as an expression of individual freedom from white-dominated society. Some women give up wearing bras, as an expression of freedom from male-dominated society. These kinds of acts dramatize the larger issues (the desire for independence and equality of opportunity) by catching the attention of the public through the mass media and, thereby, attract other adherents to the cause.

United Press International

United Press International

United Press International

In the second stage, intellectuals (writers, ministers, professors) begin to provide the movement with a lasting ideology by articulating the issues and relating them to major social values and institutions. Martin Luther King placed the American civil rights movement within the context of Christianity and related it to the church. Betty Friedan challenged traditional sex-role relationships in the family setting. In this stage, these and other leaders also begin to provide the movement with organization and structure in the form of planned meetings, demonstrations, marches, and so on.

United Press International

United Press International

In the final stage, social movements become highly structured with national (and international) organizations and formally elected leadership. This enables movements to consolidate and extend power and influence by attracting more permanent adherents, by maintaining a budget to finance actions and programs, and by operating a formal communications network. In addition, traditional organizations and groups become supportive of and a part of the movements. For example, Reverend Jesse Jackson addresses a convention of the National Association for the Advancement of Colored People, and Congresswomen Margaret Heckler, a member of the National Commission for the Observance of International Women's Year in 1975, heads a panel to hear testimony on issues of concern to women in the New England area.

to Le Bon's crowd-mind notion—is that it does not tell us much about how social movements begin and what part humans play in bringing them about. On the contrary, such a theory perceives of individuals as essentially captives of a predetermined social order, responding automatically to unrecognized social forces.

Other scholars argue that social movements are more than spontaneous behavior since they depend upon preexisting social organizations [Turner and Killian, 1957; Lang and Lang, 1961]. As Lewis Killian [1964, pp. 426–455] has observed, humans and human groups are the creators, not the creatures, of social change. Killian defines a social movement as a collectivity with a career, an emergent structure, and a culture. Therefore, social movements have the following characteristics: (1) Shared values and an ideology. (2) A sense of membership or "we-ness." (3) Norms and rules about how members of the movement should act. (4) A structure consisting of leaders and followers who interact in particular ways.

Killian, therefore, does not see social movements as distinct and separate from other forms of human experience. They develop in response to on-going society, often *emerging out of crowds and publics.* Crowds may become a vital part of a social movement, especially in its formative stages, since public debate about the issues involved is essential to continuing interest. Social movements emerge to provide people with the opportunity to express their frustrations and to develop responses to the conditions causing the frustrations. Therefore, one of the interesting questions facing social scientists is why particular social movements develop at one time rather than another.

In describing how social movements move through a career pattern from less structured to more formal forms—unlike elementary forms of collective behavior, which die out in their formative stages—Killian [1964, pp. 440–443] identifies several important stages. (1) Movements begin with vague and inarticulate feelings of dissatisfaction. Emotionally oriented leaders help dramatize issues by use of provocative actions, and a few intellecutuals usually provide a lasting ideology for the movement by writing books and essays on the central issues. (2) Those with administrative skills organize what would otherwise remain a haphazard and uncoordinated aggregate of groups and individuals. (3) An emerging structure gradually takes shape with clear delineation between leaders and followers. Both the leadership and the membership undergo changes with each stage.

At first, active members tend to be volatile and fanatic; they tend to be on the defensive and to use publically offensive language and gestures. Eric Hoffer [1951] has described this early militant leadership in his study of "the true believer." He says that most fanatical members of all movements share the general characteristics of being "frustrated, disaffected, and rejected." As a movement progresses, however, both the type of leadership and the character of the followers change: leaders emerge who are less shrill and followers emerge who respond to more rational strategy. Interaction between older and younger members of a movement brings stability and strengthens the chances for success and public support. Through such a process, a social movement may eventually become a new social institution, a basic and permanent part of the social order.

However, not all scholars agree completely with the interpretation of the evolution of social movements developed by researchers such as Hoffer, Killian, and Turner. The following study illustrates how a scholar can build upon earlier theories while modifying them to formulate new perspectives.

▶ STUDY 5

The Origins of the Women's Liberation Movement [1973][1]

Problem

Professor Jo Freeman points out that the emergence of a feminist movement in the 1960s caught many thoughtful observers by surprise. The new movement generated speculation about the sources of female discontent and why such discontent was expressed at that particular time. The sociological literature was not of much help in providing answers, since *few theorists had dealt with the origins of social movements.* Furthermore, *observers tended to ask the wrong types of questions,* focusing upon the assumed problem of frustrations and social strain rather than upon the social and cultural preconditions for the emergence of more structured forms of collective behavior. There is a more important question: *How do people come together?* That is, how do people come to share a similar view of the circumstances which compel them to political action?

Hypotheses and Study Design

Observation of six social movements, including the women's movement, led Freeman to formulate three hypotheses:

1. Masses of people acting spontaneously do not form social movements, however discontented they may be. There must be a *preexisting communications network* within the social base of a movement. Previously unorganized individuals may spontaneously form small local groups; but unless these groups are linked in some manner, protest does not become generalized and the movement will not spread rapidly. Some organization must already exist to channel new spontaneous activity.
2. Furthermore, the communications network must be one that is *co-optable to the new ideas of the incipient movement.* That is, it must be composed of like-minded people whose background, experiences, or position in the social structure make them receptive to the ideas of the new movement.

[1]Adapted and abridged from Jo Freeman, "The Origins of the Women's Liberation Movement," *The American Journal of Sociology,* 78 (January 1973), pp. 792–811. Also see Jo Freeman, *The Politics of Women's Liberation,* Chapter 2 (New York: David McKay Company, 1975).

3. Finally, *precipitating events and organizers* must trigger the birth of the new movement. A crisis may galvanize a well-framed network into spontaneous action, and/or persons with commitment and organizing ability may use an incipient network to disseminate new ideas and mobilize action.

Participant observation of the women's liberation movement was the primary research method utilized by Freeman for testing her hypotheses.

Methods of Data Collection

Professor Freeman describes her methods of data collection as follows:

> As a founder and participant in the younger branch of the Chicago women's liberation movement from 1967 through 1969 and editor of the first (at that time, only) national newsletter, I was able, through extensive correspondence and interviews, to keep a record of how each group around the country first started, where the organizers got the idea from, who they had talked to, what conferences were held and who attended, the political affiliations (or lack of them) of the first members, etc. Although I was a member of the Chicago *NOW* (National Organization for Women), information on the origins of it and the other older branch organizations comes entirely through ex post facto interviews of the principals and examination of early papers in preparation for my dissertation on the women's liberation movement [Freeman, 1973, p. 794].

Findings and Interpretations

Women's grievances did not find a voice and become an organized movement in the 1950s largely because there was no communications network—individuals were unaware of common problems and of sympathetic others. However, by the 1960s, the necessary conditions existed for a social movement. Before identifying these conditions, Freeman analyzes the important groups and activities in the women's liberation movement.

The movement has been characterized by many styles of action and organization. This diversity sprang from two distinct origins: often referred to as the "reform" and "radical" branches. However, Freeman points out that these terms are not completely appropriate, since feminists do not fit into simple right-versus-left political categories. Structure and style, rather than ideology, more accurately distinguish the two branches. Therefore, Freeman contrasts an older with a younger branch of the movement.

The *older branch* began first and the median age of its activists was higher. It contains many organizations, including the Women's Equity Action League (a lobbyist group), Human Rights for Women (a legal foundation), over 70 caucuses in professional organizations, and separate organizations of women in the professions and other occupations. Its most prominent "core group" is NOW, also the first to be formed. The activities of the older branch originally were concentrated on legal and economic problems, although they have diversified in recent years. Groups consisted of women—and men—who worked and who were essentially concerned with the problems of working women. Their style of organization tended to be traditional and formal (elected officers, boards of directors, bylaws, etc.) and all started as top-down national organizations lacking a mass base (though some subsequently developed such a base).

In contrast, the *younger branch* of the movement consists of many small groups whose contact with one another was informal at best. Freeman indicates that, contrary to popular belief, the younger branch did not begin on campuses, nor was it started by the Students for a Democratic Society (SDS). However, its activists were on the other side of the generation gap. Though few were students, all were "under 30" and had received their political education as participants in or observers of the social action and protest of recent years. The younger branch prided itself on its lack of organization. Its radical origins led it to assume that formal structures are always conservative and confining and formal leaders are usually isolated and elitist (see the discussion of Michels' "iron law of oligarchy" in Chapter 7). Therefore, the concept of "everyone doing her own thing" developed, and communication and coordination were haphazard and almost nonexistent. Thousands of sister chapters around the country were virtually independent, linked only by many underground papers, journals, newsletters, and cross-country travelers.

Like the older branch, the younger branch tended to be predominantly white, middle-class, and college educated; but, unlike the older branch, it was more homogeneous. Most small groups tended to form among friendship networks and, because of a lack of structure, it was often easier for an individual to form a new group rather than to find and join an already existing one.

The contrasting style and organization of the two branches of the movement were derived largely from their different kinds of political education and experiences. However, despite these differences, *there were similarities in the way the two branches came into being.* The forces which led to NOW's formation were initiated in 1961 when President Kennedy established the President's Commission on the Status of Women at the behest of Esther Petersen, then director of the Women's Bureau. The Commission's 1963 report, *American Women,* and subsequent publications documented how thoroughly women were still denied many rights and opportunities.

As a consequence, 50 state commissions were eventually established to do similar research on a state level. The activity of the federal and state commissions laid the groundwork for the future women's movement in several ways. It brought together many knowledgeable, politically active women who otherwise would not have worked together on matters of direct concern to women. The investigations unearthed ample evidence of women's unequal status and of their legal and economic difficulties, thereby convincing many previously uninterested women that something should be done. The reports also created expectations that something would be done.

During this time, two other events of significance occured. The first was the publication of Betty Friedan's book, *The Feminine Mystique* [1963]. It stimulated women to question the status quo, and some suggested to Friedan that a new organization be formed to attack women's problems. The second event was the addition of "sex" to Title VII of the 1964 Civil Rights Act. Freeman points out that many people thought the "sex" provision was a joke, and the Equal Employment Opportunity Commission (EEOC) refused to enforce it adequately.

Within EEOC, a "pro-woman" coterie argued that "sex" might be taken more seriously if there was an organization for women, similar to the NAACP (National Association for the Advancement of Colored People), that could put pressure on the government. They suggested this idea to many people, including Friedan.

On 20 June 1966, Representative Martha Griffiths of Michigan criticized EEOC's attitude in a speech on the floor of the House. She accused the EEOC of "casting disrespect and ridicule on the law." This speech was distributed a week later at the Third National Conference of Commissions on the Status of Women, ironically titled "Targets for Action." On the last day, Conference officials refused to allow discussion of a proposed resolution urging the EEOC to give the same enforcement to the sex provision of Title VII as was given to the race provision. The small group of women who backed the resolution had met the night before in Friedan's hotel room to discuss the possibility of a civil rights organization for women. When the resolution was vetoed, these women met over lunch and agreed to form an action organization. The name NOW was coined by Friedan, and before the day was over 28 women paid $5.00 each to join. By the time the organizing conference was held the following October, over 300 men and women had become charter members.

A year later, unaware of and unknown to NOW, the EEOC, or the state commissions, younger women began forming their own movement. Here, too, the groundwork had been laid some years before. The social action projects of preceding years had attracted many women, who were quickly shunted into traditional roles and told to make coffee instead of policy, to run the mimeograph but not the organization. They were faced with the self-evident contradiction of working in a "freedom movement" without being free themselves.

No single protest movement activity or organization was responsible for the younger branch of the women's movement. But together they created a "radical community" in which like-minded people continually interacted with each other. This radical community not only provided the necessary communications network, but its radical ideas also provided the explanation for the dismal situation in which radical women found themselves.

At least five groups in different cities (Chicago, Toronto, Detroit, Seattle, and Gainesville, Florida) formed spontaneously, independently of each other, in 1967 and 1968. Typical of the precipitating events that created the groups was an incident at the 1967 National Conference for New Politics convention in Chicago. A women's caucus met for days, but was told its resolution wasn't significant enough to merit a floor discussion. When the women threatened to tie up the convention with procedural motions, their statement was tacked to the end of the agenda, but it was never discussed. The chair refused to recognize any of the many women standing by the microphone and, instead, called on someone to speak on "the forgotten American, the American Indian." When five women rushed the podium demanding an explanation, the chairman patted one on her head and said, "Cool down, little girl." The "little girl" was Shulamith Firestone, future author of *The Dialectic of Sex* [1971] and she didn't cool down. She joined with one of the other five women who organized a Chicago meeting to tell their stories. This stimulated sufficient rage to carry the group for three months, by which time it had acquired some permanency. This group was composed primarily of women who had access to the infrastructure of the New Left—its conferences, organizations, and media. They used this infrastructure to spread the ideas of the movement. Within a year a national conference had been organized for 200 women from 20 states and the younger branch of the movement began to expand exponentially.

Conclusions and Implications

Freeman's study of the women's movement not only supports her three hypotheses about the origin of social movements, it also questions and refines earlier theories of collective behavior. *First,* both the Commissions on the Status of Women and the "radical community" created a communications network in the existing social base. This network provided a means whereby women initially interested in forming organizations and engaging in activities could easily reach sympathetic others. Such a network had not previously existed among women, since they had been historically tied to the family and isolated from one another.

In addition, this finding is contrary to much mass-society theory which argues that those most likely to join a mass movement are the most isolated, anomic, or alienated in a society [Kornhauser, 1959]. In contrast, Freeman points out that isolation has proven more of a hindrance than a help in the women's movement. Even today, those women who are most anomic (housewives) are the least likely to join a feminist group. Her findings confirm those of Pinard [1968], who studied the Social Credit Party of Quebec and concluded that, when strains are severe and widespread, a new movement is more likely to be successful among more strongly integrated citizens.

Second, not just any communication network will do. It must be one which is co-optable by the incipient movement because it links together like-minded people. For example, the 180,000-member Federation of Business and Professional Women's (BPW) Clubs appeared to be a likely base for a new feminist movement, but was unable to assume this role. Though it had steadily lobbied for legislation of importance to women, as late as 1966 BPW rejected the idea that it become a kind of NAACP for women for fear of being labeled "feminist." In contrast, the women of the President's and State Commissions and the feminist coterie of the EEOC were co-optable, because they were aware of cases of sex discrimination and conscious of the need for change. Similarly, the young women of the radical community lived in an atmosphere of confrontation and change, and they absorbed an ideology of "freedom" and "liberation" more potent than any latent "antifeminism" might have been.

Third, for a movement to develop, participants' similar perceptions must be translated into action. "Crises"—in the form of precipitating events—perform this function by providing a situation in which people feel the need for change and can exchange these feelings with others. For the older branch, the impetus to organize was the refusal of the EEOC to enforce the sex provision of Title VII and the refusal of federal officials at the conference to allow a supportive resolution. For the younger branch, there were a series of minor crises.

However, a crisis will only catalyze a well-formed communications network. If such networks are no more than embryonically developed or only partially co-optable, the potentially active individuals in them must be linked together by someone. This is the role of the "organizer." The significance of organizers in the formation of social movements is another neglected aspect of past research (see the discussion of change-agents in Chapter 13). Though leaders have been frequently studied, leadership is different than organizing. Freeman indicates that, in the early stages of social movements, organizers are more important than leaders, and the former must often operate behind the scenes (see Lowry's distinction between formal community leaders and informal mediating leaders in Study 8). Furthermore, organizers require considerable experience and skill, and, in this sense, the professional is more valuable than the amateur in supposedly spontaneous social movements.

CONCLUSION

Collective behavior emerges when there is uncertainty about norms and when strain develops in the social order. It may signify momentary insecurity, as in the case of panic, or it may represent a challenge of the old order and a desire for social change, as in the case of social movements.

Although collective behavior is the least structured and patterned group behavior, it is not entirely unpredictable since one stage of action leads to the next. Panic is most likely to occur when the social setting is appropriate and when strain, anxiety, and a triggering event are present in appropriate relationship to one another. However, behavior, even in crises, is not totally chaotic; rather, it reflects the deeply instilled commitments to family, job, and moral values.

The behavior of crowds also shows the same characteristics. Acting crowds take on an elemental structure with definite leaders, a core group of supporting actors, and a surrounding body of spectators. They go through stages of development, beginning with the milling process and moving through circular reaction, collective excitement, and on to some target activity.

Finally, social movements may include several forms of collective behavior. When the social order develops major strain and there is general unrest and dissatisfaction, spontaneous group action can emerge (as it did on the Kent State campus in 1970), generate collective protest, and initiate forms of action that change the established order.

We have seen some of the effects of status in our discussions of the blacks in Watts, and the women involved in the liberation movement. The following chapter considers various types of status groupings in detail.

REFERENCES

American Psychiatric Association. "Psychological First Aid in Community Disasters," *The American Journal of Nursing, 55* (April 1955), p. 437.

Berk, Richard A. "A Gaming Approach to Crowd Behavior," *American Sociological Review, 39* (June 1974), pp. 355–373.

Blauner, Robert. "Whitewash Over Watts: The Failure of the McCone Commission Report," *Trans-action* (now *Society*), 3 (March–April 1966), p. 3.

Blumer, Herbert. "Collective Behavior," in *Principles of Sociology,* Robert R. Park, Ed. New York: Barnes and Noble, 1939.

Caplan, Nathan S., and Jeffery M. Paige. "A Study of Ghetto Rioters," *Scientific American, 219* (August 1968), pp. 15–21.

de Beauvoir, Simone, and Betty Friedan. "Sex, Society, and the Female Dilemma," *Saturday Review, 2* (14 June 1975), pp. 12–14.

DeFleur, Melvin L., William V. D'Antonio, and Lois B. DeFleur. *Sociology: Man in Society.* Glencoe, Ill.: Scott, Foresman and Company, 1972, abbreviated ed.

Elsner, Jr., Henry. *Robert E. Park: The Crowd and the Public and Other Essays.* Chicago: The University of Chicago Press, 1972.

Firestone, Shulamith. *The Dialectic of Sex: The Case for the Feminist Revolution.* New York: William Morrow & Co., 1970.

Friedan, Betty. *The Feminine Mystique.* New York: W. W. Norton, 1963.

Hoffer, Eric. *The True Believer.* New York: Mentor Books, 1951.

Kerr, Clark. "White Paper on the Panty Raids," *The Daily Californian* (5 June 1956), p. 1ff.

Killian, Lewis. "Social Movements," in Robert E. L. Faris, Ed., *Handbook of Modern Sociology.* Chicago: Rand McNally & Co., 1964.

Kornhauser, William. *The Politics of Mass Society.* Glencoe: The Free Press, 1959.

Lang, K., and Gladys Lang. *Collective Dynamics.* New York: Crowell, 1961.
Le Bon, Gustave. *The Crowd.* London: George Allen & Unwin, 1917.
Lewis, Jerry M. "A Study of the Kent State Incident Using Smelser's Theory of Collective Behavior," *Sociological Inquiry, 42* (1972), p. 2; also, in the same issue, "Reply to Smelser."
Life Magazine. "Some Negroes Riot but Most Go Forward" (Journalistic account of the Watts riots), *Life, 59* (27 August 1965), p. 4ff.
The McCone Report. *Violence in the City: An End or a Beginning?* A report by the California Governor's Commission to study the Los Angeles riots (December 1965).
Miller, Merle. *Speaking Plainly, An Oral Autobiography of Harry S. Truman.* New York: Berkeley Publishing Corporation, 1974.
Morgan, William R., and Terry N. Clark. "The Causes of Racial Disorders: A Grievance-Level Explanation," *American Sociological Review, 38* (October 1973), pp. 611–624.
Odegard, Peter H. *Pressure Politics: The Story of the Anti-Saloon League.* New York: The Columbia University Press, 1928.
Pinard, Maurice. "Mass Society and Political Movement: A New Formulation," *The American Journal of Sociology, 73* (May 1968), pp. 682–690.
President's Commissions on the Status of Women. *American Women.* New York: Charles Scribner's Sons, 1965.
Quarantelli, Enrico L. "Images of Withdrawal Behavior in Disasters: Some Basic Misconceptions," *Social Problems, 8* (Summer 1960), pp. 68–79.
Sapir, Edward. "Fashion," *Encyclopedia of the Social Sciences.* New York: The Macmillan Company, *1937.*
Smelser, Neil J. *Theory of Collective Behavior.* New York: The Free Press, 1963.
————. "Some Additional Thoughts on Collective Behavior," *Sociological Inquiry, 42* (1972), p. 2.
Spilerman, Seymour. "The Causes of Racial Disturbance: A Comparison of Alternative Explanations," *American Sociological Review, 35* (August 1970), pp. 627–649.
————. "The Causes of Racial Disturbances: Tests of an Explanation," *American Sociological Review, 36* (June 1971), pp. 427–442.
Steinbeck, John. *In Dubious Battle.* New York: Viking Press, 1936 and 1963.
Turner, Ralph, and Lewis M. Killian. *Collective Behavior.* Englewood Cliffs, N.J.: Prentice–Hall, 1957.
Weller, Jack M., and E. L. Quarantelli. "Neglected Characteristics of Collective Behavior," *The American Journal of Sociology, 79* (1973), pp. 665–684.

- Are all people created equal, or are some people better qualified and more important than others?
- Is America an open democratic system or a closed society based upon privilege?
- Are truly classless societies possible, or are some social-class distinctions unavoidable?
- Can poverty be eliminated, or will the poor always be with us?
- Is power really shared in democratic societies, or do a few people (the elite) possess most power?
- Was Marx correct when he called religion in a traditional and Capitalist society the "opiate of the people," or is religion in these societies an important way of challenging sharp status distinctions?

How do you react to the above questions? Many people agree in part with both viewpoints expressed in each question. For example, Americans are conscious status seekers, and yet they place great value on equality. Political radicals have referred to this mixed perspective as a fundamental hypocrisy in the American capitalist system. Sociologists, on the other hand, argue that there are social and cultural reasons, not readily apparent in everyday life, for this seeming conflict in values and behavior. An understanding of the nature and function of status groupings in societies helps disclose these often hidden reasons.

6

Status Groupings

ASPECTS OF SOCIAL STRATIFICATION

As we have seen, social roles and groups are basic elements of the social order for the sociologist. All roles and groups differ from one another, particularly in terms of the division of labor in a society. Therefore, the life-style, goals, and patterns of interaction of a truck driver are different from those of a physician; similarly soldiers and automobile workers differ from each other because of the kinds of work they are required to do. Sociologists sometimes call this social differentiation. When, however, different roles and groups (1) are placed in a rank order and (2) carry with them exaggerated distinctions that go beyond a simple division of labor, differentiation becomes *social stratification.* For example, it is possible to conceive of a society where truck drivers are considered as important as physicians, and soldiers as important as automobile workers. Truck driving is a physically and mentally demanding job, and without an effective nationwide system of trucking most modern countries would experience industrial crises. Automobile workers are necessary to supply truck drivers with vehicles; truck drivers supply physicians with medical supplies; physicians help workers and drivers stay on the job; soldiers help protect the goals and working conditions of workers, drivers, and physicians; and so forth.

It is obvious, however, that this pure egalitarian model does not apply in modern life. Certain kinds of skills and knowledge come to be seen as more or less important, and this, in turn, permits people in some roles and groups to have more access to prestige, power, and wealth. Soldiers, particularly enlisted personnel, have declining prestige and power in contemporary America. Physicians are seen by most citizens as warranting more prestige than workers and drivers, and they get greater financial reward. Although workers have considerable power through labor unionization, they are less well-rewarded in terms of money and prestige than are some other occupations. What determines these differences?

Roles, Status, and Class

The concept of *status* refers to the value that a society places on different social roles. A study conducted in the early 1960s asked people to rank over 80 occupations on a scale from 20 to 100. Table 6-1 contains a sample of

TABLE 6-1 How Americans Rate Occupations

Occupation	Score	Occupation	Score
U.S. Supreme Court justice	94	Policeman	72
Physician	93	Radio announcer	70
Nuclear physicist	92	Tenant farmer	69
State governor	91	Local official of a labor union	67
College professor	90	Mail carrier	66
U.S. representative in Congress	90	Plumber	65
Lawyer	89	Machine operator in a factory	63
Dentist	88	Corporal in the regular Army	62
Minister	87	Truck driver	59
Priest	86	Clerk in a store	56
Banker	85	Lumberjack	55
Sociologist	83	Singer in a nightclub	54
Captain in the regular Army	82	Coal miner	50
Public school teacher	81	Bartender	48
Building contractor	80	Soda fountain clerk	44
Author of novels	78	Garbage collector	39
Railroad engineer	76	Shoe shiner	34
Trained machinist	75		
Undertaker	74	*Average of all rankings was 71*	

Source: Robert W. Hodge, Paul M. Seigel, and Peter H. Rossi, "Occupational Prestige in the United States, 1925–1963," *The American Journal of Sociology, 70* (November 1964), pp. 286–302.

the results and shows how Americans in the 1960s ranked—that is, made value-oriented distinctions between—various kinds of jobs. Notice that the ratings are not based solely on income. A very recent study found that, after Watergate, many Americans had more faith in local police and city garbage collectors than in senators and congressional representatives. Status thus indicates a preference ranking or an evaluation of occupations or social roles.

In a similar manner, groups can also be ranked into various social *strata* according to differences in prestige and privilege. For example, the unique character of many churches in modern communities stems from the particular strata or status level of its members. In 1941, W. Lloyd Warner and Paul S. Lunt published the first in a series of books on the social ranking and style of life in American communities. They analyzed in depth the status structure of a New England town with a population of about 17,000, which they called Yankee City (to be discussed again in Chapter 8 on "Communities"). Many of Yankee City's churches were ranked according to perceived differences in the general status of most members. Thus, although a few upper-middle-class people attended St. Paul's Espiscopal Church and some low-status families were served by an Episcopal Mission, most members of that church came from the upper class, as illustrated in Figure 6-1.

This reference to the Yankee City studies serves as an introduction to another key sociological concept used to identify groupings in a stratified social system—*social class.* This concept implies something more than a statistical aggregate of roles or groups at a particular status level. Karl Marx saw classes as groupings of people who share a common situation in the *economic* order of life, particularly in relationship to the means of production. Therefore, in an industrial society, those who own the means of production (capitalist bourgeoisie) and those whose labor is controlled by the owners (worker proletariat) form two potentially antithetical classes. In 1848, Marx and Friedrich Engels published the *Manifesto of the Communist Party,* which developed the revolutionary theme of an unavoidable conflict between the proletariat and the bourgeoisie and the ultimate evolution of a classless society.

Max Weber [1946] went beyond Marx and perceived of social stratification as being the result of two other important factors—*social* and *political*—in addition to the economic. Weber argued that economic factors give rise to social class based upon (1) what people do within the production system; (2) how they acquire goods from the system; and (3) their life-chances within the system. By *life-chances,* sociologists mean such things as life expectancy, good versus bad health, family stability, and mental health. Thus, lower-class people would be expected to die at younger ages, have worse physical health, experience more divorce and separation, and have more mental illness than upper-class people. Social factors give rise to what Weber called status groups, which are distinguished by different *life-styles* in the consumption of goods and by different forms of esteem and honor [Bendix and Lipset, 1953]. Political factors give rise to

FIGURE 6-1 Status Level of Churches in Yankee City

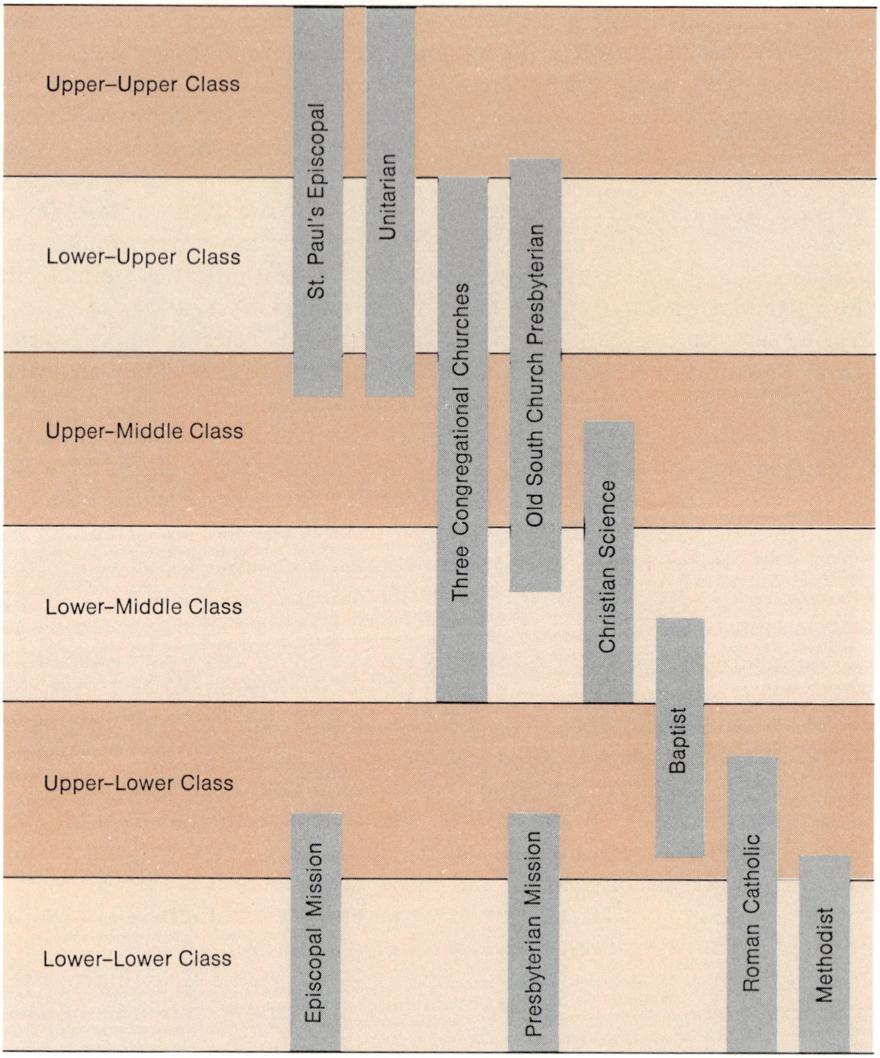

From W. Lloyd Warner, *Yankee City* (New Haven: Yale University Press, 1963), pp. 189–193.

parties, which determine the extent to which various groups have access to *power.*

The concepts of life-styles, life-chances, and power will be discussed in more detail later in this chapter. For the moment, however, it is necessary to state some cautions. Some societies have sharp distinctions in status groupings that are easily observable, for example between the very rich and the very poor. In industrial societies, however, these distinctions often become less visible because of the rise of a middle-class culture. In addition, although economic, social, and political factors are often interrelated (for example, the very rich can have much esteem and power), the acquisition of much property does not necessarily bring honor, nor do all powerful people necessarily have great wealth (military leaders).

These cautions also highlight the importance of distinguishing between different kinds of stratification systems. Some are *open* systems offering mobility to individuals and groups up and down the hierarchy. Others are *closed* and offer little or no opportunity for mobility. Still others contain elements of both open and closed systems.

Open Versus Closed Societies

There are two ways in which individuals and groups can be assigned a particular status. Status criteria may be *ascribed* (that is, based on social and physical inheritance) in which case the individual or group has little or no control over them. One's race, age, sex, ethnicity, and family background are examples. Societies based upon ascribed status tend to be closed. Conversely, in open societies, status criteria are *achieved* (that is, based on what you can do) and, therefore, the individual or group can earn a particular status. Skill, educational level, amount of income, and special knowledge would be examples of status criteria in an achievement-oriented society.

Hereditary *ascribed status* tends to be associated with premodern societies. Ascription assures that the important positions and occupations will be filled by persons reared from birth to carry on the work. A son will continue in the footsteps of his father. He is born to be a hunter, farmer, chief, or priest. There is little chance for change, and there is little chance that the positions will be left vacant. Great emphasis is therefore placed upon a man having many sons to carry on his occupation as well as his name. The advantages here may be summed up in the word "security." The society is sure of its workers; the individual is sure of his occupation. The disadvantages lie in the risk of inefficiency. The son of the chief may not be qualified as an individual for the great responsibilities of leadership, whereas the son (or daughter) of the water carrier or serf may have great personal potential for more responsible work.

Achieved status is associated with modern industrial society. Hundreds of new occupations develop that require specialized preparation. No parent can train a child for the multitude of jobs that are available in industry or the modern professions. Society attempts to provide an equality of opportunity in order to lure the best talent into the most difficult positions. The key word in modern society is "efficiency." No one deserves a job just because of family background; rather, a person must earn the right to that position. Individuals born in the slums should not be held back just because they are starting out with a relatively low social status. All members of the society are encouraged to achieve their highest potential.

An open system, however, is not without risks. One problem is the great potential for individual insecurity and uncertainty. The society can-

6-1 Is Success in American Society Achieved or Ascribed?

Many Americans believe that success is achieved; that is, that high status (money, prestige, power) is attained by individuals who possess special skills, unusual intellectual abilities, and the willingness to work hard. American history and folklore are filled with stories which seem to support this belief.

Henry Ford was born on a farm near Greenfield, Michigan, in 1863. He attended grammar school there and later became a machinist in Detroit. In 1890, he began to experiment with engines and built his first gasoline engine in 1893. In 1896, he built his first automobile in a Detroit workshop and put it on exhibit in Dearborn, Michigan. In 1903, he organized the Ford Motor Company, which, at first, made automobiles that only the wealthy could afford. Soon, however, Ford believed that every person, no matter what their income, should be able to own an automobile, and he pioneered the development of mass assembly-line techniques. From 1908 to 1917, Ford sold over 15,000,000 "Model T's."

Culver Pictures, Inc.

His early success brought him such financial rewards that, in 1914, he announced he would share his profits with his employees. At the same time, he cut the working day from nine to eight hours and established a minimum wage for every employee over 21 years of age or older of $5 per day (unskilled workers had been receiving $1; skilled workers, $2.50). Ford also believed that profits should be used to build larger factories, at a time when stockholders wanted to share the profits in the form of dividends. As a result, Ford bought out all the stockholders in 1919, and the Ford family were sole owners until 1956. In 1919, Ford's son, Edsel, took over the presidency of the company. During his remaining lifetime, Ford established Greenfield Village (a group of historical buildings and landmarks), the Edison Institute School, and the Henry Ford Museum. He donated large amounts of money and Ford Motor Company stock to the philanthropic Ford Foundation. Ford died in 1947, an example of the independent self-made man of an achievement-oriented society.

News Department, Ford Motor Company

As a mixed social system, however, American society also contains many elements of status ascription; that is, high status is attained partly as the result of family origins, inherited wealth, and so on. Within one family or one individual of the same family, success by both achievement and ascription may be evident.

Detroit Public Library, Burton Historical Collection

Detroit Public Library, Burton Historical Collection

Henry Ford II was born in Detroit in 1917, the eldest son of Edsel Ford and the grandson of Henry Ford. His early childhood was marked by all of the advantages of high ascribed status: a privileged life-style, travel, and private education (The Hotchkiss School). He attended Yale University from 1936 to 1940 and was commissioned a lieutenant (j.g.) in the United States Navy in 1941. When Ford's father died in 1943, he was released from the Navy to return to the family business at Dearborn, where he became a vice president. In 1944, he became an executive vice president, and, in 1945, he became the president of Ford Motor Company.

The inherited advantages of Henry Ford II's family background permitted him to attain early successes which might not otherwise have been possible. Nevertheless, it was also necessary for him to achieve success in terms of his own abilities and talents. In 1944, Henry II reorganized the company, bringing it back from the verge of bankruptcy and putting it on a paying basis. In 1945, he became the first manufacturer to exhibit a 1946 model automobile. In 1946, the Ford Motor Company had a net loss of $8 million, but by 1955 it had a net profit of $430 million. Henry II has served as national chairman of the Community Chests of America, as national chairman of the Crusade for Freedom, as chairman of the American Heritage Foundation, and as an alternate delegate to the General Assembly of the United Nations (in 1953).

Success by both achievement and ascription has certain strengths and weaknesses. Societies which emphasize achievement reflect the democratic ideal that all individuals, regardless of origins, should be free to utilize special and unique skills. Societies which emphasize ascription reflect the aristocratic ideal that certain specially trained individuals are more likely to accomplish the important leadership tasks which society needs. Contemporary America is a mix of both views.

not always be sure of enough qualified workers to fill certain crucial positions. For example, in America we talk about a shortage of ecology experts, skilled workers, and physicians. People cannot always make up their minds about what occupations are best for them and, thus, get the proper education and training for those jobs. Vocational uncertainty is widespread. There is also serious risk of social strain in modern society because many people never attain true equality of opportunity. We will return to this problem at the end of the chapter. For the moment, however, let us consider the differences between four basic types of stratification systems.

Types of Systems: Class, Caste, Estate, and Mixed

Sociologists call achievement-oriented societies *class* systems of stratification, and ascription-oriented societies, *caste* systems. Social classes and social castes, then, each perform different functions depending upon the total requirements of a social system. Premodern traditional societies rely upon the rigidity and exclusive character of social castes to provide continuity and stability. Modern societies depend upon social classes for flexibility and social change through individual achievement.

Some sociologists have identified a third type of stratification system referred to as the *estate* system. It has been described as having elements of both classes and castes. Status distinctions based upon the notion of estate can be found in feudal societies, which emphasize one's role and position in terms of one's relationship to the land. Those of lowest status may be slaves, who are treated as property or serfs, or tenant farmers, who must work the land and turn large portions of produce over to others who own the land. Those of highest status are the landowners and landholders; for example, the high status of the church during the Middle Ages was partly a function of its vast land holdings.

In reality, however, most societies, particularly in the modern world, tend to have *mixtures* of all the basic types of status. In the contemporary United States, many poor whites and wealthy ranchers in the South and Southwest retain characteristics of estatelike status distinctions. American blacks still live in a castelike society. Yet some blacks and many poor whites can attain some measure of personal achievement in the larger class system. This mixture of status systems often produces anxiety and strain as individuals and groups seek to orient themselves. The distinctions between these types of stratification systems are summarized in Table 6-2.

This discussion of the four basic types of stratification systems raises two crucial issues, which will be dealt with in the remainder of this chapter. First, since all the systems seem to create special kinds of functional problems—ranging from role allocation problems in closed societies to tension and hostility problems in open societies—why does stratification seem to be universal in all human societies? That is, why is it not possible to construct societies without status distinctions? Does status inevitably arise to serve some basic human need? Second, since problems can be found

TABLE 6-2 Characteristics and Examples of Stratification Systems

	Caste	Estate	Class	Mixed
Type of Society	Folk	Feudal	Purely industrial	Modern mixed
Type of Status	Ascribed	Mostly ascribed	Achieved	Achieved and ascribed
Types of Status Characteristics	Family, race, sex, religion	Relationship to land and property	Education, occupation, income	All the characteristics
Mobility	Some within castes; none between castes	Some in top estates; none in bottom estates	Open within and between classes	Open between classes; closed between castes
Examples	Traditional India; American and British black–white relations; Protestant–Catholic relations in Northern Ireland	Medieval China, Europe, and Japan	Most of white American society	All of American society, including white, black, Chicano, Indian, and so on
Problems	Lack of freedom, rigidity, no guarantee of best qualified	Similar to caste systems	Anxiety, insecurity, class conflict	All the problems of both open and closed societies

in all systems, how do societies go about managing these problems in order to maintain social stability and equilibrium? In particular, why has the Marxian prediction of widespread and revolutionary class conflict and warfare not yet broken out in societies like contemporary America?

IS STRATIFICATION NECESSARY?

That stratification seems to be inevitable in all human societies is dramatically illustrated by what has happened in Communist countries, where egalitarian ideology has been most pronounced. In some, the traditional Communist slogan—"From each according to his ability, to each according to his needs"—has been given a new ending—"to each according to his work"—indicating that some kinds of work are considered more important than others. In Iraq, in 1958, revolutionary crowds dragged the bodies of the king and his chief advisor through the streets, protesting feudalism and imperialism. Since then, the Iraqi Socialist Party has nationalized about 90 percent of the country's oil producing industry. Contrary to the democratizing aims of the socialist revolution, however, a new class of rich bureaucrats and property owners has been created, the members of which build luxurious homes on land costing as much as $100 a square meter and purchase imported cars at from $15,000 to $45,000 each as status symbols [Onis, 1975, pp. 43, 46]. Russian social scientists admit the existence of at least three classes in the Soviet Union: workers, peasants, and the privileged intelligentsia. American sociologists distinguish at least 100 different classes and castes in the Soviet Union, including party officials, military officers, scientists, Ukranians, Cossacks, Armenians, and Jews. Therefore, the United States is not the only country in which a gap exists between an ideal of egalitarianism and the reality of sharp status distinctions.

Are there fundamental reasons for this stratification that seems to be present in all human societies? The continuing debate about whether stratification is necessary is based upon two conflicting theories in contemporary sociology: the "conservative" *functionalist view* and the "radical" *conflict perspective.*

The "Conservative" Functionalist View

As we saw in Chapter 1, functional theory emerged early in the development of sociology, starting with the work of Auguste Comte and Emile Durkheim, and continues today in the studies of American sociologists. Functionalists focus upon social order, integration, and equilibrium; that is, they generally tend to view rapid change, conflict, or deviance as forces that threaten the orderly operation of a social system. A functionalist would argue that a system of social stratification is merely *one of the many ways in which societies try to maintain some form of stability.*

Functional theory starts with the assumption that people in a society share a consensus view of major goals and values, that is, of what is good and what is bad. Since all societies possess limited resources and rewards (wealth, power, prestige, and so on), the problem is to assign the limited rewards to those roles that can most effectively use the limited resources to attain the desired goals. In other words, functionalists argue that the greatest status goes to those roles that (1) are considered most important; (2) require the hardest training; and (3) involve the most demanding work. Kingsley Davis and Wilbert Moore [1945, pp. 242–249], leading exponents of the functionalist view, put it this way:

> Inevitably, then, a society must have, first, some kind of rewards that it can use as inducements, and second, some way of distributing these rewards differentially according to positions. The rewards and their distribution become a part of the social order, and thus give rise to stratification. . . .
>
> If the rights and perquisites of different positions in a society must be unequal, then the society must be stratified, because this is precisely what stratification means. Social inequality is thus an unconsciously evolved device by which societies insure that the most important positions are conscientiously filled by the most qualified persons. Hence every society, no matter how simple or complex, must differentiate persons in terms of both prestige and esteem, and must therefore possess a certain amount of institutionalized inequality.

Thus sociologists like Davis and Moore find the fact that physicians are highly rewarded in contemporary society both understandable and natural. The work of a physician is most important. Without modern medical knowledge and practice, not only would the universal goal of good health and long life be unattainable, but industrial society would also suffer the problems resulting from illness, plagues, and accidents. In addition, premed students must study long and hard at great personal expense to become members of this occupation. Finally, the life of a physician is demanding and difficult. She or he must work with death, pain, disease, in difficult situations, at all hours of the day and night. Therefore, without the rewards of high status, few individuals would be attracted to this role, and the modern social order would be threatened.

In short, functionalist theory is oriented toward social integration by arguing that stratification guarantees that the best qualified and most motivated individuals will be attracted to the most important roles. Furthermore, status distinctions insure a general sense of security in so far as people know what rewards to expect, what kind of esteem and honor they will receive from fellow citizens, and what kinds of working conditions they will face.

There are a number of unresolved problems with the functionalist view. First, as Louis Wirth points out [1953–1954, pp. 279–303], this perspective takes "the democratic value of equality of opportunity for granted." Second, the functional view seems applicable only to class systems, which are more open. Third, even within class systems, functionalism leaves unanswered some major questions and issues. For example, the claim that status distinctions attract the best qualified to the more important roles assumes that all or most citizens have an equal opportunity to gain access to these roles. This is obviously not the case in castelike social systems. Even in class systems, race and sex can limit opportunity. Blacks and women are underrepresented in the medical profession, despite the fact that, given equal opportunity, there is no reason to assume that either group is inherently less able to become physicians. Indeed, research shows that being the child of a physician, a caste or estatelike characteristic, is a better guarantee of access than individual skill or ability. Furthermore, what crucial social goal is achieved by paying professional athletes and entertainers extremely high salaries? Is garbage collection a less important job than law in modern urban centers? Citizens of New York, after a garbage collectors' strike, would argue that it is not.

What these criticisms suggest is that functionalist theory is most applicable to the middle ranges of achievement-oriented class systems, where reasonable opportunity exists, and it is least applicable to status systems based upon ascription [Pease *et al.*, 1970, pp. 127–137]. The way in which the Rockefeller family, for instance, inherits money and power, and the way that the poor inherit poverty and dependency, are examples. As a consequence of these criticisms, a second major theory has arisen to challenge the functionalist view.

The "Radical" Conflict Perspective

Radical conflict theory had its origin in the work of Marx and Engels, particularly as it applies to social stratification. For many decades, however, Western sociologists generally ignored or denounced this view, as a result of anti-Communist beliefs. As indicated in Chapter 1, conflict theory has experienced a recent revival in sociology and is beginning to play a more important role.

Marx argued that status, particularly in the form of social classes, arose to serve two purposes. First, status distinctions were a way in which one class could oppress another. Such oppression allowed *the ruling classes to maximize their access to limited resources and rewards* and, at the same time, to maintain their power (influence and authority) over the ruled classes. For example, a Marxian analysis of the medical profession would argue that physicians deliberately limit access to the profession by establishing criteria such as race, sex, and family background. In this way, physicians maintain an artificial shortage for their services, thereby guaranteeing higher salaries and better working conditions, as well as honor and prestige. In other words, citizens are willing to pay almost any cost and offer almost any reward to physicians because their limited services are so badly needed. At the same time, this high status maximizes the power of physicians, who use that power to achieve their own, rather than society's, goals (for example, their opposition to a nationwide medical health plan).

Second, Marx also suggested that, ironically, status distinctions could become the basis for a collective consciousness that would lead to a revolution against oppression. Specifically, the existence of imposed social classes could lead to the development of class consciousness among the oppressed. Revolutionary leaders could mobilize this consciousness and try to bring about a truly classless society. For example, to bring about major changes in contemporary American medical practice, consumer advocates like Ralph Nader have attempted to organize citizens by making them aware of their inferior status and the problems that arise because of status distinctions.

The revolutionary class consciousness predicted by the latter part of Marx's theory seems not to have developed in class societies like the United States for several reasons. The existence of a large, generally unaware, and fairly confortable middle class acts as a buffer between the highest and lowest classes. Appeals by activists like Nader are more attractive to this nonrevolutionary middle class than to the most oppressed. In addition, oppressors and rulers in contemporary society have a variety of ways in which they can co-opt or redirect revolutionary fervor. Corporations sometimes try to intimidate or blackmail the Naders. Federal and local governments can provide minimal health plans, thereby draining off some antagonism and hostility. Control of the mass media by members of the ruling classes maximizes their ability to combat revolutionary ideologies. More will be said about other ways in which societies manage the potential conflicts in status systems in the last section of this chapter.

Just as functionalist theory applies best to middle-class achievement-oriented societies, Marx's notion of class conflict seems to be most relevant to developing non-Western nations in contrast to modern Western settings. Nevertheless, the notion of status as a mode of repression is playing an increasingly important role in contemporary sociological analysis. As a consequence, modern sociology seems to stand somewhere between the two conflicting theories with regard to whether some form of stratification is necessary.

Where We Stand

Most sociologists seem to agree that, although some status inequality may be functionally necessary, extreme differences between roles and groups are not. Presidents and vice-presidents of leading business corporations are paid from $200,000 to $300,000 per year in salary. In addition, they receive additional income in the form of bonuses, stock options, and fringe benefits. This can represent from 10 to 50 times more financial reward than other employees of the corporation. Some social scientists refer to these differences as invidious distinctions, that is, excessive and unnecessary ones. Since other organizations run as effectively and efficiently with much smaller status distinctions between employees (for example, public service agencies, educational institutions, the military), there is no reason to believe that these differences are any more than special privilege for a few.

Indeed, some research shows that many citizens are motivated to select roles, even difficult ones, for personal or altruistic reasons unrelated to traditional status symbols. Many choose college teaching because of the individual freedom and a long summer vacation; many choose law out of a desire to change the way things operate in contemporary society; free-lance writers and artists often live at a near-poverty level motivated only by aesthetic satisfactions. There is no theoretical reason why a relatively statusless society could not develop these kinds of motivations in relationship to many important jobs.

In all societies, particularly modern mixed systems, large numbers of people are generously rewarded even though they may not perform important tasks. Furthermore, some are rewarded who actually perform undesirable tasks. Criminal activities, price fixing in industry, stock manipulation, publication of worthless but lurid stories, these and a host of other activities can bring both fame and fortune. Contemporary political life is an example of this dilemma. Although modern societies reward politicians with many of the economic, social, or political aspects of high status, an increasing number of citizens question whether these rewards attract the best qualified to those roles.

In reality, what seems to be inevitable in society is not just the existence of specific status differences but the use of status for purposes of self-aggrandizement. Once people attain money, prestige, and power, they will do everything possible to protect and enhance these rewards. There-

6-2 The Functions and Dysfunctions of Status Rewards

All status systems, particularly in modern achievement-oriented societies, offer multiple rewards as a way of attracting the best qualified talent into the most needed or prized roles.

Donald Dietz, Dietz/Hamlin

Financial reward enables individuals to purchase larger homes and automobiles. It permits them to live "the good life" in a home of their own with a beautiful view. People will strive for these benefits by training for and performing the most needed and difficult roles. In addition, their purchase of desired goods and services creates work for others, who, in turn, can then avail themselves of some of these rewards.

United Press International

Some roles are also rewarded with prestige and honor, rather than with money. Shown here are silver medalist Dianne de Leeuw of Holland, gold medalist Dorothy Hamill of the United States, and bronze medalist Christine Errath of East Germany (left to right) at the Olympic awards ceremonies for women's figure skating in 1976. Popular acclaim for athletes emphasizes the importance of the value of individual achievement. In addition, widespread spectator interest in sports is considered an important unifying device in mass society.

Societies which emphasize money and prestige as rewards, however, may encourage some individuals to use any means in order to achieve these goals. Rewards can become dysfunctional when the scramble for monetary success encourages illegitimate or deviant behavior, or when the desire for fame encourages the seeking of notoriety.

United Press International

In 1972, author Clifford Irving and his wife admitted that a biography of Howard Hughes they had written, allegedly based upon personal interviews with the multimillionaire recluse, was a hoax. They had fooled book publishers, the press, and the public. Some observers charged that, by so doing, they had weakened the integrity of the publishing industry and the press in the eyes of the public.

fore, much contemporary sociological research has focused upon trends towards authoritarianism and oligarchy (see the discussion of the "iron law of oligarchy" in Chapter 7). Other researchers concentrate upon what can be done to bring about a more equitable distribution of society's limited resources. This latter orientation is the subject of the following section.

LIFE-STYLES AND LIFE-CHANCES

How inequitably do status distinctions distribute the limited resources of contemporary societies? As indicated earlier in this chapter, the concept of *life-chances* provides a partial answer. In addition, the concept of *life-styles*—the extent to which high status groups have access to the advantages and privileges of a social system—also provides an answer. Studies of poverty and inequality in American society illustrate the use of these two concepts.

Poverty and Inequality: The American Case

Social scientists have been interested in four major types of questions concerning poverty and inequality in the United States.

1. Is the American situation better or worse than the economic conditions of other nations?
2. Have poverty and inequality increased or decreased in recent years?
3. Which social groups are most affected by poverty and inequality?
4. In terms of life-styles and life-chances, what is the impact of poverty and inequality upon particular groups?

The difficulty with most research designed to address these kinds of questions is that economic measures tend to be used, primarily annual income of individuals and families. As we have already seen, wealth is not always accompanied by other aspects of status, such as honor, prestige, and power. Furthermore, economic measures create special difficulties in data collection and analysis. For example, real income may vary considerably from earned and recorded income for various groups. Comparing income data for different nations (with different currencies) and ethnic groups (with different degrees of purchasing power) is extremely difficult. Inflation has a different impact on various social groups in terms of changes in purchasing power. Nevertheless, it is possible to summarize briefly the results of recent research as a background for the discussions to follow.

How does America compare to other nations? According to American mythology, the most industrialized economies tend to be the most equal, whereas, according to Communist ideology, the classless socialist societies are most equal. An interesting attempt to test these beliefs [Lydall, 1968] disclosed that there was a partial truth to both views. Using only earned income data, Lydall classified 25 countries according to five categories ranging from the most to least economically equal. Australia, Czechoslovakia, Hungary, and New Zealand—a mix of democratic, socialist, and Communist nations—appeared in the most equal category. Brazil, Ceylon, India, and Mexico, among others, appeared in the least equal category. The United States appeared in the second most equal category together with Austria, Belgium, Canada, Denmark, Great Britain, Poland, Sweden, West Germany, and Yugoslavia. The study concluded that *egalitarian distribution of earned income was related to both political ideology and degree of industrial development.* The Communist countries tended to be more equal than the non-Communist, if the comparison was made between countries at similar levels of industrialization. At the same time, among non-Communist countries, more economic equality was associated with a higher level of industrial development.

Have poverty and inequality increased or decreased in recent years in America? Again, according to American mythology, economic inequality has decreased substantially since almost all status groupings have shared to some extent the economic prosperity experienced from the 1940s to the 1970s. Once again, this belief is a half-truth. At the end of World War II, the median (most frequent) income for all American families was slightly over $5000. By 1970, the median income had increased to just under $10,000, and by 1974 it was over $12,000 per year. During the same time, the percentage of American families with very low incomes dropped by almost one half [Bureau of the Census, 1975]. These figures would lead one to conclude that shared prosperity was generally the norm. However, during this same period of time, there was little or no change in the proportion of total income going to relatively poor versus relatively wealthy families. In other words, the poor stayed poor, and "them who had, got."

In fact, the upper 5 percent of all American families received about 14 percent of all annual income, compared to the lower 20 percent who received about 5 percent. The middle 60 percent of all American families receive slightly more than 50 percent of all income. Therefore, only in the middle ranges can one say that there is something approximating economic equality in contemporary America. Indeed, the upper 20 percent of American families receive about 40 percent of all available earned income. Thus, *the problem of relative economic inequality is a more persistent condition in American society than the problem of the degree and extent of absolute poverty.* This becomes even more evident when one examines data comparing income on a social and ethnic basis.

Which social groups are most affected by poverty and inequality? Not surprisingly, though social-class distinctions play some role, *those groupings identified by castelike features suffer the most.* In 1974, all males earned a median income of $11,840, whereas females earned $6770 [Bureau of the Census, 1974]. Table 6-3 illustrates the same kinds of differences, according to status, for various racial, religious, and language groups. This table strikingly illustrates the impact of color, as a form of racial iden-

TABLE 6-3 Unequal Distribution of Income in the U.S. in 1974 for Major Caste Groupings

Caste Groupings	Median Income for a Family of Four	Percentage Below Poverty Level
All Whites	$13,360	9
Total Population	12,840	12
Latin American	11,410	14
All Spanish	9,560	23
Mexican	9,500	24
Black	7,810	32
Puerto Rican	7,630	33

Source: Bureau of the Census, *Current Population Survey* (Washington, D.C.: U.S. Government Printing Office, 1975). Figures have been rounded off for ease of comparison.

tification, upon status, and, therefore, upon poverty and economic inequality. When racial identity combines with other special characteristics (recent migration, different language, unusual culture), the impact upon a group can be substantial. For example, in 1972, when the median family income for whites was $10,236, it was $5279 for blacks and less than $2000 for Native Americans. Caste, therefore, remains a very real part of the American status system.

In terms of life-styles and life-chances, what is the impact of status distinctions? As indicated before, economic data alone disclose only a part of the problem. Low income means low educational opportunities, which in turn mean poorer jobs, which in turn lead to the perpetuation of low income. In this manner, *both caste and class criteria combine to establish a cycle of poverty and inequality for some groupings in the society,* a cycle that can last for many generations. Furthermore, the life-styles and access to basic benefits of these groups are influenced. In 1970, the life expectancy for all white males was about 67 years, whereas for black males it was 60 years. In 1970, infant mortality for native Americans was 50 percent higher than the rate for the total population; for Mexican Americans, it was almost 100 percent higher. In California, Mexican Americans averaged slightly over two visits to a physician per year in 1970, while all citizens of that state averaged almost six visits during the year. Studies of broken families (divorce, separation), admission rates to institutions for mental psychoses, and the like show the same disparities in life-styles and chances by class and caste. Low-status citizens have higher rates of marital problems, mental illness, and other problems than do high-status groups.

As important as economic factors may be in determining life-styles and life-chances, Max Weber and other scholars have suggested that power and influence may be more significant. These two variables can lead to a clearer understanding of the workings of status systems than can traditional concepts like the distribution of economic rewards.

Power and Influence

Power can be defined as the ability of someone in a social relationship to influence the will and actions of others [Weber, 1957, p. 152]. In other words, power involves *making decisions about what other people think and do.* Power also involves determining the life-styles and chances of those who do not possess power.

Power can take one of two forms in society. The first is characterized by *force, coercion,* or *repression;* that is, the will and actions of people may be influenced without their full consent. A criminal who points a gun at someone's head and demands, "Your money or your life," is exercising this type of power. Most people feel they have no choice in this situation; they give their money out of fear for their lives. However, this form of "naked" power is ineffective as a basis for stable long-lasting social systems. Force will eventually be met by counterforce. Furthermore, even when counterforce is not available, the powerless may refuse to cooperate. For example, "your money or your life" could not become the basis for a system of widespread voluntary taxation. Large numbers of citizens could refuse to pay, requiring the powerful either to back down on the threat of force or to carry out mass executions. In either event, the *legitimacy* of the powerful (the right to be powerful) would be quickly eroded. In other words, for power to be effective it requires legitimacy in the form of *authority* (see Chapters 7 and 14 for a discussion of types of authority).

The second form of power—authority—arises when *people agree to abide by the dictates of the powerful.* James Kimberly [1970, pp. 73–101] has summarized sociological theory relating status and power as authority as follows:

1. *Status differences are a result of authority differences.* Those who are powerful in a society are granted high status partly as a reward for their skilled leadership [Homans, 1961].
2. *Authority requires status differences.* When social changes demand people with special skills, those who can solve new problems are rewarded with special status [Bales, 1950].
3. *Status differences for those in authority are accepted without question.* Most people believe that things are better that way and that leaders deserve to be given higher status [Blau, 1964; Thibault and Kelley, 1959].

These are the most common sociological views about the relationship between social status and power, and they reflect the functional perspective. They have merit but tend to apply more to traditional societies than to modern ones. In the former, wealth, status, and authority more frequently go hand in hand. Most citizens consider it correct that the rich should be accorded high status and the authority to make decisions influencing the life-styles and chances of all citizens. When struggles for power occur in traditional societies, they often involve only special interest groups already at the top of the status structure. For example, revolutions and coup d'etats in many developing nations of the contemporary world often take the form of battles between the corporate elite, army colonels, traditional political rulers, units of a naval or air force, and the like. In Latin America, this has been referred to as the tradition of "palace coups."

In contrast, in modern societies, the trend has been toward the separation of status and power, the diffusion of power, and the resulting erosion of authority. For example, as we have already seen, traditional status criteria may no longer necessarily reflect power. Military commanders may possess power (as potential force) because of the military's monopoly of weapons of mass destruction rather than as a result of accumulated wealth. Early corporate leaders (the original Rockefellers, Mellons, and Fords) possessed power as a result of wealth and ownership of the business, whereas leaders of modern corporations are experts in bureaucratic management. Although these managers may be paid high salaries for their knowledge, their power stems not from the salary but rather from their bureaucratic roles. Indeed, corporate ownership is often widely dispersed and fragmented by individual and organizational shareholding.

What such changes have created is a *crisis of authority* (discussed at greater length in Chapter 8). Citizens are no longer able or willing to grant unquestioned authority to specifically identifiable groups. Vested interests must often rely upon implied or threatened coercion and repression to maintain power. For example, the Watergate disclosures gave evidence of the way in which some contemporary leaders use spying, police agents–provocateurs, manipulation of public information, threats of income tax investigation, and the like to protect their power since they may feel that their rightful authority is eroding.

The Consequences of Powerlessness: Blacks and the Ku Klux Klan

This developing perspective, which examines the relationship between status and power, has become the basis for recent sociological research that analyzes the powerless rather than merely studying the powerful. An analysis of the changing position of American blacks provides a good example of how the new research illustrates differences between status, life-styles, life-chances, and power.

A recent Census Bureau report showed that, during the 1970s, American blacks made important gains in education and in election to public office, but at the same time they suffered substantial loss of income and jobs [*The Boston Globe*, 1975, p. 9]. In that period, black joblessness was 13.7 percent, compared to 7.6 percent for whites. Some of the consequences of this deprivation can be seen by the fact that in 1973 the average life expectancy for black males was 61.9 years and for black females it was 70.1 years, compared to 68.4 for white males and 76.1 for white females. Therefore, although blacks made gains in some characteristics of status, they suffered losses in others. Even more significant may be a growing *sense of powerlessness* by urban blacks in cities like Boston:

> The sleek John Hancock Building towers gracefully over the Boston skyline, a symbol of the city's economic power. But to Boston blacks, that symbol serves as a painful reminder of their lack of power. And that reminder seems always to be visible from the black community—from the Roxbury ghetto, from the upward-mobile Mattapan section of two- and three-story frame homes, and from the cozy suburbs, now home to most of the city's "black Brahmins." While they make up about a fifth of the city's population of around 650,000, blacks here seem to wield less political, economic and social power. . . . Only one black has served on the City Council and none have ever served on the Boston School Committee . . . [Delaney, 1975, p. 10. Copyright © 1975 by The New York Times Company. Reprinted by permission.]

Therefore, not just in spite of, but perhaps even *because of* gains in some aspects of status (for example, education, income), ethnic minorities may feel an accentuated sense of powerlessness.

For some subgroups in a society, feelings of powerlessness may lead to alienation and the encouragement of extremist behavior. In the 1950s, James Vander Zanden [1960, pp. 456–462] applied this type of perspective to a study of the Ku Klux Klan. Through an historical analysis of the development of the Klan, Vander Zanden identifies two interesting phenomena: (1) Unlike the White Citizens Councils of the rural American South, the Klan's strength was urban based; (2) the Klan did not arise merely as a response to other social movements favoring racial integration. Therefore, Vander Zanden suggests that one must turn elsewhere in order to discover the unique function of the Klan for its members. Although the Klan is a secret society, he was able to obtain, from charter applications, police arrests records, press reports, and police-seized membership lists, the names and occupational positions of 153 Klansmen. (See Table 6-4.)

TABLE 6-4 Occupational Status of Ku Klux Klan Members

Number	Occupational Category	Examples of Occupations
51	Skilled workers	Carpenters; garage mechanics; machinists; stonemasons
11	Marginal small businessmen	Proprietors of food markets, grills, and gasoline stations; small building-trade contractors
36	Marginal white-collar workers	Grocery-store clerks; policemen; salesmen; service-station attendants
55	Semiskilled and unskilled workers	From the following industries: aircraft, automotive, coal, construction, steel, textile, and transportation (primarily truck drivers)

Source: James W. Vander Zanden, "The Klan Revival," *The American Journal of Sociology, 65* (March 1960).

Analysis of these occupations disclosed that the first three categories are commonly ranked in both the upper levels of the working class and the lower levels of the middle class. That is, they are considered to be in an *intermediary position* between clear-cut blue-collar manual jobs and white-collar service jobs. In addition, many in the semiskilled and unskilled category feel themselves to be *marginal* in somewhat the same way. They have accepted and internalized the status success goals of the larger society but lack the means to attain these goals. Vander Zanden highlights the important attributes of members of these kinds of occupations—status insecurity; personal anxiety; and lack of the resources, skills, or education necessary to improve their life chances.

In short, Klansmen suffer from the strain of status *marginality* in contemporary society and feel powerless to do anything about it. As a consequence, extremist Klan ideology and practices act as a release from this strain in the following ways:

1. Klansmen *overemphasize patriotism* and equate it with white superiority.
2. Klan *secrecy,* stressing exclusion of all outsiders, gives members an explicit group identification.
3. What others in society would identify as personal *weaknesses are defined* by the Klan as *strengths:* "The Ku Klux Klan is the only white Christian Protestant 100 percent American organization in America today. . . . Klansmen are the cleanest and most perfect people on earth" [Vander Zanden, 1960, p. 460].
4. Klan regalia, ritual, and exaggerated titles (Exalted Cyclops, Grand Dragon, Grand Titan, Imperial Wizard) set members of the "Invisible Empire" apart as *superior to others.*
5. Feelings of personal failure and frustration are released by *attacking evil individuals* who are considered to be a part of hostile conspiracies (blacks, Communists, Jews, the FBI, the Red Cross, the Nashville School Board).

This study of the Ku Klux Klan demonstrates one mode of reaction to the social strains that develop in a society that emphasizes mobility. The origins and nature of this problem are the subject of the last section of this chapter.

▶ SO WHAT?

The concepts of life-styles and life-chances illustrate the multifaceted nature of the problems of poverty and inequality. More than the lack of money is involved. This realization has become the focal point of the continuing debate about what to do about poverty. Most sociologists agree that the poor act differently than the nonpoor. However, two conflicting interpretations have developed. One argues that some people are poor because they behave differently; the other, that some people behave differently because they are poor (see Carol Stack's study of a black ghetto in Chapter 4). Those who adopt the first view support a "services strategy" with regard to poverty. Those adopting the second view support an "opportunities strategy." The services strategy has been popular and leads to modestly reformist programs designed to change the behavioral patterns of the poor. The opportunities strategy usually involves more radical programs designed to change significantly the institutional structures that make poverty unavoidable. Existing and proposed programs are frequently criticized by advocates of alternative strategies:

Strategy	Example of Programs	Criticisms
Service	*Headstart:* Preschool training (ages 3–5) in skills lacked by children of the poor	Since this program is offered only to the children of the poor, it stigmatizes and labels them as inherently inferior.
Service	*Low-cost public housing*	The poor are concentrated into huge, institutionalized projects, which only exacerbate personal and family problems (crime, deliquency, anomie, divorce, and so on).
Service	*Guaranteed employment* (for those able to work) and *Family allowances* (for those unable to work)	Make-work programs often lead to the creation of relatively worthless jobs. Furthermore, what is important is the kind of work or job. The poor are typically trapped in unrewarding and menial occupations. Family allowances merely encourage large families, thereby making population pressures among the poor worse.
Opportunities	*Occupational retraining*	The ability to obtain employment may raise the income of poor

Strategy	Example of Programs	Criticisms
		families, but it does nothing to change illegitimacy, alcoholism, gambling, impulse buying, wife-beating, and other problems associated with the "culture of poverty."
Opportunities	*Annual minimum family income* through income maintenance or a negative income tax	Poverty is not merely a result of income insufficiency. It also involves lack of housing, educational opportunities, and political influence. Marginal improvements in income will not solve these problems.
Opportunities	*Institutional change:* Changes in the entire welfare system (extend to nonblack and rural poor); community self-help and action programs	These kinds of changes are expensive and complicated and often lead to more bureaucratization and government influence without appreciable success.

The debate continues. Many social scientists and community leaders feel that what is needed is a mix of the two strategies. However, the reluctance of the public to support such an effort makes this difficult. Furthermore, some feel that recommendations for such complex "complementary strategies" can too easily become a mask for failing to come to grips with the problem of poverty and deciding priorities. What do you think? [See James L. Sundquist, Ed., *On Fighting Poverty: Perspectives from Experience* (New York: Basic Books, 1969).]

SOCIAL MOBILITY AND SOCIAL STRAIN

As Vander Zanden's study implies, a major factor in creating strains within systems of social stratification is *mobility*. In other words, the manner in which individuals and subgroups can or cannot move within a prevailing status system can create personal and collective feelings of anxiety. This is especially true if actual mobility, or the lack of it, seems in contrast to widely accepted norms and values. For example, the rags-to-riches, Horatio Alger ideal is seldom realized, even in relatively open societies like contemporary America. The much publicized success of a few Americans simply overdramatizes the possibilities for other citizens.

As a matter of fact, our society idealizes goals that most of us will never reach. The American dream does not come true for many, which results not only in widespread frustration and feelings of failure but also in various types of deviant behavior. As sociologist Robert Merton [1938, pp. 672–682] indicates, our society sets up goals of success (measured primarily in monetary rewards) but denies the means to those goals to many of its citizens (see Chapter 12). The goals–means crisis encourages some people to resort to illegal means (traditional or white-collar crime) to try to achieve the "impossible dream." Others give up the struggle and turn to forms of escape, such as alcoholism, dope addiction, religious extremism, and living in isolated communities. Still others try to change the whole American emphasis upon success goals and the means necessary to reach them by using forms of revolutionary social action. These types of responses to strains can be better understood by first considering the various types of social mobility associated with different kinds of status systems.

Types of Mobility

Social mobility can be categorized according to whether a society's status system is based upon achieved or ascribed criteria, that is, whether the society is open or closed. At the beginning of this chapter, the distinction was made between four different types of stratification systems—the caste, estate, class, and mixed systems. Figure 6-2 illustrates the mobility patterns in each of these systems.

FIGURE 6-2 Types of Mobility in Caste, Estate, Class, and Mixed Societies

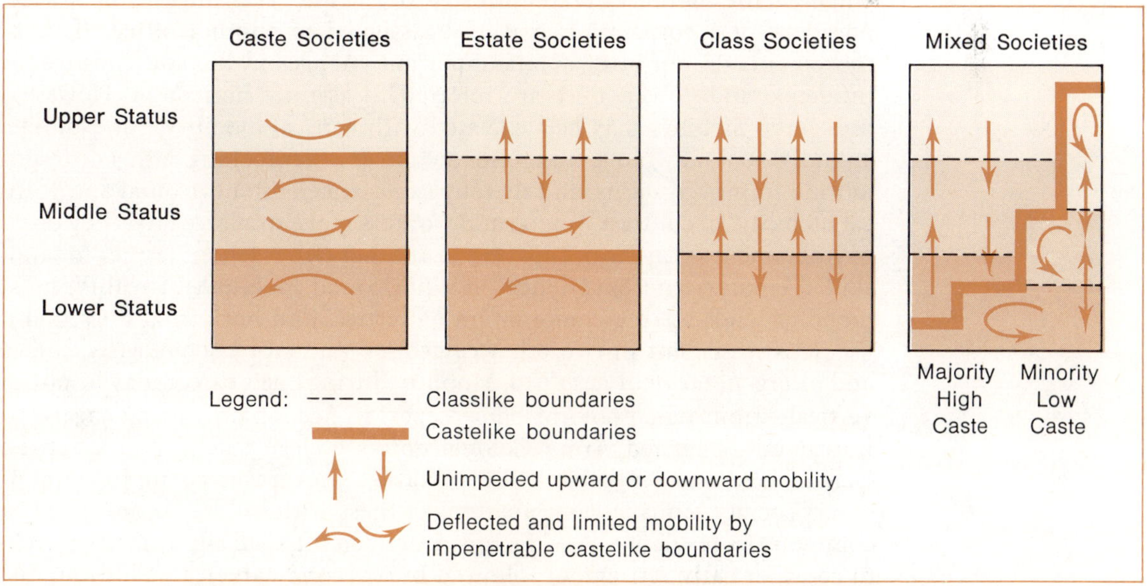

From Seymour M. Lipset, Martin A. Trow, and James S. Coleman, *Union Democracy* (New York: The Free Press, 1956).

In closed caste societies, mobility of individuals and subgroups is limited to movement only within prescribed status levels. In societies based upon estate systems, mobility is possible only in the upper statuses, while mobility in the lower status is confined to that level. Open class societies, in contrast, theoretically provide for relatively free mobility between all status levels. Finally, mixed societies, like the contemporary United States, show evidence of all of these patterns. These types of patterns are often referred to as *vertical mobility*, in which movement may be *downward* as well as *upward*. We will return to the special problem of downward mobility, sometimes called *skidding*, in the next section of this chapter.

What determines the extent and direction of vertical mobility is, of course, the degree to which individuals and subgroups can manipulate or control their assigned status characteristics. In closed societies, ascribed criteria, like family or racial origin, are difficult to alter, although to a limited degree people may marry above or below their inherited status or try to "pass" from a racial minority to a racial majority. In open societies, achieved criteria, like education and occupation, are more subject to personal control. One might be able to seek new employment or attain a higher level of formal education. One might also lose a job or find that a previously attained educational specialty is no longer needed in the job market and, thereby, experience downward mobility.

The diagram of types of vertical mobility given in Figure 6-2 also suggests a second major category—*horizontal mobility*. This is movement of individuals and subgroups from one position to another without a significant change up or down in the system of stratification. For example, an automobile worker may leave a job in Detroit, Michigan, to seek new employment in the aircraft industry of Seattle, Washington, or a vice-president of a corporation may be reassigned to another office. If these movements do not bring about important changes in income, prestige, or influence and power, they are referred to as only horizontal. However, horizontal mobility may be associated with vertical mobility. For example, an individual may move from one town to another seeking both a different job and improved status, and thereby experience both horizontal and vertical mobility. In contrast, when rural workers move to a large city, they often go from one low-paying occupation to another (from tenant farmer to semiskilled laborer) and experience only horizontal mobility. In reality, most mobility tends to be a combination of vertical and horizontal movement.

This is evident in two other categories studied by sociologists, *career* and *intergenerational mobility*. Mobility during one's career may be either vertical—from office boy, to bookkeeper, to accountant, to manager—or horizontal—a retired Army Colonel enters college teaching or a retired General becomes a member of a corporation's governing board. In contemporary society, unusual combinations of these patterns are becoming more common as a result of several factors. Extended life span allows many people to consider early retirement followed by a second career. In addition, dissatisfaction with present employment has led many people to shift occupations relatively early in their careers. For example, a Sylvania employee was offered a vice-presidency. He turned the job down, feeling that he would be "trapped" in a dull job with salary and prestige so high that he could not afford to change occupations in the future. He resigned from Sylvania, moved to New Hampshire, and became an innkeeper.

Intergenerational mobility illustrates the same fixed patterns. This concept refers to social mobility from one generation of a family to another. Studies [Bendix and Lipset, 1953, pp. 424–425] indicate that the children of unskilled and semiskilled workers are least likely to move out of their father's occupational status. In other words, they are most likely to experience only horizontal mobility and least likely to experience vertical mobility. In contrast, the children of farmers and farm laborers are likely to become proprietors, managers, and professionals, and the children of skilled workers are likely to become clerks, salespeople, and professionals. It is important to note that these findings reflect tendencies only and that some intergenerational mobility will be downward. Some of the children of semiskilled workers will become unskilled workers, as will some of the children of farmers.

Much sociological research has focused upon strains created by achievement ideologies and upward mobility. This approach originates to some extent in the tacit Horatio Alger dream that characterizes contemporary class societies. A newer perspective has developed in recent years, however, that focuses on the strains created by downward mobility or skidding.

Downward Mobility: The Strains of Skidding

In periods of relative prosperity, downward mobility has not appeared to be very significant. Yet there is evidence that a significant portion of the urban labor force, particularly the urban working class, may fall into this category. That is, they are manual workers who have nonmanual backgrounds and have, therefore, fallen from a higher to a lower social status. Other research indicates that, at any one time in contemporary American society, a third of that total work force is upwardly mobile while another third is skidding. Harold Wilensky and Hugh Edwards [1959, pp. 215–231] have suggested that the manual worker experiencing downward mobility represents perhaps a fifth of the working class of urban background and almost a tenth of all urbanites in the labor force, with larger proportions in times of recession. It is obvious, therefore, that the strains created by skidding are considerable even in apparently stable social systems.

Wilensky and Edwards studied the nature and consequences of these strains among workers in two large factories in a small Midwestern city of 15,000 population, in the fall of 1951. Questionnaires were filled out anonymously by 2499 nonsupervisory employees—virtually all of the manual workers—in the Rockwell Company. The strains of skidding were disclosed in two major findings. All skidders were more traditional in their values and beliefs regarding the American status system than were nonskidders. For example, a large proportion of downwardly mobile workers:

1. Rejected identification with the working class and aspired to a middle-class position for themselves.
2. Believed in an open class system and in ability as the proper basis for promotion.
3. Anticipated leaving the factory soon and expected their children to achieve middle-class positions.
4. Said they would accept the job of foreman if it was offered to them.

In other words, skidders did not become acculturated into their new status position and were reluctant to become a part of their new social level. They retained their preference for middle-class values and, therefore, were unlikely to join in working-class protests of the status quo or action programs for social change. Furthermore, *skidders tended to develop greater feelings of status marginality and insecurity* than did nonskidders. In addition, while younger skidders were less apt to identify with the middle class, older skidders not only tended to deny failure but also felt urgency about the limited time they had to climb back into a former status. Finally, skidders tended to be less interested in horizontal mobility as an alternative to vertical mobility, with one exception: Skidders were more likely than nonskidders to accept jobs as foremen willingly. This position symbolized the power and authority of management. Therefore, while rejecting strong ties with the working class, some skidders exhibited conflicting and vacillating attitudes with regard to the values of the American stratification system.

The findings of Wilensky and Edwards were not unlike the responses of Ku Klux Klan members in Vander Zanden's study. Downwardly mobile workers experienced strains that necessitated some form of personal adaptation. Klansmen adapted through overconformity and extremism; Rockwell Company skidders adapted through conservatism, commitment to middle-class ideology, and rejection of identification with the working class. This latter form of adaptation has both dysfunctions and functions—disadvantages and advantages—for the larger social system. On the negative side, it can help shut off criticism of the status quo and it can weaken working-class movements that seek greater influence and equality. On the positive side, it can help avoid extremist political commitment among skidding manual workers in the form of left-wing (Symbionese Liberation Army) or right-wing (Klan) activities, where such extremism could threaten other American social values and beliefs.

In a recent study, Paula Leventman [1974] went beyond previous research on skidding in several ways. She analyzed the impact of *unemployment,* as a form of "temporary" skidding, *upon high-status technical professionals.* Her sample came from the aerospace and electronics industries in the Boston metropolitan area. She estimated that about 21 percent of the professionals in these industries had experienced unemployment for varying lengths of time from the late 1960s to the early 1970s, as a result of cuts in defense spending and other changing economic policies. Leventman suggests that this type of upper-middle- and upper-class skidding may become more common as changes in the modern bureaucratic state-controlled economy become necessary.

Leventman found that her sample, somewhat unlike the Rockwell skidders, generally rejected any social class identity. About 300 respondents were studied through participant observation, and one hundred were analyzed through three hour in-depth interviews. The interviews disclosed that 53 percent refused to classify themselves using the concept of class, while 23 and 17 percent identified with the upper-middle and middle class, respectively. At the same time, 47 percent of the sample studied felt that income was the most important criteria of social differences, and 81 percent identified with managerial, professional, and technical occupations. In addition, an overwhelming proportion had high status ambitions for their children. For this group, then, although class was a relatively unimportant concept, there was a sharp awareness of status inequalities, particularly economic, in the American system.

Again, somewhat in contrast to previous studies of manual worker threatened by status loss, the downwardly mobile technical professionals exhibited marked *ambivalence* in many of their attitudes and beliefs. Political disillusionment, rather than political radicalism of either the right or the left, was characteristic. George Wallace's presidential candidacy received no support, and although they exhibited some alienation from the traditional parties, many supported Richard Nixon as a traditional conservative. There was also some support for Eugene McCarthy and George McGovern. Most blamed the economic and foreign policy programs of the federal government for the problems with the economy. There was a strong commitment to rationality, that is, to a belief that economic problems could be avoided through planned policies and through a rejection of merely playing politics in favor of rational management of social problems.

Ambivalence was also found by Leventman in attitudes about what should be done to avoid severe economic dislocation in the future. Just under half the interviewed sample of 100 (about 40 percent) supported the development of unions for technical professionals. Others rejected this option since it symbolized identification with traditional working-class interests. Many favored social services for unemployed professionals, pointing out that available government aid (food stamps, financial assistance) tended to be provided only for the lower statuses. Still others rejected these solutions, which were also traditionally associated with the lower classes. Many of the unemployed professionals formed self-help organizations (to seek other employment, to gain new training, and so on) to substitute for the lack of government assistance.

As these studies of downward mobility indicate, movement in any direction within a status system can create major strains in the form of feelings of status marginality and inconsistency. If these strains are unrecognized and adaptations are not available to those suffering from them, the consequences for society can be severe. The following sections of this chapter consider some of the ways in which societies attempt to manage social strains.

Managing Social Strain

One way in which societies manage tensions is through social mechanisms that counterbalance or soften the effect of strain. For example, ours is a society in which social welfare programs attempt to ensure that the majority of citizens have enough material goods and services to live comfortably. And while we do have many families living in poverty, they do not usually experience the kind of dire poverty where many people are born, beg, and die on the streets. Welfare programs keep the most disadvantaged from the kind of begging and suffering that is so often observable in many underdeveloped regions of the world.

Furthermore, in many ways, our middle-class culture makes the recognition of status distinctions difficult, since there are few external public symbols definitely attributable to a certain status. Everyone dresses in a similar way. We drive automobiles that are mass-produced in similar styles and take advantage of public parks and recreational services, whether we are from the working or middle class. Class lines in highly urban societies are not rigid and clear-cut. In traditional India, it was quite clear where the line was drawn between one caste and another. People dressed according to caste position and treated each other with appropriate etiquette. Similarly, in a feudal society, the behavioral distinctions between serf and nobility were clear and unchanging.

Another mechanism that has reduced strain is unionization, as evidenced by the comment: "The working man is getting more pay than I am in a white-collar job." Organized labor has increased wage and fringe benefits of blue-collar occupations so that income alone is no longer a reliable measure of differences in social class. Still another strain-reducing mechanism is our system of education, which has become more available to all status levels. Public junior and community colleges, state colleges, and universities have made advanced education financially possible for more and more youths from lower social-class levels (see the discussion in Chapter 10). Social institutions, such as welfare, labor, and education, therefore, often play a major, though indirect, role in managing the strain of status distinctions in societies. In order to examine this process in more detail, we have selected one particularly interesting illustration—religion—to discuss in the last section of this chapter.

The Special Example of Religion

Lipset and Bendix [1960], in a study of social class in industrial society, singled out two mechanisms of adaptation to strain—education and religion. As a phenomenon appearing in all human societies, religion functions somewhat differently than education. Its beliefs and practices not only reinforce the norms of the society and thereby contribute to orderly behavior and conformity but also help to make life bearable for individuals in the face of crises like personal failure, suffering, and death. Most of us feel deprived and defeated in one way or another. We may, at these times, turn to religion for comfort and assurance. When individuals feel most deprived and defeated, they are most apt to turn to some form of religious expression. The church is an institution that offers certain answers to perplexing questions about the meaning of life and death; furthermore, it can also be a kind of second family group. In the church, many feel surrounded by friends who really understand them and continue to accept them even when the stress of life is defeating. In fact, much of the time people find in the church a place of *recreation*, in the several meanings of that word (see the discussion in Chapter 10).

As we have seen, striking status differences exist among the churches in America. Some have greater appeal to people with lower levels of education and social status. These are the holiness sects which emphasize spiritual status rather than social status; their thrust is toward the final judgment day, when "the last shall be first," and the despised of this earth shall be the elite of heaven. Those who suffer economic deprivation in our society also are most apt to turn to holiness sects with this type of appeal when they go to church. By way of contrast, the more established denominations, like the Methodist and Presbyterian churches along with many Catholic and Jewish congregations, tend to appeal to people who as a rule do not suffer economic deprivation. However, even more privileged citizens in our society suffer from some sense of deprivation. One of the most common problems of urban life is that of rootlessness and loneliness. This problem is closely related to Durkheim's concept of anomie. Thus some people turn to the church as a place to put down social roots and create identity in the impersonal urban world.

To be sure, there are other forms of deprivation. Some people are troubled about their health; others are perplexed about social injustices and ethical issues; still others ask for answers to the philosophical questions of why we are here and where we are going. Although other groups help people adapt to these deprivations (hospitals, political parties, fraternal organizations), religion continues to be one of the most important mechanisms for managing the strains of deprivation. For example, Lipset and Bendix [1960, p. 263] describe the relationship between educational deprivation and religion. Religious beliefs may either (1) teach that the good rather than the rich will be rewarded in an afterlife or (2) encourage a high degree of child-centeredness, through which parents seek satisfaction in their high aspirations for their children, although their own personal goals have not been achieved. Both of these philosophies can be interpreted as different ways of safeguarding society against instability:

6-3 Are Methods for Managing Social Strain Effective?

All status systems must deal with the problem of social strain. Strains are created when individuals fail to live up to personal or public expectations, experience downward mobility, feel they are unjustly deprived of deserved rewards, or find that it is not possible for them to succeed regardless of personal abilities. A variety of social mechanisms and institutions arise to offset or counterbalance these strains. However, each method creates special problems.

Income tax regulations frequently incorporate special provisions for groups that feel they are not being sufficiently rewarded for their work. For example, salesmen and college professors can deduct travel expenses for business purposes. Problems with this method include the following: tax deductions can be misused (vacation travel becomes business travel by merely attending a meeting for a few hours); tax loopholes frequently favor those who are already privileged (oil depletion allowances).

Elsa Dorfman

The **social welfare system** is a method for cushioning the shock of downward mobility, which can be caused by loss of job because of aging, illness, or widespread unemployment. Problems with this method include the following: welfare benefits are insufficient to sustain many deprived citizens (massive unemployment during a depression); benefits do not apply equally to all needy groups (the rural poor); the system for dispensing benefits becomes bureaucratized and depersonalized (exacerbating the social strains of deprivation).

P. Hollander Gross/Stock, Boston

United Press International

Unionization and collective bargaining can provide groups who feel they are being left behind in the scramble for rewards with a feeling of unity and strength and with some economic security. Problems with this method include the following: some unions become undemocratic and leaders function to protect their own rather than members' interests (see Study 7); unionization may carry with it the stigma of permanent working-class status (for this reason some professionals, like college professors, have been reluctant to unionize); union-obtained benefits (higher wages, a strike fund) may be insufficient in times of rapid change or extreme crisis (a high rate of inflation, a protracted strike).

Evangelical religious sects and churches often cushion the shock of deprivation for members of castes by providing a sense of belonging, the feeling that an uplifted spirit is more important than material circumstances, and the belief in salvation through God. Problems with this method include the following: the emphasis upon separate identity and experiences can make it difficult to bring about required changes (Karl Marx suggested that religion can be a soporific); emotional release through enthusiastic participation may divert deprived peoples' attentions from the need for social and political action (sometimes a charismatic leader such as Martin Luther King can mobilize this enthusiasm for action).

N. Sapieha/Stock, Boston

In America, for example, the depressed strata seem to have turned to evangelical religion rather than to radical politics. . . . It is in societies of Europe and Asia where less emphasis is placed on equality of opportunity that left-wing political movements are strong among the lower strata—presumably because they teach that traditional inequalities can be done away with by changing the social system. In general, it seems to be true that the depressed and the failures who have little hope of individual success have a strong faith either in radical politics or in an emotional religiosity, so that almost nowhere are the lower classes both moderate in their politics *and* indifferent to religion.

The role of religion in managing social strain seems so important that many sociologists have turned to a scientific study of it in recent years. A provocative theoretical perspective has been developed by Glock and his colleagues. They assume that the people most likely to turn to various forms of religious expression are those who are most deprived. This assumption does not imply that religion is solely for the weak, since many devout church members appear to be strong and successful. It does imply, however, that the most deprived are most apt to be religious and that all human beings are deprived in one way or another. For example, the popularity of the recent "Jesus Revolution" and other evangelical communal religious movements among the young may relate to youthful feelings of being deprived. The following study describes the continuing research of Glock and his colleagues on this issue.

▶ STUDY 6

A Deprivation Theory of Religion [1965 and 1967][1]

Problem

Previous social research [Niebuhr, 1929; Troeltsch, 1931; Weber, 1930] has indicated that social-class differences were partly responsible for the development of two very different types of religious movements—the sect and the church. The *sect* is a religious movement arising among the lower class in protest against the established church, which has permitted status differences to arise and, subsequently, has rejected the deprived. The sect differs from the church in that it is marked by spontaneous relationships of a small fellowship-type group and emphasizes conversion and a literal interpretation of scripture. It proves functional for the economically and politically deprived by fulfilling their need for group life and

[1]Adapted from *Religion and Social Conflict,* edited by Robert and Martin E. Marty, copyright © 1964 by Oxford University Press, Inc., by permission; and Charles Y. Glock, Benjamin B. Ringer, and Earl R. Babbie, "A Theory of Involvement," *To Comfort and To Challenge,* copyright © 1967 by the Regents of the University of California, by permission of the University of California Press.

recreation, and by giving them a sense of worth. If the meek cannot inherit the earth, at least they can be first in the kingdom of heaven.

Enthusiastic preaching ensures the sect's followers that they are the spiritual elite. The promise of future rewards also has the effect of draining off discontent with earthly injustices that might erupt into aggressive radicalism. The sect phenomenon was especially evident in Great Britain among separatist movements like the Methodists, and it came to play a prominent role as revival religion on the American frontier.

As time passes, sects evolve into formalized denominational *churches*. This transformation occurs partly because sectlike qualities encourage personal disciplines that eventually lead to upward social mobility. More and more followers, therefore, come from middle or upper statuses, and they bring with them new attitudes, needs, and life-styles. An educated clergy, a more formal worship service, and more compromise with the demands of the secular world further transform the sect into a church.

Glock and his colleagues wanted to broaden this sociological theory to answer additional questions. What *specific kinds of experiences* do religions develop in order to meet the needs of those who feel deprived? Is it possible that *secular* movements and organizations can also supply such experiences? And, finally, can *the relationship between deprivation and religious behavior* be measured?

Hypotheses and Study Design

Glock and his colleagues theorized that there were *five types of deprivation* (economic, social, organismic, ethical, and psychic) that demand some form of social response, either religious or secular. All five types were seen as deriving from people's inability to meet prescribed standards. Individuals or groups could feel deprived by failing to meet either of the following:

1. *Society's Standards*: One might feel disadvantaged in contrast to other individuals and groups in terms of not living up to society's overall expectations or goals. The first three types of deprivation (economic, social, and organismic) tend to be socially derived.
2. *Their Own Standards*: One might feel disadvantaged in terms of not living up to personal expectations and goals. The last two types of deprivation tend to be personally derived.

Furthermore, the researchers felt that movements, whether religious or secular, tended to follow one of *three basic patterns*: (1) They emerged, flowered, and then died; (2) they survived indefinitely in substantially their original form; or (3) they survived in a form radically different than the original one (for example, changed from sect to church). The particular pattern would be determined by the type of deprivation, how the movement dealt with it, and the degree to which the deprivation persisted as a continuing source of anxiety.

Because of the tentative nature of the theory and hypotheses to be tested and because there was little previous research from which empirical data could be drawn, the study design varied from the usual social scientific approaches. Glock and his colleagues utilized the typology of deprivation to *explain* various types of religious and secular movements.

Methods of Data Collection

The typology, which amounts to a deprivation theory of religion, was tested both *historically and sociologically*. For example, does history show that particular sects and churches arose during periods characterized by one or more hypothesized types of deprivation? Also, according to what we know about strains in systems of social stratification, does the typology make sense?

Data were also collected during 1951 and 1952 from a nationwide sample of Episcopalians from 234 congregations, including both ministers and lay persons. A measure of religious involvement was developed that indicated how strongly Episcopalians were committed to the church's ritual, literature, educational activities, and the like. This was correlated with age, sex, and family variables to determine if those who were most deprived tended to be most committed, and those least deprived, least committed.

Findings and Interpretations

Analysis of historical records indicates that religious and secular movements are likely to arise in response to the five types of deprivation when feelings of being disadvantaged are shared, no other solutions are perceived, and leadership emerges with innovating ideas. Examples of these movements are summarized in Table 6-5.

When the source of deprivation is economic, social, or organismic, a resulting movement is likely to be religious only if the type of deprivation is inadequately understood and specific action seems hopeless. In the case of ethical deprivation, however, both religious and secular movements may be equally effective. Psychic deprivation calls for religious and secular responses involving a transcendental power, which is needed to solve the problem. Social deprivation tends to be met adequately by both religious groups and a variety of secular organizations.

In addition, history indicates that movements arising out of economic deprivation tend to be short-lived. Few sects survive as sects because economic conditions (their prime cause) change; furthermore, sects themselves help to overcome the deprivation of the followers. Likewise, organismic deprivation produces movements that last only until new knowledge about causes and treatment of mental or physical disorders is discovered. The Sister Kenny movement flourished until medical science was able to cope with polio. Ethical deprivation tends to be subject to fads. A long-term trend like secularism in urban society may call for a continuing religious movement like Unitarianism. Many citizens, however, do not suffer from ethical deprivation but accept the dominant value system. Cults that deal with psychic deprivation are also momentary movements unless, like Christian Science, they relieve social deprivation as well. The most persistent need within modern society appears to be social deprivation, which according to Glock's theory, accounts best for the continuing presence of churches in a society that is so overwhelmingly secular.

The contention that a major function of church participation is to relieve members' feelings of deprivation is made here primarily on theoretical grounds. Some empirical support, however, was found in the study of Episcopalians. Those who appeared to be most deprived and rejected by the general society were those who were most deeply involved in the church. Glock and associates found that 75 spouseless childless parishioners had the highest measure of involvement in church activities, compared to 593 married parishioners with children who had the lowest measure of involvement. Furthermore, age and sex differences played

TABLE 6-5 Religious and Secular Movements by Source and Type of Deprivation

Source of Deprivation	Type of Deprivation	Examples of Religious Responses	Examples of Secular Responses[a]
Society's standards	Economic (money, clothes, food)	Sects (symbolically revolutionary)	Consumer lobbies, unionization, extremist action groups (SLA, KKK), widespread retreatism and self-destructive behavior (crime, alcohol abuse)
Society's standards	Social (sense of belonging, involvement, and relatedness)	Churches (providing a sense of belonging)	NAACP, fraternal clubs, womens' liberation, Townsend Movement, sports organizations, occupational groups, societies for owners of trailer homes
Society's standards	Organismic (physical and mental health)	Healing cults and special groups within churches (Christian Science, Unity)	Society for the Blind, Crippled Children's Society, Cancer Society, Heart Association, Alcoholics Anonymous, Synanon
One's own standards	Ethical (concern with right and wrong, good and bad)	Religious fads and ethical movements (Zen Buddhism, Ethical Culture, Unitarianism)	Planned Parenthood League, American Civil Liberties Union, civil rights groups, communes, environmental protection movements
One's own standards	Psychic (level of consciousness and awareness)	Momentary ethical movement and fad (Theosophy, I AM Cult, Vedanta)	Momentary social fadism like Unidentified Flying Object societies, Yoga, transcendental meditation, and sensitivity groups

[a]Secular solutions are sometimes referred to as functional alternatives to religion.
Source: Charles Y. Glock and Rodney Stark, "The Origins and Evolution of Religious Groups," *Religion and Society in Tension* (Chicago: Rand McNally & Co., 1965), Chap. 5.

an important role. For men between the ages of 30 and 50, those without wives or children were more involved than those who were married and had children. Though both younger men and women (30 years and under) were relatively uninvolved, older women had consistently higher involvement than older men.

The extremes of involvement are best visualized by seeing the wealthy young man with a family at one end of the scale and the poor elderly widow at the other. Clearly, all of the rewards and gratifications that society has to offer are readily accessible to the former while they are almost wholly withheld from the latter. Furthermore, men in our society, especially in their most productive years (from ages 35 to 55), obtain many of the rewards of status outside of family and church. For women, on the other hand, feelings of deprivation can become a problem as the children grow up and move away, particularly if they do not have careers of their own. This preliminary analysis, then, seems to indicate that *those who feel most deprived tend to have a higher degree of church involvement than those who feel least deprived.*

Conclusions and Implications

The deprivation theory does not answer all the questions about why people are religious. This study, an example of on-going research, is only a beginning. Not only is the sample of respondents limited, but the measures of involvement and deprivation are not as rigorous as they ought to be. Much more needs to be done in the scientific study of religion before we can achieve an adequate understanding of this dimension of human behavior. Nevertheless, it is clear that social status is an important variable in religious behavior, especially in so far as religious institutions and movements provide channels for managing the problems of strain in a class society.

Societies provide strain-management mechanisms, in the form of social institutions and movements, in order to avoid the risk of violent conflict and extremist behavior; however, this response is not without its own risks. By reducing strain and frustration, societies may redirect human energies away from productive social reform and, thereby, perpetuate inequities in existing status systems. The challenge to most societies is to provide opportunities for both adaptation and constructive social conflict (see Chapter 14). For example, much of the current revolution in American churches such as the Catholic "underground church" movement and the involvement of Protestant clergy in the social reform activities, is an attempt to seek this effective balance [Hadden, 1970; Stark *et al.*, 1971].

CONCLUSION

This chapter has considered status groupings as a second major form of group behavior. Stratification develops when individuals and groups are differentiated and then ranked in a hierarchy. The concept of status refers to the general ranking position of a social role in the resulting system of stratification. Sociologists have identified four basic kinds of status systems—closed castes, partly closed and partly open estates, open classes, and mixed. If the criteria for ranking individuals, roles, and groups are ascribed (inherited), the system is closed. If the criteria are achieved (earned), the system is open.

Functionalists argue that stratification is necessary as one of the ways in which all societies try to maintain some form of stability. Rewarding some roles in terms of more income, power, prestige, or fringe benefits assures that the most important, difficult, and demanding tasks will be accomplished. In short, the best qualified and most motivated individuals will be atracted to the most important roles. The difficulty with the functionalist argument is that it applies largely to the middle levels of open systems, and, even in these statuses, opportunity is frequently unavailable to many well-qualified citizens.

In contrast, conflict theorists argue that stratification systems exist primarily to serve the vested interests of the wealthy and powerful. Since the resources and rewards of any society are limited at any one moment in history, it is in the interests of a few to monopolize these benefits. As a consequence, radical theorists like Marx saw class conflict as inevitable. The problem is that class warfare has not developed in many contemporary societies, and, therefore, open conflict over status differences apparently is not inevitable.

One of the reasons that open conflict does not arise is that life-styles and life-chances are not necessarily distributed throughout a society in precise relationship to other indicators of status. For example, the rich do not necessarily obtain all the benefits of high status, and the poor are not necessarily deprived of all the benefits. American blacks have made some gains in income and education in recent years, although they have made few gains in power during the same period. At the same time, possession of high status does not necessarily bring great power, and the possession of power does not necessarily bring public acceptance of authority.

Another reason why conflict is not inevitable in status systems is that societies, groups, and individuals develop ways of managing or softening the strains of status, particularly those strains created by mobility within the system. Feelings of frustration resulting from injustices, marginality, and status inconsistency are often expressed by overconformity to accepted middle-class values, extremist behavior, or participation in religious and secular movements. Indeed, societies often call upon their basic institutions, like schools or churches, to perform the function of managing status strains, as the deprivation theory of religion illustrates. The risk of this type of strain management is that it may be so effective that serious inequities in existing status systems may go unrecognized or unresolved.

This consideration of status groupings sets the stage for the next chapter—a discussion of a third major form of group behavior, associations. Not only do associations often reflect the status structure of a society, but they also frequently become ways in which people compensate for the strains they experience, as exemplified by the American predilection to "joining."

REFERENCES

Bales, Robert F. *Interaction Process Analysis.* Cambridge: Addison–Wesley, 1950.

Bendix, Reinhard, and S. M. Lipset, Eds. *Class, Status and Power.* New York: The Free Press, 1953.

Blau, Peter. *Exchange and Power in Social Life.* New York: John Wiley and Sons, 1964.

The Boston Globe. "Blacks Lose Income But Gain Educationally," (28 July 1975), Editorial.

Bureau of the Census. *Money, Income and Poverty Status of Families and Persons in the U.S.—1974.* Washington, D.C.: U.S. Government Printing Office, 1974.

————. *Current Population Survey—1975.* Washington, D.C.: U.S. Government Printing Office, 1975.

Davis, Kingsley, and Wilbert E. Moore. "Some Principles of Stratification," *American Sociological Review, 10* (April 1945), pp. 242–249.

Delaney, Paul. "Blacks are 20% of Boston But Have Limited Power," *The New York Times* (15 September 1975), p. 10.

Hadden, Jeffrey K. *The Gathering Storm in the Churches.* Garden City, N.Y.: Doubleday and Company, 1970.

Homans, George C. *Social Behavior.* New York: Harcourt, Brace and World, 1961.

Kimberly, James C. "The Emergence and Stabilization of Stratification in Simple and Complex Social Systems," *Sociological Inquiry, 40* (Spring 1970), pp. 73–101.

Leventman, Paula Goldman. "The Technical Professional: A Study in Career Disillusionment," unpublished Ph.D. thesis, Bryn Mawr College, Bryn Mawr, Pennsylvania, 1974.

Lipset, Seymour, and Reinhard Bendix. *Social Mobility in Industrial Society.* Berkeley: University of California Press, 1960.

Lydall, Harold. *The Structure of Earnings.* London: Oxford University Press, 1968.

Merton, Robert K. "Social Structure and Anomie," *American Sociological Review,* 3 (October 1938), pp. 672–682.

Niebuhr, H. Richard. *The Social Sources of Denominationalism.* New York: Henry Holt and Company, 1929.

Onis, Juan de. "Oil Wealth Building a Favored Class in 'Socialist' Iraq," *The New York Times* (6 August 1975), p. 43ff.

Pease, John, William H. Form, and Joan Huber Rytina. "Ideological Currents in American Stratification Literature," *The American Sociologist, 5* (May 1970), pp. 127–137.

Stark, Rodney, Bruce D. Foster, Charles Y. Glock, and Harold E. Quinley. *Wayward Shepherds: Prejudice and the Protestant Clergy.* New York: Harper & Row, Publishers, 1971.

Thibaut, John W., and Harold H. Kelley. *The Social Psychology of Groups.* New York: John Wiley and Sons, 1961.

Troeltsch, Ernst. *The Social Teachings of the Christian Churches.* New York: The Macmillan Company, 1931.

Vander Zanden, James W. "The Klan Revival," *The American Journal of Sociology, 65* (March 1960), pp. 456–462.

Warner, W. Lloyd, and Paul S. Lunt. *The Social Life of a Modern Community.* New Haven: Yale University Press, 1941.

Weber, Max. *The Protestant Ethic and the Spirit of Capitalism.* London: George Allen & Unwin, 1930.

————. *From Max Weber: Essays in Sociology.* H. H. Gerth and C. W. Mills, Ed. and Transl. New York: Oxford University Press, 1946.

———. *The Theory of Social and Economic Organization*. New York: The Free Press, 1957.

Wilensky, Harold L., and Hugh Edwards. "The Skidder: Ideological Adjustments of Downward Mobile Workers," *American Sociological Review, 24* (April 1959), pp. 215–231.

Wirth, Louis. "Social Stratification and Social Mobility in the United States," *Current Sociology, 2,* No. 4 (1953–1954), pp. 279–303.

- Observers have often said that Americans are "joiners." What does this mean, and why are they?
- Why is it that, in most clubs, a few people seem to run things?
- Are fraternities and sororities democratic? Labor unions? Churches?
- A few years ago, at a very large university, the students put through registration for a pet dog. They even considered carrying him through to graduation. How might this be possible and why is it so much fun for students to play such a prank?
- What is your impression of bureacracy? Of a bureaucrat?
- Do you agree with the following descriptions of bureaucrats and bureaucracy?

  Brooks Atkinson [1951]: "The perfect bureaucrat everywhere is the man who manages to make no decisions and escape all responsibility."

  Alexander Ostrovsky [1868]: "It's all papers and forms, the entire Civil Service is like a fortress made of papers, forms and red tape."
- If bureaucracy is so evil and corrupting, why do we put up with it?

7

Associations

These kinds of questions have concerned sociologists since Max Weber observed:

> The man of today is without doubt an association man (*Vereinsmensch*) in an awful and never dreamed of degree. . . . What is, qualitatively considered, the association-land par excellence? Without doubt America. . . . [Weber, 1911, pp. 52–50].

Weber goes on to observe that a fundamental task of sociology is to study those structures conventionally called "social" (*gesellschaftliche*). By this, Weber meant all those human groupings that lay between politically organized and recognized powers (states, municipalities, and established church) on the one hand, and the primarylike natural community of the family, on the other. Thus, he saw the sociology of associations—the study of the bowling club, the political party, and the religious, artistic, or literary sect—as crucial. In fact, Weber was one of the first scholars to foresee the many problems associated with modern bureaucracy. At a time when many warned against a dictatorship of the proletariat, Weber spoke of the possibility of a dictatorship of bureaucrats. In this chapter, we will consider the importance of associations as groups that stand between the *impersonal* controls of big government and other large-scale organizations and the *personal* controls of family and close friends. The following list describes this relationship:

Tertiary Controls: Top levels of impersonal control, often far removed from individual members of a society or organization.

Secondary Controls: Voluntary *associations* standing between the top levels of leadership and the grass-roots membership of a nation or a large organization.

Primary Controls: Individuals in primary groups like the family and friendship groups.

Associations can be defined, therefore, as groups that are more formal and highly organized than collectivities; perform specialized functions for their members; and combine both spontaneous and structured forms of human behavior. They are small societies made up of workers, rank and file members, leaders, and patrons. Associations may range in size from relatively small social or recreational clubs to large-scale organizations. Their diversity, importance, and complexity becomes clear when we suggest the following examples of associations:

Recreational groups (bowling, softball, bridge clubs, and leagues).

Lodges (Elks, Moose, Masons, and similar groups).

Service groups (Rotary, Lions, Kiwanis).

Political organizations (political parties, special pressure groups).

Business organizations (the local hardware store, large corporations like American Telephone and Telegraph).

Labor unions (the United Auto Workers).

Religious denominations (Baptist, Roman Catholic, Orthodox Jewish, and many others).

Involvement in an association differs according to whether one is a paid worker on the staff, an active member, or a contributing patron. Whereas patrons, members, and even directors may have nominal and loose ties with an association, a salaried employee, especially in a large association, may become part of a highly formal and complex *bureaucratic* system. An association takes on bureaucratic characteristics when much of its work is turned over to specialized administrators, who operate according to prescribed rules and regulations. Efficiency is the manifest goal of bureaucratic organization in spite of the tendency on the part of bureaucrats to become rigid and to lack initiative and resourcefulness. In other words, an association is a bureaucratic organization that becomes highly structured and formalized, while maintaining, at the same time, many elements of informality.

Later in this chapter we will have much to say about the two faces of bureaucracy—the formal and the informal—and how this duality affects group structure and behavior. The line of authority, channels of communication, and means of control in an association can be clearly delineated by the preparation of an "org (organization) chart." Such charts symbolize formal structure and rational social roles. On the other hand, human behavior does not conform strictly to formal expectations. Interaction is often spontaneous and emotional; consequently, in any study of associations, it is extremely important to analyze the unplanned primary ties and the human feelings of friendship and animosity that also play an important role.

We will begin our analysis of associations by examining their development as a major form of group behavior in contemporary society, a development so dramatic that it has been termed the "organizational revolution" by some observers. Our analysis raises the question of who has power in modern associations and whether associational groupings contribute to or undermine the maintenance of democratic processes. The final section of the chapter deals with the special problems of bureaucracy and the search for alternative forms for associational organization.

THE DEVELOPMENT OF ASSOCIATIONS

The rapid growth of associations is a recent development in human societies. About the only large-scale organizations in America 100 years ago were the churches and the Freemasons. Nevertheless, a visiting Frenchman, Alexis de Tocqueville [1835, 1840], did characterize Americans in 1838 as people who were quick to organize themselves whenever there was a task to be done. He sensed that our democracy was due in part to our emerging associations. Nevertheless, the remarkable growth of organizations, many of which are nationwide in scope, has come within the last century.

The extent, character, and general purpose of associations has been given particular attention by scholars who have analyzed community life. In the study of Yankee City by Warner and Lunt (discussed in Chapter 6), information about the community's associations was an important aspect of their analysis. With a population of about 17,000, Yankee City had a total of 357 permanent organizations, many of which were branches of larger bodies. Membership, however, differed significantly from one organization to another. Some associations attracted primarily working-class citizens, while others served citizens of higher status.

Therefore, an association owes its unique character partly to the social-class level of its members. Social status determines not only the membership of particular organizations but also which citizens will be most likely

TABLE 7-1 Percentages of Social-Class Groupings Who Were Members of Associations in Yankee City

Social-class Grouping	Percentage
Upper-upper class	72
Lower-upper class	71
Upper-middle class	64
Lower-middle class	49
Upper-lower class	39
Lower-lower class	22

Source: W. Lloyd Warner, *Yankee City* (New Haven: Yale University Press, 1963), p. 131.

to join any association. For example, Warner found that the upper-class citizens of Yankee City were more apt to belong to associations than were citizens of the lower classes. While 41 percent of the total population were members of some association, membership decreased consistently from a high of 72 percent in the upper-upper class to a low of 22 percent in the lower-lower status group. (See Table 7-1.) In addition, more of the higher-status individuals belonged to several organizations at the same time. Upper-class organizations promoted speeches and stressed formal activities, while lower-class organizations tended to emphasize ritual and the acting out of feelings in drama and talent shows.

Other scholars of community life have made similar findings. Robert and Helen Lynd [1929] reported 363 organizations in Middletown (a Midwestern American community), one for every 73 citizens. Lowry [1965] found that the Chamber of Commerce in Micro City, a far Western American town of approximately 15,000 population, included in its formal listing of organizations 98 social and recreational groups, 30 service and educational organizations, 68 occupational and professional groups, 15 veteran and military organizations, and 4 political groups. (Middletown and Micro City are discussed more fully in Chapter 8.) In addition to these officially recorded groups, there were many unlisted associations, not to mention the town's business and labor organizations. The author concludes that Micro City is "overorganized," since it has more organizations than are needed to meet the basic community needs. Because of the tendency of some people to have multiple memberships, it is even possible to imagine that many smaller communities in contemporary America may have almost as many official and unofficial associations as there are citizens of the community.

It is clear, then, that modern community life is built upon a complex network of associations through which a majority of citizens involve themselves in the community's educational, recreational, social, and cultural activities. The unique character of each association derives from the social origins of the citizens who tend to join and participate. Even supposedly

7-1 America: A Nation of Joiners

Many Americans are members of a variety of associations—groups which combine both formal and informal aspects and range from small, local peer groups to national organizations. Associations develop to meet two important basic needs for members and society: they perform tasks that might not otherwise be accomplished in a large heterogeneous society; and they also meet a variety of emotional needs for members and other citizens. (See the Introduction to Part IV.)

Elizabeth Hamlin, Dietz/Hamlin

Educational associations. Graduates of high schools and colleges hold class reunions where they renew old friendships and relive former experiences. In addition, these contacts may lead to continuing business and professional contacts. For schools, class reunions and associations provide a way in which private contributions can be obtained and a sense of cultural continuity from one generation to the next can be maintained.

P. Hollander Gross/Stock, Boston

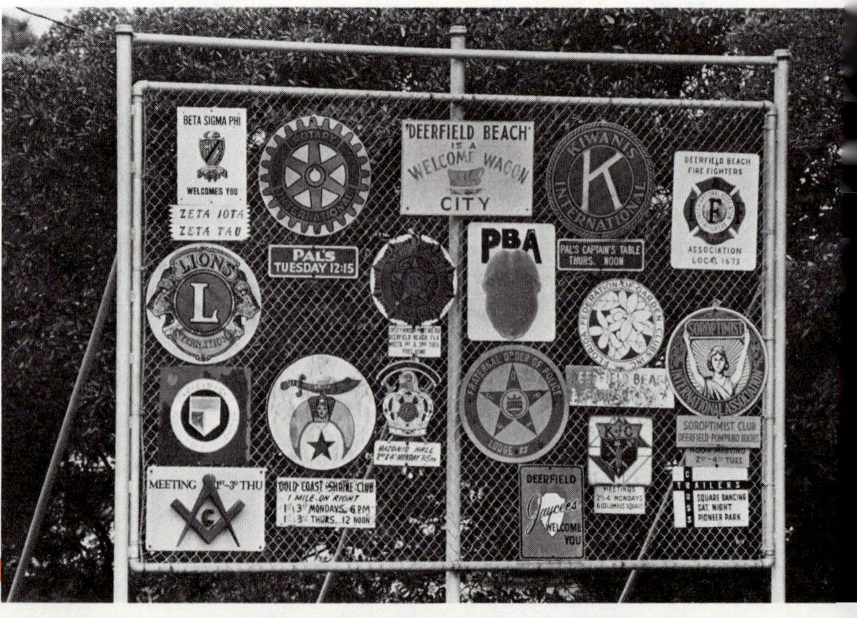

Community service associations. Almost every American town and city has literally dozens of service clubs for both men and women. These groups meet the need for a sense of belonging and help create a sense of community cohesion (see Chapter 8). They also provide staffing and financial support for voluntary community activities (in health, recreation, social service, and other areas).

Elizabeth Hamlin, Dietz/Hamlin

O. Manken/Stock, Boston

Recreational associations. Like cultural associations, sports and athletic groups provide members with a feeling of personal fulfillment, in addition to a sense of belonging. The membership is frequently drawn from specific areas of human activity (church and business bowling leagues) and reflects the social class or ethnic origins of the members (women's and men's bowling leagues; suburban Little League; inner-city basketball leagues).

Cultural associations. Members of dance, painting, writing, and other cultural groups can express feelings of creativity and personal fulfillment. These kinds of voluntary associations are particularly important in contemporary society where formal support (money and organizations) for the arts is minimal. Also important to cultural associations are patrons, wealthy philanthropists who provide the necessary money and buildings (see Photo Essay 6-1).

Occupational associations. The American Medical Association is among the most formal of American associations. In a large-scale society, these associations provide a way for members to maintain a feeling of being part of a larger professional community. They also perform a variety of political functions by considering the impact of legislation and new scientific discoveries upon medicine.

Religious associations. Religious associations can range from small spontaneous sect-like groups to large-scale bureaucratized churches. Depending upon their nature or character, they can perform different functions for the members: provide the economically deprived with a feeling of spiritual salvation; provide the socially deprived with feelings of relatedness and involvement; provide the sick and ill with a feeling of healing through God's love; and provide the ethically and psychically deprived with feelings of a concern for right and wrong and an awareness of one's place in the larger universe (see Study 6).

American Medical Association

J. Ritscher/Stock, Boston

democratic and egalitartian associations, like churches, can be classified by the social status of their members. In fact, the needs, interests, and life-style of the predominant social class of the members of an association can evolve into an unofficial criterion for membership. In this manner, free and voluntary organizations can rapidly become exclusive, and large numbers of citizens can be denied access to the associational activity of modern life. Feelings of anomie may result, causing important political consequences, both within an association and for the larger community. The following examination of the origin, sources, and nature of "the organizational revolution" forms a basis for analyzing these political implications.

The Organizational Revolution

Kenneth E. Boulding [1953] used the term the *organizational revolution* to refer to the increased number and influence of associations at all levels of contemporary society. Boulding borrowed the economic concepts of "demand" and "supply" to help account for this remarkable development. The demand for organizational life has multiplied as humans have become lost and alienated in an increasingly urbanized environment. Simultaneously, technological advances in communications have provided the means for expanding the supply of associations.

As we saw in Chapter 6 and in the introduction to this chapter, modern people have a marked need for status. Or, put another way, modern conditions create a need for status that must be met in new ways. Boulding suggests that all individuals have a profound inner need for a "place" in society. In earlier nonmodern societies, individuals could identify themselves as members of a stable family in a slowly changing, small community. In contrast, modern societies, which have great mobility and weakened family and neighborhood ties, frequently create a desperate need for identity. To become a member of an organization helps to satisfy the need of individuals to formalize their status and, thereby, gives them a sense of security.

Within modern large-scale organizations, wage earners often feel little identity with the organization; they merely sell their labor for a wage. Modern workers do not really feel a part of the productive enterprise, nor do they feel a deep sense of satisfaction in having created the product. As Boulding points out, alienation may be one of the most important forces underlying the rise of the labor movement. Having ceased to identify with the work experience itself, workers may turn to a labor union. For some members, the union fulfills a need far deeper than the economic desire for a living wage. It fulfills the need to belong and to be identified. Thus the contemporary social *demand* for organizational life reflects the need for status and social identity.

Boulding argues, however, that the major part of the explanation for the organizational revolution lies with the *supply* side of the case. Advances in technological communications have greatly increased the efficiency with which organizations can recruit and organize members. The early Methodist bishops traveled by horse through the wilderness and rarely stayed in cabins. Travel was so slow that many of them accepted voluntary celibacy because they were seldom home long enough to provide for a wife and children. Communication was limited to face-to-face contacts, since there were no electronic amplification systems to permit huge mass meetings. Printed materials were limited.

Today any American bishop can travel to a national headquarters meeting in Chicago or New York in a matter of hours, or speak across the nation instantaneously by telephone, radio, or television. In addition, other devices like the typewriter, dictaphone, and intercommunication systems facilitate more rational and formal kinds of association. Technology, then, has enabled modern organizations to become the most effective way of supplying society with many of its basic requirements.

However, technological advances alone cannot fully account for the organizational revolution. Sheer population growth has also contributed to the growth and maintenance of organizations. There are simply more people in modern urban society and more of them feel a need to join. In fact, organizational life has become so dominant in modern society that it has contributed to the creation of a distinct social type called the "organization man or woman."

Organization Men and Women

When William H. Whyte [1956] talks of an "organization man" and David Riesman and his colleagues [1950] describe an "other-directed" person, they are referring to the fact that modern people have become sales oriented, habitually selling their associations, their organizations, and even themselves.

> The past seventy or eighty years have seen a marked advance in the skills of salesmanship, not merely in commercial life, but also in the church, in the labor movement, and in almost all the other organizations of social life. Indeed as David Riesman has pointed out, salesmanship has likewise invaded the individual personality. The characteristically "inner-directed" person of an earlier day, who was content to go on producing the immutable product of his personality without any thought of "selling himself" or of adjusting himself to different environments, has given way to a great extent to the "other-directed" person, who is all things to all men, whose personality depends largely on the group around him, and who devotes so much attention to playing roles that his inner life dries up and he becomes almost pure actor who cannot "be himself" because he doesn't have any "self" to "be" [Whyte, 1956, pp. 27–28].

In other words, the nature of modern society not only increases the need for organizations but also socializes individuals to function as members of organizations. Organizations have become efficient at catering to the needs of people and, at the same time, have helped to shape the character of modern people. Organizations reward individuals who "work for the good of the team" and can sell both themselves and their enterprise.

Closely related to this phenomenon is the development of the "human relations" emphasis in modern industry. Early capitalistic enterprises paid little attention to the human element in the factory and merely bought wage workers. Before long, however, employers realized that laborers were also human beings with social and psychological as well as economic needs. It became evident, too, that the most productive worker was the happy worker. Thus, business owners and administrators began treating employees as whole persons with needs ranging from fringe benefits to social and recreational outlets such as coffee breaks, bowling teams, and even counseling facilities.

Similar tendencies characterize other organizations as well. We have already mentioned how labor unions have become much more than bread-and-butter organizations. Emile Durkheim saw trade unions, in the early stage in their development in Europe, taking on the humanistic functions of churches, insofar as they tried to respond to the basic social needs of modern people. Churches themselves have gone to great lengths to keep both their staffs and their members happy. The art of management in any modern organization—industrial, labor, church—calls for expertise in psychology, sociology, education, and other social and humanistic disciplines.

This tendency of modern organizations to interest themselves in the personal lives of their employees was illustrated by Whyte [1951] in his reference to management or corporation wives. When Whyte did his research in the early 1950s, he found that most wives of corporation employees agreed that "the good wife" adjusted to the system by conforming and curbing individuality and intellectualism. The wife was considered the unpaid member of the team, an important cocktail party appendage for the husband. Wives were frequently interviewed along with their husbands, and one's maiden name, number of marriages, community activities and reputation, and religion were considered crucial, particularly where husbands were applying for top executive positions. Much of this attitude still prevails, although there are some signs of change [Bender, 1971].

Marriage for the male executive is still considered a sign of emotional and social stability. A director of the Massachusetts Institute of Technology's Sloan School of Management has said: "We'd have to ask a 35-year-old bachelor why he isn't married" [Bender, 1971, p. 1]. Yet, there is now a Women's Liberation Collective of the Harvard Business School Wives Club, and the local chapters of the Young Presidents' Organization (an association of members who achieve company presidencies before the age of 40 years) have scrapped the fashion shows and the speech, personality, and slimming seminars that had been traditional convention activities for wives [Bender, 1971, p. 3]. These have been replaced by sessions on world problems and social issues. Still, many wives of management continue to refer to themselves as Shell, Continental Oil, or ATT wives.

One should not, however, come away from this discussion of organization men and women thinking that the rise of associations in contemporary society has led only to a loss of individual freedom and an increase in conformity. Research in a relatively new field of sociology—the study of formal voluntary organizations (FVOs)—discloses the multitude of needed functions performed by modern associations. An important characteristic of associations is that membership in them, as opposed to membership in a family, is *voluntary.* At the same time, associations are *formally organized.* The term "formal voluntary organization" thus includes the two essential characteristics of associations.

The Function of FVOs in Community Life

Early FVO studies argued that four basic factors accounted for the organizational revolution: (1) a permissive decentralized power structure, which encouraged the formation of many private interest groups; (2) an egalitarian, relatively open stratification system, with an absence of an established aristocracy; (3) a decentralized policy and economy that emphasized individualism; and (4) a local–federal type of political organization, which encouraged the activist propensity of Americans. Other researchers have argued that factors like urbanization are more important, since FVOs are most prevalent in the more industrialized countries, which are characterized by high urbanization, low agricultural population, high per capita gross national product, high literacy, and high percentage of the labor force in industry [Harp, 1973, p. 2].

Traditional theory assumed that most, if not all, citizens in an open democratic society participated widely in associational behavior. Such participation was attributed to the members' desires to achieve special goals that could not otherwise be met. Other theory argues that voluntary associational behavior primarily characterizes the more literate, well-educated, and economically privileged persons in society. This perspective assumes that associations function primarily to provide members with a variety of emotionally satisfying, leisure-type activities. The first view argues that associations are essentially *instrumental;* the second, that they are basically *expressive.* An instrumental group is one designed primarily to "get things accomplished." Chick's gang, which is described in Study 3, is an example of an instrumental group. An expressive group like Doc's gang puts more emphasis upon recreation and helping individuals to "feel good about themselves."

In reality, many associations serve both instrumental and expressive needs of members. Examples of FVOs classified according to function are given in the Table 7-2. As one might expect, expressive FVOs tend to be less structured, more primarylike, while instrumental FVOs tend to be more

TABLE 7-2 Function of FVOs

Function	Type of Organization	Examples
Expressive	Fraternal	Lodges and secret orders
	Social	Bridge and poker clubs
Instrumental	Civic	Charitable and welfare agencies
	Occupational	Work and professional organizations
Mixed	Educational	Literary and study groups
	Youth	4-H, Scouts, and the like

highly organized and secondary in character. As we saw at the beginning of this chapter, Max Weber argued that this unique mixed quality of associations—that is, the blending of the two extremes of informal and formal group structure—gives them their importance in human society.

The combination of informality and formality also creates several special problems within the context of associational life. The first has to do with political power, the second with the rise of bureaucracy and the human response to it. In the next section, we will discuss problems of authority and power within associations. In the last section of this chapter, we will consider the problems of bureaucracy in detail.

PROBLEMS OF AUTHORITY AND POWER

The informal, expressive, less structured aspects of associational life tend to support democratic processes, whereas the formal, instrumental, and structured aspects create undemocratic authoritarian tendencies. Therefore, in most associations, there is a constant tension and conflict between these two tendencies. Sociologists have long been interested in this problem since answers to it may provide insights into who has power in modern organizations and whether democracy is possible in organizational contexts.

The "Iron Law" of Oligarchy

Robert Michels [1949] studied socialist and trade-union organizations in Europe before World War I and discovered what he felt to be an inevitable and irreversible tendency toward *oligarchy*—the accumulation of greater power in the hands of fewer and fewer leaders. Since he observed this process even in organizations that purported to be democratic, he called it an "iron law." Michels hypothesized that this law was a result of the inherent nature of organizational life for both leaders and members. In order to be effective and efficient, even the most benevolent leaders must learn the skills of their office and accumulate the special knowledge and professional contacts associated with their role. In struggling to assimilate the special role skills and knowledge required of their office, leaders begin to identify psychologically with their offices and tend to feel personally

7-2 Why Has There Been An Organizational Revolution in Modern Society?

The term "organizational revolution" refers to the increased number and influence of associations in daily life. The economic concepts of demand and supply can help explain the origins of this revolution.

Marion Bernstein

The Demand for Associations. Modern society creates a number of new needs which can be met only through the creation of special-purpose associations, both informal and formal.

Many modern citizens experience feelings of rootlessness and anomie. Membership in informal cultural, recreational, communal, and religious associations can provide contexts needed for new experiences of relatedness and belonging.

J. C. LeJeune/Stock, B

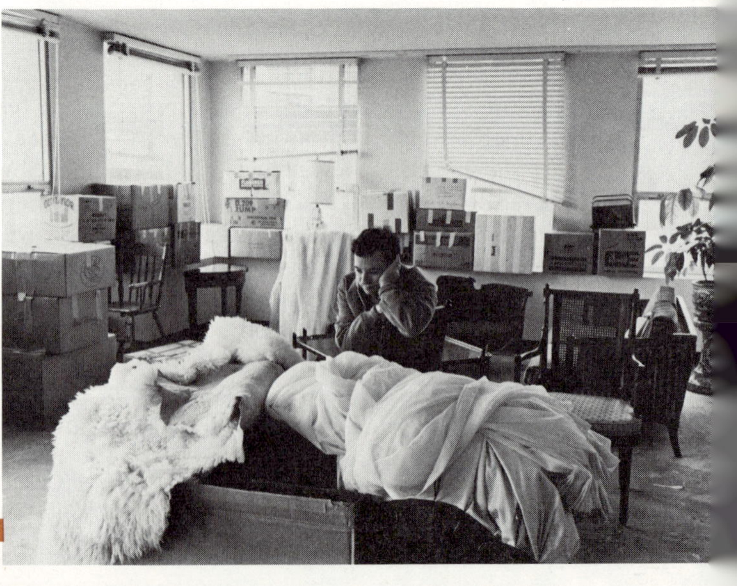

The extensive geographic and social mobility of citizens in modern society creates a need for organizational assistance. For example, some communities maintain a "Welcome Wagon" service. New arrivals are greeted by a paid representative of area merchants, who provides information about local services and products (grocery stores, laundries, interior decorators, television sets) and with gift certificates (free household plants from a nursery).

s Draper

)orfman

The Supply of Associations. However, demand alone is not sufficient. Associations must be able to recruit new members and publicize their activities by informal and formal means.

The densely settled and highly mobile nature of modern society actually facilitates face-to-face contact in some contexts. Members of voluntary associations can pass out literature to and talk with community citizens in town and city streets.

Modern technological innovations have increased the formal means which associations can use to contact people. The printing of hundreds of leaflets and posters can be supplemented by the use of the telephone and television and radio advertising.

rejected if replaced by others. Furthermore, leaders may sincerely come to feel that others could not do as effective a job, since they lack the skills, knowledge, and personal contacts necessary for the successful operation of the organization.

At the same time, the tendency toward apathy on the part of members is encouraged by such managerial specialization. "Support our President," "The boss knows best," and "Don't rock the boat" can have great appeal, particularly if leadership is apparently doing an adequate job. Moreover, members often lack the knowledge with which to criticize or challenge their leaders. They may find meetings boring and routine, since important decisions are usually made by a small group. In addition, many members may not have access to an opposition party or may have many of their personal needs met outside of the organization in other social settings.

One further trend is worth noting. Frequently, the original goals and norms of an organization are either replaced or diluted by the addition of newer ones. Alfred Vagts [1967] identifies such a process in modern military forces by distinguishing between "the military way" and "militarism." Military organizations have one major function in all societies—to develop the capability for waging war in defense of society. Sometimes, however, military forces take on paramilitary or nonmilitary duties, such as ceremonial activities or civic duties (building roads or helping in disaster situations). Such nonmilitary tasks can give rise to an emphasis upon fancy uniforms, useless rituals, sharp class distinctions, or exotic codes of etiquette and conduct. Vagts argues that these latter functions and forms of behavior tend to weaken and undermine a military organization's essential defense responsibility. Militarism, then, becomes dysfunctional both to civilian society and to the military (see Chapter 11).

Unknowingly, then, both leaders and members of an organization can lose sight of their original, social goals and become preoccupied with the internal operation of the organization. This problem becomes particularly acute in democratic associations that stress the importance of regular changes in leadership, full participation by most members, and an equal chance to participate in decision making. As an association's activities become less related to basic goals and more concerned with internal routine, the propensities toward oligarchy are strengthened. Members become more apathetic and leaders find it easier to operate behind the scenes for their own special purposes. As Michels puts it: *"Who says organization says oligarchy."*

One can also substitute the concepts of *limitation,* maintenance of the *status quo,* and *apathy* for the concept of oligarchy in the above quotation:

1. *Who says organization says limitation*—There are limits beyond which an organization cannot grow and still remain viable. For one thing, as Kenneth Boulding suggests, a growing organization will sooner or later use up its human environment. It may grow rapidly at first as it attracts new members whose needs are met by the character and program of the group, but gradually it will run out of potential members. This is as true for a religious sect as for a labor union. In addition, the larger an organi-

zation becomes, the more difficult it is to maintain effective communication and favorable internal relationships. The "iron law of hierarchy" works to bring about greater and greater distance between leaders and members of the organization. Relationships become more impersonal, and members feel manipulated rather than appreciated as persons. They no longer feel wanted or needed, and apathy inevitably results.

2. *Who says organization says status quo* on the part of leaders—One of the most common organizational problems is the breakdown of communication between executives and grass-roots members. The president of a corporation or the bishop of a church tends to surround himself or herself with advisors of similar persuasion who see and hear what the boss wants seen and heard. They must be good team people in the leader's terms. Together they proceed to manage the organization as it has always been managed, maintaining the status quo, which has been good to them and rewarded them with leadership positions. They perform as if things were the same even when they are constantly changing. At the same time, new attitudes are emerging at the grass-roots level, and new members are entering the organization, bringing with them new perspectives and demands. In an ideal situation, changing needs at the bottom would be communicated upward to the executives, and necessary changes would be made in the organization. In actuality, the organizational leader all too often becomes insulated from the members.

> The president of a corporation cannot spend much time in the shop; the president of a university finds it difficult to teach even one course; the Pope is effectively insulated from the parish; and the top labor leader or farm leader seldom spends time at the bench or on the farm. . . . [The leader] creates, as it were, a spurious environment of his own—an environment, if he is a dominant type, of yes men who reflect the executive's own wishes rather than the realities of the world around him . . . [Boulding, 1953, pp. 24, 70].

3. *Who says organization says apathy* on the part of many members—It is not only the modern labor union that has difficulty getting members to attend meetings and take an active part. Even the Roman Catholic church, which has perhaps the best record of member attendance among the large religious bodies of America, has a major problem of "marginal members," people who seldom take part [Fichter, 1951]. The larger the organization, the more critical the problem of fringe members. Core members may develop primary ties and feel a sense of personal involvement. For them, the group becomes multifunctional. A very large number of members, however, will drift to the fringe of the organization's activities and develop feelings of impersonality and indifference. As they become "backsliders" and cease to take part, the organization is no longer functional for them.

In more theoretical terms, it is possible to speak of this dilemma as one that confronts every social system [Parsons, 1951]. Even a single organization is a social system, a small society where input of energy must be comparable to the output of rewards. Usually there is a measure of both coercion and voluntary involvement behind the input of individual members. In any case, there must be significant energy expended for any social system to function effectively. If it ceases to function because energy is withheld, the organization dies. Usually, in any organization, those who put in the most energy are those who feel rewarded most by the output. They are willing to be *deprived* of time and money and to contribute skills as long as they are *rewarded.* This is partly what sociologists mean by saying that there must be a balance between input and output in a social system.

It follows that one reason some members in an organization are active and involved and others are not is because some feel rewarded while others do not. No one is going to continue to be active in any organization, even a church, unless one feels that his or her deprivations are "paying off." In a very large organization, it is virtually inevitable that many members will think it costs more than it is worth. Thus they slide to the fringe of participation and commitment or drop out altogether.

The degree of apathy of organization members depends largely on the character of the leadership and the structure of the social system. As we saw in Study 3, two broad types of leadership can be identified in human groups of all kinds—*task leaders* and *morale leaders.* Task leaders carry out the instrumental purposes of an organization (that is, they ensure that things get done). Morale leaders concern themselves with the expressive purposes (that is, with making people feel satisfied).

Task leaders have the ability to organize and get things accomplished. They may persuade others to do the work, as in a voluntary association like a church, or they may have authority to coerce others into performing, as in a military organization. The latter is more autocratic or authoritarian, the former more democratic or permissive. In both cases, however, effective leaders must achieve intended results. Certainly one kind of organizational reward that is most effective in motivating members is visible movement toward the agreed upon goals. "Nothing succeeds like success" is an adage that may be relevant here. Boulding refers to this as part of the dynamics of growth. Members feel it is all worthwhile as long as "the ball is rolling." Effective task leadership, therefore, convinces members that the rewards, in terms of goal attainment and organizational commitment are worth their expenditures of time and energy (that is, the rewards are sufficient enough to outweigh the deprivations).

On the other hand, there are other rewards, more subtle and more informal, which contribute to a viable organization. Group life helps to overcome the alienation and despair so common in urban society. As we saw in Chapter 6, the sect rewards the dispossessed person with a feeling of spiritual status and promise (in the life-to-come "the last shall be first"). The labor union can reward those people who need a sense of community insofar as they find much of their recreation and many of their primary ties in the union. The reward for membership in all organizations is partly in the form of morale. Some organizational leaders are especially adept at fulfilling this need and may well be identified as morale leaders. They are attuned to the need for members to be kept happy. They are more sensitive to the personal feelings of members than the task leaders, who are busy with the business of the organization. In other words, morale leaders are more capable of implementing the informal goals of an organization.

In short, apathy most frequently occurs when members feel that membership in an association is of no avail, and such apathy is most likely to occur in large-scale organizations. Nevertheless, more significant than sheer size is the nature of the social structure. If a complex organization is structured so that members become involved in small groups within the total associational system and are rewarded by involvements in these subgroups, then there is a greater probability of good morale and active participation. Small groups serve to mediate between the individual member and the higher levels of leadership. Thus, the large church is most viable when members within it are related to small classes, clubs, committees, cliques, or friendship circles. Such subgroups make primary associations possible within the larger secondary organization. They help to meet the perennial dilemma of fringe membership in social organizations. Furthermore, as we will see in the following section, intermediary groups within the organization play a vital role in maintaining democratic processes.

Running throughout this discussion is Michels' pessimistic view of associations. He spoke of the "iron law of oligarchy," which implies that because of the difficulty of actively involving all members in a large organization, there is an inevitable tendency for power to concentrate in the hands of a few people and for most members to become apathetic. His perspective would lead us to assume that organizational democracy is impossible even when task leaders and morale leaders are effective. Is this conclusion justified? Research since his time indicates that it is not.

Maintaining Democracy

Michels has certainly isolated a fundamental structural problem inherent in many, if not most, organizations. However, some associations seem able to counter the tendency toward oligarchy effectively. By what means do they counteract these oligarchic tendencies, and, in terms of understanding political behavior, what are the implications of their actions? As we have seen in the preceding section, small groupings within large-scale organizations are important for the morale and well-being of members. More significantly, perhaps, these same primarylike groups can be conducive to democratic processes. Ideally, a democratic organization, or society, is based upon the following characteristics:

1. Full open discussion of differing views and perspectives.
2. Persuasion as a technique of influence.
3. A balance of power between competing interest groups.

4. The fullest possible participation and involvement by most members.
5. Periodic and regular changes in leadership, that is, a circulation of elites.
6. Equal opportunity for the widest number of members to play a role in political decision making.

How can such an ideal be attained in large-scale organizations? Instruments like a constitution or declaration of purposes can be useful; however, although these may be necessary tools, they are not sufficient means for the maintenance of organizational democracy. Freedom and equality must be reflected in certain kinds of interpersonal relationships; democratic processes must be reinforced by specific types of intergroup relationships. A study of democracy in action within the organizational setting can identify these crucial relationships.

Study 7 examines the problem of democracy in an organizational setting. Lipset and his colleagues were, in effect, asking whether it was possible to find an exception to Michels' law of oligarchy. Their conclusion indicates that small associations within the larger organizational context are the keys to understanding how the spirit and the practice of democracy can be related.

▶ STUDY 7

A Democratic Union—The Printers [1952 and 1956][1]

Problem

Most associations in North American society fail to involve the bulk of their members in the social and political life of the organization. As a matter of fact, some of the most powerful and deeply rooted people's organizations in America have reached a degree of popular participation of only 5–7 percent [Barber, 1950, pp. 484–485]. This means that a large majority of members may not be involved in the political process or the decision making of many presumably democratic organizations. Such a problem has been characteristic of trade unionism.

There is, however, one case that deviates from the typical pattern—the International Typographers Union (ITU). In this organization of printers in the United States and Canada, most members seem vitally involved in social and political affairs. Furthermore, old leaders are frequently turned out of office and replaced by new leadership, representing differing views and perspectives on the organization's problems. *What factors account for this exceptional case,* a deviation from Michels' notion of inescapable oligarchy?

[1]Adapted and abridged from Seymour M. Lipset, "Democracy in Private Government," *The British Journal of Sociology, 3* (March 1952), pp. 47–65; and Seymour M. Lipset, Martin A. Trow, and James S. Coleman, *Union Democracy* (New York: The Free Press, 1956) with permission of Macmillan Publishing Co., Inc.

Hypotheses and Study Design

Lipset and his colleagues hypothesized that *democracy has the best chance of prevailing* in a private organization *when the following are present:* (1) a pluralistic social structure (or pluralism); (2) enlightened members who take pride in their role and status; (3) ample opportunity for members to associate with each other and develop a sense of community; and (4) a climate of opinion that encourages critical and responsible opposition to incumbent leadership. Current studies at the time suggested that, for a democratic political structure to be viable, a pluralistic system of strong and autonomous *intermediary associations* has to exist within the structure. These associations mediate between the individual citizen and the power center.

This theoretical insight was based upon historical theories about democracy. For example, Aristotle recognized that Greek democracy was made possible in large part because of a middle-class citizenry, in a relatively small city-state, with freedom to criticize and challenge the elites who held power and authority. Similarly, intermediary associations, representing competing interest groups, seemed to Lipset and his colleagues to be a structural way of countering mass apathy and leadership oligarchy in large-scale contemporary unions. The single *deviant case* of the democratic ITU provided an excellent context for testing the theory of the importance of intermediary associations in unions.

Methods of Data Collection

Lipset and his colleagues set out to test their hypotheses about democracy by employing several methods of research over a period of years. These included *documentary analysis, participant observation, questionnaires, and interviews.* Historical records for the ITU were particularly important since the character of an organization cannot be understood without information about its origin and development. The researchers also relied upon personal observation of and involvement in union activities. The systematic study was started in 1949 while Lipset was a faculty member at Columbia University, and the report was completed in 1956. Interviews were also a central part of the research; the early ones were unstructured and exploratory, while the later ones were systematic and followed a carefully developed schedule.

Two mailed questionnaires followed the interviews in order to get up-to-date information as to how workers voted on union issues and in national elections in 1952. Membership in the international body totaled about 100,000, and a representative sample was drawn from the overall population. However, much of the focus for the study centered in New York and in the San Francisco–Oakland Bay area, partly because of the large number of printers in these metropolitan centers. New York's local union, referred to as the "Big Six," numbered about 10,000 and served as a laboratory for much of the analysis.

Findings and Interpretations

The historical record showed that printers were among the first craftsmen to organize in European societies, and the first American printers' strike took place as early as 1776 in New York City. Soon thereafter, a two-party system and voluntary associations began to emerge within the union. The associations were not only voluntary groups, but they were also autonomous—that is, they were not controlled only from the top by leaders. The party system was in some ways even more remarkable. It reflected a distinct difference among printers: *the Progressive*

TABLE 7-3 Election Returns in the ITU from 1918 to 1950

Election Year	Percentage of All Members Voting for Union President:
1918	67
1926	81
1934	69
1942	71
1950	80

Party was made up of printers who favored militant action against employers and *the Wahneta–Independent Party* involved those who were more conservative and cautious. Furthermore, no one party was strong enough to stay in power all the time, and the "ins" were frequently replaced by the "outs." In addition, most printers voted in elections and many of them were deeply involved in the politics of the association. The table below shows the high percentages of members of both parties who voted. This means that, among printers, there is a minimum of apathy and that very few have a "let George do it" philosophy.

According to the summary of the voting record of printers given in Table 7-3 80 percent of the total union membership turned out to vote for a president in 1950. This is remarkably high and indicates that the organization is vibrant and active. Likewise in each of the two political parties in the union, the voting turnout shows vital concern not only for the office of President but also for Secretary–Treasurer, as shown in Table 7-4. When any organization has this much involvement by members consistently, the questions *Why?* and *How?* are worth consideration. The answers with respect to the printers appear to be related to the following characteristics of the ITU:

1. The printers have established and maintained a *pluralistic society* within their organization. It can be graphically portrayed as in Figure 7-1.

2. Most members are caught up in strong *secondary groups* and are involved socially and politically with other printers. As a consequence, they attend union meetings with particular zest when crucial issues are at stake. Business is not merely routine but is exciting and calls for debate and voting; in other words, it calls for active and meaningful participation by the largest number of members.

TABLE 7-4 Election Returns, by Party, in the ITU from 1918 to 1950

	Percentage of Progressive Party Members Voting for:		Percentage of Wahneta–Independent Party Members Voting for:	
Election Year	President	Secretary–Treasurer	President	Secretary–Treasurer
1918	36	36	64	64
1926	52	48	48	52
1934	57	66	43	35
1942	48	51	52	49
1950	55	58	45	48

FIGURE 7-1 Pluralistic Aspects of Printers' Organization

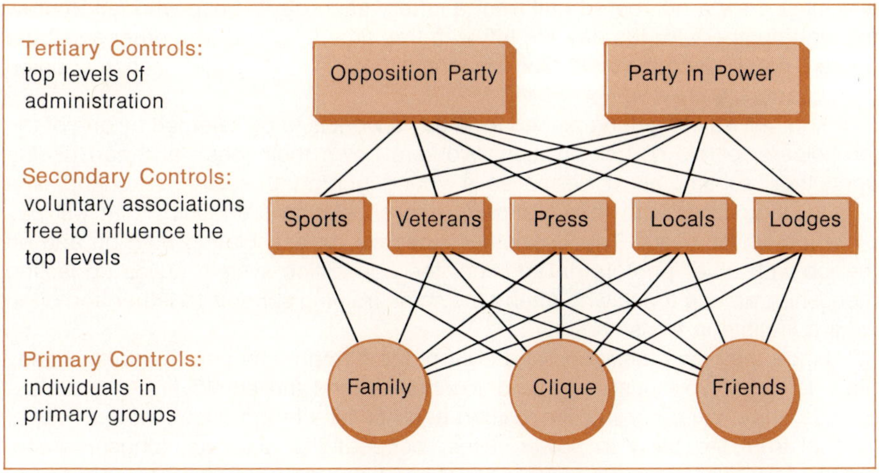

3. There are many *associations* within the union. An incomplete list of printers' organizations in New York City alone totals more than 100. These secondary associations function in several ways to encourage democratic participation: (1) They are sources of new opinions; (2) they are a means of communication about union issues; (3) they become workshops where skills of leadership are developed and encouraged; and (4) they become informal contexts for personal interaction between leaders and followers.

4. Printers associate with other printers both on and off the job. This, together with membership in associations within the union, makes for a strong *sense of community.* The researchers found that this constant printer–printer relationship helped to keep alive a continual interest in the affairs of the trade and the larger organization. They were able to account for this close association in one of two ways: (1) Work conditions among printers conspire to throw them together with each other and (2) printers are proud of their craft and think of themselves as the elite of manual workers.

One of the particularly important findings of this study was the identification of certain social and cultural variables that tend to be correlated with pluralistic social systems. The work conditions of the ITU that contributed to its solidarity included night work and the substitute hiring system. Most printers work a night shift sometime during their careers. For long periods, theirs is not a normal pattern of work, family life, and leisure. Thus, they not only have more time to socialize on the job, but when work is done they are not compelled to hurry home to the family. They are likely to spend free time with fellow workers at the local bar or bowling alley before returning home. Data show that night workers are more apt to be active in both formal and informal union social relations.

In addition, the way in which printers obtain their jobs encourages "hanging around with other printers." The demand for workers in the print shops varies greatly from day to day and from season to season. Young workers, along with those who have lost regular positions, show up daily for hiring as substitutes. They fill in on heavy work days or when regular workers must be absent. This is the way in which printers typically get their start in the craft. The system involves many workers and continues year after year. "Subs" are placed on a hiring list and must draw a numbered ball from a lottery each day. Those who fail to draw the high numbers for the day are left with free time to spend with other subs and printers not working the shift. Consequently, there is much fraternization at union headquarters and bars.

Another way of getting placed for a day's work is to be selected by one of the job-holders for his or her position. Workers "own their jobs" and can decide upon their substitutes. It behooves a young printer, therefore, to spend time getting acquainted with fellow printers and cultivating friendships that will pay off in job assignments. This is another incentive for associating both on and off the job with other printers. In addition, the apprentice system builds up lasting friendships among those who attend the same training schools together and often work a lifetime in the same city.

Since they own their jobs and control the hiring by means of a lottery, they are relatively independent of the union bosses and the employer. As a consequence, they can enter into opposition party politics in the union without fear of reprisal from the party in power. Other occupations (painters, longshoremen, entertainers) also have seasonal work schedules; however, since these workers do not have control of hiring, they are likely to be at the mercy of union officials and reluctant to enter into political activity or to oppose the oligarchy in control.

In addition to work conditions that favor the development of an occupational community, printers prefer to spend time with other printers. They have always considered themselves the "aristocrats of labor"; there is evidence to suggest that they are better educated and apt to have more middle-class tastes than other manual workers. In this sense, printers tend to be marginal people, having a social status somewhere between manual and white-collar workers. They are, therefore, strongly motivated to associate with people of equal or higher status. For example, a group of 412 printers named their "three best friends" as follows: 35 percent were printers; 21 percent professionals, business executives, and independent business owners; 20 percent white-collar or sales employees; and only 25 percent other manual workers.

In summary, then, the relatively high status of printers, their tendency to associate with other printers or those of higher status, their pride in their craft, and their strong sense of community are all related to the pluralistic social structure that exists within the union. This pluralistic structure plays a vital role in maintaining active democratic processes, as does the sense of occupational community generated within the associations.

Such a system of political opposition could lead to irresponsible criticism of those in power, disruptive conflict, and antagonism on the part of those defeated for public office. The ITU, however, provides a context for meeting these kinds of problems. Those who oppose an incumbent administration are not regarded as disloyal to the union; rather their opposition is legitimate and acceptable to the membership, thus making an election of officers a meaningful contest. Furthermore, union officers are more willing to step down from positions of power in the ITU than in many other organizations partly because it is common for a union leader to return to the shop. Such a step does not constitute a loss of status or salary. In addition, printers are proud of their occupation and do not consider shop work to be less important than work in union administration. Thus, the gap in status between union officials and shop workers is not great. As a matter of fact, it has been kept relatively small partly because of the fact that the rank and file in the union consistently reject requests for salary increases for officials.

Conclusions and Implications

Most voluntary associations in American society face the problem of fringe membership because many members are inactive and apathetic about the organization. As a result, power may concentrate in the hands of a few core members and officers. The analysis of the ITU by Lipset and his colleagues identifies those conditions under which such problems do not arise. The high degree of member involvement among the printers can be attributed in part to the existence of a pluralistic society within the union where strong secondary groups mediate between individuals and the central administration. These groups are autonomous and free from manipulation by union officials, and they are strong enough to encourage their members to take an active role in decision making. In addition, the character of printing as an occupation develops a deep sense of pride among printers and a larger sense of occupational community. Unique features of the work life play a part in the development of this ethic. *A democratic process* within organizational life, then, *exists only when social conditions are appropriate.* These conditions can act as countervailing forces to oligarchic tendencies in leadership and trends towards apathy in followers.

The problem in contemporary society is that few organizations or associations possess the unique sociohistorical and cultural features of the ITU—particularly the sense of occupational community and job pride. Therefore, one might well ask if democracy in these other contexts is as likely or even possible. In addition, other structural factors may be present that, despite conditions conducive to democratic pluralism, make that pluralism all but ineffective. Bureaucracy is an example of this type of condition. Overbureaucratization can easily pervert pluralist ideals and structures.

PROBLEMS OF BUREAUCRACY

The work of Kenneth Boulding helps to introduce the notion of how bureaucratic organization can corrupt the daily work of an association. Why is it, he asks, that in all human endeavor there is a tendency for the "letter" to kill the spirit, when we know it is "the spirit that giveth life?" Why are ethical ideals not easily put to practical use within human social systems? Boulding suggests the answer lies in the problems encountered when implementing ideals through organizational structures:

> The trouble lies, of course, in the "flesh"; that is, in organization. All bodies are corruptible, whether the body of the literal flesh or the body of the state, the corporation, the trade union, the philanthropic organization, or the church. All organizations possess laws of their own which they impose on their members, laws which may not be consistent with the purposes of these members. . . . [But] we cannot rest content in corruption, and there is a constant drive toward the less and less corruptible. In this movement the theory of organization holds great promise. Unless we understand the theory of organization, at least in some degree, we cannot hope to create organizations which serve the ends of man instead of frustrating them. And organizations—"bodies"—are necessary if the "word"—the ethical insight, the perception of good—is to be made "flesh" [Boulding, 1953, p. 67].

In other words, organizations, as small social systems, possess a life of their own, as reflected in the existence of organizational goals, rules, and regulations. Since members frequently join for diverse personal reasons, the goals and needs of individuals may often conflict with this organizational life. Such conflict grows and is made more probable because organizations rely upon secondary, formal, and rational structures, while individual members seek primary, informal, more spontaneous avenues of participation. As a consequence, leaders' interpretations of proper organizational goals may be at odds with those of the members.

A minister, for example, may feel that an outspoken idealistic position in favor of civil rights is necessary to maintain the spirit of the church. Or a business executive may feel that sponsorship of educational programs on television is necessary to demonstrate the community awareness of the corporation. However, members of the congregation and stockholders may become concerned about the controversy that develops, offering arguments such as "That is not why I joined this association," or "We should get on with our appropriate business." Appropriate business for the member of a church often consists of ministering to his or her personal needs, not the needs of the larger community. Appropriate business for the stockholder often concerns increasing dividends, not spending corporation earnings on nonprofit community service.

Furthermore, the spirit or ideals of an organization are invisible and subtle. They cannot be counted and measured, put into mimeographed communications, or incorporated clearly in organizational rules. The spirit of a school, church, or labor union cannot be successfully assessed in the annual report:

> The spirit somehow eludes the information system; hence, the "executive" is not aware of its decline and becomes increasingly aware of the external items of information which pass more easily into the information system and can more easily be influenced by the effectors [the members] [Boulding, 1953, p. 85].

Bureaucratic organization specifically involves these two problems. First, it is highly formal, secondary, and rational and, therefore, can be in direct conflict with the primary and informal needs of members. Second, bureaucratic rules and regulations cannot effectively incorporate the spirit of an organization. As a consequence, the formal aspects of bureaucracy give rise to informal response, creating special problems for the organization.

Formal Aspects: Bureaucratic Structure and Ethos

Associations tend to be called bureaucratic when they operate according to prescribed rules and regulations. Bureaucracy is not a modern phenomenon, but, with the rise of capitalism and industrial specialization, it did develop as a highly rational form for structuring organizations. The *rational systems model* is based upon the idea of ordered relationships that are clearly spelled out in explicit directives, usually written into some sort of constitution or by-laws. In addition, all jobs within the organization are similarly described in specific detail. Therefore, decisions by leaders are always made with an eye to the manual which contains the rules, regulations, and job descriptions. Impartiality is the reigning virtue.

According to Max Weber [1947, pp. 329, 340], in his summary of the essential features of bureaucratic organization and the way in which they are related, the effectiveness of legal-bureaucratic authority rests on the acceptance of the following interdependent ideals:

1. Any legal norm may be established by agreement or by imposition, on the grounds of either expediency or rational values or both. Members of the organization must obey the norms.
2. The person in authority occupies a formally described "office." In the actions associated with this office, including any orders issued to others, the bureaucrat is subject to the same impersonal rules and regulations that apply to other members.
3. The person who obeys authority does so only in the capacity as a "member" of the organization; furthermore, the person obeys only "the law," rather than the person in authority.
4. Therefore, members of the organization who obey a person in authority do not owe this obedience to an individual. They owe allegiance only to the impersonal order.

At the time Weber did his analysis, he saw these principles as fundamentally important for a new, more democratic, political order. Making both members and leaders of an organization responsible to an informal rule of law could free them from personal commitments and involvements with one another. Also, all within an organization would be equal under the same law. Finally, one's performance within the organization, regardless of position in the hierarchy, would be judged by the book, not by the personal whim of some leader.

This perception of bureaucracy described an ideal type of organization, one that might never be found in pure form in the real social world. Weber argued, however, that any rationalized organization would tend to have many of these characteristics to some degree or other. In addition, Weber went on to indicate that offices follow the principle of hierarchy in that each lower office is under the bureaucratic control and supervision of a higher one. Promotion is based upon seniority or achievement, or both, and is dependent upon the judgment of one's performance by his or her superiors. Strict and systematic discipline and control prevails for officials in the conduct of their office.

In a bureaucracy, the lines of authority and communication, the division of labor, and the coordination of activities are so clearly planned that it is possible to draw a formal chart depicting the structure. The "org chart," indicating lines of authority and the flow of communications, looks much the same for any complex organization, whether a business corporation, a school system, a labor union, or a church.

The bureaucratic character of organizations has emerged in modern society because it is functional. Sheer size and the complexity of integrating many social groupings necessitate systematic planning and exact rules and channels for activity. Only in this way can chaos be avoided and confusion minimized. Thus, following the lead of Weber, some scholars have viewed modern organizations as a liberating force, a device that emancipates people from the influence of tradition and encourages productivity and efficiency.

Furthermore, the impersonal rule of law is as essential in organizations like the corporation or the union as it is in government. Arbitrary decisions by officials may be appropriate for a premodern setting, but they are out of place in a modern democracy. The same holds true for traditional methods of filling offices and rewarding the work of members. Ascribed status by virtue of family name or sex is becoming less significant. Achieved position, which comes about through personal expertise and promotion based upon a clearly delineated career pattern, is required in a complex modern society.

In addition, there are indications that modern people are successfully putting the rule of reason to work in associational life, despite the many problems of bureaucracy. Alvin Gouldner [1959] points out that modern organizations have become increasingly dependent upon the kinds of rational information supplied by operations and market researchers, opinion pollsters, industrial sociologists, and group dynamicists. In other words, applied social science has improved the efficiency of large-scale bureaucratic organizations. Therefore, despite the familiar problems associated with it, rational organization in the form of bureaucracy can be made to work and deserves more favorable attention than it often gets in the current research. It establishes the structure within which people's spontaneous needs are expressed, and as such it sets limits to the informal dimensions of behavior within associations.

Informal Aspects: The Human Response

As we have seen, human needs are never fully met by rational efficiency, and people frequently act out of deep-seated emotional responses to their environment. Spontaneity, then, inevitably produces informal and personal patterns of interaction within an organization, and these in turn modify the highly structured bureaucracy. This perspective has been called the *natural system model* of social organization—that is, the model that takes into account the natural reactions of members.

Although Max Weber tended to underemphasize this aspect of organizational life, he, too, was concerned that the efficiency of bureaucracy might eventually destroy individual personality differences and result in dehumanizing regimentation. Alvin Gouldner refers to this concern in a 1909 speech by Weber and compares it to William Whyte's criticism of the organization man [Whyte, 1956, p. 402]. In other words, is there a danger that effective bureaucracy will snuff out personal spontaneous forms of behavior? Scholars have suggested that the following kinds of processes operate to offset this possibility:

1. Even in the most bureaucratized setting, authority can never be entirely rational. A bureaucrat is obeyed not only because of his or her formal skills and knowledge but also because of deference for the office. This deference can exist independently of rational rules and regulations. For example, all presidents of the United States tend to be accorded great prestige and honor because of historical tradition. This happens even though the Constitution provides no basis for "imperial" respect, or even when an individual president is not an effective formal leader.
2. Individual bureaucrats can transcend the formal requirements of office because of unusual qualities. Therefore, some presidents are accorded more or less prestige than others because of exceptional personal characteristics.
3. In all bureaucracies, there is a latent tendency to permit informal relaxation of rules. When rules appear to be too oppressive, leaders may relax them as reward for cooperation. Furthermore, if inflexibly applied, formal rules can be counterproductive to an organization's goals. Many people praise those leaders who can "cut red tape" and get things done in spite of formal requirements. For example, some presidents may promise not to veto legislation in order to obtain cooperation and compromise from Congress; or they may use informal bargaining and compromise to obtain desired goals, rather than relying upon formal authority such as the veto power.
4. Informal practices can develop that are in opposition to formal regulations. For example, there is a tendency for advisors to leaders to withhold or distort information they consider unpleasant or disturbing. Some military leaders and other officials manipulated information given to President Johnson (as former Commander-in-Chief of the Armed Forces) during the Vietnam War in order to maintain the feeling that the war could be won and that there was "a light at the end of the tunnel" [Adams, 1975].

In other words, these kinds of informal human responses to formal and impersonal bureaucracy constitute a natural system of social relationships found in all organizational contexts, even the most rational. They illustrate the human element in associations, the element that can never be completely controlled by rules or regulations.

The problem for social scientists is to strike a balance between rational and natural system models of organizational life. Both forms of behavior can be either functional or dysfunctional in terms of organizational goals and daily activity. For example, although certain features of rational organizations (specialization and impersonality) can lead to dehumanization

7-3 The Desirable and Undesirable Consequences of Bureaucracy

The dilemma of bureaucratic organization is that it has both desirable and needed (functional) and undesirable and destructive (dysfunctional) consequences.

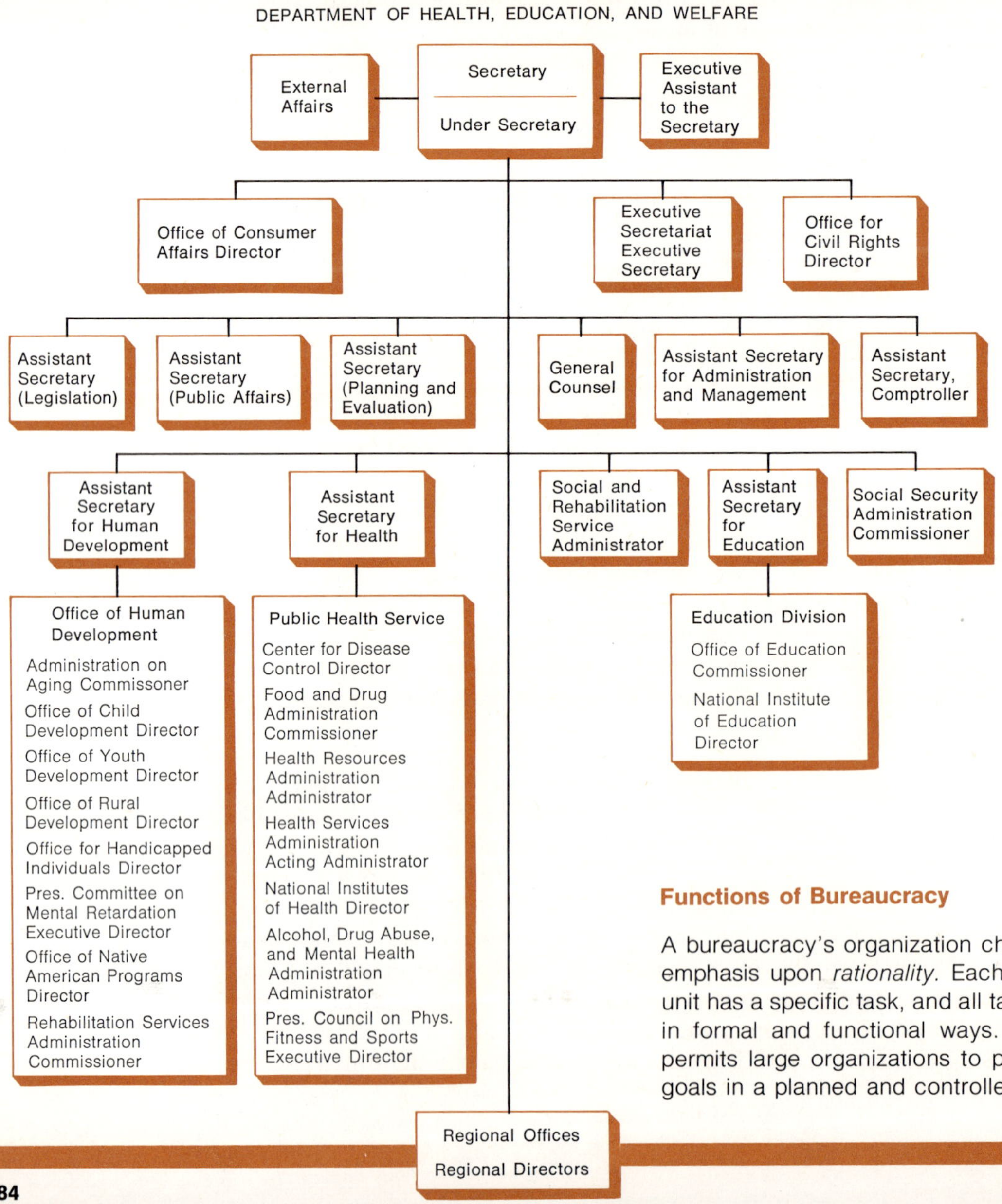

Functions of Bureaucracy

A bureaucracy's organization chart reflects the emphasis upon *rationality*. Each individual and unit has a specific task, and all tasks are related in formal and functional ways. This structure permits large organizations to pursue complex goals in a planned and controlled fashion.

E. Herwig/Stock, Boston

Bureaucratic structure also assures the most *efficient* and effective use of multiple skills and talents. Individuals are assigned specialized tasks on the basis of their ability to perform them and to assist others in the performance of different tasks.

David W. Corson from A. Devaney/E. P. Jones

Bureaucracies are more *democratic* than some other forms of human organization. Individuals can experience upward organizational mobility by demonstrating superior skills and knowledge, rather than being judged solely on the basis of ascribed criteria (sex, age, length of time in the organization, and so on).

Dysfunctions of Bureaucracy

P. Southwick/Stock, Boston

Rational organization leads to a dependence upon formal communication and contact, particularly between leaders and rank-and-file members. As a consequence, workers can become *alienated* and feel that they are nothing more than cogs in a large impersonal machine.

Donald Dietz, Dietz/Hamlin

The emphasis upon efficiency causes bureaucracies to adopt any method which enhances the operation of the organization. This leads to *a loss of spirit* or purpose. For example, means may be adopted for increasing and holding membership (church bingo) that conflict with basic goals and values (the evils of gambling).

C. Richard Read/Metamorphosis

When bureaucracies assign tasks on the basis of formally measured skills and abilities (typing speed, for example), employees feel that personal and emotional needs are not being met. *Boredom* develops from performing the same routines over and over again. The organization, therefore, loses employee spontaneity, creativity, and commitment.

and authoritarianism, other features (impartiality and coordination) can be liberating and rewarding. At the same time, some features of natural systems (informality and spontaneity) can lead to both desirable (bargaining, compromise, and the like) and undesirable (imperial deference to leaders, distortion of information, and so on) consequences. In addition, features of both models sometimes combine, as when small primarylike groups develop within large corporations.

The difficulty is that many scholars tend to focus only upon one aspect and succumb to the lure of scientific criticism. For example, Michels overlooks those formal and informal characteristics of organizational life that can lead to an "iron law of democracy." Gouldner [1955, pp. 496–507] criticizes social scientists for having become morticians, all too eager to bury human hopes, rather than clinicians, striving to further democratic potentials wherever they may be found. He suggests that a more productive focus would be an analysis of problems that stem from the interaction between rational and natural systems.

Several of these problems relate to the tensions between administrators and their subordinates in an organization. The administrator frequently must direct and evaluate experts who know far more than he or she does about their particular field of endeavor. The chemist who is a college president may have a peculiar personal view of the social sciences that may limit his ability to judge the faculty in terms of their academic qualifications. Consequently, job contracts and promotions may be approved on a human relations basis rather than upon a rigorous evaluation of faculty competence as social scientists.

A social scientist may feel more fully appreciated by other social scientists on other campuses than by his or her own university president and administrators. In fact, a faculty member must decide whether to be a "local" and win recognition within the college or to be a "cosmopolitan" and seek honors in wider circles at the risk of losing prestige at "home." Similarly, when deciding upon promotions for professors, the college must choose whether to reward loyalty to the institution or professional accomplishment. The more expert the members of the faculty, the more difficult it may be for them to maintain loyalty to the local institution. Organizational survival can be threatened either by a policy based only on the candidate's expertise or by a policy that regards loyalty as more important than ability.

Gouldner also helps us understand why widespread resentment of bureaucratic tendencies exists in modern organizations. Briefly, any organization is set within a social context. Members are socialized in the larger society and bring into an organization expectations and values that often come from traditional ways of life. Those who have traditional expectations about life will probably resent what they find within a bureaucracy. Whereas, in traditional society, authority is generally vested in older people, in an efficient organization, it is not uncommon for bright young people to be promoted to high levels of authority and to be in command over older and more experienced persons. This is part of the *line–staff conflict* depicted by Melville Dalton [1950, pp. 342–351]. Workers in the *line* are often old-timers who have been with the organization a long time and have worked their way up from the ranks. They may not have a recent or advanced education, but they do have the experience. They may resent the young "experts" just out of college or graduate school, whose up-to-date knowledge is so needed by the organization that it enables them to obtain high positions on the *staff.*

Traditional expectations also conflict with the needs of an efficient bureaucracy in other areas. For example, authority is traditionally vested in male workers rather than female; in a bureaucracy, however, skill is theoretically rewarded regardless of sex. Another area of conflict, and one most often complained about, concerns individuality. Traditionally, and especially in the family and primary associations of a rural society, individuals are treated as persons and not as instruments of production that can be freely manipulated. When members enter a large impersonal organization, they frequently resent being treated as mere cogs in a machine or as symbols on an IBM card. In summary, therefore, organizational tensions can develop when formal bureaucratic demands offend traditions and appear to threaten established, informal, and spontaneous practices.

As informal structure arises in response to the formal structure, members of an organization may engage in behavior designed to modify or subvert the formal structure or to alter the aims and goals of the organization. Sociologists are particularly interested in how formal and informal patterns of behavior within organizations support or conflict with one another. Studies of this kind have been conducted in religious and educational organizations and in mental institutions.

The Cases of the Church, the School, and the Asylum

It is possible to chart the formal organization of associations showing a hierarchy of authority, channels of control and communication, and rules of rational management. One of the largest religious denominations in contemporary American society is the Methodist church, numbering over 10 million members and reaching into almost every region and community. The organization chart for this church (as shown in Figure 7-2) depicts how the organization is supposed to work by emphasizing democratic participation of all members through elected delegates (see Chapter 10). One formal goal is total involvement of all church members, but an analysis of the informal structure reveals how there is actually a tendency toward oligarchy and apathy [Rankin, 1958].

In the contemporary Methodist church, power is latently concentrated in the hands of a few laypersons and ministers. Since most Methodists are busy with their own occupations, church decisions are left to ministers, some housewives, and a few older men who have the time to attend meetings. The laypersons who have time to attend are often the least influential (old-timers) and the most conservative. Therefore, informally the impor-

FIGURE 7-2 The Formal Organization of the Methodist Church (1975)

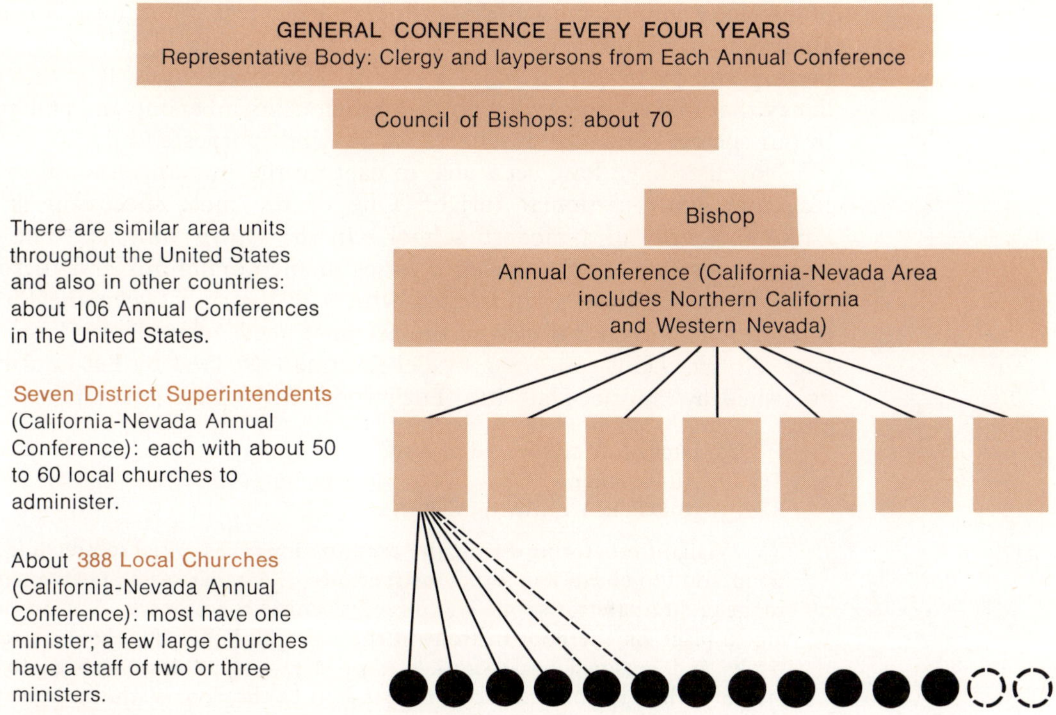

Ministers:

full connection: college degree and three years seminary training.

accepted supply ministers: may have only a high school education but are self-educated and have in-service training. They are ordained for work in a local church but are not fully qualified (not assured of a church and not permitted to vote in the Executive Session of Ministers which meets once a year to accept, ordain and retire ministers in full connection).

Lay Delegates to the Annual Conference: one layperson from each local church to balance the clergy from local churches. Laypersons have an equal vote on all policy and law except for matters pertaining to professional affairs of the ministers themselves.

tant decisions are made largely by the clergy. This is because they are more outspoken and more familiar with current church issues.

Churches may tend to subvert the ideals of the original organization by overemphasizing the things that can be measured—the size of membership, salary of the minister, new buildings, and the like. This results in the problem identified by Boulding as the conflict between the organization and the spirit. The dilemma in Methodism is especially heightened when a highly disciplined organization puts great stress upon methodical reports and when a bishop can display anger over financial accounts that show a smaller increase in donations for missionary work than in salaries and services. To a large extent, too, a minister's prestige is measured by the size of his salary, and his prestige can influence his career. Thus, ministers may attempt to minimize bad news and to maximize reports of increased membership and participation in all kinds of church activities. It is this tendency that makes statistical reports of religious membership and affiliation in our society generally unreliable for research purposes.

Novelists have long been able to capture the human response to bureaucracy with particular insight. One of the most successful is Bel Kaufman's story of a modern school, *Up the Down Staircase.* The following quotation is taken from a series of memorandums and personal notes between teachers confronted with a disparity between the formal rules of school organization and the personal needs of students [From the book *Up the Down Staircase* by Bel Kaufman. © 1964 by Bel Kaufman. Published by Prentice-Hall, Inc., Englewood Cliffs, New Jersey.]

> FROM: James J. McHabe, Adm. Asst.
> TO: All Teachers
> RE: MIDTERM EXAMINATIONS
>
> . . . Vigilant proctoring during the examinations is essential to preclude any temptation to cheat. Proctoring instructions: 1. Arrange seats in examination room in alternate rows, one seat directly behind the other. . . . 2. Students are to place on the floor in front of the room all books, notebooks, pocketbooks and personal possessions. . . . 6. If a student desires to go to the lavatory, the proctor will escort the student to the door of the examination room and summon the hall proctor, who will escort the student to the lavatory and will remain in the lavatory until the student is finished. Then the proctor will escort the student back to the door of the examination room and hand him over to the room proctor. 7. Proctors are to watch students actively throughout the examinations and be on guard for the following: eyes roving, lips moving, left arm not covering paper, bending down to tie shoe lace or pick up fallen object, blowing nose, yawning or sneezing too loudly, reaching into pocket, crumpling scratch paper into a ball, stretching legs too far out, studying nails or insides of wrists. Impress upon students the importance of high ethical standards: when they cheat they cheat only themselves. If they are caught cheating, the proctor must be blamed for lax supervision.
>
> • • •
>
> Intraschool Communication
> FROM: Room 304
> TO: Room 508
>
> Dear Bea—
>
> Just got Admiral's direction on Midterm proctoring. . . . It seems to me that—watched by hawk-eyed proctor—even if they had no intention to cheat, they'd be tempted to outwit him. Has anyone tried Honor System? I have a hunch that if they felt they were trusted, they'd rise to that trust. . . . What do I do if a kid is *not* covering with his left arm a paper which is *not* at right angles to his desk?
>
> Syl

Intraschool Communication
FROM: Room 508
TO: Room 304

Dear Syl—

You either kill the kid or yourself. Honor System would never work here—too great a premium on the Mighty Mark, which determines whether or not a kid gets into college and causes parental pressures and senior breakdowns. This is true of academic youngsters; nonacademic ones cheat pour le sport, as a matter of bravado, ingenuity or class status. Not to try to cheat is square. Trend is changing, though, from person-to-person cheating to cooperative cheating and teamwork. Some of the excuses they offer, when detected, are: altruism, good sportsmanship, and innocence—"I'm not cheating, I'm lefthanded!" . . . I'd like to know if you get any insights from their own comments on marks. You're a brave girl; we who are about to die salute you!

Bea

• • •

Dear Ellen:

It looks as if I might be fired from the school system—because I failed to provide a lavatory escort for Joe Ferone. . . . I escort him to the door—but there is no hall proctor in sight. . . . His need is urgent. We stand in the doorway for a moment, testing each other with our eyes. The situation is fraught. This may be my chance to win his trust at last. I whisper my permission for him to go alone. It is understood that he is honor-bound not to use the lavatory for any but legitimate purposes; not as a reference room, not to look up any answers that may be secreted on his person, not even for a quick smoke. He goes, and I return to my observation perch at the back of the room (so that the kids can't see *whom* I am watching: a tip from Admiral Ass!). A few minutes later, the Admiral himself appears in the doorway, white with rage, Ferone at his side. Clash of swords; two enemies face to face on either side of Ferone; the showdown—but *sotto-voce,* for we have an audience. . . .

McH: Do you realize his exam paper may be invalidated?
I: Why?
McH: He may have been looking up answers!
I: I don't think so. He told me he wouldn't.
McH: He *told* you?
I: Yes.
McH: And you believed him?
I: I believe him.
McH: Go back to your seat, young man. Miss Barrett, this is not the time and place to explain to you the gravity of your position. You had explicit instructions; you disobeyed them. You'll hear from me later. In the meantime, you will please put his paper aside when he is finished. The outcome of his examination will have a direct bearing on you. You understand that?
I: I think so.
McH: The second girl in the third row—eyes on your paper!

Exit the Admiral. Ferone and I look at each other. His face is impassive. Will he fail the exam to vindicate me? He is very bright; he has been an F student only because he chose to be. Suddenly he has become a moral issue by which I stand or fall. The incident of the lavatory has brought into focus my values against McHabe's—everything I believe in as opposed to all that is petty, degrades the dignity of my profession, and consequently, of my pupils; my desire to teach well, as opposed to bureaucracy, trivia and waste. . . . If only the McHabe's didn't keep getting in the way, I think I could move mountains. Now I have to mark, over the four-day Thanksgiving holiday, 201 papers. Each is in 5 parts. Each contains 2 compositions. . . .

Love,
Syl

• • •

Dear Miss Barrett:

Please bring to my office the examination paper of Joseph Ferone as soon as you have marked it. I understand that he has been a failing student in English for the last two terms.

Samuel Bester
Chairman, Language Arts Department

• • •

Intraschool Communication
FROM: Room 304
TO: Room 508

Dear Bea—

I've just graded Ferone's paper; he got 89%. Do you suppose I'll be court-martialed?

Syl

Rules and regulations, then, are required to ensure efficient and effective conduct of work in the school setting. In addition, regulations can act as a formal guarantee of equal and fair treatment for all students. Latently, however, regulations may become so elaborate and specified that they become conterproductive to the individual needs of students. Furthermore, teachers may rebel as they come to see the formal regulations in direct conflict with their professional ideals and standards. Teachers may stretch or ignore the rules in specific contexts, and students may develop elaborate means of redefining or justifying cheating.

Religious and educational contexts are not, of course, the only ones within which human beings learn to beat the system. When forced to live within strict formal boundaries, human beings become ingenious at modifying organizational structures regardless of context. As noted in Chapter 1, Peter Berger cites this characteristic as an indication that people never become completely enslaved to society, even though they are a product of the cultural and social setting.

Erving Goffman [1959] illustrates this same conclusion in his study of mental patients in a public hospital of over 7000 inmates and staff. Goffman found a human community in Central Hospital, similar in many respects to other social settings. Patients exhibited normal human responses to formal associational structure: that is, they learned to cooperate and participate as expected. At the same time, Goffman observed a number of other adjustments by which patients employed unauthorized means to obtain unauthorized ends. In this manner, they circumvented the organization's formal assumptions about how a "typical" well-behaved patient should act and, in essence, about what a "typical" patient should be.

Goffman [1959, pp. 171–320] found that the mental patients rebelled against the formal organization of the asylum in the following ways:

1. *Make-dos:* Unintended use of artifacts—for example, drying laundry on free-standing radiators.
2. *Work the System:* Exploitation of official routines for private ends—wrapping up first serving of food in napkins to take back to ward for a night snack; or use of therapy sessions to date girl friends or associate with nonpatients.
3. *Escape to Freedom:* Reject the close surveillance of most activities by going to free places or personal and group territories—a patch of woods for drinking or poker, or a back porch for socializing with attendants on an equal basis.
4. *Stash Belongings:* Overcome the public character of hospital life by hiding belongings under the mattress or in secret pockets (bulging pockets with concealed compartments become a symbol of status in the hospital).
5. *Undercover Transportation System:* Create independence from formal service system by developing ingenious ways of transporting one's own body, artifacts, or messages—a parole patient with canteen privileges fills the shopping lists for those in a restricted ward, smuggling goods in a cigar box.
6. *Make Use of Other Persons:* Redefine formal relationships by means of private coercion, economic exchange, or social exchange—a patient may use a subordinate to hold his chair for the movie, his exlandlady to withhold his Veterans Administration check from hospital authorities; or he may exchange favors to express appreciation with buddies, a girl friend, or an attendant.

The patients made these unauthorized adjustments for three reasons: (1) to obtain forbidden goods and services; (2) to conceal part of themselves and their activities from official recognition and judgment; and (3) to maintain their sense of personal autonomy and freedom. By the development of such an "underlife," as Goffman calls it, individuals express themselves as unique human beings within the organizational setting.

This perspective is important and deserves special comment. In Chapter 3 ("Self and Society"), we spoke about the self as emerging from and being dependent upon group life. This view alone can lead to an underestimation of the role of individual action and innovation. What Goffman is emphasizing is that individuals can be both within the group and set against the group. Just as a prisoner in a criminal institution will order a book from the library not for self-education but to make an impression on the parole board, so mental patients find ways of expressing their rejection of the formal organization that holds them captive:

> The practice of reserving something of oneself from the clutch of an institution . . . is not an incidental mechanism of defense but rather an essential constituent of the self. . . . [The individual] takes up a position somewhere between identification with an organization and opposition to it, and is ready at the slightest pressure to regain its balance by shifting its involvement in either direction. It is thus *against something* that the self can emerge. . . . Our sense of being a person can come from being drawn into a wider social unit; our sense of selfhood can arise through the little ways in which we resist the pull. Our status is backed by the solid buildings of the world, while our sense of personal liberty often resides in the cracks [Goffman, 1959, pp. 319–320].

This analysis of the importance of associations in human group life has dramatized the use of our continuum classification. It is evident that both spontaneous, less structured forms and rational, highly structured forms of behavior are present in all social relationships. Furthermore, both are required for the full development and survival of human individuals, groups, and societies.

▶ SO WHAT?

Utilizing these kinds of studies, some scholars and leaders have experimented with alternatives to bureaucratic organization, associational forms that combine elements of both the natural and rational models. The purpose is to humanize and democratize organizations without abandoning the efficiency of rational structures.

1. Professor Almond [1971, pp. 34–42] reports on the development of a *therapeutic community* in a small psychiatric unit of a large bureaucratic hospital. The unit has between 20 and 40 patients, is self-governing, and is based upon open discussion of patient problems. Staff and patients help one another in the decisions that affect their daily lives. Almond [1971, p. 36] depicts the difference between this form of organization and traditional bureaucracy (see Figure 7-3).

FIGURE 7-3 Comparison of Bureaucratized Asylum and Therapeutic Community

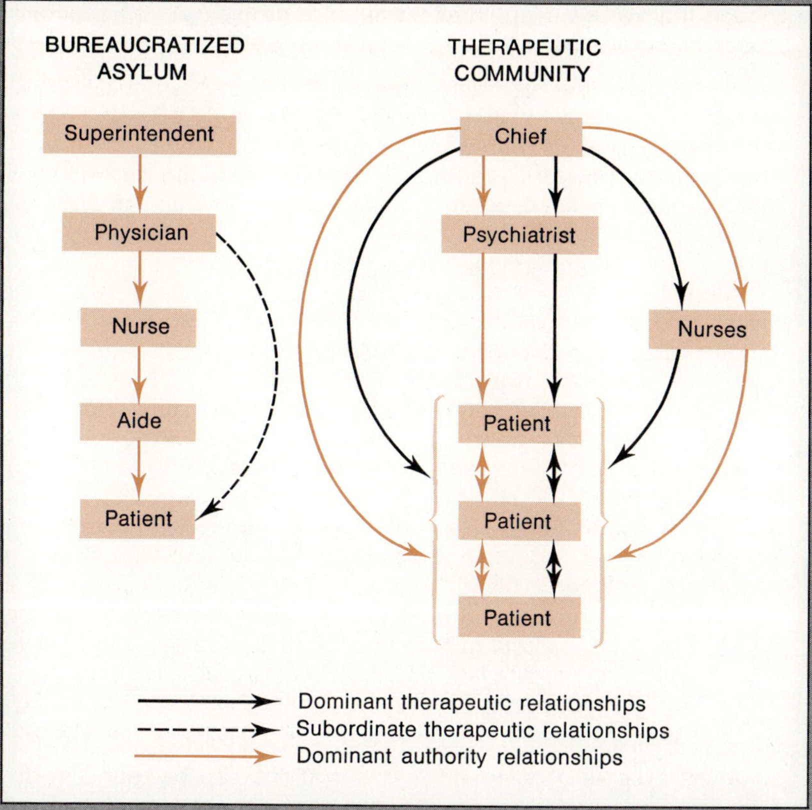

From Richard Almond, "The Therapeutic Community," *Scientific American, 224* (March 1971), p. 36.

In bureaucratized asylums, authority relationships dominate and are one-way. In therapeutic communities, both authority and therapeutic relationships involve a maximum number of staff and patients in mutual interaction. Thus, a feeling of shared problems and a sense of community are developed. One patient commented:

> I was quite taken aback when people would come up and say to me, "Why were you brought here?" I began talking with very many people, staff and patients alike. I began seeing the problems I had. . . . I was becoming more objective. . . . I had never been quite so clear about what got me into this illness.

Almond points out that similar self-help communities are used by Alcoholics Anonymous, Synanon (for narcotics addicts), and Recovery, Inc. (for former mental patients). In addition, the healing cults of primitive societies often use social involvement within the cult; they also teach new role behavior through use of primary interaction with others. Therefore, other societies, even nonmodern ones, may have models that can be adapted to alleviate the problems of bureaucracy in contemporary organizations.

2. Another society that has been experimenting with alternative organizations is Yugoslavia, where *worker self-management* has been a basic part of political theory and constitutional law since the 1950s. This concept transforms economic organizations into communities that are not committed to profit making alone; they also provide for social and political decision making by workers and management alike. A 1971 conference sponsored by the Center for the Study of Democratic Institutions reported that every Yugoslav organization has a workers' council elected by the total membership of the organization [Adizes and Borgese, 1975]. This council is an autonomous body that makes its own internal rules regarding policies, sharing of revenues, allocating of resources, and other business. Self-management differs from the bureaucratized capitalist model in that it does not rely upon outside influences to resolve conflicts (for example, compulsory collective bargaining initiated by the government). It is also based upon a "linking pin" concept of membership; each member of any community is also a member of other communities. Thus, a factory worker who is on the communal board of a municipality can represent the interests of one community within the other. This leads to the formation of comprehensive goals that relate organizational and community needs. In twenty years of self-management, Yugoslavian yearly per capita income has risen from $200 in 1950 to $700 in 1970; industrial output has increased fivefold.

3. Another example of alternative organizations can be found in the Swedish Saab and Volvo automobile factories. The Scandinavian Institutes for Administrative Research [SIAR, 1973] have helped these organizations *redesign the assembly line*. Teams of three to four workers assemble light, four-cylinder car engines at a rate of up to eight per hour, and team members decide among themselves who will work on what part of the engine [*Time,* 1975, p. 42]. Units to be worked upon by the team are mounted on separate free-wheeling tables, in place of the traditional long and unbroken assembly line. Factories are reported to be safer, cleaner, cooler, and better lighted than similar U.S. plants, and they contain more work space per person. A sense of communication and worker autonomy is created. This organization can be adapted to community needs as well; for example, Swedish workers change shifts each week to allow working spouses to take turns with household chores.

A word of caution is necessary. Because these alternatives to bureaucracy work well in one context does not mean that they are automatically applicable in another. The therapeutic community seems particularly appropriate for patients with mental problems, but it might not work for those in hospitals suffering purely physical afflictions. Some U.S. workers who have visited the Saab and Volvo factories in Sweden dislike the apparent loss of individual freedom in favor of dependence upon group commitment in the work situation. Also, changing of shifts would have little meaning in a society where household chores are not generally shared by two working spouses. A socialist and decentralized society like Yugoslavia seems more congenial to worker self-management than the highly centralized private-profit economies of many other developed nations.

CONCLUSION

Associations are organizations that combine both formal and informal —structured and spontaneous—forms of behavior. Modern society is characterized by a multiplicity of associations, many reaching vast size and complexity. Individuals in contemporary society frequently join voluntary associations since these groups act as intermediaries between the primary ties of family and friends and the secondary bonds of citizenship and occupation. This mediating activity gives associations a crucial political role in the maintenance of democratic processes. They can become a training ground for the skills of leadership since they encourage meaningful interaction between leaders and followers. They can also help check the inherent tendencies toward managerial oligarchy and worker apathy in large-scale organizations.

One of the major problems faced by all associations, particularly large-scale organizations, is the conflict between the impersonal structured character of bureaucracy and the human need for personal spontaneous (primary) behavior. Many organizations attempt to provide both formal and informal means of handling this problem, illustrated by Lipset's study of the ITU or by systems of worker autonomy in factories. In addition, individual members devise ways of fighting or beating the system, as we saw in the cases of the school, the church, and the mental asylum. Recognizing the tendency for people to fight for spontaneity within the formal system, some social scientists have sought to identify alternative forms of organization, as reflected in the studies of therapeutic communities and worker self-management in Yugoslavia. Adjustments by individuals and organizations must be made if each is to survive and continue to function in a vital and meaningful way.

This discussion of associations has implied throughout the importance of another major form of group behavior—human communities. The community context frequently determines the kinds of associations that develop, the functions they perform, and whether they are largely informal or highly structured. The following chapter discusses the way in which human communities also frequently combine more spontaneous and more rational characteristics.

REFERENCES

Adams, Sam. "CIA Cover-up: Playing War with Numbers," *Harper's, 250* (May 1975), pp. 41ff.

Adizes, Ichak, and Elisabeth Mann Borgese, Ed. *Self-Management: New Dimensions to Democracy.* Santa Barbara, Calif.: A.B.C.-Clio Press, 1975.

Almond, Richard. "The Therapeutic Community," *Scientific American, 224* (March 1971), pp. 34–42.

Barber, Bernard. "Participation and Mass Apathy in Associations," in Alvin Gouldner, Ed., *Studies in Leadership.* New York: Harper & Row, Publishers, 1950.

Bender, Marylin. "Corporate Wives Studied," *The New York Times* (21 February 1971), Financial Section, pp. 1ff.

Boulding, Kenneth E. *The Organizational Revolution: A Study in the Ethics of Economic Organization.* New York: Harper & Row, Publishers, 1953.

Dalton, Melville. "The Conflicts Between Staff and Line Managerial Officers," *American Sociological Review, 15* (June 1950), pp. 342–351.

DeTocqueville, Alexis. *Democracy in America,* Henry Reeve, Transl.; Henry Steele Commager, Ed. New York: Oxford University Press, 1947. (DeTocqueville's original work was published in 1835 and 1840.)

Fichter, Joseph. *Southern Parish.* Chicago: University of Chicago Press, 1951.

Goffman, Erving. *Asylums: Essays on the Social Situation of Mental Patients and Other Inmates.* Chicago: Aldine Publishing Company, 1959.

Gouldner, Alvin W. "Metaphysical Pathos and the Theory of Bureaucracy," *The American Political Science Review, 49* (June 1955), p. 496–507.

————. "Organizational Analysis," in Robert K. Merton, Leonard Broom, and Leonard S. Cottrell, Jr., Ed. *Sociology Today.* New York: Basic Books, 1959.

Harp, John. "Formal Voluntary Organizations: Agents of Stability and Change," *Search, 3,* No. 7 (1973), pp. 1–28.

Kaufman, Bel. *Up the Down Staircase.* Englewood Cliffs, N.J.: Prentice–Hall, 1964.

Lowry, Ritchie P. *Who's Running This Town?* New York: Harper & Row, Publishers, 1965.

Lynd, Robert S., and Helen M. Lynd. *Middletown.* New York: Harcourt, Brace and World, 1929.

Michels, Robert. *Political Parties: A Sociological Study of the Oligarchic Tendencies of Modern Democracy.* New York: The Free Press, 1949.

Parsons, Talcott. *The Social System.* New York: The Free Press, 1951.

Rankin, Robert P. *Religious Ideals and Church Administration: A Sociological Study of Methodism.* Unpublished Ph.D. thesis. University of California, Berkeley, California, 1958.

Riesman, David, Nathan Glazer, and Reuel Denney. *The Lonely Crowd.* New Haven: Yale University Press, 1950.

SIAR (Stiftelsen Foretags-administrativ Forskning). "The Problems of Large Organizations in a Structurally Changing Environment—Summary of Research Results for SIAR's First Five Years: 1961–1966" (February, 1973). SIAR, Östgötavägen 8, S-222-25, Lund, Sweden.

Time Magazine. "Doubting Sweden's Way" (10 March 1975), p. 42.

Warner, Lloyd W. *Yankee City.* New Haven: Yale University Press, 1963.

Weber, Max. "Geshaftsbericht," *Verhandlungen des Ersten Deutschen Soziologentages von 19–22 Oktober 1910 in Frankfurt a.m.* (Tubingen), 1911. Paper presented at conference. Translated for private use by Everett C. Hughes (January 1940).

———. *The Theory of Social and Economic Organization,* A. M. Henderson and Talcott Parsons, Transl. New York: Oxford University Press, 1947.

Whyte, William H., Jr. "The Wives of Management," *Fortune, 44* (October 1951), pp. 86ff.

———. *The Organization Man.* Garden City, N.Y.: Doubleday and Company, 1956.

Vagts, Alfred. *A History of Militarism: Civilian and Military.* New York: The Free Press, 1967.

- When you think of your home town, do you think of it as the physical place in which you live or as the friends you know?
- Is it better to grow up in a small town or in a large city?
- Does it make any difference where a person grows up?
- How would you describe the ideal community?
- How would you measure the quality of life in your town? When you come to the section in this chapter that deals with this topic, consider how you would improve upon the study cited. For example, how would you account for Emily's feeling about her hometown as described in the chapter introduction?

8

Communities

For the sociologist, *a community* is much more than a settlement of people in a geographical area. It is a network of human relationships that develops over a long period of time and takes on a special quality of life. When Thornton Wilder wrote the well-known drama entitled *Our Town* in 1938 he was portraying the everyday experiences of people living together from birth to death in a small town. Some of the resulting community experiences were harmonious and satisfying, while others were troubled and marked by conflict.

The tension between change and stability in community life also fascinates both the sociologist and the playwright. In Act III of *Our Town*, returning from the grave to look at her town, Emily cries out:

I can't look at everything hard enough. There's the butternut tree. There's Mr. Morgan's drug store. And there's the High School, forever, and ever, and ever. And there's the Congregational Church where I got married. . . . Life goes so fast. We don't have time to look at one another. Good-by world. Good-by, Grover's Corners. . . . Mama and Papa. Good-by clocks ticking . . . and Mama's sunflowers. And food and coffee. And new-ironed dresses and hot baths. . . and sleeping and waking up. Oh, earth, you're too wonderful for anybody to realize you. Do any human beings ever realize life while they live it . . . every, every minute? [Wilder, 1957, pp. 87–100]

WHAT IS A COMMUNITY?

The Problem of Definitions

George A. Hillery, Jr. [1955, pp. 194–204] found that, although social scientists differ in their definitions of community, they usually agree on at least three characteristics. Of the 94 definitions he identified, 69 designated *social interaction, area,* and a *common tie* (or *ties*) as fundamentally important. Christen T. Jonassen found considerable agreement on the presence of the following elements in a community: (1) a population; (2) a territorial base; (3) interdependency of specialized parts and a division of labor; (4) a common culture and social system, which integrate activity; (5) an awareness of unity or belonging among the inhabitants; and (6) an ability to act in a corporate fashion to solve problems. Jonassen [1959, pp. 20–21], therefore, arrived at the definition of a community as "a spatial group wherein the effects of interdependence and integration are made evident by the community's consciousness of unity and its ability to exercise adequate control over social, cultural, and biotic processes within its boundaries."

Nevertheless, the problem of defining and empirically identifying specific communities continues to be a perplexing one for sociologists. Roland L. Warren [1963] reminds us that it is no longer possible to draw a clear boundary between one town or city and another. Localities often overlap, some citizens going in one direction for shopping and various community services, and others going in different directions. Small communities in modern society are rarely independent of other towns or, particularly, of large cities in the region.

Warren [1963] indicates that social scientists discovered early in this century that political boundaries did not necessarily coincide with patterns of community activities (see Chapter 11). Thus, recent studies refer to the community as a *trade area* that includes a broad set of interrelated institutions and associations (industry, stores, churches, social organizations, schools, government agencies, and so on). Warren, therefore, views a community as any combination of social units needed to sustain social functioning within some locality. Locality produces particular kinds of social relationships. These, in turn, produce special kinds of social groupings, which give different communities their unique quality. This type of conceptualization has become the basis for identifying those social processes that create a community life.

What Creates Communities?

James S. Coleman [1971] says that we often speak of a locality as a community because, when people live in close proximity for a period of time and share common or complementary activities, community-generating processes arise. *Similar activities* (work, education, religious behavior, organized leisure) encourage the development of similar values, attitudes, and beliefs. In addition to similar activities, *common needs and interests* help to develop a sense of community. When people feel the need for protection against crime or for the development of a better water system, they tend to band together and establish community organizations. Communities emerge when citizens in local contexts confront common problems.

Conversely, one of the contemporary threats to community life is the tendency for many of these problems to be handled by state and federal governments rather than by local residents. When citizens do not have to cope with local events and issues, they find it increasingly difficult to develop and maintain a strong sense of community. This situation may, in fact, be circular in nature, and therefore, self-perpetuating: Community apathy leads to outside aid, which, in turn, leads to more apathy and indifference. This is precisely the sort of community problem that constantly challenges such nationwide programs as slum clearance, aid to the poor, and smog control.

Community interaction can also be based upon *dissimilar activities.* For example, the real estate dealer and the teacher are often interdependent, their occupational roles influencing one another. They both may have a genuine concern for better schools, as a way of making their community a more desirable place in which to live. At the same time, their interests may conflict. Improved teachers' salaries may necessitate higher property taxes, which, in turn, may decrease real estate sales. Hostility may then develop, resulting in conflict, which, if resolved, can encourage necessary social change and, thus, strengthen community life. Unresolved conflict, however, can become a serious threat to the community. We have witnessed this type of process in contemporary American cities where blacks and police have developed hostilities toward one another that have resulted in city-wide violence by both police and citizens.

Finally, Coleman identifies two different sources of community action—(1) identification with others or (2) self-interest. He utilizes Ferdinand Tönnies' [1957] concepts of *Gemeinschaft* and *Gesellschaft* to illustrate these two types of community action. In a small town where people have lived together for a long time and have shared many intimate group experiences, a shared identity—a *Gemeinschaft* spirit—is present. If, for example, there are loose bricks in the cornice of a hotel, a citizen may report them because of strong feelings of identity with both the hotel owner and any pedestrian who might be injured. Their fate is the citizen's fate, and the citizen is motivated to help from a sense of mutual identity.

In contrast, in a large city where relationships are much more impersonal, a citizen is less likely to report the loose bricks because of little feelings of responsibility for either the hotel owner or any pedestrians. Nevertheless, self-interest—a spirit of *Gesellschaft*—can foster community action that will lead to necessary repairs. A bricklayer will be employed by the hotel owner who is anxious to maintain a good reputation in the community and to avoid being sued by injured persons. In all communities, both kinds of motivation—identification with others and self-interest—are present in varying degrees, though *Gemeinschaft* prevails in older small towns and *Gesellschaft* predominates in newer large cities.

These, then, are some of the social interaction processes that lead to the development of communities, whether they are small villages or large cities. Urban life, however, is obviously different from rural life. Using a conceptual approach similar to Coleman's and Tönnies', Louis Wirth defines and characterizes the particular nature of urban communities. His discussion is the subject of the following section.

A Sociological Definition of the City

One of the classic essays in American sociology is Louis Wirth's "Urbanism as a Way of Life" [1939]. As a professor in the "Chicago School of Sociology" in the early part of this century, Wirth argued that a truly sociological definition of the city was needed. He criticized previous studies by pointing out that characterizing a city on the basis of population size and physical boundaries alone was misleading. Wirth began his analysis with the three demographic traits traditionally used to identify urban communities—(1) *large size;* (2) *extreme density* (number of people per square mile); and (3) *heterogeneity* (diverse occupations, races, ethnic groups, and so on). Wirth maintained, however, that these traits alone were not sufficient to distinguish the unique quality of urban life from life in small, sparsely settled, and homogeneous rural communities. As a sociologist, he raised the question of how such demographic traits affected self-conceptions, interpersonal relationships, social roles, and the cultural norms in cities.

Wirth characterized their influence as follows:

1. The superficiality, anonymity, and transitory nature of urban social relationships results in the sophisticated, cosmopolitan, and rational personality so often ascribed to residents. Urbanites relate to each other as a means of achieving their own ends.
2. In a *Gesellschaft* community, where it is impossible for residents to know one another intimately, communications must take place through indirect and formal mediums.
3. In the urban context, physical contacts are close and numerous, whereas social contacts are distant. As a result, urbanites put a premium upon visual recognition. Uniforms, both manifest and latent, become symbols of roles, and urbanites rarely recognize the

8-1 What Creates A Community?

Although social scientists disagree on many of the characteristics common to all communities, they agree that three are fundamentally important—territory, social interaction, and culture. Each of these characteristics combines to reinforce the others, whether the community is a small village, a neighborhood, a large city, or a metropolis.

Elizabeth Hamlin, Dietz/Hamlin

Lou Draper/Metamorphosis

A common **territorial base** for a population forms an area within which individuals and groups can interact with one another. In small territories, the interaction may be more primary, while in large territories it may be more secondary. In either case, a social system of interdependent individuals and groups arises.

Elizabeth Hamlin, Dietz/Hamlin

Interacting individuals and groups become related because each possesses special skills, performs different functions, or occupies different roles. These various skills, functions, and roles become interdependent in order for the population to achieve desired goals. In smaller communities, such interaction is most often informal and spontaneous—as in the case of a block party. In larger communities, it is most often formal and unemotional—as in the case of business and commercial activities.

G. Malave/Stock, Boston

Staffan Weinberg/Black Star

A social system of interdependent individuals and groups also leads to the creation of a common **culture.** By sharing similar norms and values, community residents create of feeling of mutual identity and uniqueness. In smaller communities, this identity may be expressed in the form of special celebrations involving fairs or rodeos. In larger communities, widespread support for professional athletic teams (in baseball, football, basketball, and so on) performs the same cultural function.

Charles Harbutt/Magnum

personal eccentricities hidden behind them. The world of artifacts and material elements becomes most important.

4. Because of the spirit of competition and the tendency toward exploitation, formal controls are utilized to minimize disorder and to counteract irresponsibility. Rigid adherence to routine, symbolized by dependence upon the clock and the traffic signal, are necessary for the social system to maintain itself.

In summary, if one is to survive as an individual in the city, and if the city is to survive as a social system, interaction between people must occur in partial and formal ways. Primary relationships become less appropriate and are replaced by more functional secondary relationships. The problem is that these secondary relationships may become characteristic of all interaction in the metropolitan community. Thus, the cold, impersonal and blasé attitude characteristic of many urbanites is, in fact, the result of environmental adaptation rather than the manifestation of sick or inhuman personalities.

If residents of the city were to become deeply and personally involved with everyone around them, they would—as a result of population size and density—be overwhelmed with personal crises, daily tensions, and other strains. Residents would find themselves continually involved with death, sickness, family dissolution, behavioral deviance, and mental disorder, as well as with a multitude of normal everyday encounters. Therefore, in order to protect themselves psychologically, urbanites remain aloof and disengaged, and they become accustomed to interacting in formal and partial ways.

Wirth's functional defense of urban life touches upon a major problem that has preoccupied students of community life in recent years—that is, "the loss of community" in modern society. What has really been lost is a type of community, the older, more traditional sense of intimate and personal community. Some scholars argue that as an intimate community disappears, personal insecurity, alienation, and anomie increase, and that these are the features that characterize the trend toward worldwide urbanization. Citizens then turn away from traditional communities toward other social institutions, often the nation-state, in a search for a new sense of community.

The Quest for Community

Robert A. Nisbet puts the study of communities in historical perspective. He contrasts the security of the premodern *gemeinschaftliche* communities of medieval society to the insecurities of communities in the modern Western world. He argues that we have gained new freedom as individuals by giving up the bonds of feudal caste, medieval church, and traditional kinship groupings. Yet, with the increased freedom and individualism that has accompanied capitalism, Protestantism, and democracy, there has

8-2 Functions and Dysfunctions of Gemeinschaft and Gesellschaft

Ferdinand Tonnies distinguished between two different types of communities: *Gemeinschaft* contexts are primary, informal, and personal; *Gesellschaft* contexts are secondary, formal, and impersonal. Each type of context has unique functions and dysfunctions. In addition, each type can be encouraged by designing the physical context to provide for primary or for secondary interaction.

Gemeinschaft Communities

Donald Dietz, Dietz/Hamlin

Parks or squares in towns and cities frequently become contexts within which a *Gemeinshaft* spirit prevails—a spirit based upon shared identity and mutual activities. These territories are designed so that face-to-face interaction can take place (benches facing one another, chairs around tables, etc.) and small intimate groups can form around common activities (card playing, talking, lawn bowling, and so on).

Elizabeth Hamlin, Dietz/Hamlin

Within formal organizations, such as schools, the same features are often employed to create a *Gemeinschaft* character. Classrooms may have separate cubicles and small tables with chairs, where spontaneous groups can form around similar projects (see the *So What?* box in Chapter 10). In addition, this type of context encourages independence and the release of the unrestrained "I" (watching others at play, engaging in isolated games and play, and so on).

Donald Dietz, Dietz/Hamlin

Even in highly urbanized contexts, architecture can be planned to encourage *Gemeinshaft* interaction. Hotels or business buildings may have inner and enclosed parks or malls, containing separate benches and tables that facilitate small group formation. This setting can help offset the anonimity of the larger social setting by providing an attractive surrounding where primary-like work, recreational, and friendship groups can continue their informal and different activities.

Gesellschaft Communities

Sometimes, however, a *Gesellschaft* spirit is more desirable —a spirit based upon the effective pursuit of self-interest. Airports must handle large numbers of people with different needs, and for reasons of safety the emphasis must be upon formality and efficiency. Long, sterile-looking passageways and rows of seats that are uncomfortable and do not face one another make the formation of small primary groups difficult. Furthermore, the unemotional nature of the context guarantees that people will keep moving (meeting arrivals, catching outgoing flights, etc.) and a permanent and hard to control population (drifters, beggers, the homeless, and so on) will not accummulate.

N. Sapieha/Stock, Boston

Donald Dietz, Dietz/Hamlin

In modern society, schools must train large numbers of students with different abilities and needs in the same basic skills and knowledge. A *Gesellschaft* context, emphasizing formality and motivation based upon self-interest, best meets this need. The traditional classroom with separate desks all facing the teacher makes it difficult for students to form primary groups or engage in spontaneous behavior, both of which could distract from common learning.

Similarly, most modern hotels must provide a momentary stopping place for a highly transient and diverse population. The *Gesellschaft* context emphasizes efficiency and minimizes emotional and primary-like interaction. The problem is that environments which provide only these characteristics may rapidly begin to experience conditions of anomie and alienation, both among those served by the airports, schools, and hotels and among those providing the services.

Elsa Dorfman

also come rootlessness and anomie. Ours is an age of industrialization and urbanization, and our cities and towns have taken on the *Gesellschaft* qualities of the marketplace, where people are related to others by formal contract and rational calculation. Not only are economic relationships more impersonal, but urban residents are also less likely to be intimately related to church and family or to feel a strong sense of identification with their neighborhood and community.

> This is an age of economic interdependence and welfare states, but it is also an age of spiritual insecurity and preoccupation with moral certainty. Why is this? Why has the quest for community become the dominant social tendency of the twentieth century? What are the forces that have conspired, at the very peak of three centuries of economic and political advancement, to make the problem of community more urgent in the minds of men than it has been since the last days of the Roman Empire? [Nisbet, 1953]

Nisbet finds the answer in the breakdown of many traditional institutions, in the growth of superstates and totalitarianism, and in related feelings of insecurity experienced by modern people. He believes that a truly democratic society can survive only where a multiplicity of loyalties and associations are encouraged and act as checks against centralized commitment and authority. Such a concern is reflective of pluralist political theory, which we considered in the preceding chapter on "Associations." Nisbet goes on to point out, however, that a meaningful pluralistic society can arise only within a larger *communal* context, since the emergence of political extremism and personal insecurity, with all of their attendant problems, can be attributed, in part, to the general dislocation and weakening of community life in modern society.

The quest for the essential nature of community life is not particularly new. Since the time of Aristotle, people have sought to design or devise ideal communities, that is, to develop utopian settlements that would encourage the fullest expression of human potential. This quest, however, has been marked by urgency in recent years for a number of reasons. Apparent increases in community disorganization, deviance, mass apathy, personal anomie and alienation, especially throughout the Western world, seem to signal the decline of community. Furthermore, many of the utopian schemes for the creation of national communities, particularly totalitarian fascism and communism, have not only failed to meet their ideal goals but have also often resulted in the dehumanization of populations through the curtailment of individual freedom and liberty.

The sociological notion of a "quest for community" has influenced many modern professions, including architecture. Early in the 20th century, master architect Frank Lloyd Wright criticized the dehumanizing effect of many modern cities where the human need for an "organic" relationship with nature has been ignored. The buildings he designed are examples of indoor–outdoor living, even in the heart of a large city. Wright believed that buildings could be designed that would stimulate more creative and productive encounters between residents, that is, a more *Gemeinschaft* relationship. He saw prevailing urban architecture—impersonal and wasteful skyscrapers, anonymous tract houses, and isolated urban-renewal housing that resembled prefabricated penal colonies—as reflecting only the characteristics of *Gesellschaft* life [Marlin, 1975].

A word of caution is necessary concerning the Nisbet and Wright view of modern urbanization. Some critics see this perspective as an anticity bias and a naive desire to return to the "good old days" of a rural past. They suggest that it is not very scholarly or scientific to speak of the loss of community as though it were a transition from natural rural life to unnatural urban living [Bell and Newby, 1972]. Furthermore, critics argue that the concept of a loss of community implies that cities are something less than communities rather than a different form of community. Nevertheless, all scholars agree that rural and urban communities do exhibit different qualities of life, and this distinction is important in understanding *the process of urbanization.*

The Rural-Urban Transition: Urban Revolutions

One way of tracing the history of urbanization is to contrast rural and urban societies. A rural society is one in which agriculture predominates, and most people live on farms near villages, small towns, or small cities. According to the current definition of a rural society as one in which less than 25 percent of the people live in places of 2500 people or more, there are many rural areas, even in today's world. An urban society is defined as one in which fewer and fewer people are engaged in agriculture and many are employed in extraction industries, like mining and oil drilling, or in manufacturing and human services. The shift away from agriculture means that increasing numbers of people become concentrated in larger towns and cities.

This shift is often referred to as the *rural-urban transition.* It had occurred throughout human history at a gradual rate until the last two to three centuries; since then, the transition has been extremely rapid. To be more exact, however, there have, in fact, been two historic bursts of urbanization. One led to the development of ancient cities; the other resulted in modern metropolitanization. These have been called, by Leo Schnore [1967], the *first and second urban revolutions.* The first urban revolution—the first emergence of cities—was preceded by an agricultural revolution in the form of settled agriculture. However, none of the early urban developments were agriculturally productive enough to support more than 5–10 per cent of the total population as nonfarming city dwellers. This set an upper limit on urbanization, which was not exceeded until the modern period (starting in the 17th century). In contrast, during the second urban revolution, truly urban societies developed, featuring a majority of city dwellers and city growth on a permanent basis. Schnore points out that all the major regions of the world, including those called "underdeveloped," have been influenced by this later urbanization.

Modern Urbanization

Kingsley Davis points out that urbanized societies, where people live crowded together in towns and cities, are a new and recent direction in human social evolution:

> The urbanized societies of today . . . not only have urban agglomerations of a size never before attained but also have a high proportion of their population concentrated in such agglomerations. . . . Neither the recency nor the speed of this evolutionary development is widely appreciated. Before 1850 no society could be described as predominantly urbanized, and by 1900 only one—Great Britain—could be so regarded. Today . . . all industrial nations are highly urbanized, and in the world as a whole the process of urbanization is accelerating rapidly [Davis, 1965, p. 41].

One measure of urbanization is the proportion of the population living in cities of 100,000 or more. For the world as a whole, this measure increased between 1850 and 1950 much faster than it did from 1800 to 1850. In 1800, less than 2 percent of the world's population lived in cities of more than 100,000, while, by 1950, over 13 percent lived in such large cities [Davis, 1955, p. 433]. Furthermore, Davis indicates that this proportion grew at twice the 1900 to 1950 rate from 1950 to 1960 [Davis, 1965, p. 44]. As a consequence, by the year 2000, more than half of the world's population will be living in cities of 100,000 or more people.

This world-wide urbanizing trend was partly a result of a significant shift in population from rural to urban regions, particularly in industrializing Western nations. In 1800, about 95 percent of the population of the United States was designated as rural. By 1900, 60 percent of the population was rural, and 40 percent urban. By 1970, the urban percentage had reached 73.5 [*The U.S. Census of Population,* 1970].

Definitions of what constitutes an urban or rural place vary from one society to another. Furthermore, the village of 5000 inhabitants in modern America does not have the same character as the medieval town of 5000. Similarly, a community of 10,000 in Pakistan can be highly urban, while in the United States a community of similiar size may be traditionally rural. However, statistics do serve to highlight the spectacular development of urban life as a consequence of modern agricultural, industrial, communication, and transportation technology. Modern urban communities no longer need to depend upon the immediate surrounding countryside for their survival; they can draw instead upon the resources and goods of the entire world. Countries and societies, as a result, now find themselves politically, socially, and economically dependent upon others far beyond their own borders.

Urbanization, however, has not increased unchecked in all countries or areas of the world. In addition, the historical development of urban communities varies greatly from one type of society to the next. For example, as Davis pointed out, Britain, in the early 1800s, was by far the most urbanized country in the world, some 50 years ahead of any other. In fact, the most rapid urban increase in Britain took place in the first half of the 19th century, between 1811 and 1851. The most rapid urbanization in the United States was not until the period from 1860 to 1890; in Egypt, rapid urban gains did not occur until after 1920, and in India, not until 1941.

The growth of large cities—some of them numbering several million people and some merging with others to form a huge metropolitan area (sometimes called a megalopolis)—is thus a recent phenomenon and one that is rapidly sweeping the entire world. Schnore [1967, pp. 121–122] concludes that, although no one knows for sure, it is entirely reasonable to expect that 85 to 90 percent of the world's future population may live in cities. For this reason, any complete study of communities must consider the process of urbanization. At the same time, however, we must never forget that small towns and rural areas continue to play a vital part in society; one quarter of America's population still resides in nonurbanized areas. In fact, because of the number of industries now moving to the countryside, the rural workers of today are soon likely to become predominantly blue-collar workers, as Lee Taylor [1968, p. 24] points out:

> The occupations of people in rural areas [of the United States] are changing. Farming is declining; it is now a minority occupation. Blue-collar workers now out-number farmers in rural areas. . . . Many plants can be located in small towns and open-country areas. . . . The composite result is the bringing of urbanized social organization to rural areas; the urbanization of the whole of American life.

Three special aspects of community life have been particularly influenced by the rural–urban transition. As Maurice R. Stein indicates in his book, *The Eclipse of Community* [1960], most of the recent sociological research in community has focused on these three aspects:

1. *Ecology*—The relationship of the community's structure and organization to the natural and social environment. According to Stein, studies by Robert Park and Ernest Burgess of urbanization in the city of Chicago exemplify research concerned with this aspect of community life.
2. *Quality of Life*—The impact of change upon the culture of the community. The study of industrialization in Middletown by the Lynds is cited by Stein as representative research.
3. *Leadership and Political Structure*—Changes in community political life and particularly the problem of maintaining democratic processes. Stein cites Lloyd Warner's study of bureaucratization in Yankee City.

In other words, Stein suggests that the loss of community is a result of the impact of urbanization, industrialization, and bureaucratization upon small community life. These major foci will be discussed in detail in the remainder of this chapter.

ECOLOGY: THE PHYSICAL AND SOCIAL ENVIRONMENT

In our earlier discussion of the problems of defining a community, we indicated that most sociologists agree upon the importance of locality or area. This consensus reflects their recognition of the fact that natural geographical surroundings, man-made environmental elements (buildings, roads, parks, and so on), and population can all influence the kinds of communities that develop, the patterns of interaction that arise among residents, and the basic institutions and associations that evolve.

The *ecological approach* views community life in just this way; that is, it studies how people are related to land area and resources. Essentially, the ecological approach is analogous to biological studies of how plants and animals are related to natural regions and to each other. For example, if the ferns of the rain forest die, the insects will perish. Their ability to cope with such a change is restricted by their inherent organic capacities. The human capacity for adjustment is, of course, far greater. People can live in the forest, in the tropics, in the arctic, and even in the completely hostile world of outer space. Nevertheless, the environment does influence the patterns of community life that will evolve.

Robert Park and Ernest Burgess on Urbanization in Chicago

The classic ecological studies of urban life took place in American sociology during the period of the "Chicago School." In the 1920s and 1930s, men like Robert E. Park and E. W. Burgess became interested in the theoretical parallels between plant and human communities [Park *et al.*, 1925; Park, 1952]. Not only did they employ the concepts of cooperation and competition to explain patterns of urban life, they also saw such processes as accommodation, succession, invasion, and dominance at work. Just as a species of wild grass will invade and dominate a garden over a period of time, so do various ethnic groups invade urban regions and eventually become dominant. The history of American black migration from the rural South to northern and western urban centers, as well as the outward migration to the suburbs by whites, is a case in point. What the Chicago School of sociologists wished to do was to detect and describe consistent patterns in this kind of continuing process in community life.

Perhaps the best-known study is Burgess' *concentric zone theory* [Park *et al.*, 1925], developed from an analysis of the city of Chicago. Basically, this theory views the center of the city as originating at some key point, such as the intersection of major lines of communication and/or transportation. Immediately around this point develops Zone I, a district containing financial and commercial activity and the administrative institutions of city government. Residents in this zone are transient and live in hotels; others working in Zone I are only a "daytime" population, commuting from areas farther out. As the community grows and develops, Zone I takes roughly the shape of a circle, and other zones form in the shape of concentric circles around the city center.

In Zone II, we find light manufacturing. In large urban centers like Chicago, this is most often an area in rapid transition. As a result, real-estate values and the condition of property are in a state of flux. If Zone I develops and merges at various points with Zone II, land values can increase. If not, the presence of manufacturing may bring general blight and slow deterioration to the area. The residents here, individuals who cannot afford the costs of living farther out or in the expensive hotels of Zone I, live in blighted and slum conditions. Crime and delinquency are frequent, partly because of the living conditions and partly because of the area's proximity to the targets of crime. Near Zone II, and in Zone III, subzones of "bright light" areas spring up, where night clubs, prostitution, and gambling facilities are located. It is important to remember that Burgess did his study before the mass movement of middle- and upper-middle-class groups to the distant suburbs; there is an indication in many areas today that certain crimes have moved far out from the city center—for example, during 1967, numerous child molestations occurred in the suburban villages of Connecticut—since many of the targets are now located in the suburbs.

Farther out from the city's center, Burgess found that subsequent zones consist largely of different kinds of residential areas. Zone III houses the working people, including immigrant groups "on the move." It is an area where few residents own their own homes. Commercial activity is primarily small family-owned businesses. Zone IV is an area of mixed apartments and private dwellings, a middle-class district. In Zone V and beyond are upper-class residential areas, outlying business districts, heavy industry, and distant suburban communities.

In summary, Burgess found that land values correlated with centrality (proximity of a zone to the city's central core) and that social life correlated with land values. The Chicago School focused its research upon the three most central zones—Zones I, II, and III, the areas of rapidly changing land usage.

This is, of course, an idealized picture of urban community structure, and even our discussion varies somewhat from what Burgess actually found in Chicago. Most American cities do not look like neat concentric circles, although all contain some type of ecological variation similar to that described by Burgess. Other variables may limit the circular form of expansion. Because of Lake Michigan, for instance, Chicago actually looks like a series of concentric semicircles.

The tradition of early American community planning has also played a role in structuring urban ecological areas. The 19th century towns and cities of America generally developed streets and boundaries along a grid

FIGURE 8-1 Concentric Zone, Sector, and Nuclei Theories of Urban Ecological Areas Applied to a Western U.S. Community

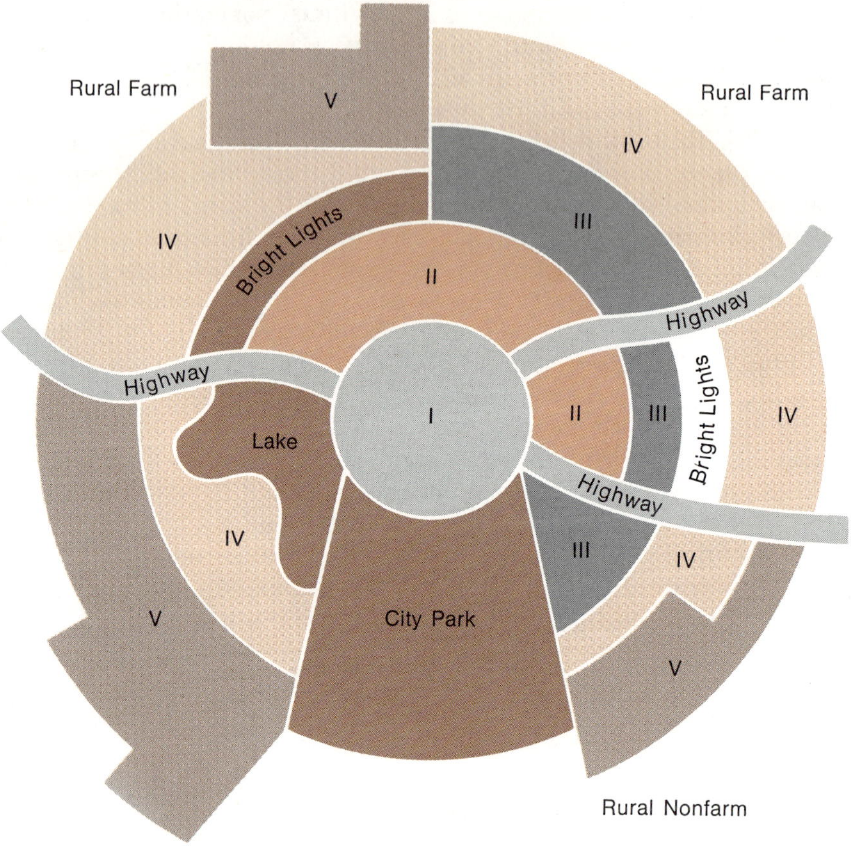

pattern rather than in a hub pattern, in which the streets radiated out, like spokes, from a central hub and intersected a series of larger concentric wheels. In communities developed according to the grid pattern—frequently a North–South and East–West grid—ecological areas tend to follow the major avenues of transportation. They most often look like truncated slices of a pie, or they may take on rectangular and other geometric shapes. These sector and nuclei approaches to ecological areas [Hoyt, 1939] seem to be more applicable to communities that have experienced very rapid growth over a short period of time and in which, as a result, various ethnic groups have not been able to establish long periods of residence in single zones. Figure 8-1 depicts a community that contains elements that illustrate the zonal, sector, and nuclei theories of ecological areas. No matter which theory is most applicable, different styles of life, resulting from adaptation to ecological variations in the environment, may be observed within any community.

The Ecology of Rural Areas and Small Towns: Industrialized Farming

Other community contexts are equally influenced by the impact of the physical environment. Writing in the 1940s, rural sociologist Carl Taylor *et al.* [1949] described the manner in which a basic crop can determine the patterns and cycles of community life, which, in turn, influence family life, recreational pursuits, education, and other activities. In looking at rural life in the United States, Taylor distinguished between six different geographical areas or regions on the basis of the fundamental crop—the cotton belt of the South; the corn belt of the middle United States; the wheat areas of the Midwest; the range–livestock regions of the West; the dairy regions of the Northeast; and specialty crop areas in the far West. He argued that distinctly different types of rural cultures and societies have arisen in each of these areas as a result of ecological adjustment to the cycle of planting, growing, and harvesting the basic crop.

For example, since cotton can be handled in a leisurely fashion, hand labor is employed with many families working as a unit. Family-owned farms and plantations utilize tenant farming and sharecropping. Use of tenant farmers has meant the development of a caste system. The church, rather than the school, has become the important social group since education often interferes with the cotton cycle. In contrast, corn dictates a demanding cycle with daily routine during planting and harvesting from 4:30 A.M. to 9 P.M. Family-owned farms become highly commercialized and industrialized. Urbanlike patterns develop; for example, many ministers and other community leaders are recruited from professional backgrounds in the city. Range–livestock areas call for "man's work," and cities become cow-town metropolises with bars, gambling, dependence on physical force, and so on. And, because of the need to transport dairy products quickly to urban markets, dairy farming is often found scattered among suburban developments and wealthy country estates. Thus, dairy farmers may live and act like suburbanites. In other words, the type of crop has an impact upon the ecology of a rural region, which, in turn, influences social and cultural life.

Large-scale harvesting by machines has recently changed some of these patterns. The appearance of intensive farming in the production of speciality crops also has stimulated social changes. For example, in one county of California, oranges, cherries, figs, prunes, grapes, livestock, poultry, olives, almonds, wheat, rice, and beets are all grown. This diversity is reflected in a population that includes Germans, Italians, Irish, Punjabis, blacks, Japanese, Chinese, Filipinos, Mexicans, Latin Americans, and Scandinavians. Some farms use industrialized agriculture, while others employ migrant farm labor. Extreme poverty and great wealth exist side-by-side, and frequent social-class conflict is not unusual. California's population increase and rapid urbanization reflect this diversity and explain in part the explosive nature of the recent social situation in that area.

Agriculture has become so mechanized in California that farms have been referred to as "factories in the fields." Farm workers have become organized into unions very much like factory workers in large cities. The early stages of this development were studied by scholars like Carey McWilliams [1939] and dramatized by novelists like John Steinbeck, who wrote *In Dubious Battle* [1936] and *Grapes of Wrath* [1939]. Rural unionization reached a critical period in the 1970s with a battle between Caesar Chavez's United Farm Workers' Union (UFW) and the Teamsters' Union. Violence erupted and the conflict was prolonged, causing bitter differences within California organizations, including both Protestant and Catholic churches. The result was a new labor law in 1975, which established a procedure for voting among the farm workers. Under this law, workers decided which union would predominate in an agricultural area. In October 1975, in San Francisco, the national labor union AFL–CIO voted to support Chavez and the UFW.

Anthropologist Walter Goldschmidt [1947] studied the impact of agricultural industrialization in three rural California communities in the 1940s and provided an ecological background for understanding the later conflict between the UFW, the Teamsters, and farm owners. Goldschmidt found that all three communities (Wasco, Dinuba, and Arvin) lost much of their rural character under the impact of industrialization. Early rural towns were small and people knew each other personally. The "hired man" on the traditional *gemeinschaftliche* farm was considered a part of the farmer's family.

As farm owners began to operate with complex machinery and businesslike organization, however, farming became rationalized and farm workers became contractual wage earners. Farm labor on a year-round basis, rather than only during harvest period, became necessary. Therefore, farm owners began contracting with migrant workers who moved up and down California following the cycle of different crops. These workers were no longer personally known in any community. They had only their manual labor to sell; otherwise, they were neither needed nor wanted. They often lived in temporary housing on the outskirts of a small town. As a consequence, rural communities lost much of their traditional intimacy and became more *gesellschaftliche.* The larger the new industrialized farms, the more impersonal became the relationships.

Goldschmidt found that the most urbanlike town was Arvin, and the least urbanlike was Dinuba. Wasco stood somewhere between these two extremes. Arvin consisted of large landholdings; Wasco had a mixture of large and small farms; and Dinuba had mostly small farms. Figure 8-2 shows Goldschmidt's [1947, p. 219] representation of these distinctions. According to the figure, the greater the percentage of large farms in the town, the greater the degree of industrialized or mechanized agriculture. Thus, Arvin was the most industrialized, and Dinuba the least.

This, in turn, had an impact upon occupational groupings in each of the communities (as shown in Figure 8-3). Arvin had the fewest farmers

FIGURE 8-2 Distribution of Farmland According to Size of Farm

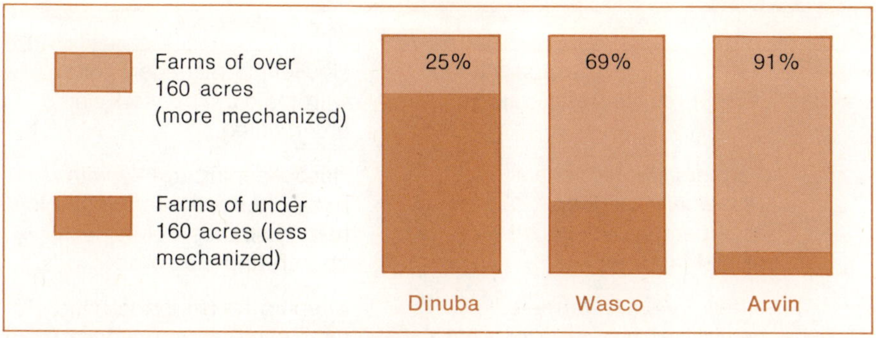

From Walter Goldschmidt, *As You Sow* (Glencoe, Ill.: The Free Press, 1947), p. 219. With permission of Macmillan Publishing Co., Inc.

FIGURE 8-3 Distribution of Employed Persons According to Occupational Status

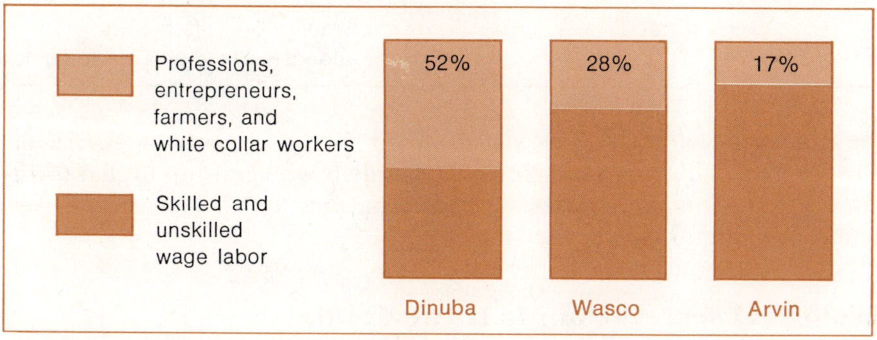

From Walter Goldschmidt, *As You Sow* (Glencoe, Ill.: The Free Press, 1947), p. 219. With permission of Macmillan Publishing Co., Inc.

and professional, white-collar, or enterpreneurial workers and the highest percentage of skilled and unskilled labor. As a result, owners of large farms in Arvin lived in the nearby city of Bakersfield and did not take part in community life to any great extent. A few entrepreneurs and small-farm owners acted as local leaders. This "nuclear group" felt strong ties to the community, in contrast to skilled and unskilled workers, who were considered "outsiders." On the other hand, in Dinuba, where farms were smaller, there was not as much social distance between land owners and workers. Since Wasco contained elements of both of these extremes, the status distinctions and life-style differences between all groupings could be found in that community [Goldschmidt, 1947, p. 91]. Wasco's various status groupings (and their associated life styles) are listed in Table 8-1.

Thus, more than merely the type of crop is involved in the ecology of community life. The mechanization of agriculture also plays an important role. These factors determine who is considered a high-status insider and who is considered a low-status outsider. Often outsiders literally "live on

TABLE 8-1 Social Status Distinctions in the Town of Wasco

Social Status		Men	Women
Nuclear Group—Insiders	Elite	Farm managers, corporate executives, professionals	Household managers, often with maids; club work and entertaining
	Middle	Farmers, professionals (especially teachers), salespersons, clerks, skilled laborers	Housekeeping, rarely with help; often work for wages to help husbands in business; church and club work
	Marginal	A few "worker-farmers," semiskilled workers (for example, bus drivers)	Keeping house is the major task; some church work
Outsiders	Permanently employed	Agricultural laborers, dairymen, tractor drivers	Housework with occasional gardening; sometimes work during harvest
	Seasonally employed	Harvest hands	Housework; often work alongside husband in the fields

the other side of tracks," as visualized in the accompanying sketch of Dinuba by a California State University student who grew up in that town (Figure 8-4). This issue raises an important question: Is ecological segregation in community life inevitable?

Ecological Segregation: Is It Inevitable?

The changes in these California communities is indicative of what has happened throughout urban society. In early rural communities, there were close bonds between people, between employees and employers, and segregation within a town was minimal. As communities have become more urbanized, as in the case of Dinuba, segregation has increased and some people have had to live "on the other side of the tracks." Some of this is to be expected as occupational specialization increases. Special areas arise for retailing, wholesaling, light industry, heavy industry, the theater, and major shopping centers.

In addition, residential sorting and shifting takes place according to social class and ethnic differences. Karl and Alma Taeuber [1965] found a high degree of residential segregation according to color characteristics in all American cities of any substantial size. It would be easy, therefore, to conclude that ecological segregation is natural, unavoidable, functional, and perhaps even desirable.

Many scholars today, however, are pointing out that residential segregation does not need to be as extreme as it is in our cities and in many of our small towns. Unlike animals, humans possess the ability to control their environments and to modify the processes of urbanization and in-

FIGURE 8-4 The Town of Dinuba

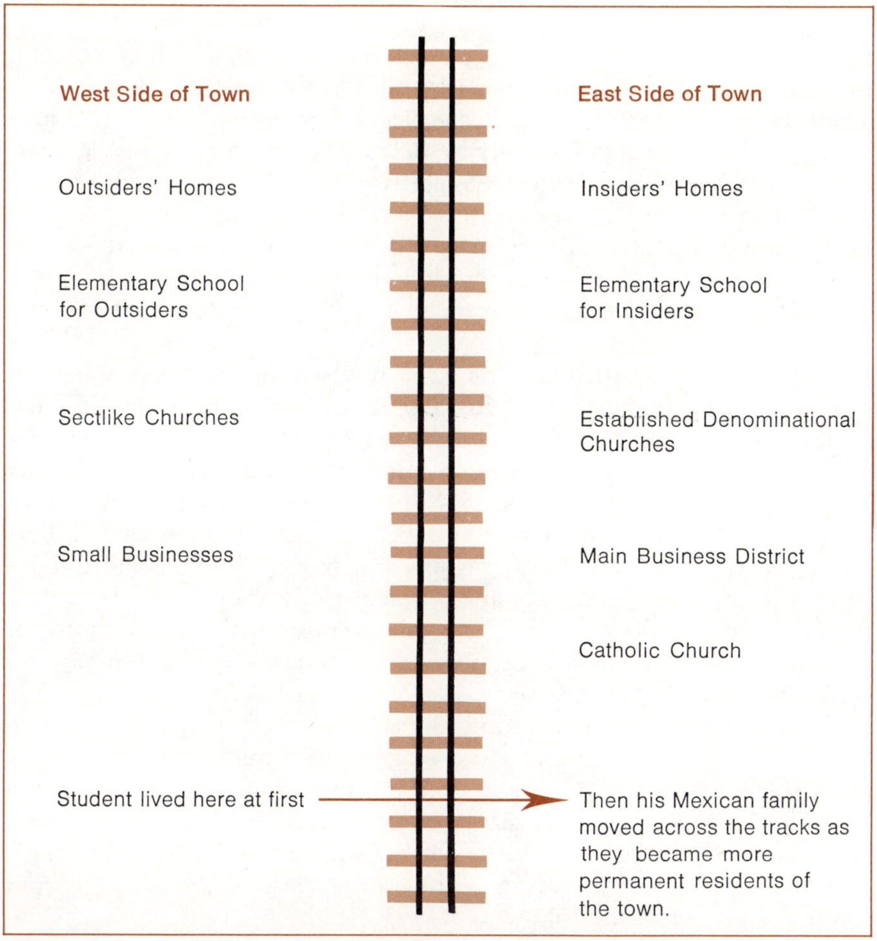

Adapted from an impressionistic study by a sociology student at California State University who grew up in Dinuba.

dustrialization. Segregation in housing, which leads to the perpetuation and exaggeration of human inequalities, deserves to be challenged. It means that many are shut out from full participation in community life; it leads to exaggerated distinctions between people often for the calculated ends of special interests and privileged groups; and it is related to many of our social problems, including the crisis over school busing and the desegregation of public schools.

The identification of distinct ecological areas within communities introduces the second major focus of recent research—an interest in the quality of life within communities. Are some communities more desirable places within which to work and live than others? What features make them so?

QUALITY OF LIFE

The Lynds on Industrialization in Middletown

Stein illustrated what he meant by the eclipse of community not only through the study of Chicago by Park and Burgess, but through the classic study of a Midwestern American city called Middletown (Muncie, Indiana). It was selected for study by Helen and Robert Lynd [1929, 1937] during the mid-1920s and mid-1930s partly because it had not gone through rapid urban growth. They wanted to assess the impact of industrial development upon a typical small city in America. One of their hypotheses was that the coming of industry, whether or not it led to population growth, created alienation among townspeople. The evidence they collected supported this hypothesis.

For example, glassmaking, the basic industry of the town, was done largely by individual craftsmen in 1890. By the 1920s, however, they had been replaced by mass-production techniques in a modern factory, the Ball Glass Company. Individual workers no longer felt pride in their own products. Instead, they felt like cogs in the wheel of a large-scale organization. They suffered alienation from their work, from fellow workers, and especially from the factory owners and bosses. They turned to labor unions for a sense of security and a voice strong enough to counter the power of management. Their ties to the community became more impersonal, and Middletown became divided into essentially two parts—*the working class* and *the business class.*

The Lynds lived in the community and observed every aspect of daily life. They singled out several dimensions of community life for study—getting a living, making a home, training the young, using leisure, participation in religion, and engaging in community activities. The dimension that seemed most important was "getting a living," and this changed radically with industrialization. Middletown's loss of the sense of community occurred in the following way:

> Between 1890 and 1924 industrialization shattered the occupational basis for craft employment by rendering skilled laborers unnecessary for most jobs. . . . Where craftsmen had formerly tended to live close to their places of employment, the development of transportation systems and the loss of attachment to their jobs meant that they could distribute themselves throughout the city. As residence patterns shifted in this fashion, working-class neighborhoods lost their cohesiveness and "visiting" declined while the number of socially "isolated" families increased. Workers who wished to maintain their own self-respect and the respect of their families were forced into the scramble for household gadgets. Their children demanded educational opportunities and this quickly became a major goal for working-class parents, since they saw in it a way of helping their children to regain the status they themselves had lost. Drastic changes in working-class family life, including acceptance of the need for wives and mothers to take jobs, were justified in terms of the new status requirements [Stein, 1960, p. 52].

Members of the business class also made changes in life-style, although on a lesser scale. These changes included an increasing emphasis upon mobility symbolized by acquisition and display of commodities, which paralleled the "scramble" for material objects occurring among the working classes. The concomitant flood of new enterpreneurial and managerial opportunities then accentuated these trends, where they were already under way.

The impact of industrialization was felt most strongly during the depression of the 1930s, when labor unions developed to gain worker recognition from the powerful and wealthy X Family (owners of the glass factory), who dominated the economic life of Middletown. As indicated earlier, the Lynds' view of the changing quality of life within small communities contains an unspoken antiurban bias. Urbanization and industrialization are seen as promoting alienation and conflict. A number of other writers and scholars have argued that urban life actually contains unique strengths, in contrast to the restraints of rural communities.

Urban Subcommunities: Kinfolk, Ghetto, Suburb

Antiurban bias is qualified by those who have studied urban subcommunities. The quality of life in these areas frequently exhibits *Gemeinschaft* characteristics, in contrast to the larger urban community, which functions mainly as a marketplace. Studies of three types of urban subcommunities—kinship groupings, the ghetto, and the suburb—illustrate this fact.

Urban families appear to be quite different from rural families. Seldom do we find the large kinship group living together in urban housing. Lack of space, emphasis upon individual freedom, and the need for mobility in the job market are some of the reasons. In fact, the urban family is usually fragmented into small nuclear units consisting of the father, mother, and their children. This, along with the fact that divorce is more common in cities, has often led to the conclusion that urbanites lack the primary ties of stable families. Recent research tends to question this conclusion. (Also see Chapter 10.)

A study of families in Cleveland, Ohio, by Marvin Sussman [1959] concluded that the so-called "isolated nuclear family" was more fiction than fact. He found that kin ties, particularly intergenerational ones, had far more significance than had been previously expected. Sussman tested the assumption (of scholars like Emile Durkheim) that the urban family was fragmented and weak since kin ties appeared to be unimportant in a person's choice of job.

When Sussman and his colleagues interviewed an adult member of 80 families, they found that "persons seeking a new job often locate where their kin are already established." They also found that many kin-related families live close to each other in the city and participate in all kinds of mutual assistance. Interfamily visitation was found to be very common, along with housekeeping assistance, care of children, care during illness, financial aid, cooperative decision making (personal and business), and celebration of ceremonial occasions (birthdays, anniversaries, holidays).

This type of assistance network is similar to what Carol Stack found in her study of a black subcommunity discussed in Chapter 4. Continued research since the findings of Sussman has led other scholars to identify a viable and functioning nuclear kin-related family system in modern urban societies [Sussman and Burchinal, 1962; Adams, 1968].

Strong primary ties can, therefore, be found in the city in spite of the impersonal character of larger urban life. As Sussman observes, it is not unusual for kin who are established in a city to attract other kin to the same city and even to the same neighborhood in order to help them get employment and housing. Newcomers to the city, therefore, are not always complete strangers. This is especially the case for ethnic and racial migrants to an urban area (for example, migrants from Puerto Rico or a specific rural area join relatives and family in an urban ghetto). In many respects, the subcommunity known as the ghetto helps individuals to maintain a sense of belonging even in the city.

Research on the origin, role, and nature of *urban ghettos* has typically combined an interest in the quality of daily life there with an examination of how the ghetto emerged as a natural ecological area. In a classic study, Louis Wirth says:

> The ghetto seems to have been originally a place in Venice, a quarter of the city in which the first Jewish settlement was located. It became, in the course of time, an institution recognized in custom and defined in law. It became, in short, not merely the place in which Jews lived, but the place in which they were compelled to live. . . . Our great cities turn out, upon examination, to be a mosaic of segregated people—differing in race, in culture, or merely in cult—each seeking to preserve its peculiar cultural forms and to maintain its individual and unique conceptions of life. Every one of these segregated groups inevitably seeks, in order to maintain the integrity of its own group life, to impose upon its members some kind of moral isolation. So far as segregation becomes for them a means to that end, every people and every cultural group may be said to create and maintain its own ghetto. . . . The ghetto, as it is here conceived, owes its existence, not to legal enactment, but to the fact that it meets a need and performs a social function. The ghetto is, in short, one of the so-called "natural areas" of the city [Wirth, 1928, pp. v–vi].

Several points are worth stressing in this conception. Wirth's view of the ghetto includes the following assumptions:

1. As Wirth puts it, ghettos represent a total way of life, a community within a larger community, and, as such, they perform important functions for the residents and the society as a whole.
2. Ghettos are not necessarily synonymous with slums. Some may have drab exteriors, as a consequence of urban physical deterioration, but a closer analysis discloses a rich and varied social structure and culture.
3. Ghettos did not initially arise as a result of formal edict or overt discrimination by church or state. They developed because of the

needs of ethnic groups in a particular context and the corresponding requirements of the larger community life.

Specifically, in the case of the medieval Jewish ghetto, segregation into separate areas was a product of the needs and practices, both religious and secular, rooted in the Jewish heritage [Wirth, 1928, pp. 28–39]. As a matter of fact, residence in the historic ghetto was frequently considered a privilege and a right and was vigorously defended when it was threatened. Jewish traditions, such as the preparation of special foods, attendance at the synagogue three times a day, and the religious obligation to participate in community life, required a high degree of community isolation.

At the same time, princes and rulers often used the privilege of ghetto life as a way of maintaining social control. Medieval cities lacked the strong central government that characterizes modern society. Rulers, under whose authority communities fell, could not provide adequate public services, in the form of police or fire protection, for the entire city. Walled ghettos allowed peoples in separate areas to protect themselves against outside attack, fire, and overpopulation. In such isolated surroundings, an esprit de corps was quick to develop throughout the community and was reinforced by the common language, customs, and social institutions.

As large numbers of Jews migrated to the New World, they carried these ghetto experiences and institutions with them, and segregated ghettolike areas soon became familiar patterns in early American cities. Other ethnic groups also settled into isolated ecological areas. America, however, provided a new and rapidly changing cultural milieu in which integration and assimilation conflicted with traditional ghetto ideals. Many ethnic groups were successful in escaping from these natural communities into the larger society.

On the other hand, nowhere are the problems associated with ghetto life more evident than in the case of American blacks. Kenneth B. Clark has recognized the duality—that is, the functions and dysfunctions—of ghetto life for urban blacks:

> America has contributed to the concept of the [historic] ghetto the restriction of persons to a special area and the limiting of their freedom of choice on the basis of skin color. The dark ghetto's invisible walls have been erected by the white society, by those who have power, both to confine those who have *no* power and to perpetuate their powerlessness. . . . The objective dimensions of the American urban ghettos are overcrowded and deteriorated housing, high infant mortality, crime and disease. The subjective dimensions are resentment, hostility, despair, apathy, self-depreciation, and its ironic companion, compensatory grandiose behavior. The ghetto is ferment, paradox, conflict, and dilemma. Yet within its pervasive pathology exists a surprising human resilience. The ghetto is hope, it is despair, it is churches and bars. It is aspiration for change, and it is apathy. It is vibrancy, it is stagnation. It is courage, and it is defeatism. It is cooperation and concern, and it is suspicion, competitiveness, and rejection. It is the surge toward assimilation, and it is alienation and withdrawal within the protective walls of the ghetto [Clark, 1965, pp. 11–12].

In discussing the continuing family ties among many urbanites and the tendency for city people to find a sense of community in ghetto areas, it becomes clear that urban life is not completely impersonal. Suburban living is still another example of a meaningful subcommunity within the urban context.

"The flight to the *suburbs*" has become a familiar phrase in 20th century America. It refers not only to the ecological movement of urbanites from central cities to outlying areas, from Burgess' Zones I, II, and III to Zones IV, V, and beyond. It refers also to a new way and quality of life. When suburban development began in America before World War II, the first to move out were the most affluent, the white-collar workers and the upper middle class. These were the people who could afford to leave overcrowded downtown housing for the open spaces of the suburbs. They were, for the most part, white and Protestant. For this reason, early suburbs were sometimes called "middle-class ghettos" or WASP (white Anglo–Saxon Protestant) communities. Residents were very much alike in background, and they were all newcomers.

After World War II, many suburbs were created as "instant" communities of mass-produced inexpensive tract homes. Schools, churches, and community centers had to be created to meet the needs of these new communities. Many suburbanites became commuters, riding trains, buses, or automobiles many miles to offices and factories located closer to city centers. Families, both parents and children, were young. All this led to a distinctive suburban way of life that has been described in the following ways [Whyte, 1956]:

Newcomers tried to "put down roots" quickly by neighboring across new yards without many fences.

Adults established friendships according to the play patterns of their children and by coming together to discuss common school problems.

Mothers were tied down with the demands of children-rearing and sought release through kaffee klatsches with other mothers in the immediate neighborhood.

Fathers were commuters all week and gardeners and golfers on the weekend with too little time for the children.

Families went to church to meet friends and to live up to the expectations of neighbors.

Churches often became "community social centers" with little emphasis upon creed or denomination.

Workers were mostly professionals and junior executives climbing the ladder of success in bureaucratic organizations and acting as "organization men."

This description, although it presents a relatively accurate picture of the early stages of development of suburban life, tended toward a stereotypical and negative view that has been difficult to erase. As industry gradually moved outward from city centers and as working-class people became more affluent, the suburbs became more heterogeneous communities. In a study of a working-class suburb in the San Francisco–Oakland Bay area, Bennett Berger [1960] found that the earlier suburban stereotype was not appropriate. Residents of this suburb brought their previous life-styles with them, including their Catholic faith and strong kinship ties. They did not become "joiners" or commuters (a Ford Motor plant had moved to the suburb). In addition, the community included diverse ethnic and racial groupings.

In a more recent systematic examination of the residents of Levittown, New Jersey, Herbert J. Gans [1966] raises serious questions about the degree to which physical environment in suburban communities influences behavior. He points out that since the late 1940s, scholars and journalists have characterized suburbanites as uniquely conformist, middle-class, lowbrow, hedonistic, conservative, hyperactive social sheep at the mercy of the builders, planners, and founders of their communities. In a participant–observer study done in the years from 1960 to 1962, Gans found that Levittowners were not an undifferentiated homogeneous mass. Informal organizations and groups arose in the community through a process of social sorting. This sorting process evolved along minority group lines—that is, according to whether people were middle or working class, whether they were members of the older population, and whether they were Jewish.

Levittowners were not a uniform community of frenetic neighbors and kaffee klatschers responding blindly to the physical environment. About half the population interviewed said they visited more in Levittown than in their former communities. However, the reasons for visiting were related to (1) changes in family structure because of the move to Levittown (formerly resided with in-laws), (2) a change in the type of residence (formerly lived in an apartment building); or (3) a desire for more neighboring which had prompted the move in the first place. Thus planners, builders, founders, and community leaders—those responsible for mass-produced suburbs—do not necessarily determine the ultimate shape of the community that evolves; the residents do.

Gans concludes his study by returning to an old, but often forgotten, sociological truism: What happens in a community is "almost always a reflection of the people who live there, especially the numerical and cultural majority." What the analysis suggests is that there are important differences between suburbs, that suburbia is a community experience within some larger social and cultural context, and that physical environment is only one of many complex and interrelated variables influencing community development.

8-3 Urban Ghettos: Myth and Reality

Most people think of urban ghettos as slums (deteriorated areas) where ethnic and racial minorities live in poverty, engage in deviant behavior, and are confined by a larger population which considers the residents a threat. Sociological studies show that this belief is a misleading myth, based upon a distorted view of reality.

Culver Pictures, Inc.

This painting by L. Knaus depicts the probable origin of the ghetto as a separate urban quarter allotted to Jews in some medieval cities. The residents felt secure from the intolerance and discrimination of others by this physical segregation, and they were able to transmit their valued traditions from one generation to the next. Officially enforced ghettos declined after the French Revolution.

A. Devaney, Inc./E. P. Jones

However, many ethnic groups continue to live, some voluntarily, in separate and distinct city subcommunities. This is particularly true of new migrants or others who possess a different language and cultural heritage. One example is the subcommunities of Chinese American citizens in many U.S. cities.

Marion Bernstein

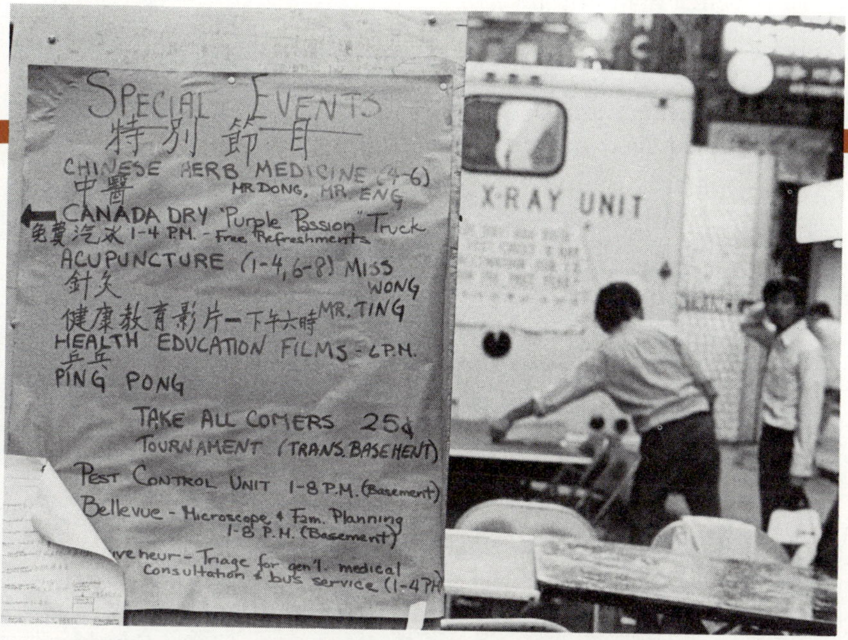

Sea Pines Company

Urban ghettos, unlike slums, provide residents with their own community services and activities. In the Middle Ages, some ghettos had separate police and fire services, in addition to separate health, educational, and recreational activities. In modern ghettos, when services are provided by the larger city government (for example, health), they may take on the special character or nature of the ghetto.

Some modern ghettos are upper-middle-class or upper-class communities where residents of similar ethnicity (usually white Anglo-Saxon Protestant) live, play, and sometimes work. These upper-status ghettos also have all needed services—stores, banks, automobile service stations, restaurants, and so on.

The Quality of Life: Can It Be Measured?

Throughout this part of the chapter, we have implied that people make value judgments, such as the following, about different kinds of communities:

Rural life is better than city life.

A small town like Middletown becomes more impersonal when industry comes.

There is more freedom and opportunity in a city, yet some parts of the city are better than other parts.

Suburbs produce conformity.

The question is: Are these just biased impressions or can we assess the quality of community life objectively and scientifically?

The Hoover Commission in the 1930s approached this question in the *Report of Recent Social Trends in the United States* [1933]. This was perhaps the beginning of an attempt to establish a regular report on the qualitative state of society using selected social factors or indicators and leading to the HEW publication, *Toward a Social Report,* in 1969. Some scholars have attempted to develop a *gross social product* (GSP) indicator, modeled after the familiar economic indicator called the gross national product (GNP).

Freshman students on one university campus took a cue from this new trend and undertook a project worth repeating in many places across the nation. They set out to measure the quality of life in the state of California according to county units. They patterned their study on David Smith's *The Geography of Social Well-Being in the United States* [1973] and centered their analysis upon six major categories of social life, each of which was measured by specific criteria. These are summarized in Table 8-2. Every California county was evaluated according to all the items in the table and assigned a composite score on an "Index of Social Well-Being"; for example, a county would receive a high score if the per capita income were high and the number of families with an annual income less than $3000 were low. Counties were then ranked into the 10 highest and the 10 lowest.

Although there were inadequacies in these qualitative measures, some guarded conclusions about the differences between one county and another could still be drawn. On the Index of Social Well-Being, the 10 counties with the highest scores appeared to have some advantages over those with the 10 lowest scores. The 10 lowest tended to be those in outlying areas, somewhat removed from the metropolitan areas of San Francisco and Los Angeles (as seen in the map shown in Figure 8-5). The 10 highest counties were for the most part near urban centers, including Sacramento, the state capitol.

This bears out the findings of other studies that suggest that cities do have advantages in health, education, welfare, income, and employment

TABLE 8-2 Categories and Measures of Community Social Well-Being

CATEGORY	MEASURES: Social well-being is present when the following measures are *high*	MEASURES: Social well-being is present when the following measures are *low*
Income, wealth, and employment	Average monthly Aid for Dependent Children payments Average monthly aid to disabled Average monthly benefit for retired workers Average monthly old age assistance Per capita annual income	Percentage of families with annual income less than $3000 Percentage of unemployed
Social environment	Median value of owner-occupied homes Number of picnic tables per 1000 people	Percentage of houses lacking complete plumbing Percentage of occupied homes without telephones
Health	Dentists per 1000 people Hospital beds per 1000 people Physicians per 1000 people	Deaths per 1000 people
Education	Percentage of population age 25 and older who have completed four or more years of high school Percentage of population age 25 and older with four years of college or more Persons attending college per 1000 people	Percentage of population age 25 and older with less than five years of schooling
Social stability	Percentage of homes with husband residing in them	Admissions to state hospitals for alcoholism per 1000 people Arrests for drunk driving per 1000 people Divorces per 1000 people Motor vehicle accident deaths per 1000 people Suicides per 1000 people
Social participation	Percentage of eligible voters voting	Drug arrests per 1000 people Homicides per 1000 people Percentage of jail inmates not convicted through criminal trial

opportunities. Cities are also cited as having such cultural advantages as music, art, theaters, and museums, although these factors were not included in the Index of Well-Being. Small towns and rural areas are able to compensate for their cultural restrictions by offering other kinds of advantages. The students found, for example, that in the category of social

FIGURE 8-5 Ratings of California Counties According to the Index of Social Well-Being, 1970

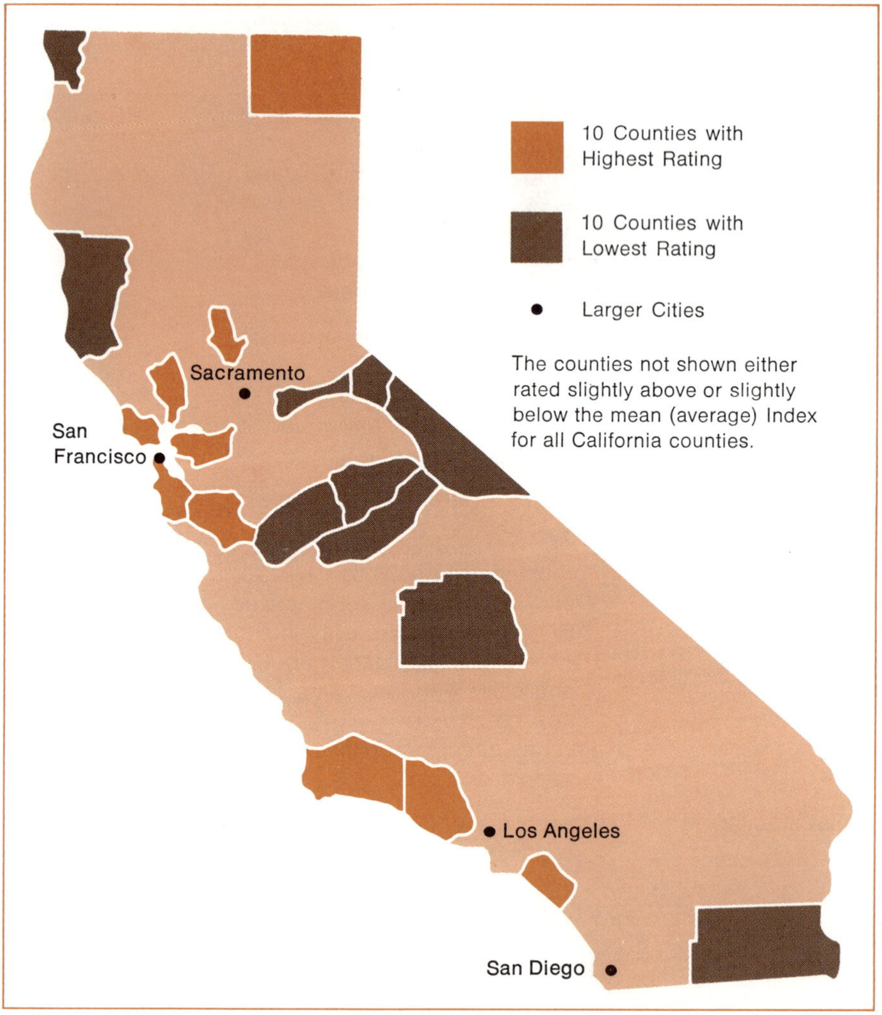

From J. W. Gurjton and J. R. Williams, *Toward a Comparison of Quality of Life in the Counties of California,* unpublished paper in the General Studies Thematic Program California State University at Chico, 1974.

stability, areas near cities tended to rank lower than counties in the outlying sections of California.

In conclusion, social scientists are trying to measure empirically the quality of life in American communities. The measures are still crude, and they apply more to material features than to subtle psychological, interpersonal, and cultural indicators of human satisfaction and fulfillment. In addition, some measures may be value-biased and inappropriate (for example, husbands residing at home as an indicator of social stability).

Furthermore, there are major gaps in information about such important items as air and water pollution, drug use, alcoholism, venereal disease, and the state of mental health. Nevertheless, the university project referred to above deserves to be followed up by students in sociology.

In the *Study Guide* accompanying this text, there is a reference to the way in which first-year students in a special program at the California State University at Chico conducted the above study [Guyton and Williams, 1974]. This could be a model for other students to use in the study of their own communities. The purpose of such studies is both academic and practical. On the practical level, hopefully measures can be developed that will help guide political policy. This practical purpose introduces the final section of this chapter, the third major focus of recent community studies—community leadership and political structure.

LEADERSHIP AND POLITICAL STRUCTURE

In the last chapter, Lipset's study of democracy in the printers' union showed that most printers voted and took part in political discussions. Leaders of two political parties vied with each other for power in the union. Individuals of all kinds belonged to printers' groups; this heterogeneity helped to minimize the sense of apathy and alienation. In addition, Lipset referred to the importance of strong autonomous associations that stood between the individuals and their primary groups on the one hand and central authority on the other. This focus upon internal processes is one way in which sociologists have studied political structure. Somewhat in contrast, scholars who study communities have focused upon leadership commitments *beyond* the local context.

Lloyd Warner on Bureaucratization in Yankee City

When Warner studied Yankee City, he found that bureaucratic leaders with allegiances *outside* of Yankee City became more and more influential, while old-timers gradually lost control. "Outsiders" replaced "locals" in the power structure. Warner's most important book in the Yankee City series was the fourth one, entitled *The Social System of the Modern Factory* [1947]. It dealt primarily with Yankee City's first major labor strike in a shoe factory, and it serves as an example of how a researcher can use a moment of crisis in a town to reveal the political structure of the community. In this case, Warner found that the strike initiated radical changes in leadership patterns.

In the early period of Yankee City's development, shoemakers had been craftsmen, and business leaders had been well-known local residents who took a personal interest in employees and the community. As the old-timers died or were replaced, absentee owners took over at the factory, many of them Jewish and stigmatized as "big-city outsiders." The new owners increased the mechanization of the factories and sent their own managers to preside over the industrial life of Yankee City. The hearts of these managers were not really in the community; their future depended upon their ability to work their way up through the impersonal corporate bureaucracy with headquarters in the big city.

In turn, workers in the shoe factory began to feel more and more as if they were mere extensions of the factory machinery, rather than individuals with indispensable skills. They had lost not only pride in their craft but a sense of being known and respected by their bosses. The result was the formation of a labor union and the strike. However, the union extended far beyond Yankee City in order to match the power of the big corporation. The big union became necessary as a counterbureaucracy through which workers as a group could improve their lot. Relationships between management and labor thus became impersonal as representatives of the two bureaucracies negotiated and jockeyed for power.

This was a typical story of the shift from traditional patterns of community authority to bureaucratic patterns. Stein summarizes the change in these words:

> The old feeling of solidarity based on a sense that everyone in the town belonged to a common community gives way to subcommunities with hostile attitudes toward each other. . . . Urban impersonality takes hold and Warner's data certainly suggest that bureaucratization with centralized absentee control over community affairs is an important step in this process [Stein, 1960, pp. 92–93].

As similar changes take place in many smaller communities today, the quality of public life is transformed. The small town is no longer the same, even if it is still relatively small. It becomes dependent upon the larger urban society and, in many respects, "its soul is not its own." Warner saw this happening in the 1940s. Vidich and Bensman [1958], authors of a study in the 1950s entitled *Small Town in Mass Society*, portrayed a similar process. In the 1960s, Ritchie P. Lowry made a similar appraisal of a small town in California, the topic of the following study.

▶ STUDY 8

Who's Running This Town? [1965][1]

Problem

The problem in Lowry's study of Micro City is not as simple as the title implies. It is not just "Who's running this town?" It is, in addition, an investigation of what is happening to the quality of public (political) life in small towns everywhere in America. Lowry is especially concerned with the problem of alienation in American communities.

> Again we find a familiar and persistent belief about American political life—the Tocquevillean assumption that modern mass society breeds alienation and apathy at the grass roots. This study considers these assumptions about

[1]Adapted and abridged from Ritchie P. Lowry, *Who's Running This Town* (New York: Harper & Row, Publishers, 1965).

community power by examining in detail the relationship between social and cultural change in a rapidly changing small community and the impact of this change upon the quality of daily public life and leadership [Lowry, 1965, p. xviii].

Lowry recognizes that community power can be studied from three different perspectives. *Elitist theories* assume that there are ruling cliques in every community and proceed to identify these. *Mass theories* imply that the quality of political life is influenced by masses of citizens who become apathetic and alienated. *Pluralist theories* focus upon the channels and techniques whereby community leaders achieve consensus in daily decision-making processes. All three perspectives are important and are used in the Micro City research. They are employed to address one central question: Is democracy more vital in the small *gemeinschaftliche* town?

Hypotheses and Study Design

Popular conceptions of democracy in the small town are expressed by Lowry in terms of *seven interrelated hypotheses.* Small town life makes the following possible:

1. Protection from social change and disorganization.
2. Meaningful interaction between people who know each other well.
3. A cooperative approach to community affairs.
4. A communal awareness of problems and issues.
5. Community-wide participation.
6. Leaders and citizens who have intimate access to each other.
7. And, therefore, community action that avoids antidemocratic processes such as alienation and apathy.

The study design for this research featured *a qualitative analysis of the decision-making process* in Micro City and a detailed study of *leadership types and interaction.* This design permitted the researcher to make discoveries as the work progressed.

Method of Data Collection

Lowry was a citizen of Micro City for about eight years and took part in many of the community activities described in the study. He was, therefore, *a participant observer.* In addition, he conducted an intensive *interview study* of citizens and community leaders. Interviews were all conducted by Lowry himself and were partly structured and partly open-ended. That is, he followed an interview schedule to ensure that he covered the same topics with each interviewee; he also asked each one to write out some of the responses. In addition, Lowry allowed plenty of time for respondents to reminisce and explore questions as he probed for insights. Over 100 community leaders were contacted either formally or informally; 77 were interviewed in depth.

An additional source of data included historical accounts of the town along with reports concerning a series of *community issues.* The local newspaper was valuable in this respect. Written accounts by local citizens and students from the college were also helpful. Many informal conversations with citizens of all ages added to the fund of information about the town and relevant events.

Findings and Interpretations

From the beginning, Lowry sensed that Micro City did not measure up to the idealistic democratic expectations for a small town. As the study progressed, he found evidence that led him *to deny every one of the seven basic hypotheses.* At the same time, he did not arrive at a completely negative conclusion about the quality of public life. He discovered a type of leader—*the mediating leader*—who offered promise for a more vital grass-roots democracy within a pluralistic community structure.

Although Micro City was relatively isolated from the urban areas of the state, it was by no means protected from social change and disorganization. Lowry cited evidence of urban blight in a small but very real slum in a low-income area of the town. Though the black population was small, the black families lived in a shanty-town section where many houses were without indoor plumbing and the streets were rivers of mud when it rained. Statistics on divorce, annulment, separation, delinquency and crime, low income and unemployment reflected urban problems that have emerged almost everywhere in American society. Most low-income citizens did not feel an integral part of the community, and many did not make use of the parks, swimming areas, and community activities.

More telling than the fact that Micro City had the usual urban problems was Lowry's discovery of a pervasive sense of alienation among the privileged citizens, including community leaders. He found that much of this alienation was because people knew each other too well. Social and political issues quickly became personalized. Leaders became stigmatized as being conservative or liberal because of their stands on one sensitive community issue. A philosophy of "he who is not with us on one thing is against us on all things" tended to predominate. As a result, there was a tendency for many actual and potential leaders to withdraw from rational confrontation on issues.

Lowry also found that the resulting sense of alienation was not confined to the liberals in a culturally conservative town. It was typical of various types of leaders, but for different reasons. Table 8-3 summarizes the six types of community leaders:

TABLE 8-3 A Typology of Community Leadership

Type of Participation in the Structure of Group Life	Type of Cultural Orientation: Conservative (C)	Utopian (U)
Local (L)	C–L	U–L
Mediating (M)	C–M	U–M
Cosmopolitan (C)	C–C	U–C

The contrast between "locals" and "cosmopolitans" is a familiar one in sociology [Robert Merton, 1968] and suggests the difference between citizens who center primarily upon local affairs and those who turn their attention largely to interests beyond the community. Lowry found this contrast in Micro City and defines the types as follows:

> *Locals* tend to be "old-timers" for the most part. However, some are *conservative–locals* (C–L) with strong emphasis upon self-determination while others are *utopian–locals* (U–L) and take a more liberal view of civil liberties, social reform, and social welfare.
>
> *Cosmopolitans* are citizens who have come to Micro City since World War II by and large. *Conservative–cosmopolitans* (C–C) reflect the business interests for the most part while *utopian–cosmopolitans* (U–C) look beyond local affairs to state and national matters as well as broad professional interests.

Another type of leader emerged in Micro City as Lowry studied the social structure, namely, the *mediating leader.* Mediating leaders differed according to political philosophy, but they had one thing in common: They held overlapping memberships in Micro City associations and acted as buffers between locals and cosmopolitans. They were people who sensed the importance of dialogue between contending forces and tried to be channels of communication. Lowry saw in these citizens the real hope for a plural society wherein local government and organizations generally could become vital units for debate and decision making with a minimum of personal animosity. *Conservative–mediators* (C–M) were especially promising, according to Lowry, because they were not a threat to a conservative community and yet they were willing to respect those with differing views. *Utopian–mediators* (U–M) were important, too, in that they could help bridge the gap between the conservative community and the alienated experts, usually the utopian–cosmopolitans, whose leadership was very much needed in the town.

For example, debate about a highway illustrated the role of mediating leaders. It symbolized the fact that Micro City was no longer isolated from the larger society and was influenced by change. State highways are planned by state authorities, and decisions are often taken out of the hands of local leaders. Warner saw this happening in the industries of Yankee City, and Lowry found this to be true in Micro City. Conservative–locals fought vigorously against the plan to cut through Micro City and its historical park with a state highway. They saw this not only as a threat to their residential properties and as a splitting of the town geographically, but also as a violation of a sacred agreement with the founders of the town who gave the land for the city park, the pride of Micro City.

Cosmopolitans, on the other hand, were quick to see that such changes are inevitable, and they were not in sympathy with the locals. It was here that the mediating leaders tried to step in and bridge the differences. They could empathize with locals, who felt threatened by the state decision, yet they knew that such changes must come. It was this mediating influence that may have helped the community through what seemed to be sheer "tragedy." Even so, mediating leaders could not keep the issue from becoming personal; some of them were accused of turning traitor to the town tradition and were for a time rejected. In fact, old-timers withdrew their business from prominent stores in town to express their fury. Lowry viewed this incident as an example of how local issues tend to become too personalized in the small town. Some of this tendency can be muted, however, by citizens who adopt the mediating role.

Conclusions and Implications

Lowry's findings could lead to a pessimistic conclusion with respect to the quality of public life in a small town. Lowry goes beyond this, however, in spelling out possibilities for effective leadership and meaningful political pluralism. Where Lipset's study of the International Typographers' Union identified mediating groups as the key, Lowry's study of Micro City argues for different kinds of relationships between leaders. Both locals and cosmopolitans are needed in a community, as well as conservatives and utopians. Mediating leaders can become the important linkages between these others, as long as the following conditions are present:

1. Associations of all kinds must become *channels* for a rational and sincere expression of diverse opinions in community life, rather than just social and recreational groups.
2. Leaders of all types must be able to find ways of *gaining access* to formal positions of power and influence in vital associations and government.
3. Leaders must be *protected* from the enormous pressures of interpersonal contact in a small town. Alienation is partly the result of a situation in which people know each other too well and tend to personalize everything. The informal structure of the community may help to mute this tendency. That is, when individuals associate with each other through informal groups, they may come to trust each other even when they differ on community issues. Herein lies the possibility for psychological protection.

The implications of the Micro City study are important with respect to the future of community life in a changing society. Small towns will continue to exist, but they will become more and more a part of the total urban society. They run the risk of being centers of arch conservatism, hostility, and alienation. On the other hand, they have the potential for becoming dynamic centers for democracy. Much depends upon the social structure and how it is used. Associations are key factors in the democratic process, but they must become more than perfunctory groups. They must become channels for debate and decision making. Furthermore, a community climate that fosters honest controversy with a minimum of personal animosity becomes exceedingly important. Only under these circumstances will effective leadership develop.

Lowry and his colleagues have continued to observe life in Micro City since his study in the early 1960s. By 1975, many changes had come about. The small college had become a large university with over 12,000 students and a faculty of almost 800. Students were coming from all parts of the state, a great many of them from urban areas and from minority groups. Faculty members were more inclined than ever to be cosmopolitans and to be very slow to become involved in local affairs. In fact, a former president of the university remarked that, today, "most professors would not even care who runs this town." There is not so much antagonism between town and gown as there is indifference between the two segments of the community. He also noted that the center of community action has been somewhat dispersed because of the rise of a major shopping mall north of the city limits. No longer is the central business district also the center of community affairs; even the central downtown hotel, which once symbolized the crossroads of activity, has been demolished. In one sense, then, Micro City is no longer a small town confronted with a problem of alienation as described by Lowry. It has become more of an urban area.

At the same time, Lowry calls attention to the fact that underlying the external changes there is an undercurrent of community life that is much the same. Perhaps more than ever, there is need to make the most of the possibilities for a vital interplay of diverse social and economic interests in the context of a plural society.

▶ SO WHAT?

Planned communities and the "new town" movement have utilized social science theories to create more democratic *gemeinschaftliche* communities and a better quality of life. The movement started in England at the turn of the century, when citizens and planners established "garden cities," which emphasized green spaces, communal participation in a variety of activities, and a mix of rural and urban lifestyles. Today, some of the best known planned communities in the world are Columbia (Maryland), Cumbernauld (Scotland), Jonathan (Minnesota), Reston (Virginia), and Tapio (Finland). These communities are attempts to help people leave the deteriorating conditions of urban life and settle in new towns where workers and jobs are integrated.

British and American planned communities are somewhat different [von Eckardt, 1971, pp. 21 ff]. Cumbernauld, near Glasgow, was begun in the late 1950s and stressed three things—separation of cars and people, abolition of isolated neighborhoods, and urban services to communities with low population density. Cumbernauld is built around one big town center with shops, apartments, meeting halls, neon lights, and "fish 'n' chips" stands—all straddling a superhighway. The population, projected to be about 250,000, lives in surrounding green-belt areas and is serviced by rapid transit. In contrast, Columbia is a community of about 15,000, located in the countryside between Baltimore, Maryland, and Washington, D.C. It is organized into neighborhoods, each with its own elementary school, swimming pool, and other recreational and meeting facilities. The neighborhoods contain a mixture of racial and economic statuses.

How successful are planned communities? They certainly are not free from stress and strain. Despite the attempt to attract racial and economic minorities, most blacks in Columbia are highly educated and from the middle class. In addition, one black psychologist summarized community life as follows:

> I don't know. Columbia seemed like a good idea, but I don't know. I think it all still has that concept of property values. All the American prejudices about low-rent housing are being preserved intact here. If something is stolen, everyone looks at the Interfaith [the low-income housing] kids" [von Eckardt, 1971, p. 23].

However, although many residents still fear change (falling property values because of integration), the fear seems moderated because change is planned and there is, therefore, order and predictability in community life. Most whites in Columbia do not object to racial integration as long as they know that they will remain in the majority. This attitude is racist, but it seems to be expressed in less violent and virulent forms than in unplanned cities. In addition, a University of Michigan survey reported that 25 percent of the Columbia residents in the early 1970s thought their new life was better, while only 9 percent thought it was worse. When the attitudes of Columbia residents were compared to the attitudes of residents of unplanned communities, important differences were observed [Marans, 1971, p. 21]. Only 18 percent of the former moved to Columbia because of some aspect of their new house and property; 51 percent were attracted by the idea of planning and experimentation. In contrast, 49 percent of the residents of unplanned communities moved because of a desire for better housing or property, and only 10 percent mentioned planning or other community-wide attributes. Therefore, Columbia residents seem to share a collective feeling of democratic pioneering experimentation.

Why are planned communities not more prevalent in America? It does not seem to be because of economic failure. Private industry seems anxious to prove that it can make a profit while providing a well-balanced "total living" community. Edward Logue [1971, pp. 27 ff] suggests that, in the United States, the major problem may be political, in contrast to other countries. New towns require an extraordinary amount of political coordination, administrative planning and policy integration. In a pluralistic society such as the United States, this becomes difficult—something akin to getting an acceptable resolution on a controversial issue through the United Nations. To accomplish the most basic task (for example, build a man-made lake for recreation), the following kinds of agencies and groups might have to be involved—sanitation district, water authority, waste disposal authority, fire district, state transportation department, sheriff's office, power company, telephone company, railroads, local ecology groups, and more. The success of the new town movement in America may eventually depend upon new legislation that simplifies and streamlines the politics of such projects.

CONCLUSION

In this chapter, we have defined human communities in terms of places and persons. We have been concerned with the kinds of social interaction that take place when people live together in a geographical area whether it is called a county, a town, or a city. The contrast between rural and urban places, frequently referred to in sociology as the difference between *Gemeinschaft* (self-interest) and *Gesellschaft* (mutual interest) was stressed. The human quest for a sense of community has been accentuated in the modern period as a result of the industrial revolution and the rural–urban transition.

Community studies in American sociology have made a significant contribution to our understanding of human society. This is particularly true of three early studies: (1) Park and Burgess on urbanization in Chicago; (2) the Lynds on industrialization in Middletown and (3) Warner on bureaucratization in Yankee City. These have been featured in the chapter discussions and have made it possible for us to consider communities with respect to ecology, the quality of life, and leadership.

Ecology deals with the physical environment of communities and the way in which human activities and land areas are interrelated. When sections of a town or city become devoted to special activities, the process of segregation takes place. This process is especially noteworthy in cities, but it is also found in small towns and rural areas when industrial development takes place. We saw this with respect to three California towns.

The quality of life undergoes change when industry comes to a community like Middletown. The tendency is for relationships to become more impersonal. At the same time, even in large cities, there are subcommunities where close ties and primary feelings develop. We examined the importance of kinship bonds in the city and of community associations in ghettos and suburbs.

Changes in the leadership and political structure of a community are usually indicative of major social transitions. Warner found that such changes occurred when bureaucratic leaders, as opposed to local residents, came to prevail in Yankee City, and the labor–management conflicts emerged. Lowry deals with similar changes in a small town. He gives special consideration to the problem of alienation among townspeople and the need for mediating leaders to ensure the continuation of a vital plural society.

Throughout our discussion of communities, there has been reference to a multiplicity of groups and social organizations. Kinship groups continue to be essential in large cities, as well as in small towns and rural areas. Associations stand out as especially significant for maintaining a sense of personal identity and political involvement as well as a plural society. Running through the analysis of community life is the constant reference to groups that have become particularly important in society, those that are well-established and highly organized. We are referring to community groups called institutions. We devote all of Chapter 9—"Institutions"—to the study of these forms of human group behavior.

REFERENCES

Adams, Bert N. *Kinship in an Urban Setting.* Chicago: Markham Publishing House, 1968.

Bell, Colin, and Howard Newby. *Community Studies.* New York: Praeger Publishers, 1972; also published in 1971 by George Allen & Unwin, London.

Berger, Bennett M. *Working-Class Suburb: A Study of Auto Workers in Suburbia.* Berkeley: University of California Press, 1960.

Clark, Kenneth B. *Dark Ghetto: Dilemmas of Social Power.* New York: Harper & Row, Publishers, 1965.

Coleman, James S. "Community Disorganization and Conflict," in Robert K. Merton and Robert A. Nisbet, Ed., *Contemporary Social Problems.* New York: Harcourt Brace Jovanovich, 1971.

Davis, Kingsley. "The Origin and Growth of Urbanization in the World," *The American Journal of Sociology, 60* (March 1955), pp. 429–437.

———. "The Urbanization of the Human Population," *Scientific American, 213* (September 1965), pp. 41–74.

Gans, Herbert J. *The Levittowners: How People Live and Politic in Suburbia.* New York: Pantheon Books, 1966.

Goldschmidt, Walter. *As You Sow.* Glencoe, Ill.: The Free Press, 1947.

Guyton, J. W., and J. R. Williams. "Toward a Comparison of Quality of Life in the Counties of California," unpublished paper in the General Studies Thematic Program, California State University, Chico, California, 1974.

Health, Education and Welfare, Department of. *Toward a Social Report.* Washington, D.C.: U.S. Government Printing Office, 1969.

Hillery, George A., Jr. "Definitions of Community: Areas of Agreement," *Rural Sociology, 20,* No. 1 (1955), pp. 194–204.

Hoover Commission. *Report of Recent Social Trends in the United States.* New York: McGraw-Hill Book Company, 1933.

Hoyt, Homer. *The Structure and Growth of Residential Neighborhoods in American Cities.* Washington, D.C.: Federal Housing Administration, 1939.

Jonassen, Christen T. "Community Typology," in Marvin B. Sussman, Ed., *Community Structure and Analysis.* New York: Thomas Y. Crowell Company, 1959.

Logue, Edward V. "Piecing the Political Pie," *Saturday Review* (15 May 1971), pp. 27 ff.

Lynd, Robert, and Helen Lynd. *Middletown.* New York: Harcourt, Brace and Company, 1929.

———. *Middletown in Transition.* New York: Harcourt, Brace and Company, 1937.

McWilliams, Carey. *Factories in the Fields.* Hamden, Conn.: Archer Books, 1969; originally published by Little, Brown and Company, Boston, 1939.

Marans, Robert W. "Dream Analysis," *Saturday Review* (12 June 1971), p. 21.

Marlin, William. "Frank Lloyd Wright, The Enduring Presence," *Saturday Review,* (4 October 1975), pp. 14–17.

Merton, Robert K. "Patterns of Influence: Local and Cosmopolitan Influentials," in Robert K. Merton, *Social Theory and Social Structure,* 3rd ed. New York: The Free Press, 1968.

Nisbet, Robert A. *The Quest for Community.* New York: Oxford University Press, 1953; also published as *Community and Power.* New York: Oxford University Press, 1962.

Park, Robert E. *Human Communities.* Glencoe, Ill.; The Free Press, 1952.

———, Ernest W. Burgess, and Roderick D. McKenzie. *The City.* Chicago: University of Chicago Press, 1925.

Schnore, Leo F. "Community," in Neil J. Smelser, *Sociology, An Introduction.* New York: John Wiley and Sons, 1967.

Smith, David M. *The Geography of Social Well-Being in the United States.* New York: McGraw-Hill Book Company, 1973.

Stein, Maurice R. *The Eclipse of Community.* Princeton, N.J.: Princeton University Press, 1960.

Steinbeck, John. *In Dubious Battle.* New York: Viking Press, 1936; see also the Bantam edition, New York, 1961.

———. *The Grapes of Wrath.* New York: Viking Press, 1939.

Sussman, Marvin B. "The Isolated Nuclear Family: Fact or Fiction," *Social Problems, 6,* No. 4 (1959), pp. 333–340.

——— and Lee Burchinal. "Kin Family Network: Unheralded Structure in Current Conceptions of Family Functioning, *Marriage and Family Living* (presently *The Journal of Marriage and the Family*), *24,* No. 3 (1962), pp. 231–240.

Taylor, Carl C., *et al. Rural Life in the United States.* New York: Alfred A. Knopf, 1949.

Taylor, Lee. *Urban–Rural Problems.* Belmont, Calif.: Dickenson Publishing Company, 1968.

Tönnies, Ferdinand. *Community and Society,* Charles Loomis, Ed. and Transl. East Lansing, Mich.: Michigan State University Press, 1957.

Traeuber, Karl E., and Alma F. Traeuber. *Negroes in Cities.* Chicago: Aldine Publishing Company, 1965.

The United States Census of Population. Washington, D.C.: U.S. Bureau of Census, U.S. Government Printing Office, 1970.

Warner, W. Lloyd, and Paul S. Lunt. *The Social System of the Modern Factory.* New Haven, Conn.: Yale University Press, 1947.

von Eckardt, Wolf. "A Fresh Scene in the Clean Dream," *Saturday Review* (15 May 1971), pp. 21 ff.

Warren, Roland L. *The Community in America.* Chicago: Rand McNally & Co., 1963.

Wilder, Thornton. "Our Town," *Three Plays by Thornton Wilder.* New York: Harper and Row, 1957 (originally published by Coward–McCann, Inc., New York, 1938).

Wirth, Louis. *The Ghetto.* Chicago: The University of Chicago Press, 1928; also published in 1956 by Phoenix Books, Chicago.

———. "Urbanism as a Way of Life," *The American Journal of Sociology, 44* (July 1939), pp. 1–24.

Whyte, William H., Jr. *The Organization Man.* Garden City, N.Y.: Doubleday and Company, 1956.

- Are there human needs that must be met in all societies? What might these be?
- What are the differences between basic institutions in primitive, medieval, and industrial societies?
- What do we mean by a professional person? Is a business executive a professional? A member of the clergy? A university professor?
- A newspaper advertisement reads—"DIVORCE, ONLY $70, plus court costs." What is your reaction to this ad? Does it suggest anything about social change and modern institutions?
- How have American institutions changed as a result of the automobile? How does your list of changes compare with the one later in this chapter (on pp. 353–354)?

9

Institutions

This chapter deals with social institutions, a form of human group crucial to all societies. We will consider how different institutions become important at varying stages of societal development. During much of early human history, the family was so important as a basic institution that we refer to some societies as kinship-oriented. In later stages of development, other institutions arose and competed with the family. During the Middle Ages, for example, the church emerged as an all-inclusive social group. So influential was this religious institution that we can refer to the medieval period as a sacred society. With the industrial revolution, a number of other institutions arose. Religious institutions broke into sects and denominations; nation-states became important in fulfilling the need for jobs, goods, services, and governmental control; educational and cultural institutions met health, welfare, and socialization needs. Society changed from sacred to secular.

In this chapter, we will use the church, the nation-state, and the university as examples of how social change alters institutional functions and relationships. In particular, we will focus on what happens as institutional leadership becomes professionalized in education, religion, and medicine. First, however, we must define clearly what sociologists mean by *institutions,* in contrast to other fundamental human groups.

THE NATURE AND ROLE OF INSTITUTIONS

Precisely defining the concept of an institution is sometimes difficult because scholars use several different ways of viewing the nature and role of institutions in human societies. However, two particular characteristics that are common to most definitions can be identified. Institutions can be seen as *all-inclusive* forms of human behavior, and they can be understood as groups that meet *basic needs* in a society.

The All-Inclusive Nature of Institutions

In social scientific literature, the concept of an institution is used in several ways, all of which are closely related to popular notions. Some writers speak of institutions as fundamental patterns of behavior. Harry Johnson [1960, p. 22] defines a social institution as a normative pattern of behavior associated with a particular category of interpersonal relationships. For example, marriage is sometimes referred to as a basic social institution because it encompasses a whole complex of interrelated norms and behavioral patterns. (Who is a father, a wife, a husband, a mother, a sister and so on, and how are these roles related?) Furthermore, this complex is woven into the total cultural and social fabric (the institution of marriage is intimately related to the economic, religious, political, recreational, and other aspects of life). Such a definition, then, stresses the all-inclusive character of institutions because it points to the relationship between customs, practices, social roles, and behavior.

Philip Selznick [1951, p. 330] has argued that institutions are so inclusive that they cannot be distinguished from their societal context:

> Institutions are defended, often at great cost of life and resources, because they come to reflect society's self-image. They define its aspirations and its moral commitments; they are the source and receptacle of self-respect, of unique identity. No enemy is so dangerous as he who threatens these valued principles and structures. . . . [Institutional forms of behavior] have the indirect consequence of committing the society to an integrated system of values . . . [and] valued institutions reflect the ethos of the culture, its peculiar way of self-fulfillment.

Individuals, groups, and whole societies, therefore, often identify totally with their basic institutions. For this reason, many older people have resented youth's radical challenge of many of the norms and practices of the American family system in recent years; the older people see this challenge as a threat to the very foundation of our way of life.

9-1 The Nature of Institutions

The characteristics of an institution are illustrated by the San (or Bushmen) of the Kalahari Desert of Botswana. The San are a hunting and food-gathering people of nuclear families, several of which live together in a camp or village. Their community life has the following characteristics of an institution:

R. Lee/Anthro-Photo

All inclusive. Community life encompasses members of all ages and both sexes in permanent patterns of interaction. Several San families temporarily camp in a nut grove away from their permanent waterhole.

I. DeVore/Anthro-Photo

Highly structured. Community patterns of behavior become fixed for generations by long-lasting norms and values. A San man, an excellent dancer, is supported by women singers, who clap in syncopated rhythm. His dance is for entertainment. However, when many San men dance and go into trances, the activity becomes religious and a curing dance.

R. Lee/Anthro-Photo

Long lived. All members live within the communal context from birth to death. A San daughter, mother, and grandmother roast nuts in a hearth.

R. Lee/Anthro-Photo

Multifunctional. All needs are met by diverse community activities (social, political, religious, economic, child-rearing) and all needs are intimately related to one another. A San hunter with bow, arrows, and spear is setting a trap he will check later in the day. In Chapter 11, we shall see how some primitive people wage war against other groups, using weapons and tactics that were developed for hunting. San women, carrying children on their backs, gather tubers.

M. Shostak/Anthro-Photo

An effective way of identifying institutions for the purposes of our discussion is to refer to the working typology of human groups in Chapter 2. On one extreme of the continuum, we find collectivities—that is, spontaneous groupings without much formal structure and of limited duration and function. On the opposite extreme, we find institutions, or human groups that have endured a long time and, therefore, have developed more intricate planned forms of structured interaction and fulfill multiple functions. In other words, institutions are more inclusive. Behavior within this context becomes fixed as a social habit. Thus, to change institutions and habitual behavior is to threaten society itself, as Selznick indicates.

In addition, using the typology, we can see important differences between associations and institutions. As association tends to have private and limited purposes, while institutions tend to be public and have multiple purposes. For example, the church of medieval Europe was more institutional because it was an all-inclusive center for daily life; music, education, art, architecture, social and recreational activity, as well as religion, were all in its domain. The church was not only multifunctional, but virtually everybody belonged to it. In contrast, the modern Roman Catholic Church in America is less institutional and more communal and associational. It serves only one segment of the total population and is not nearly so all-inclusive for its members. American Catholics are caught up in the associational society of our time and take part in many activities outside of and unrelated to religious involvement. This change, characteristic of many contemporary churches, has been referred to as a crisis in institutional character. We will return to this problem later in this chapter.

The Role of Institutions: Basic Needs

In addition to their all-inclusive character, institutions have been defined by other scholars as groupings that uniquely meet basic human needs. J. O. Hertzler [1961, p. 84] maintains that the functional essence of an institution can be seen in "the fact that it is a system of required, concerted, cooperative, and reciprocal practices or activities whereby the people concerned satisfy their individual and social needs." Other scholars [Etzioni, 1966, p. vii; Merrill, 1969, p. 245] have similarly defined institutions as cultural patterns grouped around the central needs of people in society. These patterns influence behavior continually: Citizens are born in hospitals, are educated in schools, work in complex organizations, and participate in religious and political organizations. This perspective suggests that certain social institutions may be indispensable to human societies. In other words, not only would we expect to find some similar institutions in all social contexts, but we would also expect these institutions to perform the same important public purposes.

One research attempt to validate this perspective was conducted by scholars at Yale University in a cross-cultural study utilizing the "Human

FIGURE 9-1 Institutional Groupings Found in All Societies and Types of Relationships Between Them

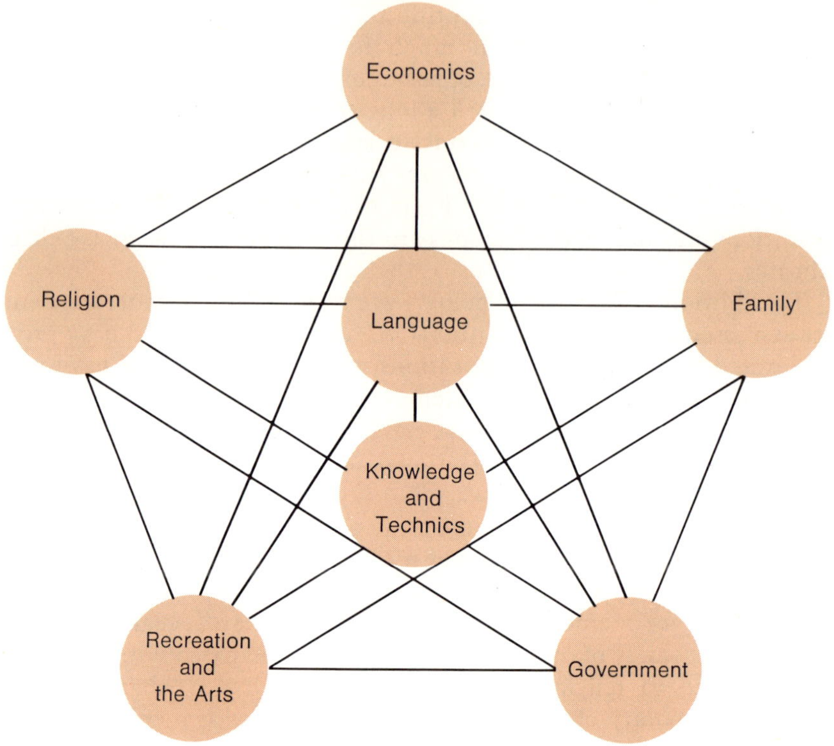

Adapted from Frances E. Merrill and H. Wentworth Eldredge, *Culture and Society* (Englewood Cliffs: Prentice-Hall, 1952), p. 87. With permission.

Relations Area Files." These files contain information on the habits, customs, practices, and behavior of hundreds of societies and cultures throughout the world. By analyzing these data, the researchers were able to construct the accompanying chart (Figure 9-1), which shows the institutional groupings found in all societies.

The researchers argue that every society must provide for human needs in the following broad spheres of activity—economics, family, government, recreation, the arts, religion, language, knowledge, and technics. In some societies, most of the needs may be met within one large institutional context, such as the kinship groupings among premodern people or the church in feudal periods. In modern societies, the function of meeting needs tends to be distributed among many institutions, each of which takes on a more specific and prescribed role.

At the same time, all human needs and the appropriate social institutions tend to be interrelated and interdependent (as depicted by the lines in Figure 9-1). These interrelationships form a network of a larger social fabric. Therefore, changes in one institutional area will bring about changes in many or all others. An especially fascinating example of this process is the impact of the invention and development of the automobile on contemporary life. The automobile was developed in the economic sphere of society following discoveries in the knowledge and technics sphere (the development of assembly-line production). Table 9-1 is an adaptation from a summary by Merrill and Eldredge [1952, pp. 119–120] and depicts ways in which the automobile prompted changes in the several institutional spheres other than the economic sphere.

TABLE 9-1 Changes in Institutional Spheres Brought About by Development of the Automobile

Institutional Sphere	New Needs To Be Met ⟶	New or Changed Functions To Perform
Family	Automobile expense	Altered family budget
	Different work patterns	Changed family roles, especially husband–wife; decline in the importance of neighborhood and extended kin
	New recreational and social patterns	Dating and courtship by car; automobile as a status symbol; new child-rearing patterns and discipline, especially for teenagers
Government (federal, state, and local)	Automobile safety	Different laws and regulations
	Highway construction	More taxes
	Growth in cities and suburbs	New forms of government
	Mobile farm workers	Low-cost rural housing; new health and welfare services
	Migration of urban workers	Unemployment and underemployment assistance
	Mobile warfare	Tanks; *Blitzkrieg* strategy
	New forms of deviance (bank robbery, kidnapping)	National police (FBI); national kidnapping law
Recreation and the Arts	New recreational patterns	Automobile races; the Sunday family outing; National Park system; motels and trailer camps; roadside businesses (hot dog stands)
Religion	More mobile churchgoers and migration of population	Changed relationship of church to parish
	New recreational patterns	Golfers' mass; Friday and Saturday night mass
	Previously isolated communities	Revivalists travel in trailers; church missions to isolated areas
	The automobile city with its secular and materialistic values in an age of science and advanced education	Scientific study of scriptures and religious tradition, led to liberal creed, ritual, and ethical practices.

Source: Adapted from a summary by Frances E. Merrill and H. Wentworth Eldredge, *Culture and Society* (Englewood Cliffs, N.J.: Prentice–Hall, 1952), pp. 119–120.

In addition, of course, the automobile had a profound impact upon the institutional spheres within which it was developed (economics, knowledge, and technics). Population dispersion and different work patterns gave rise to new types of technical schools, consolidated school systems and busing, and commuter colleges. Drivers' education and automotive shop were taught in the schools, and mobile students created new problems of discipline and traffic control. New businesses were created (gasoline stations, perfection of the internal combustion engine for aircraft, the trucking industry, taxis), and related businesses were influenced (insurance, oil exploration, the stock market, hotels and restaurants).

This type of complex interdependence is particularly common in modern societies and helps to emphasize the unique role of institutions in meeting the basic needs of individuals. In premodern societies, the pattern is somewhat different. There, single institutions, like the family or the church, tend to predominate. A comparison of institutions in premodern, feudal, and modern societies makes the unique nature and role of institutions clearer.

INSTITUTIONS THROUGHOUT HISTORY

Kinship in Premodern Society

The human family predominates in the societies of early peoples. It is the single social institution not only in nomadic hunting and food-gathering communities but also in most preindustrial societies. Virtually all basic needs are fulfilled within the kinship group, as illustrated in Figure 9-2. This diagram is based on the circle chart in Figure 9-1, and it illustrates how one predominant institution can perform a variety of functions and meet a variety of needs.

As Lenski [1970] points out, human groups moved about as nomads, hunting and gathering their food in the earliest societies. Kinship (blood-related) organization performed the function of meeting all needs—economic, governmental, religious, recreational, and the like. A simple division of labor prevailed between male–female, old–young, and headman–shaman. Honor and respect were given to three kinds of people: (1) those who were older; (2) those endowed with supernatural power; and (3) those with valued personal qualities (skill in hunting and warfare or possession of a generous and kind temperament, free from bad temper).

The role of the headman (in governance) and the shaman (in religion) illustrates the manner in which all segments of the premodern society were intimately interrelated. Holmberg [1950, pp. 59–60] describes the headman in a hunting and gathering society as nominally the highest official of the group. His authority depends upon personal leadership qualities, and there is no obligation to obey his order and no punishment for noncompliance. Actually, little attention is paid to what the headman says unless he is a member of one's immediate family. Like any other man in the group, he must make his bows, arrows, and tools, and he must hunt, fish, collect, and plant gardens. He may offer advice about migrations and hunting trips,

FIGURE 9-2 The Institution of Kinship in Premodern Society (This diagram is based on the circle chart in Figure 9-1 and it illustrates how one predominant institution can perform a variety of functions and meet a variety of needs.)

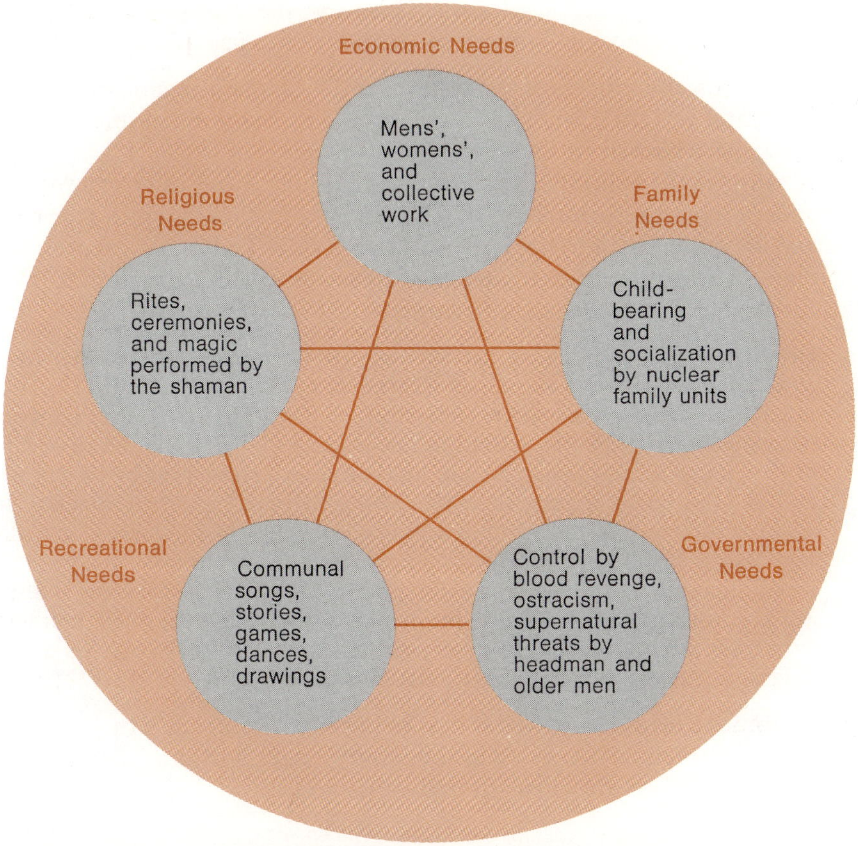

but this advice is not always followed by others. In short, the government of the earliest societies was simple and direct. Political needs could be met informally, and there was not a great distance between the headman and the people. The headman's authority existed as long as he could perform his individual tasks satisfactorily.

In premodern societies, the entire group participated in the control of human behavior. Three means were used: blood revenge, ostracism, and supernatural threats. Religion played a major role in this social control. Those individuals who possessed special gifts for communicating with the spirit world were highly respected and could take a place of authority along with the headman:

> Because of their role, shamans [priests] usually command respect and are often more influential than headmen. Sometimes as with the Northern Maidu in California, the headman "was chosen largely through the aid of the shaman

> who was supposed to reveal to the old men the choice of the spirit." The role of the shaman tends to be profitable, since others are usually happy to offer gifts in exchange for his help or to maintain his goodwill. . . . Though the shaman is normally a man, a woman might become one if she had the requisite experiences and if, like other shamans, she could prove her power through the healings and other feats [Lenski, 1970, pp. 183–184].

In other words, the spheres of economic, family, religious, recreational, and governmental activities were all interrelated. Furthermore, all members of the group participated in these various activities.

Kinship as the primary institution can still be found in contemporary premodern communities, like the Australian Bushmen, and in preindustrial areas of Africa, Asia, and South America. The family is probably the oldest human institution, and only in recent history have other institutions developed to challenge its functions:

> Historically, kin groups have been the matrix from which every other form of social organization evolved. . . . This could not last. In order for societies to grow in size and complexity, relationships had to be established between individuals who were not related to one another. . . . While the functions of kin groups began to change thousands of years ago, no type of society has ever gone as far in altering their role as our modern industrial societies. In agrarian societies, the family was still the basic unit of production and the state was normally the property of the royal family. Education, too, was still predominantly a family responsibility; most boys learned the male role by assisting their fathers, and girls the female role by assisting their mothers. Even when a boy was apprenticed to a master craftsman, he lived in his household in a kind of pseudo-familial relation [Lenski, 1970, pp. 416–417].

During the medieval period, a new major institution arose that adopted many of the functions formerly in the family's domain. This institution—the church—is the subject of the following section.

The Church in Medieval Society

In Western Europe, from about 500 to 1500, the institution that eventually became the Roman Catholic Church was all important. Although its primary function was to deal with spiritual needs pertaining to the unknown, the Church also became the focus for learning, music, and art. In addition it was involved with land ownership and other economic activities, and it shared political power with secular rulers. This diversity of functions enabled individuals, as Christians, to become more than merely family members or participants in a social system of feudal allegiances. Eventually, the Church helped prepare individuals for new roles in the world, specifically, the roles of citizen and merchant. The involvement of the Church in many different activities is depicted in Figure 9-3. This adaptation of the circle chart in Figure 9-1 illustrates the beginnings of the distinction between different institutional spheres and activities. The Church, however, predominates; overlapping areas in the figure show the

FIGURE 9-3 The Institutional Role of the Church in Medieval Society

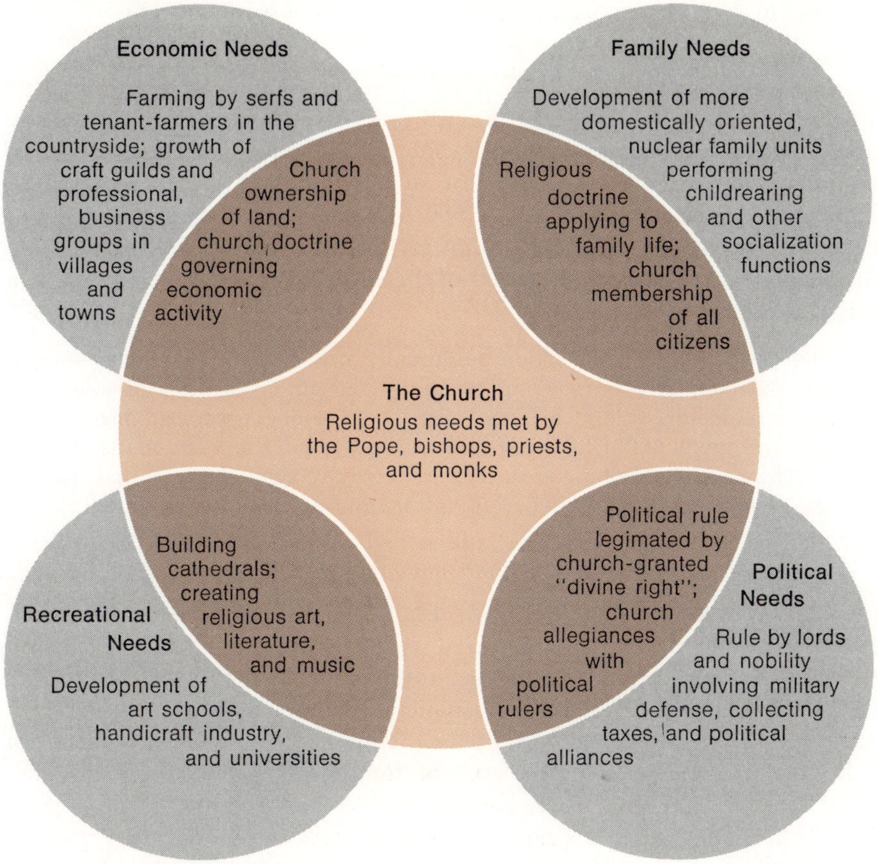

Church's influence in all aspects of life. Some scholars have called this kind of overlapping relationship the "medieval synthesis" [Nisbet, 1953].

In a study of the history of the Western family, Carle C. Zimmerman [1947] points out that before the Western world could modernize, traditional kinship society had to be transformed. Great families were in complete control of social activities in the tribal societies of Western Europe, and powerful kinship groups were constantly at war with each other. The Church emerged as a counterforce and, together with government, was successful in dominating much of human life for about 1000 years. Kenneth Clark [1969, pp. 29–31] writes:

> . . . At the end of the tenth century there was a new power in Europe, greater than any kind of emperor: the Church. If you asked the average man of the time to what country he belonged, he would not have understood you; he would have known only to what bishopric. And the Church was not only an organizer; it was a humanizer. . . . [It contributed to] humanity's moral

> sense and belief in the authority of a higher power. By the year 1000, the year in which many timid people feared that the world would come to an end, the long dominance of the barbarian wanderers was over, and Western Europe was prepared for its first great age of civilization.

Clark also points to the 11th century as a time when human culture made a great leap forward in achievement. The accomplishments of this period paralleled in many ways the development of Greek and Ionian science, art, and poetry in about 500 B.C. and the birth of the ancient Egyptian, Mesopotamian, and Indian civilizations in about 3000 B.C. The medieval creative activity, like that of the earlier periods, was inspired by a religious institution:

> In every branch of life—action, philosophy, organization, technology—there was extraordinary outpouring of energy, an intensification of existence. Popes, emperors, kings, bishops, saints, philosophers were all bigger than life, and incidents of history [such as the Crusades and the martyrdom of St. Thomas à Becket] are great heroic dramas, or symbolic acts, that still stir our hearts. . . . The evidence of this heroic energy, this confidence, this strength of will and intellect, is still visible to us [in the cathedrals erected by the people to the Glory of God]. . . [Clark, 1969, p. 33].

Clark points out that these kinds of changes required a new social and intellectual milieu; they required wealth, stability, technical skill, and the confidence necessary to push through long-term projects. There are many reasons why these characteristics suddenly appeared in Western Europe, but the Church certainly played a major role. The Church did not suffer from some of the problems of feudalism (for example, divided inheritances), and, therefore, could conserve and expand its properties. The Church also became a powerful, integrative, and stimulating force in other ways. People of intelligence naturally and normally took holy orders and could rise from obscurity to positions of influence. Although a number of bishops and abbots came from royal and princely families, other factors determined one's success as well, including administrative skill, diplomatic ability, and intellectual competence. In this sense, the Church was both bureaucratic and democratic. Finally, Clark points out that the Church was international in orientation and interests (as, for example, modern science is today).

One of the medieval Church's achievements was the modification of the influence of the powerful kinship groups that had dominated tribal societies. The Church's influence was eventually modified, beginning in the early 1500s, the time of Luther and the Protestant Reformation. During this period, often cited by scholars as the time of transition from the medieval to the early modern era, the Church was challenged by Protestantism and secular princes. This challenge and the changes it brought had to occur before the modern nation-state could develop to its present form.

The Nation-State in Modern Society

"Big government" is a term used frequently today to emphasize the importance of the state in the lives of all citizens. The term refers partly to the fact that modern governments perform many essential services previously provided by other institutions. In fact, some contemporary states attempt to meet the needs of most citizens from the cradle to the grave (see Chapter 11).

For this reason, we say that, in the modern period, the one institution that epitomizes an all-inclusive social institution is the nation-state. It is not only long lived, highly structured, and bureaucratic, but it also performs multiple functions for all its citizens. In the world of modern states, a person's nationality is a fundamental aspect of one's social identity. One's way of life is determined in large part by the kind of state in which one lives, whether democratic, totalitarian, or some modification of the two.

The modern nation-state is the sovereign unit of social control over life within a given territory. It holds a monopoly on the exercise of legitimate force in the name of police protection and national defense. No matter how democratic a society is, the political arm of the state reaches into the lives of every citizen and private group in a variety of ways.

> Although other institutions have played dominant roles in the control and direction of society at various times in history, most thoughtful observers would agree that today in advanced technological societies characterized by urban concentration of great populations, government has assumed the predominant role. Government is generally the institution to which people turn when great problems arise. If the economy manifests serious symptoms of weakness, the typical citizen reacts immediately with an outcry that the government "ought to do something about it" [McDonagh and Simpson, 1969, p. 181].

There is similar reaction with respect to rising crime rates, the crisis of the cities, the threat of nuclear war, and the depletion of natural resources. This citizen response is ample indication of the assumed influence and power of modern governments.

It is important to emphasize the relationship between *society* and the *state.* Society and state should not be thought of as separate and distinct entities. As we have seen, there is no differentiation of institutions in premodern societies. Virtually all basic functions are performed within the context of the larger kinship group. There is no separate governmental organization; political rule takes place through a council of older citizens with a patriarch as leader. This is a homogeneous society with emphasis upon interrelatedness, consensus, and a collective consciousness.

A similar homogeneity exists in feudal society, where kinship groupings, the church, and political institutions support, complement, and restrain one another. However, under the impact of the religious reformation and the industrial revolution, marked differentiation occurred. Not only was the single church challenged by the emerging Protestant groupings, but the kinship family also gave way to many conjugal units, and princes asserted their independence from loose confederations of empires. Nation-states began to evolve. There was no longer uniform consensus throughout Western society; instead conflicts arose between the many subunits of larger society.

Classic debates between philosophers developed about the appropriate role of the state as the governing body in society. Some, like Karl Marx, argued that the state had to be limited or abolished so that the fabric of society might be strengthened through consensus. Others, like Hegel, insisted upon the sovereignty of the state over society's disparate elements; only through a strong central power could there be consensus in a society of conflicting interests. According to Lipset [1960, pp. 23–24], there was a basic error running through both kinds of arguments:

> [This error lay] . . . in dealing with state and society as two independent organisms, and asking which was the more important or preferable. Political sociologists now argue that the state is just one of many political institutions, and that political institutions are only one of many clusters of social institutions; that the relationships among these institutions and clusters of institutions is the subject of a sociology of politics. In debating with political scientists about the credentials of political sociology, sociologists have held that the independent study of the state and other political institutions does not make theoretical sense.

The state, then, cannot be adequately understood sociologically apart from its place in the total fabric of society. However, the practical political problem of the desirable balance between conflict and consensus within the sociopolitical structure still remains.

The French scholar Alexis de Tocqueville proposed a theory that took a middle ground between the views of Marx and Hegel. The very same social units that made for conflict—different governmental structures (federal, state, and local), the courts, the Congress, the presidential branch of government, as well as the private associations representing diverse interests—could also contribute to social integration. There can be unity in diversity, argued Tocqueville, as long as the state is not the only and total center of power and authority. There is, of course, the possibility that the modern state can become a "leviathan," coercing individuals and groups into consensus. Nevertheless, Tocqueville saw hope for a balance, in a plural society between two potential institutional areas—local self-government and voluntary associations. Insofar as these social units could effectively meet many of the basic needs of citizens, they could become the foundation for social consensus; at the same time, they could act as competing interests among one another and as constraints upon centralized national authority. (For a detailed discussion of the political roles of voluntary associations in a pluralist democracy, see Chapter 7.)

These classical theorists set the stage for a continuing debate among modern Americans as to how big and multifunctional government should become. Views range from one extreme to another. The idea that "the best government is that which governs the least" is a part of the laissez-faire folklore. It was exemplified by President Cleveland in 1887, who said, as he vetoed a bill appropriating $25,000 to buy seed for distressed farmers suffering from a Texas drought:

> I do not believe that the power and duty of the general government ought to be extended to the relief of individual suffering which is in no manner properly related to the public service or benefit. . . . Though the people support the government, the government should not support the people [Fabricant, 1952, pp. 6–7].

In contrast, many Americans today approve of the fact that the federal government insures half of all newly constructed dwellings, provides most of the investment opportunities for commercial banks, finances over 75 percent of all schools and colleges, and assists a variety of other individual, corporate, and private interests [Weinberg and Shabat, 1965, pp. 443–444]. This kind of involvement in meeting diverse basic needs has led to complex relationships—both supportive and competing—between government and other basic institutions.

Modern Government and Other Institutions

The impact of the nation-state can be understood by considering the various functions that the nation-state has taken over partly or wholely from other institutions. Merrill and Eldredge [1952, pp. 466–467] point to the way in which the following functions have been transferred to the state:

1. From the family:
   a. Physical protection of the home.
   b. Economic support of the unemployed.
   c. Care of the sick.
   d. Custody of the aged.
   e. Treatment of the insane.
   f. Support of widows and orphans.
   g. Formal education of the children.
2. From economic institutions:
   a. Fixing of prices.
   b. Limited control of wages.
   c. Control and manipulation of credit.
   d. Settlement of labor–capital disputes.
   e. Regulation of securities exchanges.
   f. Guarantee of bank savings.
   g. Production of electricity.
   h. Monopoly of atomic research and production.
   i. Commercial recreation.

3. From the church:
   a. Education of children.
   b. Diversion of emotional loyalties.
   c. Regulation of conditions of marriage.
   d. Jurisdiction over divorce.
   e. Rise of secular over canon law.
   f. Maintenance of poor relief.
   g. Separation of church and state.

This list could be greatly expanded by including laws on abortion, children's rights, sexuality, death and dying, and many other life experiences. It suggests how much we have come to depend upon the institution of government.

As Lipset and Weber have pointed out, this increasing role of government in modern life cannot be satisfactorily explained by liberal versus conservative politics. A better explanation lies in terms of overall changes in institutional relationships in modern America, brought about by industrialization and urbanization.

> As families decreased in size, each child was valued more as an individual. Parents demanded more and better education for their children, and this demand required larger expenditures by government. The average life span began to grow longer and longer, but society did not provide the economic means for increasing numbers of old people; so government was called upon to provide old-age assistance and other benefits.
>
> The closing of the western frontier underscored the fact that the country's natural resources were limited. . . . Cries arose for the government to conserve our natural resources.
>
> Expanding technology also added to the roles of government. Automobiles required better roads; even Adam Smith—back in 1776—had approved of government expenditures for public works such as roads. And increased car travel brought demands for more state and national parks [Weinberg and Shabat, 1965, p. 445].

In other words, government has become increasingly involved with the economic, familial, recreational, and technological institutions of society. As a consequence, the modern nation-state has also become more bureaucratized, rationalized, and all inclusive in scope and functions. This process can be summarized as the *institutionalization* of government. It has resulted in many of the crises that confront modern institutions, particularly the problem of institutional character.

INSTITUTIONAL CHARACTER AND CHANGE

Every institution develops a character, and its original goals and purposes play a part in shaping this character. Yet, the goals change over the years and are constantly compromised in the actual day-to-day operation of the institution. As we have seen in discussing associations (Chapter 7), there are forces both within and outside organizations that compete for its soul or spirit as reflected in organizational purposes or goals. These factors give rise to processes of institutionalization or deinstitutionalization and account for the fluctuation between these varying directions.

Institutionalization as a Process

As we have seen in discussing associations, some organizations gradually became increasingly institutionalized over time while others became deinstitutionalized. The characteristics of the process of institutionalization are summarized in Table 9-2. Institutionalization is represented by movement from left to right in the table; deinstitutionalization, the opposite. For example, sects can become churches, a radical labor union can grow to be wealthy and respectable, a small private college can develop into a large public university, or a family owned and operated business can become a national corporation.

TABLE 9-2 The Process of Institutionalization

Characteristics	From Less Institutional →	To More Institutional
In group structure and organization	Small and regional; loosely structured organization with few formal rules	Large scale and widespread; highly bureaucratized with many regulations
In leader-led interaction	Primary ties; intimate communication; little difference between the leaders and the led	Marked gap between officials and members; hierarchy of authority
In type of leadership	Emotional commitment to a cause; leaders feel "called"	Matter-of-fact concern for the "cause"; preoccupation with routine and tradition
In member commitment	Members feel deprived by the world; engage in dissent and criticism	Members gain privileges and come to accept the larger world; engage in compromise and accommodation

Ernst Troeltsch [1931] examined institutionalization in religious movements. He found that cults and sects are zestful new religious groupings bent upon withdrawing from the sinful world and maintaining a simple life, faithful to the spirit of a unique founder. They are dissenting associations that reject the imperfections of the world. Through the process of institutionalization, however, they may gradually become churchlike

9-2 The Church and the Process of Institutionalization

As institutions, such as the church, come into being, they go through specific phases of development. They develop a unique character as their structure and goals change to meet new needs and problems. The history of Christianity illustrates this process of institutionalization.

In the earliest pre-institutional period, a charismatic Jesus preached and taught before spontaneous crowds and small groups in informal settings. Adherents to this early social movement (see Chapter 5) were drawn from those who felt deprived and, consequently, the emphasis in early Christianity was upon dissent from and criticism of prevailing norms and values and the seeking of new norms and values.

The Bettmann Archive

The Bettmann Archive

As the movement grew in size and influence, there was a need for more structured organization and formal ideology. When Jesus said to Peter: "I give you the keys to heaven," the Disciples became endowed with the authority to act as leaders and to preach a more specific ideology involving concepts such as heaven, hell, salvation, and so on.

As Christianity prospered, the Medieval Church began to reflect the major values and norms of society. Leadership became formalized, and roles such as (1) Pope, (2) Cardinal, (3) Canon, and (4) Archbishop involved specific duties and authority. A marked distinction developed between leaders and members of the Church.

The Bettmann Archive

The Bettmann Archive

At the same time, the Church became bureaucratized, as characterized by an Ecumenical Council meeting at St. Peter's in Rome. The Church became involved with all aspects of daily life, and leadership meetings became formal and routine. The Church had become highly institutionalized.

The Protestant Reformation brought about denominationalism, whereby many new Christian sects and churches sprung up, meeting new and different needs of various people in an urbanizing world. As a result, a process of deinstitutionalization sometimes took place as membership declined. Though some outward signs of formality remained (in church architecture, seating, leadership dress), churches found it necessary to seek out new and more informal roles and goals (see the *So What?* box at the end of this chapter).

E. Herwig/Stock, Boston

large-scale organizations with a complex structure and substantial wealth. In contrast to a sect, a church welcomes into its membership the more successful citizens of a society and, in so doing, broadens its perspectives and compromises its initial goals. In seeking to influence the larger society, the church is, in turn, influenced by society. When a religious group transforms from sect to church, it confronts the dilemma of every human institution: How to keep its original zest and purposes while gaining prestige through compromise and bureaucratization (see Study 6).

One aspect of this dilemma is reflected in changes in organizational leadership and authority. Amateur leaders are especially well-fitted for the early stages of institutional development. They emerge spontaneously from the grass roots; they are close to the members and identify with them and their needs. The first leaders are set apart, not because they have formal training or an advanced education, but because they have the gifts of leadership and unique personal qualities. Members frequently revere these leaders and attribute to them special, sometimes even superhuman, qualities. These leaders are personally called to the task, and they embody the spirit of the cause. They often become symbols of revolt against the established institutions of society. In fact, new movements frequently spring from frustrations and conflicts experienced in dealing with old and established institutions.

As the institutionalization process unfolds, however, leaders do not remain amateur for long. They soon learn the skills of office and begin to enjoy the status and privilege of their new positions. Responsibilities tend to set them apart from the membership, and there is inevitable pressure for them to become formally trained. An educated leadership becomes more and more important for the organization, and the leadership becomes bureaucratized. In the final section of this chapter, we will discuss this dilemma of institutional leadership in greater detail. In essence, though, the dilemma of institutionalization arises from the fact that, while institutional character depends upon the degree of involvement, commitment, and personal enthusiasm of both the leaders and followers, some aspects of institutionalization make this spontaneous character difficult to maintain.

The contemporary university is a case in point. Crises have developed on American campuses from Berkeley, California, to New York City, and in many foreign countries. One early explanation of what has been happening to the modern university was developed by Dr. Clark Kerr [1963], while he was President of the University of California. His lectures at Harvard have been published in a book entitled *The Uses of the University.* The following discussion is based on Kerr's book and subsequent studies.

Institutional Change: The Modern University

Centers of higher learning have always been important in Western society. They have become increasingly so as modern people have come to realize that knowledge is essential to survival as well as to enriched living. Modern higher education is increasingly supported by the state and federal funds (rather than by private organizations like churches) and is increasingly involved with all segments of society. Colleges and universities have become sources of vital information for contemporary industry and government.

> Basic to this transformation is the growth of the "knowledge industry," which is coming to permeate government and business and to draw into it more and more people raised to higher and higher levels of skill. The production, distribution, and consumption of "knowledge" in all its forms is said to account for 29 percent of gross national product, according to Fritz Machlup's calculations; and "knowledge production" is growing at about twice the rate of the rest of the economy. Knowledge has certainly never in history been so central to the conduct of an entire society. What the railroads did for the second half of the last century and the automobile for the first half of this century may be done for the second half of this century by the knowledge industry: that is, to serve as the focal point for national growth. And the university is at the center of the knowledge process.
>
> The University historically has been growing in concentric circles. It started with philosophy in Greece, and a library—the first great one—at Alexandria. It spread to the ancient professions, and then to science. It permeated agriculture and now industry. Originally it served the elites of society, then the middle class as well, and now it includes the children of all, regardless of social and economic background [Kerr, 1963, pp. 87–88].

Not all Americans attend major universities, although more are going on to a college education of some kind. In the narrow sense, then, the university does not directly educate all the citizens. In a broad social sense, however, the university is a public institution involving and influencing the entire citizenry. It is often supported by taxes and under partial control of a legislature or under direct control of a board of laymen, who set policy. In addition, the university is under strong pressures from public opinion, as was evident during the Berkeley Student Revolt of the 1960s and other campus disturbances of that period. The results of most university research have an increasing impact upon the total society, and professors are called into consultation in growing numbers by government and industry. As Clark Kerr [1963, p. 115] points out: "The campus and society are undergoing a somewhat reluctant and cautious merger."

In many different ways the modern university has been experiencing the process of institutionalization, and this has brought about an accompanying crisis in institutional character. What are the bases and forms of this crisis?

The precipitating factor has been an increase in size. From 1924 to 1963, Harvard doubled its number of buildings, increased its faculty fivefold and its budget fifteenfold, and entered into increasingly sophisticated areas of research (including radio telescopes, masers and lasers, and equipment for interplanetary exploration). By 1974, Harvard had a student body of 22,000. Major state universities have been subject to even more dramatic expansion. In the United States as a whole, the number of university and college students, many of them in junior colleges, increased approximately 3 million in the 1960s, an increase equal to the growth of the previous 300 years, that is, from the founding of Harvard until 1960. It has been estimated that enrollments in higher education will reach almost 10 million by 1980 [U.S. Commissioner of Education, 1974]. There was a growth in the number of colleges, universities, and professional schools in the nation from 2008 in 1960 to 2665 by 1973. Furthermore, many campuses have grown in size, some of them very rapidly. Major state universities, like the University of California at Berkeley, often reach a student body of 27,500 and more. Even smaller state universities like the one in Micro City (see Study 8 in the previous chapter) began as tiny normal schools to train public school teachers. The Micro City campus had only 3500 students in 1960, but it had increased to over 12,000 students by 1976.

This increase in number of students has, of course, led to larger faculties, larger classes, more impersonal campuses, and a larger administrative staff. Kerr points out that the managerial revolution that we have seen in industry has also occurred in the large university. Skilled and trained administrators are now needed to manage a university; this is in sharp contrast to those earlier days when the role and importance of a rector or dean of the faculty tended to be minimized. This situation, in turn, has added a new dimension to the traditional conflict between faculty and administrators. Although the university president and other administrators receive a higher salary than most classroom professors, the latter have continued to think of themselves as having the highest academic status. In addition, professors have continued to be skeptical of the abilities of administrators and have struggled to retain decision-making powers that affect the central teaching–research purposes of the university.

In other words, as universities have grown in size and complexity, differing views and perspectives have become more frequent. These have led to internal tension and conflict. This conflict tends to focus upon two specific institutional crises that tend to characterize many other modern institutions as well—the crises of changing purposes and changing personnel.

Institutional Crises: Changing Purposes and Personnel

The crisis in the modern university is partly related to a struggle for new meaning and purposes in education. As Kerr [1963, pp. 8–9] puts it: "The university is so many things to so many different people that it must, of necessity, be partially at war with itself." It is customary to speak about a "community of scholars" when referring to an academic institution. There is a measure of truth in this concept. Intellectuals in any society do have many interests in common. Furthermore, when a university is small in size and there is communication among all the faculties across subject-matter boundaries, a measure of unity is possible. However, diversity and separation are more common today, especially in the larger universities.

This has been caused by both the increase in size of faculties and the growth of academic specialization, which makes communication between scholars increasingly difficult. In fact, communication is often difficult even within the same subject-matter discipline. The potential for this diversity has always been present in centers of learning because professors are required to perform three different tasks—teaching, research, and public service.

But the problem has been exacerbated in recent years because there seems to be no public agreement about what education ought to be or about what professors should really do. Traditional schooling, mostly taught in the conventional classroom, is not satisfying to many students, nor is it a fulfilling experience for many instructors. Yet, despite the discontent expressed in recent years, many educational institutions are apparently still committed to traditional beliefs and practices. In a study of eight institutions with sixteen campuses throughout the nation, Warren Martin [1969] found that they were all devoted to academic professionalism and to conventional standards of excellence, although the institutions differed in size, organization, and character. Even on the most innovative campuses, administrators, faculty, and students still believed in the value of achieving cognitive skills and training the mind. Martin indicates that academic professionalism leads to:

1. The measurement of institutional success by the effectiveness of student ability to use scientific concepts and special academic code words. This stress upon language skills alone encourages institutions to raise admission standards as a way of improving quality.
2. The loss of a spirit of community among scholars and students. Departmentalization fragments the student learning experience, and student–faculty relationships become formal and partial.
3. Greater emphasis upon academic freedom and the freedom to teach and research as an individual faculty member pleases. This results in further departmentalization, as the teaching–learning experience becomes less integrated, and in increased academic expense, as teaching hours are reduced to add time for research.

Martin concludes that American higher education is characterized by conformity at a time when diversity is needed. Educators have become more concerned about personal career matters than about institutional character. For example, he found that when new faculty members were recruited for teaching positions, they talked more frequently about departmental affairs and the guild activities of the academic discipline than about their educational philosophy or the academic goals of the institution. Martin also found that students experienced the same problem. Those entering the institutions he analyzed often knew very little about the educational status and character of the institution, although this was less true of students entering the new innovative campuses.

Nevertheless, Martin found some evidence that both students and faculty were generally supportive of the need for innovation in higher education. There was a strong inclination toward more discussion and independent study, more chance for an integrative curriculum across departmental lines, and more flexibility in grading and examinations. On some campuses there was a new spirit emerging that challenged more conventional views.

The institutional crisis in modern universities is partly a result of changing personnel, both students and faculty. Both state universities and private institutions have opened the field of higher education to youth of all social classes. What was once a privilege of the middle and upper classes in our society has now become accessible to almost everyone. This diversity in the student body is also characterized by the emergence of different and conflicting student subcultures. Burton R. Clark and Martin A. Trow [1966] have suggested four student classifications—the collegiate, the vocational, the academic, and the nonconformist.

The collegiate subculture has prevailed on many campuses since the turn of the century with its emphasis upon athletics, fraternities, sororities, and other social and recreational activities. Many campuses have also been characterized by a strong vocational or academic orientation. These student subcultures were challenged by nonconformist subcultures and political activism in the 1960s. An interest in recreation, vocationalism, or academic work, however, seems to be returning to many campuses in the 1970s, as economic conditions become uncertain.

Perhaps even more important than the fact that students can differ in subcultural orientation is the fact that they all face the dilemmas of campus freedom. Kerr points out that the modern campus is a confusing place because it is highly competitive and offers such a vast range of choices. It is no wonder then that "the casualty rate is high. The walking wounded are many. *Lernfreiheit*—the freedom of the student to choose courses or programs based upon his interest, and to stay or to move on—is triumphant."

Faculty members also have much to do with the institutional character of the university, since they, too, can reflect change and diversity. In early American universities, professors, like the students, were drawn largely from the more privileged levels of society. Today many of them come from working- or lower-middle-class origins. They are often the "serious students" who have gone on to graduate school and emerge as bright young faculty. Not all are content to be "ivory tower scholars" in the old tradition, remaining largely aloof from the world of social action. Many have become involved with industry and government as a result of the increasing public demands for problem-solving research. Some are sympathetic with the nonconformist student subculture and become involved in social issues and activism. There is some evidence that the faculties are beginning to develop a combination of detached scholarship and involved leadership in society. One clue to the changing character of the occupation is the recent unionization movement to bring about collective bargaining on the part of many college and university professors [Haehn, 1969; Gerth and Haehn, 1971; Ladd and Lipset, 1973].

In addition, just as the students have great freedom of choice, professors have *Lehrfreiheit*, the freedom to teach as they please. Professors may adopt traditional teaching roles, or they may move toward other roles such as research entrepreneurs and consultants. In some cases, professors become administrators. Kerr refers to these new nonteaching roles as those in which "the higher a man's standing, the less he has to do with students." Kerr [1963, p. 43] also points to a threefold status distinction in faculties: "In one university I know, the proportions at the Ph.D. level or its equivalent are roughly one researcher to two teachers to four who do both." Many professors are hired for their research abilities. They may not teach at all, and, therefore, they may not be fully accepted members of the academic community by other colleagues.

Professors show the same ambivalence and diversity on the issue of power and authority in the university. They do not all agree about the appropriate degree of faculty participation in decision making because of competing academic demands. Some still look longingly back to the European tradition when the faculty ran the institution and the administrative officers followed faculty dictates. Other professors, however, are busy with their own academic affairs and are willing to see more control move into the hands of expert administrators. Most agree on the importance of faculty influence in the areas of appointment and retention of professors, academic promotion, academic freedom, admissions, approval of courses, examinations, and the granting of degrees.

Not only has the importance of administrators in the university increased, but the role of public authority has also grown. The distribution of power now includes governmental leaders, lay boards of control, and the "public," which has great informal influence through subtle pressures upon the university.

> The solution to this dilemma in American universities has been to let power lodge where it may, to let it "roll free" to be taken into whatever hands are capable of exercising it, and to permit situations to "decide themselves" in the absence of specific rules for the attachment of authority to particular positions. . . . In this sense universities are lawless organizations. . . . One result is that a great deal of arbitrary and often capricious power may be assembled and wielded by persons without any institutional responsibility for it: witness the "robber baron" chairman or dean (or professor). . . . Another result is that the institution itself . . . moves by fits and starts in many directions in a kind of evolutionary anarchy [McGee, 1962, pp. 111–112].

In conclusion, the modern university is an example of a major social institution in crisis. It has a long history of development and has become intricately interrelated with other major institutions, especially the modern nation-state. The modern university is a large-scale organization with a highly formalized structure whose basic purpose has traditionally been the maintenance and transmission of fundamental knowledge, skills, norms, and values. At the same time, universities as basic institutions are increasingly expected to fulfill the function of creating new ideas, values, and knowledge, as the student body and the faculty become more diverse. Conflicts over institutional goals about teaching versus research versus public service are intensified.

As the preceding discussion implies, an important question must be asked. How do institutions in crisis attempt to respond to and contend with the problems of changing purposes and personnel? We suggest that answers to this question lie in the nature of institutional leadership. Not only are there different kinds of leaders, but some leaders in modern society become professionals. We turn now to a consideration of types of authority and the process of professionalization.

LEADERSHIP RESPONSES TO CHANGE AND CRISIS

Leaders in any social or group situation possess *power.* As we saw in Chapter 6, power can be defined as the ability to impose one's will and inclinations upon the behavior of other persons—that is, it is the potential to influence the thoughts and actions of others [Bendix, 1962, Part III]. In this sense, power is a natural part of most, if not all, social interaction. It is, of course, an essential aspect of effective leadership.

The power of leadership, however, is a reciprocal relationship insofar as it involves interacting human beings. It depends upon the willingness of individuals to acquiesce to the commands of their leaders. In other words, followers must see leadership as legitimate; this obviously does not always happen. Some politicians are unable to mobilize popular support for their programs despite the power of their office. Kings have frequently been overthrown because their rule is seen as illegitimate. Similarly, the possession of sheer physical force and superior weaponry does not necessarily legitimize total dominance by leaders; police can arrest and apprehend, but only courts can make judgments and determine punishments. One of the most provocative sociological questions dealing with the question of leadership is the following: What are the different bases by which leader domination can be legitimized?

From Charismatic to Bureaucratic Authority

Max Weber identified three basic types of dominance—charismatic (religious and political heroes), traditional (headmen, kings, and queens), and legal-bureaucratic (officeholders like the Pope or an American president). According to Weber, the authority of the charismatic leader lies in personal, extraordinary qualities. This leader seems to possess magical powers for followers. In this sense, *charismatic authority* is nonrational and potentially revolutionary. It is unstable and temporary and must constantly prove itself by repeated demonstrations of the miraculous. As we saw in our earlier discussion of the processes of institutionalization, charisma is common to social movements during their early, first-generation stages.

In contrast, *traditional authority* is more permanent and is based upon custom and accepted practice. Traditional leaders exercise authority through inherited status, and followers obey because of unquestioned acceptance of this status. Traditional leadership, however, still provides for elements of personal power. By justifying their rule in terms of traditional authority, leaders can inject an element of personal arbitrariness into commands and decisions. Charismatic and traditional authority, then, are related. For example, once a social movement becomes established and organized activity begins, life can no longer be lived in the high pitch of emotional commitment to the "miraculous" cause. Charismatic authority, therefore, inevitably gives way to more traditional forms of authority.

Finally, dominance can be based upon *legal–bureaucratic authority:*

> Our modern "associations," above all the political ones, are of the type of "legal" authority. That is, the legitimacy of the powerholder to give commands rests upon rules that are rationally established by enactment, by agreement, or by imposition. The legitimacy for establishing these rules rests, in turn, upon a rationally enacted or interpreted "constitution." Orders are given in the name of the impersonal norm, rather than in the name of a personal authority; and even the giving of a command constitutes obedience toward a norm rather than an arbitrary freedom, favor, or privilege [Gerth and Mills, 1958, pp. 294–295].

Whereas authority of tradition can be nonrational (the patriarch can exercise arbitrary favor within the established system of norms), the authority of "office" is rational and impersonal, reflecting the legitimacy of the legal system rather than the powerholder. It is by virtue of this authority, *ex cathedra,* that the Pope has spoken with infallibility from his official position or the president of the United States is commander in chief of the armed forces during wartime. Therefore, as institutional settings bureaucratize, different bases are required for legitimizing leadership. Charisma may become routinized into traditional forms, and tradition may be transformed into legal forms. To put it another way, the moment an emerging organization begins to establish a budget to finance its operation, routinization is under way. Changes then occur in every aspect of the movement including the character of the leadership.

A special problem faced by modern large-scale institutions is that all three kinds of authority may be required for many leadership positions. For example, professors and administrators in the university are expected to possess unique personal qualities, technical skills, and knowledge, and to uphold and transmit the basic traditions of society. Physicians and politicians are likewise expected to have charismatic appeal to their patients and constituents, commitment to the fundamental traditions of society, and occupational competence. In an attempt to meet the demands of institutional leadership in modern society, a form of occupational adaptation known as professionalization has arisen.

Professionalization is an attempt to combine the altruistic "spirit of the calling" with the highest level of technical competence and rational objectivity. There is obviously a measure of contradiction in these goals. The scientific detachment of a physician or lawyer can be interpreted by clients as indifference or a loss of calling. Yet, this very objectivity enables the professional to serve clients with effective altruism. It is to the client's benefit that the professional refuses to become too emotionally involved with the problem.

Professionalization is playing an increasingly important role in many of today's institutions. When it does, both professions and institutions undergo change. "While many professions are becoming bureaucratized, many bureaucracies are also becoming professionalized" [Etzioni, 1966, p. 265]. Thus, new forms of institutions are emerging partly as a result of the impact of professionalization.

Professionalization

In the late Middle Ages, only a few occupations (law, the clergy, university teaching, and, to some extent, medicine) could be characterized as professions [Carr-Sanders, 1928, 1933]. With the coming of the industrial revolution and occupational specialization, professionalization began to spread until today there are perhaps 30 or 40 occupations that exhibit the following professional characteristics [Cogan, 1953, pp. 48–49]:

1. Altruistic service to clients and society.
2. A basic liberal education followed by professional and technical training. The professional role is related to a specialized body of theory and research.
3. Licensure by the state. The state uses this power for the protection of the public. The criteria for licensure and practice, however, should be drawn up with full reference to and consultation with practitioners representing the profession.
4. The competence of professionals is judged by other professionals. The layman is not in a position to make such judgments.
5. Professional practice is continually directed by the body of theory and research relevant to the field of specialization. This excludes the possibility of fraud or dangerous and purely mechanical practices.
6. A code of professional ethics. This code should be continually developed, corrected, and enforced by the profession itself.

In other words, a professional person tries to combine an altruistic spirit with technical competence. That is, the physician or lawyer is ex-

9-3 Professional Altruism Versus Professional Efficiency

Professionals are characterized by altruistic commitment—the desire to meet the special and intimate needs of their clients without concern for personal reward or achievement. At the same time, professionals are expected to dispense skilled services effectively and efficiently without concern for client preference. These two characteristics frequently compete with one another, as can be seen in the case of modern medicine and teaching.

Elsa Dorfman

Some physicians practice medicine from small mobile clinics which can be taken to rural and urban areas where medical care is usually not available. They may donate their services free of charge or they may charge moderate fees. This practice, though giving expression to the altruistic commitment, may make it impossible for the physician to meet the different needs of many citizens while utilizing the best available techniques and equipment.

Herbert Robinson/Metamorphosis

In contrast, physicians serving many patients from permanent offices in or near hospitals can serve large numbers of patients. They can also maintain the costly equipment necessary to meet multiple needs effectively. This context, however, often transforms the doctor–patient relationships into an anomic and formal contractual tie. As a result, the altruistic commitment can erode and physicians can become interested in the size of fees, the number of patients served, the ability of patients to pay for services, and the like.

Elizabeth Hamlin, Dietz/Hamlin

In a small, intimate classroom teachers can meet the many different spontaneous needs of individual students. The teacher feels altruistically involved in the teaching–learning relationship. However, an informal context sometimes makes it difficult to transmit basic skills and knowledge in a formal, sequenced fashion to large numbers of students.

Donald Dietz, Dietz/Hamlin

In contrast, modern technology (teaching machines, computers, television) makes it possible to transmit knowledge to many students in widely separated areas. However, the teacher may be completely removed from the classroom setting and, thereby, may come to feel only like a technician or performer.

pected to render service even if he is not paid for it. Indeed, the professional fee is not considered a normal market price since, theoretically, the services rendered are worth more than money can buy. A professional has knowledge that cannot be fully imparted to a layman; hence, the client is at the mercy of the professional. Professionals could take advantage of clients, but they will not do so if they are "true" professionals with an altruistic commitment to service.

Free professionals is the term that emphasizes the importance of occupational autonomy. The professional must be free from irresponsible or unknowledgeable control by nonexperts. Only the physician knows what it is to be an acceptable doctor. However, this traditional perspective of free professionalism is rapidly changing, as more professionals begin to work within large-scale bureaucratized institutions. The developing relationship between professional and bureaucratic cultures has resulted in mixed organizational forms. Many professionals no longer practice privately; many have become employees within organizations, ranked according to seniority, and controlled by organizational rules and regulations. This change has influenced professions and institutions alike.

Professionalism and Institutions

As Wilensky [1964] indicates, professionalism has altered institutional structure in three important ways. *First,* institutions tend increasingly to be run by professionals who become administrators. In churches, universities, law firms, and hospitals, leaders are professionals first and, secondly, heads of departments and chief executives. For example, many professors insist that university presidents be scholars in their own right. University presidents who are only skilled managers and not academicians often experience great difficulty with their faculties. As a consequence, institutions tend to take into account the unique character of professions and use management principles that involve professional autonomy and the service ideal. By means of these changes, professionals in institutional contexts attempt to assure that they do not work for lay leaders.

Second, professionals share the power in many institutions. In a university, professors organize into an academic senate and, as a corporate body, they demand that many decisions be theirs. To be sure, they must share the authority with lay boards and administrators. Yet they assert themselves within the institution and claim that in many respects they alone are qualified to decide. In other words, they refuse to be mere employees.

Third, professionals maintain their ties with and responsibilities to professional associations, which extend beyond any one institution. One characteristic of professionals is that they are colleague-oriented—that is, only their peers can judge and reward them. Thus even though they become salaried employees of an institution, they continue to take their cues from and render allegiance to a professional body of peers. This means that the institution does not gain complete control over its employees. However, an institution like the university may well gain in reputation by having on its staff a scholar–scientist who wins national and international acclaim. In other words, more and more professionals today are working in institutions rather than working alone. This is part of the overall trend toward bureaucracy. And when this happens, both institutional character and professional practice are affected.

One important aspect of this trend has to do with the question of professional altruism. There is always the risk, in our highly competitive society, that professionals will put concern for their own success and reputation above that for their students, clients, patients, and so forth. This risk is perhaps greatest when professionals work in large institutions. In this situation, there may be a loss of professional altruism, or, in other words, *an attentuation of the calling*. The following study examines this problem by comparing several pieces of research that deal with the institutional experiences of physicians and clergy.

▶ STUDY 9

The Loss of Professional Altruism: Physicians and Ministers [1954–1965][1]

Problem

In current studies of modern institutions, there is evidence that the character of leadership changes as organizations go through different phases of development. Changes also seem to characterize the career cycle of individual professionals. How do these changes come about and what factors help to account for them? *How are these changes related to Wilensky's thesis that, when professionals become more involved in bureaucratic institutions, both institutional character and professional practice are affected?*

Hypothesis and Study Design

The technique employed in this study involves *comparing the research* of different academicians *from two areas of professional and institutional life:* medicine and the clergy. The objective is *to test Wilensky's hypothesis* that professional altrusim suffers significantly when professionals—in this case, physicians and ministers—must work in institutionalized settings.

[1]Adapted, abridged, and based upon several different studies and articles on physicians and the clergy, including Talcott Parsons, "The Professions and Social Structure," *Essays in Sociological Theory* (New York: The Free Press, 1954); Howard S. Becker and Blanche Geer, "The Fate of Idealism in Medical School," *American Sociological Review, 23* (February 1958), pp. 50–56; Samuel Blizzard, "The Minister's Dilemma," *The Christian Century* (25 April 1956), pp. 508–510; Robert P. Rankin, "Religious Ideals and Church Administration: A Sociological Study of Methodism," (1958), unpublished Ph.D. thesis, University of California, Berkeley, Calif.; and "The Ministerial Calling and the Minister's Wife," *Pastoral Psychology, 11* (September 1960), pp. 16–22.

Methods of Data Collection

This adapted study begins by reviewing research based upon *observation* of, and *interviews* with, medical students in the 1950s. In particular, Talcott Parsons' analysis of the risk of commercialism among physicians is examined. The findings from the area of medical sociology are then compared to research results from another rapidly developing specialty, the sociology of religion.

Samuel Blizzard gathered data from a complete sampling of Protestant ministers who were graduates of five major theological seminaries, including Union Theological Seminary in New York City. He relied largely upon the results of *mailed questionnaires,* which investigated how ministers adjust as they move from their formal training out into the parish and on through various stages of their careers. Rankin's study of Methodism is then utilized for comparative purposes. His research was based upon *participant observation* in the California–Nevada Annual Conference of the Methodist church and upon interviews with both the nonclergy and the ministers in church administration. The results of this comparative analysis are in part exploratory and suggest additional hypotheses that require further testing.

Findings and Interpretations: Medical Professions

Physicians have long been classified among the professionals. Ideally, all the major requirements of professionalism—a liberal arts degree as well as professional training, licensing by a professional body of colleagues, a mandate to serve, commitment to professional ethics, altruistic service to clients without primary emphasis upon reward, and confidentiality—are fulfilled by physicians. There is evidence, however, that physicians a generation or two ago were more committed to the professional ideals of medicine and were more willing to render altruistic service through house calls and long work hours without undue concern for income. Recent trends indicate that medicine is becoming increasingly businesslike, and physicians are under criticism from patients and the public for becoming more commercial.

Talcott Parsons tries to single out those social forces that have contributed to this trend. In most normal work situations, occupational success depends on (1) *achievement* by technical competence and (2) *recognition* by one's peers in the occupational group. The same two elements are at work whether a person is in business or is a physician. Consequently, even though the two occupations promote different behavior patterns—acquisitiveness on the one hand and altruism on the other—these behavioral differences cannot be accounted for in motivational terms. In other words, business people are not inherently acquisitive; they are simply working in an acquisitive setting that defines their career pattern. Physicians are not inherently altruistic; they are merely working in a professional setting and respond to what is expected of them. Parsons suggests that business occupations institutionalize acquisitiveness and self-interest, while professions institutionalize altruistic disinterestedness.

It follows, then, that the altruism of physicians and other professional people is not so much motivational as it is institutional. Thus, when strains and conflicts develop in the institutional setting, professionals may resort to deviations from the norm of altruism. Physicians may turn toward commercialism if the larger society does not recognize and reward them for their professional competence and disinterestedness. They, too, live in the acquisitive society where money can buy the symbols of recognition. Hence, there is a tendency for physicians to lose a measure of the calling in favor of redefining medicine as a career or job.

This initial hypothesis can be clarified even further when we examine what happens to medical students during training. In theory, professionalization should begin here. Findings, however, suggest that the early idealism of young medical students undergoes a change in professional schools. Becker and Geer conclude that this idealism is not so much lost as it is transformed into a more realistic form that may appear to be cynical. Their conclusion is based upon a field study of students at the University of Kansas Medical School in the 1950s.

Becker and Geer discovered that disillusioning experiences began for medical students as soon as they started their professional preparation and continued throughout the long training period. They summarized this process as follows:

1. Freshmen found that they were not going to be dealing with patients. Their required courses were not as good as some other college courses. They were also shocked and frustrated to learn that there was more medical knowledge than they could ever learn.
2. The sophomore year continued many of the same problems. The pressure to pass examinations resulted in further frustration.
3. Clinical years of training brought new forms of frustration. Contact with patients began, but under circumstances which made it difficult to fulfill the student ambition to help people. Student physicians had to cope with a steady stream of patients, yet without the authority to make important decisions. Demands also made it impossible to pay primary attention to patients as individuals.
4. As the students neared graduation, however, they still talked about wanting to be good physicians and helping people, particularly when they were alone and away from their peers.

In summary, there is evidence that, although student physicians go through stages of cynicism in their professional schooling, they do not surrender their idealism. Rather it is postponed or translated into a more *pragmatic professional idealism.* Furthermore, a seemingly detached attitude toward patients is not necessarily because of a loss of interest in clients. It may well be a function of striving for greater efficiency, which, in turn, will benefit the most people. What looks like heartless cynicism to patients may be an effort to practice medicine with integrity. The idealism of the professional has become more informed, although no less selfless.

Findings and Interpretations: Professional Clergymen

In contrast to physicians, there is evidence that *disillusionment among the clergy takes place during the early years of adjustment in the parish.* Samuel Blizzard studied a large sample of Protestant clergymen of all denominations and discovered that young men entering the ministry had a primary commitment to service as a preacher and pastor. Seminaries trained them for this service through courses in theology, Bible, ethics, homiletics, and church history. The occupational shock occurs when a minister takes charge of the first church and discovers that most of the work time is spent directing or administering the organization. Thus, Blizzard suggests that one problem for the modern minister relates to the confusion about what is to be expected of him (or her) in the occupational role. There is considerable disillusionment among ministers after they leave school.

Ministers rate the roles of preacher, priest, pastor, teacher, counselor, and administrator in that order, from most to least important. However, the church as a social organization demands that the minister allocate work time almost in reverse order. Thus, administration takes the most time, whereas preaching is considered most important.

In his first church, the minister learns that he must be first of all an administrator of an organization with unique problems of self-maintenance. Therefore, he is faced with the dilemma of how to strike a balance between "a calling" and "a career." The minister is traditionally called to serve the spiritual needs of individuals, but he may find himself overly involved in the career obligations of an organization man. He must eschew the charismatic role and become overly concerned with what is good for the operation of the institution rather than what is best for the spirit of the movement. For the clergy, this represents a change from an amateur spirit to a professional orientation.

The process of professionalization, involving both commitment to a career and a calling, is represented in Table 9-3.

TABLE 9-3 Career Pattern of Methodist Clergy

Commitment To a Career	Commitment to a Calling: Present	Commitment to a Calling: Absent
Present	STAGE C: *Providential and Ecclesiastical Call* The minister becomes a professional fully ordained by the church.	STAGE D: *Loss of Secret Calling or Its Attenuation* The minister may lose the call in stressing success in the career: May drop out of church. → May drop out of ministry.
Absent	STAGE B: *The Secret Call* The minister is called to preach but is not yet fully educated or ordained.	STAGE A: *Call to be a Christian* The minister starts here as a lay church member.

The arrows indicate possible progress through the career from Stage A, to B, to C. Most ministers intend to maintain professional life at Stage C, which combines trained expertise with the altruistic spirit. Some move on to Stage D under pressures within the institution.

Source: Robert P. Rankin, "Religious Ideals and Church Administration: A Sociological Study of Methodism" (1958), unpublished Ph.D. thesis, University of California, Berkeley, Calif.

When the Methodist religious movement emerged within the Church of England in the 18th century, most ministers were laymen (at Stage A) who felt a "secret call" to preach (and moved toward Stage B). They were working-class men who stood out in small meetings as persons with special charismatic talents and enthusiasm. They were unlettered and thought of their ministry as a calling to service without thought of personal advancement. As the new church took form, it set up an institutional process for formally approving the authority to preach. Laymen who felt called to preach had to fulfill requirements of reading and preaching and be ordained as local preachers. Assigned to a local church, they became "supply pastors" (Stage B). Supply pastors are still used in Methodist churches today, usually in small rural churches, when a shortage of fully qualified ministers exists. They serve, however, without full ordination.

In the 20th century, as the church became one of the largest Protestant denominations in America, and as Methodists became, for the most part, educated middle-class citizens in white-collar occupations, the trend towards a professionalized ministry accelerated. Institutional requirements for full ordination and membership in a Methodist Conference now include an A.B. degree; seminary training; the B.D. or M.A. degree; a three-year trial period under supervision; screening by a board of professional ministers, who frequently make use of psychological testing and interviews for ministerial candidates and their wives; and a formal vote by the Executive Session of Professional Ministers "in full connection." In other words, most ministers today must move from Stage A, through B, to C. It is not enough to feel a secret call; the institution must approve and confirm persons with the "Providential Call" (they have the talents) and the "Ecclesiastical Call" (they have the blessing of the church). As professional ministers, they are expected to commit themselves to a full-time career. Ideally, the profession should include both a calling and a commitment to career (as at Stage C).

The risk of professionalization is that the process will not culminate at Stage C but will move on toward Stage D. In fact, some observers feel that there has been a gradual transition toward Stage D for the whole church, as it has become increasingly involved with organizational self-maintenance. As mentioned earlier, there is evidence that ministers tend to be so caught up in administrative and organizational work—the career path—that they have lost the original sense of mission.

This is sometimes expressed by ministers themselves in comments like the following:

> When I was a young minister, we were proud of the fact that our salaries were so low—lower than most other professional people. Today, I find that a young minister just out of seminary will bargain for the highest possible salary, indicating that he has a "better offer" in some other conference. We have become more "professional" [Rankin, 1958, p. 319].
>
> • • •
>
> I sense that our ministers today are better men than ever before in all ways (education, ability, and the like) except for spiritual depth and that personal touch and love for persons. A really effective minister is one with something more profound than the ability to keep the Methodist machinery running smoothly. He is able to relate to people so as to make them feel important and loved rather than "used" to make an institution function [Rankin, 1958, p. 324].

Conclusion and Implications

This analysis of two professions suggests that a common problem does exist as professions become institutionalized. *The early sense of individualism and altruistic calling gradually becomes weakened, modified, or lost completely as it comes into conflict with an organizationally based career.* The resulting tensions lead to necessary adaptation between the organization and the professional, including a compromising of the original spirit and purpose of the profession.

The form this adaptation process takes may vary significantly from one profession to another, depending upon the particular organizational and institutional environment. For physicians, cynicism occurs early in the training period and results primarily in a redefinition of the calling or a postponement of altruistic ideals until private practice is reached. On the other hand, for ministers who must work in large-scale organizational settings, disillusionment and cynicism occur later in their career, and the opportunities for effectively redefining their professional ethics are often not available.

These kinds of studies are examples of how social scientists have started to grapple with the question of institutional adaptation to the crises of change. Further research is needed to indicate how institutional settings can be effectively restructured and reorganized to lessen the resulting problems. As institutional leaders, professionals can play an active role by recommending changes in hiring and promotion procedures; by suggesting different administrative practices; by developing meaningful ways of measuring commitment to professional goals, and so on.

An additional career problem for clergy in our society is also related to professionalization. It is a role crisis: Should a minister be primarily a pastor who comforts individuals (the *comforting priest*) or should he or she be a social reformer who challenges churches to become instruments of change (the *challenging prophet*)? This role conflict is a familiar one in the history of Western and other religions and was dramatically evident in the United States during the civil rights struggle of the 1960s (see Chapter 10). Catholic, Protestant, and Jewish clergy marched as challenging prophets in demonstrations led by Martin Luther King and other black leaders. Those clergy who took part were, for the most part, highly educated and professionalized. They often participated in demonstrations in spite of strong objections from members of their local churches, who wanted them to perform only comforting clerical roles.

This tension between clergy and laity highlights an important aspect of religion as a basic social institution. It can become a conservative force that resists change, or it can become a force that encourages rapid change, as we saw in Weber's study of the Protestant ethic and the development of capitalism. In the same way, professionalization can lead to either conservative, comtemplative roles, or radical action-oriented behavior. Jeffrey K. Hadden [1969] studied 7441 clergy from six denominations in America and found that many of them faced a crisis of role identity. This was especially true for what he called "the new breed" of clergy—those who tended to be young and to view the church as an instrument of social change. Their involvement in radical causes and social action created a backlash among many of the more conservative laity in the churches. The result was that many young ministers in the 1960s either left the church or looked for jobs other than in the parish ministry.

In a recent study, Rodney Stark and his colleagues [1971] surveyed Protestant ministers from nine major denominations in California. They found that most did not speak out on social and political topics in their sermons; only about 6 percent of the sermons given in California Protestant churches in 1967 were devoted mainly to these topics. Ministers tended to avoid speaking about social and political issues because they were committed to the comforting role and believed that salvation of the individual was the only solution to social problems. On the other hand, about one third of the ministers surveyed exhibited a concern about social action similar to that expressed by Hadden's "new breed" of minister. They appeared to avoid controversial topics only when they lacked the support of the laity.

In spite of the conservative trend in American churches in the 1970s, activists (both ministers and liberal laity) continue to find ways of participating in social action. The ministry to migrant labor in California, which supported Caesar Chavez's United Farm Workers, is one example. Another example is the fact that church money and leadership helped to bring about the court trial of National Guardsmen following the shooting of Kent State students (see Chapter 5). Furthermore, some church people continue to speak out on issues like the arms race, poverty and pollution, the risk of nuclear power plants, and so on. Sociologists will continue to analyze these kinds of religious involvements, as well as the more traditional ones discussed in the following chapter.

▶ SO WHAT?

Study 9 indicated that professional individualism and altruistic commitment frequently become weakened in institutions by commitments to organizationally based careers. Furthermore, our discussion of the university indicated that institutional crises are often caused by changing membership size and needs. Finally, we have seen how some scholars identify the crisis in institutional leadership as a conflict between comforting and challenging roles. Can these sociological concepts and theories be utilized to identify ways in which both professionals and institutions might be able to adapt to crises and change? Newly emerging ministerial roles in the contemporary church provide a partial answer to this question:

1. *Individualism and Altruism Outside the Formal Institution*—For many years, Reverend David Beebe of Medfield, Massachusetts, was active in the Baptist parish ministry. He performed traditional institutional roles—preaching on Sundays, marrying, burying, visiting the old and sick, and counseling those with personal problems. By 1976, the 55-year-old Reverend Beebe was full-time director of a nutrition program for the elderly at the Age Center in Worcester, Massachusetts, and he no longer drew a paycheck for a pulpit position. Reverend Beebe may represent a new ministerial role of the future: The

worker–priest earning a living and carrying out an altruistic role in the secular marketplace [Longscope, 1976, pp. 25, 38]. Such new roles could release professionals from the constraints of institutionally oriented careers.

2. *Response to Changes in Membership Size and Needs*—In the Massachusetts diocese of the Episcopal Church, because of a shortage of church leadership roles, more than 100 of the 400 canonically resident priests are in secular jobs, including real estate, school guidance, and welfare work. Other churches have been similarly influenced; for example, Jesuit priests have entered business and politics (Rev. Robert F. Drinan, S.J., U.S. Representative from Massachusetts' 4th Congressional District). However, many of these former church leaders have been able to carry their altruistic commitments and life-styles with them, even though they perform purely secular roles (Governor Jerry Brown of California). In addition, secular roles provide ways of meeting new needs that the older institutional roles could not provide. Catholic Jesuit priests in Boston's South End neighborhood have run schools for labor organizers, teaching them how to establish a shop and set up collective bargaining procedures. Other Jesuits have helped citizens fight government agencies over issues like potholes in streets or broken street lights [Bicknell, 1976, pp. 23 ff].

3. *New Roles Combining Comforting and Challenging Aspects*—Roles that are more secular provide ways in which comforting and challenging tasks can be combined. Harvey Cox [1965] has headed a group known as The Boston Industrial Mission, an organization that encourages business people to think about practical solutions to value problems, such as poverty, war, and civil rights. During the Vietnam War, for example, the Mission provided professional advice to industries on economical and organizational ways of converting from war-related production to peace production (from the production of electronic components for nuclear missiles to components to be used in urban mass-transit systems).

Is the newly emerging, more secular ministry an adequate institutional response by the church to crisis and change? Will it be a meaningful way of combining older and newer roles and duties, while maintaining individualism and altruism? Further analysis is needed to answer these questions. There are some signs of weakness in these new roles. Without the daily support of a formal institutionalized church, many secular ministers feel isolated and alienated from denominational life. Many resent having been trained for parish jobs that no longer exist. Others feel new organizational pressures to adapt to secular demands in economic and political life. Nevertheless, sociological theory does indicate that some form of adaptation may well be possible, enabling the institution of the church to survive and thrive by adapting to crisis and change.

CONCLUSION

In defining institutions, we noted that societal norms and values become channeled and regularized into social habits by social groupings that we call institutions. These forms of group behavior give permanence and stability to human societies. Institutions represent long-lived and highly structured ways of organizing daily life, in contrast to the collective outbursts of human action that emerge in pioneering social movements.

The human family is one example of an institution that is found in all societies and that fulfills basic human needs. Religious institutions are also present in every society, and in feudal Western civilization the Church emerged as a predominant force. In contrast to the family and the church, the nation-state is a relatively new phenomenon, which arose to meet the needs of more specialized industrial societies. One of the central issues of our time has to do with the increasing size and all-pervading character of big government. The modern state influences the lives of all citizens within its territory in a variety of ways, both material and nonmaterial.

In stressing the permanence of institutions, we have not implied that they are unchanging. On the contrary, several problems of modern institutions result from their dynamic character. The changing character of the modern university is an example. In addition, the processes of institutionalization and professionalization play a role. Many human groupings are constantly going through transition from less institutional to more institutional forms. They become more highly structured; their normative patterns become more firmly established and formalized; and their leaders become more formally trained and professionalized.

Many occupations in modern society actively strive for the high status of a profession. Most, of course, are not likely to achieve more than a kind of semiprofessional character. This is true largely because a professional occupation requires both specialized expertise, which comes from long training, and the spirit of altruism, a commitment to service without concern for profit. There is evidence that professional altruism is changing even in the oldest and best-established professions such as medicine and the ministry. One reason is the fact that more and more professionals are working within institutions. The institutional setting tends to place a new emphasis upon career goals, which often run counter to older professional aspirations. Thus professional life undergoes transformation as it interacts with institutions, and institutions are changed as professionals make new demands upon them.

This chapter on institutions is a fitting transition from Part 3 to Part 4. It has introduced the concept of institutions, by indicating their importance and changing character. In Part 4, we will examine the way in which institutions are interrelated in both a supportive and competing manner. Chapter 10 deals with socializing institutions (family, school, and church) and Chapter 11 deals with power institutions (the state, military, and technology).

REFERENCES

Bendix, Reinhard. *Max Weber: An Intellectual Portrait.* New York: Doubleday and Company, 1962.

Bicknell, Stan. "Jesuits: The Church's Shock Troops Move into the Modern World," *Boston Sunday Globe* (15 February 1976), New England Section, pp. 23 ff.

Carr-Saunders, A. M. *Professions: Their Organization and Place in Society.* Oxford: Clarendon Press, 1928.

———, and P. A. Wilson. *The Professions.* Oxford: Clarendon Press, 1933.

Clark, Burton R., and Martin A. Trow. "Determinants of College Subculture," in T. M. Newcomb and E. K. Wilson, *The Study of College Peer Groups.* Chicago: Aldine Publishing Company, 1966.

Clark, Kenneth. *Civilization.* New York: Harper & Row, Publishers, 1969.

Cogan, Morris L. "Toward a Definition of Professions," *Harvard Educational Review, 23,* No. 1 (1953), pp. 48–49.

Cox, Harvey. *The Secular City.* New York: The Macmillan Company, 1965.

Etzioni, A. "Professionals and Complex Organizations," in Howard M. Vollmer and Donald L. Mills, Ed., *Professionalization.* Englewood Cliffs, N.J.: Prentice–Hall, 1966.

Fabricant, Solomon. *The Trend of Government in the United States Since 1900.* New York: National Bureau of Economic Research, 1952.

Gerth, Donald R., and James O. Haehn. *An Invisible Giant: The California State Colleges.* San Francisco: Jossey–Bass, 1971.

Gerth, H. H., and C. Wright Mills. *Max Weber: Essays in Sociology.* New York: Oxford University Press, 1958.

Hadden, Jeffrey K. *The Gathering Storm in the Churches.* Garden City, N.Y.: Doubleday and Company, 1969.

Haehn, James O. "A Study of Trade Unionism Among State College Professors" (1969), unpublished Ph.D. thesis, University of California, Berkeley, Calif.

Hertzler, J. O. *American Social Institutions.* Boston: Allyn and Bacon, 1961.

Holmberg, Allan. *Nomads of the Long Bow: The Siriono of Eastern Bolivia.* Smithsonian Institution: Institute of Social Anthropology, 1950.

Johnson, Harry M. *Sociology: A Systematic Introduction.* New York: Harcourt, Brace and World, 1960.

Kerr, Clark. *The Uses of the University.* Cambridge, Mass.: Harvard University Press, 1963.

Ladd, Everett C., Jr., and Seymour M. Lipset. *Professors, Unions, and American Higher Education.* Berkeley, Calif.: Carnegie Foundation for the Advancement of Teaching, 1973.

Lenski, Gerhard. *Human Societies.* New York: McGraw-Hill Book Company, 1970.

Lipset, Seymour M. *Political Man.* New York: Doubleday and Company, 1960.

Longscope, Kay. "Clergy Find Jobs Scarce in Churches," *Boston Sunday Globe* (14 March 1976), pp. 25 ff.

Martin, Warren M. *Conformity: Standards and Change in Higher Education.* San Francisco: Jossey–Bass, 1969.

McDonagh, Edward C., and Jon E. Simpson, Ed. *Social Problems: Persistent Challenges.* New York: Holt, Rinehart and Winston, 1969.

McGee, Reece. *Social Disorganization in America.* San Francisco: Chandler Publishing Company, 1962.

Merrill, Frances E. *Society and Culture: An Introduction to Sociology.* Englewood Cliffs, N.J.: Prentice–Hall, 1969.

————, and H. Wentworth Eldredge. *Culture and Society.* Englewood Cliffs, N.J.: Prentice–Hall, 1952.

Murdock, George P., *et al. Outline of Cultural Materials.* New Haven: Human Relations Area Files, 1942.

Nisbet, Robert A. *Community and Power.* New York: Oxford University Press, 1962; also published as *The Quest for Community.* New York: Oxford University Press, 1953.

Selznick, Philip. "Institutional Vulnerability in Mass Society," *American Sociological Review, 16* (January 1951), pp. 320–331.

Stark, Rodney, Bruce D. Foster, Charles Y. Glock, and Harold E. Quinley. *Wayward Shepherds: Prejudice and the Protestant Clergy.* New York: Harper & Row, Publishers, 1971.

Troeltsch, Ernst. *The Social Teachings of the Christian Churches.* Olive Wyan, Transl.; with an introduction by Charles Gore. New York: The Macmillan Company, 1931.

United States Commissioner of Education. *Annual Report of the U.S. Commissioner of Education.* Washington, D.C.: U.S. Government Printing Office, 31 March 1974.

Weinberg, Mayer, and Oscar E. Shabat. *Society and Man.* Englewood Cliffs, N.J.: Prentice–Hall, 1965.

Wilensky, Harold L. "The Professionalization of Everyone," *The American Journal of Sociology, 70* (September 1964), pp. 137–158.

Zimmerman, Carle C. *Family and Civilization.* New York: Harper & Brothers, 1947.

▶ KEY CONCEPT REVIEW

To aid you in mastering the basic concepts of Part 3, we have organized key terms into convenient and logical conceptual networks. Refer to the study procedure recommended for the clusters and Key Concept Reviews in Part 1 and follow the same procedure here.

CLUSTER 6
Social Groups, Systems, and Mobility

- Group
- Primary Group
- Secondary Group
- Social System
- Social Mobility
- Open Society
- Closed Society

CLUSTER 7
Human Group Behavior—More Spontaneous Forms

- Collectivity
- Panic
- Craze
- Fashion and Fad
- Crowd
- Expressive and Acting Crowds
- Social Movement

CLUSTER 8
Human Group Behavior—Mixed and Variable Forms

- Class
- Caste
- Association
- Democracy
- Community
- Ecological Area
- Ghetto

CLUSTER 9
Human Group Behavior—More Structured Forms

- Institution
- Institutionalization
- Profession
- Bureaucracy
- Oligarchy
- *Gesellschaft* (as contrasted to *Gemeinschaft*)

6. Social Groups, Systems, and Mobility

	Definition	Example
Group	Two or more persons who identify in some way and who take each other's behavior into account. People who share some common characteristic (age, sex, race, wealth) but do not have a sense of shared identity and do not interact in some fashion are referred to as an *aggregate*.	All nearsighted sociologists constitute an aggregate (shared characteristic), but when they begin to recognize their similarity and interact with each other, they become a group (for example, they establish SNS—Society for Nearsighted Sociologists).
Primary Group	Any group where the members interact on an intimate, spontaneous, and total basis. Strong feelings of mutual identification and cooperation characterize primary-group life.	The family is the classic example of a primary group. Family life, particularly in traditional societies, is characterized by shared identity and informal intimate relationships involv-

	Definition	Example
		ing the total personality of all members. Peer groups (juvenile gangs) and small work groups are other common examples.
Secondary Group	Any group where the members interact on an impersonal, formal, and partial basis. Relationships are generally task-oriented and often stereotyped in secondary-group contexts.	In large *bureaucratic* organizations, like IBM or the U.S. Department of Health, Education, and Welfare, most employees interact with each other and their clients in a limited, impersonal, task-oriented fashion—a contractual relationship. Most employees in such organizations do not even want to know each other beyond the formal contexts of their job.
Social System	Any social unit (group, society) comprised of interdependent parts that interact with each other in order to perform the basic functions needed to maintain the unit. Each unit may, in turn, be part of a larger unit. When discussing the internal aspects of a social *group, community,* or *society,* one refers to it as a system; when discussing it in terms of a larger unit of which it is a part, it is called a *subsystem.*	The nuclear family can be viewed as a social system. Mother, father, and children together comprise a family unit in which each member is an interacting part, contributing to the long-term maintenance of the family as a whole. When interacting with other families in the community, it becomes a subsystem within the larger community social system.
Social Mobility	Vertical or horizontal movement within the *stratification* system—that is, within the *status* structure of the social system. *Vertical* movement represents a change of status, whereas *horizontal* mobility represents a change of occupation or physical location at the same status level. Both types of mobility characterize *open class societies,* but only horizontal mobility is possible within *closed caste societies.*	When a Vietnam veteran decides to go to college on the G.I. Bill, he exchanges his soldier status for that of college student. This represents primarily horizontal mobility. After obtaining a master's degree in electrical engineering, he joins an aircraft manufacturing firm (upward mobility) and later is promoted to a management position (further upward mobility). If he loses his job because of economic cutbacks, he experiences downward mobility or *skidding* (pp. 241–244). If he retires early and decides to teach at a state college, he experiences horizontal mobility.

	Definition	Example
Open Society	A social system in which it is possible for an individual to move from one *status* level to another. Open societies are characterized by *class-like* groupings.	The existence of a "Horatio Alger" myth (poor boys can make good by hard work) within a society is evidence that the society believes it is an open one.
Closed Society	A social system where there is little or no opportunity for an individual to move from one *status* level to another. Closed societies are characterized by *castelike* groupings.	In medieval society, children born into peasant families had virtually no chance to ever move up in the status system. Likewise, children of the nobility could rarely experience downward mobility. Everyone has his or her place assigned (by *ascribed status*) from birth.

7. Human Group Behavior—More Spontaneous Forms

	Definition	Example
Collectivity	A human group that is transient, temporary, spontaneous, and has little formal social structure. Sometimes collectivities develop into long-lasting *social movements.*	Persons gathered about a street-corner preacher or curiosity seekers gathered at the scene of an accident are examples of elementary forms of collectivities. Members of the group come and go, have little or no identity and only emotional interaction, and disperse entirely after a short time. However, if the preacher is successful in attracting permanent adherents, a social movement may develop in the form of a religious *cult* (pp. 364–366).
Panic	A form of collective behavior in which people feel threatened and entrapped and seek escape in highly individualistic ways. Collective emotion circulates through the group, building as it goes, and frequently leads to *nonrational* (p. 64–65) counterproductive behavior.	Passengers aboard an airliner, upon hearing of a bomb threat, might begin to cry, scream, pray, think of family, write a will, or simply sit tight and wait (all individualistic responses). Those who cry and scream might well induce similar (nonrational) behavior in others, thus raising the general level of fear throughout the plane (circulating emotion).

	Definition	Example
Craze	A form of collective behavior that appears and disappears suddenly, tends to be obsessive among its practitioners, and is often seen as foolish or outlandish by the general population.	Famous crazes of the past have included flagpole sitting, crowding into telephone booths, swallowing live goldfish, and dance marathons. Crazes enable participants (1) to involve themselves with others in group activities and (2) to stand out as individuals who perform bizarre acts that most people would not do.
Fashion and Fad	Forms of collective behavior that are less unusual, more widespread, and less subject to change than a craze. Fashions and fads are also less individualistic than crazes.	Styles of dress (length of hemline on dresses; size and shape of lapels on mens' coats), modes of speaking (''right on,'' ''getting it on,'' ''bug-off''), and membership in exotic groups (''Jesus freaks,'' Moonies) are examples of fads and fashions.
Crowd	A loosely organized group that forms around some mutually interesting object or event and which is usually rather short-lived. In crowds, people interact with one another in emotional ways; *norms* and *roles* begin to emerge along with the collective mood; and the crowd may eventually take action as a group.	Persons waiting in long lines for World Series tickets to go on sale are a crowd. As they wait, they talk to one another and develop norms about butting into line, holding someone's place, blocking the sidewalk, and so on. Leaders may emerge if the group stays together long enough.
Expressive and Acting Crowds	Expressive crowds are those where group interaction revolves around emotional expression and release; whereas, in acting crowds, interaction takes the form of collective action aimed at some specific target or goal.	The spectators at a football game represent an expressive crowd. As the game concludes, their expressive behavior (shouting, pennant waving) may be replaced by collective action (tearing down goalposts, carrying a hero from the field, chasing the referees from the field). If so, they have then become an acting crowd.
Social Movement	Long-lasting collective behavior, involving large numbers of people held together by shared beliefs, goals, and ideologies. Social movements may lead to the formation of *associations* and social *institutions.*	The Womens Movement (Freeman, Study 5), American labor organization, and civil rights organizations are all examples of or the results of social movements.

8. Human Group Behavior—Mixed and Variable Forms

	Definition	Example
Class	A *status* grouping largely determined by achievement of the members, in terms of occupational *role,* amount of income, and amount of educational training. Class systems are usually described as consisting of three levels: (1) upper (prestigious occupations, highest income, most education); (2) middle (*white-collar* and upper *blue-collar* occupations—for example, a foreman); and (3) lower (lower blue-collar or working-class occupations).	*Functionalists* argue that class societies are the most *open* and that classes ensure that the hardest working, most capable people will fill the necessary and important jobs. *Conflict theorists* (like Karl Marx) argue that class societies provide a way in which the elite can dominate and oppress the poor by gaining a monopoly of the limited rewards (income, education, honor, land, and so on).
Caste	A *closed* social system, where *status* is allocated on the basis of *ascribed* criteria such as family origin, race, or religious affiliation. A rigid system of *stratification* (pp. 215–216) restricts social interaction to the *life-styles* and *life-chances* associated with one's hereditary caste.	In pre-World War II India, society was divided into different castes, each with its "place" and purpose in Indian society. It is often argued that racial minorities in the United States, particularly black Americans (pp. 231–232), are castes.
Association	Special purpose groups organized to pursue some common interest of the members. Associations contain elements of both spontaneous (*primary-like*) and structured (*bureaucratic*) forms of behavior.	Numerous types of associations could be cited, including, among others, lodges (Moose, Elks); community service organizations (Rotary, Lions); recreational clubs (bowling and softball leagues); and occupational groups (labor unions, the American Medical Association).
Democracy	Democracy has been defined in different ways. Sociologists speak of democracy as a type of social structure characterized by *pluralism* (many competing associations) and *mediating groups* (associations that mediate between governmental leaders and individual group members).	Lipset's analysis of the ITU (Study 7) disclosed a rich array of associations that mediated between the rank-and-file membership and the leaders of the union's two major parties. Lowry's study of Micro City (Study 8) examined the important role of mediating leaders, that is, those with multiple associational ties and commitments. Mediating groups and leaders serve as links between society's primary (personal) and tertiary (impersonal) levels of control.

	Definition	Example
Community	A geographical concentration of people who interact long enough to establish a common bond in terms of shared interests and needs. As a consequence, communities eventually develop a special quality of life, which may be found in either *Gemeinschaft* or *Gesellschaft* forms.	Communities vary in type and size and include small, isolated rural villages; self-contained suburban neighborhoods (with housing, churches, a school, a shopping center, and so on); innercity *ghettoes* (Harlem, Greenwich Village); major urban centers (San Francisco, Los Angeles, Detroit); or large metropolitan regions that are trade and cultural areas (New York–New Jersey megalopolitan region).
Ecological Area	An area within which sociologists study how people and their activities adapt to land, natural resources, and other physical features. Such a study is similar to the way in which biologists study the relationship between animals, plants, and their natural environment (including weather, topography, and so on).	Burgess' concentric zone theory of Chicago in the 1920s is an example of a study of ecological areas. Because of the intersection of lines of communication and transportation, business and industrial activities concentrated in one ecological area. Other activities (working-class residences, middle-class homes, bright-light activities) naturally concentrated in other zones.
Ghetto	An ecological area where people of similar characteristics tend to concentrate, in which they find a sense of belonging and a measure of *Gemeinschaft.* Typically, ghettos contain their own services and activities (fire protection, police, small businesses, newspapers, and so on).	This term was first applied to a Jewish community in Medieval Venice (Wirth's study, pp. 326–327), but it is now used more generally to refer to the ghettolike character of white middle-class suburbs, to the student ghetto near a college campus, and so forth. Some ghettos are a result of voluntary action by the residents (middle-class white suburbia); others result because people are forced to live in them by others (black ghettos of urban cities). A ghetto may or may not be "slumlike."

9. Human Group Behavior—More Structured Forms

	Definition	Example
Institution	As used in this text, any highly structured (formal *norms, values, roles*), long-lived (many generations), all-inclusive (affects all or most members of society), and multipurposed human group.	The modern nation-state perhaps best fits our institutional criteria. Other major institutions have included family, church, school, military establishments, and technological systems (universities and think-tanks as knowledge producers).
Institutionalization	The process of formalizing and perpetuating the structure (norms, values, roles) of successful and important social groups. The group grows larger as new members are recruited, and it becomes multipurposed as its *power* and influence spread (see Chapters 10 and 11).	The Roman Catholic Church began 2000 years ago as a small deviant cult (*collectivity*) with a specific purpose, went through an *associational* stage of development during Peter's time, and, by the medieval period, had become one of the great institutions in human history. Its membership included virtually everyone in the society (all-inclusive). It controlled and influenced virtually all aspects of life (multipurposed). It had already endured 1000 years (long-lived), and it had developed a very elaborate system of norms, values, beliefs, and roles (social structure and culture).
Profession	An occupation that combines an *altruistic* motive with expertise based upon formal training (a liberal arts degree and specialization).	Medicine is a classic example. A doctor is expected to render services, not for wages but for a fee, which may vary according to the patient's ability to pay, and which is secondary to altruistic service.
Bureaucracy	A highly *rational* (organized and goal-oriented) form of group structure, featuring a clear-cut division of labor among members and a hierarchical chain of command that coordinates specialized activities according to precise formal rules. In theory, bureaucracy maximizes efficiency and effectiveness in complex organizations that require extensive coordination of different activities.	Dropping a course at a large university usually requires filling out one or more official forms and obtaining one or more official signatures authorizing the drop. These formal procedures have been planned according to a fixed pattern and sequence. Any deviation requires authorization "from above." In theory, this system protects students from dropping courses when they should not, and it protects the university, which must keep precise records of student enrollment.

	Definition	Example
Oligarchy	The tendency within formal organizations for *power* to concentrate into the hands of a few leaders who acquire the specialized skills connected with their office and develop a deep personal attachment to the office. At the same time, grass-roots members generally lose touch with their leaders, and their organizational commitment gives way to mass *apathy* or individual *alienation.*	Many local churches and labor unions are controlled by a small group of old-timers who are emotionally identified with their own office and the other office holders, but who are not sensitive to the needs and desires of the rank-and-file membership. As a consequence, a high turnover in organizational membership can result.
Gesellschaft (as contrasted to *Gemeinschaft*)	*Gemeinschaft* communities feature a high degree of stability and social cohesion (shared identity and commitment) based on a broad consensus regarding norms and values. Social interaction tends to have a *primary* quality even beyond the family and peer group. *Gesellschaft* communities feature the rational pursuit of self-interest, little social cohesion, and impersonal *secondary* relationships.	A formal *Gesellschaft* spirit of noninvolvement is *functionally* necessary in large urban cities, like New York, where intimate relationships with many others would lead to excessive strains and anxieties. Self-interest works to maintain the social system: for example, bus drivers and bus passengers effectively go about their roles without being intimately involved. However, in pluralist urban communities, this can become a problem when many competing self-interests develop. For this reason, many Americans blame the *Gesellschaft* spirit in New York City for vandalism, street crime, uncontrollable general strikes, citizen unwillingness to report crimes, and the like.

PART 4

Institutions and Their Interactions

In Chapter 9, basic institutions and their interrelationships were depicted in a circle chart. It was pointed out that institutions come into being as a means of meeting certain needs inherent in social living. Whether particular institutions flourish or perish depends on their ability to continue satisfying these basic social needs. Various scholars [Bales 1949; Parsons, 1951; Parsons and Shils, 1951] have identified four functional problems that must be solved by all societies. Every society and group must do the following:

1. *Produce* the goods and services necessary for survival.
2. *Distribute* its goods and services in a manner that encourages cooperation and ensures efficiency in the pursuit of major social goals.
3. *Socialize* its members, especially the young, into the social and cultural heritage.
4. *Integrate* its members (individuals and groups) so as to create a sense of social solidarity and cohesion.

The production and distribution of resources can be considered *task-oriented* needs, while socialization and integration can be viewed as *emotionally oriented needs.* In Whyte's analysis of street-corner society (Study 3), two kinds of gang leaders were identified—the task leader (Chick) and the morale leader (Doc). Chick helped his gang develop activities that were efficient in getting tasks accomplished. In contrast, Doc helped his gang enter into activities, many of them recreational, that led to a strong sense of solidarity and group morale. Every human group and society has a need for both task and emotional fulfillment.

In other words, one of the most interesting ways of studying social institutions is in terms of how they function, alone and in concert with other institutions, to fulfill the basic needs of society. The chart opposite provides an overview of this perspective.

Although most institutions tend to have a primary orientation and one or two primary functions, most of them overlap with other related institutions in their pursuit of basic social needs. For example, the family not only plays a major role in socialization, but it also is the fundamental institution for providing human resources through reproduction and it contributes to social solidarity and integration. In some societies, particularly rural, the family may also be the basic unit for the production and distribution of goods and services.

Therefore, institutions, particularly in the modern world, tend to compete and conflict with one another in the performance of their functions. The modern centralized state may take over the emotional tasks (socialization and integration functions) previously performed by the family and religious organizations. This process is most evident in totalitarian societies. Military institutions frequently erode the ability of civilian states to meet task needs (for example, distribution). The post-World War II debate over "guns versus butter" illustrates this conflict. Schools sometimes play a more important role in socialization than families or churches, as the recurrent disputes over allegedly radical or irreligious ideas in textbooks in American communities illustrates.

Furthermore, social institutions are miniature societies concerned with maintaining themselves in addition to performing tasks for the larger society. Therefore, each institution tries to provide for the four basic needs of its members. Military organizations must adapt to the environment around them; must socialize

Institution: Type and Orientation	Basic Need or Institutional Function	Rationale
Economic (Task)	Production	Since no one person or group can perform all the required production tasks, a division of labor develops to determine who does what kind of work. This is reflected in and supported by economic institutions.
Political (Task)	Distribution	The goals of a society must be achieved through cooperation and a balance of power. When a conflict of interests exists, political institutions determine who gets what.
Familial (Emotional)	Socialization	The skills, knowledge, and values of a society must be taught to all members; the family and related institutions typically perform this function. In addition, these institutions often provide outlets for personal hostilities and tension that would be disruptive.
Religious (Emotional)	Integration	Members of all societies need to feel that life is just and meaningful. In addition, they need to feel a sense of solidarity and relatedness to others. Religious institutions perform this function by renewing a sense of common loyalty to the traditional values and norms of the society.

members for unusual and unique roles and values; must distribute internal resources so that talents are mobilized to meet outside threats; and must provide for internal integration and esprit de corps. Often these internal demands are in conflict with the same functions being performed in the outside society. For example, military obedience conflicts with civilian values in democratic societies, and new military technology may threaten civilian society even though it provides a way in which the military can survive in a changing world.

As with all concepts and typologies used in this book, this depiction of needs and functions is an oversimplification. It is, however, a useful device for analyzing the supportive and conflicting relationships between social institutions, one of the more important forms of human group life. The following two chapters will utilize this perspective to consider the sociological theories and research that deal with institutional interrelationships.

Chapter 10 deals with familial, educational, and religious institutions, since these are primarily concerned with socialization and integration. Chapter 11 considers military, political, and technological institutions, since these tend to focus upon production and distribution-oriented goals. What is of special interest, however, is the way in which all of these institutions interact with one another, sometimes supporting each other and at other times competing or conflicting.

- Which of the following things are determined for you by your family, by your school, or by your church: political attitudes, occupational choice, religious values, economic skills, and beliefs?
- Do you think it is possible to create a society without the typical father–mother–children family form? What about communes?
- Do you think the school should be used to bring about social and political changes, such as integration or improving the environment? Why?
- Should the school leave moral training to the family and church? Or should the school reinforce major values like brotherhood, justice, and equality? What about opposition to abortion or birth control?
- Do you think the church should take on more secular kinds of functions (political action, social services, and so on), or should this institution remain essentially a religious support for those experiencing life crises (birth, death, marriage, sickness, and so on)?

10

Morale-Building Institutions: Family, School, and Church

In Chapter 3, we saw that each individual must be prepared for human society by the process of socialization. Individuals must be taught to conform to the goals and norms of society. Social roles must be learned, and cultural values must be internalized. This process continues throughout one's life. In addition, societies must provide for ways in which individuals and groups can develop a common sense of interrelation and participation in cooperative activities. In other words, the socialization process also leads to social integration and solidarity.

Socialization and integration can be considered emotional needs common to all societies. These needs are met by *morale-building institutions,* three of which—the family, the school, and the church—play a particularly important role. The family is most important in the socialization of children. As a basic primary group, it also contributes to social integration in most societies. Similarly, the school is instrumental in preparing children and teen-agers to assume needed social roles and in promoting commitment to important goals and values. Finally, the church frequently assists in these processes by reaffirming and reinforcing the values considered crucial in a society.

At the same time, however, these three morale-building institutions can also perform task-oriented functions. For example, the family and the school both influence the occupational choice of members, thereby affecting production and distribution in the larger society. The school transmits and creates new knowledge and necessary skills, and the church, especially in contemporary society, has been called upon to become involved in political activities (for example, integration of schools). Therefore, morale-building institutions may support or conflict with one another in the performance of both emotionally oriented and task-oriented functions.

This chapter begins with a consideration of the way in which the three morale-building institutions sustain or compete with each other in meeting the basic needs of society. Each of the institutions is then considered separately. In each case, we will consider what is happening to the basic functions and structures of the family, school, and church, with particular emphasis upon contemporary society. The modern family, school, and church will be analyzed from the standpoint of functional and dysfunctional characteristics. That is, we will consider whether the modern form of these institutions is desirable or undesirable in terms of meeting basic human needs, especially emotional needs. Finally, each section will deal with the way in which these institutions might adapt to the conflicts and changes that influenced their development.

CHANGING FUNCTIONS OF MORALE-BUILDING INSTITUTIONS

As societies modernize (become industrialized), processes of social change often bring about transitions in human groups and behavior from more primary spontaneous forms to more secondary structured forms. As a consequence, basic morale-building institutions like the family may become smaller and more specialized in carrying out their traditional socializing and integrating functions. Other institutions, such as the school and church, may become increasingly functional in order to transmit basic cultural goals, values, and a sense of social solidarity to the young.

Task-oriented functions may also change. In premodern societies, the family was the basic economic unit of society. Not only was it used as the basis of reproduction, but it also served as the center of economic activity (hunting, gathering, farming) and training. In the modern family, however, work is no longer centered in the home and, consequently, the school has become the primary training ground for an increasingly mobile and specialized work force. As the "So What?" box in Chapter 9 indicates, the modern church has likewise begun dealing with social and economic issues.

TABLE 10-1 Functional Interplay of Morale-Building Institutions

Institution	Emotionally Oriented Functions	Task-Oriented Functions	Consequences
Family	Child-rearing practices influence how children behave and achieve in school; parents expect other institutions to support their values in the training of children.	Reproduction and birth rates determine the need for classrooms and teachers, and family practices influence religious behavior.	The school must take on new and expanded functions to meet new needs and problems; the church may find itself in opposition to changing family values (for example, some Catholics favor birth control).
School	Teachers are expected to transmit patriotic commitment to national goals and values; in democratic societies, religious training is expected to be nondenominational.	Schools are required to prepare students for specific jobs, inculcate basic skills (the three Rs, drivers education, sex education), and train students for participation in political life.	Nondenominational training may weaken religious values transmitted by the church; patriotic commitment (for example, support for the Vietnam War) may please some parents and anger others; training in certain basic skills (sex education) may lead to conflict rather than cooperation with other institutions (family and church).
Church	The church can strengthen family traditions by hallowing norms and values regarding baptism, marriages, burial, and so on. At the same time, many families may turn to other institutions to perform these functions (marriage by a justice of the peace; burial by an undertaker).	Modern churches have become involved in sex education, alcohol and drug abuse programs, and political action (see "So What?" box in Chapter 9).	While the church takes on new task-oriented functions, its ability to perform older emotionally oriented functions may weaken.

Therefore, modern morale-building institutions are characterized by changing (expanding or narrowing) functions. This functional interplay is of special interest to sociologists. Table 10-1 contains selected examples of expanding and narrowing functions for the three basic morale-building institutions in contemporary society.

The following comparison suggests several general trends that will be the focus of the remainder of this chapter:

1. The modern *family* has generally experienced a *narrowing* of both emotionally oriented and task-oriented functions. As it has become

less multifunctional, its structure has also undergone change. Some scholars interpret these changes as evidence of the diminishing importance of the modern family, while others see them as healthy specialization, allowing concentration on the most crucial emotional functions.

2. The modern *school* has generally experienced a *broadening* of both emotionally oriented and task-oriented functions. Emotional needs are increasingly met through peer group commitments (the youth culture), and task needs are increasingly met by school achievement (degrees bring jobs). Some scholars have seen its increasingly multifunctional role as evidence that the school is becoming a more important institution, while others view this as an unhealthy dissipation of its traditional objectives.
3. The modern *church* has dual and *conflicting* functions. It must transmit and encourage conformity to traditional norms and values and, at the same time, it must be ready to challenge society when society fails to achieve the goals of justice, equality, and brotherhood. In other words, the church sometimes performs a conservative role and, at other times, a dynamic and challenging role. This necessity to fluctuate between differing functions causes conflict within religious groups and between churches. Most scholars feel the church is effective when it can strike a balance between the two roles; others feel a balance is difficult if not impossible to achieve.

Which of these conflicting views about the changes in morale-building institutions are appropriate? The next section begins to respond to this question by considering the implications of the narrowing functions and changing structure of the modern family.

THE FAMILY

In the previous chapter, we noted how the family was a multifunctional institution in most premodern societies. It was represented as a large circle encompassing almost every phase of human experience, from reproduction and child rearing to education, religion, economic activity, political participation, recreational life, and so forth. Stuart Queen and Robert Habenstein [1974, p. 98] speak of the traditional Chinese family as a classic example of the ancient multifunctional family.

Until the recent changes in modern China, the old kinship system had prevailed for centuries in the form of an *extended family,* which included all relatives and met all needs. Three or more generations (often 20 to 30 persons) lived in a single household presided over by a patriarch. The traditional Chinese family was based upon *familism,* a cultural spirit that included the following characteristics:

1. Emphasis upon the father–son relationship and filial piety.
2. Family pride.

3. Encouragement of the large family, especially many sons.
4. A cult of ancestor worship.
5. Common ownership of all property by the family.

Religion and education acted as supports to the family system. As Queen and Habenstein [1974, pp. 100–101] point out, ancestor worship and filial piety were the most important characteristics. Confucianism, as a family-oriented religion, emphasized the importance of the son's obedience to his parents, especially the father, and his commitment to have many children, particularly sons, in order to continue the name of the family. At the same time, much of the schooling of the children was carried on in the home. When teachers outside the home were used, they merely reinforced the values of the family:

> Boys are tutored or attend school. Schooling tends to be rigorous, demanding, and given over mostly to rote learning. Teachers have unquestioned authority over the pupils and may punish them severely without fear of parental interference. Training in filial respect and obedience continues apace. The boys are likely to receive many beatings from the schoolmaster and father before moving on to the next age group. Girls in the custody of the mother are spared some of the harsher discipline [Queen and Habenstein, 1974, p. 111].

This traditional family form is now being transformed, in the Peoples' Republic of China, to a narrower form whose structure and functions are characteristic of contemporary families in other societies.

Narrowed Function and Structure

Modern, particularly urban, families tend to have *fewer and more specialized functions.* Murdock [1949] suggests that familial functions have gradually narrowed down to the pursuit of four basic needs—reproduction, socialization, affection giving, and status ascription. Other functions formerly centered in the family (education, politics, work, recreation, religion) have increasingly been turned over to other more specialized institutions such as the school, the church, businesses, and political parties.

Among the remaining family functions, affection giving appears to be increasingly important in the eyes of many scholars, since so much of urban life today is characterized by impersonality and formality. Likewise, the modern family determines where children begin their careers in an achievement-oriented society. Family status may largely determine where young people go to school, how they adjust to the educational process, what neighborhood they live in, what experiences they are exposed to, and what occupations they enter.

In addition to its changing functions, the modern family can be contrasted to the traditional family by changes in structure. The traditional Chinese family was *consanguine*—that is, it was an all-inclusive group encompassing virtually all the blood kin. The consanguine family consisted of several conjugal units (father–mother–children) responsible for reproduction and child rearing, all located in or near the household of the larger kinship family. Sons remained within the father's orbit following marriage, but wives were brought into the family from other extended families.

In consanguine families, wives were carefully selected by parents in order to assure their worthiness and commitment to the new family. A new wife who experienced marital problems had only two options, either to return in disgrace to her family or to commit suicide. Some variation could be found in this traditional family pattern; for example, in feudal Japan, marital problems were frequently resolved by divorce [Goode, 1966, p. 498]. Nevertheless, the importance of the larger consanguine group and the father–son relationship characteristically determined the structure of the traditional family.

Modern families are organized as separate conjugal units termed *nuclear* families; that is, when a son marries, he usually moves out of the father's household and begins a new nuclear family with his wife. This family structure arose partly because of the Western emphasis upon individual freedom in courting and mate selection, as opposed to the parental selection of wives in the traditional family. As a consequence, nuclear families in contemporary society are frequently quite isolated physically and emotionally from their kinfolk. The contrasts between traditional and modern family forms are depicted in Figure 10-1. This diagram indicates

FIGURE 10-1 Comparison of Consanguine and Nuclear Family Structures

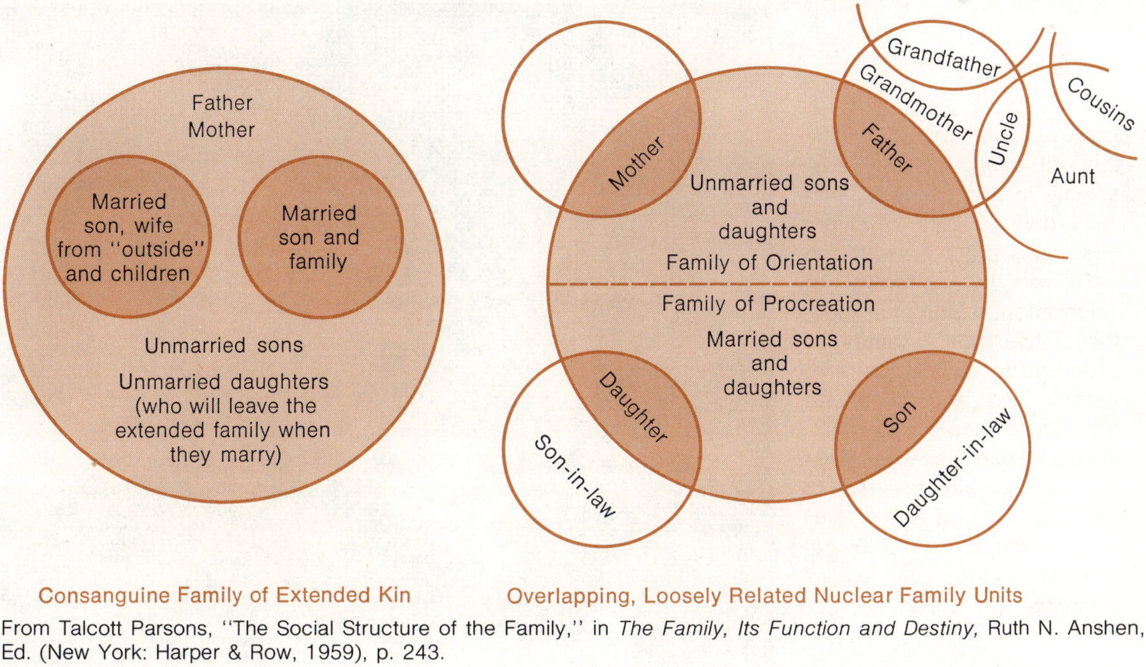

From Talcott Parsons, "The Social Structure of the Family," in *The Family, Its Function and Destiny*, Ruth N. Anshen, Ed. (New York: Harper & Row, 1959), p. 243.

10-1 Types of Families

Most modern people think of families as consisting of father, mother, and children. However, this type of family represents only one of many family forms in contemporary society.

Modern families are organized around separate conjugal units called **nuclear families.** This form arose with the emphasis upon individual freedom in courtship and mate selection. Emphasis in the nuclear family tends to be placed upon the emotional needs of affection-giving and socialization and the task needs of reproduction and status ascription.

Marc Rattner/Black Star

However, members of the modern family actually participate in two different families during their lifetime. Individuals are born into and socialized by a **family of orientation.** Upon marriage, they move into a **family of procreation** for purposes of reproduction and continued affection-giving. Lasting linkages between these two families can create feelings of family pride and larger kinship, similar to the traditional extended family of earlier societies.

Donald Dietz, Dietz/Hamlin

P. Simon/Stock, Boston

Throughout American history, religious, political, and youth groups have experimented with **communal family forms.** Groups of people, not necessarily blood-related, share a common culture (religion, political beliefs, life-style, etc.) and common ownership of property. The familial commune attempts to meet more needs than the nuclear family, including education of the young and old alike, recreation for all members, collective work and jobs, and so on.

C. S. Wolinsky/Stock, Boston

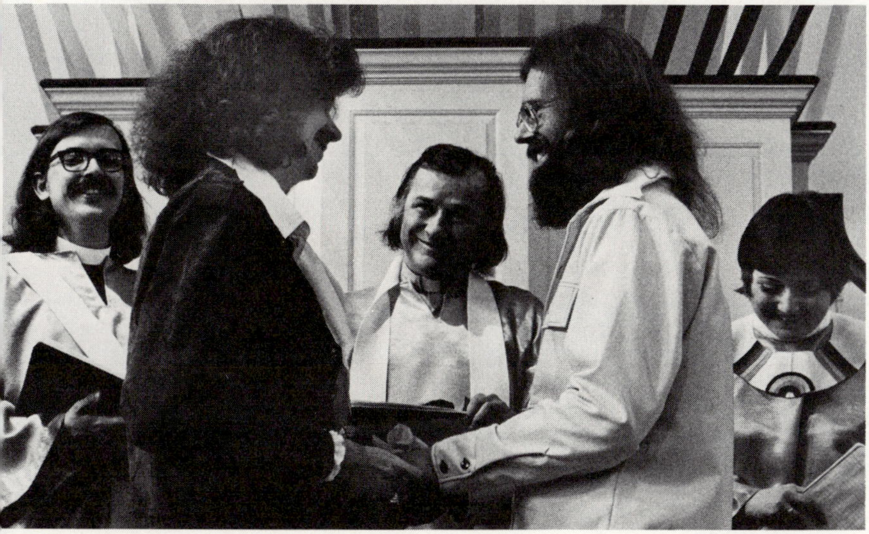

A number of **unusual family forms,** such as gay (homosexual) marriages, attempt to provide familial contexts for meeting the needs (affection, status ascription, and so on) of those who do not conform to the approved norms of society. Gay marriages are considered deviant by many because they do not perform what are seen as essential family functions (for example, reproduction). As a result, members of these types of families face special problems.

that members of the modern family actually tend to be participants in two different kinds of families during their lifetimes. The *family of orientation* is the nuclear unit into which one is born. The *family of procreation* is the nuclear unit into which one marries in order to have children. As we pointed out in Chapter 2, these two forms of the modern family can become important primary groups for members.

Functions and Dysfunctions of the Modern Family

Are the new narrowed family functions and structure desirable or undesirable? Traditionalists argue that the modern nuclear family is often *dysfunctional.* When parents have only one or two children and live with them as a closely knit and isolated unit, the children may be overindulged and, frequently, the close primary relations create ambivalent feelings of both love and resentment. Furthermore, constant mobility (from families of orientation to families of procreation) can produce a sense of rootlessness. Jobs may take both the father and the mother away from the home, weakening the family's ability to perform emotional functions. If a crisis is experienced (death of a parent, divorce, serious sickness), children and the surviving spouse are not surrounded by a host of kinfolk who can provide emotional and task supports.

Even the freer, more spontaneous mate selection process in modern society has disadvantages. It may increase the economic and social risks of marriage, when planning has been insufficient or nonexistent and the future is uncertain. In addition, mixed marriages across social and cultural boundaries (Catholic–Protestant, black–white, upper class–lower class) often create hostilities between families of orientation and procreation. Finally, pregnancy outside of marriage may force a couple to marry, since the isolated nuclear family system does not provide adequate ways of caring for illegitimate or parentless children.

Somewhat less obvious are the *functional advantages* that the modern nuclear family possesses, particularly for meeting the special needs and problems of urban society. Specifically, the contemporary family structure is desirable for the following reasons:

1. It tends to be kept small and mobile, thereby checking population growth and minimizing such problems as environmental pollution and deterioration (see Chapter 13).

2. It provides an opportunity for close personal relationships between parents and children, thereby countering the anomic rootless characteristics of modern life.

3. It is highly mobile since its basic needs (housing, transportation, and so on) can be easily met. This contributes to an achievement-oriented society, which emphasizes geographical movement and career advancement.

4. It enables family members to enjoy a higher standard of living and to obtain the cultural advantages (for example, education) necessary for a rapidly changing and developing society.

The modern family also encourages freedom and individual expression for all family members, as reflected in the patterns of mate selection. Such values help promote the kind of innovative and adaptive life-style necessary for modern life. For example, research [Macklin, 1972] is beginning to indicate that, when unmarried couples live together, their relationship may be seen as an attempt to adapt to the demands of modern living. Other experimental family forms include single parenthood, childlessness, adopted children of different races and ethnic groups, marriage contracts that are periodically renewed, and life as a single unmarried. Many of these experiments may lead to successful resolutions of contemporary problems (population pressures, illegitimate children, death of a spouse, and so on). Without the spirit of innovation encouraged by the modern family, some of these new family forms might never have been attempted.

This innovative experimental spirit is evident within the nuclear family as well. Richard Clayton [1975, pp. 400–404] identifies this with regard to male–female parental roles. Traditionally, fathers have not been considered as important as mothers in terms of socializing the children. In research and writing about American families, there has been much attention to the mother's socializing role but little to the father's. In fact, most men have tended to think of their occupation as primary and their family commitments as secondary. They have devoted their attention primarily to their career and to their role as breadwinner, while their family role has received relatively little attention. At best, the role of husband and father has been ambiguous and confusing. However, the movement to redefine women's roles is helping to bring about concern for men's roles as well:

> The new American male is being socialized to be sensitive, "cultured," gentle, and less pugnacious. . . . The last 25 years of this century will likely produce a more "unisexual" definition of the parental role. Fathers and mothers will be performing more and more of the same parental tasks. . . . If this does occur—and many social scientists think it will—the result will be a better quality of family life [Clayton, 1975, p. 403].

However, these changes are not without their own problems. Divorce and remarriage after divorce are becoming widespread; thus, an increasing number of married couples have former family members still living. This raises the question of visiting rights for children, who must divide their lives between two sets of parents, each set containing a natural and a stepparent. Current research [Renne, 1970] is investigating the impact this may have upon families in Alameda County, California, where one in every five marriages is a remarriage after divorce.

Single-parent families may develop from divorce, from illegitimate birth, or from the death of a spouse. Will single-parent families be free of

10-2 Is the Modern Family Functional?

Scholars agree that both the structure and functions of the modern nuclear family have narrowed, but they disagree on whether this is functional or dysfunctional for the family and society.

Traditional social scientists argue that when parents have only one or two children, they may overindulge them. In addition, the close primary relationships of the nuclear family can stifle individualism and creativity for all members. In contrast, modern social scientists argue that intimate relationships in small families offset the anomie of contemporary urban life. Furthermore, primary relations encourage the family to concentrate upon its most important functions—socialization and affection-giving.

Dorothy Gloster

Dorothy Gloster

Traditionalists argue that jobs in the nuclear family often take the father far away from home, thereby increasing feelings of rootlessness and anomie and making the family unimportant economically. Modernists maintain that the modern family is more mobile and achievement-oriented. Therefore, it is better able to meet the needs of its members while, at the same time, adapting to the ever-changing occupational requirements of contemporary life.

Dorothy Gloster

Traditionalists argue that the narrowed structure of the nuclear family may encourage mothers to work and seek an independent career. Therefore, the family's ability to perform basic emotional functions is weakened. Modernists maintain that new roles for wives and mothers are more appropriate for a society which emphasizes sexual equality. When the wife works, the family also can enjoy a higher standard of living and better adapt to the problems of modern life (for example, increasing expenses and costs of living).

Dorothy Gloster

Traditionalists argue that the nuclear family has given up many roles, such as education of the children, to other social institutions, such as the school or daycare center. This narrowing of functions erodes the family's importance as the most basic institution. Modernists maintain that the complexity and diversity of skills and knowledge in contemporary society can only be transmitted through special institutions. When children attend school, their individual and different needs are better met, the work requirements of larger society are more adequately fulfilled, and the whole family's cultural experiences are enriched.

marital tensions between husband and wife but lack the complete family structure traditionally associated with an effective socialization process? Furthermore, where the single parent is the mother, might not the necessity to work create special problems for child rearing? These kinds of questions have prompted some communities and societies to consider whether the family, in any form, is really necessary.

Can Societies Function Without Families?

American history is marked with various attempts to substitute communal life-styles for traditional family life. If religiously oriented groups like the Shakers and counterculture groups such as those of the 1960s prove to be successful with their communal experiments, then perhaps the family is not a social necessity, as some scholars have claimed. However, since the Shakers have almost died out and since it is still too early to assess the long-range impact of the counterculture experiments, some scholars have selected the Israeli kibbutz as an example of a communal experiment in radically new "family" functions and structures. The kibbutz has existed long enough and has played an important enough role in the development of Israel to justify an analysis of it in order to throw light on the question of whether the family is a social necessity. One such study was conducted by Melford Spiro.

▶ STUDY 10

Is the Family Necessary?— The Israeli Kibbutz [1954][1]

Problem

Murdock [1949] defines the human family as the social group that is characterized by common residence, economic cooperation, and reproduction. Marriage consists of the relationships within the family that combine sexual privilege and economic interdependence. He argues from an analysis of families in many societies that *marriage and the family are universal;* that is, they are to be found in all societies because they perform such basic functions and meet such basic needs. Spiro questions this conclusion in the light of his studies of the Israeli kibbutz. There are over 300 agricultural collectives in Israel dedicated to complete communal living, including common ownership of property and the communal rearing of children. These kibbutzim provide a laboratory for testing theories about the universality of the family.

[1]Adapted and abridged from Melford E. Spiro, "Is the Family Universal?" *The American Anthropologist, 56* (October 1954), pp. 839–846 (reproduced by permission of the American Anthropological Association from *The American Anthropologist 56(5)* 1954); "Addendum 1958," in *The Family,* Norman W. Bell and Ezra F. Vogel, Ed. (New York: The Free Press, 1960), pp. 64–75; and *Kibbutz: Venture in Utopia* (New York: Schocken Books, 1970).

Hypotheses and Study Design

This study is based upon an intensive analysis of one kibbutz, where marriage and family as defined by Murdock do not seem to exist. This community seemed to function *without a marriage* that combined both sexual privilege and economic interdependence and *without a parent–child family unit* to support and socialize the children. In short, Spiro hypothesized that there may be functional alternatives to marriage and family as traditionally defined.

Spiro's study design is of particular interest methodologically. He uses what is called the method of *deviant–case analysis.* In other words, a kibbutz in Israel is selected for study precisely because it seems to violate the general theory of institutional universality and indispensability, using the specific institution of the family as the test case. This technique of studying deviant cases contrasts with the usual approach of the social scientist, who attempts to select cases that lend support to the original theory or hypotheses. In other words, although scientists are fundamentally interested in developing theories that are universally applicable, they must also constantly seek out and identify exceptions.

One caution with regard to the use of single–case analysis is necessary. Conclusions must necessarily be tentative and qualified since an examination of one deviant case does not necessarily invalidate Murdock's general theory.

Method of Data Collection

The author and his wife spent 11 months as participating members of one Israeli kibbutz. Although their primary assignment was to study the children, they took their places as working members of the community and observed it from the "inside." They made no attempt to employ formal questionnaires or interviews. Rather, they "questioned" residents in the context of daily interaction. They were *participant observers,* and theirs was a type of *clinical study* that made use of the case method. They acknowledge the limitations of such a research technique, but they go on to suggest that it does have one marked advantage over other more formal methods: It catches the spontaneous conversations and behavior patterns of people who do not set up defenses as they frequently do in formal interviews or questionnaires.

Findings and Interpretations

A "couple relationship" does exist in the kibbutz. It includes a socially approved sexual relationship but not the basic economic cooperation about which Murdock speaks. Sexual behavior is carefully controlled in the following ways:

1. Premarital sexual relations are permitted after high school graduation as single adults visit each other in their respective living quarters. At this stage, the couple are considered "lovers."
2. Adult couples who make a formal request for a room in the living quarters do so because they are "in love" and thus declare their intention to be a "couple." Their union is sanctioned when the community grants their request for a room. This is assumed to be a permanent monogamous relationship and is usually *exogamous,* the mate being selected from another kibbutz. Furthermore, when pregnancy occurs, the couple is married according to the laws of the state so that the child will be legitimate and have legal rights.

3. The desire to marry in the kibbutz comes from the need for physical and psychological intimacy. The couple relationship is, therefore, a unique one in the community.

4. The economic arrangements for each party, however, do not change. There is no breadwinner in the new union; rather husband and wife both continue their jobs in the commune, contributing not to their own budget but to the good of the whole community. There is no change in the legal or social status of either party. The woman keeps her maiden name and her official registration card separate from that of her "friend" (*chaver*), the term used to designate spouses.

In the kibbutz, then, there is a couple relationship, but there is no marriage as defined by George Murdock. Similarly, there is a parent–child relationship, but, according to Murdock's criteria, there is no family. Soon after a child is born, he or she is taken into a nursery to be reared by nurses and teachers. The mother may return to feed the child and the father to visit, but not until the age of six months can the child spend an hour a day with the parents in their dwelling. As the child gets older, an increasing amount of time is spent with the parents, usually just before the evening meal. Most of this time, however, is spent in the children's house or at the communal school. An all-day parent–child outing is possible on Saturdays. The attachment of child to parents may be very close and, accordingly, it may thus provide the security, love, and identification that are basic to psychological growth. At the same time, parents are not directly responsible for the child's economic maintenance, physical care, or socialization. In this sense, then, *there is no family.*

Conclusions and Implications

The Israeli kibbutz does appear to be an example of a community that has been functioning successfully without traditional marriage and family arrangements. The essential sexual, economic, reproductive, and educational functions are being taken care of in other ways. This seems to negate the generalization that the family is universal and indispensable.

On the other hand, this conclusion cannot be accepted without a number of very important qualifications:

1. *A kibbutz is relatively small in numbers of residents.* It is not a complex society but rather an intimate face-to-face community, which takes on characteristics of an extended family, that is, a kinship grouping. In fact, members of the community think of themselves as kinfolk: Each child belongs to all adults just as every member shares all things in common. Children are indulged by the community, since adults want the new generation to remain in the kibbutz voluntarily. Furthermore, when a person selects a mate for the couple relationships, the incest taboo appears to function for the entire community, and the choice is made from another kibbutz. This is indeed a folk society—a *Gemeinschaft.* In the absence of a specific social group—the family—to whom society delegates the functions of socialization, reproduction, and the like, the entire society responds by becoming a large extended family. It would seem probable, therefore, that only in a "familial" society, such as the kibbutz, where members perceive of each other as kin, is it possible to dispense with the family. In other words, *family and community become one.*

2. Additional questions can be raised about an appropriate definition for marriage and the family. Why must we say, as Murdock does, that marriage com-

bines both sexual and economic interdependency? In the kibbutz, there is a relationship between an adult male and female that is unique, both structurally and psychologically. Husband and wife are set apart in a common domicile, not only with sexual privileges but with a higher rate of interaction and intimacy than in any other relationship in the commune, and they decide deliberately to have children. If we define marriage as *any socially sanctioned relationship between non-blood-related cohabiting adults of the opposite sex that satisfies felt needs,* then marriage does exist in the kibbutz.

3. Furthermore, is it not possible that the unique group of father–mother–children in the kibbutz might be considered a family? Parents plan for their children. Children clearly identify with their parents and consider the parents' domicile as home. The parent–child interaction is different from and more intimate than any other interaction the child may have in the commune. The psychological ties are more intense. In addition, the parents take part in designating the nurses and teachers who are to rear the young. Parents contribute economically to their own children by working for the economic welfare of the entire community. A definition of the family broad enough to include this kind of a relationship would lead us to conclude that *there is a family in the Israeli kibbutz.*

Spiro's study, then, represents an attempt to test empirically the ideas of institutional universality and indispensability, using the family and marriage as his unit of analysis. His qualified conclusion still leaves some of the basic questions unresolved, and further research is needed. To Spiro's own qualifications can be added the fact that recent informal observation of the Israeli kibbutz suggests a growing recruitment problem. The very young and the aged residents seem to adjust well to the communal kinship living pattern. In contrast, those in the highly productive ages between the late teens and the early 30s show a propensity to leave the kibbutzim for the greater personal independence and opportunity available in more urbanized environments. This trend, if continued, could signal important changes in this social experiment; however, further data are required to substantiate these additional observations.

In addition, other societies and subcultures also have incomplete or partial family systems according to traditional definitions. Examples can be found among the Nayars and Todas of India, the Arabs in parts of the Moslem Middle East, utopian religious communities in the Western world (for example, the Amana and Shaker communities), and those who practice common-law marriage in Jamaica. To some extent, the incomplete family units among American blacks are examples of the absence of familial institutions in traditional terms. We must conclude, then, that there are a significant number of instances of deviance from Murdock's general definition of marriage and family. Furthermore, these deviant forms frequently work well in meeting basic needs.

What Spiro's study of the kibbutz shows is the tendency for familial functions, both emotional and task, to be transferred to other institutions in contemporary society. In the case of the kibbutz, the larger community takes over some traditional familial functions. What happens, however, in less democratic contexts, where the role of the national state might be particularly important? A recent study of the family in the Soviet Union provides an answer to this question.

The Family's Role in the Soviet Union

Ludwig Liegle [1975] used original sources inaccessible outside the Soviet Union when he spent several months studying the family in Russia. His analysis goes beyond earlier studies [Geiger, 1968; Mace, 1963]. He concludes that, in spite of the "communist" society's intention of rearing "new persons" committed to collectivist goals as a result of their state-controlled schooling, "the Soviet family has remained that social group which continually influences the child from birth to maturity. It is the individual family, and not an organized children's collective, which generally determines the crucial development phase of early childhood when the personality is most malleable" [Liegle, 1975, p. xii]. Liegle compares this with the Israeli kibbutz and concludes that, even in a large, complex, and authoritarian society like the Soviet Union, society cannot dispense with the family and rely totally upon collective child rearing in communal nurseries and schools.

For one thing, *it would be an overwhelming task for the state to take over the familial roles* of rearing, educating, and supporting all children. The parental role in every society is emotionally and financially demanding. In addition, *parents are in a strategic position* as the first educators of their children. They interact with them from infancy onward and are intimately involved as role models, sources of affection, and providers of information.

Early Soviet leaders were apparently not fully aware of the importance of the family in the societal process. In accord with Marxist ideology, they tried to treat family life as a "private affair" of individuals, for which state control was unnecessary. Children were to be educated largely by state institutions beginning with nurseries and preschool activities. A radical minority among the Soviets predicted the "dying off of the family under communism." The elimination of the family, however, was never intended by most Marxists, nor was it the purpose of the early family policy from 1917 to 1936 in Soviet Russia. Rather, steps to change the family were directed against traditional male dominance since the woman was considered "enslaved" in the domestic role. In hopes of emancipating women and freeing them for productive work outside the home, Soviet family policy at first permitted easy divorce, encouraged full employment of women outside the home, legalized abortion, and legally freed youth from the conservative influence of their parents and grandparents. Soviet leaders desired a new family that would transmit collectivist values and ideology. They also expected the schools to play a major role in this educational process.

By 1936, there was a realization that the family could no longer be viewed as a "private affair." It was a social asset, and governmental controls were necessary to prevent family disintegration. A stable family was seen as essential for reproduction and socialization and was treated as an integral part of the whole educational planning process. To strengthen the family was to strengthen the society. Therefore, bold steps were taken to control divorce, to encourage marriage and the bearing of children, and to guide parents in their roles as educators committed to the goals of collectivism. Legislation included a 1968 law increasing the husband's material and moral responsibility for a pregnant wife or young mother or for an illegitimate child. Parents were charged with the education of children "in the spirit of the moral code of the builders of communism" [Liegle, 1975, p. 16]. A *Pravda* editorial on the 1936 decree described the new family policy, and concluded:

> We alone have all the conditions under which a working woman can fulfill her duties as a citizen and as a mother responsible for the birth and early upbringing of her children. . . . We must safeguard our family and raise and rear healthy Soviet heroes [Liegle, 1975, p. 10].

Therefore, ambivalence characterizes the Soviet stance toward the human family. The family is seen as a necessary partner of the Soviet state, but it is considered an unreliable partner, according to Liegle [1975, p. 152]. Its educational importance is increasingly emphasized and public statements praise the family. At the same time, Liegle concludes that the Soviet family continues to be "the most dangerous opponent of the authoritarian communist regime" [p. 153]. He suggests that the family has not lived up to expectations as a partner in Soviet education because the family in Soviet society is influenced by tradition and social-class differences.

In other words, the Soviet ideal for family–state cooperation is not being fully realized because the actual condition of the Soviet family includes the following problems:

1. Most Soviet women (75 percent in a 1967 study of 427 workers' families) still bear the full burden of household chores along with full-time employment.
2. Many families are broken as a result of illegitimacy (every ninth child is illegitimate) or divorce (in 1966, there were 9 marriages and 2.8 divorces for every 1000 people in the population).
3. Only about one fourth of the children have preschool education outside the home, and there is a great shortage of nurseries as well as preschools.
4. Children from the families of blue-collar workers are handicapped in school by lack of motivation and by insufficient basic skills and are less inclined to go on to higher education.
5. Atheistic education, a part of Soviet ideology, is also neglected in many families, especially in rural areas (in industrial centers, 25

to 50 percent of the families have had their children baptized) [Liegle, 1975, pp. 45–46, 52, 56, 77–78, 99, 103].

Liegle concludes that the Soviet family is partly dysfunctional relative to state goals. When the family is left with the responsibility for educating and supporting the children, individualistic attitudes and aspirations are bound to compete, unintentionally, with the Soviet goal of creating persons who are completely committed to the collective society.

> In the USSR, as in Western societies, the child's early and crucial socialization phase is determined almost exclusively by the family. Since the child's earliest emotional tie is directed toward one person, the mother, and then to other adult members of the family, and since in most cases he remains an only child [in about half of Soviet families], the formation of a "collective ego" cannot take place during the early socialization process. . . . [Family life] is characterized by great intimacy and a certain isolation vis-a-vis society. On the whole, the child's personality development is determined more by individual identification with his parents . . . than by his identification with the organized age group or youth collective [Liegle, 1975, pp. 149–150].

This identification with the family is reinforced by the fact that children are financially dependent upon their parents until their first job. Also, despite communist theory proclaiming a "classless" society, a class status system does exist (see Chapter 6); thus, the social status of different children is ascribed according to the economic and social position of their parents. Their access to education and to high status depends largely upon their parents. As a result, both parents and children seek to achieve for themselves as well as for the collectivity. As Liegle [1975, p. 150] puts it: ". . . young Soviet citizens see fulfillment and happiness less in the collective than in their own families."

Therefore, in the cases of both the Israeli kibbutz and the Soviet family, we see the narrowed family functions identified by Murdock being performed by some form of kinship grouping. In the Soviet case, however, we also see the special role that other institutions can begin to play in morale-building functions, particularly the modern school.

THE SCHOOL

As family functions have narrowed, school functions have broadened to meet the diverse needs of large heterogeneous societies. In premodern societies, most people did not attend schools. As we saw in the case of the traditional Chinese family, education was a function of the extended family. Formal tutoring was an opportunity available only to the privileged, often restricted to sons, and carefully controlled by the family. As societies began to modernize, however, schools became increasingly important. Formal education became a necessity for the development of an industrial society. Modern education at first emphasized basic skills in order to provide a more literate population; later, the school began to take on a number of other functions to meet a variety of emotional and task needs.

Broadening Functions and Structure

The history of education provides an example of the developing relationship between formal multifunctional schools and industrialization. American schools have passed through four stages of broadening functions, each influenced by a different social or cultural factor:

1. *A religious stage, stressing basic learning skills.*
2. *An early industrial stage, stressing technical skills.*
3. *A later industrial stage, stressing status achievement skills.*
4. *A contemporary leisure stage, stressing social participation skills.*

The first compulsory school attendance law was established by Massachusetts in 1852; and, by 1918, all states had some legislation of this type [Edwards and Richey, 1963, p. 490]. Robin Williams [1970, pp. 316–317] suggests that the initial encouragement for universal elementary education in America came from a Protestant emphasis upon reading and interpreting the Bible. Since most sects required their members to learn the Bible, many religious denominations founded schools and colleges for this purpose. Harvard University was established to train clergymen and was at first a state-supported Congregational Seminary. Thus, religion seems to have been a dominant influence in initiating compulsory education in America, and the initial school function seems to have been to teach the fundamental reading and writing skills.

Not until industrialization, however, did public education begin a period of accelerated development. Compulsory elementary education was achieved by the end of World War I. By World War II, compulsory secondary education had become the norm. In rural America, where many people were involved in farming and farm-related occupations, necessary skills could be learned "on the job" within the extended family. As work shifted from farm to factory, however, new skills were required that could only be supplied by formal schooling. These technical skills, which often involved complex machinery, could only be taught by specially trained individuals. Thus, the second stage of development was clearly a consequence of early industrial expansion.

The third stage of expanding school functions accompanied the period of later industrialization. New occupational categories, including white-collar and professional activities, created jobs that depended upon formal school training. In addition, society in which status was based upon one's family of orientation was changing toward a more open society, where status was based on mobility and achievement. No longer could family members, particularly the young, be content to accept the ascribed status of their family of orientation. The school had to function as a means of personal achievement. Not only did school diplomas guarantee access to better jobs, but the school also informally transmitted those aspects of culture (correct speech, dress, manners, and so on) needed to gain entry to upper status levels.

These new status and economic functions of the school are dramatized in the following tables:

1. In 1958, the average annual income of American males between the ages of 45 and 54—the peak income earning years of life—differed according to the amount of education they had received as follows:

Education Received	Average Annual Income (in dollars)
Some elementary schooling	3,008
Completed elementary school	4,337
Some high school	4,864
Completed high school	6,295
Some college	8,682
Completed college	12,269

Source: Miller, H. P. "Annual and Lifetime Income in Relation to Education: 1939–1959," *The American Economic Review, 50* (1960), pp. 962–986.

2. In 1960, the proportion of people in various occupations was influenced by their level of educational achievement as follows:

Occupation	Percentage with Some College
Professional and technical	75
Proprietors and managers	29
Clerical or sales	22
Skilled labor	8
Semiskilled labor	4
Service workers	6
Farmers and farm workers	5
Unskilled labor	3

Source: U.S. Department of Labor, *Manpower: Challenge of the 1960s* (Washington, D.C.: United States Government Printing Office, 1960), p. 17.

During the third period of development, then, schooling became important at the college as well as at the elementary and secondary levels. From 1870 to 1890, less than 10 percent of the U.S. population between the ages of 14 and 17 years were enrolled in high school. By 1930, this enrollment had increased to over 50 percent; by 1940, to over 70 percent; and by 1970, to almost 95 percent. For the same years, the percentages of the population between the ages of 18 and 21 years enrolled in colleges and universities were less than 5, over 10, over 15, and over 50, respectively. This dramatic growth in the functional importance of the school is depicted in Figure 10-2. In short, all levels of education—elementary, secondary, and advanced—were rapidly becoming universal. And this growth in the school population was accompanied by a broadening of both the functions and structure of schools.

The final period of development began in the late 1950s and early 1960s and continues to the present time. Citizens and special interest

FIGURE 10-2 Percentage of Persons 17 Years of Age Who Graduated from High School, 1870–1970

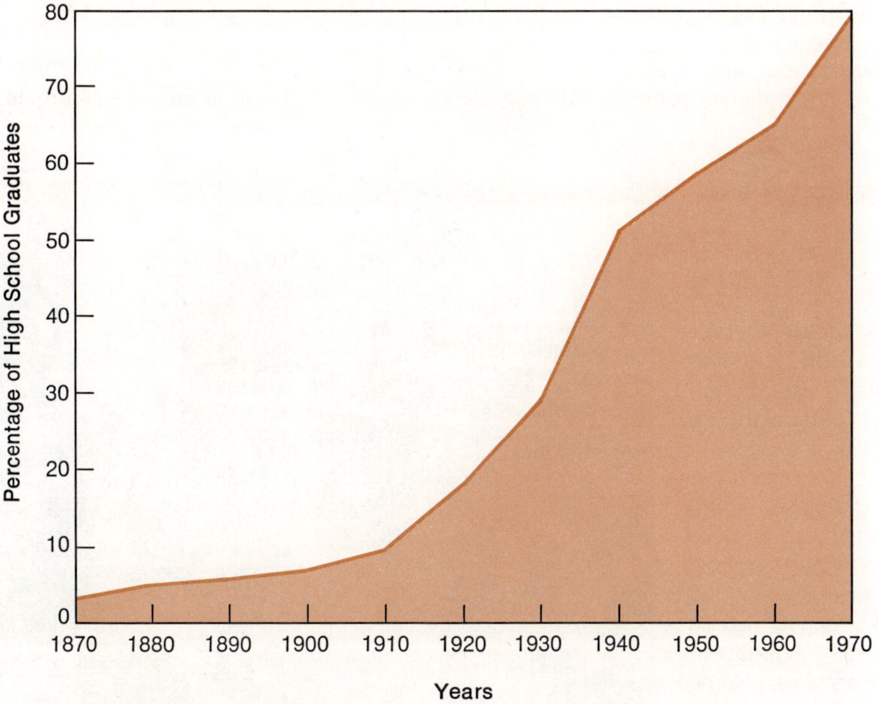

From U.S. Department of Health, Education, and Welfare, *Digest of Educational Statistics* (Washington, D.C.: U.S. Government Printing Office, 1974), Table 65.

groups have increasingly made demands upon schools to prepare people for a postindustrial society, where leisure and social participation will be as important as formal work and jobs. Indeed, many argue that with a shorter work week, increasing automation, and improving welfare benefits (health care, unemployment insurance, and so on), an increasing number of citizens will have to turn to other tasks to live full and meaningful lives. In response, schools have introduced courses that deal with leisure pursuits (sensitivity groups, hobbies, recreation) and social issues (environmental courses, courses in women's studies and black studies, courses dealing with local or state politics).

A Crisis in Modern Education?

According to some scholars, the rapid, almost uncontrolled, expansion of school functions and structure have created a crisis in modern education. This crisis has two major characteristics. (1) The school increasingly conflicts with, rather than supports, the contemporary family; and (2) the school's attempt to perform such a variety of morale-building and task

10-3 Broadening and Conflicting Functions of the Modern School

The modern school has experienced a broadening of both task and emotional functions. As a result, it sometimes supports and sometimes conflicts with other social institutions.

In premodern societies, the simple task function of the school was the teaching of basic literacy skills. This function supported the family, particularly in its emphasis upon reading the Bible. In industrial society, the school began to teach job-related knowledge which could no longer be transmitted by rural or unskilled families. To these functions, the contemporary school has added a variety of "life-experience" skills (sex education, drivers education, alcohol abuse, and so on). Some scholars see these newer functions as conflicting with traditional moral and religious training by the family.

Elsa Dorfman

The modern school has also taken on a number of emotional functions. Organized athletics provide youth with primary-like, peer-group experiences and socialize them to important cultural values (achievement, competition, team play). These types of functions support some institutions by preparing youth to enter a competitive occupational or political society. However, they can conflict with the family by providing emotional experiences unrelated to family life (youth may no longer have time to be with parents) or cultural values unacceptable to some parents (aggressive competition).

Marion Bernstein

L. Freed/Magnum

The modern school has become increasingly important in transmitting political values and training youth in social-action skills. This is particularly evident in the case of the Israeli kibbutz. Commitment to collective and communal life is encouraged and equality (for example, of sex roles) is emphasized. This function supports the aims of the larger community or state, but it also can undermine the importance of the nuclear family (as Spiro found in Study 10). In politically heterogeneous societies, such as America, indoctrination of the young by the school is considered by some citizens to be inappropriate and dangerous.

Elsa Dorfman

As the modern school has become a more important institution, it has inevitably been involved in more social problems and issues. Busing to achieve racial integration is an example. Advocates of busing argue that this technique is one of the few ways available to defeat residential segregation and discrimination. Opponents argue that busing threatens community and neighborhood control of schools and destroys the family's ability to meet the child's emotional and status-achievement needs. Advocates counter by arguing that, in a democracy, neighborhoods should not control the content of what is taught in schools and a child's achievement should not be determined by family-status criteria (race, religion, social class, and so on).

functions may simply dilute its ability to deal effectively with any one of them.

The family–school conflict is a consequence of several factors. The modern school is required to prepare citizens for jobs by supplying the necessary skills and knowledge needed to function in an increasingly complex and technical society. At the same time, the modern school is expected to socialize the young with appropriate values, norms, and beliefs in a rapidly changing culture that emphasizes the importance of diversity. In other words, the school must perform important task and emotional functions, both of which were major family functions in earlier periods of history.

Parents today turn to the schools to train their children in the technical skills that can no longer be taught at home. They also expect the school to assist in preparing young people to cope with the social and emotional demands of living in a complex pluralistic society. This parental expectation was more easily met in the more homogeneous early American communities. Small rural towns were largely Protestant, and teachers identified with the norms and values of the larger community. The Protestant ethic, which emphasized hard work, thrift, and sobriety, was taught both in the family and in school. For example, in the 19th and early 20th centuries, bank days were a common part of school activities. On these days, children were encouraged to save their earnings, as a reflection of the common ethic that prevailed in American culture [Herberg, 1955].

However, much of this situation has changed today. Communities are now urbanized and heterogeneous. Diversity in occupations, religious beliefs, ethnic identities, racial consciousness, and life-styles prevails. Schools still oriented toward traditional Protestant and middle-class values may have become dysfunctional for young people from other backgrounds. Therefore, many families find themselves in continuous conflict with the attitudes and values reflected in their schools. We will return to the question of the dysfunctionality of the modern school in the next section of this chapter.

The second aspect of the crisis in modern education has been highlighted by the decreasing job opportunities for school graduates in the mid-1970s. Fred Hechinger [1976] argues that many Americans are losing confidence in school and the educational process as a means of obtaining better jobs and of developing more effective solutions for social problems related to race, poverty, or crime. Attacks upon the modern school come from extremists on both sides of the political spectrum. Conservatives say that schools have become too permissive and are neglecting the teaching of basic literacy skills. Radicals, on the other hand, criticize the modern school for teaching irrelevant skills and values that only promote the existing society and all its problems. As Hechinger [1976, p. 11] puts it:

> Revisionist ideologues, such as Edgar Z. Friedenberg and John Holt, lashed out against what they considered the coercive aspects of universal and com-

pulsory schooling. They denounced the schools for Americanizing diverse ethnic groups and fitting them into an essentially middle-class socioeconomic pattern or, as they would put it, mold. Revisionist researchers, such as Christopher Jencks, measured the existing American society against their own ideals of the socialist state in which they expected all distinctions between affluence and poverty to vanish. Taking that blueprint as the yardstick, they proclaimed American education's failure in the war against poverty and economic inequality.

As a consequence of these multiple attacks on both the emotional and task functions performed by the school, Hechinger sees a possible threat to American democracy. Schools may become less concerned about meeting the general needs of many citizens and more interested in meeting the special needs of some citizens. Hechinger calls this *a trend toward a new educational elitism.*

This elitism may come about in the following ways. As educational costs and expenses increase, for both individuals and school districts, many citizens may withdraw their support from education that emphasizes a general and well-developed personality in favor of education that deals only with job opportunities. There is already evidence of a new vocationalism in many colleges and universities and a corresponding decline of enrollments in liberal arts and humanities courses. One risk is that young people may be trained for careers that will vanish in a few years. For example, New York's Aviation High School graduated 515 students in 1975, but only six of them found jobs in the aviation industry [Hechinger, 1976, p. 16]. Another risk is that the neglect of "general education" will deprive society of the broad, fully socialized citizens necessary for democratic participation.

Furthermore, education at all levels, particularly college and university, may become available only to those from upper statuses, and the educational experience itself may train people only for higher-status occupations. In 1973, census figures showed that 53.7 percent of the children from families with annual incomes of $15,000 or more were attending college, compared to only 12.7 percent of the children from low-income families. From 1973 to 1975, the percentage of low-income children in college fell even lower. In addition, the educational attainment of a child's parents can play an important role, as Table 10-2 indicates. Thus, as we saw in Chapter 6 on "Status," one problem in contemporary America is the tendency for the rich to get richer as the poor get poorer. Accompanying this trend is the tendency for the children of the better educated to continue their educations and for the children of the less educated to terminate their educations.

In summary, most observers agree that there is a growing crisis in education, but they differ over the causes and consequences of the crisis. The debate about the modern school, then, really involves the question of whether the school is functional or dysfunctional in meeting the needs of contemporary citizens.

TABLE 10-2 How Father's Education Influences Son's Education[a]

Education of Son	Education of Father: Not a High School Graduate	High School Graduate	Some College	College Graduate
Not a High School Graduate	43%	10%	7%	4%
High School Graduate	34%	36%	24%	8%
Some College Attendance	23%	44%	70%	88%

[a]These figures apply to the 1960s for sons between the ages of 20 and 24 years.

Source: Adapted from Murray Gendell and Hans L Zetterberg, Ed., *A Sociological Almanac for the United States*, 2nd ed. (New York: Charles Scribner's Sons, 1964), p. 80.

Is the Modern School Functional or Dysfunctional?

Some observers argue that in order for schools to respond adequately to the diverse needs of a heterogeneous and rapidly changing society, *diverse functions and complex structure are necessary.* For example, in Chapter 9, we referred to Clark Kerr's analysis of the modern university. While recognizing the problems faced by the university, he argued for what he called "the multiversity" on the grounds that complexity was necessary in order to meet all kinds of needs.

Most critics of the school, however, tend to adopt the view that much of modern education is dysfunctional. As we have seen, traditionalists generally argue for a return to the teaching of basic literary and computational skills. The modern school is seen as dysfunctional because of its failure in teaching these skills. In contrast, reformists tend to concentrate their criticism upon characteristics considered dysfunctional in all formal human groupings, not just the school (for example, bureaucratization and impersonalization). Finally, radical critics see the school as dysfunctional because it perpetrates an elitist perspective. These differing perspectives are summarized in Table 10-3.

Of particular interest are some of the recent radical criticisms of the school. Johnathan Kozol [1967, 1975] argues that schools today no longer educate; rather they indoctrinate and reward conformity. They do so in a multitude of ways, both obvious and subtle. Cultural heroes like Henry Thoreau, Helen Keller, and Martin Luther King are idealized because they were popular leaders, but their roles as social radicals who challenged the

TABLE 10-3 Traditional, Reformist, and Radical Perspectives of the Modern School

	Traditional	Reformist	Radical
Problems of the Modern School:	Has taken on too many functions; no longer meets basic skill needs of the young; is being used to promote political programs	Bureaucratization; impersonalization; weaknesses in traditional teaching; overprofessionalization of teaching	Functions only to support the interests of the privileged and powerful; is also a way of controlling younger, potentially threatening citizens
Trouble with Most Courses Taught:	Irrelevant because they deal with useless matters (how to date, how to get along with others); dangerous because they conflict with family and societal values (sex education)	Standards of grading have declined recently; grades have become higher as student abilities have become lower	Irrelevant in avoiding the critical issues (racism, imperialism); dangerous in reinforcing the prevailing system that causes the problems
Types of Courses That Should Be Taught:	Basic skills: "the three Rs—reading, 'riting, and 'rithmatic"	Mixed: traditional knowledge plus preprofessional and occupational training	How to experience and influence life: new philosophies for viewing the world, participation in community affairs, political activism
Where Curriculum Should be Taught:	Small schools with faculty highly trained in basic courses; school should be supportive of the family and community; local control	Large-scale complex schools will sometimes be necessary to handle variety of functions	"Outside" the school, within the community; the school as a separate and powerful institution should be abolished; only a skeletal structure for minimal administrative purposes should remain
Examples of Kinds of Programs That Should Be Instituted:	Return of political authority to the local community; cancel "frill" courses	A moderate mix of the various proposals from each political extreme	Interdisciplinary courses on major problems (war and peace); field study experiences; work experiences; student-initiated courses; independent study

prevailing system are played down. In other words, schools teach a distrust and suspicion of deviance, innovation, or experimentation, although these forms of human behavior may be the only way to bring about needed changes and responses to serious problems (see Chapter 12).

Schools also "teach" or reinforce conformity and the avoidance of innovation by the way teachers respond to the work of students. Herbert Kohl [1966, pp. 1–2] gives an appropriate illustration. Two school children submitted the following poems to their teacher:

Shop With Mom

I love to shop with mom,
And talk to the friendly grocer,
And help her make the list.
Seems to make us closer.
—*Pamela*

The Junkies

When they are in the street they pass
it along to each other but when they
see the police they would just stand
still and be beat so pity ful that they
want to cry.
—*Marie*

The teacher praised Pamela's poem, particularly the rhyme in "closer" and "grocer" and the fact that she "said a great deal" in only four lines. In addition, Pamela's poem expressed a pleasant and healthy thought, and, therefore, it was accepted by the school paper. In contrast, Marie's poem was rejected because she could not possibly know what a junkie was and the other children would not be interested in such a topic anyway. Furthermore, there were no rhymes in Marie's poem and no clearly discernible meter; "pitiful" was misspelled and incorrectly split; "be beat" was not proper English. And, finally, the teacher felt that Marie must be disturbed to write about such an unpleasant topic. Kohl [1966, pp. 1–2] concludes:

> Under these circumstances it is not surprising that Marie refused to perform in school and allowed herself to become the disturbed girl she was presumed to be. Children won't write if they fear that honesty will be punished, and too often they learn to distrust teachers. They have had too many school experiences where staff loyalty and the institutional obligations of teachers have taken precedence over honesty. They have seen too much face-saving and too little respect for justifiable defiance. This is dramatically true in slum schools where the pressures of teaching are increased by understaffing and a vague uneasiness about race is always in the air.

In other words, schools can also label children and thereby influence their behavior and performance. According to Kozol, such labeling also teaches children to compartmentalize their emotions. The splitting of the school day and the academic material into time units and subjects also teaches students to atomize their thoughts and attitudes. In addition, schools further dehumanize human beings and social issues by avoiding emotional discussion of subjects like love, hate, and death, and by emphasizing a detached scientific objectivity.

Radical critics, then, see *the many functions and the formal structure of the modern school as dysfunctional,* that is, as being irrelevant to the personal needs of individual citizens. This same kind of irrelevance can be seen at work in other social and cultural contexts. In a study of population information programs in Mexico, Adrienne Germain [1975] points out how inappropriate such formal programs are to the personal needs of Mexican women. Formal programs are carried out through health clinics, schools, and other institutions, where contraceptive information is provided to a selected population of women in order to reduce fertility. The justification given is the improvement of national economic and social welfare.

Individual Mexican women, however, want birth-control information in order to avoid full-time motherhood. In addition, they seek information and emotional support from a network of women's organizations and peer groups rather than from formal educational clinics. In other words, once education is formalized (whether it is about birth control, how to read or write, or how to become a machinist or physician), it may begin losing touch with the special needs of its intended audience and, consequently, become increasingly irrelevant and dysfunctional.

Finally, some critics have suggested that modern education is dysfunctional because it tends to be used as *a means of social control.* Schools may be used as a means of forcing conformity to middle-class values, thereby homogenizing the population and minimizing potentially threatening differences. Kluckholn and Leighton [1962] have described this misuse of education in the case of the American Indian. From 1800 to 1871, the United States government used the military to force various Indian tribes to cede almost a billion acres of valuable land. In the late 1800s, however, warfare became a less viable technique, and the school was seen as a new nonviolent method for continuing the government's expansionist policy. In 1879, for example, the Carlisle Indian School in Pennsylvania was established by General H. R. Pratt, a former Indian fighter. The purpose of the school was to separate the Indian child from the reservation and family and to replace tribal language and norms with middle-class American language and norms [U.S. Senate Committee on Labor and Public Welfare, 1969, p. 148]. Carlisle became a model for Indian education for the next 50 years. The problem was that, when most Indian students returned to their families and reservations, they found they could no longer take part in local life since they did not possess the necessary language, customs, or skills. As a result, Indian culture lacked trained leadership and began to decline. In addition, many Indians were forced off the reservations into large urban centers where they experienced racial and ethnic hostility.

Many radical critics have indicated that modern schools do exactly the same thing to other ethnic groups, particularly blacks and Spanish-speaking Americans. By stripping them of their prior cultural heritage, the school makes survival of the subculture impossible, and it also drives them "off the land" into the poorer paying jobs in urbanized communities. Therefore, the functions provided by the school are both irrelevant and undemocratic. In summary, then, most critics of the school see much of modern education as dysfunctional, and they differ only on the basis of what they think the school ought to be doing for society. Given this general agreement that education faces a crisis, are there ways in which the school might respond?

Theories of Educational Reform

It is impossible to review here all of the proposals for educational reform that have been offered in response to the contemporary educational crisis [Riesman, 1974, pp. 81–110]. However, as a means of determining new functions and structure for the school, one recent analysis distinguishes between three different theories of education. Lay and Dopyera [1977] point out that current educational theory reflects three competing views—environmentalist, maturationist, and interactionist—of the teaching–learning process.

According to the *environmentalist view,* the teacher is the central source of information and knowledge. In addition, the classroom should be a highly structured environment that directs the child's learning toward traditional academic subjects. The student is seen as a relatively passive learner who must be taught basic academic skills in a carefully sequenced fashion by a highly trained teacher. Furthermore, children must be systematically rewarded for their academic progress by praise, grades, privileges, and the like. Punishment is also necessary to discourage behavior that is not directed toward the academic goal.

Environmentalists tend to see educational technology as a positive contribution to an efficient learning environment. Computers, teaching machines, and various other types of programmed instruction are used to carry students from one carefully sequenced lesson to another. Those committed to this approach argue that it is especially appropriate for disadvantaged children who must be taught to achieve. If they are not, they may set their own slow pace and find that they fall far behind students who come from achievement-oriented homes.

In contrast, *maturationist and interactionist views* stress the importance of permitting students to learn voluntarily by actively exploring the environment in a personal and creative fashion. *Maturationists* use the model of personality development we discussed in Chapter 3. Minimal direction—similar to the way in which the mother or father gently restrains the uncontrolled "I" in the young child—is required at certain points in the learning process; but care must be taken to avoid either inhibiting or pushing the child. The child will develop most effectively if allowed to proceed according to his or her own internally controlled maturation schedule. *Interactionists* argue that students' natural interaction with their environment (including other persons) is the key to their development. Teachers should thus provide them with a rich environment and assist their natural exploration of that environment. In this way, learning will become relevant to their personal needs and wants.

Obviously, both the role of the teacher and the physical nature of the classroom will vary greatly according to one's view of the learning process. Environmentalist perspectives tend to prevail in most contemporary schools, as reflected in the traditional classroom structure:

Blackboard and Clock

Teacher

Teacher's Desk

pupil	pupil	pupil	pupil	pupil
pupil	pupil	pupil	pupil	pupil
pupil	pupil	pupil	pupil	pupil
pupil	pupil	pupil	pupil	pupil
pupil	pupil	pupil	pupil	pupil

In such an arrangement, the teacher becomes the central figure in the learning environment. By sitting behind a desk, or standing on a raised platform, the authority of the teacher and the teacher's message is accentuated while student-to-student interaction is minimized. There may be some periods of the day when students are free to move to the teacher's desk or to other classrooms, but most of the day is as formally structured as the physical context in which the classes occur. The entire school may be as formally structured as individual classrooms. Special learning centers, laboratories, and auditoriums usually emphasize individual separation and specialized activities.

If Kozol and other radical critics are correct, however, such segmentation of learning can become dysfunctional. Is it possible to redesign the structure of the classroom to reflect the views expressed by maturationists and interactionists? The accompanying "So What?" box deals with this question.

▶ SO WHAT?

In contrast to the environmentalist classroom depicted on page 433, a maturationist or interactionist classroom might look like the room depicted in Figure 10-3. In a classroom like this, children often sit on the floor, sometimes on pieces of rugs that they have brought to school. While one group of five to six students may be reading with the teacher

FIGURE 10-3 Maturationist Classroom

FIGURE 10-4

FIGURE 10-5

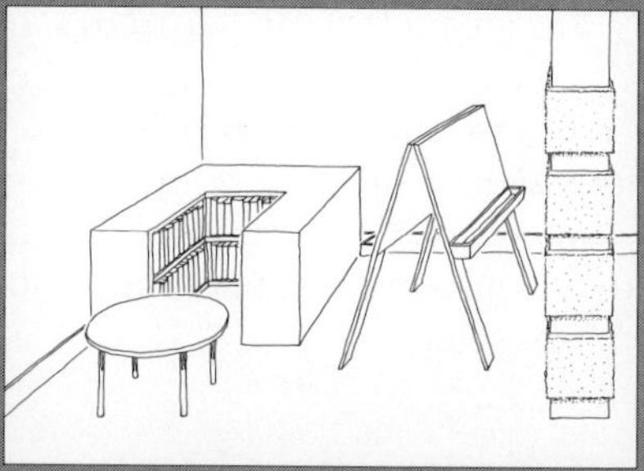

at a table, another small group of students can be helping each other with writing or art. Still other students may be studying by themselves. Therefore, such a classroom provides the opportunity for a variety of different learning experiences simultaneously. A rug placed in a corner becomes a place for teacher-led group discussions. Curtains at windows add cheerfulness and act as sound absorbers. (See Figure 10-4.) The arrangement of shelves and tables divide a reading area from an art area. The use of carpeting on a column helps absorb sound. (See Figure 10-5.) In this type of classroom, the teacher will often have a teacher's aid or a parent to help with the varied activities. The context is designed to encourage play and enjoyment as a natural part of the learning process. In addition, it is designed to encourage individual differences in learning. Although critics of this kind of classroom often argue that a "no frills" room of desks in a row is less expensive, the cost of this type of classroom can be quite reasonable. Many desks and chairs from the traditional classrooms can simply be rearranged in a manner more appropriate to the desired environment. Many of the furnishings and much of the equipment (for example, the rugs) can be donated by families, thereby promoting a sense of community and family involvement. (Figures adapted from Sabaroff and Hanna, 1974.)

Although most American classrooms continue to be structured and continue to function according to the traditional environmentalist model, an increasing number of new schools and classrooms (particularly elementary) are being constructed to fit the maturationist and interactionist models of education. The increased attention to all phases of student development (intellectual, social, and emotional) that such open classrooms permit reflects the tendency of modern industrialized societies to make the school into a broader, more multifunctional institution. Do you approve or disapprove of this trend?

Throughout our discussion of the family and the school, we have seen the relationship of these two morale-building institutions with a third—the church. If the family's functions and structure are narrowing and the school's function and structure are broadening, what is happening to the church's?

THE CHURCH

In this section, we begin by considering the universal nature of religion and the reason why religious institutions are found in all societies. Because they are so important, churches frequently are required to pursue conflicting goals. We will consider the changing functions and structures of the modern church that arise as a result of this conflict. Religious institutions also compete with other morale-building institutions. We conclude the chapter with an example of the way in which family, school, and church sometimes support and sometimes conflict with each other in modern society.

The Universality of Religion

Religious behavior is universal; it is found in some form in all societies. Religious institutions develop knowledge and practices which enable people to develop a sense of *social and cultural control* over their personal and public lives (see Study 6). Some scholars have suggested that the institutions of magic and science also appear in all societies, since they serve social control purposes as well. In Table 10-4, magic, religion, and science are compared in terms of this common purpose in primitive and modern societies.

These three types of institutions overlap and compete with one another. As we have seen throughout this book, scientists may begin to act like primitive shaman (magicians and medicine men), arguing that they possess occult and mysterious knowledge which cannot be comprehended by the untrained citizen. In this case, science may be worshipped by citizens and practitioners alike as a new form of religion that can provide all of the answers to ultimate human problems and miseries. Therefore, though magic, science, and religion are usually seen as opposing one another, they can become interrelated in complex and unusual ways. This relationship partly explains the continually shifting and changing functions of modern religion.

Changing and Competing Functions

To assess whether the contemporary functions of the church are narrowing or broadening is extremely difficult. Part of the reason is that religion in all societies tends to perform dual functions as it serves the purpose of control: (1) *it promotes important cultural values* by challenging people to achieve them and (2) *it comforts people by appealing to tradition* when pursuit of these values creates crises [Glock, Ringer, and Babbie, 1967]. As we saw in Chapter 9, two types of leaders emerge, corresponding to these two functions of religion. Religious *prophets* exhort people to strive relentlessly after such values as justice, peace, and equality, while religious *priests* seek to comfort them in times of sorrow and to celebrate with them in times of joy. Prophets are usually radical and change-oriented, whereas priests are usually conservative. It is the prophet who speaks out against social injustice and oppression, but it is the priest who performs the rites

TABLE 10-4 Similarities and Differences between Magic, Religion, and Science[a]

	Magic	Religion	Science
Purpose	Deals with the occult and mystic aspects of human experience	Deals with the supranatural aspects, which are seen as partly mystic (heaven and hell) and partly empirical (good and evil behavior in the secular world)	Deals with the rational and empirical aspects of human experience; denies the existence of the mystic and occult
Goal	Direct control of highly personal gods and spirits (good and bad) who live in the immediate environment but work in unseen, mysterious ways; encourage the gods to intervene to help	Develop an understanding of the transcendent nature of universal forces and power (God) in order to assist individuals in controlling their own lives and experiences	Control of the natural (social and physical) forces in the immediate environment in order to make human life better and solve human problems
Functions	Bring about cures in crisis situations (sickness, drought, injury, floods, madness); also define good and bad totems (objects, places, or people) and taboos (norms)	Two competing types (1) comforting (priestly role) which assists individuals through crisis situations by transmitting the social and cultural heritage; (2) challenging (prophetic role) injustices by reaffirming commitment to major values and restating rejection of evil	Generation of new knowledge to improve life conditions; also transmission of traditional scientific knowledge from one generation to the next
Methods and Techniques	Personal, unique rituals by a shaman; sometimes community members participate, usually they merely observe and judge the success of the ritual; shaman often does not have special training, but is selected because of charismatic qualities	Elaborate public rituals performed by a priest or minister with participation by community members; in sects, no special training required for leadership; in churches, formal training may be required	Rational, highly structured procedures performed by a specially trained scientist, very often in private

[a]*Note:* This comparison is adapted from a variety of sources. The most useful is Malinowski [1948].

TABLE 10-4 (continued)

	Magic	Religion	Science
Consequences	Magic is slow to change; knowledge tends to remain exclusive to the shaman or members of a secret cult	Can be either (1) a conservative force which hallows the status quo or (2) a force for rapid change by challenging a corrupt status quo; though priest may possess exclusive knowledge, shares some of this with members of the sect or community	Can be either (1) a conservative force which produces value-free knowledge to be used to maintain the status quo or (2) a force for producing new knowledge which radically questions the status quo; scientist possesses exclusive knowledge of proper procedures but is supposed to share substantive information discovered with the public
Potential Dysfunctions	Really doesn't solve problems (cure disease, bring rain, etc.); discourages innovation in new knowledge and procedures	Continuing conflict between comforting and challenging roles within the sect or church and the larger society; can often become more magical than religious (praying to God to help with a personal problem)	If too value-free, potential for misuse by others is maximized; if too value-relevant and social-action–oriented, can become a kind of secular religion; frequently procedures and knowledge take on magical aspects (participant observation comes to be seen as a mysterious technique which discloses strange and occult knowledge about human nature)
Examples: From Primitive Society	Painting an eye on the front of the canoe so that the good spirit of the boat can see and avoid the bad spirits of the sea	Rituals which bless the voyage of the canoe before a group sets sail to seek new food supplies	Design of a canoe which can sail hundreds of miles into the open sea with passengers and provisions
From Modern Society (athletics)	Wearing the same clothes before every important game; not stepping on the chalk marks; wearing a special charm or ring while playing	Praying before a game; blessing a game as an expression of important cultural values (spirit of brotherhood at Olympic Games)	Calculating the speed of a baseball; measuring body functions during long-distance races; taking into account angles and distances when shooting a basketball or hitting a hockey puck off of the boards

of marriage and burial. Both roles are necessary if people are to develop a sense of control. They must be able to adapt to change and crisis, but, at the same time, they must be able to preserve and hang onto old traditions and beliefs in order to maintain a feeling of stability in the face of rapid change or extreme crisis.

The problem is that the dual functions of challenging and comforting, and the dual roles of prophet and priest, may either support or conflict with one another; and the church may be either strengthened or weakened as a result. Prophets are needed (1) to reaffirm the church's commitment to ideal values and (2) to stimulate both the church and society into action against social problems in the name of these values. In fact, the very survival of a church or a society may depend upon the presence or absence of prophetic leaders such as Gandhi or Martin Luther King.

However, prophetic roles may also interfere with the church's ability to perform comforting functions. Prophets do not comfort; they are more likely to anger and to promote anxiety. In addition, prophets are frequently denounced by the leaders of a society or by church members, particularly if they criticize the church for complicity in social injustices (as Christ criticized established religion and King criticized white American churches). Furthermore, as we saw in the "So What?" box in Chapter 9, the desire to perform comforting as opposed to challenging roles may create major problems for church leadership. Frequently, in times of great crisis and stress, both church members and the larger society may pressure church leaders to concentrate upon comforting roles in order to lessen conflict and to enhance social solidarity and integration (for example, churches frequently support nationalistic wars). At other times, church leaders may be pressured to perform prophetic and challenging roles in the name of neglected social values such as equality, brotherhood, and humanitarianism.

Actually, priestly (comforting) religion tends to predominate in most churches. This is one reason why religion so often appears as a conservative force, hallowing the status quo, and why radical critics like Karl Marx have called religion "an opiate of the people." On the other hand, religions and churches can be a latent revolutionary force capable of promoting major change. Max Weber (see Chapter 4) demonstrated how the Protestant ethic encouraged the replacement of feudal society with capitalism and industrialization. These dual functions of churches are also reflected in different types of structures.

Contrasting Church Structures

Broadly speaking there are two types of church structure—(1) *the congregational* and (2) the *episcopal.* The former is found in institutions that are autonomous and free from external bureaucratic control, while the latter is part of a large denominational structure that may be national or international in scope. A small Baptist church, which splinters away from a major Baptist denomination and insists upon being free to control its own

10-4 Multiple Roles of the Church

The dilemma of the church is that it is frequently called upon to perform multiple roles which are constantly changing and in conflict with one another.

B. Hrynewych/Stock, Bostc

Priestly roles. A traditional role of the church is to comfort people as they face crises or problems in pursuit of their goals. The rituals and traditions of the church reflect this role. The priestly role must often be performed in unusual contexts far removed from the formal church, as illustrated by a motorcycle blessing in the town of Enfield, New Hampshire. Some church members feel that this is not a proper use of ritual, while others feel that it carries the church's mission into society.

D. Dietz/Stock, Boston

Ole Lokensgaard/University Lutheran Church

Prophetic roles. Another traditional role is the promotion of cultural values, such as equality and brotherhood, by challenging people to achieve them. Prophetic roles often conflict with priestly roles. For example, as women increasingly demand a place in the pulpit and in church leadership many members of the congregation object because this represents a sharp departure from tradition. Others feel that challenging people to live up to the highest ideals is the most important thing the church can do.

Combined roles. Many churches attempt to combine priestly and prophetic roles. For example, the University Lutheran Church is a mission congregation which works in the university community of the Boston, Massachusetts, area. It provides a variety of functions and services including worship, music, art, and Christian education. These activities also serve socialization and integration purposes for people who might otherwise feel alienated in urban society. Some people feel that multiple roles weaken the church's ability to perform priestly functions.

Elizabeth Hamlin, Dietz/Hamlin

Educational roles. The church's concern for promoting basic values and for comforting people in the face of crisis ultimately involves it in a variety of educational roles. Sex education is an example. Sexual behavior involves important moral issues and raises particularly troublesome personal problems for youth. Some people believe the church should leave teaching to other institutions and concentrate upon preaching, while others believe that education is a natural extension of basic roles.

C. Wolinsky/Stock, Boston

Political roles. Through the ages, the church has been involved in political roles and social action. Prophetic roles based upon traditional norms often conflict with changing public values. For example, when the church emphasizes a reverence for life by opposing abortion, this stance conflicts with those who believe population must be controlled by mothers who have the individual freedom to determine their own life-chances.

affairs, is a congregational type of structure. It often results in a sectlike church (see Chapter 9) of low-income, relatively uneducated people, who feel uncomfortable in the larger church with its more affluent members. They engage a minister who is not professionally trained but who can comfort and reassure church members who need to feel that "the last shall be first in the kingdom of God." The congregational structure is simple and tends to minimize differences between church members and the minister, who is paid from voluntary contributions to preach "the old time priestly religion."

This minimal church structure, and its relationship to the family, can be depicted as follows:

	Minister	
Committee	Committee	Committee
Family Family	Family Family	Family Family

The closeness of the minister to church members means that leaders can be removed if they displease others by preaching prophetic sermons or by engaging in challenging actions. The congregational type of church structure, therefore, emphasizes local control.

In contrast, the minister in a church with an episcopal structure has greater freedom from the congregations accompanied by greater commitment to an elaborate and formal denominational hierarchy. In the United Methodist Church, for example, the minister is appointed from outside the local church by a bishop who consults with a cabinet of district superintendents. This is a church with hierarchical control in a centralized bureaucracy. The highest positions are those of the bishops, who are episcopal leaders and the source of final authority. The highly structured United Methodist Church in America is depicted in Figure 7-2 on page 289.

The structure of the United Methodist Church tends to stress the importance of the entire connectional system rather than emphasizing local control by individual churches. Members of the local congregations are organized into committees to raise local budgets to pay the minister's salary and other expenses. They may consult with higher authorities about what minister is to be assigned to the local church; however, church members have little direct control over what the minister says and does. Methodist ministers, therefore, are protected to some extent by the church structure and are freer to speak out on controversial issues. Consequently, in both small and large Methodist churches, prophetic religion is more likely to be found in addition to priestly religion.

Research on the involvement of ministers during the civil rights demonstrations of the 1960s tends to bear out these observations about church social structure and prophetic religion. Campbell and Pettigrew [1959] studied ministers in Little Rock, Arkansas, during the racial crisis that erupted over the admission of black students to an all-white high school in 1957. They discovered that ministers of all denominations were very sensitive to the feelings of their local congregations. This was true even in denominations with the episcopal type of organization that had taken a strong stand in favor of civil rights and school integration. Many ministers were silent about the school crisis because they argued they would lose their jobs and, therefore, be unable to play any role at all. Even Methodist ministers tended to be inactive in the racial crisis in Little Rock.

At the same time, there were some Methodists among the few ministers who did speak out for school integration. A number did, in fact, lose their jobs; however, this was less serious for the Methodists than for other ministers since they were assured of some job elsewhere within the episcopal structure of the church. Some time after the Little Rock crisis (in January 1963), 28 Mississippi Methodist ministers signed a document opposing discrimination because of race, color, or creed. Not only did they feel strength in unity, but they also felt support from the social structure of their church. Even so, by mid-1965, only nine of these native Mississippi ministers remained in the state, and only two occupied the same pulpit [Hadden and Rymph, 1966]. Prophetic ministers often find speaking out on controversial issues to be costly, yet they are more likely to do so if they have some protection from the social structure of the church.

Therefore, any attempt to understand the contemporary church must take into account both its dual functions and its dual structure. Comforting roles maximize social solidarity but minimize needed changes, while challenging roles minimize comforting functions and maximize conflict and change. Congregational-type structures emphasize local control and autonomy but may limit the performance of challenging roles. Episcopal-type structures provide more freedom for ministers but may generate commitments to career and hierarchy. Therefore, the modern church is frequently marked by internal conflict regarding its proper role in relation to the larger society. The final section of this chapter considers one example of the way in which church, family, and school interact and compete with one another.

Church, Family, and School Conflict: The Textbook Controversy

In 1974, a "holy war" over the introduction of some controversial textbooks broke out between the rural citizens of the Appalachian mountains—miners and marginal farmers for the most part—and the Kanawha County School Board, which represented both the urban schools of metropolitan Charleston and the surrounding rural schools. Historically, there had been a close relationship between these rural families, the school, and their sectlike churches. In fact, the first frontier schools were established by these churches. Thus, as a result of this tradition, parents in rural areas expected schools to reinforce their fundamentalist values and interpretations of religion and life.

With the development of large-scale mining and the introduction and growth of industrialization, these Americans soon became economically disadvantaged and voiceless and powerless in the face of big corporations and urban institutions. Their schools and churches then became the only places where they still had some control over their own affairs. Religion not only helped them cope with their deprivations, but it was one of the few experiences that gave meaning and purpose to their lives. For sect-oriented people, the church serves as the center of their social lives. One Appalachian writer explains how functional their religion has been for them:

> Many social reformers . . . view the local sect churches as a hindrance to social progress. What they fail to see is that it was the Church which helped sustain us and made life worth living in grim situations. Religion shaped our lives, but at the same time we shaped our religion. Culture and religion are intertwined. The life on the frontier did not allow for an optimistic social gospel. . . . One was lucky if he endured. Hard work did not bring a sure reward. Therefore the religion became fatalistic and stressed rewards in another life [National Education Association, 1975, pp. 110–111].

The nature of the textbook controversy is summarized in the *Inquiry Report* [National Education Association, 1975], written by a panel of scholars representing the National Education Association. The conflict was between rural Americans with marginal jobs and modest education and the School Board, which seemed to them to represent the big city and its worldly churches. Ten clergy from the larger denominations spoke in favor of the controversial textbooks and modern trends in education. They were viewed by the rural residents as godless liberals.

The School Board had tried to involve the rural parents in selection of textbooks; however, this procedure had not been successful and the ruralites felt left out of the deliberations. They welcomed the views of one Board member, a woman who had spoken out on several occasions against sex education and what were considered offensive parts of the English curriculum, including selections by several prominent black writers. They welcomed the support from outsiders representing the Ku Klux Klan and the John Birch Society, both conservative groups of the extreme right. Confrontations were not confined to School Board meetings. There were violent outbursts and shootings at school buses, and a climate of fear prevailed in classrooms, where students spied and reported upon teachers.

In short, the Kanawha County crisis was one of cultural conflict involving diverse perspectives and the three basic morale-building institutions—the family, school, and church. *The Inquiry Report* recognizes that the crisis is not over in this county nor in many parts of America today. An uneasy peace will probably prevail for quite some time.

The report closes with the recommendation that parents be respected as consultants to the schools but not as censors of textbooks and classroom teaching. It also points out that there is need for continued consultation in

American communities with respect to the purposes of education in our society. Certainly the schools cannot impose any one value system or religious perspective upon children in the public schools. Neither can they take a neutral stance and neglect the responsibility to explore diverse values, philosophies, ideologies, and religious beliefs. Controversial issues must be confronted in the classrooms. Traditional methods and materials in education have their place alongside more liberal and innovative teaching. Nevertheless, the purposes of education must go beyond the transmission and conservation of old values and beliefs. The schools must provide free and open exploration of new values and changing perspectives in the modern world.

The case of the church–family–school interaction in West Virginia illustrates the ways in which religion can be both functional and dysfunctional at one and the same time. It can be comforting and reassuring to deprived families living under great stress, but it can also cause conflict and misunderstanding, which can inhibit needed social change in the schools and community. Continued consultations across the lines of church, family, and school are essential in order to strengthen the process of socialization and integration in our society. A final point of interest is that a religious leader in West Virginia, a Methodist bishop, was the person chosen to serve as mediator throughout the Kanawha County controversy, the person who tried to keep the lines of communication open.

CONCLUSION

Earlier in this chapter, we saw how the modern nuclear family with its limited functions and narrow structure had evolved from the multifunctional extended families of premodern times. We also found that, although these changes possessed some disadvantages, they were generally functional for life in modern urban societies. Freedom and mobility for individuals is enhanced by the nuclear family. A smaller, tightly knit family also can provide personal intimate relationships for individuals who might be alienated if they were alone in large impersonal environments.

Similarly, we saw that the expanding functions and structure of the modern school were also responses to the demands of modern urban life. In addition to individualizing the academic development of students, modern schools have increasingly broadened their program objectives to include the social-emotional and physical needs of students as well. This broadening of school functions has led to school structures that involve (1) larger and more complex staffs (teachers, aides, administrators, therapists, counselors, nurses, subject-matter specialists, coaches, and so on) and (2) more personalized classrooms, where various activities (reading, dramatics, science, and so on) can take place simultaneously and where student–student interaction is encouraged rather than curtailed.

In the Preface and in the introduction to Part 3 of this book, we pointed out that one of our major themes was the issue of human conformity versus human freedom. The functional and structural changes of both the family and the school can be interpreted as an expression of the desire for greater freedom within a context that continues to provide needed conformity to generally accepted norms, values, and behavior patterns. Interestingly, the changing modern church, as a third important morale-building institution, appears to be influenced by the same general trend.

In the older medieval church, the need for collective conformity was maximized, and individual freedom was discouraged. Members were expected to adhere strictly to prevailing norms and to remain committed to major values. Leaders were likewise expected to transmit, strictly and uncompromisingly, traditional norms and values. As a consequence, all morale-building aspects of medieval society (essentially the extended family and the all-inclusive church) emphasized stability, continuity, and resistance to change. However, the needs of modern society are entirely different. Change, innovation, and individual freedom are required for the survival of both individuals and the community in urban industrialized contexts. Just as the family had to adapt by assuming narrowed functions and structures, and the school had to adapt by expanding its functions and structures, the church has had to respond by alternating or shifting between its conflicting functions and structures.

The continuing conflict between priestly and prophetic roles provides a context within which leaders of the church can sometimes experience greater freedom while also performing traditional functions. Competing church structures (congregational and episcopal) also provide leaders with the opportunity for both conformity and freedom. Where congregational structures maximize membership control of leadership and minimize leader's freedoms, episcopal structures minimize membership control and maximize leader's freedoms. In a similar manner, the tension between comforting and challenging functions meets the dual needs of members for commitment to both traditional norms and values and to open-minded questioning, which can lead to newer, more desirable forms of commitment.

In conclusion, both members and leaders of the three major morale-building institutions are seeking ways to provide more personal and meaningful expression of the individual self. The narrowed family, the expanded school, and the shifting church are all attempts to provide such a context. Within the Catholic Church, for example, some priests have replaced the traditional impersonal confession with a more personal and intimate interaction. The priest no longer sits in a confessional, isolated by a partition from the confessor. Rather, the confessor and the priest talk with one another in close interpersonal contexts. Other Catholic groups have experimented with encounter group contexts that become a form of "public confession" and exploration of new attitudes. Small discussion groups allow each participant to share with others personal problems and anxieties. Members begin to feel that others are responding to them as individuals with special needs and wants. At the same time, the priest and other participants can fulfill the role of passing on traditional values and beliefs. Thus, the needs for both conformity and freedom are being met in new and unusual ways in all of the morale-building institutions.

In addition, the needs for conformity and freedom are being met by institutions that perform important task functions in contemporary society. The next chapter examines the role of power institutions—particularly the state, military, and technology—in both meeting task needs and enforcing conformity while enhancing freedom. We will see how the functions and structures of these institutions also have been changing in response to competing and conflicting purposes.

REFERENCES

Bales, Robert F. *Interaction Process Analysis: A Method for the Study of Small Groups.* New York: Addison–Wesley, 1949.

Campbell, Ernest Q., and Thomas F. Pettigrew. *Christians in Racial Crisis: A Study of Little Rock's Ministry.* Washington, D.C.: Public Affairs Press, 1959.

Clayton, Richard R. *The Family, Marriage, and Social Change.* Lexington, Mass.: D. C. Heath and Company, 1975.

Department of Health, Education, and Welfare. *Digest of Educational Statistics, 1973 Edition.* Washington, D.C.: U.S. Government Printing Office, 1974. Table 65.

Edwards, Newton, and Herman G. Richey. *The School in the American Social Order,* 2nd ed. Boston: Houghton Mifflin, 1963.

Geiger, H. K. *The Family in Soviet Russia.* Cambridge, Mass.: Harvard Univ. Press, 1963.

Gendel, Murray, and Hans L. Zetterberg, Ed. *A Sociological Almanac for the United States,* 2nd ed. New York: Charles Scribner's Sons, 1964, p. 80.

Germain, Adrienne. "Women at Mexico: Beyond Family Planning Acceptors," *Family Planning Perspectives,* 7, 1975.

Glock, Charles Y., Benjamin B. Ringer, and Earl R. Babbie. *To Comfort and To Challenge.* Berkeley and Los Angeles: University of California Press, 1967.

Goode, William J. "Family Disorganization," in Robert K. Merton and Robert A. Nisbet, *Contemporary Social Problems.* New York: Harcourt, Brace and World, 1966.

Hadden, Jeffrey K., and Raymond C. Rymph. "Social Structure and Civil Rights Involvement: A Case Study of Protestant Ministers," *Social Forces, 45,* (September 1966), pp. 51–61. Reprinted in Charles Y. Glock, *Religion in Sociological Perspective: Essays in the Empirical Study of Religion.* Belmont, California: Wadsworth, 1973, pp. 149–162.

Hechinger, Fred M. "Murder in Academe: The Demise of Education," *Saturday Review* (20 March 1976), pp. 10–18.

Herberg, Will. *Protestant–Catholic–Jew: An Essay in American Religious Sociology.* New York: Doubleday, 1956.

Johnson, Harry M. *Sociology: A Systematic Introduction.* New York: Harcourt, Brace and Company, 1960.

Kluckhohn, Clyde, and Dorothea Leighton. *The Navaho.* Garden City, N.Y.: Doubleday and Company, 1962.

Kohl, Herbert. "The Literature of Children," *The Urban Review, 1* (July 1966), pp. 1–11.

Kozol, Jonathan. *Death at an Early Age.* Boston: Houghton Mifflin Company, 1967.

———. *The Night is Dark and I Am Far from Home.* Boston: Houghton Mifflin Company, 1975.

Lay, Margaret, and Dopyera, John. *Becoming a Teacher of Young Children,* Lexington, Mass.: D. C. Heath and Company, 1977.

Liegle, Ludwig. *The Family's Role in Soviet Education.* New York: Springer Publishing Company, 1975.

Mace, David, and Vera Mace. *The Soviet Family.* Garden City, N.Y.: Doubleday and Company, 1963.

Macklin, Eleanor D. "Heterosexual Cohabitation Among Unmarried College Students," *The Family Coordinator, 21* (October 1972); also reprinted in Arlene Skolnick and Jerome H. Skolnick, *Intimacy, Family, and Society.* Boston: Little, Brown and Company, 1972.

Malinowski, Bronislaw. *Magic, Science and Religion.* New York: The Free Press, 1948.

Miller, H. P. "Annual and Lifetime Income in Relation to Education: 1939–1959," *The American Economic Review, 50* (1960), pp. 962–986.

Murdock, George. *The Social Structure.* New York: The Macmillan Company, 1949.

———. "World Ethnographic Sample," *American Anthropologist, 59* (August 1957), p. 686.

National Education Association, Teacher Rights Division. *Inquiry Report: A Textbook Study in Cultural Conflict.* Washington, D.C.: National Education Association, 1975.

Parsons, Talcott. *The Social System.* New York: The Free Press, 1951.

———, and Edward A. Shils. *Toward a General Theory of Action.* Cambridge, Mass.: Harvard University Press, 1951.

Parsons, Talcott. "The Social Structure of the Family," in Ruth Nanda Anshen, *The Family, Its Function and Destiny.* New York: Harper & Row, Publishers, 1959.

Queen, Stuart, and Robert W. Habenstein. *The Family in Various Cultures.* New York: J. B. Lippincott Company, 1974.

Reisman, David. "Notes on Educational Reform," *The Journal of General Education, 23* (1971), pp. 81–110.

Renne, Karen S. "Correlates of Dissatisfaction in Marriage," *Journal of Marriage and the Family, 32,* (February 1970), pp. 54–67.

Sabaroff, Rose, and Mary Ann Hanna. *The Open Classroom.* Metuchen, N.J.: The Scarecrow Press, 1974.

U.S. Department of Labor. *Manpower: Challenge of the 1960s.* Washington, D.C.: U.S. Government Printing Office, 1960.

U.S. Senate Committee on Labor and Public Welfare. *Indian Education: A National Challenge.* Washington, D.C.: U.S. Government Printing Office, 1969, Report No. 91-501.

Williams, Robin M., Jr. *American Society: A Sociological Interpretation,* 3rd ed. New York: Alfred A. Knopf, 1970.

- Are modern governments powerful because they possess force (the military) and authority (traditions) or because they perform so many important functions for citizens? What does the state do *to* and *for* you?
- Do you think the power of large multinational corporations (such as General Motors, Shell Oil, IBM) is desirable (for economic development) or undesirable (because of economic repression)? Why?
- Is a powerful military establishment a threat to world peace, or is it a necessary guarantee of national defense and, therefore, of world stability?
- Has modern technology become "the master" or is it still "the servant" of human institutions and societies?
- What can the seemingly powerless individual citizen do to combat the force of the state, the military, and the large corporation? Do you feel alienated and helpless, or do you believe we can control these power institutions?

11

Power Institutions: State, Military, and Technology

In the Introduction to Part 4, we pointed out that task-oriented and emotionally oriented institutions arise in all societies to meet the four basic social needs of production, distribution, socialization, and integration. As we saw in the preceding chapter, modern families, schools, and churches are concerned with socializing people into the basic skills, roles, norms, and values of a society, thereby integrating them into the larger social order. The modern school, however, in addition to its socializing and integrating functions, helps in the production of new knowledge and in the distribution of human resources to various occupations. In other words, as we have stressed previously, institutions often overlap and frequently compete with one another. At other times, they become dependent upon one another; for example, when Russian parents indoctrinate their children with official ideology at the request of the Soviet state, the family is supporting a major function of the Soviet school.

As this last example indicates, there is another important type of institution that interacts with and influences the morale-building institutions of family, school, and church—the *power institution* of the state. The power of the modern state is one reason why the functions of the modern family have narrowed, the modern school often becomes an adjunct of the state, and the modern church sometimes feels helpless to challenge state authority. Therefore, we begin our discussion by examining the role of power in the expanding functions of the state.

Although the state is the central power institution of contemporary society, it is frequently dependent upon and challenged by other power institutions, particularly the military and the multinational corporation. We will examine this dual supportive–competitive relationship in some detail. Finally, since the state and the military are both dependent upon the technology produced in corporations, universities, and think tanks, the chapter will conclude by examining the relationship between technology and the power institutions of society. We will consider whether technology has become the master or the servant of power institutions and societies. Throughout the chapter, the problem of controlling competing power institutions will be a central issue.

EXPANDING FUNCTIONS OF POWER INSTITUTIONS

In Chapter 9, we listed a variety of functions that have been transferred from familial, economic, and religious institutions to the modern state. This transferal indicates that the state has begun to assume responsibility for meeting all human needs; consequently, its functions have expanded to the point that it simultaneously supports and competes with other institutions.

The concept of *power* helps explain the growth of states. As we saw in Chapter 6, power is the ability to influence the actions or attitudes of others. It can take one of two forms—involuntary coercion (*force*) or voluntary obedience (*authority*). In Chapter 9, we saw how authoritative power can have a charismatic, traditional, or legal–bureaucratic basis. People willingly accept all three types of leadership, conferring on leaders the right to determine both their actions and their beliefs. A third important distinction is that power may have either personal or social goals. Personal power involves the ability to influence one's own immediate lifestyle, while social power is the ability to influence the lives of others.

The fact that modern societies are, for the most part, large, heterogeneous, and oftentimes composed of alienated or fragmented groups gives the state an advantage in acquiring and controlling all forms of power in the following ways:

1. *Force and Coercion:* In most modern societies the state virtually monopolizes the means of repression and coercion—weapons, police, surveillance networks, and so on.

2. *Charismatic Authority:* Through manipulation of the mass media, political leaders can create charismatic images for themselves. At the same time, charismatic antistate leaders can be denied access to the media, can have a negative image projected to the public, or can be eliminated by arrest or assassination.
3. *Traditional Authority:* In modern socieites, as other traditional sources of authority weaken (church, family), the state gains a monopoly of the symbols associated with this type of power. Later in this chapter, we will see how the military plays a role in giving the state traditional authority through parades, ceremonies, and the like.
4. *Legal–Bureaucratic Authority:* In modern heterogeneous societies where legal and bureaucratic power becomes important, there is a tendency for people to turn to the state to resolve problems. State law is utilized to guarantee freedom, justice, and equality. State bureaucracies are constructed to combat crime, pollution, famine, poverty, and other social problems.
5. *Personal Power:* Even in societies with a relatively high standard of living, citizens feel less able to control crucial aspects of their own lives (for example, economic or health crises in their family). They tend to withdraw into private affairs or they look to the state as the only adequate response.
6. *Social Power:* Among modern organizations and institutions, only the state possesses the ability to mobilize the extensive resources needed to resolve large-scale social problems. The state can raise great sums of money through taxation, can mobilize vast numbers of people (drafting during wartime), can enlist necessary expertise (asking scientists during World War II to build an atomic bomb), and so forth.

In other words, in large-scale contemporary society people tend to feel powerless; consequently, they voluntarily and involuntarily turn to the state in times of crisis and rapid change. As a result, the state takes on a greater and greater number of functions, which eventually become assimilated into the state's normal role. In a similar fashion, other power institutions have expanded their functions and have thus become more important. The military, for example, does not just fight wars. It is sometimes called upon to repress domestic disturbances, to build dams (the Army Corps of Engineers), and to generate a sense of state authority (parades). Likewise, technological institutions are called upon by the state to provide the knowledge, trained personnel, and organizational resources needed to meet a variety of modern problems.

A word of caution is needed at this point concerning the power of the state. First, although citizens often *feel* powerless, they may actually possess considerable *potential* power. In Chapter 14, we will discuss the theory of nonviolent action, which argues that citizens can combat state authority by withholding obedience through such means as mass strikes and demonstrations, refusal to pay taxes, or refusal to serve in the armed forces or to fight in wars. Second, the power and authority of the state is dependent upon other institutions such as the military, the church, or the scientific community. These institutions may also withhold support, or they may actually engage in power struggles with the state. This kind of process is a central theme in the following discussions.

THE STATE

What is a state? This important type of human group has the following attributes:

1. The basic characteristics of any institution.
2. Power as its major resource.
3. Maintenance of the social order as its primary purpose.
4. A common culture that helps unify all citizens.

States are referred to as institutions because they are long lived, formal, highly structured, and all inclusive, and they have a variety of public purposes. States are also political institutions; that is, they utilize power to balance the many conflicting special interests within society.

Max Weber [1957] maintained that the state possessed a monopoly of physical force and violence in order to maintain the social order. However, many modern states either rely upon other power institutions (the military) when force is required or they utilize nonphysical forms of power (authority).

Finally, anthoropologist Ralph Linton [1936] has identified states as those social groupings that have a common culture and social order. Shared values, norms, and roles develop a sense of unity among all citizens. The concepts of "nationalism" or "nationhood" reflect this definition. Greer and Orleans [1964] describe the nation as that group which is inclusive of all persons and behaviors within identifiable boundaries. All social behavior within this context must conform to approved norms under penalty of state-imposed sanctions. In this sense, the state is conceived of as the chief custodian of the social order, and it acts as a monitor, controller, and judge of human behavior.

Types of States: Geographical and Functional

Most people think exclusively of national governments when the term "state" is mentioned. There are, however, many types of states, all of which can be categorized as either *geographical* or *functional.* In other words, some states (federal, regional, state, or local governments) are determined by the geographical distribution of the population served, while others vary according to the functions performed (religious, economic, or military states). Examples of these various types of states are summarized in Table 11-1. Although all states possess the same four characteristics [*institutions* (1) that utilize *power* (2) to *maintain order* (3) and to *create a*

TABLE 11-1 Types and Characteristics of States

Characteristic	National Governments	Regional and State Governments	Local Governments	Religious Governments	Corporate States	Military Forces
Institutional:						
Long lived	Yes	Yes	Yes	Yes	Yes	Yes
Formal and structured	Yes	Yes	Sometimes less formal	Yes	Yes	Yes
Public purposes	Many for all citizens	Many but limited by geography	Many but limited by geography	Serve public interests	Serve public interests	Serve public interests
All inclusive	For all citizens	For all citizens in region	For all citizens in community	For all members, and they attempt to extend to others	For all members, and they attempt to extend to others	For all members, and they expand functions to serve others (dam building)
Use of Power: As force	Through the military	Through regional police forces	Through local police	May have quasi-military forces	May have private police forces	Usually limited by civilian authority
As authority	All types	All types, but more limited than national	All types but more limited than regional	Emphasize charisma and tradition	Emphasize legal and bureaucratic	All types
Function to Maintain Order	For all citizens	For all regional citizens	For all local citizens	For all members, and they attempt to extend to others	For all citizens by means of economic activity	Usually by direction of civilian authority
Common Culture and Social Order	Expressed as nationalism or nationhood	Expressed as regionalism or statehood	Expressed as a sense of community in village, town, or city	Expressed as "nation" of Islam or "community" of Catholics	Expressed as corporate "family" or community of Shell Oil, General Motors, and so on	Expressed as militarism or military "community"

common culture and social order (4)], there are important differences between them that help to explain their complex supporting and competing relationships.

For example, regional, state, and local governments are all power institutions similar to national governments. However, their power and functions apply to a more limited geographical area. Regional, state, and local governments all maintain police forces empowered to keep order by enforcing legal norms (laws), but the influence of these laws and the power and duties of the enforcement agencies are normally restricted to a limited territorial base. In addition, a common culture often pervades these smaller geographical states. In the United States, for example, one can find regional pride (Dixie), statehood (the Golden State of California), or community identity ("I'm a Bostonian"), as well as national patriotism.

One problem connected with the variety of geographical and functional states in contemporary society is that their roles and functions often overlap in a complex and bewildering manner. States are more often competitive than supportive in their interactions, especially in metropolitan areas. In the "So What?" box for Chapter 8, we indicated that one major barrier to the success of planned communities in the United States is the difficulty of coordinating the many different aspects of competing governments, taking into consideration such things as the sanitation and water districts, the incorporated towns, local and state police, fire districts, water and telephone companies, and the like.

In addition to overlapping and competing roles, some states are so specialized or so limited in their power that they are unable to respond to sudden change or crisis. In a study of small rural communities that suddenly became "energy boom towns," John Gilmore [1976, p. 535] suggests that these small localized states are simply unable to handle their sudden industrialization without federal assistance:

> The energy boom town in the western United States is apt to be a bad place to live. It's apt to be a bad place to do business. This is a problem for more than the people in the boom town. It also affects federal agencies seeking to increase energy resource production in the Rocky Mountain West, as well as firms building and operating energy resource extraction and conversion facilities. The situation can be frustrating for local and state governments charged with protecting the health, safety, and welfare of their populations. The problems result from the traditional, business-as-usual boom in which unmanaged growth is the cumulative result of many different corporate, governmental, and individual decisions, mostly made in total isolation from each other. (Copyright © 1976 by the American Association for the Advancement of Science.)

When an energy resource (coal or natural gas) is suddenly discovered in a rural area far from towns or cities, a boom town quickly appears, featuring mobile homes, bars, a variety of quick service facilities (coin launderettes, small groceries, and so on), and heavy equipment sprawled across the countryside. In this first phase of development, there is enthusiasm and excitement over anticipated population and economic growth.

11-1 Types of, and Relationships Between, Modern States

Modern states can be found on local, national, or international levels of society, and they can be found in religious and economic life. These different types of states are sometimes supportive and at other times competitive.

National states reflect a common culture by the use of flags, traditional buildings, and so on. They also function to maintain the social order as a monitor, judge, and controller of behavior by the use of laws and regulations.

United Press International

George M. Gardner

In modern urban society, local governments (states, regions, and cities) often conflict with one another and with national states over where legal jurisdictions begin and end.

nited Press International

International states, such as the United Nations, face special problems because of the different cultures and jurisdictional aspirations of member nation-states.

Charles Harbutt/Magnum

Religious states, such as the Vatican, may support governmental states (give moral approval for wars against fascism) or they may conflict with them (oppose legislation permitting abortion).

An Exxon Photo

In the twentieth century, multinational corporations, such as Exxon, have become corporate states independent from national authority (control of oil exploration, processing, and distribution), with a culture of their own (flags, headquarters buildings), and demanding special commitment from their members (profitmaking and monopoly).

However, population growth is usually so rapid in Western boom towns (oftentimes 15–25 percent per year) that the initial period of enthusiasm rapidly gives way to uncertainty and panic over developing problems. Uncontrolled growth leads to institutional breakdowns in the labor and housing markets and in the system for financing local public facilities. School classrooms, retail inventories, and the supply of physicians and lawyers do not grow as rapidly as the population. Old-timers and newcomers alike become alienated and suspicious and look for someone in authority to blame. Mental health clinic case loads increase, as individual deviance (alcholism, marital problems, and so on) increases. Construction hiring increases the school dropout rate; worker productivity falls; local officials argue about proposals for land-use planning and zoning. Citizens are bewildered by the varied special interests in their town—land speculators, lawyers from mining companies, government and corporate consultants and researchers, representatives of state and federal agencies, a *New York Times* correspondent doing a feature story, and so forth. As social cohesion deteriorates, local services and facilities begin to decline. Such community disintegration makes it difficult to attract and hold permanent residents and a stable labor supply. And the boom begins turning into a bust.

Gilmore's suggestions for managing boom town growth highlight the problem of the relationship between states. There is a necessity for planned cooperation between competing levels of government (local, state, and regional) and between geographical and functional states (particularly, the corporation). In addition, federal assistance may be needed to supplement the more limited resources of these other states.

Functional states also support and compete with one another. Religious states (such as the Vatican), corporates states (such as Standard Oil or General Motors), and military states (branches of large armed forces) all resemble the prototypical state—a national government. They usually possess flags, large headquarters buildings, and other symbols of their power and common culture. They may even maintain quasimilitary forces: The Vatican has a ceremonial Vatican Guard; corporations frequently have internal police forces.

As a consequence, functional states often compete with each other and with national states. Later in this chapter, we will discuss the threat that the military and technology pose to national states. At this point, we turn to a consideration of how nation-states, often assisted by military intervention, compete with one another. In short, is there a worldwide trend toward increasing conflicts between geographical states (toward fragmented and unstable nationalism), or one toward a new, unified, global government (toward stable internationalism)?

Is the Modern Nation-State Stable or Unstable?

Some scientists who have studied revolutionary processes and coups d'etat tend to conclude that *governmental instability has increased in recent*

TABLE 11-2 Changing Types and Functions of Latin American Coups, 1935–1964

Types and Functions of Coups	Percentage of Coups for Yearly Periods: 1935–1941	1935–1944	1945–1954	1955–1964
1. Reformist; dedicated to changing the status quo		50 →	23 →	17
2. Essentially using nonviolent means (often called "palace" revolutions)	81 →			33
3. Purpose of overthrowing a constitutional government		12 →		50
4. Occur around election time; for purpose of preventing the election of a reformist president		12 →		56

Based upon Martin C. Needler, "Military Coups in Latin America," *trans-action, 4* (December 1966), pp. 5–6. Published by permission of Transaction, Inc. from *trans-action.* Copyright © 1966 by Transaction, Inc.

years. They maintain that existing national states are toppling at an increasing rate and that, consequently, more new nation-states are coming into being each year. In an attempt to discover the sources and nature of this process, Martin Needler [1966, pp. 5–6] studied military coups in Latin America. He found that the governments of the 20 independent nations of that area had been overthrown by military intervention 56 times in the 30 years from 1936 to 1966. There were two to three coups per year on the average, ranging from a high of six in 1944 to a low of none in 1942. Significant changes in the types and functions of Latin American coups occurred during this period and are summarized in Table 11-2.

Needler found that earlier coups appeared to be more democratic in purposes, more peaceful, and carried out within the context of constitutional authority. In contrast, he describes the typical recent coup as one that starts with a small conspiracy of leaders, frequently military officers, who are bitterly opposed to an existing reformist regime. As the reformist administration continues in office, resentment increases and more leaders from different groups join the opposition until, finally, the conspiracy reaches the point where a respectable leader or faction is enlisted to lend public support and prestige to the revolt.

Other scholars studying the anticolonial independence movements in Asia, Africa, and the Middle East have described similar processes at work. For example, when the charter that established the United Nations was drawn up in 1945, 50 nations signed it on June 26 of that year. By the end of 1950, 10 more nations had joined the roster of the organization, and by the end of 1960, 100 nations were members. By the early 1970s, the United

Nations included 135 nations, many of them newly established following wars of independence.

William Kornhauser [1969, pp. 404–442] studied revolutions that occurred from 1917 to 1966 in all European, Asian, Middle Eastern, and Latin American nations with populations of over 1 million. He defined a successful revolution as the overthrow or abrupt change of a national government by extrainstitutional means. In other words, when a government had been expelled from territory over which it had jurisdiction or when its rulers were removed, a successful revolution was considered to have taken place. Kornhauser found about 200 successful and 185 unsuccessful, although important, revolutions during the 50-year period—an average of one successful or unsuccessful revolution per nation every 8 years or one successful revolution per nation every 16 years. He discovered three periods of peak revolutionary activity: 1917–1921, 1930–1934, and 1945–1949 (the last being the greatest). These corresponded to periods of massive worldwide stress. Two world wars had eroded traditional authority, with military defeat often leading to a loss of confidence in existing leadership. In addition to the two wars, the period from 1930 to 1934 featured worldwide economic depression, a stress that many governments were incapable of handling.

Kornhauser suggests that revolutions have three different characteristics and outcomes:

1. *Transformation* of whole societies, including establishment of a new nation and modernization of social institutions. This involves extensive social, political, and cultural change and the creation of new institutions and new definitions of political legitimacy.
2. *Polarization* of social forces within the society, often leading to "internal war." Although the resulting conflict and violence may be illegitimate, the revolutionaries may be seen as legitimate because those in power are violating basic values and practices.
3. *Mobilization* of large numbers of people under the banner of a revolutionary ideology. A social movement arises for the purpose of redistributing power, instituting programs of development, or creating a new national identity.

These three characteristics may occur independently of one another. Radical transformation may take place without much mobilization (the Meiji revolution in Japan), and mobilization may occur without transformation (Peronism in Argentina). Furthermore, governments may be changed without polarization, mobilization, or transformation (the early palace revolts of Latin America). Using this approach, Kornhauser identified eight different types of revolutions that characterize the modern world. These are described in Table 11-3.

Such studies have led many scholars to conclude that contemporary governments are extremely vulnerable to crises and inherently unstable,

TABLE 11-3 Types and Examples of Revolutions by Presence (+) or Absence (−) of Transformation (T), Polarization (P), and Mobilization (M)

Types of Revolutions	Characteristics T	P	M	Definitions and/or Examples
1. Mass	+	+	+	From 1917 to 1966, 31 mass revolutions occurred, of which 13 were successful. Examples: Mexico succeeded without extreme totalitarianism; Russian and Chinese revolutions required totalitarian controls.
2. Imposed	+	−	+	Foreign states transform another society without polarization. Example: Changes brought about in Communist satellite regimes in Eastern Europe from outside (Soviet) authority.
3. Elite	+	+	−	Transformation of a society from above without mobilization. Example: Ataturk in Turkey. From 1917 to 1966, 19 elite revolutions occurred, of which 11 were at least partially successful.
4. Orderly	+	−	−	Example: Gandhi's strict adherence to nonviolence in India. However, conflict may be difficult to control. Even Gandhi was not able to prevent some polarization and violence from breaking out.
5. Nationalist	−	+	+	Goal is independence and identity, rather than change. From 1917 to 1966, there were 12 cases. Example: Algeria.
6. Co-opted	−	−	+	Incorporation of revolutionary leaders and members into existing government. Example: German revolution of 1918.
7. Communal	−	+	−	Attempt to obtain responses from government by turmoil and violence. From 1917 to 1966, about 12 percent of all revolutions against national governments were communal. These are usually defeated because of lack of mobilization. Example: Urban revolts against repressive regimes.
8. Palace	−	−	−	Replacing one elite with another without changing basic institutions. From 1917 to 1966, 70 percent of all revolutions were palace revolts; 60 percent of these occurred in Latin America, usually in the form of a military coup. Example: Greece in 1970.

Based upon William Kornhauser, "Revolutions," in *A Survey of Military Institutions, Volume 2,* Roger C. Little, Ed. (Chicago: The Inter-University Seminar on Armed Forces and Society, University of Chicago, 1969), pp. 411–418.

and they cite the inability of these governments to meet changing human needs as a major cause. Other scientists, however, suggest that such a conclusion is not necessarily valid. When one examines revolutionary activity and military coups, the tendency for them to be concentrated in certain regions of the world (for example, in Latin America in contrast to North America or Central Europe) becomes apparent. This implies that in some regions nations create a "tradition of couping," whereby leadership naturally changes hands through military or revolutionary activity. In contrast, historically stable constitutional democracies (such as the United States or Great Britain) are able to avoid these sudden transformations by incorporating changes into the institutional structure through *orderly processes of leadership transformation* (popular elections).

In addition, critics point out that a government's ability to remain legitimate *does not necessarily depend upon its effectiveness* in combating problems, meeting crises, or managing rapid change. Again, the United States and Britain are used as examples. Extreme economic crisis (inflation and unemployment), the loss of a war or colony (Vietnam or India), and continuing social and political turmoil (the black American and North Irish movements) have not resulted in the overthrow of either of these governments.

Finally, critics point out that even where dramatic changes in leadership do take place, *power is usually transferred nonviolently to new leaders.* From 1969 to 1975, there were more than 50 major changes at the highest levels of American government (including six Attorneys General, four Secretaries of Defense, three CIA Directors, three FBI Chiefs, four Directors of the Office of Management and the Budget, and the like). Some of these changes involved extraconstitutional processes (appointment, rather than election, of one President and two Vice-Presidents). Nevertheless, normal governmental structures and processes remained intact.

These types of observations lead critics to conclude that although some of the world's geographical states seem unstable, most—particularly, the largest and most highly developed—are extremely stable. Some scholars maintain that this basic stability may lead eventually to a new sense of world internationalism. The modern multinational corporation, a new form of economic state, is seen as playing an important part in this process.

Nation States and the Multinational Corporation

Christopher Tugendhat [1972, p. 1] has pointed out that modern governments must decide soon what to do about the great multinational companies that have grown up in the last 25 years:

> Their emergence is one of the most dramatic developments of the period, and of more than just economic and industrial significance. Their position profoundly affects the role of governments in the exercise of their responsibilities, and the relationships between states.

This influence was evident during the Arab–Israeli War, when the U.S.-based and partly U.S.-owned Aramco (Arabian American Oil Company) refused to sell fuel to the United States Sixth Fleet in the Mediterranean because U.S. foreign policy was pro-Israel and anti-Arab at that time. If an individual American had taken such an action, a trial for treason would have resulted. The threat of corporate power to the authority of traditional nation-states is obvious. At the same time, other scholars have argued that such actions by multinationals may be a force for world stability. Aramco's policy may have prevented serious military escalation in the area (confrontation between pro-Israel U.S. naval units and pro-Egyptian Soviet naval units).

Large-scale international economic organizations are not new. The ancient Mesopotamians had international trading companies, and there was extensive worldwide banking in the Middle Ages. During the reign of Queen Elizabeth I, the British East India Company ruled India, and, by the end of World War II, many of today's large corporations were operating throughout the world. However, the modern multinational, as a type of power institution, is different from these historical examples in several important ways.

As indicated in Table 11-4, many modern corporate states are *larger and more influential than the world's smaller or less developed nations.* Furthermore, multinationals *no longer operate only from the world's largest and most powerful nations.* In 1970, approximately one half of the multinationals were American based, but those with other countries of origin were growing rapidly (for example: the Swedish SKF, manufacturers of ball and roller bearings; Italian Olivetti, typewriters; German Bayer, drugs). In 1976, the U.S. partners in Aramco—Exxon, Mobil, Texaco, Standard of California—sold the remaining 40 percent of their shares to the Saudi Arabians. Multinationals thus play an increasing economic, political, and social role in all nations, large and small. In contrast, the

TABLE 11-4 Economic Comparison of Selected Multinational Corporate States (Total Sales) with Selected Nation-States (Gross National Product) in 1969

Nation or Multinational	Country Base of Multinational	Billions of Dollars[a]
Holland	. . .	28.2
Sweden	. . .	27.9
General Motors	United States	24.3
Switzerland	. . .	18.8
Standard Oil of New Jersey	United States	14.9
Ford Motor	United States	14.8
Austria	. . .	12.5
Royal Dutch/Shell	Holland–United States	9.7
Greece	. . .	8.4
IBM	United States	7.2
Unilever	United Kingdom–Holland	6.0
Ireland	. . .	3.4
Hoechst	Germany	2.3
Alcan Aluminium	Canada	1.2

[a]The growth rate of multinationals is faster than that of many nations; therefore, these figures are only approximate measures of size. In addition, national accounting records vary, and some multinational data are simply not available to the public.

Adapted from Christopher Tugendhat, *The Multinationals* (New York: Random House, 1972), pp. 1–4.

influence of the British East India Company was confined essentially to colonial and undeveloped areas of the world, and it was headquartered, at that time, in a nation that was the center of a world empire.

In addition, where the East India Company carried British imperial ideology into undeveloped regions, modern multinationals separate themselves from nationalism and *develop an independent ideology and identity* (Jay, 1967; Tugendhat, 1972). In Nazi Germany, the government required companies to swear that they were "pure German" and not under "foreign, Jewish, or Marxist" control. This can be contrasted to the unique philosophy expressed in a 1968 speech by Max Gloor, Director of the Swiss-based Nestlé Alimentana:

> We cannot be considered either as pure Swiss, or as pure multinational, i.e., belonging to the world at large, if such a thing does exist at all. We are probably something in between, a breed on our own. In one word, we have the particular Nestlé *citizenship* [Tugendhat, 1972, p. 4] [italics added for emphasis].

Furthermore, the East India Company's colonial branches possessed some independence from the home office and some degree of local control, whereas the modern multinational emphasizes *concentration of power at the center.* This has been partly the result of modern travel (jet airplanes), communication (the telex system), and computer storage and processing of information. In the days of sailing ships and mailed communication, decentralized authority, decision making, and information gathering was unavoidable and essential.

However, centralization of power also reflects the fact that the power of the modern multinational is partly organizational [Perrow, 1972]. Multinationals look like governments, having not only a President and several Executive Vice-Presidents (for finance, operations, production, and so on), but also Chief Administrative Officers in charge of special bureaus (legal, public relations, technical activities, personnel, stockholders' accounts, and so on). In addition, the organization chart contains political and administrative units that specialize in particular areas of the world (Latin American, Europe, the Far East, and so on), similar to regional managers in the U.S. Department of State.

The organizational power of the multinational is also reflected in the process of mergers, which may take place by agreement or by takeover. Figure 11-1 depicts how British Leyland Motor Corporation, manufacturers of every type of English automobile, grew from 10 independent companies in only 8 years. Mergers do more than enlarge a corporation's sales base; they are also a means of obtaining needed technological skills. In an age of increasing specialization, merger becomes an efficient means of increasing an organization's financial and technological assets. However, merger does not necessarily guarantee economic success. In 1975, British Leyland was nationalized because it was losing 1 billion dollars per year.

FIGURE 11-1 Mergers That Led to the Creation of British Leyland Motor Corporation

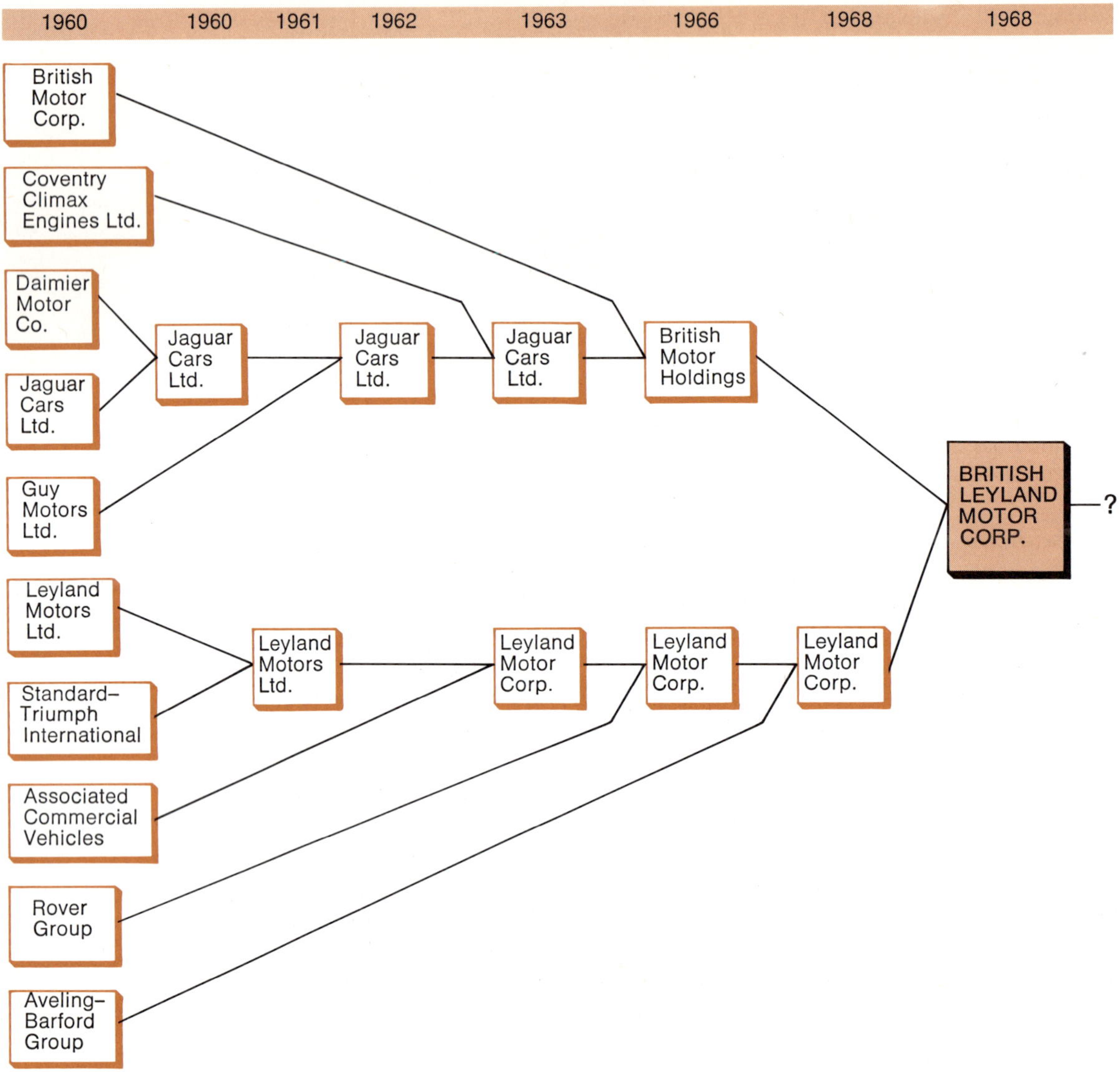

From Christopher Tugendhat, *The Multinationals* (New York: Random House, 1972), p. 59.

Richard Barnet and Ronald Muller [1974] suggest a final way in which the multinational state differs from earlier international companies: They argue that the power of the multinational, which they call a "global or planetary enterprise," derives from the *control of specific types of knowledge* about production, marketing, and finance capital. Table 11-5 lists some of the affiliates and subsidiaries of the multinational Standard Oil of California. This corporation accrues power, by means of these organizational alliances, by monopolizing knowledge about exploration, production, transportation, refining, and marketing of a variety of different products throughout the world.

In meeting the needs of society, therefore, multinationals try to monopolize certain types of specialized knowledge required to mass produce and

TABLE 11-5 Organizational and Functional Activities of Standard Oil of California and Some of Its Subsidiaries and Affiliates, 1975

Company[a]	Activities	Areas of Operations
Standard Oil Company of California (Parent company)	Exploration, producing, transportation, refining, and marketing of oil	Western U.S.
Standard Stations, Inc. (100%)	Service station operation	Western U.S.
Chandeleur Pipe Line Company (100%)	Gas transportation	Louisiana and Mississippi
Chevron Oil Company (100%)	Refining, exploration, and marketing of oil	Eastern, Central, and Southern U.S. and Canada
Chevron Shipping Company (100%)	Marine transportation management	U.S. and foreign
Vectra Corporation (100%)	Synthetic fibers	Eastern U.S.
AMAX Inc. (20%)	Minerals and metals	U.S. and foreign
Chevron Asphalte Limitée (100%)	Asphalt emulsions	Canada
Chevron Chemical Pan American Company (100%)	Agricultural and industrial chemicals	Mexico, Central and South America
Chevron Oil Latin America, Inc. (100%)	Marketing management	Central America and Puerto Rico
Arabian American Oil Company (see text reference, p. 463)	Exploration, producing, and refining	Saudi Arabia
Iran Chevron Oil Company (100%)	Ownership of 7 percent interest in Iranian oil operations	Iran
P. T. Caltex Pacific Indonesia (50%)	Exploration and producing	Indonesia
Chevron European Companies (100%)	Refining and marketing	Belgium, Denmark, Italy, Luxembourg, Switzerland, United Kingdom, Netherlands, and West Germany

[a]Percent of parent company interest appears in parentheses.

Based on *1975 Annual Report* of Standard Oil Company of California, San Francisco, California, pp. 42–43.

distribute cars, food, energy resources, drugs, clothing, housing, recreation, and the like. They form alliances with banks and manipulate money markets. They can also manipulate supply and demand. For example, some consumer advocates have charged that the U.S. energy crisis was manipulated by oil multinationals in order to create an artificial shortage, thereby forcing the U.S. government to permit price increases.

Barnet and Muller conclude that, as a consequence, geographic states, especially nations of the developing Third World, are relatively helpless. Multinationals maintain controls over patents and technology and often prohibit their use in needed areas. They create false wants rather than meeting actual needs (for example, encouraging malnourished peasants to drink Coca Cola) and manipulate information about profits and costs to obtain special favors from governments (tax incentives). Therefore, government controls are either irrelevant or ineffective. In short, Barnet and Muller claim that, since many governments do not have the necessary knowledge to formulate and administer effective economic policy, multinationals are more powerful than nation-states.

Other scholars accept the distinctions between multinationals and other power institutions, but they reject these conclusions. Supporters of multinationals argue that these new corporate states are the only way in which rapid and extensive development, requiring massive economic and technical resources, can be brought to needy areas of the world. We will consider criticism of this view at the end of this chapter. In addition, some scholars, as we have seen, maintain that multinationals are a force for world stability since old-fashioned international hostility (in the form of warfare) and governmental instability (in the form of couping) can be "bad for business." More radical scholars argue that the modern state is not all that puny and defenseless. States can force or encourage advantageous agreements [Bruyn, 1971, pp. 53–70]. They can also take over offending multinationals by force:

> The Canadian (once Czechoslovak) shoe firm Bata was expropriated in Tanzania after refusing to negotiate with the government; when a similar situation arose in Uganda, it had learned its lesson and negotiated a 60 percent share for the government. . . . There are also grounds for suggesting the hard-line approach of the Council of the Americas and ITT has worked against the interest of all American multinationals in Latin America [for example, Anaconda Copper in Chile and sugar companies in Cuba were expropriated]. [An attempt by Bechtel] to set up a fertilizer project in India [was aborted by the government because of] overambitious demands, attempts to push the Indian authorities too fast, and the company's association with the United States government at a bad time in United States–Indian relations . . . [Turner, 1973, p. 113].

Thus national governments do possess considerable power in their relations with corporations and with other states. One source of this power is the military, the topic of the next section of this chapter.

THE MILITARY

As in the case of national states, the military has expanded its functions in recent years. Not only does the modern military establishment continue to execute the four traditional roles listed below, but, as we shall soon see, it is sometimes employed by the state for nonmilitary nation-building activities. However, our examination of the military begins with a discussion of the four traditional roles performed by the military in all societies and in all periods of history:

1. *Defense:* Defend the society against external aggression once it is launched.
2. *Deterrence:* Possess sufficient power to deter other societies from launching aggressive actions.
3. *Offense:* Conduct offensive actions (a) during a defensive war or (b) for aggressive purposes to obtain needed resources from other societies.
4. *Maintaining Order:* Enforce civil law and order within a society.

As we will see, there is nothing particularly new about any of these military roles. Primitive tribes sometimes arm to deter would-be aggression or to defend the community. In the same manner, modern armies may maintain a nuclear missile force for deterrence or traditional ground forces for defending the homeland if attacked. However, the manner in which different societies prepare for and wage war determines which military roles will become important.

Changing Warfare and the Role of the Military

In a classic two-volume survey and analysis of war throughout human history, Quincy Wright [1942] identified three major types of warfare—primitive, historic, and modern. The primary function of *primitive warfare* was the maintenance of clan or tribal solidarity and order. By directing hostile and aggressive actions against a common enemy, potential in-group hostility and deviance was diverted into group harmony and commitment to the group's norms, values, and roles. For example, since strong taboos against in-group murder characterized most primitive societies, war became a justifiable outlet for personal aggression. Personal drives, such as sex and hunger, were frequently given free expression during primitive combat (the conquered people and their material goods were often taken as rightful booty).

Primitive warfare was often justified in terms of a group's natural rights to some territory and all its resources (game, crops, water, and so on). The enemy was generally perceived as less than human and, therefore, as undeserving of the same rights. Hans Speier [1952, pp. 223–229] characterizes this form of warfare as *absolutist.* An enemy is seen as absolutely different, completely evil, and totally threatening to the community as a whole.

Furthermore, the preparation for and the waging of war in primitive society was a community-wide activity. Although role distinctions such as "warrior" usually reflected individual abilities, all members—including women—participated in some fashion (making weapons, carrying supplies, and so on). In addition, primitive war was not a highly organized and specialized activity widely separated from other community activities. Traditional warfare reflected traditional behavioral patterns associated with hunting.

Thus, in its function as a means of promoting social stability and in its absolutist character, primitive warfare was a conservative force; consequently, it was relatively slow to change in form or in weaponry. This type of conflict characterized most societies until the beginning of the great civilizations and can still be found in undeveloped regions of the world today (for example, in certain areas of Borneo).

In contrast to primitive warfare, Wright suggests that *historic warfare* was completely different in function and character. This type of war predominated from the time of the Egyptian and Mesopotamian civilizations to about the 15th century. The primary function of historic war was to promote social change, and the result was the disintegration of many civilizations. The release of tightly controlled personal drives and frustrations during combat gave way to warfare that served the private interests and aims of ruling elites and cliques. War lost its communal character, as mercenary soldiers and colonial armies became commonplace (samurai warriors in medieval Japan, knights of medieval Europe, colonial armies of the British Empire).

Speier [1952, pp. 223–226] indicates that historic wars were highly *instrumental* (goal directed). The total defeat and subjugation of an enemy, rather than merely random looting or annihilation, became the primary goal. Instrumental wars were waged to obtain valuable enemy resources such as the following: political resources (strategic frontiers and important sea lanes); economic resources (markets and natural resources); religious resources (populations with a potential for conversion). Historic warfare provided the necessary foundation from which modern warfare emerged.

Wright indentifies four early periods in the development of *modern warfare.* From about 1500 to 1650, religious wars were waged because people considered military force and politics (power) an accepted instrument of religion (the Church). From 1650 to 1800, politics became secularized, and war was waged for reasons of state or for political principles. From 1800 to World War I, political purposes were joined by economic ones (imperial expansion wars against Indian tribes in the United States). Finally, from 1914 to the 1940s, the two world wars symbolized a merging of religious, political, and economic purposes, and the beginning of war waged in the name of international values and beliefs.

From the time of the Renaissance, the world has been influenced by the philosophies of humanism, liberalism, pragmatism, and relativism.

Although originally developed as instruments of peace and progress, these philosophies provided belligerents with ideological justifications for expanding their conflicts. War began to be waged by all combatants to "make the world safe for democracy," "save the free world," "bring about a decent socialist society," "establish a superior and more fulfilling 1000-year Riech," and the like. Pragmatists argued that warfare was an inescapable aspect of contemporary life, and relativists argued that wars sometimes perform important social functions. Once again, Speier [1952, p. 224] suggests that warfare took on an absolutist character as *ideological* wars created a crusading spirit in belligerents. This characteristic transformed wars from isolated battles between special states with small armies into conflicts involving the entire world and mass armies. As modern warfare expanded and became international in scope, nations began expanding both the size and the functions of their military establishments.

The Modern State and Expanding Military Functions

According to Morris Janowitz [1957, pp. 9–18], modern international conflict and competition is characterized by (1) the legitimation of warfare in terms of national interest; (2) the appearance of a specialized occupation—the profession of soldiering; and (3) the replacement of a war–peace perspective with a hot- versus cold-war perspective in international relations. As a consequence, the military has become a *permanent* and much *expanded* social institution. In a hot- versus cold-war world, when enemy attack can come within seconds as a result of pushing buttons, modern nations no longer disband and then remobilize their military forces. Instead, they feel they must maintain a large, permanent, technologically up-to-date military establishment capable of performing simultaneously *all* the traditional roles during periods of both peace and war.

In addition to these traditional and purely military functions, many modern states have increasingly used military institutions for more civilianlike roles. States can use the military as a *mark of sovereignty* when conducting ceremonies aimed at strengthening nationalistic feeling or popularizing specific rulers. The military can also be used in *nation-building* roles to construct roads, operate factories, staff government agencies, run schools, or dispense medical treatment. Within the military, training for civil affairs or civic action roles prepares military personnel to engage in a variety of nation-building activities. Some of these are summarized in Table 11-6.

A number of scholars [Daalder, 1962; Janowitz, 1960; Johnson, 1962; Moskos, 1970] have pointed out that the military often has a unique potential for performing these kinds of civilian roles. In almost every society, the military, especially the army, is *labor-intensive* in technology and

Table 11-6 Types and Examples of Nation-Building Roles for the U.S. Military

Civil Affairs and Civic Action Roles	Types of Activities	Examples
1. Provide services for civilian populations	Supply water, food, transportation, medicine, communication systems, and so on	Use of Green Beret units in Vietnam to assist in improving village life
2. Ameliorate conditions under which civilian populations (one's own or others) live	Projects may include programs similar to the Peace Corps, VISTA, Project HOPE, CARE, the Agency for International Development, the Ford Foundation, the World Bank, social action by religious groups (the American Friends Service Committee), and so on	U.S. Army operation of the Civilian Conservation Corps in the 1930s; U.S. Army Corps of Engineers flood control studies and projects
3. Prevent civilian interference with military operations	Relocate and rehouse civilian populations	Relocation of Japanese Americans from the West Coast during World War II; assistance to South Vietnamese forces in relocating villagers; in both cases, operation and maintenance of "camps" or "relocation centers"
4. Provide government functions and services	Staff and operate government and political agencies and bureaus	U.S. military occupation government in Japan at the end of World War II; participation in Allied government of Germany
5. Provide for civil defense	Draft plans, conduct tests, and maintain safe areas	In the 1950s, construction and maintenance of shelters and planning for mass evacuation of urban centers, in the event of nuclear war
6. Engage in psychological operations	Disseminate propaganda favorable to own forces and unfavorable to enemy forces	Program (including actions and leaflets) to "win the minds and hearts of the people" during the Vietnam War

Source: Adapted from Harry L. Coles and Albert K. Weinberg, *Civil Affairs: Soldiers Become Governors,* Volume 6 of "The United States Army in World War II: Special Studies" (Washington, D.C.: U.S. Government Printing Office, 1964); Alfred Hausrath, "Civil Affairs and Military Government," in Roger W. Little, Ed., *A Survey of Military Institutions, Volume 2* (Chicago: Inter-University Seminar on Armed Forces and Society, University of Chicago, 1969), pp. 250–287; Peter B. Riddleberger, *Military Roles in Developing Countries: An Inventory of Past Research and Analysis* (Washington, D.C.: Special Operations Research Office, American University, 1965).

personnel; that is, it constitutes a ready reservoir of the technical and human resources necessary to build roads, operate schools, run medical clinics, and so on. In some less developed nations, the military may represent the only institution capable of providing for such basic social needs since the other institutions (family, church, corporation, and so on) are often unskilled or weak. At the same time, the *authoritarian* and highly *bureaucratized* character of many military forces enables them to mobilize these resources easily. Emphasis upon esprit de corps, internal cohesion, and unified command guarantee rapid and effective response to problems.

In less developed nations, military elites often constitute the most qualified management pool for handling complex diplomatic and government duties. In the most developed nations, military elites, within a service such as the Air Force, may develop a relative monopoly over the use of certain sophisticated forms of electronic and technical information. Once out of the service, both military elites and rank-and-file personnel may contribute to what has been called *the multiplier effect,* where elites fill needed positions of civilian leadership and ex-soldiers return to local communities where they become teachers and innovators.

Finally, the military commitment to *nationalistic symbols* and ritual can be utilized in times of general disruption to create a sense of social solidarity and continuity. For example, the Japanese people generally applauded the ceremonies accompanying General Douglas MacArthur's military rule after World War II, since those ceremonies acted as an effective substitute for the former regal rule of the Emperor.

These are the ways, then, in which the military can support the state by assuming civilianlike roles. However, some scholars [Janowitz, 1964] have indicated that, despite the military's technical ability to execute these nonmilitary roles, the end result of their deployment to civilian activities can be undesirable. Military culture, which involves *overt violence, repression of nonconformity, and authoritarian ideology,* can inhibit or even discourage civilian support for military-run programs. Civilian elites are used to relying upon the power of persuasion, and citizens are accustomed to individual freedom. This basic incompatibility between civilian and military cultures is reflected in the demand of many citizens that the military be removed from civilian affairs (dam building) and "stick to the kill biz."

The apparent success of military organizations in training raw recruits to perform difficult and unusual tasks often leads military leaders to overestimate the extent to which civilian populations can be quickly and effectively mobilized by force or coercion to solve social problems. When frustrated in the performance of their roles, military leaders often blame uncooperative civilians rather than themselves and may, as a result, resort to force or political overthrow of state authority [Morgan, 1971]. This can lead to political instability and a loss of legitimacy for both the state and the military.

11-2 Competing Roles of the Military

The major role of the military is to maintain a monopoly of the means of violence in order to provide the national state with the power to use force if necessary. In addition, the military can be used to perform a number of nonaggressive nation-building roles. These competing functions present special problems for both the national state and the military.

United Press International

Defense or deterrence. The military is expected to maintain sufficient force to defend a country against aggression or to deter other countries from launching aggressive actions. However, an unending arms race can become a threat to peace and it can weaken the military's ability to prepare for traditional offensive warfare.

United Press International

Offense. The military is expected to be able to conduct offensive actions either during a defensive war or for purposes of obtaining needed resources from other societies. However, a strong offensive capability may encourage the state to engage in continual aggression against other societies.

Courtesy of the *Boston* Globe

Maintain civil order. The military is often used to enforce civil law and order within a society. However, this gives the state the ability to squash legitimate civil dissent, and the military's force can be turned against the state itself.

Mark of sovereignty. The military is used by civilian leaders to lend authority and legitimacy to their rule. However, this use erodes the distinction between civilian and military roles and may encourage civilian leaders to act militaristically and military leaders to become involved in civilian politics.

United Press International

Civil affairs or civic action. The military is often used to operate welfare and public service programs, such as dispensing medical services in underdeveloped regions or after disasters. However, this function detracts from the military's ability to concentrate upon its primary role (fighting) and it also undermines the authority of legitimate civilian institutions (civilian health agencies).

U.S. Marine Corps Photo

Furthermore, military organization and ideology may lead to *over-bureaucratization,* reliance upon personal and organization *secrecy,* and *ethnocentric commitment* to one's special unit or leader. These qualities can interfere with both the execution and the assessment of civilian programs. For example, U.S. civilian advisers in South Vietnam found that the results of many civilian aid programs operated by the U.S. military were either consciously or unconsciously distorted. Military commanders operated these programs far from the source of state control and transmitted information concerning results back to civilian leaders through military channels. In addition, since military leaders are military *professionals,* they often judge civilian activities ultimately in terms of what is good for the military effort. The common military complaint—"You can't fight a war with one hand tied behind your back by civilian leaders"—expresses this view. Every activity must contribute to the "winning of the war," even if the acts are politically undesirable.

In short, changing and expanding military roles, in both small and large nations, can lead to either supportive or competitive relationships between the state and the military. Judging the impact of this increased interaction between state and military is not easy. Some scholars argue that both supportive and competitive relationships are bad since they make civilian control of the military difficult. Other social scientists argue that they are good since they guarantee civilian involvement and, therefore, civilian control. The next section considers these conflicting views.

Can Civilian States Control the Military?

Janowitz [1957, pp. 9–18] identifies four types of relationships between political and military elites—aristocratic, democratic, totalitarian, and garrison state. Each involves different forms of civilian control. The *aristocratic model,* which characterized Western nations before industrialization, involves the integration of civilian and military leaders on the basis of a common social background. For example, important families give one son to the military, one to the church, and one to politics. The fact that top level military appointments are made on the basis of civilian pedigree guarantees civilian dominance. Also, the fact that military leadership within this model requires little specialization means that civilian authority can supply most of the military leadership that is needed. At the same time, military leaders follow orders and fight because they feel that *they* are really issuing the orders [Janowitz, 1957, p. 10]. Janowitz calls this *subjective control* by civilian society.

In contrast, civilian and military elites are sharply differentiated in societies based upon the *democratic model,* typical of Western nations in the first half of the 20th century. Here the military relies upon a small and highly specialized professional leadership, which functions under a set of formal bureaucratized rules and regulations. Military personnel fight because fighting is their profession, and they are socialized to believe that political involvement is incompatible with the professional role. Janowitz calls this *objective control* by civilian society. Military leaders follow the orders of civilian leaders, since their primary commitment is to their career *within* the military.

Aristocratic traditions can lead to the development of a totalitarian model, as well as a democratic model. The *totalitarian model* is based upon a mixture of subjective and objective controls, as in the case of the Soviet Union. A revolutionary political elite utilizes a number of different techniques to guarantee civilian dominance. These can include (1) a secret police who observe military personnel; (2) infiltration by state party members into the military organization (particularly the hierarchy); (3) manipulation of important symbols (rewards and honors); and (4) direction of officer selection and training. In totalitarian societies, the military fights and follows civilian orders because there are no other alternatives.

Both totalitarian and democratic models may lead to the final form of state–military relationship [Lowry, 1970, pp. 3–16]. The *garrison-state model* [Lasswell, 1941, pp. 455–468] may develop when there is a weakening of civilian dominance. Status and authority distinctions between the civil and military sectors of society become blurred. Civilian leaders issue military orders, and military leaders make civilian decisions. Obligatory military service for all or most of the citizenry further blurs the differences between the civilian and military ways of life. Professional and career commitments give way to fighting for the sake of national glory or duty. The military becomes a permanent institution, intimately related and similar to all aspects of social, economic, and political life, rather than a special-purpose organization providing for defense or deterrence. Both democratic and totalitarian societies in the contemporary world (China, Israel, United States, the Soviet Union, and so on) face the potential threat of garrison-state military systems, particularly as war (hot or cold) becomes a more natural and inescapable aspect of everyday life.

In his farewell radio and television address to the American people on 17 January 1961, President Eisenhower warned about the dangers of a "military–industrial complex." Although Eisenhower was essentially concerned about the latent role the military might be playing in a free-enterprise economy, this concept referred to all of the problems associated with a garrison state. The speech stimulated much social scientific research [Sarkesian, 1972] and popular debate concerning a number of questions. Was the modern military playing too great a role in basically civilian affairs? If so, what accounted for this development? What were the consequences for both the military and for civilian society? In the last several years, Charles Moskos has focused upon these kinds of issues, attempting to provide answers to the questions raised. The following study is based upon his extensive research on the U.S. military.

▶STUDY 11

The Changing U.S. Military: Civil, Traditional, or Plural? [1970 and 1973][1]

Problem

Philosophical and political views of the American armed forces have always fluctuated between two extremes. Some believe the military should reflect dominant civilian values and be entirely dependent upon the orders of civilian decision makers. Others view the military as essentially different from civilian society and believe the military should exert an independent influence on the state. However, the question of the appropriate relationship between the military and the state is not necessarily related to one's political philosophy. Supporters of the military have argued both for and against greater relationships between military and civilian societies. Likewise, the harshest critics of the armed forces have claimed that the military is either too isolated from or too integrated with civil society.

Moskos raised a number of questions about these different views of the military–state relationship in the United States: *What has happened to the U.S. military; has it become more dependent upon or more independent of civilian society? What are the implications for continued civilian control? Is an independent or an involved military establishment more desirable?*

Hypotheses and Study Design

Moskos hypothesized that, in the period from World War II to the end of the Vietnam War, *the United States military passed through several different periods of civilian–military relationships which partly explains the existence of conflicting political views of the military.* For example, during World War II, the American military was held in high esteem in a popularly supported war. But, in the wake of the Korean War, unfavorable views of the American serviceman were propagated by right-wing spokesmen, who charged collaboration with the enemy, surrender under fire, and the like. Liberal commentators, however, generally defended the qualities of the American armed forces. Finally, during the war in Southeast Asia, the military was generally defended by political conservatives and severely attacked by liberal observers.

Therefore, shifting political views on the part of both liberals and conservatives actually reflect changes in the relationships between the military and the state. The goal of Moskos' research, then, was to identify the form and nature of these changing relationships. In addition, he stated that *a meaningful political position regarding the state–military relationship would have to be based upon*

[1]Adapted and abridged from Charles C. Moskos, Jr., *The American Enlisted Man: The Rank and File in Today's Military* (New York: Russell Sage and Basic Books, 1970); "The Emergent Military: Civil, Traditional, or Plural?" *Pacific Sociological Review, 16* (April 1973), pp. 255–280, and in *National Security and American Society: Theory, Process, and Policy,* Frank N. Trager and Philip S. Kronenberg, Ed. (Lawrence: University of Kansas, 1973); and "The Military," *Annual Review of Sociology* (Palo Alto, Calif.: Annual Reviews, 1976).

a sociological understanding of their relationship, not just an ideological reaction to the rightness or wrongness of a war.

The study design involved *the construction of developmental models,* which reflected the history, the current trends, and the probable future direction of civilian–military relationships. Moskos' approach reflects a classic sociological technique. As we have seen throughout this textbook, other scholars have frequently employed developmental models (folk–feudal–urban society, charismatic–traditional–bureaucratic authority, and so on).

Methods of Data Collection

In order to construct developmental models, Moskos employed a variety of methods for data collection. He relied upon *historical records and studies* to describe earlier forms of civilian–military relationships. Furthermore, Moskos employed information and experiences gained from *personal observation and participation* in the U.S. military to generate insights into the contemporary changes taking place. In the late 1950s, he served as an enlisted man in the U.S. Army; in 1965, he made field trips to Germany, Korea, and Vietnam; and, from 1966 to 1967, he did *field research* in the Dominican Republic, Germany, and Vietnam. During his field research, he lived with the men of the 173rd Airborne Brigade, 82nd Airborne Division, and First Infantry Division.

Findings and Interpretations

Historical analysis disclosed that from World War II to the present the American military has passed through several distinctive phases. Prior to World War II, the U.S. military constituted less than 1 percent of the male labor force and consisted exclusively of volunteers, most of whom were career soldiers. Enlisted personnel were almost entirely drawn from Southern, Protestant, middle-class origins. Within the military, manual labor or combat roles predominated. Socially and culturally, the military *was separated from civilian society* and was characterized by tradition, ceremony, and hierarchy.

World War II brought mass mobilization, and by 1945 there were close to 12,000,000 persons in uniform. *Although the military was now more representative of American society, its internal organization still contrasted sharply with civilian roles, relationships, and norms.* Following World War II, there was a 16-month period during which there was no conscription at all, but, by the time of the Korean War in 1950, the draft had already been reinstituted. The Korean War was a period of partial mobilization with slightly over 3,600,000 personnel serving at the peak of hostilities. *Organizationally and culturally, the armed forces closely resembled those of World War II.*

The Cold War military took shape after Korea, averaging around 2,500,000 personnel and again relying upon the pressures of a draft for recruitment. During the 1950s and 1960s, in contrast to the earlier periods, technical specialization became important throughout the military. *The proportion of personnel assigned to combat or service duties declined, and the proportion assigned to electronic and technical specialties increased.* These trends were most obvious in the Air Force, less so in the Navy, and least evident in the Army and Marine Corps. During this time, *the military also became embroiled in political controversy* about the nature of military leadership and the institutional role of the military. The military was charged with being soft on Communism in both the

Army–McCarthy hearings of 1954 and the 1962 hearings that followed Major General Edwin Walker's relief from command for sponsoring troop "indoctrination" programs with an extremely conservative content. At the same time, intellectuals on the left began to attack the military for its role in a developing military–industrial–political complex.

Finally, the Vietnam War ushered in another phase in civilian–military relationships. Troop strength increased, reaching a high of 3,500,000 in 1970. The role of the Air Force and Navy declined, as the Army and Marine Corps bore the brunt of the conflict in Indochina. In 1966, entrance standards were lowered to allow the induction of persons previously disqualified because of low scores on intelligence tests. This led to an overrepresentation—particularly in combat roles—of blacks and persons from lower-class backgrounds. In 1968, the personnel pool was enlarged again by terminating draft deferments for recent college graduates, largely middle-class whites. The membership of the armed forces *once again bore some resemblance to the social composition of the larger society.*

However, with the end of the Vietnam War, the cessation of the draft, and the introduction of the all-volunteer armed forces, other changes began to occur. Some studies show that enlisted personnel are becoming increasingly black and poor, and that a volunteer service in peacetime attracts primarily *school dropouts from older impoverished urban areas.* At the same time, other studies indicate that a growing number of officers are coming from the service academies and have, once again, Southern, rural, and military backgrounds. Not only is the military becoming less like civilian society, but within the military there is a growing discontinuity between the social and cultural characteristics of officers and enlisted personnel.

From this analysis, Moskos constructed two developmental models, summarized in Table 11-7. Those who study the U.S. military, focusing on the period between the Korean and Vietnam Wars, maintain that military and civilian forms of social organization are *converging* and becoming more similar. This is partly a result of more sophisticated weapons systems and the need for technical proficiency. In addition, leadership positions require greater managerial and bureaucratic decision-making skills.

The convergent model also sees military norms and values as shifting away from traditional military authoritarianism toward a more democratic persuasive leadership. For example, the introduction of VOLAR (the volunteer Army) in 1969 brought reforms in hair styles, abolition of reveille, fewer personal inspections, and more privacy in barracks on a growing number of Army posts. In the early 1970s, Chief of Naval Operations Admiral Zumwalt issued "Z-grams" alerting commissioned and petty officers to concern themselves with the personal problems and needs of sailors. The Air Force issued a new regulation in 1971 specifying broader standards for political protest. Human relations councils of black and white service personnel were formed in all branches of the armed forces to cope with racial strife.

In contrast to this model, those who focus on the U.S. military during World War II and during the period from the end of the Vietnam War to the present maintain that military and civilian culture and forms of social organization are becoming more *divergent* and dissimilar. Ideologically—the military is hostile to a civilian society that, they feel, has been unfairly critical of the military. Socially, the military is becoming more isolated as both officers and enlisted personnel become less

TABLE 11-7 Convergent Versus Divergent Models of the United States Military

	Convergent Model	Divergent Model
General Trend	Toward a civilianized military, increasingly a part of and similar to the larger society (that is, management skills of officers and technical skills of enlisted men are easily transferred to civilian jobs)	Toward a traditional military, increasingly separate and distinct from larger society (that is, isolated military communities have own PX and commissary, medical care, quarters for married noncoms, legal and real estate advice, and so on)
Periods of Greatest Change	Between the Korean and Vietnam Wars	From the end of the Vietnam War to the present
Primary Reason for Change	Development of technologically sophisticated weapons systems requiring new knowledge and skills	Feeling that the military was made a scapegoat for Vietnam; disillusionment with mass media and intellectuals who are seen as undermining the honor of military service and fostering dissent within the ranks
Basis of Authority	Managerial philosophy stressing persuasion and individual initiative (human relations councils of black and white enlisted personnel; councils of junior officers and enlisted personnel); relaxation of traditional military discipline and ritual (length of hair, political activity); more democratic and responsive	Return to traditional "domination" and obedience to authority ("Duty, God, and Country"); conventional, conservative, and authoritarian
Organizational and Command Structure	More rational and bureaucratic (like civilian bureaucracies); increase in number of nonacademy graduates at highest levels	More castelike distinction between officers and enlisted personnel ("officers and their ladies" versus "enlisted men and their women"); increasing monopolization of military elite positions by academy graduates

	Convergent Model	Divergent Model
Membership:		
Officers	Broader social origins to include more representative sample of the country's regional and religious groups	Narrowing social base; more new officers coming from rural backgrounds, more cadets at academies coming from military families
Enlisted	More representative of larger population in racial and social class origins; increasing level of skills	All-volunteer service has decreasing representation of upper and middle classes; growing discrepancy between educational level of officers and enlisted
Roles and Functions	More civilianlike (officers—managerial, personnel relations, international relations; enlisted—technical and white-collar jobs)	Automation of technical jobs and use of civilians for support roles leading to increase in traditional combat roles

Source: Adapted from Charles C. Moskos, Jr., "The Emergent Military: Civil, Traditional, or Plural?" *Pacific Sociological Review, 16* (April 1973), pp. 267–275.

representative of the larger population. The downgrading of the National Guard, reserve units, and ROTC programs accelerates this divergence and indicates the disappearance of the "citizen-soldier" concept.

Symbolic of this trend is the increasing isolation of military family life. On-post privileges (PXs, commissaries, housing for families, free medical care) have been expanded, and assistance activities have been introduced to provide more services for military families (real estate advice, family counseling, baby-sitting, employment for wives, loans for household furnishings, and so on). As Moskos puts it, where the pre-World War II military was a total institution for bachelors, the post-Vietnam military is a total institution for the entire military family.

What are the implications of these two developmental models of civilian–military relationships? One model sees the emergent military as more *civil;* the other, as more *traditional.* Some view the civil military as a threat to state control, since it can lead to a garrison state, while others feel that its democratic trends and interaction with civilian society ensure civilian control. Likewise, some critics of the military see the traditional military establishment as a threat, envisaging a society of the future where a separate and uninvolved military wages private uncontrollable wars or becomes so disenchanted with the civilian state that it engages in couping. However, supporters of the traditional military maintain that a separate force is easier to monitor and to control and that it will have the necessary esprit de corps and commitment fo fight effectively when called upon to do so by the civilian state.

Conclusions and Implications

How, then, do we resolve the dilemma of which model is more appropriate and desirable? Moskos responds to this problem by proposing that the emergent U.S. military is probably *both convergent and divergent.* Furthermore, he argues that a mix of the two models would provide for more control of the military by the civilian state. In short, he concludes by constructing a third developmental model—the *plural military.*

The plural model is not merely a random mixing of opposing trends; rather it is a compartmentalization of these trends. In other words, the future military will probably converge toward civilian society in some areas while diverging from it in other areas. For example, by reason of their different roles and functions, the Air Force will move toward civilianization, while the Marine Corps will continue to uphold traditional procedures and regimentation of personnel. In short, combat forces, labor-intensive support units, and some elements of senior command will most likely follow the divergent model. In contrast, the convergent model will most likely predominate where military roles deal with clerical administration, education, medical care, logistics, transportation, construction, and other technical tasks.

Several different forms of state–military relationships could develop from this combined trend. "Two militaries" might emerge, each organized for entirely different purposes. The *civil military* might encompass a host of nonmilitary nation-building activities (job training, restoring ecologically devastated resources, providing health care, and so on), while the *traditional military* prepares for and wages military actions. Another alternative can presently be found in the Canadian military. The unification of the Canadian Armed Forces has resulted in the complete separation of support and administrative functions from the combat arms (which are now referred to as "land, sea, and air elements" in Canadian nomenclature).

Moskos concludes that neither the convergent or divergent models alone are appropriate, since each contain disadvantages for both the military and the civilian state. It is the plural model, with its compartmentalized segements within the military, that seems to offer the best promise for the future. This model could provide an armed force with organizational effectiveness to wage war, if required, and yet be a part of civilian society under the control of the state.

In this study, the special role of technology has become evident. This is particularly true in the case of the convergent model of state–military relationships. According to this model, the development of more sophisticated weapon systems led to major changes in the social and cultural life of the military and to changing relationships between the state and the military. The last section of this chapter, then, discusses *technology* as a third form of power institution, one that has a profound impact on other institutions.

TECHNOLOGY

Elements of technology have played an important part in the following discussions in this textbook:

In Chapter 1, the scientific method.

In Chapter 4, the material aspects of culture.

In Chapter 7, bureaucratic forms of organization for work.

In Chapter 8, types of human communities and industrialized agriculture.

In Chapter 9, changes in the medical profession.

Furthermore, in this chapter, we have already seen the importance of the multinational corporation as a power institution that monopolizes technological knowledge. In the discussion of change in Chapter 13, we will examine the role of both material and social inventions.

All of these references indicate that technology can be seen as much more than just physical objects or machines. We begin this last section by discussing the characteristics of technology as a human institution. In particular, we analyze the power of technology in relationship to the state and the military. This power has led to a continuing debate over whether modern technology is the servant or master of human society. Finally, we conclude the chapter by pointing to studies that suggest ways in which technology might be controlled.

Technology as a Power Institution

When talking about technology, most people think of the *material aspects of culture* that humans create to cope with their physical environment. Used in this way, the concept of technology refers to tools and machines—shovels, hammers, engines, automobiles, nuclear missiles, printing presses, television, and the like. Certainly these are important parts of human life, but technology, as an institution, includes much more.

In Chapter 9, we depicted the circle diagram used by Merrill and Eldredge to show the relationship between seven basic types of social institutions. One of these types was "knowledge and technics." We are using the concept of technology in that sense—as *a clustering of roles, relationships, types of groups, and norms and values, which taken together constitute and stimulate the knowledge and techniques used by humans to meet their basic needs.* For example, Kranzberg and Pursell [1967, pp. 3–11] point out that certain social roles and role relationships are an important part of technology. As we indicate in Chapter 13, the inventor can be viewed as more important than the invention, since without the inventor, there would be no invention. Therefore, all societies provide for formal and informal roles that encourage innovation (scientist, engineer, magician, innovative deviant, technocrat, and so on). These roles are frequently taught and sustained within larger social groupings or organizations (colleges and universities, think tanks, multinational corporations).

In addition, technology consists of nonmaterial culture—that is, important norms, values, and ideas that can encourage the development of

11-3 Is the American Military Divergent or Convergent?

Some scholars argue that the modern U.S. military establishment is **divergent**—that it differs in culture (uniforms, symbols, values) and social organization (authoritarian structure) from civilian society. Other scholars argue that it is **convergent** and increasingly resembles the democratic culture and organization of civilian society. Still other scholars argue that the U.S. military is both divergent and convergent and that both trends have advantages and disadvantages.

U.S. Army Photograph

In 1943, General Dwight D. Eisenhower was named Supreme Commander of the Allied Expeditionary Force in Europe, and, on June 6th, he led the Allied invasion of Europe. In 1944, Eisenhower was promoted to General of the Army, and, in 1945, he became Army Chief of Staff. During his career, Eisenhower was the exponent of a divergent military. He argued unsuccessfully for a slow rate of military discharge after World War II and for some system of universal military service to guard against future surprise attacks by enemies. When he retired from active duty in 1948, Eisenhower turned down attempts by both the Republican and Democratic parties to draft him for the presidential nomination. He maintained that "lifelong professional soldiers" should not enter civilian politics. Some observers felt that this kind of separatism deprived civilian society of available talent and led to an independent and hard-to-control military elite.

D. C. Heath Files

In 1952, Eisenhower gave in to increasing pressure and campaigned for the presidency as a Republican, retiring from the Army without pay or benefits. After he won the election from Adlai Stevenson, some scholars thought the country might be endangered since a simple change of outward symbols (uniform, medals, and so on) did not alter Eisenhower's lifelong commitment to military values and goals. In 1954, Eisenhower urged Congress to pass a series of internal security laws which outlawed the Communist party, provided the death penalty for spying in peacetime, and initiated widespread investigation of alleged subversive infiltration in government. But, retiring in 1961, he was the first major leader to warn the American people of some of the dangers of the military–industrial complex. As president, he was also reluctant to use U.S. military force in foreign policy.

tools and techniques to meet human needs. The perspectives and the methodology of science offer the most obvious example in contemporary society. However, as Kranzberg and Pursell [1967, p. 5] point out:

> To limit the definition of technology to those things which characterize the technology of our own time, such as machinery and [scientists], would be to do violence to all that went before. Indeed, a good case can even be made for considering magic as a technology, for with it primitive man attempted to control or at least influence his environment— . . . [the] goal of all technology. If we now feel that our ancestors used their magic without *successful* technology. The past abounds with failures [and so does the present]. . . .

Technology, then, refers to the way in which humans collectively engage in organized work (manipulate their natural and created environments) in order to satisfy their basic wants and needs. As a consequence, the purpose of technology is to understand and subsequently to control the environment. Institutions of technology, therefore, need to use power in two ways: (1) Power is necessary to stimulate the collective action needed to create the required tools, social organizations, or ideas; (2) power is also needed when technology is used to alter or control the environment. Technological institutions, therefore, frequently support or conflict with other power institutions.

For example, societies must encourage some people to become scientists or to become witch doctors by manipulating important status symbols (money, honor, prestige, or power). Societies must also influence others to support these technological roles by means of federal funding through taxation or through gifts of food and other services. Special group contexts must be provided that will maximize individual freedom to think and do creative, and sometimes deviant, things. (See the discussion of the problems of "free" professionals in bureaucratic organizations in Study 9.) Therefore, the moden state often levies, with public approval, substantial taxes to support public colleges and universities. However, at other times, the state or citizens may disapprove of innovative and deviant acts, and universities find themselves in conflict with other institutions. This was especially true in the United States in the late 1960s, when some college students and faculty were protesting the Vietnam War.

Similarly, when new tools or ideas are created, their application usually must await the support of other economic or political power institutions. For example, if the state had not provided public highways and traffic control procedures when the automobile was invented, this innovation would have remained a "plaything of the rich."

In the case of some innovations, attempts at application may result in social conflict. With the invention of the nuclear-powered submarine, Admiral Hyman Rickover recommended that traditional U.S. naval vessels be replaced by this new weapons system. He argued that nuclear weapons had made battleships, heavy cruisers, and possibly even aircraft carriers easy targets in future naval warfare. Only the far-ranging and submerged submarine, armed with nuclear weapons, was safe from detection and quick destruction. At that time in the early 1950s, many senior naval commanders resisted, not because they necessarily disagreed with Rickover's assessment of the changing nature of naval warfare, but because they did not want to lose their traditional ships. Standing on the deck of a battleship engaged in a close-quarters bombardment with an enemy ship was a "heroic command." To be stuffed in a small submarine many fathoms below the sea's surface was not so heroic. Rickover finally persuaded the U.S. Congress to support the development of a nuclear submarine fleet and, in the process, made many enemies in the traditional Navy hierarchy.

Technology: Servant or Master?

The incredible growth and development of modern technology in all its forms (new ideas, inventions, forms of social organization, and so on) has led to an increasingly spirited debate between those who consider technology the servant of humans and those who consider technology the master. This debate provides a convenient vehicle for quickly reviewing the multiple characteristics and functions of modern technology.

Those who *oppose* further unrestrained technological development maintain that it has become too *big,* too *complicated,* often *uncontrollable,* frequently *worthless,* and highly *susceptible to misuse* for personal, rather than public, benefit. These arguments and the opposing views are summarized in Table 11-8. For example, many persons believe that both strip mining and nuclear weapons technologies have outgrown the original goals they were designed to serve and, consequently, their continued use can only be counterproductive to human society. Related to this argument is the view that much modern technology is so complicated that people cannot understand or control it.

The San Francisco–Oakland Bay Area Rapid Transit System (BART) is an example frequently used by these critics [Lindsey, 1975, pp. 17 ff]. This 71-mile rapid transit system was opened in 1972 to provide residents of San Francisco, Oakland, and Berkeley with an attractive alternative to the family automobile. Both underground and surface stations are high-ceilinged buildings with murals and large plazas, and the trains are comfortable and quiet. The system is totally automated, the speed of each train, the opening and closing of doors, the purchase of tickets all being handled by electronic and mechanical equipment.

BART was *supposed* to be the "aerospace" industry's contribution to resolving pollution, urban overcrowding, migration of city residents to the suburbs, wasteful consumption of energy, and poverty. But by the time BART was opened, it was already three years behind schedule and its cost had doubled because of inflation. Because the system was so electronically complex, it was continuously plagued by equipment breakdowns. Management was forced to put an attendant at each station to inform the station behind that the train had passed and it was now safe to send another train through. In an average day, only half of the 450 cars can be used at any one time because the rest are in the repair shop.

Critics maintain that blind faith in the aerospace industry's ability to build perfect equipment led planners to overlook the need for spurs for disabled cars. In addition, to repair the brakes of a car, its wheels must be removed. Furthermore, when something goes wrong, the complex organizational relationships make it almost impossible to find out who is responsible (management, major contractors, subcontractors, suppliers, planners, and so on). Labor unions objected to the automation because it removed jobs from the economy. Finally, blacks and other poor urban residents do not seem to be using the system to seek new employment, since they do not have marketable skills, and the Bay Bridge is still clogged with private autos.

Some critics indicate that BART and similar technologies are examples of the fundamental weakness of modern technology: Nothing new is invented or discovered; things are simply made more complex. Coupled with this argument is the view that technology can become completely worthless and uncontrollable. Are more Xerox machines really needed to duplicate everything in sight [Morrison, 1976, pp. 69–70], when the current information explosion is already beyond human control? Is the SST really needed to shorten transoceanic flights, when there are risks of severe environmental damage [Wilford, 1976, p. 1]?

Finally, critics of technology argue that, because of its complexity and uncontrollable nature, it can be too easily misused for private or special purposes that are opposed to the public interest. In one case, some observers maintained that cloud-seeding operations in Rapid City, South Dakota, in 1972, caused a subsequent flood [Reed, 1973, pp. 676–684]. In another, a young dermatologist, working at the Sloan–Kettering Institute for Cancer Research, faked a skin transplant on a laboratory mouse with a felt-tipped pen [Hixson, 1975]. He felt enormous pressures to succeed in his research for the sake of the Institute. Federal grants, guaranteed jobs, and scientific prestige went to those who were on the verge of a major discovery, while others received little support for their work. Thus, the young scientist felt an obligation to show how close to success his work might be, even if this involved faking the results of an important experiment.

Some of these criticisms are overstated, and the opposing arguments are presented in Table 11-8. However, they do raise the important issue of the control of technology. As the table indicates, even the supporters recognize the necessity for human controls and for careful application of new inventions and ideas. It is impossible to discuss this topic thoroughly here, but several examples will illustrate the direction of contemporary research and study concerning the control of technology.

TABLE 11-8 Arguments For and Against Modern Technology

Those Against Modern Technology Argue That It Is:	Examples	Those for Modern Technology Argue That:
1. *Too Big*—Technology has become so large-scale that it often simply overwhelms and destroys human society.	Strip-mining techniques and equipment; nuclear warfare strategy and missiles. Strip mining irretrievably destroys the natural environment, and nuclear warfare could destroy all human civilization.	"Bigness" is not necessarily bad, and sometimes it is needed. Strip mining is the only way to obtain coal to ease the oil shortage. Nuclear weapons deter aggression and guarantee no major world wars.
2. *Too Complicated*—Technology is so complex that it can no longer be understood by most people, and it frequently does not work.	The San Francisco–Oakland Bay Area Rapid Transit System (BART); the East Coast blackouts and brownouts of electrical power. BART often stops running and does not make money. Electrical power systems are overloaded because people use electrical toothbrushes, nail polishers, dehumidifiers, air conditioners, and so on.	Complexity does not cause technology to be misunderstood or to break down. What is needed are more innovations, a better educated and trained citizenry, and newer ideas; in other words, more technology, not less.
3. *Too Uncontrollable*—Technology often seems to have a momentum of its own over which humans have little or no control.	The new electronic battlefield for warfare. The military blindly adopts any new device simply because it is new; such technology, therefore, not only becomes an increasing threat to peace, but it cannot win wars.	When an innovation first appears, it takes humans some time to learn how to control it. Studies are now underway to determine how wars of the future may be fought electronically. This could lead to fewer human casualties.
4. *Too Worthless*—Technology is often worthless, serving no purpose at all.	Xeroxing and the SST. There is no need to copy everything in sight. More speed in air travel is useless.	The problem is for humans to apply technology in useful ways. New technology often has far-reaching unanticipated results. Copying has lead to the spread of information and education. Faster international travel could lead to a greater sense of world community.
5. *Too Susceptible to Human Misuse*—Technology can be and usually is misused for personal or private purposes, not for the benefit of the public.	Cloud seeding, which can cause floods; cheating on research results for personal gain.	The misuse of technology simply reflects human frailty, rather than something wrong with technology itself. In addition, many claims of misuse are exaggerated and scientifically unwarranted (for example, cloud seeding).

11-4 The Functions and Dysfunctions of Technology

Those who consider modern technology functional argue that it can be used to solve most of the world's major problems.

United Press Intern

Nuclear weapons, such as the Minuteman missiles at Vandenberg Air Force Base, can bring about world peace by providing a reliable deterrence to aggression.

Atomic Electric Company

United Press International

Nuclear power plants, such as this facility of the Yankee Atomic Electric Company, can resolve the energy crisis by providing an alternative to diminishing fossil fuel supplies.

Radioisotopes can be used to test the thickness of eggs. The thickness can then be increased by changing the diet of chickens, thereby lessening losses due to breakage. Such techniques can end the world food crisis by improving the quantity and quality of products.

Those who consider modern technology dysfunctional argue that it has become too complicated and uncontrollable, too big to serve its basic purposes, that it is often worthless and destructive, and is subject to potential misuse. Technology produces more problems than it resolves.

United Press International

Warfare experiments with complicated chemical and biological agents can lead to accidents which threaten humans, animals, and the natural environment. In Skull Valley, Utah, Army lethal nerve gas killed 7000 sheep in 10 days.

United Press International

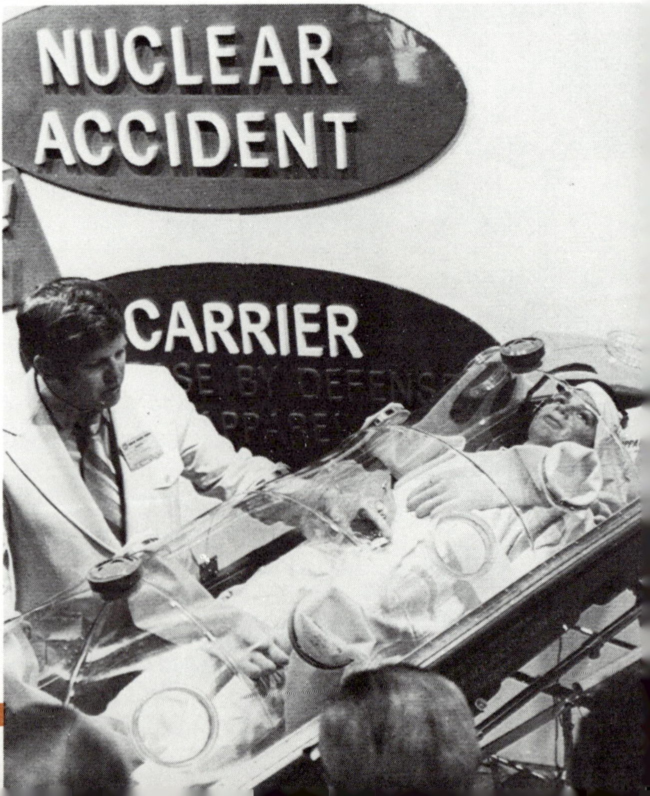

Nuclear devices can cause accidents which lead to long-term and unpredictable effects (birth defects, genetic mutation, and so on). As a result, new methods of handling victims of radiation contamination must be developed which completely isolate the patient from the immediate environment.

United Press International

Nuclear warfare is both unjustified and unnecessary since the resulting destruction does not guarantee lasting peace and it destroys only civilian populations and nonmilitary property. This 1947 photo shows the destruction in Hiroshima where only the shell of the Museum of Science and Industry was left standing.

The use of electronically directed bombardment or defoliation in war only needlessly destroys the environment and does not win the war. In 1968, the consequences of war technology for the natural environment could be seen in the Ashua Valley of Vietnam.

Philip Jones Griffiths/Magnum

United Press International

Technology can no longer be controlled by publicly accountable leaders; individuals can misuse it for their own purposes (for example, start a nuclear war). The command post of the Strategic Air Command Headquarters near Omaha, Nebraska, has 16 computer consoles manned by military personnel in its subterranean center.

Can Technology Be Controlled

The control of technology rests upon an understanding of its social and cultural nature. Control is not merely a matter of limiting or prohibiting the development and use of tools and machines. It also involves creating and managing *social roles, social relationships, groupings, and norms and values.*

The work of John Raser [1970, pp. 105–124] on the problem of controlling nuclear weaponry represents this broader perspective. Raser examined the research on human behavior in crisis situations and applied the findings to the problem of nuclear weapons design and the theory of military deterrence. He looked at the following research:

1. *Laboratory decision-making games* involving international affairs. At various stages in the games, experimenters introduced crises that threatened to block the players' (military officers) goals. As the crises became more intense, the officers became less able to evaluate information or to consider alternative courses of action. Their ability to cope with threat decreased.
2. *Computer analysis* of international communications during the six-week period preceding the outbreak of World War I. As the crisis intensified, key governmental decision makers of Austria–Hungary, Germany, England, France, and Russia saw fewer alternatives for action, distorted their positions (thought them worse or better than they were), lost the ability to think in long-range terms, and focused attention entirely on immediate problems.
3. *Analysis of records* covering 40 years of research on human physiological responses to crisis situations. As fear and anger increase, adrenalin shoots into the bloodstream, the heart speeds up, muscles expand, strength becomes greater, and individuals become superb fighting machines (if the threat is immediate and physical).

Raser concludes that threat, fear, and rage (crises) stimulate humans physically but impair their mental abilities.

Yet complicated modern weapons systems are based upon the concept of rational cautious human response in crisis situations. As Raser puts it:

> Forty-one . . . Polaris submarines prowl the depths of the oceans, each carrying more explosive power than has been expended in the history of warfare [each carries 16 nuclear missiles with the explosive power of at least 1 megaton each]. Each is linked to headquarters by radio waves. Each is commanded by officers chosen for their reliability. In 1964 some strategists began to question that reliability, suggesting that it might be safer if there were some kind of electronic lock-up of the missiles . . . that could be released only by radio signal from headquarters. . . . The Navy's response was an outraged assertion that these officers had been carefully selected, painstakingly trained, and continually tested, and that they could be totally trusted to behave responsibly—*never* to fire unless ordered to and *always* to fire if ordered to [Raser, 1970, p. 113].

However, the research cited above would seriously question this view. What would happen if an isolated commander of a U.S. missile submarine lost radio contact with headquarters during a crisis (like The Bay of Pigs incident) and believed that he was under enemy (Soviet) fire or that the United States was being attacked?

As a result of this concern, the military has introduced some "fail-safe" systems. On the Polaris, only after receiving a coded sequence of radio signals is a submarine commander supposed to fire missiles to predetermined targets. This firing requires that several individuals perform coordinated tasks. Since the captain must direct the efforts of a group of subordinates in order to fire nuclear missiles, the assumption is that others will retain their judgmental ability, even if the captain loses his, and a mistaken firing will not take place. Thus, the control of nuclear military technology is based upon assumptions about certain kinds of roles and relationships. Once again, however, the above research raises serious questions about the reliability of these roles and relationships under stress.

Raser proposed an alternative method of control in 1965. He suggested that Polaris submarines retain 1200-mile-range missiles and not be given new 2500-mile-range missiles. At the same time, they should be kept "off-station"—that is, out of range of their targets by several hours' sailing time. This would mean that the submarines could be used as retaliatory threats (their official role) without being in the provocative position of being able to strike first or to have an accidental firing start a nuclear war. This policy would also make the U.S. nuclear threat appear less aggressive. However, decision makers did not adopt his suggestions, and modern Polaris submarines carry very-long-range missiles and patrol up to the very borders of the Soviet Union (for example, in Mediterranean waters).

New technology has also led to the production of MIRVs—multiple, independently targeted, reentry vehicles. (Each missile can now carry more than one warhead so that the 16 missiles of one Polaris submarine will be able to deliver 30–50 nuclear warheads on 30–50 different targets.) This unchecked technological growth has had the following social consequences: (1) The arms race has accelerated as the Soviets develop a MIRV capability to meet that of the U.S.; (2) international military hostility and distrust increases, since both U.S. and Soviet submarine forces now have an aggressive, first-strike capability, despite official claims by both sides that the primary mission is deterrence.

Nuclear warfare technology has gone beyond the point of necessary defense. Some experts maintain that there are only 50 to 100 important targets in either the United States or the Soviet Union, yet each side presently possesses anywhere from 6000 to over 10,000 defensive nuclear weapons based on land, in the air, and under the sea. The possibility of dangerous nuclear accidents also increases as more and more nations obtain these capabilities. Some scholars claim that the authority of the modern state is less meaningful since small nations or terrorist groups can now threaten nuclear destruction of important civilian and economic targets throughout the world [Steiner, 1976, pp. 65–66].

In summary, even the most complex modern technology—the weapons and systems of nuclear warfare—could be controlled if new values, human relationships, and devices were adopted. The accompanying "So What?" box illustrates how another social scientist is putting these ideas to work in the area of industrial technology.

▶ SO WHAT?

E. F. Schumacher was economic advisor to the British Control Commission in post-World War II Germany and later the head of planning at the British Coal Board. He is also founder and chairman of the Intermediate Technology Development Group, which specializes in creating small-scale tools, machines, and production methods for developing countries.

Schumacher argues that modern technology must be compatible with a country's social structure and culture. The tendency of modern industrialized nations to associate technological bigness automatically with efficiency and the social good must be reexamined according to Schumacher. For instance, is efficiency served when the U.S. industrial system uses 40 percent of the world's major resources to supply less than 6 percent of the world's population? Is a developing African nation benefited by the presence of a foreign-sponsored textile factory whose technology is too advanced for local labor, whose end product is unsuitable for local markets, and whose raw materials are imported from other regions? Is Egypt efficiently served by the operation of the world's largest dam (Aswan Dam), which was built with Russian money and technology, which produces far more power than the country can use, and which blights the environment and destroys local agriculture in the process?

In short, large-scale complex technologies can often be counterproductive to the social good in Schumacher's opinion. Planned production efficiencies often have unintended, negative side effects: a displaced or degraded labor force, increased subjugation of the poor to the rich, foreign controls, and so on. In Spain, Tahiti, and many Carribean Islands, for example, international tourism brings jet airports, high-rise hotels, and new roads, but the native population end up as bellhops, maids, desk clerks, entertainers, or souvenir sellers. The proudest local traditions deteriorate into grotesque caricatures.

Why does this happen? Schumacher seeks to answer this question by constructing a three-stage model of technological development that he uses to analyze national development.

Type I Societies: Based on native technology (simple hand tools such as hoes and shovels); low worker cost and output; jobs are plentiful but difficult.

Type II Societies: Based on intermediate technology (simple tools and machines such as animal-drawn plows and hand-operated coffee grinders); moderate worker cost and output; jobs are still plentiful and work is easier and more meaningful.

Type III Societies: Based on advanced and complex technology (computer-operated machines); high worker cost and output; jobs are less plentiful and work is routine and unrewarding.

The problem is that many developing societies attempt to move directly from Type I to Type III technologies and incur problems like those mentioned above in the process. As a consequence, people in these externally developed Type III societies become completely dependent on large, powerful, and oligarchic foreign states—both national states and multinational corporations. What is needed is the design and implementation of more intermediary Type II technologies that provide what Schumacher calls a "middle way." Examples of middle-way technologies include:

1. Small-scale desalinization plants for separate clusters of villages or towns in Africa, rather than one giant plant for a large region.
2. Solar cells to provide individual homes and small businesses with power, rather than one giant power station.
3. Small plows pulled by simple engines that can be maintained by individual farmers and will not force unemployed farmers from their land, rather than complex harvesting equipment that drives many farmers off the land and can only be maintained at high cost by multinational farm-equipment corporations (such as International Harvester).
4. Medium-scale business organizations featuring worker participation and a constitution defining the tenure and election of officers, the maximum size of the enterprise, the proper use of profits, and the economic and social goals of production. Schumacher is a director of such a business—the Scott Bader Company, producers or polyester resins, alkyds, polymers, and plasticizers.
5. Communities with limited sizes so that adequate services can be provided for all residents. For example, Schumacher feels that a modern city should not have more than 500,000 inhabitants. See the reference to the Northern California town of Petaluma at the beginning of Chapter 13 (page 559).

Some critics of Schumacher claim that these alternatives are too utopian and could not be applied to modern society. Supporters of Schumacher argue that once people abandon the concept of "the larger-the-better," a middle-way technology is possible even in advanced societies. What do you think?

Based upon Edward Cornish, "Think Small," *The Futurist, 8* (December 1974), pp. 276–284; and E. F. Schumacher, *Small Is Beautiful: Economics As If People Mattered* (New York: Harper Torchbooks, 1973).

CONCLUSION

In this chapter, we have seen that the functions and influence of contemporary power institutions, particularly the nation-state, are expanding. This is a consequence of both their institutional nature (growth is sought by all institutions) and their use of power (force and authority) as a means of growth. The growth of these power institutions is often at the expense of traditional morale-building institutions such as the family or church. At the same time, power institutions can either support or conflict with one another.

The modern state often depends upon the military, not only for traditional roles (like defense or deterrence), but also for newer nation-building roles. Although the modern military seems to possess a special capability to perform these civilianlike roles, it also has limitations. Its authoritarian, secret, and ethnocentric character may make performance of civilian tasks (road building, running schools, staffing government agencies, dispensing medical care) difficult, and military ideology may arouse the suspicions and hostilities of civilians. As a result, the legitimacy of both the civilian state and the military may be threatened. Furthermore, military establishments may overthrow states by force (especially where a tradition of couping develops), or they may become so intimately involved in civilian activities that a garrison state begins to emerge.

The military is not the only threat to national authority. The new multinational corporation, which develops power by monopolizing various kinds of important technological knowledge, can also either support or challenge state power. Developing nations frequently become totally dependent upon the skills and information such corporations possess. Multinationals can also manipulate markets, thereby creating false needs and wants. However, states are not powerless and they may use nationalization or expropriation as ways of getting multinationals to respond to local needs.

While power institutions like the state, the military, and multinational corporations can act as checks and balances against one another, the problem for individual citizens is more difficult. For example, how does civilian society maintain control of the military? Must citizens always turn to the centralized state for answers to critical problems? Is the citizen totally dependent upon the products and services of the corporation for survival? A number of scholars have suggested new kinds of roles, relationships, and values that might be appropriate responses to these questions.

According to John Gilmore, rapidly developing, boom town communities need comprehensive local planning to regulate the overlapping interests of the various types and levels of states. Charles Moskos suggests that the modern military might be controlled by a model where the military converges toward civilian roles in certain areas and diverges away from civilian roles in other areas. Finally, E. F. Schumacher offers middle-way technologies as an alternative to incompatible large-scale technologies.

This chapter, with its emphasis on institutional relationships, is a fitting transition to the last part of the textbook, which discusses processes of social dynamics. Shifting relationships between institutions give rise to processes of individual and collective deviance, change, and conflict. These are the processes that give human society its dynamic character. However, there are both undesirable and desirable aspects of deviance, change, and conflict. Is it possible, therefore, to control these processes, utilizing the theories and empirical findings of social scientific research?

REFERENCES

Barnet, Richard J., and Ronald E. Muller. *Global Reach: The Power of the Multinational Corporations.* New York: Simon & Schuster, 1974.

Bruyn, Severyn T. "The Multinational Corporation and Social Research: The Case of the United Fruit Company," *Social Theory and Practice, 1* (Fall 1971), pp. 53–70.

Coles, Harry L., and Albert K. Weinberg. *Civil Affairs: Soldiers Become Governors.* Volume VI of "The United States Army in World War II: Special Studies." Washington, D.C.: U.S. Government Printing Office, 1964.

Cornish, Edward. "Think Small," *The Futurist, 8* (December 1974), pp. 276–284.

Daalder, Hans. *The Role of the Military in the Emerging Countries.* The Hague: P. H. Klop, 1962.

Gilmore, John S. "Boom Towns May Hinder Energy Resource Development," *Science, 191* (13 February 1976), pp. 535–540.

Greer, Scott, and Peter Orleans. "Political Sociology," in *Handbook of Modern Sociology,* Robert E. L. Faris, Ed. Chicago: Rand McNally & Co., 1964.

Hausrath, Alfred. "Civil Affairs and Military Government," in *A Survey of Military Institutions. Volume II,* Roger W. Little, Ed. Chicago: Inter-University Seminar on Armed Forces and Society, University of Chicago, 1969.

Hixson, Joseph. *The Parchwork Mouse.* New York: Anchor/Doubleday, 1975.

Janowitz, Morris. "Military Elites and the Study of War," *Journal of Conflict Resolution, 1* (March 1957), pp. 9–18.

———. *The Professional Soldier: A Social and Intellectual Portrait.* New York: The Free Press, 1960.

———. *The Military in the Political Development of New Nations.* Chicago: University of Chicago Press, 1964.

Jay, Antony. *Management and Machiavelli: An Inquiry into the Politics of Corporate Life.* New York: Holt, Rinehart and Winston, 1967.

Johnson, John J., Ed. *The Role of the Military in Underdeveloped Countries.* Princeton: Princeton University Press, 1962.

Kornhauser, William. "Revolutions," in *A Survey of Military Institutions. Volume II,* Roger C. Little, Ed. Chicago: The Inter-University Seminar on Armed Forces and Society, University of Chicago, 1969.

Kranzberg, Melvin, and Carroll W. Pursell, Jr. *Technology in Western Civilization. Volume I.* New York: Oxford University Press, 1967.

Lasswell, Harold D. "The Garrison State," *The American Journal of Sociology, 46* (January 1941), pp. 455–468.

Lindsey, Robert. "Mass Transit, Little Mass," *The New York Times Magazine* (10 October 1975), pp. 17ff.

Linton, Ralph. *The Study of Man.* New York: Appleton–Century–Crofts, 1936.

Lowry, Ritchie P. "To Arms: Changing Military Roles and the Military–Industrial Complex," *Social Problems, 18* (Summer 1970), pp. 3–16.

Morgan, Arthur E. *Dams and Other Disasters: A Century of the Army Corps of Engineers in Civil Works.* Boston: Porter Sargent Publisher, 1971.

Morrison, Donald M. "What Hath XEROX Wrought?," *Time* (1 March 1976), p. 69.

Moskos, Charles C., Jr. *The American Enlisted Man: The Rank and File in Today's Military.* New York: Russell Sage and Basic Books, 1970.

Needler, Martin C. "Military Coups in Latin America," *Trans-action, 4* (December 1966), pp. 5–6.

Perrow, Charles. *Complex Organizations: A Critical Essay.* Glenview, Ill.: Scott, Foresman and Company, 1972.

Raser, John R. "The Failure of Fail-Safe," in *Peace and the War Industry,* Kenneth E. Boulding, Ed. Chicago: Aldine Publishing Company, 1970.

Reed, Jack W. "Cloud Seeding at Rapid City: A Dissenting View," *Bulletin of the American Meteorological Society, 54* (July 1973), pp. 676–684. This reference also includes sharp rebuttals by other scientists of Reed's criticism of cloud seeding.

Riddleberger, Peter B. *Military Roles in Developing Countries: An Inventory of Past Research and Analysis.* Washington, D. C.: Special Operations Research Office, The American University, 1965.

Sarkesian, Sam C., Ed. *The Military–Industrial Complex: A Reassessment.* New York: Russell Sage, 1972.

Schumacher, E. F. *Small Is Beautiful: Economics As If People Mattered.* New York: Harper Torchbooks, 1973.

Speier, Hans. *Social Order and the Risks of War: Papers on Political Sociology.* Cambridge: MIT Press, 1952.

Standard Oil of California. *1975 Annual Report.* Standard Oil of California, San Francisco, Calif.

Steiner, Arthur. "Sovereignty and Technology," *Bulletin of the Atomic Scientists, 32* (February 1976), pp. 65–66.

Tugendhat, Christopher. *The Multinationals.* New York: Random House, 1972.

Turner, Louis. *Multinational Companies and the Third World.* New York: Hill and Wang, 1973.

Weber, Max. *The Theory of Social and Economic Organization.* New York: The Free Press, 1957.

Wilford, John Noble. "Is Infinite Speed Really an Imperative?" *The New York Times* (8 February 1976), Sect. 4, p. 1.

Wright, Quincy. *A Study of War.* Chicago: University of Chicago Press, 1942 (in two volumes).

▶ KEY CONCEPT REVIEW

To aid you in mastering the basic concepts of Part 4, we have organized key terms into convenient and logical conceptual networks. Refer to the study procedure recommended on page 73 and follow the same procedure here.

CLUSTER 10
Morale-Building Institutions

Emotional Needs (or Functions)
Family (of Orientation and of Procreation)
Consanguine Family and Familism
Nuclear as compared to Extended Family
School (and Education)
Educational Elitism
Churches (Congregational and Episcopal Types)
Prophetic as compared to Priestly Roles

CLUSTER 11
Power Institutions

Task Needs (or Functions)
Power
Authority (as contrasted to Force)
Geographical and Functional States
Multinational Corporation
Military (Convergent and Divergent)
War as compared to Revolution
Technology

10. Morale-Building Institutions

	Definition	Example
Emotional Needs (or Functions)	All societies have two basic emotional needs: socialization and integration of members. Morale-building institutions arise to meet these needs (to perform socialization and integration functions).	Modern families socialize and integrate members of all ages. Modern schools teach skills, knowledge, and values to children and young adults. Modern churches transmit major social values from one generation to the next and provide a feeling of belonging (integration) for the aged, lonely, disadvantaged, and the like.
Family (of Orientation and of Procreation)	An institution that combines common residence, economic cooperation, and reproduction and is basic to and found in some form in all societies. Families are primarily responsible for the production (*task need*), socialization, and integration of the present and succeeding generations. The family of orientation is the family into which one is born. The family of procreation is the family created by marriage.	In modern societies, families usually consist of small mother–father–children units. However, families can also be found in other forms: the Israeli kibbutz, communes, childless couples, spouseless mothers or fathers, and so on. The modern child is born into a family of orientation and later creates through marriage a new family of procreation.

	Definition	Example
Consanguine Family and Familism	A family where all members are related by descent from a common ancestor or by "blood." Consanguine families are characterized by familism—filial piety, importance of having many sons, ancestor worship, and common family ownership of property.	The large family units of premodern societies tend to be consanguine. However, elements of familism can still be found in some modern families that take pride in ancestors, stress the commitment of children to parental authority, and emphasize the value of having many sons (for example, the Rockefeller and Kennedy families).
Nuclear as compared to Extended Family	The typical nuclear family consists of a married couple and their children living together. Extended families exist where two or more nuclear families, related by blood, live together.	The modern nuclear family maximizes freedom and independence for all members, whereas the extended family requires conformity and obedience to traditional norms and authority. However, the extended family can provide emotional support at times of crisis (death, sickness, and so on), whereas the isolated nuclear family must often turn to outside social agencies for assistance and support.
School (and Education)	Formal institutions that teach the skills, knowledge, and values of one's culture. The process of education also consists of informal experiences within the classroom setting.	All societies seem to have some system of formal education. In premodern societies, this is related to and controlled by the extended family; sons are trained in necessary skills by tutors selected by the parents. In modern societies, schools perform a growing number of emotional and task functions, separate from the influence of the nuclear family.
Educational Elitism	The tendency for schools to become less interested in meeting the different needs of many citizens and to become more interested in meeting the special needs of only some citizens.	The educational system of premodern societies was characterized by elitism. In modern mass societies, however, there has been a movement toward the meeting of many different needs. Some scholars fear that modern attacks upon the school's ability to perform many functions effectively may lead to a narrowing of functions and a new form of elitism—an education for only the bright and privileged.

	Definition	Example
Churches (Congregational and Episcopal Types)	A formal religious organization with relatively fixed doctrine and ritual and trained leadership. Churches with a congregational structure stress local autonomy and are often *sect*-like in character. Churches with episcopal structure tend to be highly bureaucratized and international in scope.	Newly formed sectlike churches often adopt a congregational type of structure. However, large established denominations, such as the American Baptist church, also sometimes encourage local autonomy. On the other hand, Methodism and the Catholic Church have a bureaucratized hierarchy with bishops presiding over an episcopal type of structure.
Prophetic as compared to Priestly Roles	For religious leadership, all churches contain a conflict between *roles* that challenge members to live up to the highest ideals (prophetic) and those which comfort members in times of crisis (priestly).	Martin Luther King was a priestly clergyman when he performed marriages and burials. He was a social prophet when he led demonstrations and spoke out against segregation and racism.

11. Power Institutions

	Definition	Example
Task Needs (or Functions)	All societies have two basic task needs: the production and distribution of goods and services necessary for growth and survival. Power institutions arise to meet these needs (to perform production and distribution functions).	Modern states regulate production and distribution by laws, tax incentives, financial assistance, and so on. States may also nationalize industries, universities, and the like in order to directly perform these functions.
Power	Institutions involved in production and distribution functions utilize power—the ability to influence the actions and attitudes of others.	Power institutions encourage desired actions and attitudes by rewards of honor, recognition, financial success, and so on (for example, tax incentives for oil companies to seek new energy resources). They discourage undesirable actions and attitudes by sanctions of legal punishment, political harassment, *force,* and so on (for example, prosecution by the Justice Department for price fixing or violations of the antitrust laws).

	Definition	Example
Authority (as contrasted to *Force*)	Force is power in the form of involuntary coercion, whereas authority is power in the form of voluntary obedience. The authority of leaders may be based upon *charisma, tradition,* or *legal–bureaucratic* roles and rules.	The nuclear arms race is an example of power as force—major nations attempt to coerce other nations into desired actions and attitudes. President John Kennedy often utilized charismatic authority, reflected in a dynamic personal life-style and dramatic speech making, to influence citizens and other leaders. The office of the presidency automatically conveys traditional authority to American leaders; citizens feel they ought to obey the president. This office also possesses legal and bureaucratic authority, since its powers are defined in official documents, including the Constitution.
Geographical and Functional States	States are those institutions that use *power* in order to maintain the *social order* and unify citizens with a common *culture.* Some states meet the task needs of citizens within specific geographical boundaries, while others perform specific types of functions in terms of task needs.	Power institutions like the church often combine both geographical and functional characteristics. The Church in medieval Europe relied upon traditional and bureaucratic authority to get citizens to build cathedrals, compose music, work as tradesmen or farmers, and so on, for "the glory of God." The medieval Church sometimes supported military forces for protection and to open up regions for Christian conversion.
Multinational Corporation	Modern multinational corporations are more than international economic organizations. They develop an ideology and identity which is independent from the state. They utilize centralized authority and power that derives from a monopoly of knowledge about production, marketing, and finance capital.	During the "oil and gasoline shortage" of the early 1970s, many citizens and world political leaders felt relatively helpless against the power of oil multinationals. Centralized authority made it possible for the oil companies to act in their own interests (to control supply in order to increase demand and raise prices). The oil companies possessed the necessary knowledge about the availability, development, and marketing of world oil supplies. In contrast, historic international economic organizations (the British East India Company) were dependent upon national states for their continued success.

	Definition	Example
Military (Convergent and Divergent)	That power institution with a monopoly of the means of *force* and violence and the functions of defending a society against aggression, deterring aggression, conducting offensive warfare, or maintaining civil law and order. Convergent military forces are those that become more interrelated with and similar to civilian authority. Divergent military forces are those that become more separate from and dissimilar to civilian authority.	All societies, both democratic and totalitarian, face the problem of maintaining civilian power over military forces, particularly since the military has a monopoly of force. Some societies maintain civilian authority by civilianizing the military (deemphasize military values and ritual, have the military perform civilian functions), thereby making the military's functioning dependent upon civilian roles and values. Other societies attempt to keep the military separate and distinct from civilian society.
War as compared to Revolution	Wars involve the clash of opposing military forces. In contrast, revolutions may take place with or without violence. Revolutions may be extensive transformations of whole societies, polarization of political forces within a society, and/or mobilization of large numbers of people under the banner of a revolutionary ideology.	Both wars and revolutions may lead to little or extensive social and cultural *change. Primitive warfare* contributed to clan solidarity and reinforced prevailing norms for many generations, whereas *historic warfare* resulted in the disintegration and creation of many empires and civilizations. In the same way, *mass revolutions* (the Russian and Chinese) may bring about extensive transformation, polarization, and mobilization, while *palace revolutions* (Latin American coups) may involve only change in individual rulers of a society.
Technology	Refers to more than the material aspects (techniques) of a *culture.* Technology is the clustering of *roles, relationships, groups,* and *norms* and *values* that constitute and stimulate the knowledge and techniques necessary for a society to meet its basic task needs.	Power institutions depend upon technology for the performance of their functions. The modern military needs sophisticated weapons systems, and the multinational corporation requires highly developed knowledge and means of mass production. As a result, technological institutions—such as universities, think tanks, research agencies, experimental laboratories—become interrelated with power institutions. Modern technology can sometimes begin to determine the functioning of these institutions (nuclear weapons encourage the arms race despite political desires for disarmament).

PART 5

Social Processes

SOCIETY is never static; it is always undergoing change and is always in *process.* One way of studying social processes was developed in Part 3. We saw that collectivities are the early stages of groups coming into being and that they are most apt to emerge in time of crisis and change. Social status differences are never fixed, and in open societies the characteristics of working- and middle-class styles of life are constantly changing. Associations develop bureaucratic tendencies, which, in turn, are modified and transformed by the dynamic quality of the human response to formal organization. Communities are in a constant state of flux from rural, to urban, to suburban forms. Even the most permanent of institutions in modern society are influenced by a multitude of changes and challenges, such as professionalization. In other words, social processes can be studied by using the typology of five basic forms of human group behavior.

We have also suggested a second approach to the study of social processes—the examination of the changing functions of basic institutions. In the previous section, Part 4, we saw how institutions arise in various social contexts to meet basic needs. Thus, the family has traditionally performed a socializing function; the state, a distributing function; the church, an integration function; and so on. However, both societies and institutions change through time. As they do, one institution may either complement or erode another institution's ability to meet basic needs of individuals and groups. The modern nation-state and school have taken over many functions previously performed by the family. The church and the state may either support (religious approval for a war) or conflict with (religious opposition to warfare) one another. Therefore, human institutions are always in process in so far as they are interrelated and interdependent.

This final section of the book will discuss a third way in which social processes may be studied. Sociologists have identified three basic types or forms of social processes: *deviance, change,* and *conflict.* These are of particular interest because they represent tendencies in opposition to society's natural predisposition towards conformity, stability, and cooperation. Therefore, like many of the dual and dichotomous sociological concepts we have employed throughout this book (primary versus secondary relationships, rural versus urban communities, *Gemeinschaft* versus *Gesellschaft* society, and the like), the following three chapters will consider the problems associated with the tension between deviance and conformity, change and stability, and conflict and cooperation.

Chapters 12, 13, and 14 will consider deviance, change, and conflict, respectively, from the standpoint of their sources, their nature, and their control:

1. *Sources:* Why do social processes arise in human societies? For example, although socialization emphasizes conformity, why do some people deviate? How is change possible in highly stable systems? If societies depend upon cooperation for their survival, why is so much conflict evident, especially in the modern world?
2. *Nature:* What are the major theories about the form, characteristics, and consequences of social processes? In particular, are devi-

ance, change, and conflict desirable or undesirable, functional or dysfunctional?

3. *Control:* Since most societies consider processes disruptive, especially in extreme forms, how can deviance, change, and conflict be controlled? At the same time, these processes can also be valuable to a society: Some forms of deviance encourage creativity; changes are necessary for a system to adapt to new conditions; conflict may be required for survival. Therefore, do societies have a means of managing social processes that surpasses mere control; that is, is there a method by which these processes can be directed into productive channels and toward desired purposes?

In addition, each chapter will focus primarily upon one major example of each type of social process. Chapter 12 on deviance will use studies of crime and delinquency to illustrate concepts and theories. Chapter 13 on change will use studies of demographic processes and population. Chapter 14 will focus upon conflict between ethnic groups, frequently referred to in sociology as minority group conflict (conflict between minorities and majorities). We will refer to these particular examples of social processes for purposes of clarity and brevity only. A complete treatment of deviance, for example, would also consider many other studies of mental disorder, alcohol or narcotics abuse, sexual deviation, and the like. However, the same general perspectives developed in the following chapters can be applied to social processes that differ from the ones used as illustrations.

- Which of the following people do you think deviated from accepted norms, and which merely conformed to certain values more than the rest of us: Daniel Berrigan, Joan of Arc, Leon Trotsky, Martin Luther, and Mohandas Gandhi?
- Are deviants inherently defective or are they striking out against deviant societies?
- Is "law-and-order" a necessary response to crime?
- Are all juvenile gangs whose members engage in delinquency alike?
- Why do the agents of social control (FBI, local police) sometimes deviate (use illegal violence, spy on citizens, encourage criminal behavior)?

12

The Dynamics of Deviance: Delinquency and Crime

In this chapter, we will be concerned with what happens when human behavior deviates from expected forms. Social order and integration obviously depend in large measure upon conformity to norms and acceptance of basic values. At the same time, order is never fixed or unchanging. Orderly processes in society are constantly subjected to criticism by creative individuals and challenged by the deviant behavior of special subgroups. Furthermore, behavior that departs from expected norms is not always destructive and dysfunctional, as was illustrated in our previous discussions of marihuana addiction and slum communities in modern urban environments. Marihuana use and slum environments were seen to be functional (to meet basic needs) for some people.

Deviant behavior, then, can play a positive role in social organization.

It enhances the possibility for social change, and change can give rise to new and vital forms of social reorganization. Deviance can take a variety of forms, many approved and encouraged by a society (for example, heroic fighting in war). These forms can sometimes bind individuals together and promote social solidarity. This complex character of deviant behavior—the potential to contribute to both social and cultural disorganization and reorganization—makes deviance analysis and theory construction an unusual challenge for the social scientist.

We will begin this chapter by considering the sources and nature of deviant behavior, particularly the idea that social control can never be perfect. We will then compare older and newer theories—the older arguing that most, if not all, deviance is a result of individual pathology, whereas the newer theories stress the fact that much deviant behavior can be functional for both individuals and society. Finally, we will conclude with a special focus upon the question of how deviance might be controlled effectively. Throughout we will use studies of crime and delinquency to illustrate concepts and theories.

SOURCES AND NATURE OF DEVIANCE

The fact that some deviance occurs in all human societies indicates that the social control of human behavior can never be perfect, even in the most authoritarian and restrictive contexts. A major source of deviance then is the imperfect nature of social control.

Sources of Deviance: Imperfect Social Control

Most behavior conforms to social expectations for several reasons. For one thing, conforming is less painful than nonconforming. The infant recognizes this very early in the socialization experience. When a child is good, the parents are pleased and reward the child with attention and approval. When bad, the child suffers rebuke. Mothers may use positive sanctions to encourage desired actions—a kiss, a proud smile, a plaything. Fathers may use negative sanctions to discourage undesirable behavior—a frown, a spanking, withholding a privilege. This never-ending process of reward and punishment causes the developing self to internalize the values of society. Social conformity becomes the basis for self-approval. Not only do we become a part of society, but society becomes a part of us.

> For most of us, the yoke of society seems easy to bear . . . because most of the time we ourselves desire just that which society expects of us. We *want* to obey the rules. We want the parts [roles] that society has assigned to us. . . . Society not only determines what we do but also what we are. In other words, social location invoices our being as well as our conduct [Berger, 1963, pp. 93–94].

Thus, humans learn to control their actions in accordance with what they perceive is expected of them. As we saw in the discussion of George

Mead's theory in Chapter 3, the "me" cautions the "I" against outrageous acts, and a person controls his or her actions in anticipation of unfavorable responses from the group. When an individual acts according to the norms, the group functions smoothly and society benefits from cooperative behavior. There is a high degree of predictability, as one member knows what to expect of another. Conformity contributes to group morale and performance and makes for personal satisfaction and social solidarity. Why then, does deviance often arise in society?

One answer, to which we have already alluded, is the imperfect nature of social control. Two characteristics, one related to the social self and the other to social organization, make perfect social control an impossibility. For one thing, the dynamic unrestrained "I" within the social self represents a reservoir of energy that constantly threatens to break the bounds of control. Young children, bubbling over with energy, are constantly testing boundaries to see how far they can go without getting punished. As they grow older, behavior patterns (habits) develop that conform to social expectations most of the time. Yet the latent potential for individuals to deviate is always present, especially when they are under strain. For example, a person might drink alcohol to excess or take illegal drugs in order to escape the pressures of a job; or, in anger and frustration, one might punch a friend.

In addition, *normative conflict,* which characterizes most modern heterogeneous societies, makes social conformity difficult to achieve. To conform to the norm in one subculture is to become a deviant in another. Youth in our society face this problem in an acute way. Adolescents may live up to parental expectations when at home but be under pressure to behave quite differently in the presence of peers. Furthermore, what is defined as deviant by family standards (marihuana use, sloppy styles of dress) may be looked upon as required conformity or normal behavior in the peer group. Thus, the same behavior can threaten the structure and solidarity of one group while reinforcing these elements in another group context.

In other words, the difficult-to-control "I" and normative conflict are two major sources of deviant behavior, and they account for the imperfect nature of social control. Thus, no group or society can expect complete or absolute conformity, and all societies must provide for a margin of error—that is, for a degree of nonconformity. In every human group, there are limits to freedom, and within these limits some deviation is generally tolerated.

The Complex Nature of Deviance

One can readily see that deviant behavior has a complex nature and character. It can be relative—that is, seen as desirable in one context and undesirable in another. It can also result from human error rather than devilment, or it can remain hidden or undiscovered. These multiple features of deviance have made its scientific study particularly difficult, a problem that has been the focus of recent sociological theory.

For example, Stanton Wheeler [1967, pp. 605–606] points out that the imperfect nature of social control makes deviant behavior *hard to define:*

> Deviant behavior, ordinarily, is defined as conduct that runs afoul of social norms. But norms are not blueprints outlining in compulsory detail how people should act; they are abstract standards of conduct that people are expected to *approximate* in their daily activities. . . . In this sense, the norm itself is a midpoint in a range of behavior, and when we say that someone has violated the norm we are saying that this behavior has passed over some cut-off point at the edges of the norm's jurisdiction. . . .

Wheeler uses the example of public drunkenness, which is generally considered to be improper in our society. This moral sentiment, therefore, is backed by legal ordinances and other sanctions. However, there is no precise delineation of the degree of intoxication that qualifies individuals for official censure. A moderate degree of drunken behavior is considered more serious in Salt Lake City, Utah, than in Las Vegas, Nevada; or among Christian Scientists than among Irish Catholics. Similarly, an intoxicated clergyman is subject to far greater censure than a drunken merchant seaman. In other words, in a complex society, definitions of deviance vary according to such social and cultural criteria as area of residence, occupation, social class, and religious beliefs.

In addition, many people may deviate *unintentionally or accidentally.* Some laws are so complex, and so many informal norms conflict with one another, that a person may violate standards without being aware of any transgressions. Judith Blake and Kingsley Davis [1964, p. 468] have illustrated this by pointing to four possible relationships between people's behavior and their motives. In all societies, many people want to conform, and they do so; others want to deviate, and they do so. At the same time, there are some people who want to conform, but they deviate; and there are some who want to deviate, but they conform. The interrelationships of motives and behavior, as seen by Blake and Davis, are shown in Table 12-1.

This typology by Blake and Davis has important implications for the question of the social control of deviance (to be discussed in detail at the end of this chapter). For example, the unintentional deviant (conforming motives but deviating behavior) may deviate for three reasons—error, lack of knowledge about rules, and/or social situations that require deviation from accepted norms. In these cases, more laws, greater punishment, or quicker application of justice may be ineffective. Studies have shown that a significant proportion of "welfare abuses" are caused by bureaucratic rules so complex that even welfare administrators may not be able to understand or apply them properly. Another example is the businessman with a family to support who finds that his boss expects him to cheat, as in the case of American business firms who have bribed foreign governments to procure contracts.

Table 12-1 Possible Relationships Between Conforming and Deviating Motives and Behavior

Motives	Behavior: Conforming	Behavior: Deviating
Conforming	Citizen honestly pays income tax; motorist drives at the speed limit; credit card owner pays debts on time	Gang members does not know how to solve personal problems without violence; motorist is unaware of the speed limit; businessman's boss considers cheating good business practice
Deviating	Citizen wants to cheat on taxes but doesn't know how; middle-class youth wants to steal but is afraid of family disapproval; motorist wants to speed but thinks he may be caught	Businessman embezzles company funds to pay gambling debts; politician buys votes to win an election; thief becomes an expert at breaking and entering

Similarly, those who want to deviate but do not (deviating motives but conforming behavior) are deterred by three factors—the desire for social rewards, the fear of social sanctions, and/or the lack of opportunity to deviate. The individual who does not have the tools or the knowledge cannot become an expert thief. Advocates of gun control argue that people who cannot obtain guns will not kill by those means. At the opposite end of the status system, the businessman who cannot gain access to the company's books or computer records cannot embezzle. Furthermore, desire for social approval and other rewards can, in some cases, be as important in deterring deviant behavior as fear of punishment.

The scientific study of deviant behavior is further complicated when one realizes that deviating motives or behavior may be *unrecognized and undiscovered.* Therefore, whether one is perceived of as being a deviant by others can be as important as whether they are actually deviant. Labeling theorists, like Howard Becker [1963, p. 20], have suggested four possible categories of deviance based upon actual behavior versus the perceptions of that behavior by others (see Table 12-2).

The falsely accused category is especially important to labeling theorists in terms of social action. They argue that as long as society continues to view people from lower-status ethnic groups as inherently deviant, they will have little opportunity to become conforming members of larger society. More importantly, they may actually begin to deviate, not so much because they personally wish to do so, but because they gradually begin

TABLE 12-2 Actual Conformity and Deviance Versus the Perceptions of Others

Perceptions of Others	Actual Behavior: Conforming	Actual Behavior: Deviating
As Conforming	*Conformist:* Those judged to be and who are straight, good, and correct in their behavior according to accepted standards	*Secret Deviant:* "Closet" homosexual; housewife who drinks at home all day; politician who commits adultery
As Deviating	*Falsely Accused:* Lower-class youth who conforms but is considered a "thug" by the middle class; some American soldiers thought South Vietnamese males were "queer" because of different cultural habits	*Deviant:* The known, apprehended, and prosecuted criminal; one who is convicted for a crime that he or she actually committed

to accept and internalize the deviant image falsely applied to them by others. Social scientists advocating prison reform frequently use this theory. They maintain that what prisons really do is to label inmates as incorrigibly deviant. Inmates, in turn, accept this self-label and begin to act according to its definitions (for example, they act tough, violent, tricky, and the like).

The Problems of Studying Crime and Delinquency

The complex nature of deviance is evident in the study of crime and delinquency. To begin with, the problem of reporting deviance is complicated by three interrelated problems.

1. *Measurement is difficult.* What should we measure—the number of arrests, recorded cases, or those judged to be guilty?
2. *Collection of information for social research purposes involves a multitude of social variables,* such as class, sex, age, race, urban or rural residence, and the like. How can we be sure that some of these variables will not be more important than others or that certain ones, such as race, do not distort information collected as a result of political persuasions?
3. *Some deviant acts are judged to be more serious and threatening to the social system than others.* How can we measure these degrees of importance? In the conduct of social research on deviance, these three questions tend to become interrelated.

12-1 Sources of Deviance

People conform when they adopt accepted goals and use approved means (norms) for achieving these goals. In other words, deviance is absent when people play by the approved rules of the game. However, the rules or norms of a society may be unknown or unavailable to some citizens, in conflict with other norms, rapidly changing, or seemingly inappropriate for achieving some goals. When these conditions exist, deviance results.

Marion Bernstein

Normlessness and labeling. Some citizens may become deviants because they feel alienated from society. They experience a condition of anomie and feel that they are alone in the world. Their deviant behavior (seeking food in garbage cans, alcoholism, excessive drug use, and so on) seems to be the only means available for personal survival. The extreme nature of the behavior causes others to label them as deviants and, thereby, alienation is increased and the deviant behavior continues.

Culver Pictures, Inc.

United Press International

Positive versus negative deviance. Killing in civilian society is considered negative deviance and is punished, whereas killing in warfare is considered a necessary means to a desired goal (winning the war). When Sergeant Alvin York single-handedly killed more than 20 German soldiers and forced 132 others to surrender in one action during World War I, he was awarded the Congressional Medal of Honor. However, even in war there may be normative limits to deviance. When Lieutenant William Calley led an attack upon the village of My Lai during the Vietnam War, 22 South Vietnamese men, women, and children were killed. He was later court-martialled for premeditated murder. President Nixon intervened in the case when many citizens argued that Calley's behavior was not negative deviance but was merely the unavoidable result of a guerrilla war which involved innocent civilians.

Anthony Barboza/Metamorphosis

Wide World Photos

Goals–means disparity. Deviance may result when acceptable means for achieving approved goals (such as wealth, fame, and power) do not seem to be available. This disparity is a consistent problem for groups which are exposed to racial and economic discrimination in contemporary society. Deviance may also result when unacceptable means are seen as the only way of achieving desirable goals. When the members of the Symbionese Liberation Army kidnapped Patricia Hearst and later robbed the Hibernia Bank in San Francisco, they argued that these acts were necessary to dramatize the corrupt nature of capitalist society and to bring about the necessary changes for resolving major problems (poverty, hunger, financial greed, and so on). Furthermore, they argued that capitalists had consistently used violence to protect their own interests at the expense of others who were less privileged.

J. C. LeJeune/Stock, Boston

Culver Pictures, Inc.

Normative conflict. Deviant behavior may arise when norms and values conflict with one another. During war, each side depicts the other as the personification of all evil and their own society as the personification of all good. This stereotyping can justify the use of any means (gas warfare, bombing of civilian cities, use of atomic weapons) in order to defeat evil. Domestic minority-group conflict involves the same process. Advocates of white supremacy label integrationists as Communists and queers and see themselves as protectors of basic Christian values and patriotic norms. Integrationists see groups such as the Ku Klux Klan (see Chapter 6) as exponents of racism, fascism, and violence, and they see themselves as standing for the most important religious and political values (equality, humanitarianism, brotherhood).

Some criminologists refer to the "inverted pyramid of crime" to depict these problems. This concept is illustrated in Figure 12-1, which visually depicts (1) various crimes, categorized according to their place within the criminal justice system; (2) why each step in the system involves fewer crimes and criminals; and (3) the major social groups and institutions involved at each step. The relative size of each step of the pyramid is only approximate, since accurate data simply do not exist in many cases. What Figure 12-1 indicates is that the "crime problem" is both more, and less, serious than is popularly believed. For example, no one really knows the total extent of crime and delinquency, since many deviant acts are accidental, hidden, or unreported. Rape is an example where relatives and victims may be reluctant to report the crime for fear of its social consequences or because the rapist was a friend or relative. Perhaps as few as one half of certain types of deviant acts are ever detected and recorded in official crime statistics and scientific study. At the same time, most official reports of crime and delinquency (like the annual FBI reports) fail to weed out cases where false reports may have been made, where the crime is never solved, or where an arrested individual is later judged to be innocent. Therefore, *underestimates* and *overestimates* can occur.

Furthermore, the "peak" (top) of the inverted crime pyramid indicates that the heart of the crime and delinquency problem cannot be attributed to permissive courts and prisons, since most criminal activity never even reaches the courts. Although overcrowded courts certainly play a part, the inability of police to make arrests, the unwillingness of citizens to report crimes, and the invisible nature of much crime also play a large role in the seeming "breakdown" of the contemporary justice system. Furthermore, *no system of social control can be effective simply in terms of apprehending and prosecuting large numbers of deviants.* As we have already seen, effective control depends also upon such factors as *promises of rewards* for conformity and *fear of disapproval* for deviance.

Legal definitions of criminality also present special problems. Raab and Selznick [1964] note how serious this problem is with regard to delinquency. A committee of the National Probation Association defines delinquency not only as a *violation of an adult law* but also as behavior that indicates *potential criminality.* Nonadults who are wayward, habitually disobedient, or show improper deportment may be identified as delinquent because they are considered "precriminal." Such persons are assumed to be in need of rehabilitation as a preventive measure. Raab and Selznick question this legal concept because it fails to account for pseudo-delinquency—temporary waywardness caused largely by expressive behavior that may be normal during adolescence. For example, there is evidence to show that much delinquency is not potential criminality. An estimated 65 percent of all the children who appear in juvenile court do not repeat their delinquencies, as compared to the high rate of recidivism for adult crimes (over 50 percent of the former inmate population of some adult prisons continue to engage in crime).

FIGURE 12-1 The Inverted Pyramid of Crime

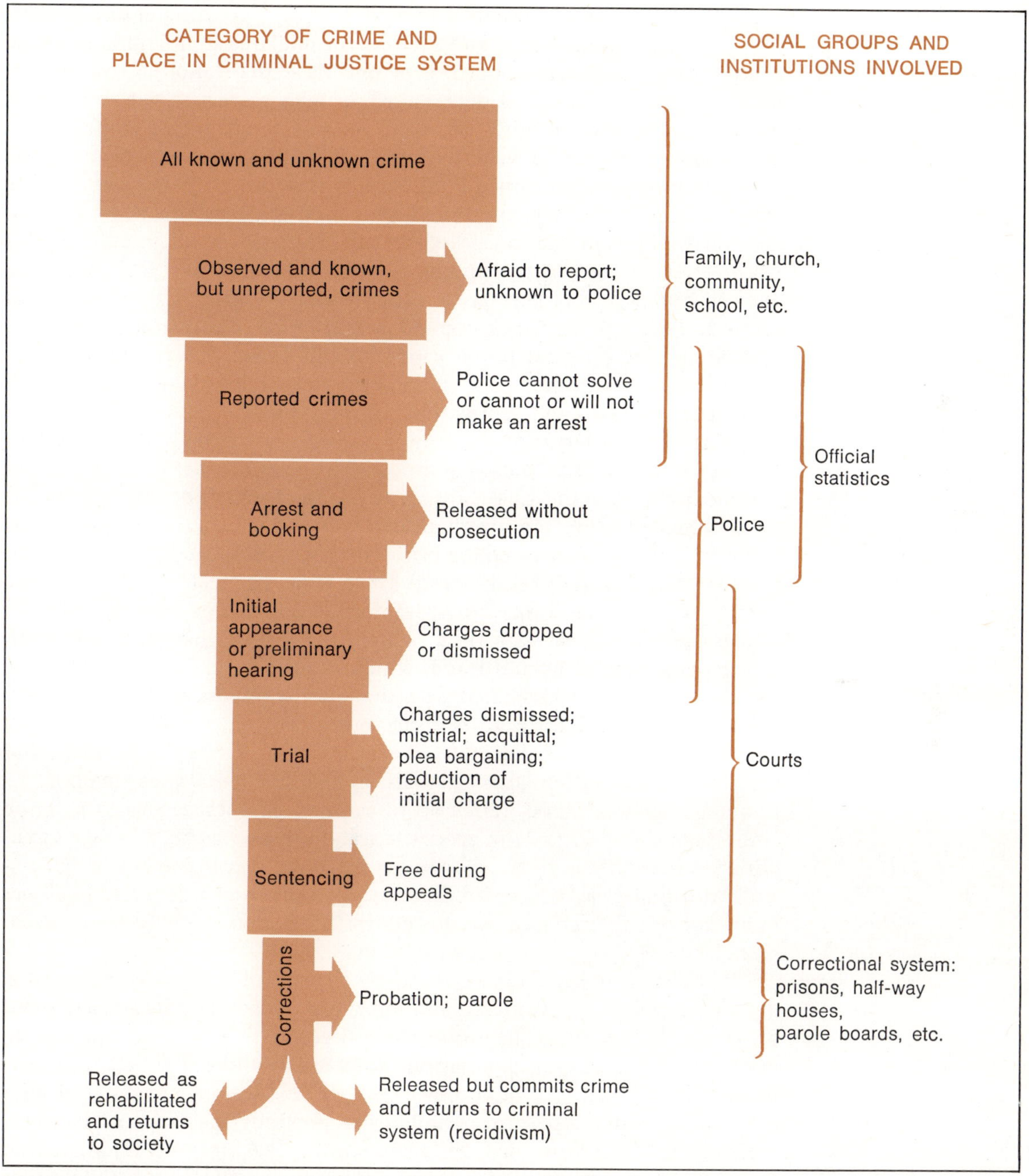

From the President's Commission on Law Enforcement and Administration of Justice, *The Challenge of Crime in a Free Society* (Washington, D.C.: U.S. Government Printing Office, 1973). This source contains a more detailed version of this figure.

Furthermore, official statistics on juvenile delinquency are subject to the same limitations that qualify the validity of criminal statistics, in addition to the special limitations just described. Reporting of deviant acts may be more conscientious and accurate in one area than another (urban ghetto versus upper-class suburb), at one time than another (periods of prosperity versus periods of depression), or with respect to one social class or racial group than another (for black youths versus white youths). Law enforcement officials may be willing to look the other way when some youths commit technically illegal acts. Furthermore, in the eyes of the court, juvenile offenders are joined with their families and receive different treatment than that accorded to individual adult offenders. For this reason and because of the emphasis upon rehabilitation, the courts are allowed a great deal of permissive interpretation. Finally, statistics on both crime and delinquency are compiled primarily for administrative purposes and often have political implications. In this sense, the recording of delinquency may tell more about the behavior or biases of officials than about the activities and motivations of offenders.

With these reservations in mind, we can draw upon available reports in order to summarize the contemporary distinctions between crime and delinquency. Since the 1950s, arrests of young people under 18 years of age have increased more rapidly than arrests of older persons. Young people come to the attention of police primarily for crimes against property, for juvenile offenses such as running away from home ("runaways") and curfew violations, and for vandalism. Exceptions to this "youth trend" in crimes against property are those white-collar crimes like embezzlement, forgery, counterfeiting, and fraud, which require special skills and higher social status and are associated with the older segments of the population.

In 1963, offenders 16 years of age outnumbered the offenders in any other age category. Furthermore, the proportion of female offenders has been increasing, although males still outnumber females as juvenile delinquents. Around 1900, the ratio of boys to girls appearing in juvenile courts was about 60 to 1; in recent years, the ratio has been about 5 to 1. Girls are more likely to be arrested for behavior that involves sexual deviance, running away, incorrigibility, and delinquent tendencies. They are more commonly referred to the courts by parents, relatives, or social agencies.

In addition to age and sex, there are significant variations in recorded delinquency by race, ethnicity, and social class. Black youths are estimated to have a delinquency rate from two to five times higher than would be expected on the basis of population. They are also likely to be committed to custodial institutions at younger ages, for less serious crimes, and with fewer prior court appearances and fewer previous institutional commitments than white children. Cohen and Short [1966, pp. 84–135] argue that this may result not only from racial prejudice but also from the fact that children from poorer homes are more likely to be labeled precriminal and, therefore, more likely to be handled by the court than by their own families and communities. There may be a similar explanation for high rates of reported delinquency among Puerto Ricans, Mexicans, and American Indians. Children of foreign-born parents have also had records of high incidence of delinquency, but these children make up only about one fourth of the total offenders because the flow of immigration into this country has been sharply restricted since the 1920s.

Ecological differences have often been the focus for studies of delinquency. Rural–urban contrasts often reveal lower rates in rural areas and small towns. Yet the contrast may not be so great as implied by official statistics: There may be less accurate reporting in rural areas, where less serious offenses are customarily handled by parents, ministers, and teachers. When cases do reach the rural courts, however, a higher proportion of the offenders are sent on to correctional institutions than in urban areas, according to Cohen and Short.

Within cities, delinquency rates are much higher in low-income areas than in other parts of the city. Delinquency areas in a city are often located in transitional zones, near the downtown or industrial sections, where land use is in a state of flux, property is rundown, and population densities are high. Official delinquency rates in these areas are deceiving, however, as Cohen and Short point out. A high reported rate of 25 percent does not mean that only one quarter of the boys in an area are engaged in deviance. There can be much hidden delinquency. Thus, in high-rate areas, probably a sizable *majority* of boys will be officially designated as delinquent at some time during their period of residence.

The problem of studying and reporting crime and delinquency, therefore, is related to the complex nature of deviance. Despite these difficulties, however, sociologists have utilized official reports to formulate theories of crime and delinquency. As the reporting and understanding of deviance has improved and become more sophisticated, older perspectives have been challenged by newer views.

THEORIES OF DEVIANCE

Deviance As Pathological

Older, more conservative theories [Gibbs, 1966, pp. 9–14] assumed that there was something *inherent* in deviants that distinguished them from nondeviants. Historically, criminals were viewed as biologically distinctive in one way or another and, therefore, fundamentally defective, dependent, and delinquent. In other words, deviance was considered to be a *pathological trait* located within individuals. A more recent liberal variation of this notion of pathology has been identified by Jack Gibbs as the "analytical conception." Rather than assuming that criminals are inherently deviant, this view assumes that deviant acts are *inherently injurious to society;* thus, in this variation, there is a shift from an interest in the character of deviant actors to an interest in the characteristics of their acts.

The pathology perspective has been used by conservatives, liberals, and radicals alike, and examples of it abound in sociological research. In Chapter 8, we considered a zonal theory of urban areas of disorganization. This theory argued that certain areas of modern cities were characterized by high rates of crime and delinquency because of other characteristics associated with these regions (high mobility of the population, slum conditions, criminal and "bright light" activities, and so on). Much recent radical theory is based upon the view that modern society is itself pathological, which, in turn, causes citizens to act in deviant ways. Values and attitudes that encourage militarism, racism, and authoritarianism, and institutions like capitalism and the military–industrial complex, which encourage aggression, competition, and violence, are all assumed to lead to higher rates of criminal deviance within the population.

A number of criticisms of these theories of pathology have been developed. Some scholars point out that deviant behavior is not necessarily injurious. In some cases, deviance may make positive contributions to parts of the social order. Furthermore, as we have seen, deviance is a relative concept; what is wrong in one society or at one time is not necessarily wrong in another or at a different time. One of the pioneers of this perspective was William Graham Sumner in his book on *Folkways.* He set out to show that almost any form of human behavior is normative somewhere in the world. Monogamy, for example, as a norm for marriage, is the rule in many societies. Deviation from this norm can be punished severely. In other societies, however, monogamy is permitted, but polygamy is preferred and may be a mark of status. Conformity in one culture may be deviance in another. "Social groups create deviance by making the rules whose infraction constitutes deviance and by applying those rules to particular people and labeling them as 'outsiders'" [Becker, 1963, p. 9].

In other words, deviance is not a quality of the act that someone commits but rather is the normative perception of that act by others. Deviants are those who have been labeled as such; therefore, much depends upon whose rules we are considering. Certainly, all rules are not universally accepted, especially in a heterogeneous society. The ones that prevail and are used are the ones insisted upon by the most influential people in a society. Those with the power and prestige establish the prevailing norms; those who do not live by these norms are considered deviants. For example, older citizens set down rules for youth; male citizens set down rules for women; white Anglo-Saxon Protestants set down rules for immigrants; middle class for working class; whites for blacks. Whether an act is pathological, therefore, depends upon how other people define and react to it and, to be more specific, *which* other people react to it.

These criticisms of the older pathology perspective of deviance were developed primarily by labeling theorists like Howard Becker. Jack Gibbs points out, however, that the critics, in turn, are not free of criticism. For example, he indicates that they do not make clear what kind of reaction is needed to define a behavioral pattern as deviant. If public reaction to some form of deviance is mild (like moderate cheating on income tax), does this mean that most income tax cheaters are not deviant? How harsh must a reaction be before the behavior can be defined as deviant? In addition, Gibbs claims that critics of the pathology perspective are not always consistent. To be consistent, they would have to insist that behavior contrary to a norm is not deviant unless it is discovered and then causes a particular kind of response or reaction.

> Thus, if persons engage in adultery, but their act is not discovered and reacted to in a certain way (by members of a social unit), then it is not deviant! Similarly, if a person is erroneously thought to have engaged in a certain type of behavior and is reacted to "harshly" as a consequence, a deviant act has taken place . . . [Gibbs, 1966, p. 13].

This is another example of the provocative interchange between scholars that leads to new definitions and conceptualizations. Gibbs suggets that better deviance theory must concentrate upon three questions:

1. Why does the incidence of a particular deviant act vary from one population to another?
2. Why do some persons commit this act while others do not?
3. Why is the act considered deviant (pathological) in some social and cultural contexts but not in others?

Recent studies of juvenile delinquency have developed another theory that attempts to address these questions while avoiding the value biases of earlier pathology theory. We refer to E. H. Sutherland's [Sutherland and Cressey, 1955] theory of *differential association* which has become the basis for much contemporary scholarship.

Deviance and Differential Association

Sutherland argues that people learn all forms of behavior, including criminal behavior, through interactions with other people within specific social situations. In other words, learning occurs within the context of a *socialization process.* This theory attempts to recognize the importance of *both* the individual actor and the milieu within which the action takes place. When an individual associates with other people, some encourage conformity to accepted norms while others encourage violation of the norms. This is what is meant by differential association.

Thus a person's delinquent or criminal behavior can be attributed to that person's overexposure to situations favorable to violation of the law coupled with underexposure to situations unfavorable to violation of the law.

> [When people become criminals,] they do so because of contacts with criminal behavior patterns and also because of isolation from anti-criminal behavior. . . . [In addition] the situation is not exclusive of the person. . . . In an area where the delinquency rate is high a boy who is sociable, gregarious,

active, and athletic is very likely to come in contact with other boys in the neighborhood, learn delinquent behavior from them, and become a gangster; in the same neighborhood the psychopathic boy who is isolated, introverted, and inert may remain at home, not become acquainted with other boys in the neighborhood, and not become delinquent. In another situation, the sociable, athletic, aggressive boy may become a member of a scout troop and not become involved in delinquent behavior [Sutherland and Cressey, 1955, pp. 74–81].

In other words, both the characteristics of the individual and the nature of the social situation interact with one another to determine whether deviance or conformity will result.

Critics have argued that this theory is far too general an explanation of deviant behavior. Sutherland and Cressey point out, however, that it is more than a simple "bad companions" explanation. There must be an *overabundance of associations* with criminal patterns of behavior; furthermore, some of the associations that make up this adverse ratio may even be with persons who are not themselves criminals. For example, while a certain boy's parents may teach him that "honesty is the best policy," they may inadvertently give him an example of behavior that is just the opposite (by cheating on their income tax). Thus, how one perceives both the attitudes and the behavior of others determines to some extent how he or she will be socialized; clearly, then, these perceptions play a role in socializing someone into deviance, as we have seen in previous studies in this book involving marihuana users, illegitimacy, suicide, and extremist behavior in social movements.

Other scholars have applied this theory of deviance as a consequence of association to the provocative analysis of specific problems. Ruth Cavan [1961, pp. 243–258] maintains that laws relating to juvenile delinquency are of little use because they refer only to serious adult offenses. Laws defining juvenile delinquency tend to be vague and varied. Illinois law has defined a delinquent child as one who is incorrigible or who is growing up in idleness, one who wanders about the streets in the night without being on any lawful business, or one who is guilty of indecent or lascivious conduct. New Mexico law has rested its definition on the word habitual—A child who is habitually disobedient, uncontrolled, wayward, truant from home or school, or injurious to self or others is delinquent. The federal Children's Bureau has referred to conduct that is so seriously antisocial as to interfere with the rights of others or to menace the welfare of the delinquent or of the community. The Children's Bureau definition is used by Cavan as a tentative starting point, since it relates juvenile delinquency to the social structure.

Cavan suggests a theory that visualizes juvenile behavior as falling along a continuum ranging from extreme forms of underconformity to extreme forms of overconformity. She then draws a bell-shaped or "normal" curve to depict the extent of the various types of behavior in any society (see Figure 12-2). The behavior of most juveniles falls around the midpoint

FIGURE 12-2 Continuum of Types of Deviance: The Example of Juvenile Delinquency

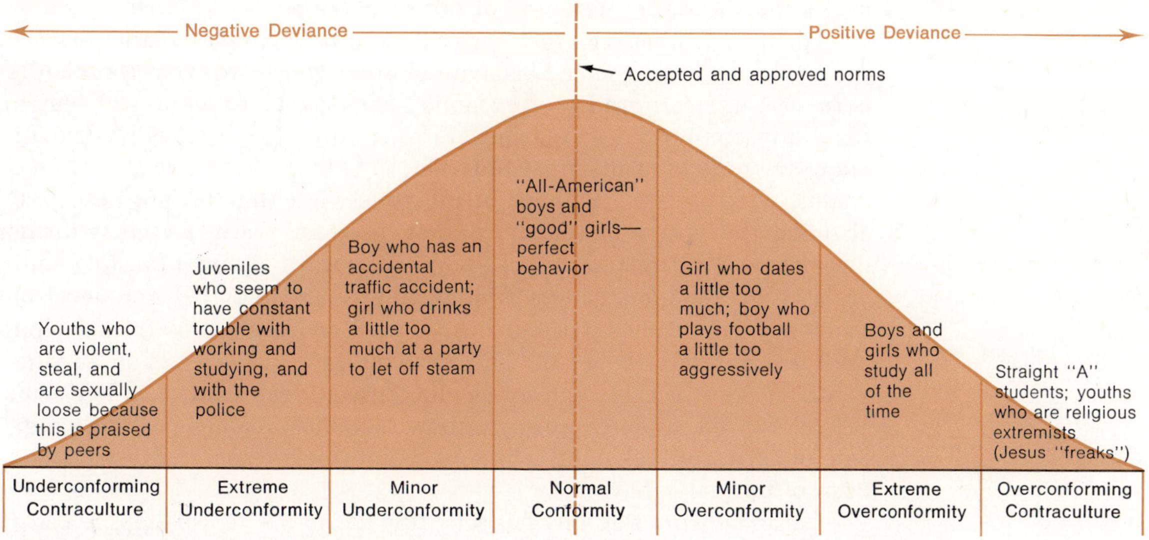

From Ruth Shonle Cavan, "The Concepts of Tolerance and Contraculture as Applied to Delinquency," *The Sociological Quarterly, 2* (October 1961), pp. 243–258.

of the continuum and involves *normal conformity, minor underconformity,* or *minor overconformity.* Here we find behavior that is most highly rewarded and praised by society, including the behavior of "All-American" boys and "good" girls. Minor deviance from accepted norms is frequently considered to be a result of accident, momentary passion, or lack of awareness of specific norms. Juveniles who drive carelessly while drunk, hit someone when mad, or become a little aggressive while pursuing accepted goals are examples.

In contrast, Cavan argues that a small portion of the juvenile population will deviate in very extreme ways in both positive and negative directions. These forms of behavior represent more than simple deviation from accepted norms; they constitute detachment from and opposition to the prevailing culture. Youths participating in these forms of deviant behavior are a part of *underconforming* or *overconforming contracultures,* which have distinct norms, hierarchies of statuses and roles, and internal methods of social control. The "hard core" delinquents deviating in a negative direction are applauded by their peers for stealing, chronic truancy, sexual promiscuity, or fighting. Since they are condemned by the rest of society, they may enter into an adult criminal contraculture. Youth deviating in a positive direction may be considered by others as "sissies," "teachers' pets," "brains," "squares," or "freaks." Youth from this extreme may also enter adult contracultures and become conscientious objectors to war, rejectors of scientific medical care, members of utopian communities, and the like. Behavior at either extreme is considered "wrong" since it undermines the routine functioning of the social system.

Finally, lying between these two extremes of behavior—that is, between these contracultures—is the behavior of other youths who engage in either *extreme underconformity* or *extreme overconformity* while still remaining partly committed to the prevailing culture. These types of deviance are characteristic of marginal individuals. Underconformists are often in trouble with parents, teachers, or the police, but they do not necessarily abandon the norms of society. Rather, they are warned against further deviance and are encouraged to reform their ways. Overconforming youth are also on the outer fringes of acceptability and may be excluded from many normal social activities. However, here too adults may try to encourage them to "have more fun" and "become involved." As a consequence, youth in both of these categories alternatively feel wanted and rejected. When rejected, underconformers show their hostility by stealing, vandalism, or aggressive behavior, while overconformers resort to excessive criticism of normal behavior.

Cavan's theory not only has scientific merit, but it also helps to clarify several practical problems related to delinquency. It suggests the need for a new perspective on differences in social-class morality. Behavior that the lower class would regard as normal conformity, and therefore to be tolerated, might be considered minor or extreme underconformity by the middle class, and therefore not to be tolerated. Permissive sex relations by lower-class youth might be accepted as normal (or even as approved overconforming behavior) by gangs but looked upon as delinquent by higher-status parents, teachers, and policemen. In contrast, the petting that some middle-class youth substitute for intercourse is regarded as hypocritical and prudish overconformity by lower-class youth. This perception helps to explain why some delinquent behavior by middle-class youth seems to be often overlooked or excused: Authorities consider these deviant acts to be less serious than those of the lower classes. Thus, in one sense, the authorities are not actually (or consciously) giving the middle-class youths preferential treatment; rather, these youths are benefiting from the fact that they and the authorities both conform to basically the same values. Therefore, juvenile probation and parole might be more realistic and successful if lower-class youth were not expected to conform rigorously to middle-class standards.

Cavan's approach to delinquency has advantages and disadvantages. It is one way of showing how delinquency varies in degree and direction, and it suggests that similar variation may exist in other forms of deviation. Her conception, however, may seem to be an oversimplification of delinquency. A chart or a continuum can never take into account or convey all the subtleties and complexities of human behavior. We can make use of such a diagram only for purposes of abstract analysis. Cavan's concept of overconformity is perhaps the most questionable aspect of her approach. According to Cavan, there are always some individuals who tend to be scrupulous to a fault and who have a compulsion for perfection and absolute commitment to a norm. The theory implies that this is neurotic rather than normal behavior. Cavan might have qualified her interpretation by pointing out that, in some cases, extreme commitment to moral goals can be considered exemplary.

This criticism of Cavan's theory highlights a continuing debate in sociology about the nature of deviance. Deviant behavior is commonly thought of as "bad" and conformity as "good." Many social scientists have tended to imply that deviance is a sign that something has gone wrong in the social system. When norms conflict and a social context called "anomic" or "disorganized" prevails, people are considered to be more likely to deviate. In other words, wrongdoing is seen as a basic sign that social conditions are inadequate.

> It is common practice in sociology to picture deviant behavior as an alien element in society. . . . [It] is described almost as if it were leakage from machinery in poor condition: it is an incidental result of disorder and anomie, a symptom of internal breakdown [Erikson, 1965, p. 457].

In opposition to this view is the concept that deviance is "normal" behavior and can often be *functional.*

Deviance As Functional

According to Sutherland, deviance can be considered normal in that it is learned behavior, and it can be understood in terms of the social setting in which it takes place. Kai Erikson draws upon an insight from Emile Durkheim in order to explain the more positive view that deviance is often a product of stable institutions, an important social resource that is guarded and preserved by many social organizations. In other words, deviance is not just a measure of the breakdown of the social system; *deviance is useful to the social order and, therefore, may be perpetuated by the community.*

When a deviant challenges the norms of a community, citizens rally in defense of the prevailing social order. In rejecting crime, delinquency, and other forms of deviance, people are drawn together in mutual anger and indignation. This collective experience promotes group cohesiveness and a sense of mutual solidarity.

> We have only to notice what happens, particularly in a small town, when some moral scandal has just been committed. [Citizens] stop each other on the street, they visit each other, they seek to come together to talk of the event and wax indignant in common. From all these similar impressions which are exchanged, for all the temper that gets itself expressed, there emerges a unique temper . . . which is everybody's without being anybody's in particular. This is the public temper [Durkheim, 1947, p. 102].

In other words, deviance performs the function of helping to keep the social system intact. It does not merely disrupt the system; in fact, it may also work to preserve it. Deviant behavior functions to maintain the

12-2 Is Deviance Desirable or Undesirable?

Various types of deviant acts—behavior which is seen as extreme, bizarre, different, or highly individualistic—can be considered both desirable and undesirable. In other words, the same type of deviant act may have both functional and dysfunctional consequences for society.

D. S. Brody/Stock, Boston

Public nudity is often a simple release from the boredom and anxiety which characterizes contemporary urban life. To others, however, this behavior may seem to be an outrageous attack upon traditional norms of decency.

Donald Dietz, Dietz/Hamlin

Public gambling and burlesque can become a controlled safety valve for the pent-up frustrations of a Puritan culture, which emphasizes thrift and saving and sexual behavior confined to monogamous family relationships. At the same time, however, gambling and burlesque threaten and erode these traditional values.

Newsweek, Inc.

To the consumer, illegal bribery, monopoly, and price fixing by corporation executives constitute deviant behavior. However, to some leaders of industry these same acts may appear to be necessary for corporate survival or merely an expression of smart business practices.

The Bettmann Archive

Individual acts of defiance, such as Luther's nailing his theses on the church's doors, may seem to be a necessary attack upon institutional evils and a call for new norms and values. To others, such acts represent inexcusable threats to important social institutions.

The Schlesinger Library, Radcliffe College

Some acts of deviance, such as the public demonstrations by members of the early women's movement, are calls for a reaffirmation of basic values like freedom and equality. To many men, these same acts challenged crucial values of family life based upon assumed male superiority and dominance.

F. W. Owen/Black Star

Public leaders often believe that they must have greater freedom than other citizens to engage in and order extreme behavior to protect national security and interests. However, this assumed freedom can also encourage leaders to use illegal or extralegal means (spying, intimidation, blackmail, terror) to enhance their own power.

normative boundaries of a social system. This *boundary-maintenance function* takes place as citizens confront the deviant act and debate and argue about it. As Erikson [1965, p. 461] puts it: The mere act of condemning deviance "sharpens the authority of the violated norm and declares again where the boundaries of the group are located." Furthermore, enforcing the law by punishing the deviant restates normative boundaries. At the same time, condemnation and punishment may involve *redefinitions* of older norms. These processes provide a way in which societies can respond to changing conditions. The contemporary debate in many churches over abortion and homosexuality—how to define these acts and how to deal with those who commit them—both restates old commitments and redefines new boundaries.

Society's "need" for deviants is indicated by the fact that deviant activities often seem to receive support from the very agencies designed to suppress them. Institutions ostensibly created for control or rehabilitation (mental hospitals, prisons) give the institutional residents an opportunity to teach one another the special skills and attitudes necessary for a deviant career. The resident's sense of alienation and isolation from outside society also tends to promote a continuation of deviant behavior. The problem of recidivism in crime (criminal repeaters) reflects this process of socially approved reinforcement of deviant subcultures.

In addition, a community may provide ceremonies that symbolically transfer a person from a normal position in society to a deviant role, such as a trial, psychiatric case conference, formal and publicized verdicts, or formal commitment to a mental institution. These are dramtic rituals that attract widespread public attention. On the other hand, there is no comparable ceremony when the deviant returns home later as a rehabilitated or cured citizen. In fact, the former deviant is suspect as a potential recidivist or as one who might relapse and is, therefore, treated as a permanent deviant:

> Police departments could not operate with any real effectiveness if they did not regard ex-convicts as an almost permanent population of offenders, a pool from which to draw suspects [and informers]; and psychiatric hospitals could not do a responsible job in the community if they were not alert to the fact that ex-patients [allegedly] are highly susceptible to relapse [Erikson, 1965, p. 462].

Erikson emphasizes that not *all* societies regulate movement in and out of normal behavior in the same way. In some societies, the former deviant may go through ceremonies designed to reintegrate the individual into acceptable society without stigma. In some premodern societies, the young are expected to deviate (for example, sexual experimentation may be permitted), but when they move through public rites of passage to adulthood (which can involve circumcision, subincision, or scarification), they are expected to give up their deviant career (channel sexual behavior into approved familial patterns). Other societies permit deviation on special days or in special group contexts (one can drink to some excess on holidays or at a cocktail party), and the individual can gain legitimate passage back to normal society by merely leaving those contexts.

In addition to boundary maintenance, Lewis Coser [1962, pp. 172–182] suggests that deviance is functionally related to the problems of tolerance, boredom, and group leadership in four specific ways. *First,* the level of tolerance toward deviant behavior influences both internal and external group relations. When the group is intolerant and rejects the deviant, it may redefine normal behavior and strenghen the common loyalty to established norms. At the same time, if the group is too rigid in its demands, as in fanatical religious and political sects, it may lose so many members that group size and influence are diminished and weakened. There is, however, still another possibility: A group may value tolerance and refuse to reject the deviant. Coser refers to the illustration of the Quakers, who value tolerance as a central component of their ideology. This group practices what it professes; in fact, the group needs social objects toward whom tolerance can be directed to provide an opportunity for practicing and reaffirming this important group value. The Quaker practice of tolerance tends to enhance the group's image in the eyes of the outside world and thus makes more effective ingroup–outgroup relationships possible [Webb, 1975].

Second, boredom and apathy may be created in a social system where there is sustained conformity. Repetitious and monotonous rituals of conformity can lead to patterns of interaction that encourage social fatigue. Thus, the deviant who shocks the community from complacent conformity, especially the innovator who demands a new morality or the restoration of an old and neglected morality, helps to break the spell of apathy. John Dewey said that conflict can set society to contriving and can create the appropriate context for reflection and ingenuity (see Chapter 14 for a discussion of the functions of conflict). Many civil rights leaders and antiwar advocates have seen their roles to be the challenging of the social boredom and apathy that permit racism and militarism to persist.

Third, deviants may be innovators who alert the community to imperfections and strains in the social system. They may be the marginal people of society who are registering the pain that comes from being on the periphery of the status quo. For example, during the ghetto uprisings of the 1960s, many American blacks argued that they were rebelling against the economic imperfections of society, not merely engaging in criminal deviance (looting, vandalism). Leaders are also marginal in so far as they occupy a high status level in group life. They are charged with the responsibility of seeing that the group is able to make adjustments to change and to remain flexible. When leaders meet with outgroups, they are on the boundaries of the ingroup and are often given license to deviate and violate group norms in fulfilling their roles. Thus, American presidents and secretaries of state claim that they must be free to use clandestine tactics, threats of warfare, economic bribery, and other behaviors considered to be deviant in domestic politics in order to protect the national interests when dealing with potential enemies.

Fourth, since leaders have highly prized qualities, they are permitted to deviate in ways that would be intolerable for the ordinary group members. Presidents may disclose national secrets with impunity, whereas a Daniel Ellsberg is prosecuted for publication of *The Pentagon Papers.* This process may partly explain why members of the Teamsters' Union accepted James Hoffa in spite of his many deviations, or why Sammy Davis' mixed racial marriage was generally tolerated by the society as a whole. In other words, some deviants have high status and take advantage of their privileged positions.

The functional approach to deviance, then, can contribute special insights to a scientific analysis of problems like crime and delinquency. Of particular value is the way in which deviance can be viewed as an integrated and related aspect of the larger social fabric, contributing to the maintenance of the social system as a whole. There is, however, a problem with the functionalist perspective. Deviance does tend to be related to various forms of disorganization, particularly personal alienation and social anomie. A purely functional approach can obscure these important characteristics. Therefore, one final theory—Robert Merton's attempt to account for various forms of social anomie within a larger functional framework—is worth discussing at this point.

Social Structure and Anomie

Arguing that some, but not all, deviance can give support to the social system, Merton [1966, pp. 808–811] distinguishes between *aberrance* and *nonconformity.* The aberrant person knows and accepts the norms of society but seeks to violate them to his or her advantage. In contrast, the nonconformist knows the norms of society but considers them unjust and violates them openly in an effort to bring about change. Aberrant behavior, then, is irresponsible negative deviance (many forms of crime), whereas nonconforming behavior is responsible positive deviance (Gandhi's civil disobedience). Aberrance can be destructive to society, while nonconformity can be constructive in the long run. As Merton indicates, sociologists have given more attention to the study of aberrant forms of deviance (called by Alexander Liazos [1972] the sociology of "nuts, sluts, and perverts") than to more functional forms.

Focusing upon nonconformity, Merton [1938, pp. 672–682] points out that "some social structures exert a definite pressure upon certain persons in the society to engage in nonconformist rather than conformist conduct." For example, in America, we value success in terms of money, status, and style of life, and we urge success as a goal for all citizens, not just a privileged few. We also say that all people can succeed if only they will apply themselves (the Protestant ethic). Yet, for many citizens, the social *means* of attaining cultural *goals* are not available. Social conditions

TABLE 12-3 Differentiation of Various Forms of Behavior with Respect to Acceptance or Rejection of Means and Goals[a]

Form of Behavior	Culturally Approved Goals	Socially Accepted Means	Examples
Conformity	+	+	Most behavior that strives for approved goals by accepted means.
Innovation	+	−	Turning to crime in order to obtain monetary rewards; using civil disobedience to achieve racial equality
Ritualism	−	+	The superpatriotic activities of Ku Klux Klan members; bureaucrats who follow every rule of the organization to the letter
Retreatism	−	−	Withdrawal in the form of vagrancy, alcoholism, drug addiction, isolated living, psychoneurosis, and the like
Rebellion	+/−	+/−	Revolutionaries who reject old goals and means and create new goals and means

[a]A plus sign means acceptance; a minus sign means rejection.

exist that can deny certain people access to education, occupations, medical care, the development of self-confidence, and the like.

As a consequence, some citizens will reject the goals of society or create new goals. Others will adopt unacceptable means for achieving approved goals. Table 12-3 indicates the way in which Merton differentiates various forms of conformist and nonconformist behavior according to their acceptance or rejection of basic cultural goals and the social means for achieving these goals. He refers to these forms of behavior as five logically possible, alternative modes of adjustment or adaptation by individuals within societies. Most people are *conformists* and fall into the first group, accepting both the goals and the prescribed means of achieving these goals. By way of contrast, *innovators* accept the fundamental goals of a society but seek new or unconventional means of obtaining those goals. *Ritualists* tend to give up the struggle for goals that may seem impossible for them to achieve, but they cling to respectability. In other words, they modify their ambitions to a level that they can more easily reach, even with limited means. At the same time, they take great pride in abiding by conventional means. On the other hand, *retreatists* withdraw from both the struggle to be successful and the struggle to be respectable. Defeatism and resignation often mark their perspectives on life. Finally, *rebels* are characterized by a revolutionary spirit as they replace old goals and means with new ones.

Merton's reference to anomie in the title of his essay needs special clarification at this point. A state of anomie tends to prevail in many societies, such as ours, where goals of success are so exalted that all members feel compelled to compromise the means for attaining the goals. There is a tendency to believe that "anything goes" as long as a person gains the appropriate prestige symbols (for example, Watergate participants). After an individual acquires significant status, we often tend to overlook the means he or she may have used to achieve this position. In this sense, there is a lack of rules, or, to be more specific, a state of anomie—a lack of coordination between means and ends.

Merton's thesis has become a kind of contemporary classic. To be sure, it has been criticized and modified by Merton himself and by others. Some scholars question whether all Americans feel themselves under pressure to achieve the cultural goals of success. Others point out that there have been significant steps in our society to open the avenues of social mobility to children of the lower class, especially through college education. Still other critics note that, while Merton's theory may suggest why many individuals turn to innovation, it fails to deal with those who might be motivated to deviate but who do not find the opportunity to do so. Nevertheless, the concept of anomie as developed in this context by Merton remains fundamental to sociological thought. Its greatest limitation, perhaps, is that it remains at a very high level of abstraction. Researchers have found that empirical testing of the types of deviance identified by Merton is an extremely difficult task; nonetheless, much scholarly work has been stimulated by his theory. We will now turn our attention to several studies of juvenile gangs that are intellectually indebted to Merton, as well as to the other theories we have considered.

Studies of Juvenile Gangs

The work of Albert Cohen [1955] on delinquent boys was influenced by Merton's theory. He was concerned primarily with working-class boys who engage in deviant behavior as a result of the goals–means strain in our society. According to Cohen, delinquent behavior can be understood in large part as a result of the gap between what seems to be expected of boys by a middle-class world and what they realistically see themselves accomplishing in a lower-class subculture. For example, some may become deviants because their parents had difficulty in school and have passed on their negative school attitudes to their children. In addition, school stands for middle-class values and is often conducted by middle-class teachers who cannot relate easily to lower-class boys. The boys' language is not "nice" and their dress and manner are not "dignified."

Furthermore, working-class boys are ambivalent toward middle-class values. They feel that they cannot possibly live up to these standards. They generally lack both the skills and the finesse to perform very successfully; the hostile responses of teachers then reinforce the feelings of inadequacy and impossibility. As a consequence, although they want many middle-class goals (money, status, prestige), lower-class boys may turn completely and compulsively against middle-class standards. Psychologists in the Freudian tradition have called this a *reaction formation*. The individual actually rejects the very thing he or she most wants. Such rejection often takes the form of extreme deviance and can become a way of "getting even" with a society that encourages impossible expectations.

> Cohen explains the content of the subculture as determined in part by compulsive opposition to middle-class norms. The middle class values property: the delinquent subculture shows its contempt for property. The middle class places value upon working toward the deferred goal of success: the delinquent subculture despises school and abandons the goal of middle-class success, along with all the discipline and decorum required to achieve it [Johnson, 1960, p. 672].

Cohen suggested that Merton's theory, although useful, does not account adequately for the nonutilitarian character of many destructive and violent acts committed by working-class delinquents. Those youths Cohen studied often stole clothes they could not wear and toys they could not use. Therefore, they were not merely using illegitimate means to achieve the desired symbols of success. Malicious and negativistic behavior was simply a means of striking back at the conventional world, which allows an impossible goals–means gap to develop:

> In homelier language, stealing "for the hell of it" and apart from considerations of gain or profit is valued activity to which attaches glory, prowess and profound satisfaction. A group of boys enters a store where each takes a hat, a ball or a light bulb. Then they move on to other stores to continue the game indefinitely. They steal a basket of peaches, desultorily munch on a few of them and leave the rest to spoil [Cohen, 1955, pp. 24–32].

Where Cohen focused upon what working-class boys are *against*, other scholars, like Walter Miller [1958, pp. 5–19; 1959, pp. 97–107], have emphasized what they are *for*. Miller sees working-class boys as living up to the expectations of their subculture, which values trouble, smartness, excitement, fate, luck, and autonomy. In expressing these values, boys engage in activities and develop personalities that lead to delinquency. They are socialized into this way of life by their parents and their peers. For example, overly masculine behavior may reflect the rebellion of a boy reared in a female-based household. At the same time, toughness may be functional because it prepares working-class boys for the kinds of manual occupations into which many of them will go. According to Miller, delinquency among slum boys is not related to the goals–means crisis; rather, it is more the outcome of socialization into the American slum subculture.

Cloward and Ohlin [1960] utilize both perspectives and identify three different types of youth gangs: *criminal, conflict,* and *retreatist*. The structure of the neighborhood determines what type of gang emerges. In a fairly stable community, where crime is well-organized and often related to conventional groups and institutions (police, businesses, the political structure, the courts), youths develop criminal gangs. These gangs socialize members who possess innovative skills for a life in the underworld. Opportunities are provided to learn the illegitimate means for achieving accepted goals (like monetary success) and to enter the world of professional crime. Adult criminals who are successful, powerful, and active in the conventional institutions of the community (the church, politics) are admired.

In disorganized communities with weak and ineffective institutional controls (police, church, family), conflict gangs arise. These fighting gangs give members a feeling of achievement in terms of peer values and goals. Although conflict gangs are likely to be found in all slum neighborhoods, they tend to prevail in the most transient unstable areas, those characterized by massive housing projects (where residents are strangers to one another) and by rapidly changing land use (residential areas that are being encroached upon by commerce and industry). Conflict gangs arise to offset the social anomie created by the transient and unstable community life.

Finally, some lower-class youth cannot succeed in the world of crime and turn to retreatist gangs. These gangs contain the "double failures"—those who fail in both the conventional world and in organized crime. The gang provides group support and a sense of achievement as members enter into a subculture of drug users and prostitutes. In retreatist gangs, members seek escape from the burden of failure.

As can be seen, much of the research on delinquency has placed an emphasis upon social background, and high delinquency rates have been correlated with slum life. Social-class position, race, and economic deprivation have been considered important variables. In other words, research has suggested that deviant behavior occurs among youth when anomic conditions prevail and when there is a marked degree of family disintegration and social disorganization.

In contrast, sociologists Short and Strodtbeck [1965] felt that they could discover more about delinquency by analyzing the *processes of interaction within gangs and between gangs and society* than by focusing upon social conditions. From June 1959 to August 1962, they studied both black and white gangs involved in the YMCA Program for Detached Workers in Chicago. Although they set out to test the theories of Cohen, Cloward, Ohlin, and Miller, they also designed their research to permit formulation and discovery of new and unanticipated information. Many of the familiar hypotheses about anomie and delinquency were found to be valid. In addition, Short and Strodtbeck also discovered diverging evidence that suggested additional processes at work.

There was no indication that lower-class boys, black or white, rejected middle-class values—that is, there was no evidence of any exaggerated reaction-formation behavior or of any strong commitment to an alternative subculture. The boys generally aspired to a stable family life and were quick to note how important it was for a father to have a reliable job. Most felt they should do everything possible to make their own boys want to go to school. Boys in all categories rated middle-class life-styles equally high. A large percentage aspired to achieve at least some college, even those who had been unsuccessful in their educational careers. Thus, when gang members showed such obvious strong support for middle-class norms, Short and Strodtbeck had to wonder what could account for higher rates of delinquency?

Their most provocative finding was that *gangs provide a strategic functional context for deviant behavior.* Not all gang boys became delinquent, nor did all nongang boys conform. There was, however, a greater *risk* of delinquent behavior within gangs. This risk developed because of the member's urgent need to keep his place and reputation within the group. In other words, gang boys would willingly run the risk of delinquency in order to achieve and maintain status in the gang.

Some boys became delinquent because they were more highly exposed to the risk of becoming illegitimate fathers, having to fight, or having to use a knife or a gun. For example, constant sexual intercourse was the norm among lower-class boys, and it was a form of behavior that received much support from adults in the subculture. A boy who was successful with girls often emerged as a gang leader. Sexual activity was one way to maintain status, and this reward outweighed the risk of parenthood and punishment by society when illegitimacy resulted. In addition, since most of the gangs studied were conflict gangs, the importance of fighting was evident. Fighting, too, was related to status management within the gang and between the gang and the larger society. Analysis of a gang fight that broke out one night at an athletic event led to the conclusion that it all started when a 21-year-old gang leader was reprimanded by a detached worker for wanting to buy beer at an event sponsored by the YMCA. The leader lost face in the eyes of his peers. The worker ordered the whole gang to leave the scene, and this was a status threat to the group as well as to the leader. As a result, the shamed gang started a fight with other gangs.

Lewis Yablonsky [1962] found similiar processes in his study of gangs in New York. A boy gradually entered a group by hanging around the corner, the bar, the poolroom, or other informal meeting places. At the same time, the tenuous and temporary nature of gangs created uncertainty and insecurity. Commitments were shallow and transitory. Boys had to prove themselves constantly to others and continually reaffirm their status within the gang. In this sense, gang boys are no more free of normative conflict and ambivalence than are other members of urban society, and delinquent acts can be viewed as resulting from this conflict and its frustrations.

In summary, these studies of juvenile gangs have utilized all the basic sociological theories of deviance; that is, the studies have moved from a focus upon social background factors to an interest in the relationship between delinquent youth and the larger society. The latter perspective serves to introduce the question of the social control of deviance, the final topic of this chapter. Specifically, what are the various ways in which societies attempt to control deviant behavior? How effective are these different methods? And what are some of the special problems associated with the social control of crime and delinquency?

CAN DEVIANCE BE CONTROLLED?

The social control of deviant behavior follows the same general principles in all human societies. Three methods are utilized—self-internalization of norms, informal approval or disapproval by others, and formal detection and punishment by agents of social control.

Methods of Social Control

The most fundamental method of social control is the *internalization of norms* that takes place through socialization. Most people conform to conventional standards of behavior because they personally identify with the society in which they have been reared, and they discipline their behavior accordingly. One generally feels *shame, guilt,* or *anxiety* when one fails to conform [Riesman *et al.*, 1950]. In traditional societies, individuals are reluctant to deviate because deviation would bring shame upon themselves and upon their family, friends, and community. In societies that stress individualism (the Protestant ethic), people feel personally guilty or uncomfortable when they violate approved norms. They become dissatisfied with themselves. In contemporary society, many individuals conform in order to lessen general feelings of anxiety. One can never be sure exactly what kind of social disapproval deviant behavior will arouse. In all of these cases, the identity of the social self with socially approved standards of behavior leads individuals to reject deviance in favor of conformity.

As we saw in our discussion of socialization (Chapter 3), the human self does not exist apart from relationships with others. Therefore, *informal processes* of social control operate in all societies. These processes are subtle ways in which other people show approval or disapproval of behavior. This method works most effectively in a closely knit group or society where individuals know each other well and come to depend upon one another intimately. For example, in small towns, informal controls may operate for the entire community, and there may be little need for formal policing of behavior. People continually say and do things, by insinuation or by impugning someone's motives, that are designed to bring deviants back "into line" [Parsons, 1951, p. 303]. Informal controls can involve a frown, tactful disagreement, prolonged silence, or sarcastic humor in response to an individual's deviant act. In this way, self-control and informal control become interrelated.

When these methods fail or are ineffective, societies may have to depend upon *formal methods* of social control. This is particularly true in heterogeneous and complex societies. In this context, informal controls

12-3 Methods for Controlling Deviance: Strengths and Weaknesses

Societies attempt to control behavior which might deviate from approved norms by both personal and impersonal means.

When the unrestrained "I" leads the young child to commit deviant acts, adults warn or scold, thereby inducing feelings of shame, guilt, or anxiety. Since these feelings are unpleasant, the child alters behavior to conform to expectations which will encourage adult praise and affection. This type of control, however, is essentially negative and can inhibit individualism and creativity. Adults also help form the child's concept of "me" by instructing them in the traditional cultural values. This instruction is particularly important when it involves potentially threatening deviant behavior; for example, sexual conduct. However, an excessive "me" can lead to unthinking conformity and the inability to alter behavior when change requires new forms of response; for example, when changing sex roles require new types of male–female relationships.

Jamyl Smith/Metamorphosis

Elsa Dorfman

The Bettmann Archive

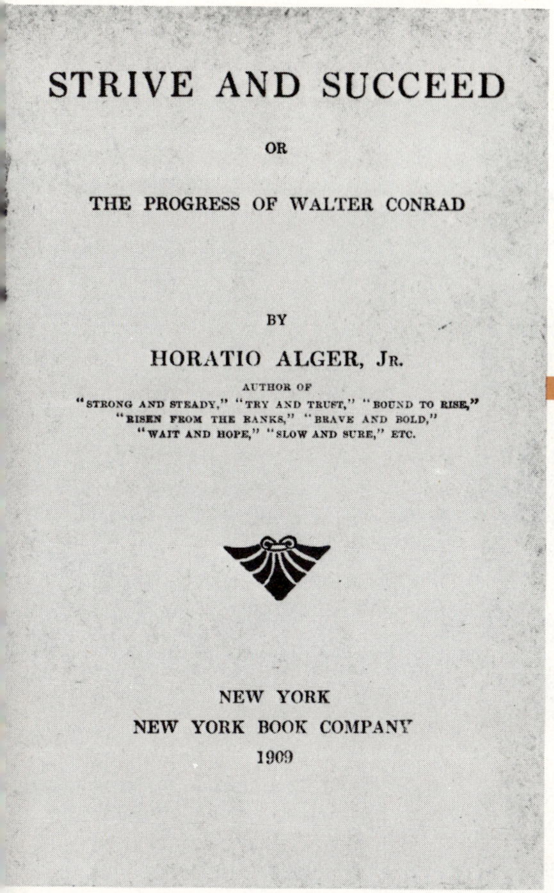
STRIVE AND SUCCEED

OR

THE PROGRESS OF WALTER CONRAD

BY

HORATIO ALGER, Jr.

AUTHOR OF
"STRONG AND STEADY," "TRY AND TRUST," "BOUND TO RISE,"
"RISEN FROM THE RANKS," "BRAVE AND BOLD,"
"WAIT AND HOPE," "SLOW AND SURE," ETC.

NEW YORK
NEW YORK BOOK COMPANY
1909

Humans also identify personally with the norms and values of conforming behavior and, thereby, internalize them. Cultural heroes, such as Horatio Alger, play an important role in this socialization process. However, unquestioning adoption of heroic roles may become dysfunctional; commitment to monetary achievement can become expressed as individualistic greed. Once norms and values are internalized, people are reluctant to deviate when they are aware that others may observe their actions and will disapprove. Therefore, stores have had success displaying ''Thieves Beware'' signs, even when cameras or guards are not utilized. However, this method of control does nothing about the basic conditions which may have led to the deviant behavior. Shoplifting may be the result of poverty and the need for food.

P. Hollander Gross/Stock, Boston

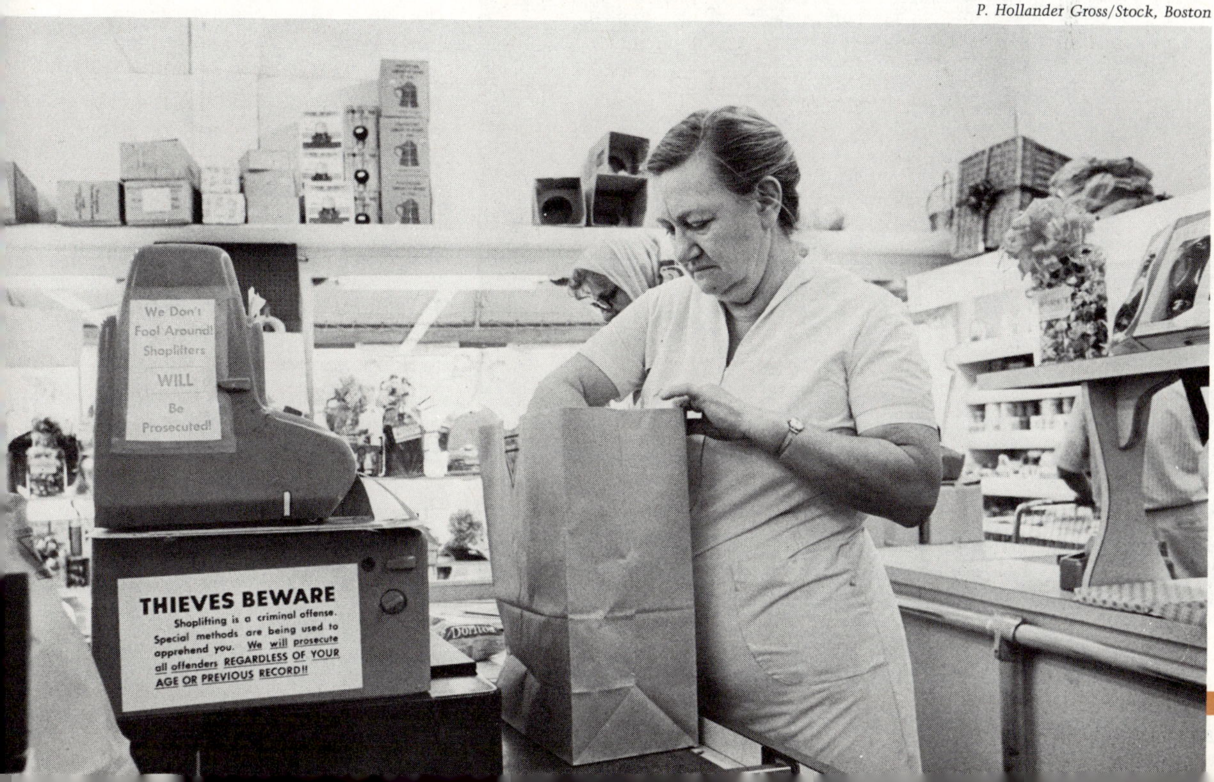

E. Herwig/Stock, Boston

Wide World Photos

Modern societies rely upon formal systems of control, such as courts and prisons which enforce norms expressed as laws. However, there are limits to the law-and-order approach to deviance. Laws may become complex and difficult to enforce. In addition, prisons do not get inmates to internalize approved norms, and courts and prisons do not resolve the original causes of the deviance. As a result, deviant behavior may continue in prison. Shown lower left are the inmates at Attica Prison, after the riot in 1971, as they discuss where, when, and how to negotiate with New York State prison officials. The inmates are wearing cloaks and football helmets, and in the center is a local TV station cameraman. Because of the limitations of formal systems of control much discretion must be used by police, judges, and others in the detection, apprehension, processing, and disposition of those who commit criminally deviant acts. For example, some crimes are overlooked, some sentences are shortened, and so on.

are insufficient because people in the same community do not know each other well and do not always take individual responsibility for controlling each other's behavior. There is much anonymity and impersonality. Some citizens, therefore, are designated as specialists in the making, interpreting, and enforcing of norms, and the norms become formalized as laws. Reliance upon formal control can become pronounced:

> The public police are second only to teachers in the number of service persons that are on the typical public payroll. And the average citizen, after leaving school, is probably more likely to have contact with the police than with any other single branch of public officials. There are also vast numbers of private police, of course, who perform detective and other functions related to the private sector. A great bulk of all employee theft and theft from commercial establishments such as department stores is processed by private policing mechanisms [Wheeler, 1967, p. 654].

The distinction between these three methods of social control helps identify a major problem of controlling deviant behavior in modern societies. Self-control, combined with informal methods, is the most effective way of guaranteeing conformity to accepted norms. In contrast, formal methods of control are expensive, complex, and difficult to implement. Yet most modern societies must of necessity rely upon formal systems. For example, crime and delinquency require an elaborate criminal justice system (see the discussion of the inverted pyramid of crime, pages 522–523), which involves complicated relationships between professionals, citizens, and deviants at each stage of the process. In addition, as we saw in our discussion of bureaucracy (Chapter 7), no formal organization works well unless it permits exceptions to the rule and the possibility of an informal human response.

In the case of the criminal justice system, the notion of *discretion* is critical. If every criminal or delinquent were discovered, reported, arrested, charged, given a trial, found guilty, and sent to an institution, the entire system would collapse. Furthermore, exceptions must be provided for those who are discovered to have been unjustly accused and for changing definitions of what constitutes serious crime or delinquency. The use of discretion by everyone involved in the system helps meet these important needs. Citizens may choose not to report certain kinds of crimes. Police may choose not to make arrests in some cases. Prosecutors may engage in plea bargaining to reduce or dismiss certain charges. Judges and juries often have some leeway in determining degree of guilt and the extent of punishment.

There is, however, a dilemma. Discretion can be misused and abused. Some citizens will not report crimes because they fear becoming involved. Some police will treat certain people and groups more leniently than others. Private prejudices and self-interest can play a role throughout the criminal justice system at all stages of detection, prosecution, sentencing, and treatment. This problem—the misuse of discretionary authority—has been the focus of much recent sociological research. The final sections of this chapter discuss several examples.

Social Status and Crime

One major factor influencing the use of discretion in the contemporary criminal justice system is social status. A person's chances of committing a crime, of being apprehended for the crime, and of being punished for the crime are all related to social-class differences. Sociologists have identified three major types of crime—traditional, victimless, and white collar. *Traditional crime* refers to those types of deviant activities that involve forced violence to persons or property. Such crimes tend to be committed by lower-status persons who lack the skills and knowledge to attain desired goals either through legitimate channels or through more sophisticated criminal activity. These are the acts that most politicians refer to as "the contemporary crime problem" or "crime in the streets"—burglary, mugging, rape, robbery. The Federal Bureau of Investigation and other governmental agencies publish annual reports that deal primarily or exclusively with traditional crimes.

In contrast, *victimless crime* refers to those activities that, although legally criminal, do not characteristically involve a victim in the traditional sense. Such activities include prostitution, drug use, and gambling. The relationship between the individual dispensing the "service" (the criminal as prostitute, drug pusher, or bookie) and the user of the service (the citizen as John, drug user, or gambler) is a voluntary one. Therefore, the user is seen as a contractual customer, who willingly participates in the relationship, in contrast to the nonvoluntary victim of a bank robbery. Because of the voluntary nature of the act, victimless crime is typically considered to be devoid of force or violence.

Criminologist Edwin Sutherland [1949] was the first to identify the importance of *white-collar crime* in contemporary society. As the concept implies, these are criminal activities commited by upper-status, often powerful and influential, members of society. Income tax evasion, price fixing and other monopolistic practices, embezzlement, and business fraud and bribery are examples. It has been estimated that white-collar crimes may cost as much as 40 to 50 billion dollars per year, or half as much as the yearly U.S. defense budget. Yet these crimes are in some ways the hardest to detect, the easiest to commit and get away with, and the least prosecuted following apprehension. There are several reasons for this contrast with traditional crime.

White-collar crimes, like victimless crimes, are nonviolent and are, therefore, looked upon as "clean" crimes. Furthermore, abstract companies and corporations are frequently the "victims," in contrast to the individual persons who are victims of traditional crime. In addition, white-collar criminals need both access and special knowledge and skills to commit their acts. Embezzlement requires access to a corporation's records and special knowledge of accounting techniques. Income tax evasion and business fraud require knowledge of loopholes and evasive tactics. The various political crimes committed by the members of the Nixon White House required access to the major institutions of power in America and an awareness of the way in which these institutions usually worked.

White-collar criminality is often rewarded and honored in American folklore. Americans romanticize the lovable confidence man portrayed by W. C. Fields or George C. Scott's characterization of *The Flim-Flam Man.* Groucho Marx received laughs for his ability to bilk unsuspecting wealthy widows, and Robert Preston conned a whole Midwest town in *The Music Man.* Polygraph lie-detector tests in industry have indicated that as many as 7 of every 10 employees in some retail stores steal from their employer, considering this theft a "natural" right to the available goods. One can purchase towels, ash trays, and other similar articles displaying the name of famous hotels and resorts, thus implying to one's friends that they were stolen from these spots during a vacation stay. In reality, many high-status visitors do steal items from hotels. As a consequence, police and the courts often cannot cope with white-collar criminality. Indeed hotels "budget" for such thefts and may even "welcome" the informal advertising achieved when stolen items are shown to one's friends. High status brings influence and power, and the pressures not to prosecute may be irresistible, in addition to the view that high-status people are not really criminal. Gerald Ford's pardon of Richard Nixon is an illustration of these unique characteristics.

Table 12-4 illustrates the distinctions between the three different types of crimes. *Low-status traditional crime* is the most observable and the most frequently punished. *Middle-status victimless crimes* constitute a gray area, where purveyors of the criminal activity are sometimes punished (the prostitute, the drug seller, the professional gambler), but the customer is rarely if ever detected or punished. *High-status white-collar crimes* are the least observable, and when they are detected the individual criminal is often pardoned or excused. All three types require special access and knowledge. For example, the traditional criminal needs access to the means of violence and knowledge of its proper and most effective use. The middle- and upper-status customers of the prostitute or gambler also need access and knowledge to find and obtain the desired services. Furthermore, in terms of apprehension and punishment, crime does pay—especially middle- and upper-status crimes.

This use of the concept of status distinctions to analyze crime in contemporary society has several important implications, both philosophical and practical. Philosophically, the stereotyped beliefs that criminality is confined to lower-status groups or that traditional crime constitutes the greatest continuing threat must be reexamined. In addition, this typology suggests that the simplistic view that contrasts certain lower-status criminal elements with the rest of society, which is seen as straight and law abiding, is unwarranted. Indeed, many traditional criminals argue that they are only doing what most everyone in our society does. They claim they are singled out for punishment only because they are black, or poor, or uneducated.

The necessity to use discretion in formal systems of criminal justice, therefore, can be complicated by discrimination on the basis of social class.

TABLE 12-4 Social Status and Types of Crimes

	Low Status	Middle Status	Upper Status
Traditional Crime	Automobile theft as a business Burglary Mugging Rape Robbery Theft	Automobile theft as "joy riding" Selling drugs to college classmates Vandalism as "horseplay"	Counterfeiting Forgery
Victimless Crime	Prostitution and pimping Drunkenness as a "wino" Using and selling drugs	Intoxication Professional gambling	Gambling customer Prostitution customer Using drugs
White-Collar Crime		Employee theft Minor shoplifting	Computer crime Embezzlement Bribery Business fraud (Fraudulent advertising) Kickbacks Stock manipulation Violations of civil liberties by officials of government
	← Most Observable and Punished →		← Least Observable and Often Excused →

Furthermore, the gap between official definitions of deviant behavior and informal reactions to that behavior also plays a role. One final factor is worth considering. Discretion may be misused when there is confusion over what constitutes acceptable methods of social control. Public demands to enforce conformity may create a situation whereby agents of social control find themselves engaged in deviance in order to control deviance.

Controlling the Controllers

This final problem associated with the control of deviance in contemporary societies has received increasing attention in recent years. Disclosures that the FBI, local police, CIA, Internal Revenue Service, Watergate Plumbers, and other groups in positions of authority, have used spying, blackmail, provocation, and other illicit and disapproved tactics have raised the question of how to control the controllers. One of the classic studies of this problem is William Westley's analysis of the social conditions that encourage police to resort to extralegal forms of violence.

▶ STUDY 12

The Misuse of Violence by Police [1953 and 1970][1]

Problem

Police are engaged in an occupation that sometimes calls for physical force and violence in order to control deviance. Violence is a property of the state on loan to the police officer as an agent of law enforcement. In the performance of their role, however, police sometimes resort to brutality, the third degree, or intimidation. Is there something in the nature of their occupation that encourages the extralegal or illegal use of violence? Under what conditions does this situation occur?

Hypothesis and Study Design

The distinction between legitimate and illegitimate uses of violence is important. The legitimate use of violence refers to the necessary and expected use of force by police in the line of duty. The use of a club or gun is justifiable when force is necessary to make an arrest or when use of such implements is unavoidable. In other words, police have the authority to enforce the law, defend themselves, and maintain the peace. However, any use of violence beyond these purposes can be considered illegal or extralegal power. Westley hypothesized that *unique pressures in the occupational setting can encourage the illegitimate use of violence by police.*

In order to identify these pressures and the contexts within which they occurred, the *study design* involved an intensive analysis of *one case,* the police force of a Midwestern city of about 140,000 population. The city had a large slum area, a black population with a history of friction with the white population, a high crime rate, an organized political machine, and extensive gambling and vice activities.

Methods of Data Collection

Westley used *participant observation* as his primary research method. Involvement ranged from walking the beat and cruising in squad cars to observation of raids, interrogations, and the training at the police school. In addition, Westley conducted *intensive interviews* with policemen drawn from all ranks and constituting approximately 50 percent of the force. Of special interest were the personal attitudes and feelings of police as they went about their daily activities. The study focused upon how police perceive their role in contrast to the views of the larger society and how police justify the use of violence.

Findings and Interpretations

The interviews disclosed that the policemen tended to transfer violence from a legal resource to a personal resource under certain conditions. Less than 33 percent gave legal reasons for the use of violence when asked, "When do you think a policeman is justified in roughing a man up?" In contrast, almost

[1]Adapted and abridged from William A. Westley, "Violence and the Police," *The American Journal of Sociology, 59* (July 1953), pp. 34–41; and *Violence and the Police: A Sociological Study of Law, Custom, and Morality* (Cambridge, Mass.: The MIT Press, 1970).

50 percent of the policemen gave illegal reasons, and 22 percent gave reasons that stressed the law-enforcement role but constituted extralegal (excessive) use. Of particular interest, 37 percent, the highest category of responses, stressed purely personal ingroup reasons (when disrespect for the police had been shown).

Policemen's Justifications for the Use of Force[a]

Reason Given	Number	Percentage
Legal Uses:	*(23)*	*(31)*
Only when impossible to avoid	17	23
To make an arrest	6	8
Extralegal Uses:	*(16)*	*(22)*
To obtain information	14	19
When you know a man is guilty	2	3
Illegal Uses:	*(34)*	*(47)*
When there is disrespect for police	27	37
For the hardened criminal	5	7
For sex criminals	2	3
Totals:	*73*	*100*

[a]Many respondents gave more than one reason for the use of force. This table, adapted from Westley's study [1953, p. 38], includes the one reason given most emphatically or as the primary explanation by each policeman interviewed.

Westley suggests four processes at work that account for these responses. First, *the desire to make good in one's career is a major and constant concern.* Living in the public eye, the policeman is continually criticized. Of the policemen Westley interviewed, 73 percent believed the public hated them. The policeman's status is low and his salary is small. While the public is quick to criticize brutality, it is equally vocal in its demand for efficient arrests. Therefore, personal prestige and approval goes to the policeman who makes the good pinch. Since this requires quick arrest and conviction of a suspect, there is strong pressure on the policeman to use extralegal force in order to obtain a confession, particularly before detectives step in and get the credit for solving the crime.

In addition, the patrolman finds fulfilling the heroic role that the public often demands especially difficult—for example, in the case of sex crimes. Victims of sex crimes are reluctant to admit their involvement or to cooperate with the police. Many reports of sex offenses are vague and false (''Peeping Toms''). Because the public demands immediate protection from molesters, exhibitionists, and rapists, the officer is under pressure to find a suspect and ''throw the book at him.'' One interviewee stated: ''Now, in my own case, when I catch a guy like that I just pick him up and take him into the woods and beat him until he can't crawl'' [Westley, 1953, p. 37].

Furthermore, occupational pressures encourage illegal violence. A rookie officer summarized the policeman's attitude:

> [Most policemen] feel that it's okay to rough a man up in the case of sex crimes. One of the older men advised me that if the courts didn't punish a man we should. . . . In extreme cases like rape . . . if a man is guilty he

ought to be punished even if you could not get any evidence on him [quoted in Westley, 1953, p. 38].

Second, *colleague attitudes are important.* Although individual officers vary in their use of extralegal and illegal violence, policemen do not condemn each other, either privately or publicly. This is part of an occupational code of ethics. Even those policemen who eschew violence and choose desk jobs refuse to condemn others openly. This collective sanction of violence permits those men who are so inclined to employ violence without fear. Those policemen aware of the risks involved in the misuse of violence will minimize these risks by roughing up a victim in secret or by covering up his abuse by accusing the victim of resisting arrest.

Third, *differential treatment of citizens is a common aspect of the policeman's daily role.* In dealing with middle-class citizens, the officer is much less likely to utilize force. In contrast, ethnic minorities and slum dwellers are assumed to respond only to fear and rough treatment. This attitude is more than prejudice on the part of the police. It also reflects the attitudes of the larger society. The policeman is expected to perform two different roles—law officer and peace officer. When a policeman deals with high-status citizens, law enforcement, usually involving arrests for minor deviations (traffic violations), is his primary duty. However, when he deals with lower-status citizens, maintaining the peace becomes important. This role is not clearly specified in the law, and police may resort to an excessive show of force in order to maintain control. Other citizens generally approve of this behavior since they want low-status citizens to "stay in their place." (See the reference to Egon Bittner's study of the police on skid row in Chapter 14, p. 645.)

Fourth, *one of the most important uses of violence by police is to coerce respect.* Resorting to a tough-guy stance is a defensive reaction by the officer who is sensitive to the pressures of his occupation. Two rookies told how they must make others respect them in order to perform their roles.

> "For example, when you stop a fellow for a routine questioning, say a wise guy, and he starts talking back to you and telling you you are no good and that sort of thing. You know you can take a man in on a disorderly conduct charge, but you can practically never make it stick. So what you do in a case like that is to egg the guy on until he makes a remark where you can justifiably slap him and, then, if he fights back, you can call it resisting arrest."
>
> "If there is any slight resistance, you can go all out on him. You shouldn't do it in the street though." [quoted in Westley, 1953, p. 39]

Conclusions and Implications

This study of one police department suggests that the use of illegitimate violence by police often takes place because of the unique characteristics of the occupation in relationship to the expectations of larger society. Career pressures tend to encourage the use of violence and to transfer it from the state to the occupational group. This process is more likely to occur when the policeman identifies his career as low status, under constant and critical public demands, and subject to resistance and disrespect by deviants. There is an absence of collective sanction against the use of excessive violence among police themselves; more importantly, there is ambivalence in the public's demand for fair play *and* for resolution of the crime problem.

Westley's research has become a benchmark for the continuing study of deviance by the controllers of deviance [Graber, 1975; Marx, 1974, pp. 402–441; Skolnick and Currie, 1970]. By examining more recent information about illegal activities by police, these newer studies suggest additional factors that might be important. For example, organizational pressures require police agencies to *anticipate, manage,* and, sometimes, *manipulate intelligence* (information) about actual and potential criminal groups and activities in society. Police agencies, like other modern corporations, need organized intelligence to anticipate demands that may require action. This is functionally necessary for the survival and autonomy of the organization. Therefore, the fact that control agencies (FBI, CIA, etc.) utilize spying, infiltration, and other covert techniques to collect needed information is not surprising.

Anticipation, however, is not sufficient. Having learned of actual or possible deviant acts, police agencies are often tempted to manage and manipulate this information to their benefit. These activities may involve the following: mass detention and other forms of preventive action; espionage and subversion in the form of secretly undermining groups or movements considered to be dangerous; bribery, blackmail, and other forms of intimidation; provocation that encourages groups and individuals to commit illegal acts that can result in arrest. In other words, much as the automobile company executive attempts to anticipate (through consumer preference studies), manage (through advertising), or manipulate (through creation of new consumer needs) the public's desire for automobiles, representatives of control agencies can become preoccupied with the nature of their "market"—criminal and deviant behavior. This protects them from being a purely "reactive" force, constantly responding to the whims of their "clients" or "targets."

Formal systems of control, then, bring with them a host of problems that transcend the behavior of deviants themselves. Both internal and external pressures operate to make the controllers of deviance engage in acts of deviance in the name of enforcing conformity.

▶ SO WHAT?

So many different "solutions" to the problem of crime have been suggested that to consider many of them in detail would be impossible. For purposes of simplicity, we can categorize these recommendations into three groups. The debate about crime has tended to be polarized into those who argue for law and order (harsher laws and penalties, stronger and larger police forces, and so on) and those who favor radical changes in the criminal justice system (decriminalization of many laws, abolition of most of the traditional prison system, and so on). Standing between these two extremes are those who favor reform of the existing system (mandatory sentences for some serious crimes, police reform, and so on). Each group utilizes various aspects of sociological knowledge to support their position and to criticize opposing recommendations. Below are some examples of these recommendations.

Recommendation	Strengths	Weaknesses
Harsher laws and penalties—for example, the death penalty for kidnapping, skyjacking, or killing a policeman	The certainty of harsh punishment will deter serious deviance by others and will also remove dangerous criminals from public life.	Research is inconclusive: There is no discernible correlation between the use of the death penalty and a decrease in serious crimes. The most effective means of control is personal and informal, not formal and institutionalized. Unreasonably harsh laws might cause officials to exercise even greater discretion in prosecuting crimes.
Mandatory sentences—for example, life in prison without parole for recidivists of felonies	This will delimit the discretion that is often misused by officials for personal or political reasons. Also, some offenders simply cannot be rehabilitated.	No formal system can work without substantial discretion, especially for judges and police. Mandatory sentences would require more prisons and greater expense, and they ignore the importance of the issue of human rehabilitation.
Police reforms, including community relations programs, professional training, and citizen review boards for complaints	Professionalized police would have greater pride and commitment to the occupation. Training in how to deal with ethnic minorities would reduce some of the special interpersonal pressures police face. Citizens, rather than the police themselves, should review allegations of misconduct.	As we saw in Chapter 9, professionalization can create strains and problems. For example, this might create a militarylike police force distinct from civilian society. Police should be trained to enforce the law, not to become involved in human relations. Citizen review boards often increase feelings of insecurity in the police. Furthermore, police are better able to determine when conduct is inappropriate.
Deciminalization, particularly for victimless crimes and crimes against morality (drug use, prostitution, and so on)	Police should not be asked to control deviant behavior where there is no victim, and no threat to society as a whole, and where voluntary behavior by ordinary citizens is involved. Control here should be left to other institutions (church, family, and so on).	Crimes against morality threaten the public order. Also, innocent victims are often involved in drug use, sexual deviance, and so on. Where do we draw the line with decriminalization? For example, should some types of robbery (to feed one's hungry family) be decriminalized?

Can you think of other examples of solutions and the sociological findings that would either support or question these solutions?

CONCLUSION

This chapter has introduced deviant behavior as one aspect of social dynamics. Orderly processes of society require a high degree of conformity to established norms and respect for dominant cultural values. At the same time, deviation from norms is bound to occur in all societies. Some forms of deviation are not a threat to the larger social order. In fact, there is a good deal of tolerance of minor departures from normal behavior patterns, and in some cases deviance becomes institutionalized, as in New Year's Eve celebrations in our society, or praised as in heroism on the battlefield. Furthermore, a strong case can be argued for the functional significance of deviance. Deviant behavior helps to establish the boundaries for legitimate behavior, rallies community support for the norms, and contributes to a sense of group solidarity. More than this, moral pioneers or prophets who deviate from model forms of behavior in the direction of societal ideals of justice often shock the community into necessary steps toward social change.

Robert Merton and others have pointed to the significance of the social and cultural context in determining the nature of deviance. When success goals are held out to everyone in society, while, simultaneously, the means to attain these goals are denied to many citizens, some individuals turn to various forms of deviant behavior. At the same time, deviance must be studied not only from the standpoint of individual actors but also in terms of the larger social setting within which it occurs. Delinquent behavior may be learned through differential association. Furthermore, delinquency and crime may be the result of special risk factors in gang contexts, the functional need to manage feelings of anomie and status frustrations, and the unique relationships of gangs to larger society.

Finally, control of deviance is effected through both informal and formal means. However, control becomes more difficult as a society becomes heterogeneous, complex, and highly structured. At all levels of formal systems of control, discretion plays an important role; this is necessary to a certain extent, but it can create special problems. For example, police sometimes find themselves under pressure to resort to illegitimate violence as a result of unique occupational problems. In fact, all modern agencies of control, not only the police, respond to organizational demands that can lead to the use of deviance to control deviance.

This discussion of deviance is closely related to another aspect of social processes—the dynamics of change. As we have seen, deviance is not always synonymous with anomie, disorganization, and pathology. As a basis for social and cultural change, deviance may act as a force toward a new social order. In the next chapter, we will consider the process of change as illustrated by studies of population problems and demography.

REFERENCES

Becker, Howard. *Outsiders: Studies in the Sociology of Deviance.* New York: The Free Press, 1963.

Berger, Peter L. *Invitation to Sociology: A Humanistic Perspective.* Garden City, N.Y.: Doubleday and Company, 1963.

Blake, Judith, and Kingsley Davis. "Norms, Values, and Sanctions," in *Handbook of Modern Sociology,* Robert E. L. Faris, Ed. Chicago: Rand McNally & Co., 1964.

Cavan, Ruth Shonle. "The Concepts of Tolerance and Contraculture as Applied to Delinquency," *The Sociological Quarterly,* 2 (October 1961), pp. 243–258.

Cloward, Richard A., and Lloyd E. Ohlin. *Delinquency and Opportunity: A Theory of Delinquent Gangs.* New York: The Free Press, 1960.

Cohen, Albert K. *Delinquent Boys.* New York: The Free Press, 1955.

———— and James F. Short, Jr. "Juvenile Delinquency," in *Contemporary Social Problems,* Robert K. Merton and Robert A. Nisbet, Ed. New York: Harcourt, Brace and World, 1966.

Coser, Lewis A. "Functions of Deviant Behavior," *The American Journal of Sociology, 68* (September 1962), pp. 172–182. Reprinted in *Social Problems: Persistent Challenges,* Edward C. McDonagh and Jon E. Simpson, Ed. New York: Holt, Rinehart and Winston, 1965.

Durkheim, Emile. *The Division of Labor,* George Simpson, Transl. New York: The Free Press, 1947.

Erikson, Kai T. "The Sociology of Deviance," in *Social Problems: Persistent Challenges,* Edward C. McDonagh and Jon E. Simpson, Ed. New York: Holt, Rinehart and Winston, 1965.

Gibbs, Jack P. "Conceptions of Deviant Behavior: The Old and the New," *The Pacific Sociological Review, 9* (Spring 1966), pp. 9–14.

Graber, Edith E. "Police Undercover Agents: The Anticipation and Management of Demand," unpublished paper, Washington University, St. Louis, Mo.

Johnson, Harry M. *Sociology: A Systematic Introduction.* New York: Harcourt, Brace and World, 1960.

Liazos, Alexander. "The Poverty of the Sociology of Deviance: Nuts, Sluts, and Perverts," *Social Problems, 20* (Summer 1972), pp. 103–120.

Marx, Gary T. "Thoughts on a Neglected Category of Social Movement Participant: The Agent Provocateur and the Informant," *The American Journal of Sociology, 80* (September 1974), pp. 402–442.

Merton, Robert K. "Social Structure and Anomie," *American Sociological Review,* 3 (October 1938), pp. 672–682.

————. "Social Problems and Sociological Theory," in *Contemporary Social Problems,* Robert K. Merton and Robert A. Nisbet, Ed. New York: Harcourt, Brace and World, 1966.

Miller, Walter B. "Lower-Class Culture as a Generating Milieu of Gang Delinquency," *Journal of Social Issues, 14,* No. 1 (1958), pp. 5–19.

————. "Preventive Work with Street-Corner Groups," *The Annals of the American Academy of Political and Social Sciences, 322* (March 1959), pp. 97–107.

Parsons, Talcott. *The Social System.* New York: The Free Press, 1951.

President's Commission on Law Enforcement and Administration of Justice. *The Challenge of Crime in a Free Society.* Washington, D.C.: U.S. Government Printing Office, 1973.

Raab, Earl, and Gertrude J. Selznick. *Major Social Problems,* 2nd ed. New York: Harper & Row, 1964.

Reisman, David, Reuel Denney, and Nathan Glazer. *The Lonely Crowd: A Study of the Changing American Character.* New Haven: Yale University Press, 1950.

Short, James F., Jr., and Fred L. Strodtbeck. *Group Process and Gang Delinquency.* Chicago: University of Chicago Press, 1965.

Skolnick, Jerome H., and Elliott Currie. "The Police," in *Crisis in American Institutions,* Jerome H. Skolnick and Elliott Currie, Ed. Boston: Little, Brown and Company, 1970.

Sutherland, Edwin H. *White-Collar Crime.* New York: Dryden Press, 1949.

——— and D. R. Cressey. *Principles of Criminology,* 5th ed. Philadelphia: J. B. Lippincott, 1955.

Webb, Jane K. "The AFSC—A Quaker Experiment in Social Change and Organizational Innovation: A Study in Value Conflict," unpublished Ph.D. thesis, Boston College, Chestnut Hill, Mass., 1975.

Wheeler, Stanton. "Deviant Behavior," in *Sociology: An Introduction,* Neil J. Smelser, Ed. New York: John Wiley & Sons, 1967.

Yablonsky, Lewis. *The Violent Gang.* New York: The Macmillan Company, 1962.

- If you had the chance to work in a less developed country (for example, for the Peace Corps in Tanzania, Africa), what changes would you try to bring about to help the people? How would you do this?
- How would you account for the following example of rapid change? In 1972, when Senator George McGovern was running for President, he was criticized by his opponents for advocating more liberal marijuana laws; but, in 1976, most presidential candidates advocated similar policies and received little criticism.
- With which of the following conflicting sentiments do you agree: "You can't change human nature" or "Things always change"?
- Most people agree that population growth threatens less developed nations, but do we have a population crisis in the United States? Does it affect you?
- In 1976, the small Northern California town of Petaluma attempted to limit population growth by restricting home construction. Real estate and other business leaders objected. Does a town have the right to "prohibit" population growth and immigration of people into the town in this way?

13

The Dynamics of Change: Population and Demography

Change is inevitable. This fact seems obvious whether we are studying nonliving things such as the geological history of the earth over millions of years or the human societies that have populated the earth. Social scientists' fascination with the subject of social and cultural change has led them to focus on the following kinds of questions. How does change come about? What cause change? Do we have the responsibility to encourage, limit, or direct changes?

This chapter begins by considering the sources and nature of change in human society. Fundamental to this discussion is the dynamic character of the social self as reflected in social roles, norms, and interpersonal relationships. Next we examine the special role that technological innovation plays in stimulating social change. This is illustrated first in premodern society, where agricultural innovation was a major change agent, and then in modern society, where industrialization has become paramount.

Next we examine some of the theories that try to explain the direction and form of change. Early social scientists attempted to develop global theories of change that would apply to whole social systems. They argued about whether change was evolutionary or cyclical. Recently, theorists have begun to abandon these perspectives, finding them too abstract and oversimplified and have instead begun to analyze change as the product of multiple processes. We will use the study of demography and population to illustrate this multiple theoretical approach. Finally, we will consider those theorists who have developed cultural theories of change.

The final section of this chapter will be concerned with the problem of control. Here, too, we will focus our discussion around the modern world's population "explosion." The problems associated with population control will be considered, and the control techniques used by different societies will be compared. In particular, we will see how population control poses different problems for undeveloped and developed countries.

SOURCES AND NATURE OF CHANGE

The Dynamic Character of Human Life

Most people associate change with instability and lack of permanence. This view obscures one of the ironic aspects of change: its *permanence* and *persistence.* Change is a permanent, ever-present aspect of human group life, even in the most traditional and isolated communities. Part of the reason for this is the dynamic character of the social self.

As we saw in Chapter 3, the social self emerges through the interaction connected with the socialization process. Social interaction, moreover, means constant change. *No two persons or groups interact in exactly the same way, nor do their established relationships follow a static unchanging pattern.* For example, as parents and children grow older, their role relationships and patterns of interaction alter. As we saw in the discussion of parent–youth conflict, youth grow up in a world that is somewhat different from that of their parents. Values and behavior change so rapidly in modern society that parents quickly become "old fashioned" and, thus, out of step with what is happening in the world of youth. This dynamic and ever-changing interaction between the generations not only brings a measure of conflict and misunderstanding, but it also creates a rich variation in human life.

Francis Merrill [1969, p. 332] reminds us of this variety of interaction in the following way:

> Human beings never take each other into account in exactly the same way twice. There is always some element of novelty, evolution, and change in each human relationship. This dynamic aspect of society was grasped by social thinkers as far back as the ancient Greeks, who regarded the eternal flux of man and his institutions with attitudes ranging from resentment to resignation.

In fact, *social stability and integration (social equilibrium) would be impossible without some change.* Human societies must adapt to new threats and challenges from the social and natural environments (floods, famines, warfare, disease, and so on). In doing so, relationships alter, new roles emerge, and values change, thereby establishing a new, more viable social order. As Georg Simmel points out, change is not a disturbance [Hughes, 1955, p. 9]; rather it is natural and normal. However, although the fact of change is permanent, its source and nature may differ from one context to another.

In premodern societies, changes in traditional roles and values may be so slow or slight as to be almost imperceptible through many generations. In contrast, modern societies frequently experience sudden and precipitous change as seen in the recent civil rights and women's movements. However, this does not mean that the process of change is unpatterned or unpredictable. *Patterns of change evolve out of the nature of group life.* For example, although some changes in modern society (for example, new sexual behavior and methods of warfare) may appear "shocking" or unanticipated, they nevertheless have some continuity with the past. New sexual relationships evolved out of changes in the traditional family. New forms of warfare evolved from changing relationships between the state and the military (as we saw in Chapter 11). Perhaps this is why our folklore contains such contradictory statements as "You can't change human nature" and "Things are always changing." Such conflicting statements reflect the two aspects of change— (1) its traditional roots and (2) its innovative end result.

Finally, to say that change is inevitable and patterned is not to imply that it is constantly unfolding in all contexts in exactly the same manner. *Change usually moves in an uneven manner,* particularly in modern contexts. Once again, this is related to the nature of group life. As women seek new freedoms and occupational opportunities, some men may be reluctant to change either their traditional roles or attitudes. Conversely, other men may willingly take on the child-rearing roles traditionally associated with women, even though their wives may not immediately reciprocate by taking on the economic or social roles traditionally associated with the husband or father.

William Ogburn [1922] was one of the first sociologists to point out the uneven nature of change. He also argued that *technological change tended to precede changes in social roles and cultural norms.* This view has become one of the major perspectives used in analyzing the source and nature of change in human society.

Technology and Cultural Lag

When the automobile was introduced in America soon after the turn of the century, there was resistance from many people who were accustomed to the horse-and-buggy society. Some said the gasoline engine would never

13-1 Television and Cultural Lag

Often changes in social and cultural aspects of society occur some time after changes in technology. Culture, in the form of norms and values, tends to lag behind other changes most of all. The development and use of television is an example of this phenomenon of cultural lag.

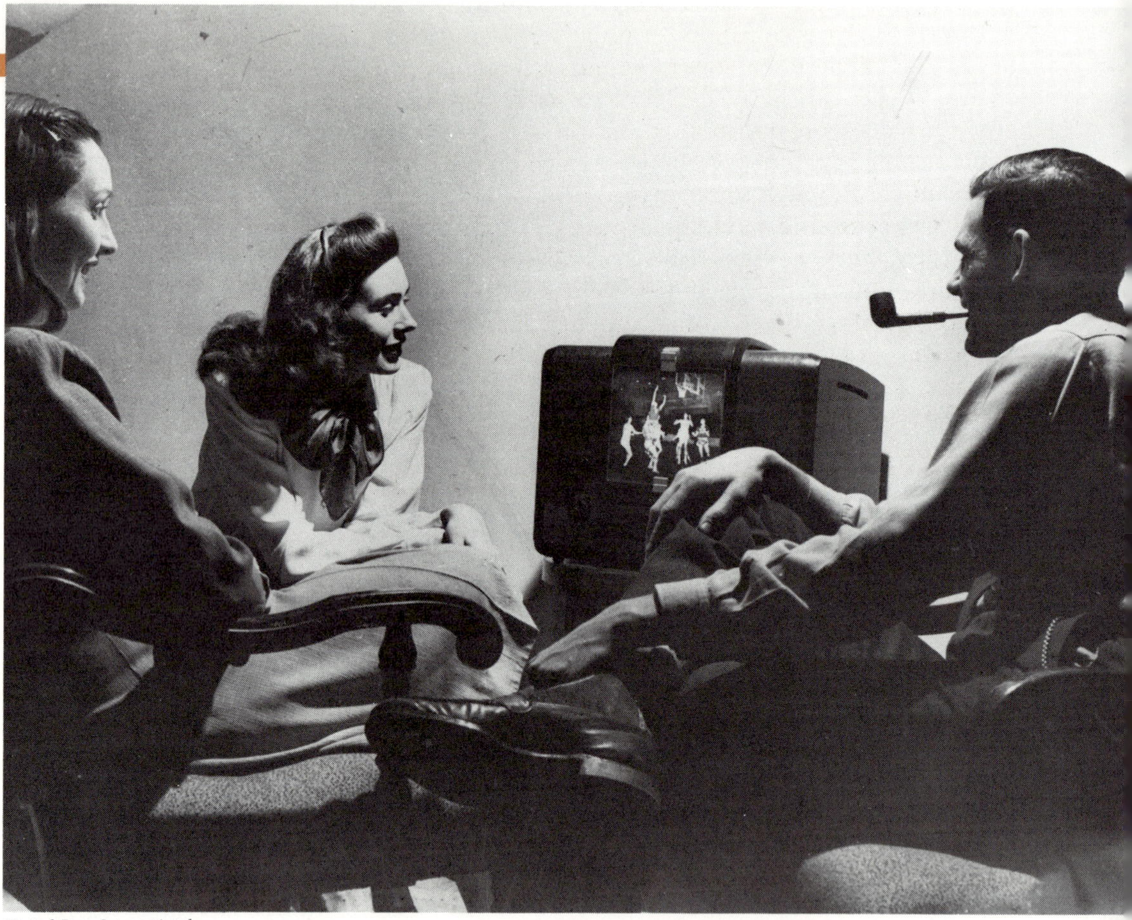

United Press International

Actually, scientific discoveries enabling the development of television were made in the late 1800s, but it was not until the 1930s that an experimental station and a regular commercial channel were put into operation in the United States. Television production was discontinued during World War II and started again in 1946. By 1950, television had become a new major source of news and entertainment. Slowly it began to have an impact upon social relationships and values in professional athletics.

Wide World Photos

Television revenue from advertising became substantial, causing an economic impact on many sports. In professional golf, prize money skyrocketed. For example, in April of 1974, Johnny Miller received a check for $40,000 for winning the Tournament of Champions at La Costa Country Club, pushing his earnings for that year to $192,877.

United Press International

Television also reached audiences numbering in the millions. This enabled athletes to promote individual and collective causes to many people simultaneously. In 1973, Bobby Riggs, self-styled sports "hustler," challenged women tennis professionals to matches in order to prove the "superiority of male athletes." In the Astrodome before a nationwide television audience, tennis pro Billie Jean King beat Riggs in a $100,000 winner-take-all match, thereby improving the image of women athletes and assisting the aims of the women's movement.

United Press International

United Press International

As the salaries of athletes increased and the availability of television to dramatize grievances became more evident, the tactics and organization of union–management relations moved from industry to athletics. In 1974, seven veterans of the Chicago Bears' football team, members of the striking National Football League Player's Association, picketed along a county road adjacent to their training camp in Indiana. Inside the camp, 56 draftees and free agents had started practice for the upcoming season.

These types of social, economic, and political changes also led to changes in the laws governing professional athletics. In 1970, baseball star Curt Flood talked with his attorney, former Supreme Court Justice Arthur Goldberg, during a break in his trial in New York. Flood was testifying in a suit against the major league baseball owners to overturn the reserve clause when he was suddenly traded by the St. Louis Cardinals to the Philadelphia Phillies.

take the place of the horse. Before long, however, American society embraced the automobile as a fundamental necessity for daily life. Today, the prospect of doing without our cars is virtually unthinkable, even though they bring noise, congestion, and pollution into the environment.

For most Americans, acceptance of the family car as a means of transportation was much easier than acceptance of the cultural changes that followed. Such trends as unsupervised dating outside the home, a decrease in home-centered recreation, and the employment of women and youth outside the home are still not totally accepted by many older citizens. Ogburn [1957, pp. 167–174] refers to this phenomenon as *cultural lag*. Certain aspects of the culture, usually norms and values, tend to lag behind changes, usually resulting from technological innovations, in other areas of the culture. The result is a tension or maladjustment that can sometimes create social problems. We will presently discuss in detail one of the major social problems of our time, the population explosion. Central to this discussion is the concept of cultural lag. People have been quick to accept modern medicine and public health measures, which bring about fewer deaths, but they have been slow to accept birth control techniques and the desirability of smaller families. Death is seen as bad, and, therefore, it must be controlled; birth is seen as good, and, therefore, it must be encouraged. Many people fail to see that when death rates decline at the same time birth remain high, the resulting population growth is so dramatic that human survival, not to mention the quality of life, is seriously threatened. Changes in our life-sustaining technology are outdistancing corresponding changes in our norms, values, and institutions. The resulting cultural lag could become critical.

The importance of technology in bringing about change has been used by social scientists to contrast premodern with modern societies. Those scholars who focus upon premodern societies point to the role of agricultural innovation, while those who focus upon modern societies tend to deal with the role of industry. The following two sections compare and contrast these perspectives.

Agriculture in Premodern Society

The remarkable leap from medieval to modern society in the Western world within the last 400–500 years has been the subject of much scholarly analysis. What brought about modernization, and why did it occur first in the West rather than in other parts of the world where ancient civilizations flourished long before our own? Although most scholars recognize that many factors contributed to this major transition, they tend to emphasize the crucial role played by agricultural innovation. Lynn White [1962] points out the degree to which agriculture predominated in premodern society:

> From the Neolithic Age until about two centuries ago, agriculture was fundamental to most other human concerns. Before the late 1700's there was probably no settled community in which at least nine-tenths of the popula-

tion were not directly engaged in tillage. Rulers and priests, craftsmen and merchants, scholars and artists, were a tiny minority of mankind standing on the shoulders of peasants. Under such circumstances any lasting change in climate, soil fertility, technology, or the other conditions affecting agriculture would necessarily modify the whole of society: population, wealth, political relationships, leisure, and cultural expression [White, 1962, p. 39].

Yet scholars, according to White, have neglected the study of premodern peasants and their methods of land cultivation. His research reveals a remarkable development in medieval agriculture involving three new technologies—the heavy plow, the use of horse power, and three-field rotation of crops. Each of these innovations had a profound impact upon medieval life and prepared the way for the industrial revolution that followed. Together the new technologies produced the following changes—a better diet, population growth, freedom for some serfs to enter alternative occupations, development of small cities and industries, and the emergence of a new spirit of "modernization." Thus, changes in agricultural technology led to social and cultural change.

The impact of the new technologies is summarized by White as follows:

1. *The new plow*—featuring wheels, heavy knife, flat plowshare, and moldboard—replaced the old scratch plow, which had been used for centuries and is still in evidence in some regions. The old plow was little more than a digging stick that did not turn over the soil and, therefore, required a cross-plowing of square fields. The new plow was much heavier and its ability to turn the soil made cross-plowing unnecessary, thereby saving labor. However, it required a team of perhaps eight oxen or strong horses.

Cooperative farming and the medieval manor or village emerged from the use of the heavy plow because a single farmer could not afford to own eight oxen. The result was a new social structure, which included a powerful village council of peasants. Moreover, the improved method of plowing led to a rearrangement of the fields; instead of square plots of ground, they became oblong. With the old scratch plow and one-family subsistence, humans were still largely dependent upon nature. However, with the new heavy plow and related innovations, humans became capable of exploiting the land for surplus food and fiber.

2. *The discovery of horse power* for agriculture and transportation made use of the new plough more efficient and enlarged the possibilities for trade and transportation. The use of horse power encouraged the invention of two additional technologies: (a) *The nailed horseshoe* was essential for prolonged plowing and transportation (this invention appeared about the end of the ninth century); (b) *the horse collar* was, perhaps, even more important (horses were stronger and faster than oxen, but the yoke of oxen choked horses when they were pulling a heavy load; the collar harness equipped a team of horses so that they could pull heavy loads rapidly). This development led not only to a more efficient agriculture but to freedom and mobility for some peasants, and thus to the subsequent rural–urban migration.

3. *The three-field crop rotation* plan led to a more profitable use of the land and to improved nutrition for both animals and humans. Horses, unlike oxen, must eat grain as well as grass. Old two-field agriculture meant that half of the land lay fallow while the other half was planted with winter grain. This made the growing of sufficient surplus grain for horses difficult. Hence, the use of horse power had to await the Northern European three-field plan, which came into being about 1100 A.D. and made the following system of crop rotation possible: one third in autumn to winter wheat and rye; one third in spring to oats (feed for horses), barley, peas, lentils, or broad beans; and one third fallow for rest and replenishment of the soil. As a result, Northern European peasants could choose between the ox and the horse as a plow beast, whereas the peasants of Southern Europe had no choice; they were stuck with grass-eating oxen since the two-field crop rotation system did not provide a sufficient surplus of grain for horses. In addition, the new three-field crop rotation provided a large amount of vegetable proteins, thus improving the quality of food in the Middle Ages from the 10th century onward.

In summary, as agricultural technology began to change, other social and cultural changes were set in motion, changes that eventually culminated in the industrialized world of today. Improved tillage led to more and better foods, which simultaneously produced population growth and food surpluses. This, in turn, permitted some people to migrate to the cities and enter into such nonagricultural occupations as merchants, artisans, and scholars [Pirenne, 1925]. These early merchants were the forerunners of modern industrialists and middle-class entrepreneurs. Henri Pirenne points to the way in which they created new norms and values that challenged the feudal nobility and the clergy. This spirit of modernization called for a new kind of city with freedom for people:

1. To leave the lord's manor.
2. To become free citizens in towns with city charters, laws that applied equally to all, and secular schools.
3. To work for wages in jobs of their own choosing or to travel as merchants and charge interest on their money.
4. To establish guilds to control and protect their jobs from the interference of the nobility and clergy and to begin elementary industry by working in homes and small shops.

In other words, an accumulation of sociocultural changes were spurred by technological innovations. Eventually this produced today's modern industrial society, where changes take place with great rapidity as inventions are transported from one place, or context, to another.

Industrialization in Modern Society

Industrialization appeared first in Northern Europe and Great Britain as machines replaced animals and human beings as sources of power and production. Just as the horse had become more efficient than the ox for plowing, the tractor and other mechanized farming equipment eventually became more productive than the horse. Although horses are still used in some parts of the world today, even relatively poor farmers are likely to be seen plowing behind a small inexpensive gasoline engine. A tractor may be too costly for some, but even a simple machine is better than an animal. As a consequence, agriculture in modern countries needs very few farmers since most of the work is done by machines. In Chapter 8, we saw the dramatic impact that industrialized agriculture can have upon the social and cultural life of a community.

Industrialization of a society, however, means more than just technological improvements in agriculture. When we speak of developed countries today, we refer to countries where most of the workers have left the farms for nonagricultural jobs in urban areas. Many are blue-collar workers in factories, while others pursue white-collar occupations that provide support to the factory system (secretaries, accountants, and so on). Still others occupy service jobs in health, education, and welfare.

What can account for this change from an agricultural to an industrial society? While the sources of modernization were (and are) many and complex, among the most important factors was *the need to accumulate enough technical innovations to build a wide technological base* for modern society. The base was gradually developing throughout early human history, beginning with inventions like the wheel and fire, but its development accelerated in the Middle Ages. As we saw in the previous section, the horse collar was invented about 800 A.D. but could not be widely used until about 1100 A.D., when the three-field rotation of crops came into being and horses could be fed. The windmill and water power were other important inventions, which, in turn, were followed by steam- and gas-driven engines. Fuels like coal, oil, and gas had to be on hand to power the machines. Workers had to be transported from rural to urban settings near the factories. Raw materials had to be imported, and finished products exported to distant markets.

After 1500 A.D., inventions proliferated, some appearing almost simultaneously in different places. Change, however, involved *an accumulation of social as well as technological inventions.* For example, Edward Rose [1948, pp. 255–272] cites a collection of 2498 technical innovations and 3263 new social and cultural activities in America between 1540 and 1935. Table 13-1 illustrates the numerical accumulation of these social and technical inventions. By social inventions, Rose is referring to major new cultural events and ideas, such as Benjamin Franklin's book of insurance.

Therefore, technical know-how alone cannot explain the explosion of industrial society. These developments had to be coupled with appropriate social and cultural innovations. For example, although the number of scientific inventions in the world doubled from the 14th to the 15th century, and tripled in the 16th century, not all societies participated equally in the growth of science:

> Not even those who had contributed significant scientific inventions [participated equally in the growth of science]. Scholars are still seeking a full

TABLE 13-1 Number of Technical and Social Inventions in America, 1540–1935

Years	Technical Inventions: Number During Years	Technical Inventions: Accumulated Total	Social Inventions: Number During Years	Social Inventions: Accumulated Total
1540–1549	2	2	2	2
1550–1599	11	13	11	13
1600–1649	84	97	91	104
1650–1699	67	164	82	186
1700–1749	70	234	85	271
1750–1799	260	494	335	606
1800–1849	500	994	639	1245
1850–1899	844	1838	1114	2359
1900–1935	660	2498	904	3263

Adapted from Edward Rose, "Innovations in American Culture," *Social Forces, 26* (March 1948), pp. 255–272.

> explanation of why the Industrial Revolution should have reached its culmination in the last half of 18th century in England rather than somewhere else. It was certainly not because all the great inventions had occurred there. A partial explanation may lie in the fact that technological change in England was coupled with changing ideas of the individual and society [DeFleur *et al.*, 1972, p. 192].

Therefore, just to create new technologies was not enough; the technologies had to be put to work. This required new group arrangements, such as the factory and the corporation; new social roles, such as bureaucratic specialists; and new interpersonal relationships, such as dual careers for husband and wife. The societies that are most receptive to these kinds of social and cultural innovations are the ones that seem to experience the most rapid industrialization.

Finally, accumulated technical and social innovations must stimulate each other and encourage further change and invention. A society's capacity to recognize and take advantage of changes explains the emergence of major new social systems like industrialization. Benjamin Higgins [1968] points out that the land enclosure system in England hastened the movement of farmers from agriculture to industry. As sheep became profitable, there was a need for larger plots of land, and small farmers, recognizing their vulnerability, migrated to the better paying jobs in the cities, thereby accelerating the growth of the factory system.

Other scholars [Rostow, 1956] have pointed out that sometimes unanticipated threatening changes, in conjunction with technological innovations, can contribute to growth and development. For example, agricultural improvements led to a food surplus that permitted labor to leave the fields and seek work in the new towns of early medieval society. [White, 1962, p. 40]. At about the same time, the plague of the Black Death occurred, greatly reducing Europe's population and permitting the accumulation of surplus capital for investment in factories, larger farms, and urban services such as medicine, schools, roads, and sanitation. In other words, a decline

13-2 What Causes Change in Industrial Society?

When people think of modern society, they usually think of technology. However, rapid change in industrial society depends upon more than just technical invention.

Accummulation of technical inventions. Enough technological innovations must be accummulated through the years in order to provide a wide technical base for modern society. When Henry Ford constructed his first "horseless carriage" in 1896, he built upon the accumulated work of dozens of scientists and inventors. These included: a Jesuit missionary who built a steam-powered car model in 1678; a French Army officer who built the first self-powered road vehicle in 1769; an Englishman who built a steam carriage in 1829; an American who built an electric-powered vehicle in 1836; and an Austrian who built a four-wheeled, gasoline-powered auto in 1864.

Courtesy of Mr. Henry Ford

Development of other related devices. In 1909, America had only 190,000 miles of surface roads and many highways were needed if the automobile was to become something more than a "plaything for the rich." In 1908, the first concrete road was laid in Detroit, and by 1924 America had 31,000 miles of concrete roads. After World War II, road building boomed when machinery was developed which could mix, spread, and finish asphalt, cement, and crushed-stone roadways rapidly and over great distances.

Elsa Dorfman

Accumulation of social innovations. Society must also accumulate enough social innovations so that technological inventions can be put to work easily. The small, highly mobile nuclear family of modern society, consisting of father, mother, and one or two children, was such an innovation. The freedom of both the wife and husband meant that each could use an automobile to pursue their individual interests. In addition, the isolated nuclear family as a unit needed transportation to move from one community activity to another, from one job to another, from home to recreational areas, and the like.

Elsa Dorfman

Changing roles and relationships. Technical and social innovations must encourage new social roles and relationships. These, in turn, must relate to the potential uses of the innovations. The nuclear family led to greater freedom in dating and courtship patterns for young adults. Gasoline-powered transportation, in the form of automobile or motorcycle, lent itself to the expression of these new family and peer group relationships.

Elsa Dorfman

Discovery of natural and social resources. Change in modern society depends upon the discovery of natural resources, such as fossil fuels to power the automobile's engine. It also depends upon the discovery of social resources, people to service autos, work as mechanics, and operate assembly lines. In this process, changes in social roles and cultural values play an important part. During World War II, women demonstrated their ability to operate factory assembly lines. As a result, other occupations, such as service station attendant, have recently opened up to women, thereby giving industrial society an important new social resource.

Elsa Dorfman

Innovative uses of technology. People in modern society must be able to recognize the potential for and take advantage of innovations. Sometimes this requires unusual adaptations not readily apparent when a technology is invented. Bookmobiles are particularly effective in bringing library resources to areas and neighborhoods which might not otherwise be able to obtain these services. In this manner, the automobile assists modern education.

in the population meant that medieval society had a surplus large enough to feed its people and still support those other activities that accelerated industrial growth.

Certainly industry was encouraged by the discovery of natural resources throughout the world (gold, silver, oil, coal) and the development of transportation of raw materials, finished products, and population migration. But here, too, social adaptation was needed to produce benefits from these new discoveries. As we saw in Chapter 4, the "spirit of capitalism" and the Protestant ethic developed at precisely the right time to motivate individuals to "make all" they could and "save all" they could. As a result, profits were reinvested in important economic and cultural activities.

In summary, although some scholars tend to emphasize the fundamental importance of technology as the primary source of change, most scientists point to a multitude of complexly interrelated factors. Neil Smelser [1968, p. 126] has suggested that four different variables are important. Drawing upon studies of premodern and modern societies, he maintains that major change takes place when the per capita income of the population begins to increase, as a result of the following alterations in the following variables:

1. *Technology*—Transition from simple traditional techniques to the application of complex scientific knowledge (see Chapter 11).
2. *Agriculture*—Evolution from subsistence family farming to specialized commercial production of cash crops, with resulting purchase of nonagricultural products in the market and introduction of agricultural wage labor (see Chapter 8).
3. *Industry*—Change from the use of human and animal power to industrialization, which involves humans operating power-driven machines and working for monetary return.
4. *Population*—Movement from the farm and village to urban centers.

Our discussion to this point has focused on explanations of the sources and general nature of change. In addition, other scholars have formulated theories about the *direction* and *form* of change.

THEORIES OF CHANGE

As indicated in the previous discussion, the various patterns (direction and form) of change have interested scholars for hundreds of years. Is human society evolving, or is it declining? Is change cyclical, or does it follow relatively unbroken and continuous patterns of development? These kinds of questions imply not only a scientific curiosity about change but also latent value judgments about the basic nature of human society.

We cannot possibly summarize the extensive literature on theories of change in one chapter. We must, for example, omit most of the current economic theories that emphasize the importance of increasing capital, labor skills, foreign trade in underdeveloped countries, and change in the social structure from an agricultural economy to an industrial one. Economists insist that these are the most important factors in the change process. Instead, we have selected other kinds of theories in order to present a sociological view within a historical perspective. We begin by comparing evolutionary and cyclical theories of change. Those who adopt evolutionary models generally view the human condition as improving and change as desirable. In contrast, those who develop cyclical models conceive of change as sometimes positive (indicating possible improvement in the human condition) and sometimes negative (indicating possible decline in the human condition).

Early Theories: Evolution or Cycles?

As we noted in Chapter 1, Auguste Comte [1877], the founder of sociology, compared the growth and development of human societies to the biological model of change. He maintained that all organisms, including societies, go through the same life cycle—from birth to maturity to death. In contrast, Herbert Spencer [1896] theorized that societies, like animal species, evolved from the simple to the complex. Emile Durkheim [1949] also utilized an evolutionary model by arguing that the division of labor in human societies evolved from simple forms (in premodern societies) to more complex forms (in modern societies).

A brief profile of these early evolutionary and cyclical theories is presented in Table 13-2. The theory of social *evolution* was appealing because it embraced the "idea of progress" as a natural part of all social change. More complex and heterogeneous forms of social and cultural organization were considered to be higher or better forms of human life. In addition, evolutionary theories tended to utilize single variables as explanations of change. Thus Marx saw economic organization as playing the major role, Emile Durkheim focused upon the division of labor in societies, and Edward Tylor identified religious beliefs and institutions as paramount.

As a consequence, evolutionary theories tended to be oversimplified and much too optimistic; a further inadequacy was their inability to explain why some societies seem to collapse or decay under the impact of change. Cyclical theories arose in an attempt to counteract these disadvantages. Cyclical theorists saw processes of change as following rising and falling patterns from one generation to another. Societies were seen as constantly developing new ways of combating crises and challenges. As these new ways arose, they, in turn, created different problems to which the society had to adjust. Sometimes this adjustment was successful, and the society moved on to the next natural stage. However, when the adjustment was inadequate, the society might begin to decline and might eventually die out, ultimately to be replaced by a new social order.

An example of cyclical theory is Pitirim Sorokin's [1937] concept that the major problem faced by all societies is the tension between the human senses and the human spirit. He suggests that a study of Western

TABLE 13-2 Evolutionary and Cyclical Theories of Change

	Evolutionary Theory	Cyclical Theory
Direction, Form, and Quality	"Upwards" in a single unbroken line that represents improving conditions, from worse to better	A curved line, sometimes "upwards" and sometimes "downwards," that represents the constant shifting of the human condition between good and bad
Types of Social and Cultural Transitions	From simple to complex; primitive to advanced; undeveloped to developed; savagery to barbarism to civilization; animism to monotheism	Repeating cycles from sacred to profane; folk to feudal to urban; low culture to mass culture to high culture; ideational to idealistic to sensate cultures; less rational to more rational societies; *Gemeinschaft* to *Gesellschaft* societies
Strengths	Optimistic view of human society; simple and easily understandable	Can account for social and cultural decline; allows for a degree of complexity
Weaknesses	Oversimplifies complex processes and change; assumes each successive stage of development better and more desirable than preceding stage	Oversimplifies complex processes of change; depends upon value judgments about whether a stage of development represents advance or decline
Theorists	Emile Durkheim, Georg Hegel, Karl Marx, Lewis Morgan, Herbert Spencer, Edward Tylor	Auguste Comte, Robert Redfield, Pitirim Sorokin, Oswald Spengler, Ferdinand Tönnies, Arnold Toynbee, Carle Zimmerman

history from the time of Christ to the present discloses that each major cultural epoch went through a cycle involving ideational, idealistic, and sensate periods. The *ideational period* stressed ascetic and spiritual pursuits (for example, the early Middle Ages in Europe when the Church predominated). Eventually, under the impact of new challenges and changes, this ideational period gave way to an *idealistic period,* where ideas and values, although still important, become more closely related to mundane daily needs and problems. For example, Sorokin argues that, where ideational music would honor the "Glory of God," idealistic music would reflect the human potential for violence and passion in addition to love and beauty.

Finally, Sorokin maintains that all societies eventually change to a *sensate period.* Emphasis in these contexts is placed upon satisfying the

FIGURE 13-1 Evolutionary and Cyclical Theories Applied to American Society

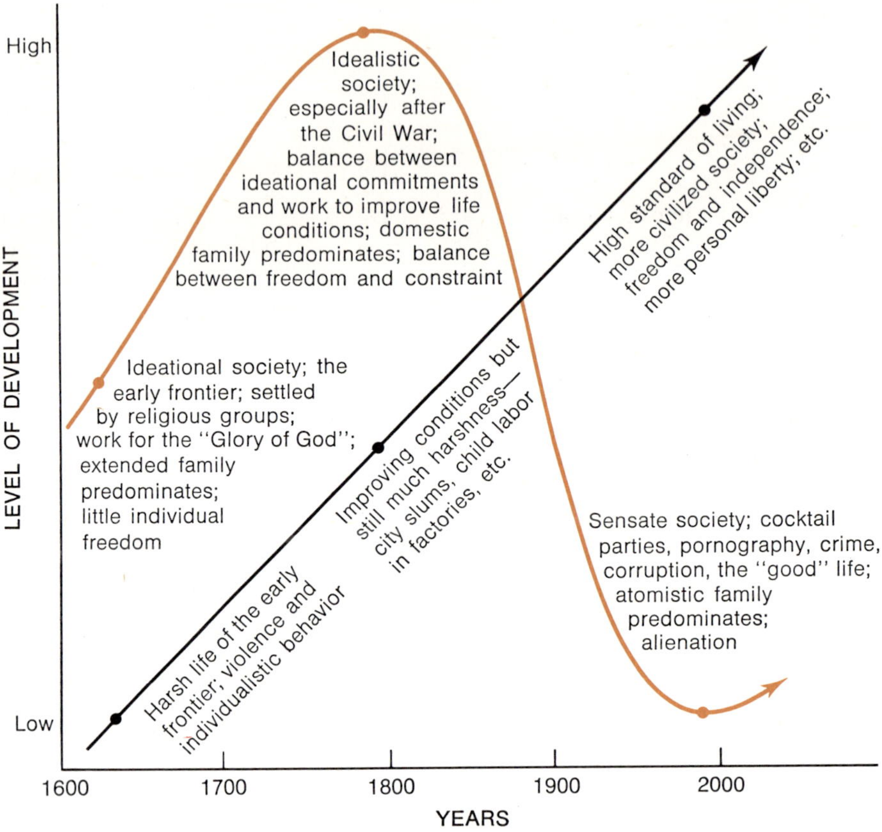

human senses (eating, drinking, sexual behavior), and the culture reflects this new orientation (*Playboy* and *Gourmet* magazines; rock music). However, sensate societies tend to be relatively unstable and they rapidly give way to idealistic periods (a balance between sensate and ideational), and the cycle begins to reverse itself.

Carle Zimmerman [1947] employed a similar approach in identifying cyclical changes in the family throughout Western history. He maintained that the Greek, Roman, medieval, and modern family have passed through three similar stages of development. The earliest stage is the *trustee family,* consisting of an extended kinship group religiously tied to both their ancestors and to the yet unborn members of the family system (the consanguine family, discussed in Chapter 10). New changes and challenges force the trustee family to alter its form, and the *domestic family* develops, a tightly knit primary group focused around the daily life-sustaining activities of the household (the nuclear family, discussed in Chapter 10). However, further change causes this form to give way eventually to *atomistic families,* consisting of fragmented and highly individualistic members (broken, incomplete, or isolated families). Once again, though, the cycle may begin to repeat itself. When the atomistic Roman family was no longer able to sustain itself, it gave way to the early medieval trustee family.

Figure 13-1 visualizes how evolutionary and cyclical theorists might analyze recent American history. The inherent value judgments in each theory are evident (which view do you think is most appropriate?). Both theories are provocative and have become the basis for much social scientific research. However, both tend to look for overall patterns of social and cultural change where none may exist. Other scholars, therefore, have argued that usable theories of change must incorporate and relate a variety of important social processes.

Recent Theories: Multiple Processes

Because of the inadequacies of both evolutionary and cyclical theories of change, more recent perspectives have been based upon the idea that change can take multiple forms and directions. These theories maintain that change must be studied in terms of *relationships between different aspects of reality* rather than as a single global phenomenon labeled "change." This approach is best illustrated by studies of what has been called the "demographic transition or revolution."

Demographers identify three variables that determine changes in population:

1. *Fertility* is usually measured by the crude birth rate:

$$\frac{\text{registered births in a year}}{\text{midyear population}} \times 1000 = \text{crude birth rate.}$$

   The crude birth rate is usually low in modern societies (in the United States, it declined from 25.3 in 1957 to 15 in 1973) and high in less developed nations (in 1975, it was 47.0 in Tanzania, 42.8 in India, and 36.6 in China).

2. *Mortality* is usually measured by the crude death rate:

$$\frac{\text{registered deaths in a year}}{\text{midyear population}} \times 1000 = \text{crude death rate.}$$

   The crude death rate is also low in modern societies (9.1 in the United States in 1975) and higher in less developed nations (in 1975, 22.0 in Tanzania, 16.7 in India, and 13.1 in China).

3. *Migration* has taken two major forms throughout human history. In the 19th and early 20th centuries, more than 50 million people migrated from one country to another, mostly from Western Europe to the new areas of the Americas. Since World War II, internal migration of populations from rural to urban regions has been substantial, particularly in developed nations (from 1950 to 1960, 3,234,000 people migrated to California, followed by another 1,845,000 from 1960 to 1970).

As we have already indicated, technological changes in agriculture together with industrialization tend to have a dramatic impact upon death rates, which drop rapidly as a result of improved food supply, better diet, medical innovations, and the like. Birth rates, however, decline more slowly as societies modernize. As a consequence, a substantial gap may exist between the number of births and deaths in a society for a period of years or even decades. It is this gap that causes the "population explosion."

The *theory of demographic transition* has identified three specific stages (in terms of the relationship between births and deaths) through which societies tend to move. These are shown in Table 13-3. Stage I societies represent a situation of high growth potential since both birth and death rates are extremely high. Deaths may fluctuate because of drought, famine, or pestilence, over which the society has little control. In Stage II societies, a transition takes place as deaths rapidly decline but births remain relatively high. In Stage III societies, birth rates finally fall so that they remain either slightly higher than deaths or about equal to them. These societies, therefore, can have either stationary populations or populations that could be subject to decline (if some catastrophe suddenly raised the death rate). This theory is visually depicted in Figure 13-2.

Thus, to understand the nature of demographic processes one must consider the relationship between two different types of change (births and deaths) in various social and cultural contexts. The situation becomes even more complex when the impact of migration is included. We might expect large-scale migrations to lower, or at least to stabilize, birth rates in both the old and new countries, especially if substantial numbers of young (marriage age) males and females are involved. However, such a result does

TABLE 13-3 Stages of Development in Demographic Transition

		Stages	
Characteristics	I	II	III
Type of Society	Preindustrial, primitive, or agricultural	Early and beginning industrialization; mixed economy	Modern, urban, industrialized
Type of Birth Rate	High (45 per 1000 population)	Gradually begins to decline after a period of remaining high	Low (around 20 per 1000 population)
Type of Death Rate	High (35–40 per 1000 population); subject to sharp fluctuations due to disease, famine, natural disaster, and so on	Rapidly declining	Low (about 10 per 1000 population); under control with modern medical technology
Type of Demographic Process	High growth potential	Transitional	Incipient decline or stationary

FIGURE 13-2 Relationship of Birth Rate to Death Rate in Three Stages of Demographic Transition

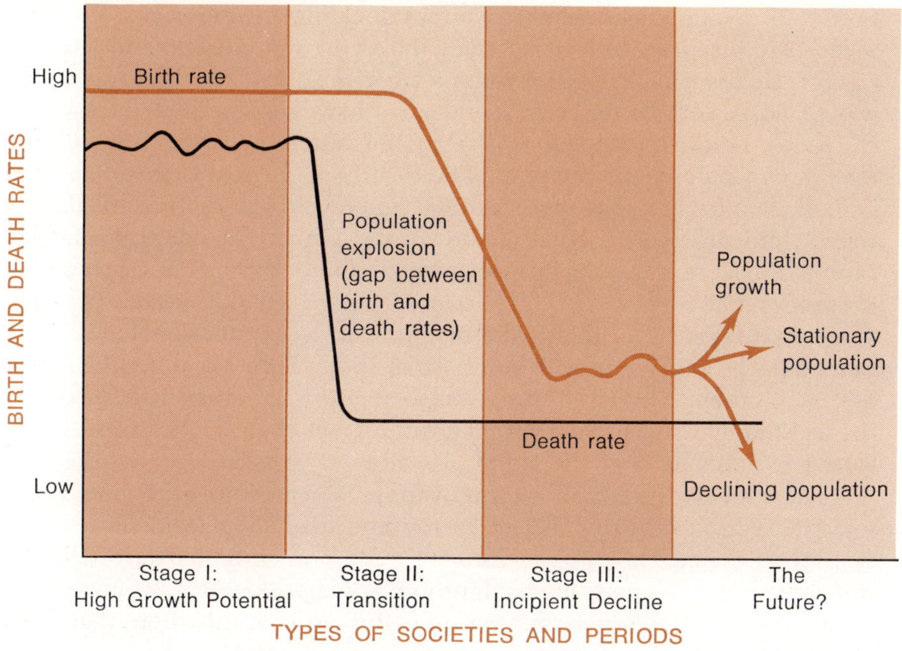

not necessarily occur. Very often migrating groups find the host country or area amenable to large families (a frontier, rural society). Similarly, inhabitants of the home countries may find that, after the migrants move away, previous social and cultural restraints to early marriage and child rearing are moderated or removed [Petersen, 1960, pp. 334–347]. Therefore, migration can play an important role in population growth.

Multiple theories, then, attempt to avoid the problems of evolutionary and cyclical theories by looking at the changing relationships between a number of different variables. The disadvantage of such an approach is that it involves complicated research methodologies and complex perspectives that are difficult to depict clearly. This becomes a special problem when scholars who study change want to move from the areas of understanding and prediction of change to its control. We will return to the question of the control of change in the last section of this chapter. At this point, we shall consider one final type of theory—cultural change—which differs in several ways from those previously considered. *Cultural theories* attempt to identify cultural processes (changing norms, attitudes, and values) that play a major role in stimulating social change. Cultural theorists also frequently try to identify specific change agents (individuals and groups) within a society who actively initiate programs of planned change.

Cultural Theories: Inventors and Change Agents

We have already considered those scholars who see technological innovations and inventions as primary sources of change. Other social scientists argue that the *inventor,* rather than the invention, creates and sustains change; that is, change occurs when a creative individual discovers a new way of doing something because old ways have become ineffective.

Ralph Linton [1936, pp. 313–316] illustrates the importance of the inventor in premodern societies. The outrigger canoe was invented by a Gilbert Islander in about the year 1900, to prevent the theft of his fishing canoe from the beach. Social change in the Gilbert Islands had changed canoes from community to private property, and traditional priest watching of canoes had disappeared. Therefore, canoes were valuable personal property susceptible to theft. The inventor devised a detachable outrigger that could be easily removed and carried to his home, making the canoe useless to others. This innovation was so appealing to other fishermen that the technique was gradually adopted throughout the islands. Eventually it spread to other parts of the world as well.

The process by which an innovation is spread to other areas and societies is called *diffusion.* People borrow and adapt ideas from one another as cultural contact takes place through trade, war, intermarriage, scholarship, travel, and the mass media. Linton [1936, pp. 325–327] estimates that about 90 percent of American culture is the result of diffusion, that is, of borrowing from other cultures:

> An American citizen awakens in a bed built on a pattern which originated in the Near East but which was modified in Northern Europe before it was transmitted to America. He throws back the covers made of cotton, domesticated in India, or linen, domesticated in the Near East, or wool from sheep, also domesticated in the Near East, or silk, the use of which was discovered in China. . . . He takes off his pajamas, a garment invented in India, and washes with soap invented by the Ancient Gauls. He then shaves, a masochistic rite which seems to have been derived from either Sumer or ancient Egypt. . . . On his way to breakfast he stops to buy a paper, paying for it with coins, an ancient Lydian invention.

Furthermore, Linton points out that single acts can involve multiple traits borrowed from other cultures. For example, smoking is an American Indian custom, involving a plant, domesticated in Brazil, used in a pipe imported from the Antilles by way of Spain or in a cigarette derived from Mexico:

> While the American smokes he reads the news of the day, imprinted in characters invented by the ancient Semites upon a material invented in China by a process invented in Germany. As he absorbs the accounts of foreign troubles he will, if he is a good conservative citizen, thank a Hebrew deity in an Indo-European language that he is 100 per cent American.

In addition to technical inventions, social inventions can be borrowed through diffusion as well. Nonviolent tactics like the sit-in (see

Chapter 14) were borrowed and adapted by Martin Luther King from Gandhi, who, in turn, based some of his philosophy of peaceful conflict upon Jesus. Within American society, diffusion of nonviolent tactics spread from civil rights groups, to demonstrators opposing the war in Vietnam, to Gay activists, to the women's movement. At the same time, other groups have traditionally employed different nonviolent means of confrontation with authorities—for example, the use of the strike and sick-in by labor. Indeed, diffusion has become so important in contemporary society that one can no longer speak of a completely unique culture, created and sustained by only the members of that society.

Thus, inventors create technical or social innovations, which are spread by diffusion. However, two questions remain: What characterizes and motivates inventors? What kinds of people and groups act as the lenders and borrowers in the diffusion process? Both of these questions deal with the concept of *change agents.* Social scientists theorize that people and groups possessing particular traits (attitudes and values) tend to become crucial by acting as the agents of change within a society. They are not only more likely to create new objects and ideas, they are also more likely to use them and to influence others to adopt them. Two different types of studies have been conducted to try to identify the characteristics of change agents.

Social psychologists, like David McClelland [1957, 1962], argue that individuals who have high achievement motivation are more inclined to strive for success. Therefore, he hypothesized that societies that cultivate high achievement motivation will have more economic development and social change than will other less achievement-oriented societies. In order to test this hypothesis, he asked children to write imaginative stories. The number of ideas related to achievement motivation in these stories were then recorded for each child. McClelland then compared children's achievement scores (number of achievement ideas in the stories) from over 50 countries with the economic growth rates for those same countries. A sample of his findings are contained in Table 13-4.

McClelland's data seem to indicate that national economic development depends upon having a number of individuals who behave in an entrepreneurial fashion. Entrepreneurial behavior appears to be motivated by a strong desire for achievement. There is reason to believe that poor countries have fewer individuals with high achievement motivation than rich countries and, therefore, they have slower rates of growth and change. There are some difficulties with this type of approach to the question of change agents. McClelland's data could well obscure other more important variables. In addition, children in countries with high growth rates might demonstrate high achievement motivation because they are growing up in rapidly changing environments, rather than the other way around. As a consequence, other studies of change agents tend to focus upon different characteristics.

In contrast to such psychological approaches, sociologists look for

13-3 Cultural Diffusion and Change-Agents

When new inventions and innovations are spread from one society to another, the process is called diffusion. People borrow and adapt ideas from one another as contact takes place through trade, travel, personal communication, mass media coverage of events, and so on. Individuals with special idealistic and achievement characteristics play an important role as change-agents in the creation and spread of innovations through diffusion.

United Press International

Mohandas Karamchand Gandhi was born of parents who were members of the merchant caste in 1869. He studied law in London and moved to South Africa in 1893, where he built a prosperous practice. However, he increasingly spent his time defending the rights of the Indian minority in South Africa, and he developed the idea of *Satyagraha,* or peaceful defiance of government. His philosophy was influenced by Jesus and by American author Henry David Thoreau. Gandhi returned to India, where, in 1919, he began his movement for Indian freedom and independence from British colonial rule. His people called him the *Mahatma,* or "Great Soul," because he lived simply, ate no meat, wore only a loin cloth, and taught the power of love. Mahatma Gandhi's nonviolent philosophy and tactics were later adopted by American civil rights and antiwar groups (see Chapter 14).

Culver Pictures, Inc.

Christopher Columbus was born in 1451, the son of a wool weaver. As a boy, he helped his father at the loom, but he always wanted to go to sea. In 1471, he shipped aboard a Genoese galley and almost lost his life in an attack by a hostile fleet off Portugal. In 1482, the king of Portugal refused to finance a plan by Columbus to try to find a short sea route to the Indies. However, by 1492 Columbus was able to persuade Queen Isabella of Spain to support a fleet of three vessels for an expedition. After over two months at sea, over twice as long as anyone had sailed in one direction out of sight of land, Columbus landed on a small island in the Bahamas, which he thought was in the Indies near Japan or China. Thus, the native inhabitants became known as Indians. Columbus not only accidentally discovered a new world, thereby encouraging trade and political expansion, but his voyages encouraged other explorers and his discoveries provided new knowledge for scientists.

TABLE 13-4 Achievement Scores in Children's Stories Compared with Economic Growth Rates of Countries

Countries	Rank Order of Children's Scores in 1925[a]	Rank Order of Economic Growth Rate of Country from 1938 to 1950[b]
High-Achievement-Level Countries		
Canada	1	2
England	2	3.5 (same rate)
Denmark	3	3.5 (same rate)
United States	4	1
Low-Achievement-Level Countries		
Germany	5	5
Belgium	6	7
France	7	8
Holland	8	6

[a]Ranked according to number of achievement ideas in children's stories (rank of 1 indicates highest; 8, lowest).
[b]Average annual gain in real national product per capita (rank of 1 indicates highest; 8, lowest).
Adapted from David C. McClelland, "Community Development and the Nature of Human Motivation: Some Implications of Recent Research," paper presented to the Conference on Community Development and National Change, Massachusetts Institute of Technology, Center for International Studies, Cambridge, Mass. (December 1957); *The Achieving Society* (Princeton, N.J.: Princeton University Press, 1962).

special types of interpersonal relationships that characterize change agents and account for their special roles, attitudes, and values. Charles Loomis [1967, pp. 875–890] selected a representative sample of 5800 adults (male and female), including influential leaders, from over 300 villages in India. He questioned them regarding their interest in, knowledge of, and adoption of new techniques and ideas, such as chemical fertilizer, improved seeds and better tools, vaccination for smallpox, and birth control. He then compared the findings for influential leaders with the findings for the general population.

As expected, leaders, as compared to the general population, were found to have adopted, or were in the process of adopting, more of the new practices. They also had more cosmopolitan and rational attitudes and values and were more actively linked to official agents of change in India (representatives of public and private agencies). For example, whereas 75 percent of the leaders had adopted chemical fertilizer on their farms, less than 50 percent of the general population of males had done so. Over half of the leaders used insecticides, almost 90 percent had been vaccinated for smallpox, and about 10 percent practiced family planning (used birth control), while the percentages for the general population were 25, 75, and 4, respectively. However, Loomis also found the paradoxical character of change to which we referred earlier—the coexistence of persistence and innovation, of oldness and newness. Over half of those sampled believed that evil spirits caused disease or said that they would go to a religious leader or temple for treatment of smallpox.

Nevertheless, three major factors seemed to account for the differences between leaders, who acted as influential change agents, and the general population:

1. *Aspiration for education and new experience:* This characteristic is similar to McClelland's high achievement motivation. Leaders sought new learning experiences and, therefore, tended to become innovators and early adopters of new techniques and knowledge.
2. *Linkage with other leaders, experts, and agents:* Motivation and open-mindedness were not sufficient. Leaders also had many contacts with professional health and agricultural specialists, lesser trained village-level workers, elected local officials, and the like.
3. *Exposure to the mass media:* One additional ingredient was also necessary—awareness of alternative norms, values, and social systems. Exposure to the media functioned to supply this awareness.

In other words, Loomis found that the Indian village change agents did two things: they acted as innovators and inventors themselves by adopting new ideas and techniques; and they also played a major role in the diffusion process as both lenders and borrowers, by means of their contact with key individuals, groups, and the mass media. Studies of change agents have specific implications for the question of the control of change. What Loomis was interested in was the possibility of identifying important villager leaders so that new programs of birth control or agricultural development could more readily be introduced into local life.

The accompanying "So What?" box gives an example of the use of change agents in Tanzania and, at the same time, points to the importance of other social and cultural factors in the process of change. The above discussion and the "So What?" box serve to introduce the final section of this chapter—the control of social and cultural change.

▶ SO WHAT?

Economist William Peek [1976] has spent several years in Tanzania, Africa, working with the Masai tribes, nomads who maintain small herds of cattle. Traditionally, the Masai have not been landowners, and as a consequence, neighboring tribes often encroach upon their grazing land and threaten the life of the tribes. This threat has led the Tanzania government to establish programs, with the assistance of experts like Peek, to encourage changes that will preserve, not eliminate, the Masai people. Ranching associations provide the Masai with new methods of agriculture, and a program for marketing cattle has attempted to create surplus capital to improve herds and to permit the Masai to purchase land and settle permanently.

In an attempt to bring about these changes, Peek enlisted the aid of two young Masai men, identified by Catholic missionaries as among the most resourceful and creative among the tribes. Lakara and Nginga were young and unmarried, and they were willing to experiment with new life-styles. They were persuaded to exchange their traditional clothing for Western-style dress. The traditional Masai wear a free-swinging blanket, which exposes their nakedness; consequently, they are not permitted in the cities of Tanzania. Dressed in pants, shirts, and shoes, Lakara and Nginga were able to go to the large city of Dar es Salaam, where they could buy and sell cattle. Although at first they were inclined to pay too much for better animals, they eventually learned to obtain good bargains on behalf of their marketing association. This resulted in surplus capital for their community, near the town of Arusha, which was used to construct water development projects, dips for cattle suffering from tick-borne diseases, new methods of castration, fencing of grazing areas, and bull ranches for breezing.

Thus, Peek and others were able to introduce changes by using innovators like Lakara and Nginga, native deviants who were willing to break with tradition. This use of change agents was not without problems. The two young men also learned to misuse their position to divert association money to their own benefit. In an effort to counteract this tendency, Peek used some of his own money to have the young men enrolled in missionary school.

Thus, major change may sometimes depend upon the willingness of several innovators to put on shoes and a pair of pants.

CAN CHANGE BE CONTROLLED?

As we saw in our discussion of deviance (Chapter 12), the question of controlling human dynamics involves both personal value judgments and adequate scientific knowledge. This section begins by considering the questions of whether change *should* and *can* be controlled. We will examine this debate as it relates to one of the most crucial areas of change in today's world—population trends.

Many scholars see the control of change and growth as absolutely necessary in order to achieve a better world in the future. They view unchecked and unanticipated change as dangerous. In contrast, newer views, reflected in the recent ecological movements, claim that human-assisted growth and change have been the cause of many of the world's problems. Therefore, they argue for less control and human involvement in the processes of change.

This section concludes by considering the major aspects of the population problem throughout the contemporary world. In particular, we compare the nature of the problem in underdeveloped and developing nations with the problem in more developed nations. The advantages and limitations of various techniques of population control are contrasted.

Problems of Control

The spirit of rationalism that has pervaded the world since the industrial revolution has led many people to believe that technological and economic change are good and desirable because they lead to more affluent life-styles. Recent awareness of the world's disappearing natural resources, increasing populations, and dangerous pollution, however, has led others to denounce technology and economic development as threats to human life. This situation has aroused, or renewed, a major and still unresolved debate about whether change *should* be consciously controlled by human intervention.

There is nothing particularly new about this debate. Social scientists have long argued about whether they should intervene in the life and cultures of other people. Some maintain that, since humans are goal-directed creatures, scientists have a moral responsibility to apply their knowledge to the attainment of those goals. Countering this view is the belief that to interfere in the life of another culture is to "play God." Social scientists may observe their own and other societies, but such observation must be combined with a "hands-off" respect for different values and behavior patterns.

This debate over values makes the question of controlling change a difficult one. It is our view that both the "interventionist" and the "hands-off" perspectives have merit. However, since both world leaders and social scientists *are* actively involved in manipulating change, our task is to understand the advantages and limitations of each position. This can be done without prejudicing the question of whether one should consciously intervene in specific situations.

The problem of control, as opposed to that of determining whether control should be exercised, is, in many ways, even more complex. In the beginning of the chapter, we identified some of the major characteristics and sources of change. Each of these presents special problems for the scientist interested in control:

1. *Change is inevitable:* Since change is an inevitable ever-present aspect of human life, how can the scientists interested in control locate its essential source or cause? Sociologists respond to this question by examining change, not as some bizarre aberration, but as the natural consequence of group life—as the product of roles and role relationships, norms and normative conflict, and the like. For example, Loomis analyzed change in terms of the roles of village leaders.
2. *Change is variable and uneven:* Since change takes place in different ways at different times, which social and cultural variables are most important from the standpoint of control? As we have seen, social scientists look for patterns of change, not overall patterns necessarily, but for relationships between different kinds of change. For example, sociologists examine the impact of technological inventions upon social institutions and values.

3. *Change contributes to both dynamic and stable processes:* Since change can bring about new conditions while simultaneously contributing to the maintenance of social stability, how does the scientist assess the impact of change? Sociologists investigate both the dynamic and the integrative consequences of different kinds of change. For example, while recognizing economic changes in the life of the Masai tribesmen ("So What?" box), Peek was also able to identify processes of disruption (the tendency of his change agents to learn new techniques of cheating).

Thus, despite the special value-oriented and scientific problems associated with change, the study of its control is possible. The remainder of this chapter utilizes the above perspectives to examine the debate about how population changes in contemporary society can best be controlled.

The Progrowth Versus Antigrowth Debate

The modern concern for population problems was initiated by the work of Thomas Malthus, published in 1798 as *An Essay on the Principle of Population.* Utilizing perspectives from classical economics, sometimes called "the dismal science," Malthus became concerned about the consequences of unchecked population growth. He observed that among plants and "irrational" animals, unchecked growth could lead to a doubling of the total population every generation, eventually producing dangerous pressures in the competition for food and living space. Malthus argued that similar processes could be observed in the case of human societies. However, two kinds of checks upon growth—"natural" and "conscious"—were present in the case of humans.

Natural checks, which Malthus called *positive checks,* included nonconscious events such as food shortages, disease, and warfare. He labeled them "positive" because of their direct and immediate check in population growth by suddenly increasing the death rate. Malthus was concerned, however, because he felt that such checks often stemmed from irrational excesses in human behavior and, consequently, might symbolize social and cultural decay. Also, writing from his 18th century perspective, he felt that such natural checks could never be totally controlled by humans. He felt that humans were both technologically and intellectually limited in their ability to increase the food supply or to control war.

In contrast to such positive checks, Malthus identified a number of conscious checks, which he called *preventive checks.* Humans could employ moral restraints to limit sexual intercourse, postpone marriage to later ages, or utilize various forms of sexual vices to reduce birth rates (birth control and abortion). However, here, too, he was pessimistic. He felt that few societies willingly adopted such techniques, and he judged birth control and abortion to be morally evil. As a matter of fact, he felt that birth control might be dysfunctional to vigorous economic activity, since it could reduce potential markets, diminish available labor supplies, and the like.

Nevertheless, Malthus reasoned that population growth, the resulting competition for space and food, an increase in positive checks, and the deliberate use of preventive checks might all become interrelated. A larger population might lead to shortages in food supply, which would increase positive checks (wars for more space or starvation). This, in turn, could encourage some societies to adopt morally approved preventive checks, such as the postponement of marriage, which would lead to smaller families and a decrease in birth rates. Malthus suggested that this type of pattern could be observed in the lower-social-class levels of industrializing populations of his time. As a consequence, the society might have time to increase food production and living standards in order to meet the needs of the population.

From our perspective in the latter half of the 20th century, Malthusian theory contains many limitations and difficulties. Research indicates that positive checks, such as war, may have a momentary depressing effect upon population (for example, the Soviet Union in World War II), but long-range growth may actually increase as societies attempt to readjust after the war (U.S. population after World War II). In other words, a momentarily high death rate may eventually encourage an extended period of high birth rates.

In addition, although many wars are started in the name of population pressures (the Nazi search for *Lebensraum*), other factors, such as national wealth and prestige, seem to be far more important. Only in special societies (for example, in religious communities) have people seemed willing to practice abstinence from sexual intercourse as a matter of long-term communal policy. In these cases, moreover, factors other than population pressures (for example, religious commitments) seem to control behavior. Furthermore, recent shifts in world attitudes indicate that practices such as birth control and abortion are no longer considered to be universal moral evils [Petersen, 1969, pp. 141–171]. And, finally, as we have already seen, technological innovations in agriculture have had a far greater impact than Malthus anticipated. Malthus failed to anticipate remarkable increases in food production. He could not foresee the extent of improvements in agricultural technology and science. In other words, Malthus' greatest limitation was that he could not realize that, while land is limited, human innovation would continue to lead to new fertilizers (including chemical fertilizers), seeds (such as miracle rice), pesticides, and farm equipment for planting and harvesting.

Despite these inadequacies, Malthusian theory sets the stage for the continuing debate about population changes. His general perspectives have been adopted in a more sophisticated and reliable form by contemporary advocates of the "limits-to-growth" philosophy. These people argue that

TABLE 13-5 The Antigrowth and Progrowth Philosophies

Beliefs About:	Neo-Malthusians (*"There are limits to change"*)	Superindustrialists (*"There are no limits to change"*)
1. World's Resources	The world has a *limited environment;* there are only so many resources. If resources are not redistributed, the rich will grow richer and the poor, poorer.	The world has a *limitless environment;* no one knows exactly what the earth holds. The more that is produced, the more that can be produced.
2. Technology and Capital	New technology and capital investment simply increase pollution and exhaust resources. Technology and capital have reached a point of *diminishing returns.*	New technology and capital investment are *absolutely necessary* to increase production, improve the environment, keep costs low, and provide an economic surplus for other activities.
3. Ability to handle problems by rational decision making	The rapidity of change, the complexity of the problems created, and the resulting conflict between special interests will lead to a *failure* in rational decision making. What is needed is a deceleration of change.	A combination of public regulation, international cooperation, and rational management will lead to *success* in decision making
4. Results of current growth and change	Current growth and change are uncontrolled, exponential, and cancerous. For example, world population is doubling every 33 years. The result is *instability.*	Current growth and change are presently both functional and controllable. For example, world population could well level off to about 15 billion in the 21st century. The result will be a transition to a new *stability.*
5. Impact of invention and innovation	New discoveries merely postpone the need for drastic action. Such postponement makes eventual collapse more severe; therefore, reliance upon invention and innovation is *a trap.*	New discoveries bring about *major improvements* in problem solving, efficiency, and the quality of life.
6. *Long-range outlook and needed response*	*The current emergency is total.* Unless *revolutionary changes* are made soon, the 21st century will see the greatest catastrophe since the Black Death, including starvation, pollution, and wars. Billions of people may be ruled by authoritarian governments. Major and radical measures are required to avert this situation.	*Things are going reasonably well.* The 21st century is likely to see a world where poverty, anxiety, and physical suffering are minimal. Continued *rational and humanistic methods* for managing change must be employed to bring this about.

Adapted from Herman Kahn and William Brown, "A World Turning Point and a Better Prospect for the Future," *The Futurist, 9* (December 1975), pp. 335–338.

the human potential to sustain ongoing growth is severely restricted. In contrast, advocates of development in all its forms (technological, social, and cultural) see continued, even accelerated, change and growth as necessary if human society is to survive and prosper. These conflicting philosophies are summarized in Table 13-5.

Which view most adequately reflects the nature, quality, and impact of contemporary change, especially population growth? As we have seen with other opposing perspectives throughout this book, each view represents a reliable assessment of different aspects of demographic change and industrial growth in contemporary society. In general, many scholars and leaders in the more prosperous developed nations are inclined toward the superindustrialist position, which sees no inherent limits to change as long as it is rationally managed. Conversely, those who are worried about the deprived position of the less prosperous undeveloped nations are inclined toward the neo-Malthusian position, which argues that the potential for functional change is severely limited. The opposing views tend to reflect the difference between the white, affluent peoples of the world and the nonwhite, poor peoples. The latter feel that the "haves" (the more prosperous nations) want to restrict the populations of the "have nots" (the less prosperous nations) without compromising their own privileged position. Therefore, underdeveloped nations view the problem as one requiring the rich to help the poor improve levels of education and economic development. In short, the population problem has global implications which are clearly expressed in the contrast between the antigrowth and progrowth philosophies. In addition, population changes have a different impact in underdeveloped societies than in developed societies.

The World Population Explosion: How Can Countries Respond?

Understanding and controlling the world population problem involves several different considerations. To begin with, *the world's total population has increased exponentially in a short period of time.* Demographers frequently make reference to the "J-shaped curve" of world population growth, depicted in Figure 13-3. This diagram illustrates three important periods in world history.

For thousands of years, the total population of the world was relatively stable and almost unchanging. In this first period, the number of births was cancelled out by number of deaths, and migration was limited to traveling by canoes on water and by foot on land. However, around 6000 B.C., with the emergence of the New Stone Age culture, modest improvements in agriculture and hunting and a more settled community life led to a modest increase in population. During this second period, technological, social, and cultural changes were able to keep pace with the small excess of births over deaths.

FIGURE 13-3 J-Shaped Growth of World Population

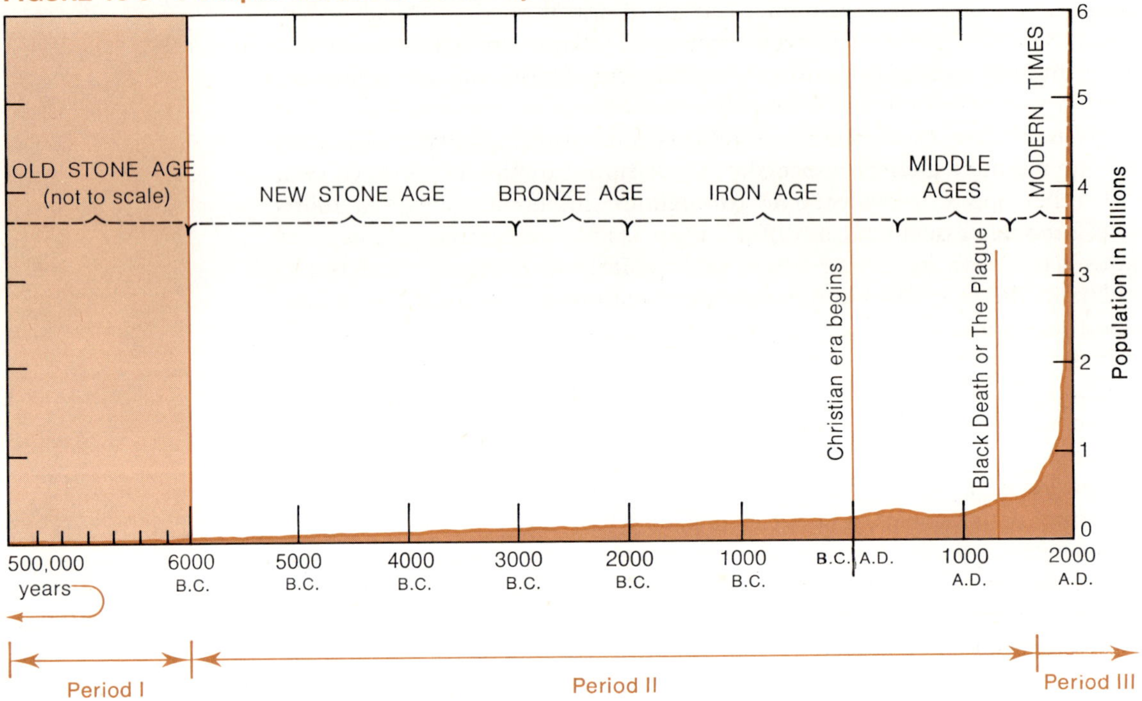

From the Population Reference Bureau, "How Many People Have Ever Lived on Earth?" *Population Bulletin, 27,* No. 1 (February 1962), p. 5.

From 1600 to 1800 A.D., however, modernization began to have a dramatic impact upon death rates, and the population growth rate turned sharply upward. Also, as we have seen, mass migrations relieved pressures on birth rates in both the home and the recipient countries, thereby prolonging drops in the birth rate for long periods of time. As the Population Reference Bureau puts it, it took hundreds of thousands of years for the human population to reach 2 billion, but it will take only 40 more years for the population to grow to 6 billion. (According to the Population Reference Bureau, world population reached 4 billion on 28 March 1976.) Furthermore, if the Old Stone Age period on the left in Figure 13-3 were in proper scale, its base line would actually extend 35 feet to the left. Thus, the world's population has truly exploded in the third period, which constitutes only a fraction of human history.

Paul Ehrlich [1971] has called the contemporary situation a "population bomb" ready to explode and bring catastrophe to human society. The ability of societies to provide the basic needs for such a rapidly growing population has already started to fall behind. Millions of people in the world are already beginning to die of starvation, with the nations of Africa being especially hard hit. The Population Reference Bureau [April 1971] and other experts have estimated that 25 million people (the approximate population of the U.S. states of California, Oregon, and Washington in 1970) may die of starvation during the 20th century. In contrast, 10 million (the approximate population of Ohio in 1970) died of starvation during the 18th century. In addition, one fourth of the world's present population is always hungry and one tenth is on the brink of starvation.

Apart from the food problem, other needed services and facilities are deteriorating throughout the world, even in the most advanced nations. Schools are overcrowded; housing and police protection are inadequate; meaningful jobs and work are disappearing; governments and private businesses are going bankrupt. As a consequence, internal turbulence (see Chapter 5) and international conflict (see Chapter 11) have increased within and between many countries of the world. Unless the rapid rate of population increase can be slowed or stopped (the aim of those who advocate ZPG—zero population growth), the results will be severe, according to those who focus upon the total numbers and increasing rate of population [Population Reference Bureau, 1974].

However, the population problem involves much more than simply the growing number of people in the world. It is also *a result of the process of demographic transition,* discussed earlier in the chapter. This theory highlights the different character of the population problem for different nations of the world (see Table 13-6). We saw that dramatic population increases take place during Stage II of the demographic process—that is, during the transitional periods, when birth rates remain high but death

TABLE 13-6 Comparison of Population Base, Period of Demographic Transition, and Population Increase for Areas of the World, 1973

Area	Total Population	Crude Birth Rate	Crude Death Rate	Birth Rate–Death Rate Gap	Yearly Increase In Population (Percentage)
Developed					
Europe	472,000,000	16	11	+ 5	+0.5
United States	210,000,000	15	9	+ 6	+0.6
Developing					
Soviet Union	250,000,000	18	8	+10	+1.0
Japan	108,000,000	19	7	+12	+1.2
Underdeveloped					
Asia (except Japan)	2,100,000,000	38	14	+24	+2.4
Africa	375,000,000	46	19	+27	+2.7
Latin America (Tropical)	265,000,000	38	8	+30	+3.0

Adapted from Ronald Freeman and Bernard Berelson, *The Human Population,* a Scientific American Book (San Francisco: W. H. Freeman, 1974), p. 11.

13-4 Means for Controlling Demographic Change

Can change be controlled? Unchecked world population growth gives a special urgency to this question. A number of different means are now available for controlling demographic processes, but each has weaknesses as well as strengths.

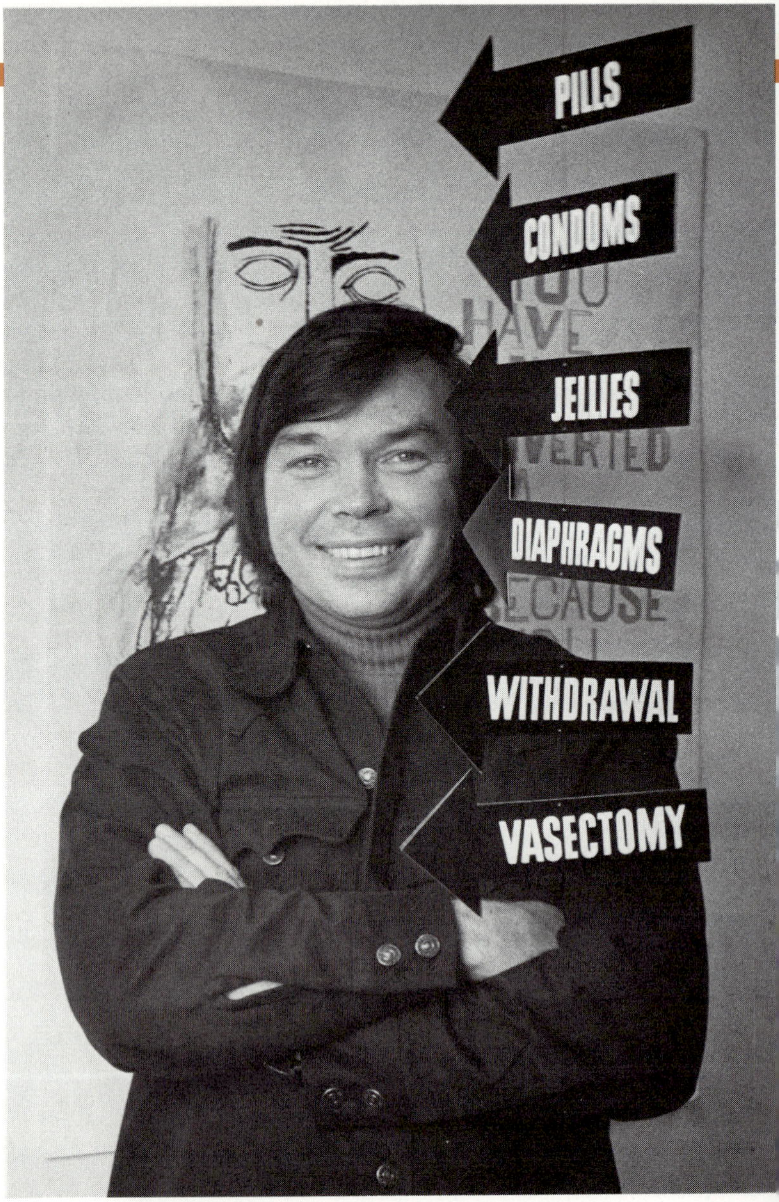

E. Herwig/Stock, Boston

Technological Means. One of the factors determining demographic change is fertility. Devices, medicines, and surgical procedures can be readily adopted by societies to bring about a rapid and significant drop in birth rates. For many years, birth control advocate Bill Baird has promoted the use of these techniques in America. However, social and cultural barriers to the use of these means often include lack of public knowledge about proper use of devices (condoms, diaphragms), the cost of surgical procedures (abortions, vasectomies), unpredictable and possibly dangerous side effects (pills, IUDs), or moral sanctions against any form of mechanical control.

D. Brody/Stock, Boston

Informal Peer Group Means. The more subtle norms and values can often be changed by informal peer group contact. Women may attempt to get other women to redefine their traditional roles, values, and norms. Such value modification through secondary contact in women's organizations, political action groups, and community service associations is often very effective in industrial societies. However, in developing nations, experiencing severe population pressures, many women are usually not members of such groups and extensive means for mass communication and influence are unavailable.

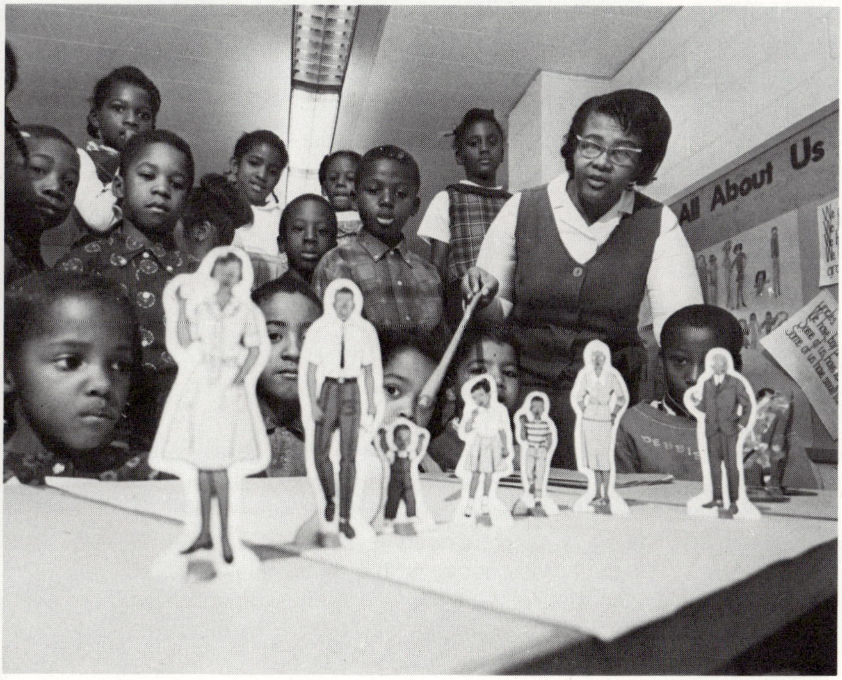

Wide World Photos

Formal Educational Means. Some of the barriers to birth control, such as lack of knowledge of the population problem and how to contend with it, are sometimes counteracted through formal instruction. Sex education courses inform the child his or her sexuality and the complex emotional and physical problems lying behind relationships between the sexes. However, moral beliefs are diverse in modern society, and this often limits the school's ability to teach specific birth control information. Furthermore, formal training does little about more subtle cultural factors which may sustain high birth rates: for example, beliefs which measure fatherhood by numbers of sons or motherhood by number of children produced.

P. Southwick/Stock, Boston

Elsa Dorfman

Economic Means. One of the most effective means for decreasing fertility is the social and geographical mobility which characterizes industrial society. Increased mobility and personal freedom permit women, both in and out of marriage, to seek permanent work and pursue careers, thereby limiting family sizes. However, industrialization also leads to a rapidly declining death rate due to better economic conditions and an improving standard of living. In addition, developing nations may experience an immediate drop in death rates followed by a long period of slowly declining birth rates. If this takes place with a large population base, serious population problems can result.

Social and Political Means. A variety of social and political means (welfare benefits, tax incentives, social security) are also available for controlling population changes. However, the consequences of these means are often unpredictable. For example, an adequate social security program might encourage couples to have fewer children and at an earlier age so that they can retire while still relatively young. Social security also makes large families unnecessary in order for parents to make certain that their children can support them in their later years. At the same time, though, social security may decrease the death rate and prolong the life span, thereby adding to population pressures and creating new population problems (care of the aged).

rates fall rapidly. This stage is particularly important for the following reasons:

1. About two thirds of the world's countries have yet to pass fully through Stage II. For example, India and China are presently in this transitional period, and many of the new nations in the world (in Africa and Asia) are just beginning industrial development. Therefore, if the population growth for these countries is as great as it was for Western nations, the result could be catastrophic for everyone.
2. Some countries presently in the transitional period (China and India) have a population base numbering in the hundreds of millions. Any significant gap between births and deaths, therefore, would cause far greater numerical growth than was experienced during Western industrialization, when nations began growing from relatively small population bases.
3. Stage II frequently seems to involve long periods of time. Actually, passage through Stage II may take longer for non-Western nations than it did for those in the West. Different social and cultural contexts, some hostile to Western-style industrialization, may limit the rapidity of demographic transition in these nations. Therefore, greater numbers of people will be involved for longer periods of time in explosive population growth.

This view of the population problem suggests that, in addition to controlling the size of populations, some nations need assistance in bringing about industrial and urban transformation more rapidly. This would not only help in decreasing birth rates more rapidly, but it would also bring technological, social, and cultural improvements to needy nations.

There is a final aspect of the world population problem that is as important as numbers of people or the stage of demographic transition; this is *the impact of population changes upon the quality of life.* This is the aspect that most frequently concerns the developed nations. As we have seen throughout this chapter, change in one part of a society or culture brings about changes in many other parts. Therefore, even modest fluctuations in birth rates, death rates, or patterns of migration can influence family life, occupational roles, norms and values, and the like. Adequate responses to the problems created by these kinds of changes often call for different programs and policies than those intended for dealing with population size or stage of industrial development. The following study is adapted from the work of President Nixon's Commission on Population Growth and the American Future. The committee, chaired by John D. Rockefeller III, was appointed in 1970 to analyze the impact of population changes upon American life and to recommend appropriate governmental policy. The study indicates that even advanced nations are experiencing a population problem.

▶ STUDY 13

Is There a Population Crisis in the United States? [1972][1]

Problem

In 1969 and 1970, pressures were brought to bear upon the White House and Congress, by environmental groups and John D. Rockefeller III, to study the impact of continued uncontrolled growth of U.S. population. This growth was seen by many as leading to higher rates of consumption of natural resources and to the use of technologies that threatened the environment. In addition, concern was expressed that the United States, by virtue of its wealth, consumed a grossly disproportionate share of the world's resources, thereby depriving other nations of resources. Thus, growth in U.S. population was seen as increasing American "exploitation" of developing countries.

As a consequence, in July 1969, President Nixon delivered a message to Congress, in which he raised a number of important questions:

> Where . . . will the next hundred million Americans live? . . . Are our cities prepared for such an influx? . . . Are there ways, then, of readying our cities? Alternatively, can the trend toward greater concentration of population be reversed? What of our natural resources and the quality of our environment? . . . How will we educate and employ such a large number of people? . . . [or] provide adequate health care? [Westoff, 1975, p. 45]

The speech was called comprehensive and eloquent by many citizens. In March 1970, Congress enacted a statute creating the Commission on Population Growth and the American Future for a period of two years.

Since President Nixon's message to Congress had emphasized the need for planning in order to accommodate the next 100 million Americans, the task of the Commission was (1) to explore the course of population growth and internal migration to the year 2000; (2) to assess the implications of probable changes on the public sector of the national economy; and (3) to evaluate the significance of these findings for the activities of federal, state, and local governments.

Under pressure from part of the U.S. "population lobby," the House of Representatives included two additional, and more controversial, mandates: (1) to assess the implications of population growth for natural resources and the quality of the environment and (2) to consider the various means "appropriate to the ethical values and principles of this society by which our Nation can achieve a population level properly suited for its environmental, natural resource, and other needs." It was the addition of these purposes that led the Commission to interpret its basic charge as that of recommending a national population policy rather than developing a master plan to prepare for continued population increase. In short, *the Commission saw the problem as the need to develop interventionist strategies to control population growth,* rather than the need to develop strategies to accommodate continued uncontrolled growth.

[1]Adapted and abridged from The Population Reference Bureau, "Population: The Future Is Now," *The Population Bulletin, 28* (April 1972); and Charles F. Westhoff, 'The Commission on Population Growth and the American Future: Its Origins, Operations, and Aftermath," in *Sociology and Public Policy: The Case of Presidential Commissions,* Mirra Komarovsky, Ed. (New York: Elsevier Scientific Publishing Company, 1975), pp. 43–59.

The Commission members formulated *two hypotheses:*

1. U.S. population can be stabilized within 50 to 60 years.
2. If this goal is achieved, American society will be better able to cope with the social problems stemming from uncontrolled fertility—birth of unwanted and illegitimate children, families living at poverty levels, women overburdened with domestic responsibilities and deprived of career opportunities, environmental deterioration, and the like.

A proposed two-year *study design* involved the gathering and assessing of data dealing with population growth and its impact upon the quality of American life. Furthermore, the study design entailed collection of data that could be used to develop national strategies for controlling population growth, strategies based upon methods of control that were both effective and culturally acceptable.

Hypotheses and Study Design

Typical of official investigative agencies, the Commission used a number of different methods of data collection. Scholars, including demographers, were appointed to the commission, together with businessmen, politicians, a physician, Catholics, a Mexican-American woman, and a 19-year-old student. The members of the Commission, therefore, acted as *personal resource people.* In addition, five *public hearings* were held, in Washington, D. C., and other cities. These open meetings allowed Commission members to question citizens directly influenced by the problems of poverty, illegitimacy, inadequate educational opportunities, and so on. Representatives of churches, lobbies, health organizations, businesses, and the like participated.

The Commission also analyzed the results of *written documents* and scientific studies dealing with the kinds of problems that were relevant to their hypotheses. Material was circulated among Commission members, and often outside experts or staff members were asked to lecture on specific topics. Finally, *research was contracted* with appropriate scholars on special topics of importance. For example, one such project was a national opinion poll to gauge public knowledge about population and to obtain public attitudes toward population-related matters (such as city size, immigration, abortion, and methods of birth control).

Methods of Data Collection

The Commission concluded that their first hypothesis was confirmed. *American population growth could be stabilized* for the following reasons:

1. The trend in average family size had been downward for a number of years.
2. The birth rate had declined over the past decade from about 24 per 1000 in 1960 to about 18 per 1000 in 1970.
3. At the same time, there had been increasing employment of women and changes in the conventional role of wife–homemaker–mother.
4. Citizen awareness and concern over population growth had increased.
5. The family size preferences of young people presently in the child-bearing ages were significantly lower than the preferences reported by older citizens when they were at the same stage in the life cycle.

Findings and Interpretations

6. The technical quality and reliability of contraceptives had increased greatly in the last decade.
7. Abortion had been legalized in a few states.
8. The experience of other countries indicated that a ZPG birth rate that merely sustains replacement levels (two children for two married adults) was feasible.

In other words, the Commission concluded that *the two-child family was coming into being in the United States.* This would have the effect of decreasing the rate of population growth from about 1 percent per year in 1970 to about 0.7 percent per year in 2000. The importance of this change is indicated in Figure 13-4.

The Commission also dealt with the social and cultural barriers that might impede the trend toward smaller families. *Norms and values frequently reflect either a conscious or inadvertent probirth policy.* For example, income tax exemptions for each new child in a family can encourage large families. Traditional values honor the "woman's place in the home." Therefore, new norms and values would be necessary to encourage women to seek educational and occupational opportunities, thereby encouraging fertility control.

In addition, the Commission found *an inadequate level of understanding about population,* the reproductive process, methods of birth control, and the like. For example, one survey disclosed that 60 percent of those questioned did not know or could not guess within 50 million people the actual size of the American population. A survey found that only 20 percent of sexually active unmarried teen-age girls reported using any contraceptive regularly. However, data also disclosed that nearly two thirds of the public approved of high schools offering information to teen-agers on ways of avoiding pregnancy, and half the public felt that abortion ought to be a matter decided solely between individuals and their physicians.

Therefore, the Commission recommended that better sex education be made available to schools and families, particularly contraceptive information for sexually active youth. The Commission voted 19 to 5 in favor of open abortion policies that would permit women to consider termination of a pregnancy in consultation with their physician. This was one of the most controversial aspects of the report. Advocates pointed to the fact that about 15 percent of all American children are born unwanted and, consequently, are apt to be either deprived or abused.

The Commission also highlighted *the role of poverty and deprivation* in sustaining higher birth rates. While the white middle-class majority bears the primary responsibility for population growth, the failure of American society to bring racial minorities and the poor into the mainstream of life has impaired their ability to implement small-family goals. Fertility control comes about when families are upwardly mobile and have the opportunity to obtain better housing, income, education, and jobs.

Reminiscent of the debate between neo-Malthusians and superindustrialists, the Commission also criticized the American *ideological addiction to growth*—that is, they questioned the assumption that the economy would falter if the population of potential consumers did not increase. The Commission argued that, in reality, society would be better off if population growth were brought under control, since resources could then be more effectively managed.

In addition, the Commission made several other important recommendations.

FIGURE 13-4 Difference in Two-Child and Three-Child Families in the United States, 1970–2070 (An average of three children per family would increase the U.S. population to about 400 million people by the year 2014; an average of two children per family would result in a population of 100 million fewer people, or 300 million.)

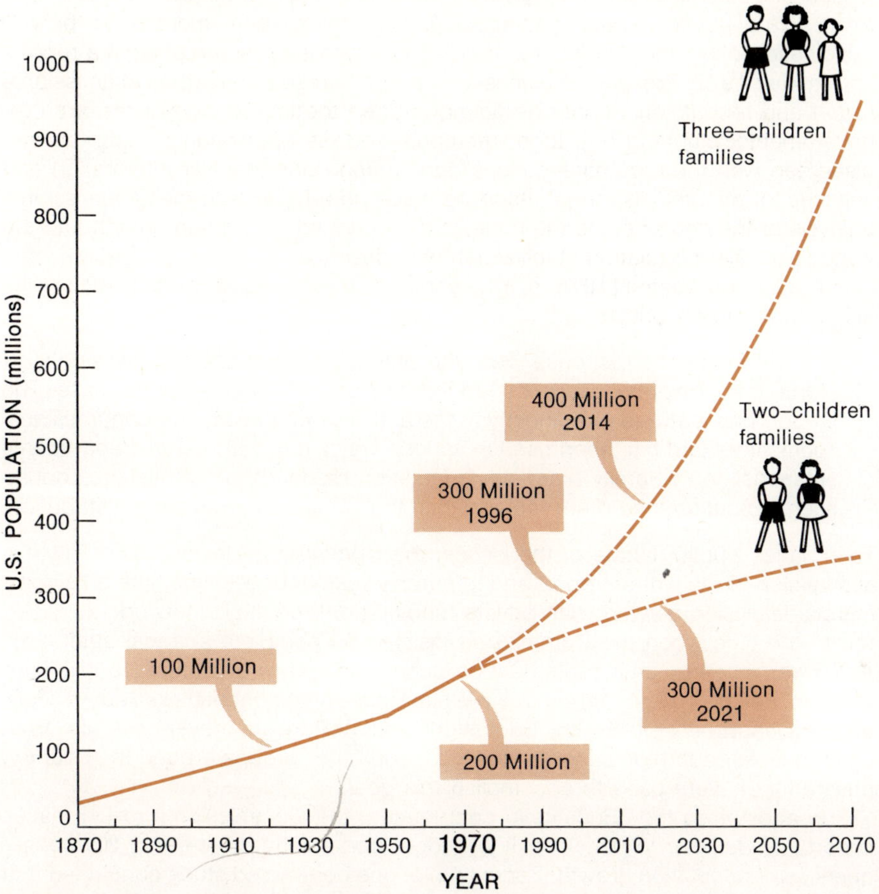

From the Population Reference Bureau, *Population Bulletin, 27* (June 1971), p. 9; originally contained in the "Report" of the Commission on Population Growth and the American Future.

Vital statistics about population should be improved, and more funding for research in fertility control should be made available. Attention should be given to problems relating to immigration and emigration, even though these processes no longer involve large numbers of people. Specifically, illegal immigration should be stopped, and internal migration from rural to urban areas and within urban areas should be closely monitored. Finally, the Commission pointed out that, if the United States with comparatively low population growth rates tried to stabilize growth, other nations might be encouraged to adopt a similar policy.

Conclusions and Implications

This study represents another type of "research" that is increasingly popular in contemporary society—the officially commissioned Presidential committee. Reports of this type differ somewhat from typical social scientific research, although official Commissions often utilize similar perspectives and methods. Somewhat unlike scientific research, however, *governmental reports are often designed to stimulate public debate and social action,* rather than merely to "prove" hypotheses. How, then, does one assess the success or failure of such a report?

In May 1972, President Nixon issued a formal response to the Commission's report and recommendations. He acknowledged the importance of research for governmental planning but, then, reemphasized his opposition to abortion and disagreed with the recommendations concerning contraceptive information and services for minors. His formal response made no reference to the Commission's analysis of the costs versus the benefits of continued population growth and the conclusion that population stabilization was desirable.

As Charles Westoff [1975, p. 58], who had served as Director of the Commission's Staff, points out:

> If the President's response were the only criterion of the Commission's efforts, then it would have to be judged a failure. But that is not the case. The report has featured prominently in the activities of at least one congressional committee and has been used in various ways in governmental departments responsible for family planning, population research and statistics, population education, and other topics within the subject of population distribution.

To enhance public debate of the issues, the Commission decided to produce a film version of the written report and to purchase an hour of prime time on a commercial television network with private funds. The three major networks declined to sell the time when the Commission insisted on complete editorial autonomy. A film was made by an independent producer and shown on national public television in the fall of 1974. Although the White House subsequently exerted pressure on the Department of Health, Education, and Welfare to prevent the film from being circulated to high schools, colleges, and other groups around the country, private funds were used to accomplish this goal.

In addition to the educational contribution, the Commission's report makes important additions to scholarly knowledge, particularly concerning the consequences of population growth. For example, one contracted study concluded that population growth plays a minor role in resource depletion and environmental deterioration in the short run (30–50 years) when compared to the impact of technological, economic, and governmental policy. In the longer run, however, population growth becomes increasingly important. Thus, serious questions can be raised about *both* long-term population growth and contemporary environmental policies.

Finally, the Commission's work represented an important effort by an advanced country to develop a national population policy based upon controlled growth to maximize the quality of life. Even though this effort was not officially adopted, it became a model for other countries. A similar panel in Great Britain drew upon the findings of the Commission's report, and contacts were made with groups in Australia and the Netherlands. As a Latin American official put it: "Your report may have more influence in the rest of the world than it will in your own country." [Westoff, 1975, p. 59].

This study, then, vividly illustrates the problems associated with the control of change that we discussed at the beginning of this section. Competing value judgments about what constitutes the best or most appropriate methods of control make the study of change and recommendations for action difficult. In addition, the Commission's findings indicate the difficulty associated with scientifically identifying the precise causes and consequences of change, especially population trends. The best that scientific studies and official commissions can do is to recommend alternative roles, relationships, and norms, based upon an assessment of present conditions. The final determination of which methods or techniques of control are most appropriate will depend upon subsequent public debate and compromise.

Before we leave the general topic of change and the specific topic of population change, an additional word about methods of control is necessary.

A Final Note on Techniques of Population Control

Although some Americans, including President Nixon, thought that the recommendations of the President's Commission were too "radical" or unacceptable, other scholars and scientists have been even more critical of prevailing policy, especially in the United States. For example, some demographers have proposed that the government impose luxury taxes upon diapers, baby bottles, baby foods, and other probirth products in order to discourage large families. They have also recommended that birth-control education be made mandatory in the public schools, and that federal funds be used for fertility control in conjunction with studies of environmental protection [Population Reference Bureau, 1972]. Furthermore other scientists argue that foreign aid should be given only to other countries that are making serious attempts to lower fertility rates. Even seemingly humane food exports (for example, grain for India) can become harmful if they are not coupled with permanent policy to control fertility. More food to meet an immediate crisis may only postpone attempts by the receiving nation to control long-term population growth.

However, not all demographers agree that such drastic actions are required. Other scientists maintain that there is no reason to believe that all underdeveloped or developing nations will go through precisely the same patterns of demographic transition that were experienced by Western countries. Although death rates seem to fall rapidly in Stage II, there is some indication that birth rates, once they start down, may fall more rapidly than expected. Contemporary Stage II nations can call upon the experience and expertise of developed nations for help in controlling birth rates by using available birth-control technology. For example, Taiwan and South Korea seem to have lowered their birth rates significantly before industrialization reached an advanced stage.

Some studies indicate that the Western pattern, where economic development precedes social and cultural change, does not seem to apply to all developing nations today. Because of cultural diffusion and social contact between nations, social and cultural changes frequently appear to come first, causing birth rates to decline before economic development is very advanced.

In addition, there are hopeful signs in nations like India and China. India was the first nation to establish a national population policy, and its government is promoting fertility control in spite of the continuing emphasis upon large families in villages and rural areas. According to the latest reports, China is also taking drastic steps toward fertility control, as witnessed by public condemnation and censorship of sexual promiscuity and by recent efforts of the state to restrict or control marriage. Such steps are especially effective when they are implemented by authoritarian governments, such as characterize a number of today's developing nations [Population Reference Bureau, December 1971]. This last trend indicates once again the sociological irony that typifies much human behavior. The resolution of one problem (fertility control by authoritarian methods) can create other problems (the loss of democracy and individual freedom).

CONCLUSION

In this chapter, we have considered the sources and nature of change. The fact that change is an inevitable and permanent aspect of all human life is attributable, in part, to the dynamic nature of the social self. Relationships between social roles, institutions, groups, and conflicting norms and values also vary according to external circumstances. In addition, change itself is variable and uneven. This presents problems for the social scientist, who often looks for overall patterns and forms of change. Sociologists resolve this dilemma by identifying different kinds of change (technological, social, and cultural) and by examining their relationships.

Technology, particularly inventions and innovations, has played a major role in theories of change. Those scholars who study premodern societies tend to identify agricultural improvements as the primary cause of change, while those who study modern societies tend to focus upon industrial innovations. Sociologists argue that no single variable can be isolated from the larger web of social experience. What is important is the relationship between technological developments, the social order (new roles and relationships), and culture (new norms and values).

Early theories of change attempted to identify global patterns of change, such as those that viewed change in terms of evolutionary development or cycles. Although these theories are often provocative (for example, Sorokin's idea of cultural decline in sensate societies), they tend to obscure more complex processes at work. Therefore, newer theories have examined the relationship between different patterns of change involving a number of variables. For example, demographers study the relationships between changes in birth rates, death rates, and patterns of migration, and the impact that these changing relationships have upon family life, occupational roles, and intergroup relationships (for example, differences between social classes).

Cultural theorists study the identifying characteristics of those individuals and groups (change agents) who play a key role in bringing about change. Psychological studies maintain that certain kinds of attitudes (for example, high achievement motivation) are crucial. In contrast, sociological studies look for important social linkages between these change agents and the general population, linkages that encourage both borrowing and lending in the process of cultural diffusion.

Finally, we considered the problems associated with the control of change. Perhaps, more than any other topic in social science, the issue of controlling change is influenced by value judgments concerning both the ethics and the methods of intervening in the life of societies and cultures. The control of change is further complicated by its complex nature and its multivariate origin. In general, two major philosophies of change have developed in contemporary society. Neo-Malthusians argue that there are limits to functional growth and change and that the contemporary worship of growth must be replaced by a respect for natural and social resources. Superindustrialists argue that invention and innovation can be encouraged to resolve the problems facing human society, and, therefore, there are no real limits to growth or change. As we have seen, the actual world situation probably lies somewhere between these two extremes, depending upon the region or nation being studied.

We concluded by considering the population problem in terms of these two competing philosophies of change. Some scholars believe that a worldwide population crisis exists and that only the harshest and most extreme responses will save the world from major catastrophes (such as war, famine, disease). Others maintain that more modest governmental programs and policies will lead to the eventual control of population growth.

This area of disagreement is an appropriate introduction to the next chapter, which discusses the third major form of human dynamics—conflict. Increasing concern for the population crisis will most probably encourage additional conflict over competing values, norms, and special interests. Will such conflict be disadvantageous to a successful resolution of the population problem, or is human conflict sometimes functional and desirable? This question is a major concern of Chapter 14.

REFERENCES

Comte, Auguste. *System of Positive Polity.* London: Longmans, Green, 1877.

DeFleur, Melvin L., William V. D'Antonio, and Lois B. DeFleur. *Sociology: Man in Society,* Brief Edition. Glenview, Ill.: Scott, Foresman and Company, 1972.

Durkheim, Emile. *The Division of Labor in Society,* George Simpson, Transl. New York: The Free Press, 1949.

Ehrlich, Paul. *The Population Bomb,* rev. ed. New York: Ballantine Books, 1971.

Higgins, Benjamin. *Economic Development,* rev. ed. New York: W. W. Norton & Company, 1968.

Hughes, Everett. "Foreward" in Georg Simmel, *Conflict and The Web of Group-Affiliations,* Kurt H. Wolff and Reinhard Bendix, Transl. New York: The Free Press of Glencoe, 1955.

Kahn, Herman, and William Brown. "A World Turning Point and a Better Prospect for the Future," *The Futurist, 9* (December 1975), pp. 330–338.

Linton, Ralph. *The Study of Man.* New York: Appleton–Century–Crofts, 1936.

Loomis, Charles P. "In Praise of Conflict and Its Resolution," *American Sociological Review, 32* (June 1967), pp. 875–890.

Malthus, Thomas. *Population: The First Essay.* Ann Arbor: University of Michigan Press, 1959; Malthus originally published his essay in 1798.

McClelland, David C. "Community Development and the Nature of Human Motivation: Some Implications of Recent Research," paper presented to the Conference on Community Development and National Change, Massachusetts Institute of Technology, Center for International Studies, Cambridge, Mass. (December 1957).

———. *The Achieving Society.* Princeton, N.J.: Princeton University Press, 1962.

Merril, Francis E. *Society and Change.* Englewood Cliffs, N.J.: Prentice–Hall, 1969.

Ogburn, William F. *Social Change.* New York: B. W. Huebsch, 1922.

———. "Cultural Lag as Theory," *Sociology and Social Research, 41* (January–February 1957), pp. 167–174.

Peek, William W. (Personal communication, 1976).

Petersen, William. "Demographic Transition in the Netherlands," *American Sociological Review, 25* (June 1960), pp. 334–347.

———. *Population,* 2nd ed. New York: The Macmillan Company, 1969.

Pirenne, Henri. *Medieval Cities: Their Origins and the Revival of Trade.* Princeton, N.J.: Princeton University Press, 1925.

Population Reference Bureau. "How Many People Have Ever Lived on Earth?" *Population Bulletin, 18,* No. 1 (February 1962).

———. "Man's Population Predicament," *Population Bulletin, 27,* No. 2 (April 1971).

———. "Toward a U.S. Population Policy," *Population Bulletin, 27,* No. 3 (June 1971).

———. "China: Population in the People's Republic," *Population Bulletin, 27,* No. 6 (December 1971).

———. "Abortion: The Continuing Controversy," *Population Bulletin, 28,* No. 4 (1972).

———. "World Population Projections: Alternative Paths to Zero Growth," *Population Bulletin, 29,* No. 5 (1974).

Rose, Edward. "Innovations in American Culture," *Social Forces, 26* (March 1948), pp. 255–272.

Rostow, W. W. "The Take-Off into Self-Sustained Growth," *The Economic Journal* (March 1956), pp. 25–48.

Scientific American. *The Human Population.* San Francisco: W. H. Freeman, 1974.

Smelser, Neil J. *Essays in Sociological Explanation.* Englewood Cliffs, N.J.: Prentice–Hall, 1968.

Sorokin, Pitirim. *Social and Cultural Dynamics.* New York: American Book Company, 1937.

Spencer, Herbert. *The Principles of Sociology.* New York: D. Appleton and Company, 1896.

White, Lynn. *Medieval Technology and Social Change.* Oxford: Oxford University Press, 1962.

Zimmerman, Carle C. *Family and Civilization.* New York: Harper, 1947.

- Are animals and humans aggressive for the same reasons (for example, because of drives or instincts for hunger, fear, sexual intercourse, and so on)?
- It has been said that "violence is as American as apple pie." What do you think?
- Is it possible to have competition without conflict, and conflict without violence?
- How would you explain the seemingly unending conflict between whites and blacks in America, Protestants and Catholics in Northern Ireland, French and English in Canada, and Arabs and Israelis in the Middle East?
- Are terrorist groups and societies (Symbionese Liberation Army, Popular Front for the Liberation of Palestine, Japanese Red Army, Nazi Germany, premodern Zulu civilization, Soviet society under Joseph Stalin) a sign of social and political disorganization?
- Which of the following is the most effective way of controlling conflict?
  1. Repression (more and stronger police and laws).
  2. Co-optation (redirecting conflict into acceptable channels, such as political action).
  3. Voluntary or compulsory bargaining (such as labor–management relations).
  4. Nonviolent action (Gandhi, Martin Luther King, the Berrigan brothers).
- What are the strengths and weaknesses of each technique?

14

The Dynamics of Conflict: Minorities and Ethnic Groups

In addition to deviance and change, the concept of *conflict* has been used by sociologists to analyze social dynamics, in contrast to social order. In the 1960s, social conflict was "rediscovered" by a new breed of sociological "radicals" (see the discussion of sociological theories in Chapter 1). "Old" sociology was categorized by the new critics as esoteric, exclusive, and ethically detached. The new radicals called for more adventurous and activist roles by scientists, pointing out that change and conflict, rather than stability and cooperation, characterized modern society [Gouldner, 1970]. The older sociologists responded by accusing the new critics of being innovative romanticists who utilized scientifically shoddy methods and unsupportable hypotheses. This creative tension between old and new perspectives has led to a renewed interest in the origins and consequences of human conflict.

This chapter begins by considering various theories that have attempted to identify the sources and nature of conflict. We consider the argument between those who see aggression and violence as a result of biological factors and those who see conflict arising because of societal variables. We also discuss the debate between those who view conflict and violence as dysfunctional and those who argue that violent conflict can be functional—that it can lead to much needed change, vitality, and creativity.

Two major sociological theories, which attribute conflict to either cultural or societal causes, are then considered. In particular, we contrast more recent sociological perspectives, which view conflict as stemming from feelings of status deprivation among minority and ethnic groups, with traditional theories, which explain conflict in terms of different norms, values, and social relationships in the larger society. Finally, the chapter concludes by comparing various views of how to control or manage conflict most effectively. The traditional liberal-democratic approach assumes that conflicting interest groups must be made to bargain and compromise. A newer, more radical approach states that conflict can be carried out by nonviolent means.

SOURCES AND NATURE OF CONFLICT: BIOLOGICAL OR SOCIAL?

The study of the sources of human conflict and aggression is characterized by a multitude of competing theories. Consequently, to summarize all of these theories and still to do justice to each one, all within a single chapter, is an impossibility. In this section, we have selected several perspectives that, together, illustrate the major debate regarding human conflict—whether it is biologically or socially determined. Some scholars see conflict as natural, genetically determined response patterns within humans, as an instinctive means of coping with the physical and social environments. Others argue that social and cultural factors (socialization, patterns of interaction, norms, and so on) determine whether humans will become aggressive in specific situations.

In addition, proponents of each perspective have viewed conflict as being both good and bad, as follows:

	Biological Theories	Social Theories
Conflict is Good	Individual aggression operates to control and redirect collective violence and killing.	Conflict leads to needed innovation and change.
Conflict Is Bad	Aggression is a result of the fact that humans are carnivorous killers.	Conflict disrupts the normal functioning of the social system.

The first sections of this chapter briefly consider examples of these competing perspectives.

Is Human Aggression Biologically Determined?

The widespread anxiety about violence and aggression in today's society is evidenced by the popularity of recent books, ranging from the journalistic treatments in Desmond Morris' *The Naked Ape* [1969] and Robert Ardrey's *The Territorial Imperative* [1966] to the reasoned scientific work in Konrad Lorenz's *On Aggression* [1969]. All of these approaches share the same assumptions: Human behavior is, to a considerable extent, genetically determined (like all animal behavior); and, within our genetic patterns, there is an instinctive drive toward violence, which often impels us to attack and destroy each other, other animals, and the natural and physical environment.

In comparing animal and human aggression, some scholars focus on a *single biological cause*. For example, F. S. Perls [1969] argues that much aggression stems from hunger and the accompanying urge to bite. In contrast to other animals, civilized humans suffer from insufficient ways of redirecting this urge into nondestructive channels. Perls and other writers recommend that competitive games and vigorous physical activities be developed as effective alternatives to individual and collective aggression. In addition, personal acts of sublimation (for example, grinding teeth together when angry) can redirect potentially destructive behavior. Advocates of this perspective often point to human language as evidence of the biological origins and aggressive nature of human behavior: We talk about attacking problems and getting our teeth into them, mastering and digesting ideas, struggling with and overcoming difficulties.

Other scholars adopting this perspective have identified *multiple biological sources* of aggression. For example, W. M. S. Russell [1964, pp. 710–712] argues that a variety of stresses, particularly population pressure, give rise to animal violence and conflict. He theorizes that surviving communities of social animals represent two different lines of evolution. At one extreme, we find high fertility species, such as ant communities, where individual lives are expendable. As a result, ants engage in collective warfare for the purpose of exterminating or enslaving neighbors or intruders, regardless of casualties. At the other extreme are low fertility mammalian species, like monkeys and apes, where individual life is important in terms of community survival and, consequently, is highly valued and duly protected.

Using this view, Russell criticizes earlier theories that assumed that certain animals labeled "wild" were always violent. He indicates that 19th century studies were typically confined to captive animals in zoos. Their wild behavior, he argues, was more a consequence of confinement than of basic biological drives. Later research on animals in their natural surroundings disclosed that monkeys, baboons, gibbons, and apes exhibited either little, or highly controlled, aggression towards one another. Russell suggests that this indicates conflict is not somehow more inherent in some primates than in others. Rather, it indicates that all primates, including humans, seem to be peaceful in some contexts and violent in others.

Other researchers, still utilizing a biological approach, sought to identify those *environmental factors* that account for peace and conflict. The question that interested scholars like Lorenz was: Why are some animals often individually aggressive while remaining collectively peaceful (they do not engage in mass warfare and killing)? For example, sea gulls seem to be notorious thieves, since they constantly eat each other's eggs. In this context, how is a social order maintained? Observation discloses that gulls stake out territorial boundaries defining the limits of their *turf* and engage in aggressive behavior to maintain these boundaries. They peck at the ground and puff up when an intruder appears. This *language of threat* is common to all species. Fish puff up, change color, or raise their fins in threatening gestures when their territory is invaded; cats and dogs bare their teeth, show their claws, and raise the hair on their bodies.

The language of threat communicates positions of dominance (territorial owner) and submission (territorial invader). Animals feel secure when at home and afraid when in unfamiliar environments, and this feeling influences their communication and their willingness and ability to fight. What results is a *balance between aggression and fear.* Animals frequently fight, but rarely do they fight to the death. The usual response is eventual retreat to a familiar territory by an invader. At other times, an invader will instinctively assume a submissive role in response to threats (by lying down and exposing its throat or stomach). When a territorial owner loses a fight, the loss can usually be attributed to old age or illness. Social primates like apes apparently maintain social order by means of these same processes. For example, no group members challenge the dominant male while he is eating food in his personal territory; they retreat and wait for leftovers.

Although useful, biological theories of conflict must be used with care. Leonard Berkowitz [1970, pp. 59–60] points out that these theories often fail to present adequate evidence for their generalizations. Flat statements tend to be based upon oversimplified observations, loose analogies, and curious reasoning. Much of the evidence presented is in the form of word usage. A human's smile is called "an appeasement gesture" (response to the language of threat). The "aggressive salesman" is assumed to be motivated by the same drives (territorial dominance) as aggressive animals. Berkowitz continues:

> Employing the well-known psychoanalytic ploy, Perls lets us know that failure to agree with him probably stems from defensive resistance to his truths. "If you find yourself belittling the importance of the chapters on the hunger instinct," he says, "you can take this as an indication that you have dental inhibitions and deep-seated neurotic attitudes" [Berkowitz, 1970, p. 60].

Consequently, without neglecting the importance of biological factors, most social scientists see human conflict and aggression as primarily determined by *social variables.* Whereas animals merely respond to the natural environment, humans, as cultural beings, can create a variety of meanings for turf, threat, aggression, and fear. For example, although all human societies have an elaborate ritual of social distance, which prescribes appropriate behavior by one group, or one individual, towards another, the idea of what constitutes the *correct distance* changes from one context to another. Pinching, standing too close while talking, or kissing strangers in public is usually considered an invasion of personal privacy—a violation of personal turf—in American society. In contrast, hugging and kissing others, even of the same sex, is acceptable in many Southern European societies [Hall, 1959].

Similarly, capitalist societies have defined private property or territory as a major value, but communal societies consider community property sacred. When competing athletic teams confront one another, the host team is considered to have a "home field" advantage, and impolite or discourteous behavior by the visiting team is interpreted as "unsportsmanlike" conduct. Yet, the home team is usually given greater latitude to play aggressively and act hostilely towards referees and judges. The political dialogue between major international powers is typically filled with the language of threat, which may include such diverse symbols as pounding a shoe on a table, displaying nuclear weapons, or raising a clenched fist. However, these symbols can also have other meanings. Display of weapons may simply be a ceremonial aspect of a peaceful ritual (in a Fourth of July or Memorial Day parade); a raised fist may signify ingroup solidarity or a ritualized salute.

Therefore, although human conflict often seems motivated by the same biological and natural variables that influence the behavior of other animals, what really determines whether human interaction is essentially aggressive is the *social and cultural context.* We will consider the role of symbols in human bargaining and nonviolent conflict in the final section of this chapter. At this point, to balance our discussion, we will examine several theories that maintain that social and cultural variables are the most important sources of human conflict and aggression.

Social Sources of Conflict

In our earlier discussions of social roles and cultural norms, we saw that both roles and norms can be either complementary or conflicting. In the same manner, social groups may interact in either supportive or antagonistic ways. Sociologists have identified three basic types of intergroup relationships.

The most basic form of intergroup process is *cooperation,* whereby social groups work together in pursuing common and shared needs and goals. This process accounts for the group structure of society. Acting as isolated individuals or as members of small groups, humans would be helpless. Therefore, they band together and interact cooperatively to meet the potential threats of the physical and social environments—famine, pestilence, war, and so on. Thus, the complex set of cooperative relationships between families, residential communities, the medical profession, religious institutions, and occupational groupings provide modern people with effective and efficient ways of meeting the challenges of daily life.

However, in their attempt to control and manipulate the environment collectively, humans inevitably compete for limited resources; and, consequently, *conflict*, a second fundamental form of intergroup relations, results. In every society, available benefits and rewards are limited. Severe social conflict between groups may break out when agreement concerning long-range goals is replaced by disagreement concerning the methods for obtaining these goals. For example, the American civil rights movement has enlisted the aid of many different groups who conflict with one another almost as frequently as they unite to fight segregation and discrimination. Much of this conflict has concerned the question of the most appropriate tactics and strategy for obtaining the goals of freedom, equality, and justice for ethnic minorities—that is, should they try to obtain these goals by means of ethnic pride and identity, by dependence upon the courts, by demonstrations and confrontation, through politics, or separatism, or long-term programs of education and training? Since conflicting groups depend upon public acceptance and support, particularly in a political democracy, for their continued existence and success, they may fight each other for public recognition and approval.

Finally, a third basic form of intergroup relations, which represents a combination of cooperation and conflict, may develop. *Competition* arises when groups share an understanding about the basic rules that govern the limits of their competitive interaction. Frequently, other social groups act as mediators, judges, or referees for competitive relationships. The most obvious illustration of this process can be found in organized sports. However, competition in other human activities also possesses these attributes. Labor and management may agree not to resort to violence, or they may be prohibited by law-enforcement agencies from doing so. Students competing for a place on the honor roll may be on the honor system or they may be strictly proctored during examination. Both laws and public attitudes govern the limits to which Democrats or Republicans may go in seeking public office. In a sense, competing groups "agree to disagree" in a prescribed fashion within certain limits over specified issues and goals.

Therefore, the *means and goals that humans share or over which they compete* determine the kind of intergroup relationships (cooperative, competitive, or conflicting) that develop. A study based upon this perspective was Wilson Record's [1964] analysis of the failure of the American Communist Party (CP) to take over the national Association for the Advancement of Colored People (NAACP). Record found that, when two groups interact, the resulting relationship is determined by the organizational structure, goals, and means of each group.

From the 1930s to the 1950s, many white American segregationists believed that the NAACP and the CP were allied organizations, sharing the same goals and employing the same tactics. In addition, some Communists deliberately cultivated this myth in order to exaggerate their claims to be "the only true spokesmen" for black Americans. Record found both these views to be incorrect:

1. *Structure:* The NAACP was structurally more appropriate to Amercan society. It was a loosely organized group emphasizing democratic processes and permitting a good deal of local autonomy. In contrast, the CP was a highly structured and disciplined group with a centralized leadership.
2. *Goals:* The NAACP's major goal was black integration into the American system. The CP's goal was overthrow of the American system and black separatism. The NAACP emphasized meeting immediate needs for jobs, housing, and voting rights. The CP stressed foreign policy and world revolution.
3. *Means:* NAACP tactics were usually more appropriate than those of the CP. This was especially true after the NAACP gave up its early courtship of only "the Talented Tenth" (the 10 percent of the black population possessing the highest education or most developed skills) and began to make a place for the disadvantaged as well. In contrast, the CP debunked traditional black institutions (for example, the black church) and politically manipulated incidents.

   For example, in rural Alabama in 1931, nine black youths, some very young boys, were accused of raping two white girls while traveling in an open freight car. Though the girls had bad reputations and gave conflicting testimony, a local court found the boys guilty and sentenced eight of them to death. The trial for this "Scottsboro case," as it was called, took less than three weeks. The NAACP had relied upon the support of "responsible" southern judges and other "decent" white elements in fighting for the boys, and, therefore, the court decision was a serious defeat.

   As the NAACP appealed the convictions to higher courts, the International Labor Defense (ILD), a Communist legal organization, stepped in. The parents of the Scottsboro boys entrusted the case to the ILD, which used the incident to vilify the NAACP and criticize the Amerian way of life. However, by 1935, the Scottsboro case became a liability for the CP. Blacks began questioning noisy talk, aggressive gestures, and appeals for money, without concrete results (the defendants were still in prison pending final appeals).

   Partly as a consequence, CP strategy shifted from separatist, revolutionary action to "united front" efforts with moderate, leftist groups. A Scottsboro Defense Committee was formed, a coalition of the American Civil Liberties Union, the Methodist Federation for Social Action, the Socialist League for Industrial Democracy, the Church League for Industrial Democracy, the National Urban League, and the NAACP and ILD. Conflict and competition between the NAACP and CP led to an uneasy cooperation and to a modification of CP means and goals. The united front effort eventually resulted in freedom for most of the Scottsboro boys. [Adapted from William C. Record: *Race and Radicalism: The NAACP and the Communist Party in Conflict.* Copyright © 1964 by Cornell University. Used by permission of Cornell University Press.]

Record points out that this was perhaps as close as the NAACP and CP ever came to intergroup cooperation, but this brief coalition did not lead to a period of peace and harmony between the two organizations. The NAACP viewed the change in CP strategy and tactics with skepticism. Black leaders feared CP efforts to infiltrate NAACP local branches, to form local fronts to court NAACP members, and to gain respectability by alliances with more moderate groups. As a consequence, the NAACP continued to broaden its structure. By the 1960s, the NAACP had about 350,000 members in 1400 local branches. Less than 5 percent of the members were white. Middle-class professional men no longer dominated, and black members and leaders included women, older people, and skilled, semiskilled, and service workers. The NAACP's greatest legal victory came with the 1954 Supreme Court decision on desegregation of schools. During the same period, the Amerian CP had all but died out as an effective, social action organization.

Cooperation, Competition, and Confiict in the Amana Colony

The study of group interaction, especially the social changes that result from competition and conflict, transcends scientific and sociological interest. Utopian idelogies such as Marxism and many religious faiths have been based upon the belief that a totally cooperative society devoid of competition and conflict is both possible and desirable. Is this view justified? Analysis of religious communities, and the way in which they must compete for survival within a larger social order, provides an excellent social laboratory for answering this question. One such community is the Amana colony located in the rich Iowa corn and alfalfa fields [Schiffer, 1961, pp. 24–27].

This community was originally established by a group of devout German refugees, who had decided to share their property in common at a time when the open plains of 19th century America offered room and isolation for such utopian experiments. The religious society began as a protest against the Lutheran church in the German province of Hesse in 1714. The participants organized themselves into a "Community of True Inspirationists" and maintained that they received divine revelations. They took the first step toward communism, or communalism, when they banded together for self-protection while still in Germany. After moving, in 1842, to eight thousand acres of Seneca Indian land near Buffalo, New York, they could not decide how to divide, among themselves in an equitable way, the property they had bought. One of their religious leaders (a *Werkzeuge* or "tool of God") then testified that a divine revelation had decreed that they live communally, the land belonging to all. This became known in the society as "communism by revelation."

In 1855, increasing population forced the society to move to their present location. The first village was settled in the Iowa River Valley, 20 miles southwest of Cedar Rapids, and others were subsequently located "two hours by oxen" apart and were named by compass and by topography (Amana, Middle Amana, High Amana, East Amana, West Amana, and Homestead). In 1859, they incorporated as a nonprofitmaking religious and benevolent organization and as a church brotherhood, holding common property. Their economy was basically agrarian, supplemented by small woolen mills, cabinet shops, and other crafts. All produce was shared equally. All members of the society were provided with shelter, medical care, clothing, and old-age benefits. Idleness was not tolerated. Men worked in the fields, women in the community kitchen. Education stopped at 14. Marriage required permission, and brides wore black. Only when the colony needed another doctor, teacher, or pharmacist was a boy—never a girl—allowed to leave and obtain an education in Iowa City or Cedar Rapids.

By the turn of the century, Amana began to feel the impact of social change for the first time. Original settlers were dying out, and some of their ideals went with them. Workers began to hire outside help to do the chores, and secret bank accounts were opened in Cedar Rapids. During the 1920s, the young people of Amana began to acquire an interest in clothes, cars, baseball, the telephone, and dancing. In 1935, dancing came to Amana High School, and Amana homes were electrified in 1937. By 1940, most members of the colony had radios and automobiles, and boys were playing baseball, once banned as too worldly; one of them, Bill Zuber, became a pitcher for the New York Yankees.

The depression of the 1930s had a major impact upon Amana's life. Although the colony was faced with bankruptcy, most members were not willing to give up. By a nine-to-one vote of the entire society, they decided to make a last effort at survival, not as communists but as capitalists, stockholders, wage earners, and individual property owners, all under the umbrella of a cooperative corporation. Voting and nonvoting stock at $50.00 a share was issued to each Amana adult. Community kitchens were shut down, and everyone went back to work at jobs paying about 10 cents per day. By the time the depression was over, Amanans had one of the highest standards of living of any similar rural community in the United States, and many members were able to purchase homes, furnishings, and other items they had never possessed before.

By the early 1960s, wages were over $2.00 an hour, and the $50.00 stock of 1932 was worth over $4000 a share. The colony's business life had become a curious mixture of collectivism, religion, and capitalism. Amana was known to most Americans for its freezer industry and as a multimillion dollar corporation operating 32 business enterprises. However, the villages still looked much the same as they did in the past, most of them composed of one- and two-story gabled structures of timber, sandstone, and homemade brick. Some of the streets were paved, and a few neon lights and signs hung over several restaurants and tourist spots. As an annual report to the stockholders stated:

> As individuals we should all realize we are merely cogs in a machine God has seen fit to guide and keep this far. Thus may He also see fit to guide and keep us throughout the future, one group, indivisible, with one for all and all for one. . . . The success of the corporation, after all, reflects on us as individual stockholders and the good of the corporation should be paramount to individual interest [Schiffer, 1961, p. 26. Portions reprinted by permission of The Reporter Magazine Co., Curtis Brown Ltd., and the author. Copyright © 1961 by Robert L. Schiffer.]

By comparing village life in the 1960s with the society's early history, one can see in what ways the Amana colony changed and adapted itself as a result of (1) internal competition between members and (2) external conflict with a larger society that possessed different practices and beliefs. Peter Stuck, Society Secretary (a kind of mayor) since 1932, described the situation in the 1960s as follows:

> After our experience with communal life, we could tell the Russians a thing or two. It's just not practical, this business of one for all and all for one. It's against human nature. We don't want to be an example for anyone, but we're the best proof there is that man must be perfect to lead an unselfish life [Schiffer, 1961, p. 24].

Henry Moershel, President of the Amana Society, commented at the same time:

> You must remember that to some extent all family life is communistic, and our society was like a large family sharing everything, just like the first Christian community. If you have a deep religious conviction and love for your fellow man, communism is possible. Today, everyone makes the mistake of thinking of communism in Russian terms only. But they forget there is a difference between communism based on the Bible and a communism based on the bayonet. One contains love, the other fear [Schiffer, 1961, p. 27].

In summary, conflict and competition appear unavoidable, even in utopian societies that attempt to eliminate or minimize these processes. Furthermore, conflict and competition are not necessarily undesirable. Sometimes competition and conflict lead to ways in which societies, like the Amana colony, can adapt creatively to internal instability and external change. This example serves to illustrate the fact that conflict can be considered as both functional and dysfunctional.

When Is Conflict Functional?

Both conventional wisdom and early social theory tend to associate cooperation with social integration and cohesion, and conflict with disintegration and instability. As we have begun to see in the case of the Amana

TABLE 14-1 Functions and Dysfunctions of Cooperation and Conflict

	Cooperation	Conflict
Potential Functions	1. Contributes to social cohesion and integration between interacting groups	1. Strengthens bonds within conflicting groups
	2. Maintains social stability and order in society	2. Clarifies issues and goals within conflicting groups
	3. Encourages cultural consensus and compromise on major social issues	3. Lessens individual deviance and anomie within conflicting groups
		4. Encourages creativity and innovation in society
Potential Dysfunctions	1. Inhibits great change and variation in society	1. Leads to oversimplfication and stereotyping of issues and goals within conflicting groups
	2. Makes response to unanticipated social crises or threats difficult	2. Encourages collective deviance
	3. Maximizes collective conformity and discourages individual creativity	3. Makes maintenance of social order and stability difficult

colony, this perspective is not necessarily valid. Recent research, especially in the area of war and revolution (see Chapter 11), has indicated that conflict, even in extreme and violent forms, often functions to meet important human needs. Conversely, cooperation can sometimes be dysfunctional. Sociologists, like Lewis Coser [1956], have suggested that cooperation and conflict can be either functional or dysfunctional depending upon their impact upon the social and cultural context. These relationships are summarized in Table 14-1.

This is not an exhaustive listing of all the functional and dysfunctional aspects of cooperation and conflict, but it does indicate that conflict, like cooperation, can be socially valuable. For example, conflict can solidify and strengthen the bonds and structure *within* the interacting groups. *Intragroup* differences and hostilities are lessened; issues and goals are clarified; common commitment and mutual support are stressed. During periods of warfare, research has disclosed that some measures of social disorganization such as crime (usually traditional), suicide (other than altruistic), and divorce fall to their lowest levels. As a society mobilizes to combat an external foe, internal solidarity and cooperation are increased.

At the same time, however, warring groups oversimplify and stereotype issues and goals, depicting themselves as personifications of good and the enemy as totally evil. This may make ultimate resolution of the conflict,

14-1 The Functions and Dysfunctions of Conflict

Most people assume that cooperation is desirable and conflict, especially in extreme and violent forms, is undesirable. Cooperation is seen as enhancing social integration and cohesion, whereas conflict is seen as leading to social disintegration and instability.

Library of Congress

Conflict leads to oversimplification and stereotyping of issues and goals between conflicting groups. Enemies are seen as dangerous and deviant, friends as good and conforming. Extreme nationalism and ethnocentrism played a role in the outbreak of World War I. Some countries had war cults which glorified conflict and insulted neighboring peoples, who quickly took offense. Warmongers sneered at foreign and different ways of doing things.

United Press International

Jamyl Smith/Metamorphosis

Conflict encourages collective acts of deviance which are defined by the perpetrators as a necessary means to resolve a dangerous situation. In 1945, hundreds of Jewish prisoners were burned alive by German S.S. guards as the U.S. 12th Armored Division approached the Landsberg Concentration Camp near Munich. After the area was occupied, Lt. Col. Seiller, head of the Military Government Section of the Division, forced 200 German civilians to tour the camp and view the horrors.

Conflict leads to the unrestrained release of pent-up aggressions and hostilities. For example, racial graffiti may be scribbled on walls and buildings. This spontaneous expression of hatred is hard to control, and it tends to inflame others to engage in extreme individual acts.

However, conflict, together with cooperation and competition, is also a basic process in all societies. As such, it is often functional and serves important purposes both for people in conflicting groups and for society as a whole.

Conflict strengthens bonds and relationships within conflicting groups. In 1971, the riot by inmates of Attica Prison in New York led to five demands which emphasized the sense of inmate solidarity and identity in the face of severe threats. The inmate statement in part said: "The incident that has erupted here at Attica is [the result] of the unmitigated oppression wrought by the racist administration network of the prison . . . WE are MEN! We are not beasts and do not intend to be beaten or driven as such. . . ."

Wide World Photos

United Press International

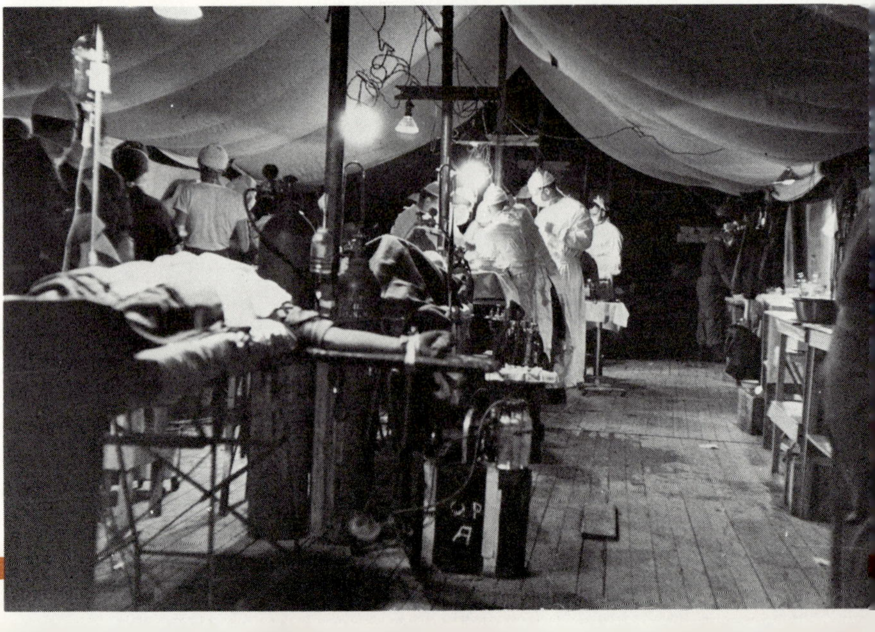

Conflict encourages creativity and innovation in society as groups attempt to adapt to new crises and threats. During the Korean War, the Army Mobile Surgical Hospital, the subject of the motion picture and television program M*A*S*H, was developed. This "Tent of Mercy" utilized technological and social innovations in medicine to get intensive operating-room care near the front lines of battle.

Culver Pictures, Inc.

Culver Pictures, Inc.

Conflict clarifies issues and goals within conflicting groups. The nature of life, death, heroism, freedom, patriotism, and the like are often given special consideration by creative artists, such as Ernest Hemingway, as a result of human conflict. Many of the issues in Hemingway's novels were inspired by warfare, starting with *A Farewell to Arms* (1929). In the 1930s, he went to Spain to report on the Spanish Civil War and later wrote *For Whom the Bell Tolls* (1940). From his experiences as a reporter during World War II, Hemingway wrote *Across the River and Into the Trees* (1950).

short of mutual annihilation, extremely difficult. Also, conflict encourages collective deviance, such as when massive bombing of defenseless civilian populations with inhumane weaponry (nuclear or chemical) is widely applauded and supported. Conquering troops may rape, pillage, and loot captured populations, believing them to be less than human, as we saw in the case of absolutist or idealogical wars in Chapter 11.

Conflict can, however, also create a context within which social, intellectual, and technological creativity are enhanced. Conflict within and between groups in a society can prevent interaction from becoming overly habitual and ritualized. Coser [1957, pp. 197–198] points to the contrast between the "frozen" world of the Middle Ages and the burst of creativity that accompanied the thaw that set in with Renaissance civilization. Citing another example—the history of labor–management conflict—he suggests that:

> Conflict not only generates new norms, new institutions . . . it may be said to be stimulating directly in the economic and technological realm. Economic historians often have pointed out that much technological improvement has resulted from the conflict activity of trade unions through the raising of wage levels. A rise in wages usually has led to a substitution of capital investment for labour and hence to an increase in the volume of investment. Thus the extreme mechanization of coalmining in the United States has been partly explained by the existence of militant unionism in the American coalfields. . . .

On the other hand, the problem with conflict-initiated innovations is that they are not always easily applied to the cooperative contexts that follow or transcend the conflict. Developed in a conflict situation, innovations may be seen by most people as applying only to that context. For example, warfare frequently encourages advances in medical technology because of the need to treat serious and unusual wounds immediately. The Korean and Vietnam wars encouraged the development of the mobile surgical hospital (dramatized in the movie and television series M*A*S*H). Its development involved a number of interrelated technologies (sophisticated medical equipment, highly trained staff, well-equipped operating rooms, rapid transportation via helicopter) designed to get intensive care and full-operating-room units to the front lines of combat. However, this development has not yet been applied throughout civilian society, where MASH-type units could assist in traffic accidents, after natural disasters, and the like.

The functional approach to conflict also has social policy implications. Following his analysis of labor–management relations, Coser raises questions about the manner in which contemporary labor negotiations have become ritualized and about the tendency of modern managers to rely upon a "human relations" approach to personnel problems:

> The "human relations" approach stresses the "collective purposes of the total organization" of the factory, and either denies or attempts to reduce

> conflicts of interests in industry [by studying ways in which workers can be given better physical working conditions, fringe benefits, or complaint channels so that they will not strike for higher wages or for worker participation in management decision making]. But a successful reduction of industrial conflict may have unanticipated dysfunctional consequences for it may destroy an important stimulus for technological innovation [which could lead to improved corporate performance and higher profits] [Coser, 1957, p. 198].

We will return to the question of the policy implications of various perspectives of conflict toward the end of this chapter. For the moment, Coser's criticism of the human relations philosophy in industry serves to focus upon the question of those factors that tend to cause conflict in human societies. The following section considers selected examples of sociological theories that have attempted to identify the social and cultural variables leading to conflict.

CULTURAL AND SOCIAL CAUSES OF CONFLICT

Whereas some theorists argue about whether conflict is biologically or socially determined, perspectives employed by social scientists tend to differ according to three broad, but related, categories. Those who employ *cultural theories* claim that conflict is essentially a result of norms and values that encourage and reward aggressiveness, violence, or terrorism. In contrast, those utilizing *communal or societal theories* maintain that conflict arises within social systems when roles, interpersonal relationships, and social institutions operate to encourage conflict rather than cooperation. Still other social scientists single out specific aspects of the communal or societal order as fundamentally important. For example, many scholars have used *status theories,* arguing that conflict is a result of frustrations and anxieties experienced within class and caste societies. All of these theories tend to be most interested in the *causes,* in addition to the nature and consequences, of human conflict.

Cultural Theories of Conflict and Violence

The popular expression—"violence is as American as apple pie"—reflects a belief that cultural *norms* and *values* play a major role in creating contexts within which individual and collective conflict becomes unavoidable. This view has been the subject of some social scientific research. Richard Brown [1969, pp. 43–80] identified 13 major types of violence throughout American history. Table 14-2 suggests that in each case a particular form of violence is caused by the presence or absence of norms. For example, America's historical commitment to informal norms based on individualistic aggressive action has tended to encourage criminal and political violence, whereas, at other times, a lack of formal norms (and formal authority) has led to lynching and vigilanteeism. Furthermore, violence in all its cultural forms can be seen as functional. That is, it has been as-

TABLE 14-2 Cultural Origins and Functions of Violence in American History

Types of Violence	Historical Examples	Cultural Origins	Cultural Functions
Criminial—Individual or Gang	Jesse James, Wyatt Earp, John Dillinger; gang battles of the 1920s in Chicago and Detroit	Frontier pioneer ethic and organized crime of the 18th century	Symbolizes the aggressive individual against a hostile world
Feuds	The Hatfields versus the McCoys	Family conflicts over territory	Family solidarity in the face of threats
Lynching	During Revolution to punish British sympathizers; on the frontier for horse thieves; later to terrorize blacks in the South	Virginia Quaker Charles Lynch who opposed killing but supported punishing Tories with tar and feathering, lashing, or fines	Taking the "law" into one's own hands to administer "quick justice"
Free-Lance Murder	Harpe Brothers (1798–1799), the Boston Strangler (1966), Charles Manson	Uncontrollable behavior in a free and weakly integrated society	Public fascination with bizarre, cruel aspect of human behavior
Political Assassination	Most recently, national personages; earlier in local big-city politics	Frontier principle of "rule of the gun"	Individuals seeking public recognition or political conspiracies
Revolution	American Revolution	Self-determination principle	Traditional American antigovernment values

sociated with desirable values (self-determination in the case of civil and Indian wars; expressing just grievances in the case of revolution and urban disturbances).

This cultural theory views *violence as a special form of conflict.* Brandeis University's Lemberg Center for the Study of Violence has defined this form of conflict as extreme aggression aimed at the serious injury or destruction of persons, objects, or organizations and involving characteristics of explosiveness. The quality of explosiveness refers to behavior that is usually spontaneous, sudden in origin, and massive in nature (see Chapter 5).

Violence generally develops in two types of social contexts:

1. It can arise in situations that are interpreted by the participants as survival contexts requiring massive and rapid response in order to eliminate an immediate and deadly threat. In such cases, violence may be seen as the only available action, short of surrender or defeat.
2. It can also arise as a response to a seemingly incurable frustration that has reached potentially destructive proportions. In this case,

TABLE 14-2 (continued)

Types of Violence	Historical Examples	Cultural Origins	Cultural Functions
Police Violence	Repression of early labor movement; killing of Black Panthers; Kent State	See Study 12	Public desire to maintain order at any cost; police anxieties and frustrations
Civil War	North–South Civil War	Self-determination versus union principles	Expression of self-determination and union principles
Indian Wars	Throughout the 1800s; then movement of Indians to "concentration camps"	Control of land and other natural resources	Control goes to the strongest; imperial expansion
Agarian Uprisings	Populist revolts of the late 1800s; recently farmer destruction of goods to maintain prices	Collective action to influence political policy	Right of aggressive collective action when all else fails
Labor Violence	Throughout history	Influence political policy	When all else fails
Vigilanteeism	In early West; recently by ethnic groups in urban centers	Lack of formal controls	Maintain "law and order"
Urban Disturbances	World War I draft riots; 1960s black rebellions	Feelings of frustration and deprivation	Dramatic communication of anxieties; a collective "cry for help"

Adapted from Richard Maxwell Brown, "Historical Patterns of Violence in America," in *Violence in America* (Report of the National Commission on the Causes and Prevention of Violence), Hugh Davis Graham and Ted Robert Gurr, Ed. (New York: The New American Library, 1969), pp. 43–80.

violence is used not so much as a means of resolving a problem; rather it becomes a way of releasing anxieties or gaining the attention of authorities who can relieve the frustrations.

Several implications follow from a perspective that views all forms of violence as functional. With the possible exception of individual or group hysteria or extreme psychosis, there is no such thing as "senseless" or "irrational" collective violence. Violence is a form of structured meaningful interaction, with cultural origins and content, and with specific goals or purposes that range from attempts at communication (urban black rebellions of the late 1960s) to physical confrontation with authority (labor and agrarian violence).

Violence, however, is not the special province of poor disenfranchised individuals or groups. It also permeates the culture of the establishment (as when police are given license to "shoot to kill" and thereby encouraged to be violent). As a matter of fact, studies at the Lemberg Center and elsewhere have estimated that close to 75 percent of all violence in American history has been committed by the forces of legitimate authority—that is, by the establishment. In short, the outcome of violence is equally dependent upon the norms of both those who initiate violence *and* those who respond to it (see the study of police violence in Chapter 12).

A cultural theory of conflict, then, can be used to formulate important conclusions about the nature, cause, and control of violence. However, there are limits and disadvantages to this theory. Although some recent research shows that very young children who have been exposed to television violence begin to act aggressively, no reliable correlation has yet been established between the presence or absence of certain norms and values and particular forms of adult violence. The unresolved question is the issue we discussed in Chapter 4. Is culture a cause or a consequence? Are we aggressive because we live in a violent culture, or does our culture reflect violence because aggressiveness is useful in meeting the basic needs of our society?

An attempt to resolve this issue was E. V. Walter's [1971] study of the rise and fall of the Zulu Empire from 1808 to 1879. The Zulu Empire is one of the very few recorded cases of the transformation of a preliterate society into a terroristic empire and one that can be compared to the modern German experience under Hitler. Walter suggests that, in the early stages of premodern societies, conflict resulting from population growth (caused by social and technological change) can be resolved by migration. Violence, therefore, is sporadic. Once the frontier disappears and population pressures continue to rise, however, terror can become a leadership tactic for purposes of domestic social control and continued empire building.

If a "crisis of integration" begins to threaten a fragmented society, rulers may adopt a regime of terror as a means of enforcing solidarity. Terror is used to dissolve all resistance and conflict in a cultural climate of fear. Eventually, terror or violence achieve their own legitimacy and become accepted almost as normal, even by the people who are subject to it. Violence comes to be accepted with resignation, as a kind of natural disaster like recurrent earthquakes, or it becomes valued as a positive strategy for resolving social conflict. Thus, Walter suggests that cultures of violence grow out of rapidly changing social situations, such as the Zulus faced. In his view, therefore, cultures of conflict are the product of social variables operating within societal contexts.

Societal Theories of Conflict and Violence

In an analysis of political violence, H. L. Nieburg [1969] criticizes those who explain violence in the United States by reference to "American traditions" or to mass-media programming. He points out that these cultural factors play a role only if they strike a responsive chord in people. Aggressive conflict results when competitive interaction between groups leads one group to conclude that violence is the most efficient and economical means of achieving its goals. Even when groups are materially weak (few weapons, little physical defense), they may be tempted to test their spiritual strength (loyalty, conviction, and indignation) against others. In short, Nieburg believes that conflict results when people assess the relationship of means to goals within the context of *community and societal interaction.*

Using this perspective, James Coleman [1957] has suggested that community conflicts can be an indication of desirable qualities in community life. Rather than taking a negative view of increasing community conflict in recent years (involving issues like fluoridation, school integration, sex education, high property taxes, prayer in the schools), he suggests that these conflicts may have resulted from greater involvement in political affairs, awareness of important issues, and feelings that problems can be resolved by community action. In short, community conflict can increase as democratic roles and relationships become more pronounced. Furthermore, despite the fact that community conflict seems to involve a variety of issues (economic, power, values, and attitudes towards others), Coleman maintains that it tends to follow the same general social processes in every case.

Coleman's [1957, pp. 9–10] research indicates that "it is the peculiarity of social controversy that it sets in motion its own dynamics; these tend to carry it forward in a path which bears little relation to its beginnings." As community conflicts evolve, original issues and organizations change as in Table 14-3.

TABLE 14-3 Evolution of Community Conflicts

	From:	To:	Example
Community Issues	Specific conflict	General conflict	A conflict in Scarsdale, New York, began with an attack upon books in the school library and evolved into a criticism of the entire educational system.
	Original disputes	New and different disputes	
	Disagreement	Antagonism	
Community Organizations	Democratic, overlapping relationships	Polarized relationships	In Cincinnati, Ohio, a Committee of 150 for Political Morality supported a city planning director, who participated in left-wing activities and held left-wing views, by arguing against smears and personal attacks in politics.
	Existing community organizations and leaders	Ad hoc partisan organizations and extremist leaders	
	Formal communication (media, courts, and so on)	Word-of-mouth communication and rumor	

According to Coleman, there are two different sources for the diversification of issues in community conflicts. The first is *involuntary:* The emergence of conflict changes community relationships and permits residents to raise questions they would not have mentioned before the conflict. The second is *deliberate:* Antagonists raise new issues in an attempt to strengthen their positions, justify their cause, and broaden the base of their support. In addition, new ad hoc groups serve as communication, planning, and organization centers. These spontaneous organizations, and the emotional character of community conflict, require informal extremist leadership with charismatic qualities. Traditional community organizations tend to remain neutral or uninvolved, making responsible action more difficult. The media, for example, are often constrained by traditional norms from reporting gossip, slander, or unsubstantiated claims, and, consequently, residents must rely upon informal communication for the information they feel they need.

Many of these processes can be seen at work in a study of Catholic–Protestant conflict in Northern Ireland by Anders Boserup. In addition, Boserup sought to identify those communal and societal variables that cause conflict to become a permanent and inescapable aspect of some social orders.

▶ STUDY 14

The Causes of Protracted Conflict in Northern Ireland [1970][1]

Problem

The seemingly unending conflict in Northern Ireland has been analyzed and reanalyzed in a variety of ways. Many consider the conflict to be essentially religious in nature, a momentary aberration in an otherwise well-integrated society, and primarily a function of extremist leaders on both sides. Since all attempts to resolve the conflict have been based upon these views, and all have failed to this point, Boserup questions their validity. If they are inappropriate, what *alternative theory or hypotheses* could be tested to generate newer, more useful perspectives?

Hypotheses and Study Design

Boserup hypothesizes that, in a situation of protracted community conflict, *the antagonistic relationship eventually becomes the basis for a new social order,* which then determines the nature of interaction between conflicting groups. Furthermore, the new social order redefines and reshapes the nature of the original antagonism. Specifically, Boserup is interested in the *political* aspects

[1]Adapted from Anders Boserup, "The Politics of Protracted Conflict," *trans-action* (now *Society*), *7* (March 1970), pp. 22–31. Also see Anders Boserup and Andrew Mack, *War Without Weapons: Non-Violence in National Defense* (New York: Schocken Books, 1975). Published by permission of Transaction, Inc. from *trans-action,* Vol. 7, #5 and #6.

of the conflict in Northern Ireland. Religious divisions have always played a political role in Ulster (the capitol), but Boserup did not see religion as the key variable. The fundamental weakness of Ulster's political structure, he believed, lay in its *postcolonial institutions* and *ruling class,* and the resulting sectarianism and discrimination required to maintain this system.

The *study design* to test these hypotheses required a comparison of the historical development of economic, social, and political institutions and their relationship to contemporary political relationships in Northern Ireland.

Methods of Data Collection

Statistical records provided information on economic development and institutions, and *historical* studies furnished additional social and political data. To analyze contemporary political life, Boserup used *observation,* including material contained in publications, such as the newspapers of the two major political parties.

Findings and Interpretations

Like many newly emergent nations, Northern Ireland has weak native institutions because of *postcolonial dependence upon Britain.* The Irish parliament at Stormont is more like a provincial council than a national governing body. It has little freedom to fashion Ulster's policies, especially economic ones, according to special local needs. Finance and credit are dependent upon Britain. Taxes and duties are controlled by the parliament of the United Kingdom, and policies are determined primarily with British needs in mind. Britain takes an estimated 55 percent of Ulster's gross national product, and the largest Belfast paper mill is British-owned. All matters of foreign and defense policy are conducted from Westminster. The political weaknesses of the country were adequately demonstrated in the late 1960s and early 1970s when the Irish government had to rely upon outside British troops, a kind of colonial militia, to quell domestic disturbances. Other Irish institutions (the courts, the educational system, the electoral process) are either operated directly from Britain or are copies of British structures and procedures.

In addition, Boserup found that *a strong ruling class is absent* in Northern Ireland. The traditional elite, Ulster's landed aristocracy, derives its prestige from landownership rather than from any real economic and political power. Their agriculturally based economic power is steadily declining, as seen by the fact that in 1966 agriculture contributed only 9.4 percent to the gross national product of Northern Ireland. Likewise, their political power is more form than substance. This can be seen in the fact that Unionist economic policies provide large subsidies to new industries rather than to traditional ones.

In addition, both major political parties are formed on exclusively religious lines and, therefore, assemble under their banners all of the divergent social interests within each religious community. As a consequence, neither the Protestant Unionists nor the Catholic Nationalists are able to put forth a clear social or economic program for the country; vested interests within each party cannot agree upon standard policy. Therefore, *both parties must of necessity revive purely sectarian issues at each election and utilize religious prejudice to mobilize political support at the polls.*

Boserup theorizes that where political parties are founded upon differences in creed rather than social and political policy, an uncommited vote cannot exist.

The majority party can retain power only by appealing to sectarian prejudice and by subordinating issues related to political and social reform. For example, Unionist majorities at successive elections remain virtually unchanged, and the Protestants have been in office in Northern Ireland for more than 40 years. About 70 percent of the seats go uncontested at general elections. At the same time, the minority Catholic Nationalist party also survives largely through appeals to sectarian divisions, although they control only one third of the Catholic electorate (compared to the Unionist's control of some 80 percent of the Protestant electorate). Thus the major function of the Nationalists seems to be to serve as a convenient scarecrow to keep the Unionists together. As Boserup says, the two parties and their associated social organizations stand in a perfect conflict relationship to one another; they are made of the same sectarian cement; they are one another's opposites and yet neither could exist in isolation.

Conclusions and Implications

In conclusion, then, Boserup suggests that *the religious conflict* in Northern Ireland, which has been frequently violent, *is an "artificial" conflict,* in that the relationship between the two religious communities need not be antagonistic. Only the weakness of prevailing institutional structures, brought about by colonialism and a weak ruling elite, make antagonism necessary. Tragically, none of the actors in the drama, including the British, seem interested in doing more than merely restoring "law and order."

Boserup indicates that if significant change is to be brought about it must involve *fundamental alterations in the prevailing social and political structure,* so that antagonistic interaction can be replaced by less competitive and more cooperative relationships. He suggests that Britain could improve the situation by radically reorganizing and relegitimizing the Irish parliament in a way that would institutionalize the historic conflict. This might be achieved by replacing the present Senate and House of Commons at Stormont with a new bicameral parliament, one elected by Catholics and one by Protestants. In addition, a majority in both houses could be required for certain types of legislation. An example might be legislation dealing with the location of highways, for which a delay in decision is bearable, yet costly to all involved. Such an issue could force the conflicting communities into dialogue and mutual concessions. In order to give Catholics a real say in matters concerning them and to give Protestants a larger share of the total budgetary resources, Boserup further suggests that each house be given a separate budget to dispose of on its own. These budgets could cover areas like housing, schools, hospitals, and new industry. Both houses would have to coordinate their programs, but at the same time there would be a redirection of grievances inwards towards each community and its special needs.

Boserup indicates that some such system for institutionalizing the conflict in Northern Ireland might also involve a significant change in the nature of the major political parties. The Unionist and Nationalist parties would probably break up, since there would no longer be any electoral advantage in remaining as a bloc. Protestants might well continue discriminating against Catholics, but this would not become a political advantage. Political fragmentation would also create a fluctuating electorate available for mobilization over important class-related issues that transcend religious barriers.

A special word about the political-action implications of Boserup's study is necessary. When social scientists recommend programs for action, they are not necessarily describing a precise and perfect blueprint for the future. Failure to understand this qualification accounts for much public disillusionment over proposed programs that "do not work." What many social scientific proposals do is indicate how seemingly irreconcilable situations and problems may be resolved if accepted myths and assumptions are questioned. In other words, they suggest unanticipated alternatives (for example, new forms of government) that represent new ways of thinking about the impossible (for example, how to bring peace to Northern Ireland). Boserup's study suggests that conflict that has become a natural and permanent part of a social system can sometimes be institutionalized to good effect. That is, conflict can be incorporated into the social and political order so as to encourage cooperation and break the processes of polarization and extremism, which Coleman identified in his study of community conflict.

There is an additional question, however, that needs answering. To what extent is it valid to assume that conflicting groups, possessing substantially different values and life-styles, can come to live in relative harmony and stability? Will such groups be willing to institutionalize their antagonism in mutually acceptable ways? An analysis of the social and cultural life of San Francisco by Howard Becker and Irving Horowitz [1970, pp. 12–19] provides a partial answer. San Francisco is known throughout the world for its generally sophisticated and cosmopolitan acceptance of deviants of all kinds. It is a city where extremes (from far-left "freaks" to far-right "superpatriots") live in comparative peace and cooperation. This is dramatically illustrated by the fact that candidates for San Francisco's Board of Supervisors frequently make a direct appeal for the homosexual vote without automatically being penalized politically; the media report the annual "Drag Ball" (homosexual dance) held in one of the major hotels; and the following kind of incident can be viewed daily:

> Walking in the Tenderloin on a summer evening, a block from the Hilton, you hear a black whore cursing at a policeman: "I wasn't either blocking the sidewalk! Why don't you motherfucking fuzz mind your own goddamn business!" The visiting [tourist] . . . expects to see her arrested, if not shot, but the cop smiles goodnaturedly and moves on, having got her back into the doorway where she is supposed to be [Becker and Horowitz, 1970, pp. 12–13].

Many communities would not tolerate such antagonistic behavior by deviants or acceptance of "sin" by political leaders. As a matter of fact, many American cities in the late 1960s would have interpreted such acts as a total breakdown in law, order, and morality. How, then, can the special nature of San Francisco's experiment in tolerating deviance and managing conflict be explained?

Becker and Horowitz suggest that such a social context can be referred to as a *culture of civility,* an intellectual climate marked by the acceptance of deviant patterns of behavior for the rich mosaic they create and the rejection of popular stereotypes about deviance. Although most people oppose deviance on the assumption that one form of immoral or illegal behavior leads to another (the "evil equals evil" myth), common sense and research indicate that this assumption is erroneous (see Chapter 12). For example, professional criminals often express a patriotism on a par with a Legionnaire's; conventional housewives sometimes shoplift; some homosexuals marry and become good family providers; businessmen who are pillars of their communities commit billion-dollar white-collar crimes. In other words, humans are typically both deviant and nondeviant simultaneously, especially in a social context that accepts everyone's behavior openly.

To blackmail a person for being a homosexual would be next to impossible in a community where most residents know this fact and/or do not care. Indeed, in such a context, that person can hold a job without fear, be married, raise a family, and become a solid citizen in every other way. This type of relationship among diverse subgroups, Becker and Horowitz indicate, is the basis of San Francisco's culture of civility. The authors point out that not all kinds of deviation are tolerated endlessly. The police do try to stamp out vices and keep a ceiling on others. Many San Franciscans are periodically frightened by the users and sellers of hard drugs, which they associate with violence and crime. However, the line is drawn much farther on the side of toleration in that city, and the fear and madness over minor forms of deviation (in life-styles, language, dress, and so on) that has characterized so many communities is absent.

The result has been the development of a stable community life, where everyone seems satisfied enough to stay where they are for awhile. Because they have a place to stay without constant worry about harrassment, many deviants sink roots like conventional citizens, hold steady jobs, buy houses or rent apartments, make friends, vote. Also, under these conditions, deviants often find they no longer feel the need to act in overtly erratic ways. In turn, police can avoid a policy of harrassment since looking the other way can also be good policy. As Becker and Horowitz [1970, p. 16] put it:

> It is easier . . . to turn your back on the sight of open marihuana smoking than it is to charge into [a] . . . crowd and try to arrest people who will destroy the evidence before you get there, give you a hard time, make a fool of you and earn you a bad press—and have no conviction to show for it. At the same time, nothing worse is likely to happen: no muggings, no thefts, no rapes, no riots. Police, more calculating than they seem, often choose to reach just this kind of accommodation with stable deviant communities.

Thus, deviants who are allowed to live decent lives can behave decently. In turn, community leaders and authorities have an easier job of control.

Most probably, neither the deviant subgroups nor the straight community is totally satisfied by this relationship. Straights undoubtedly would prefer the absence of all deviation, and deviants most likely would prefer to make few, if any, concessions to conformity. However, since each group gives up something in order to gain something otherwise unattainable, the culture of civility functions to maintain stability and channel potential conflict into acceptable forms of interaction (for example, political). Potential conflict in San Francisco, then, has actually become the basis for building a community social system based upon cooperation and competition. Communal and societal factors, therefore, can encourage either cooperation or conflict.

Status Theories of Conflict and Violence

Some social scientists who study conflict are dissatisfied with cultural or societal theories, feeling that they are too general and abstract. As a result, they prefer to focus upon some particular aspect of the social order. An illustration of this approach can be found in those theories that argue that *status* differences and the resulting feelings of *anxiety* and *deprivation* can, under specific conditions, cause conflict. As we saw in Chapter 6, both open and closed status systems lead to anxieties and frustrations. Closed systems create frustrations because opportunity for upward mobility is virtually nonexistent, while open systems are marked by widespread anxiety over inadequate upward or possible downward mobility. Therefore, mixed societies like the United States (both closed and open), which contain many different racial, ethnic, and cultural groups, are especially vulnerable to conflict. Three concepts have played a particularly prominent role in those theories that link status and conflict: (1) frustration; (2) grievance tolerance; and (3) relative deprivation.

Some scholars, like Ted Gurr, argue that a *high level of frustration* can lead to individual or collective conflict depending upon the presence or absence of the following social variables:

1. The repressive ability and performance of authorities.
2. The credibility and legitimacy of governing authorities.
3. The ability of authorities to offer rewards for loyalty and cooperation.
4. The perceived or actual success of previous users of conflict and violence.
5. The degree of organization and commitment among the frustrated.

The frustration perspective emphasizes the relationship between frustrated individuals and groups in a society (the poor, racial minorities, antiwar groups) and the authority figures who enforce and maintain order (political leaders, courts, police, social welfare agencies). Sociologists utilizing this perspective maintain that the above factors explain why persons frustrated over the continuation of the Vietnam War in the late 1960s were

14-2 Conditions Influencing Violent Behavior

Studies show that a variety of social and cultural conditions will determine whether or not a society is characterized by little or much individual and collective violence.

The Bettmann Archive

Repressive capacity of authorities. If authority figures and leaders possess the absolute power to repress and punish violent behavior, people will be reluctant to commit violent acts. The power of the traditional school master was an example. In this case, violent means are used by authorities to deter violence by others.

Culver Pictures, Inc.

Credibility of authorities. Repressive capacity alone is not sufficient for effective long-term control. Authorities must also appear credible. That is, people must be willing to follow the directions of leaders peacefully because orders are seen as legitimate. Legitimate leaders are seen as having the right to control the behavior of others because of personal ability, tradition, or legal role, as illustrated in the dress of the Lord Justice of the Court of Appeals in 1888.

Elizabeth Hamlin, Dietz/Hamlin

Rewards for conformity. Authorities must also be able to reward nonviolent and cooperative behavior. For example, parents control the behavior of young children not only by punishing violent acts but also by approving smiles and affectionate gestures for conforming and cooperative acts.

United Press International

Cultures of violence. The degree to which a society honors or praises violent norms and values determines the prevalence of extreme conflict. For example, America has often been called a culture of violence since extreme forms of conflict and aggression are glorified in many forms of entertainment. Professional wrestling is an example, where referee Red Shoes Dugan attempts to break apart The Sheik from Big Baba.

Massachusetts Half-Way Houses, Staff Photographer

Institutional alternatives. Societies must provide group contexts which can become acceptable alternatives for those who might otherwise engage in violent behavior. Traditional prisons tend to be conflict-oriented contexts where the violence of criminal behavior is simply reinforced. As a result, ''halfway houses'' have been used as alternatives. Residents of these houses are permitted some degree of personal freedom and independence in return for behavior which shows signs of peaceful rehabilitation.

N. Sapieha/Stock, Boston

United Press International

Organization of deprived groups. The degree of organization and commitment among deprived groups determines their willingness and ability to use violent means to obtain their goals. Strong organization in groups (like the Black Nationalists) can have several consequences. First, they may be able to nonviolently resist repressive actions by others, particularly authorities. At the same time, such groups may more willingly use violence for self-defense.

Perceived success of violence. When deprived groups perceive that violence has succeeded in achieving the aims of others in the past, they will be more likely to engage in extreme forms of conflict to achieve their own goals. This may be one of the reasons why members of the American Indian Movement seized the trading post and church at Wounded Knee on the Oglala Sioux Reservation in South Dakota in 1973, after weeks of clashes between whites, local officials, and Indians. The insurgents demanded a full-scale investigation of government treatment of Indians. Aggressive action by other deprived groups seemed to have brought desired official action (for example, the problems of blacks received increased attention after the urban disturbances of the late 1960s).

willing to engage in conflict, aggression, and, sometimes, violence. As the war became more violent and apparently unwinable, the credibility (Was the government telling the truth?) and legitimacy (Did the government have the right to continue the war?) of authorities diminished. As larger numbers and different kinds of people became involved in protesting the war (priests and nuns, middle-class Americans, older women, in addition to youth), the repressive ability and performance of authorities eroded; police became more reluctant to use force and some began to question the war. There was no reward, other than intangible feelings of patriotism, for continuing commitment to the war. Furthermore, antiwar activists felt supported in their use of aggressive tactics by the success of the early civil rights demonstrators under similar circumstances.

As useful as this approach is, it does contain several limitations. The concept of a high level of frustration is vague and difficult to measure. When is frustration high? When is it low? How does one empirically measure high or low frustration? Similarly, concepts like repressive capacity of authorities, rewards for loyalty, and degree of organization are equally vague and difficult to measure. As a consequence, other theorists (for example, John Spiegel and Florence Kluckholn of the Lemberg Center) have hypothesized that aggression and conflict will result when a certain *grievance-tolerance* level is reached; that is, people are willing to tolerate frustrations until they reach a specific level, which can be theoretically measured by the number and kind of grievances. After that point, if nonviolent means are not available for the resolution of their grievances, people will engage in violent conflict. For example, women were willing to accept the frustrations of lower status so long as they were few (confined to husband–wife roles) and not too severe (ameliorated by sharing their husband's status). However, once the frustrations became multiple and extensive (inability to obtain needed jobs, education, and political power), a grievance-tolerance level was reached and aggressive behavior resulted (the Women's Movement—see Study 5).

As indicated above, this grievance-tolerance perspective also includes two other factors in its analysis of conflict: (1) the presence or absence of other means for resolving conflict and (2) the potential impact of conflict upon the larger social system. For example, the traditional extended family has multiple means available for releasing individual frustrations and containing conflict. As a primary group, intimate and emotional expression is encouraged by all members. Furthermore, conflict within a tightly knit and relatively isolated family unit has little impact upon the larger society. In contrast, since the modern nuclear family is less primary and less isolated, it is less effective in managing grievances. Thus, the development of the Women's Liberation Movement as a social-conflict organization is directly related to changes in family life.

This perspective has also been used to explain why so much crime and violence in contemporary society has familial roots and origins (battered children, wife beating, child molesting by relatives or close family friends). Zalba [1971, pp. 58–61] has indicated that the grievance-tolerance level in the contemporary family is lower than it has been in the past. In contrast, recreational contexts (as opposed to family contexts) are less likely to encourage unexpected forms of violent and aggressive behavior. Other approved means for releasing frustrations in controlled forms are available (aggressively playing the game or wildly cheering and yelling), and unacceptable conflict in this setting would have an impact upon the larger society (a riot at a football game involves many people—both those in attendance and those watching the game on television). For the same reasons, this approach claims that occupational and political contexts are the least likely to encourage violent conflict, since they offer numerous alternatives for relieving pent up frustration and since conflict in these contexts might have far-reaching consequences.

The problem with both the frustration and grievance-tolerance-level concepts is that they seem to assume a direct relationship between conflict and status deprivation—that is, the more deprived people are, the more frustrated and aggressive they should be and the lower their grievance-tolerance level should be. Yet history seems to indicate the opposite. American blacks rebelled many decades after slavery—a situation of extreme deprivation. Women rebelled after obtaining some freedoms. The Catholic–Protestant conflict became worse after certain economic and social conditions were improved in Northern Ireland (industrialization, more political independence).

In order to deal with this contradiction, the concept of *relative deprivation* has been developed. This perspective stresses the importance of the *feelings* or *meanings* that accompany actual status deprivation situations. It maintains that the more deprived an individual or group feels, the less frustrated and aggressive they tend to be. For example, highly repressed persons, such as slaves and the extremely poor, rarely feel frustrated since they possess only meager expectations and are unaware of alternatives, including violence, to their prevailing life-style. Therefore, the *relative* feelings of deprivation are crucial. James Davies [1969, pp. 671–709] maintains that conflict is most likely to result when a prolonged period of rising expectations and rising gratifications is followed by a short period of sharp reversal, during which the gap between expectations and reality quickly widens and becomes intolerable. Recent research on revolutionary processes suggests that an actual reversal of gratifications may not be necessary. Deprived groups merely need to feel that gratifications are not keeping pace with their justified expectations (see the discussion of urban disturbances in Chapter 5).

Most social scientists who study the relationship of conflict to status systems utilize theories that combine the three concepts of frustration, grievance tolerance, and relative deprivation. Figure 14-1 depicts a way in which these three concepts might be interrelated to explain a developing

FIGURE 14-1 Stages in the Development of Conflict

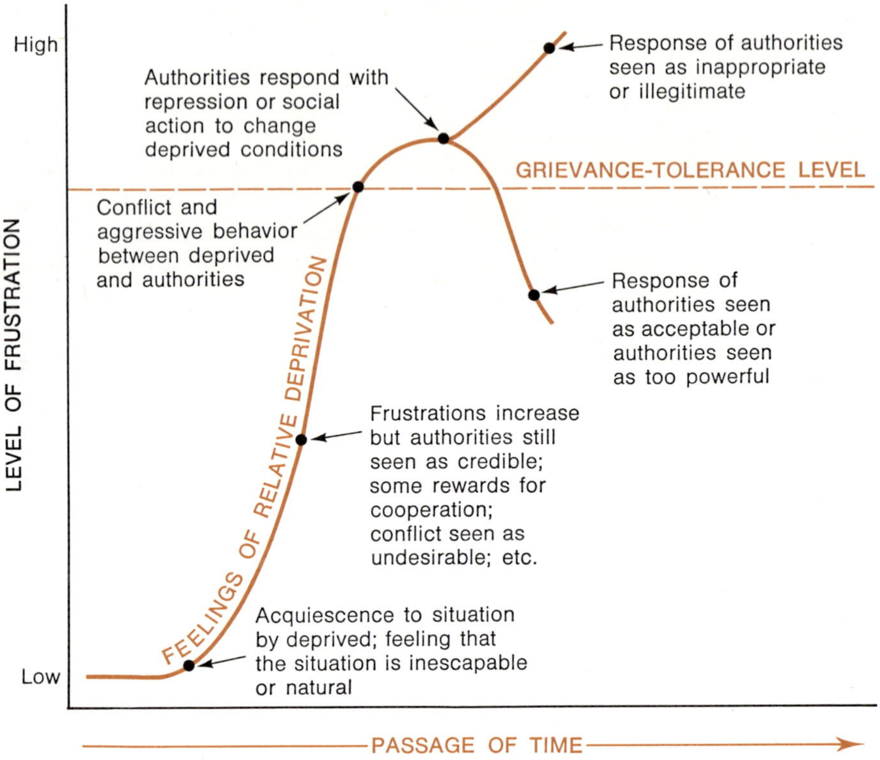

conflict between an ethnic minority and authorities representing the larger society. Such a combined approach also indicates the various outcomes that may occur at particular stages—further conflict, diminished frustrations by the deprived, improved social conditions, repression by authorities, and the like. This approach introduces the final section of this chapter, a discussion of the methods for controlling conflict in societies.

CAN CONFLICT BE CONTROLLED?

Since many people view social dynamics—deviance, change, and conflict—as potentially disruptive to the social system, the question of control of these processes is crucial. In the case of conflict, the issue is complex. This section begins by considering the distinction between the *control* of conflict and the *management* of conflict. Whereas conflict control often leads to the elimination of conflict, conflict management implies redirecting the process into deliberately planned and contained channels. Those who favor control see conflict as dysfunctional, whereas those who favor management see nonviolent competition or conflict as functional.

Next, two major theories of conflict management are considered. Traditional liberals argue for formal management systems, which encourage bargaining and compromise—a form of structured competition. In contrast, more radical theorists maintain that since conflict is natural and ever-present, a method of management that allows for *nonviolent* conflict is both essential and, under certain conditions, possible. The chapter concludes by considering the limitations of each theory and the social action implications of various perspectives of conflict.

Control Versus Management of Conflict

Those who view conflict as a problem of *control* tend to adopt one of two opposing methods—*repression* or *co-optation.* Repression involves the strict enforcement of norms by the use of force, whereas co-optation involves legitimizing the potentially threatening behavior by absorbing it into approved patterns of institutional behavior. In one case, conflict is controlled by physical containment (separating ethnic groups into isolated ghettos or camps) or by fear of reprisal (tough law enforcement). In the other case, conflict is controlled by transforming it into a part of the normal social system (labor–management conflict is taken out of the streets and put into the legal system).

Whether the control of conflict is sought through repression or co-optation, the original conflict is either eliminated or changed in nature. The threat of force deters groups from fighting. Isolation keeps conflicting groups apart, although they sometimes begin fighting among themselves or with the forces of authority. Labor leaders become a part of the system, with high salaries and prestige, whose self-interest is tied to maintaining the system through moderate demands and tactics. Therefore, the sociological problem with control is that any potentially functional aspects of the original conflict may be eliminated.

In addition, each of the two forms of control have special problems. In Chapter 12, we discussed the limitations of the problems associated with repression, that is, the difficulty of depending upon a strict law-and-order philosophy and the potential misuse of violence by police. Co-optation also has disadvantages. The attempt by many leaders and citizens to build a national ecology crusade is an illustration. Some social observers have suggested that such a crusade could lessen political polarization over other issues (race, economic, busing, and so on) by redirecting (co-opting) the previously destructive energy of the opposing groups into a common cause, the collective attack upon the problems of the natural environment. All citizens could become involved, in small ways, in a nonpartisan effort to clean up the environment, and their feelings of powerlessness, alienation, and impotence would thereby be lessened or alleviated. The difficulty is that such a strategy might lead to ineffectiveness in dealing with both the common cause crisis, in this case ecology, and the co-opted social conflicts (rich versus poor, black versus white, upper versus lower class, and so on).

14-3 Should Conflict be Controlled or Managed?

The concept of **conflict control** is based upon the notion that conflict in any form is undesirable and should be eliminated from society. In contrast, those who favor **conflict management** argue that conflict must be redirected into less violent forms, while retaining its functionally desirable aspects. Depending upon one's perception of the most effective way to deal with conflict, four general tactics can be employed.

Those who see conflict as bad, especially aggression aimed at formal laws and institutions, often advocate a law-and-order approach based upon **repression.** They assume that enforcement officials must maintain a sufficient monopoly of force in order to quickly quell any disturbance. However, the use of violence to deter violence raises important moral questions. In addition, the use of force may encourage more conflict, and it does nothing about the underlying factors which gave rise to the conflict in the first place (racism, poverty, oppressive laws, an unpopular war, and so on).

Those who see conflict as disruptive but eschew the use of force often favor **co-optation.** This control tactic involves bringing conflict-prone groups into the formal system to express their grievances through approved political procedures. The 1972 presidential campaign of George McGovern brought many previously excluded minority groups (antiwar youth, poor blacks and whites, women) into the power structure of the Democratic Party. However, the formal power structure may reject this participation, as happened when McGovern failed to obtain the backing of many traditional Democratic leaders. Too, deprived groups in the system may lose sight of their original social goals in favor of maintaining newly obtained personal advantages.

D. Brody/Stock, Boston

United Press International

United Press International

Those who see less violent forms of conflict as desirable often favor competition in the form of **structured bargaining and compromise.** This tactic for managing conflict redirects it into less aggressive paths. The debates and votes of the Security Council of the United Nations are an example. However, bargaining and compromise can take on the aspects of a meaningless game where the ritual of debate and bargaining becomes more important than its substance. In addition, eventual compromises may involve issues that are unrelated to real-world situations of conflict (verbal condemnations of aggression while warfare continues).

United Press International

Finally, those who see conflict as functional but force as undesirable often advocate various forms of **nonviolent action.** For example, in Denver, Colorado, in 1966, about 100,000 housewives boycotted five food chains because of the high price of groceries. The problem of managing conflict by the use of nonviolent tactics is that a high degree of training, organization, and commitment is usually required by those using the tactics. It is a relatively easy matter for wealthy food corporations to absorb the costs of a short boycott, or to pass the costs on to consumers in later higher prices. At the same time, families in urban society cannot feed themselves for long without obtaining food from grocery stores.

In other words, *by co-opting everyone into the fight against some universal social problem*, such as environmental protection, *leaders may unknowingly impede the ultimate solution of the problem*. For example, a pseudocommunity commitment and involvement could easily mask the extensive nature of the ecology problem [Lowry, 1970, pp. 46–48; 1971, pp. 350–359]. The world must clean up oceans, not just local backyards. In addition, a fundamental aspect of the ecology crisis is the necessity to reallocate major resources on a national and international basis. The United States claims some 50 percent of the world's resources with less than 10 percent of the population, and the country may contribute up to 60 percent of the world's industrial pollution. The real challenge is to eliminate poverty, blight, and deterioration, not just make the world cleaner and quieter. If citizens and leaders begin to address these aspects of environmental pollution, political conflict will heighten, not lessen, since the question of resource allocation will threaten established interests.

The basic causes of the ecology crisis will be addressed only when the following kinds of changes take place—changes from larger to smaller families, from obsession with consumption to a stress on public service and well-being, from marriage as a necessity for all to equal-opportunity career options for single women. However, these types of changes will *create conflicts* between traditional values and life-styles and new ones. The manner in which ecological concern challenges traditional views was demonstrated by the supersonic transport debate in Congress in 1971. Environmentalists opposing the SST argued that the noise pollution damage would harm the environment and that minor technological–economic gains were not worth the risk. Proponents argued that thousands of potential jobs, the air superiority of the United States, and the continued health of American business required the development of the SST. Thus, both sides of the debate raised serious practical and political questions, which could only be expressed within the context of conflict and confrontation politics.

The conscious avoidance of conflict by co-optation may create greater problems than the conflict itself. This is illustrated by one of the major weaknesses of American foreign policy during the Cold War period following World War II. Bipartisanship became the norm as a way of minimizing domestic turmoil and, supposedly, maximizing national security. In some cases, liberal Democrats became more "hawkish" towards international communism than conservative Republicans. This led to the acceptance of single policies and unquestioned goals by both major parties and by most citizens, regardless of partisan philosophies. This avoidance of conflict over national policies helps explain, in part, why the United States did not thoroughly consider all of the implications of an unending arms race, the use of clandestine intelligence tactics, and the development of a powerful military establishment with close ties to economic and political sectors of society.

In summary, conflict must be viewed as a natural part of any functioning social system. In some contexts, like Northern Ireland or the national ecology debate, conflict may become a crucial part of the social order. Therefore, the real question is not how to eliminate conflict, since it is unavoidable and often desirable, but how to manage it; that is, how to channel it into less destructive, more meaningful patterns of social interaction.

In a study of the role of the police on skid row, Egon Bittner [1967, pp. 699–715] describes the way in which police, recognizing the inadequacies of conflict control, develop techniques for *conflict management.* As we saw in Study 12, police work consists of two different roles. One is *law officer,* requiring enforcement of the law, or the control of deviance and conflict. The other is *peace officer,* requiring keeping of the peace, or the management of deviance and conflict. Bittner points out that effective performance of both of these roles is necessary on skid row. The first role consists of the formal activities (arrests, record keeping, and so on) that most people associate with police work. In contrast, the second role is informal and involves nonrecorded activities (giving directions, offering assistance and aid, providing information, issuing warnings, pacifying and disciplining potential deviants, rousting).

The dominant public attitude towards skid row is containment; that is, the public asks police to keep skid row residents within the skid row community boundaries. However, police recognize that they lack the personnel and other resources to completely contain the residents, so they turn their attentions to protecting the residents from one another and to maintaining the general peace. As a consequence, they develop a number of conflict-management tactics. For example, police often do not arrest persons who have committed minor offenses but use alternative sanctions instead—warnings (threats of "keeping an eye on you") or direct discipline for juveniles (that is, making them apologize or repair damage). Police may act as bargaining agents in contexts involving family quarrels or fights between friends. In dealing with people considered to be not legally or psychologically accountable for their actions (mentally ill, very aged, alcoholics), they offer advice or assistance ("Contact the social worker" or "Go to your room and sleep it off"). In dealing with owners and operators of businesses, police may be willing to "look the other way" for minor offenses since they depend on these people for a knowledge of the daily occurrences ("What's happening") on skid row, a knowledge that is necessary to maintain peace and order.

Bittner's study of the police on skid row indicates that techniques of both conflict control and conflict management may be employed in different social situations. Often, however, the management of conflict is more effective or functional, since repression and co-optation are limited and sometimes potentially disruptive. This is dramatically illustrated in the role of the police, a role that incorporates both processes. The accompanying "So What?" box gives additional examples of attempts to control and manage conflict in contemporary society. Each example is related to the concepts and theories about the sources and nature of conflict discussed in the preceding section of this chapter.

▶ SO WHAT?

All of the theories and concepts considered in this chapter have played a role in attempts to control or manage conflict in contemporary society. Below are some specific examples of how certain attempts at control reflect the theories and concepts discussed.

1. Citizen groups concerned about television and comic book content utilize a cultural perspective regarding the causes of conflict. They feel that if violence could be eliminated from programming, and emphasis upon equality and brotherhood substituted, many young viewers would become less aggressive as they mature. As a result, television producers have experimented with some less violent programs for children (for example, the recent Saturday morning programs *Shazam* and *Isis* minimize violence and emphasize sex-role equality, in contrast to older programs like *Superman*).
2. Those utilizing the work of scholars like James Coleman have attempted to create organizations that would break the natural cycle of hostility generated by community conflict. For example, many communities establish "Rumor Centers" during periods of ethnic conflict. These centers provide telephone contact for citizens and formal news releases for the media in an attempt to counteract citizen dependence upon informal and biased forms of communication.
3. Boserup's suggestion for a bicameral political structure for the government of Northern Ireland has been suggested by some researchers for American cities characterized by sharp black–white cleavages. Some American cities might consider establishing "little city halls" in black ghettoes, staffed by black leaders accountable to the local population. Some larger city governments might consider equal and competing representation and power for black and white representatives.
4. If a leader believes that frustration is a major cause of conflict, actions may be taken to diffuse or eliminate the sources of frustration. Evidence indicates that this type of reasoning played a role in the Nixon Administration's decision to abolish the draft—a policy that diffused much antimilitary sentiment in white middle-class groups.
5. The concept of a grievance-tolerance level can be utilized to implement social programs that will either eliminate grievances or raise tolerance levels. Characteristically, modern societies employ this technique, at least latently, when they establish programs of national health care, old-age benefits, food for the hungry, unemployment insurance, and the like.
6. Those utilizing the concept of relative deprivation can either design social programs to eliminate the feelings of deprivation (similar to point 5 above) or lower the expectations that are held out to dis-

advantaged groups. When Daniel Patrick Moynihan advised President Lyndon Johnson to adopt a policy of "benign neglect" toward black Americans in the 1960s, he based his recommendation partly upon the assumption that the United States government had promised black Americans advances that could not be delivered, thereby creating expectations that could not be met.

None of these examples of policy actions are without moral or political problems. Control of television programming raises issues of freedom of the press and freedom of choice for viewers. Moynihan's recommendation could be an excuse for the government's doing nothing about a serious problem. Nevertheless, each of the above actions are indebted to some sociological theory or concept about the sources and nature of conflict. The moral and political choices must be debated by all citizens.

Conflict Management: Competitive Bargaining or Nonviolent Conflict?

Since conflict control is an extremely complex issue that entails many political and moral problems, many social scientists have focused upon the study of conflict management in recent years, and one scientific journal has been established that deals explicitly with this topic (*The Journal of Conflict Resolution*). There are two competing theories of the most effective way to manage conflict in contemporary society. The *"liberal" approach* argues that processes of competitive bargaining and compromise are the most effective means of managing conflict. We have labeled those who adopt this perspective "liberal" theorists because their assumptions about human nature, human society, and appropriate forms of intergroup relations are indebted to liberal perspectives. In contrast, the *"radical" approach*—adopted by those indebted to more radical views—argues that dramatic new forms of nonviolent conflict are required. Thus, each of the two views reflects a different perception of human behavior and society and a different interpretation of the role of conflict and cooperation in intergroup relations. The important distinctions between these two perspectives are summarized in Table 14-4.

An *important* note is required here. *Radicalism* is often assumed to be associated with violence. As we saw earlier in this chapter, however, violent conflict is by no means confined to those who oppose formal authority. Furthermore, we have already considered the arguments concerning the functions of violence in the previous section. Therefore, in this section of the chapter, we have chosen to concentrate upon radical theorists who favor conflict—but in nonviolent forms.

As we have seen throughout this book, traditional liberal theorists see most human interaction as supportive (that is, cooperative or competitive)

Table 14-4 Assumptions of Liberal and Radical Theories of Nonviolent Conflict Management

Assumptions About:	Liberal Theory	Radical Theory
Character of Human Interaction	Mostly rational and supportive	Often nonrational and exploitative
Usual Type of Inter-group Relations	Cooperation or competition	Conflict
Appropriate Response	Bargaining and compromise	Nonviolent action
Nature of Power Structure	Pluralist; competing interest groups; often symmetrical or balanced	Oligarchic; power elites versus powerless; usually asymmetrical
Important Sources of Power	Social: Money, weapons, personnel	Cultural: Authority as legitimacy to rule
Most Important Resource	Threat or use of force	Threat or use of non-compliance and disobedience
Rules of the Game	Usually zero sum	Must be transformed into nonzero sum
Type of Communication Required	Verbal; often compulsory	Most often nonverbal in the form of symbolic behavior
Type of Action Required	Bilateral: Equivalent agreed-upon responses by both sides	Unilateral: Independent acts not dependent upon a response "in kind" but forcing opponent to use nonviolence

and as having the potential for rational (orderly, planned, deliberate) organization. As a consequence, they believe that conflict can be rationally managed by constructing contexts within which competing groups are forced to bargain and compromise. Such an approach is possible because power is usually distributed throughout the society between many interacting interest groups. Although different groups may possess different kinds of power (money, people, weapons, food, morality), all groups have some sort of resource that can be used in a bargaining situation. For example, although management owns the factory, labor possesses the skills and manpower needed to run the factory efficiently. Therefore, labor can ask management for high pay, and, in turn, management can ask labor for more effective job performance. This form of interaction is enforced by the threat or use of force by both sides. If labor does not get what it wants, a general strike may result; if management does not get what it wants, a lockout may result.

In contrast, radical theorists view the same human relationships and processes from a different perspective. They see conflict as a natural and ever-present form of intergroup relations, a form that contains much spontaneous nonrational interaction, such as Coleman found in his analysis of community conflict. Therefore, a different kind of response is needed, one that recognizes the actual or potential conflict running through human interaction but manages to avoid the problem of violence—namely, nonviolent action.

Radicals see power as oligarchic and power struggles as essentially taking place between power elites and the relatively powerless. For example, factory managers are seen as oligarchic bureaucrats possessing far greater wealth and influence than the workers. In a protracted strike, management can often afford to close down the factory and retire in comfort, whereas the workers and their families might starve. Therefore, advocates of nonviolent conflict maintain that the struggle cannot be in terms of traditional sources of power but must be redirected toward the question of who has the legitimate authority to control the work situation (see Chapter 11 and the discussion of authority versus power). The one strength workers possess is the ability to withhold their work, and management cannot possibly continue to survive if enough workers refuse to operate factories efficiently. Therefore, the threat or use of noncompliance or disobedience is the most important resource possessed by those who believe they are powerless.

Racial conflict has also been analyzed from these two different perspectives. Liberals feel that American blacks and whites must engage in rational bargaining and compromise in order to lessen hostilitites and violence. For example, blacks might be willing to settle for school integration, thereby gaining the education needed for future social mobility. At the same time, whites might be willing to accept school integration if they could be certain that blacks would not threaten their job seniority. Radicals counter this argument by pointing out that the black–white struggle is not one of competition between equals. Whites possess all the power and resources and, therefore, cannot be forced to bargain or compromise. Nonviolent action by blacks is the only appropriate response. When Martin Luther King led the Montgomery, Alabama, bus boycott, the white power structure of that community finally integrated buses because the city transportation system was going bankrupt. Black citizens had undermined the authority of white leaders to maintain a city service by refusing to ride on their buses.

A good deal of traditional bargaining theory is based upon the concept of *zero-sum games* [Apt, 1970]. These types of games are essentially competitive and result in one player's winnings equalling another player's losses (for example, monopoly). In contrast, nonviolent action is based upon the concept of *nonzero-sum games,* where the assumption is that all players will lose something and all players will win something. Thus, action is based upon the idea of compelling competitors to surrender some advantages (big profits or segregated schools) in order to achieve others (better work performance or a less aggressive black population).

Where liberal theory sees verbal communication—often compulsory (court-ordered arbitration)—as necessary, radical theory tends to emphasize the importance of nonverbal symbolic behavior (burning draft cards, blocking streets with human bodies, refusing to pay taxes). The latter form of behavior raises questions about the ability of authorities to govern (to operate a draft system, keep traffic moving, or collect taxes to run programs).

Finally, liberal theorists believe that bilateral interaction is required. The conflicting groups must simultaneously respond to one another by taking roughly equivalent agreed-upon actions. White leaders must agree to integrate schools while black leaders agree to stop disruptive demonstrations. Radical theorists argue for unilateral actions that are not dependent upon a response in kind from opposing forces. If the act is appropriate, no matter what the response, it will be effective. If authorities use violence against civil rights demonstrators, they run the risk of delegitimating themselves in the eyes of observers and the general public (they begin to look irrational or barbaric). If they respond with nonviolent programs or social action, the demonstrators have gained what they sought.

Limitations of Bargaining and Nonviolence

In the real world, both bargaining and nonviolent tactics tend to be used in interrelated and complex ways. Labor strikes, boycotts, slowdowns, sick-ins, and the like are all examples of nonviolent action. At the same time, modern unions depend upon highly organized systems of bargaining, related to the formal institutions of society. Ongoing research discloses that both approaches to conflict management have limitations.

The liberal approach assumes that bargaining and compromise will minimize conflict, but we find that this is not always the case. The radical approach that puts emphasis upon nonviolent action does not always get results either. These conclusions were disclosed in a laboratory study of interpersonal bargaining by Morton Deutsch and Robert M. Krauss [1970, pp. 129–162]. They observed how individuals behaved in a game which placed them in competition with each other while racing toy trucks through a complicated maze. Deutsch and Krauss found the following:

1. The players were less likely to bargain and compromise with opponents in the game when they were able to use force, or the threat of force, to win the game (closing a gate to block an opponent's truck from reaching the finish line first). When players possessed force (gates) they tended to use it increasingly throughout the game, and the originally competitive situation became more conflict-prone (increasing threats to use a gate and increasing use of gates to block an opponent's truck). This finding means that some radicals may overestimate the human ability to engage in essentially nonviolent interaction.

2. In addition, the players' tendency to use force rather than to bargain was not lessened by an opportunity to talk things over. When Deutsch and Krauss permitted the opponents to talk to one another voluntarily, they discussed issues irrelevant to the winning of the game (beating the opponent to the finish line). When Deutsch and Krauss forced the opponents to talk to one another, their communication became hostile, threatening, and combative. This finding means that some liberals may put too much stock in the ability to minimize conflict by means of bargaining and compromise.

These findings seem to reflect many of the characteristics of human competition and conflict in the real world (outside of a laboratory situation). For example, negotiations after the Korean War and during the Paris peace talks of the Vietnam War produced many verbal threats by both sides. Since each side possessed considerable military and political power, communication often became hostile. During the Paris talks, early "bargaining" involved debates about the size and shape of the negotiating table, not ways to end the continuing military conflict. In addition to these problems, formal systems for either bargaining and compromise or nonviolent action are often not easy to construct. For example, in an extensive analysis of nonviolence throughout human history, Gene Sharp [1973] points out the difficulties in creating an effective program for nonviolent conflict. Basically, nonviolent action has three possible goals—conversion, accommodation, or coercion, each one relying on a different strategy. However, the specific tactics that might be employed are diverse (see Table 14-5), and their effectiveness is often hard to assess.

For example, nonviolent protest and persuasion may be designed to *convert an opponent* to one's position, but is this often successful? In 1968, when Russian tanks invaded Czechoslovakia, citizens took to the streets and argued with the Russian soldiers. Although this action may have helped keep that situation peaceful, it seemed to have little effect on the Soviet takeover of the Czechoslovakian government. Also, tactics may sometimes have both positive and negative effects in terms of different goals. Draft-card burning and destruction of draft records were employed during the Vietnam War as a symbol of *noncooperation.* These tactics did not necessarily attempt to change people's minds about the war; rather they were aimed at getting the government to conclude that further repression of war resistance was not worth the price. Yet these tactics enraged many people, thereby possibly making later conversion more difficult.

Nonviolent *intervention* is designed to "delegitimate" authority—to compromise or discredit an opponent's legitimacy—and thereby destroy an opponent's basis of power. However, in cases where one party in a conflict possesses multiple resources, nonviolent intervention may be extremely difficult. Not until unions accumulated strike funds was labor able to use the protracted strike as an effective tactic. Management could simply

TABLE 14-5 Examples of Nonviolent Tactics[a]

Tactics →	Goal	Examples	
Protest and Persuasion	Conversion	Speeches and declarations Letters Petitions Banners and posters Leaflets and books Songs Teach-ins Silence	Lobbying Picketing and vigils Prayer and worship Protest disrobing Rude gestures Fraternization Mock funerals
Noncooperation (Social, economic, political)	Accommodation	Boycott of social, economic, and political activities Withdrawal from social situations and institutions	Strikes Refusal to pay fees, dues, and debts Blacklisting
Intervention	Coercion	Obstruction Speak-ins Guerrilla theater Seizure of land or property Blockages	Dumping or trashing Disclosing identity of secret agents Civil disobedience Seeking mass arrest and imprisonment

[a]This is a very partial list of the many nonviolent tactics that have been utilized by various groups and societies. In addition, the problem of nonviolent action is even more complex since tactics may vary according to whether they are informal or formal, or used by or against formal authorities or organizations.
Adapted from Gene Sharp, *The Politics of Nonviolent Action* (Boston: Porter Sargent, 1973), pp. 105–445.

afford to wait until workers ran out of money and had to go back to work. Therefore, intervention usually requires significant organization, alternative resources, and important commitment by those using this tactic. These are often not easy to achieve in previously deprived groups (ethnic minorities engaged in nonviolent conflict with the representatives of larger society).

Nevertheless, despite the questions that have been raised about both bargaining and nonviolence theories, these two perspectives still remain significant alternatives to violent conflict. Continuing research will identify more precisely the most appropriate social contexts within which each can be effectively utilized. The strength of both theories is that they are based upon the idea of conflict management and suggest ways of channeling conflict into potentially productive or nondestructive patterns of interaction.

CONCLUSION

In summary, we have considered the continuing debate about the sources of human conflict. Some scholars claim that it is biologically determined, that, like other animals, humans respond with genetically patterned behavior to the physical and social environments (turf, the language of threat, and so on). Therefore, conflict is seen by these theorists as natural, often necessary for survival, and largely unavoidable. In contrast, most social scientists, while not denying the possibility of biological influences, maintain that social variables play the major role. Some social scientific perspectives, typically the more traditional and older views, see conflict and competition as often dysfunctional and cooperation as the most natural and desirable form of human interaction. More recent, less conservative perspectives see cooperation as sometimes dysfunctional and conflict as sometimes functional.

Three different kinds of theories, which reflect the perspectives most often employed by sociologists, have been developed. Cultural theories locate the causes of conflict in norms and values that encourage and reward aggression and violence, as in the case of American frontier ethics. Communal and societal theories focus upon the interpersonal relationships, roles, and institutional patterns that tend to sustain conflict between interacting individuals and groups, as in the case of Northern Ireland. Still other theories look for special aspects of the social order as primary causes. Studies that examine conflict as a consequence of anxieties and frustrations caused by class and caste status systems illustrate this approach.

Each of these perspectives not only provides different ways of viewing human conflict but also can be used to plan programs of social action. Cultural theorists often argue that television programming must be changed to deemphasize violence, while those who study conflict in community life may recommend more rational forms of communication, alternative political structures, or programs by authorities to alleviate the frustrations of minority and ethnic groups.

Specifically, two kinds of approaches have been used to deal with the problem of conflict—control and management. Those arguing for conflict control see repression or co-optation as the answer. The problem with this approach is that, when it is effective, it tends to eliminate conflict altogether, thereby making any functional outcomes impossible. For example, repressing or co-opting racial conflicts (black versus white) may erase the possibility for blacks to develop pride and internal cohesion and for whites to become conscious of the problems experienced by blacks. As a consequence, newer approaches have concentrated upon techniques of conflict management.

Liberal theorists maintain that the most effective way in which conflict can be managed is by encouraging processes of bargaining and compromise—a form of structured competition. Radicals maintain that conflict is possible without violence. Each of these perspectives is based upon a different perception of the nature of power, the character of most human interaction, and the most effective tactics that can be employed by competing groups. As a result, each perspective applies to different kinds of social contexts. For example, formal bargaining often works well for modern labor–management disputes, where the relationship is one between equals (both groups possess much power). In contrast, nonviolent action seems more appropriate for much interethnic conflict, where one group (whites, for example) possesses greater power than the other (blacks).

REFERENCES

Apt, Clark C. *Serious Games.* New York: The Viking Press, 1970.

Ardrey, Robert. *The Territorial Imperative.* New York: Atheneum, Publishers, 1966.

Becker, Howard S., and Irving L. Horowitz. "The Culture of Civility," *trans-action,* 7 (April 1970), pp. 12–19.

Berkowitz, Leonard. "Tooth and Claw," *trans-action,* 7 (June 1970), pp. 59–60.

Bittner, Egon. "The Police on Skid-Row: A Study of Peace Keeping," *American Sociological Review,* 32 (October 1967), pp. 699–715.

Brown, Richard Maxwell. "Historial Patterns of Violence in America," in *Violence in America* (Report of the National Commission on the Causes and Prevention of Violence), Hugh Davis Graham and Ted Robert Gurr, Ed. New York: The New American Library, 1969.

Coleman, James S. *Community Conflict.* New York: The Free Press, 1957.

Coser, Lewis A. *The Functions of Social Conflict.* New York: The Free Press, 1956. Press, 1956.

———. "Social Conflict and the Theory of Social Change," *The British Journal of Sociology,* 8 (September 1957), pp. 197–198.

Davies, James C. "The J-Curve of Rising and Declining Satisfactions as a Cause of Some Great Revolutions and Contained Rebellions," in *Violence in America,* Hugh David Graham and Ted Robert Gurr, Ed. New York: The New American Library, 1969.

Deutsch, Morton, and Robert M. Krauss. "Studies of Interpersonal Bargaining," in *War and Its Prevention,* Amitai Etzioni and Martin Wenglinsky, Ed. New York: Harper & Row, Publishers, 1970.

Gouldner, Alvin W. *The Coming Crisis of Western Sociology.* New York: Basic Books, 1970.

Hall, Edward T. *The Silent Language.* New York: Doubleday and Company, 1959.

Lowry, Ritchie P. "The New Religecology: Salvation or Soporific?" *Social Policy,* 1 (July–August 1970), pp. 46–48.

———. "Toward A Radical View of the Ecological Crisis," *Environmental Affairs,* 1 (June 1971), pp. 350–359.

Lorenz, Konrad. *On Aggression.* New York: Bantam Books, 1969.

Morris, Desmond. *The Naked Ape.* New York: Dell Publishing Company, 1969.

Nieburg, H. L. *The Behavioral Process.* New York: St. Martin's Press, 1969.

Perls, F. S. *Ego, Hunger and Aggression.* New York: Random House, 1969.

Record, Wilson C. *Race and Radicalism: The NAACP and the Communist Party in Conflict.* Ithaca: Cornell University Press, 1964.

Russell, W. M. S. "The Wild Ones," *The Listener* (5 November 1964), pp. 710–712.

Schiffer, Robert L. "Capitalist Revolution in Iowa," *The Reporter* (5 January 1961), pp. 24–27.

Sharp, Gene. *The Politics of Nonviolent Action.* Boston: Porter Sargent, 1973.

Walter, E. V. *Terror and Resistance: A Study of Political Violence.* New York: Oxford University Press, 1971.

Zalba, Serapio R. "Crusade Against Children," *trans-action,* 8 (July–August 1971), pp. 58–61.

▶ KEY CONCEPT REVIEW

To aid you in mastering the basic concepts of Part 5, we have organized key terms into convenient and logical conceptual networks. Refer to the study procedure recommended on page 73 and follow the same procedure here.

CLUSTER 12
Types of Social Processes

- Cooperation
- Conflict
- Competition
- Change (Social and Cultural)
- Crime (and Delinquency)
- Deviance (as compared to Conformity)
- Cultural Diffusion

CLUSTER 13
Sources, Nature, and Causes of Social Processes

- Fertility and Birth Rate
- Mortality and Death Rate
- Demographic Transition
- Migration
- Relative Deprivation
- Grievance-Tolerance Level
- Differential Association
- Discretion

CLUSTER 14
Methods of Controlling Social Processes

- Internalization of Norms
- Informal Control
- Formal Control
- Conflict Management (as compared to Conflict Control)
- Co-optation
- Bargaining and Compromise
- Nonviolent Action

12. Types of Social Processes

	Definition	Example
Cooperation	An ongoing social relationship in which interacting individuals and groups join together to achieve a common goal and share the rewards of their joint activity. This basic process accounts for the group structure of human society.	By pooling and sharing their limited resources (raw materials, personnel, technology), the nations of Western Europe formed a common (cooperative) market in order to improve the economies of the participating nations.
Conflict	An ongoing social relationship in which interacting individuals and groups attempt to control or dominate each other because they disagree on the means for attaining various goals. This process is basic to all societies since both means and goals differ and are limited at any given moment in history.	The modern school has become the focus of violent conflict in recent years. Pro-busing advocates argue that the school should be used as a means for achieving racial integration. Anti-busing rivals contend that this is not a proper goal of education and that the school population should not be used as a means for achieving integration.

	Definition	Example
Competition	An ongoing social relationship in which interacting individuals and groups agree to abide by certain rules in pursuit of a commonly desired goal. This process is basic to all societies since it combines elements of both *cooperation* (over means) and *conflict* (over goals).	*Achievement-oriented* societies, like the United States, emphasize athletic events in which rival teams attempt to win the game or championship (which may bring fame or financial reward) while abiding by rules enforced by umpires or judges. Labor-management relationships and political contests between Republicans and Democrats are also examples of competition.
Crime (and Delinquency)	Crimes are those deviant acts which violate formal norms (laws). Delinquent acts are crimes committed by persons under a legal age limit and certain other deviant acts not considered criminal when committed by adults. When crimes involve forced violence to persons or property, they are referred to as *traditional crimes.* When they involve voluntary cooperative relationships, they are referred to as *victimless crimes.* When they involve acts requiring specialized occupational knowledge and access, they are referred to as *white-collar crimes.*	Evolutionary theorists argue that the *Gesellschaft* society of modern America has a more functional social structure and more complex (more advanced) norms and values. Cyclical theorists argue that American society has continuously passed through desirable and undesirable stages in its 200-year history—modern hedonistic society is a decline from earlier Puritan values.
Change (Social and Cultural)	The concept of change is used to refer to the fact that human society is in a constant state of flux. Social change refers to alterations in social roles, relationships, and the structure of society. Cultural change refers to alterations in norms and values. Some theorists see change as *evolutionary*—as from worse to better, from small to large, from simple to complex. Other theorists see change as *cyclical*—unsuccessful societal adaptation leads to social and cultural decline, whereas successful adaptation leads to social and cultural advances.	Examples of traditional crime include burglary, murder, and rape; victimless crimes include prostitution, drug use, and gambling; white-collar crimes include embezzlement, fraud, and stock manipulation. Delinquent acts include running away from home, habitual disobedience, and minor vandalism. Adults who do not pay their bills on time are often considered to be habitually delinquent.

	Definition	Example
Deviance (as compared to Conformity)	All societies require most members to conform—to act in accordance with socially approved *norms* while pursuing socially approved goals. However, much human behavior deviates from expected norms and goals. Deviance may be considered *functional* in one society at one time, and *dysfunctional* in another society at another time.	The young adult who uses "street language" is a conformist within the peer group but a deviant in the middle-class school. Polygamy is considered deviant behavior in the United States, but it is still practiced in some other societies (of the Middle East) and some contracultures (communes). Premeditated killing is labeled murder in civilian society, but it is rewarded as heroism when directed toward an enemy in wartime.
Cultural Diffusion	The process by which elements of culture (norms and values) spread from one society or subgroup to another.	*Nonviolent action* in the form of sit-ins, boycotts, and mass arrests and imprisonment became the favorite tactic of the social protest groups of the 1960s. This *social innovation* was borrowed and adapted from the civil rights tactics of Martin Luther King, who based his actions upon the teachings of Gandhi, who, in turn, based part of his philosophy of peaceful conflict upon Jesus.

13. Sources, Nature, and Causes of Social Processes

	Definition	Example
Fertility and Birth Rate	Fertility refers to the rate at which individuals are added to the population by new births. The crude birth rate—number of persons born in a given population per year per 1000 people—is usually used to measure fertility.	Highly developed societies with low birth rates provide greater freedom and opportunity for all citizens. Therefore, they may be characterized by rapid change and a variety of forms of deviance. In contrast, traditional societies with high birth rates tie people closely to work and family. However, these societies may experience social conflict as developing problems of famine, disease, and low levels of living go unattended.

	Definition	Example
Mortality and Death Rate	Mortality, as measured by the crude death rate, refers to the number of individuals in a given population who die every year. The death rate is usually calculated on the basis of 1000 people; that is, so many deaths per 1000 people in a population.	Death rates can tell us about the potential for deviance, change, or conflict within a society. For example, during periods of crisis when death rates are abnormally high (warfare, famine, plague), individual acts of deviance (such as crime) often decrease. At other times, high death rates for some subgroups can either impede necessary change (the American Indian) or encourage conflict to bring about change (American blacks).
Demographic Transition	*Demographers* (those who study the size, distribution, and composition of populations) have identified a process common to all societies experiencing modernization and industrialization. During the early periods of this change, populations grow rapidly as birth rates remain high while death rates drop quickly.	All societies experience some form of demographic transition during modernization. For countries with a small population but much land (America), the resultant population growth can be easily absorbed and utilized. However, for countries with large populations to begin with and little usable land (China), the impact of the transition can be severe.
Migration	The movement of populations from one society or country to another, or from rural to urban areas (the *rural–urban transition*). This movement may be the result of a desire to escape unfavorable circumstances, or a desire to find more favorable circumstances.	California's population has increased dramatically since the turn of the century primarily because of in-migration. People have left other states to seek a better climate and more rewarding jobs in both agriculture and industry. In contrast, Puerto Rico and Ireland have lost population, sometimes the most productive people, because of migration to American urban centers.
Relative Deprivation	A theory that argues that deviance and conflict will arise when people *perceive* themselves to be unjustly deprived, not when they are actually deprived but unaware of it.	Both the civil rights and the women's movements arose after American blacks and women had already made significant gains from their formally deprived statuses. Only after some gains were blacks and women able to perceive of their blocked opportunities and the possibilities for alternative actions and improvements.

	Definition	Example
Grievance-Tolerance Level	A theory which argues that people are willing to tolerate frustrations until they reach a specific and measurable level, after which they will engage in some form of conflict in order to resolve the frustration.	A tyrannical drill instructor in Army basic training may personally abuse and intimidate a new recruit with impunity, until, one day, he defames the recruit's mother and suddenly finds himself on the ground looking up. The recruit's grievance-tolerance level has been reached.
Differential Association	A theory which argues that deviant behavior is the product of normal *socialization* processes, carried out within contexts that encourage deviance rather than conformity.	The young child whose parents belong to a drug- or alcohol-using contraculture is likely to consider this behavior natural and conforming, rather than unacceptable and deviant.
Discretion	Since the processes of deviance and conflict are basic to and sometimes desirable (functional) in all societies, authorities must often overlook or permit acts which might otherwise be punished. The difficulty is that this necessary use of discretion may encourage further deviance and weaken prevailing norms for conformity.	Teachers will sometimes permit young boys to fight in the back of the schoolyard in order to "get it out of their system." Police on a skid row cannot possibly arrest all drunks, so they merely assure that these people "sleep it off" in a safe place. Judges and juries sometimes refuse to charge individuals with criminal offenses when the acts are deemed unintentional or were committed by people not considered to be typically criminal.

14. Methods of Controlling Social Processes

	Definition	Example
Internalization of Norms	The most effective method for controlling deviance or conflict is the process whereby individuals accept norms and values so completely that they become a part of their own self-conceptions—an internal behavioral control mechanism.	Young children are taught that it is bad to lie, steal, or cheat. Later temptations provoke inner feelings of shame, guilt, or anxiety that are usually strong enough to deter the deviant act, even if they are above.

	Definition	Example
Informal Control	Approval (of desired behavior) or disapproval (of unacceptable behavior) from members of one's primary group (family, peers, work group) either reinforces or discourages behavior.	A member of a delinquent gang who proudly announces that he received an "A" on a math quiz is brought "back into line" by frowns, sarcasm, or prolonged silence.
Formal Control	In *Gesellschaft* societies, where self and informal controls are less effective, formal systems for controlling deviance, change, and conflict develop.	For several decades, the Indian government has provided their population with birth control information in the hopes of persuading citizens to voluntarily limit the size of their families. This effort has met with limited success, because of competing norms and values (e.g., large familes are financially rewarding to peasants). In 1976, the government passed legislation that permits individual Indian states to fine parents who do not have themselves sterilized after having had two children.
Conflict Management (as compared to Conflict Control)	Theorists who view conflict as a *functional* social process believe it should be managed, that is, redirected into planned and contained patterns of interaction. Theorists who view conflict as *dysfunctional* believe that it should be controlled, that is, prohibited or eliminated.	Compulsory arbitration procedures in labor–management negotiations is an example of the application of conflict-management theory. The physical separation of conflicting ethnic groups into isolated camps or ghettos is an example of the application of conflict-control theory.
Co-optation	A method of social control that eliminates conflict and deviance by absorbing threatening groups and individuals into approved forms of behavior.	Many radical, conflict-oriented deprived groups (anti–Vietnam War, Gay Liberation, women's rights, civil rights) were incorporated into the presidential campaigns of Eugene McCarthy in 1968 and George McGovern in 1972, thereby lessening the likelihood of violent demonstrations as a means of obtaining their goals. Some radicals, like Tom Hayden in California in 1976, later ran for formal political offices.

	Definition	Example
Bargaining and Compromise	A method of social control which is based upon the assumption that conflict is dysfunctional and that competition and cooperation must be encouraged.	Relationships between the Soviet Union and the United States are based upon bargaining and compromise. Both countries continue to compete with one another in a military arms race. This is partly a result of an attempt to build up sufficient military resources (nuclear weapons, manned bombers, overseas bases, etc.) in order to be able to bargain—if one side gives up so many weapons, will the other side compromise and reciprocate by giving up so many weapons?
Nonviolent Action	A method of social control which is based upon the assumption that conflict is functional but violence is dysfunctional. Nonviolent action eschews the use of force and, instead, is based upon the withdrawal of obedience from authorities—that is the *delegitimation* of authority, thereby making it difficult for authorities to govern.	During World War II, Norwegian athletes refused to participate in sports events planned by occupying Nazi authorities as a way of building commitment and allegiance to the new regime. The Nazis found it necessary to focus upon these Norwegian civilian "reprisals" at a time when their attentions should have been directed toward the front line action in Europe and Russia.

Glossary

Note: This listing contains the more important concepts and terms used throughout this book. Terms which are more extensively defined and illustrated in the end-of-part *Key Concept Reviews* have page number references in parentheses. Additional page references for these and for the other items listed can be obtained by consulting the *Index*.

Aberrant Behavior Robert Merton's concept of behavior by a person who knows and accepts the norms of society but seeks to violate them to his or her advantage. The behavior, therefore, is considered detrimental to society.

Accommodation The process whereby interacting individuals or groups adapt to one another, retaining something of their original identity while changing to meet new demands. *See also* competition *and* conflict.

Acculturation (164) A process whereby interacting individuals or groups from different cultures each adapt elements of the other's culture. *See also* competition *and* conflict.

Achieved Position *or* Role The position or role an individual attains through personal effort and accomplishment. *See also* status.

Acting Crowd (393) A crowd in which interaction leads to collective behavior which is aimed at some target or specific goal (person, object, etc.)

Aggregate A category of individuals who share some common characteristic but who do not interact or share a social structure or culture.

Aggression *See* balance between aggression and fear *or* violence.

Alienation A condition in which individuals feel estranged from their social and cultural context and, therefore, cannot relate to others in that context.

Altruistic Suicide Emile Durkheim's concept of ritualistic, ceremonial, or sacrificial suicide, which results when people take their own lives for the sake of others because of strong ties and bonds.

Anomic Suicide Emile Durkheim's concept of suicide which results when people feel confused and ambiguous about the socially approved norms for behavior and, therefore, take their own lives as a way out of a seemingly intractable situation.

Anomie A situation of cultural confusion and ambiguity because of a lack of clear-cut rules and norms for behavior. *See also* normlessness.

Artifacts The material objects, including tools and the things made by tools, in a people's culture.

Ascribed Position *or* Role The position or role an individual attains through assignment by others, usually at birth and without relationship to personal effort and accomplishment. *See also* status.

Assimilation (164) The process whereby one group, usually a minority, gradually has its culture replaced by or merged with the culture of another, usually dominant, group.

Association (394) Special-purpose groups organized to pursue some common interest of the members and containing elements of both spontaneous and structured forms of behavior.

Atomistic Family Carle Zimmerman's concept of how cyclical change eventually causes domestic family forms to become small, isolated family units consisting of fragmented and highly individualistic members. *See also* trustee family.

Attitude A mental or psychological aspect of culture which is a product of social learning and consists of a predisposition by individuals or groups to accept or reject certain objects, people, economic systems, religions, and so on. *See also* prejudice.

Authority (507) Power based upon the willingness of people to follow the orders of leaders. Authority depends upon the consent of the governed and upon the legitimacy of leaders, rather than upon the use of force or coercion by leaders. *See also* charismatic authority, traditional authority, *and* legal-bureaucratic authority.

Autistic Children Children who suffer from a form of schizophrenia that results from extreme social isolation and emotional deprivation. Autistic behavior is the expression of an inadequately developed social self. *See also* feral behavior.

Balance between Aggression and Fear One of the environmental factors that controls conflict in animal species. Territorial owners are aggressive and dominant, whereas territorial invaders are submissive and retreat in the face of challenge. In contrast to animals, human cultures usually define fear as undesirable and cowardly and, therefore, uncontrollable and destructive conflict often results. *See also* language of threat *and* turf.

Bargaining and Compromise (661) A method of social control that is based upon the assumption that extreme conflict is dysfunctional and that competition and cooperation can be obtained by getting interacting groups to negotiate with each other and reach compromises on disagreements. Bargaining and compromise is an attempt to manage conflict by redirecting it into more rational and routine channels.

Birth Rate (657) A measure of fertility calculated as the number of persons born in a given population per year per 1000 people.

Black Power The belief of black Americans that they can attain full social, economic, and political integration by identity with one another and through their own efforts without the support of whites.

Blocked-opportunity Theory A theory that rejects "riff-raff" or relative deprivation explanations of elementary collective behavior and argues that environmental conditions cause riots when people feel that discrimination has led to their loss of opportunity for mobility and self improvement.

Boundary-maintenance Function The work done by parts of the social system which help maintain the normative boundaries of that system. For example, the act of murder can perform boundary-maintenance functions by causing people to restate important norms and values, such as prohibitions against violence and the sacred nature of life.

Bureaucracy (396) A highly rational form of group structure, characterized by a clear-cut division of labor among members and a hierarchical chain of command that coordinates specialized activities according to precise and formal rules. Bureaucracy is designed to maximize efficiency and effectiveness in complex organizations requiring extensive coordination of different activities.

Calling, Attenuation of Professionals are theoretically motivated by personal feelings of altruism and by a call to serve the special needs of clients and to support the major values of the culture. When commitment to a career in the form of concern for higher income, more clients, and the like begins to weaken this altruism, the sense of a calling becomes attenuated.

Capitalism *See* spirit of capitalism.

Career Mobility Social mobility and movement during one's career, which can be either vertical or horizontal. *See also other types of mobility* (horizontal *and* vertical).

Caste System (394) A system of stratification where status is allocated on the basis of ascribed criteria such as family origin, race, or religious affiliation. An absence of social mobility and interaction between castes limits the life-styles and life chances of individuals. *See also* closed society.

Change: Social *and* Cultural (656) Refers to the fact that human society is constantly in a state of flux. Social change refers to alterations in roles, relationships, and social structure. Cultural change refers to alterations in norms and values. *See also* cyclical change *and* evolutionary change.

Change Agent People and groups in society who possess special attitudes and values that make them the most likely creators of new technological and social innovations, the most willing adopters and users of innovations, and the most likely to influence others to use innovations.

Charismatic Authority (507) Nonrational and potentially revolutionary authority based upon the personal and extraordinary qualities of the leader. Charismatic leaders possess power as a result of special skills or sacred attributes associated only with them.

Church: Congregationalist and Episcopal Types (506) A formal religious organization with relatively fixed doctrine and ritual and trained leadership. Congregationalist church structures stress local autonomy and are often sectlike in character. Episcopal church structures are highly bureaucratized and international in scope. *See also* sect.

Class System (394) A system of stratification where status is allocated on the basis of achieved criteria such as amount of income and educational training. Social mobility and interaction between classes is relatively free and unrestricted. *See also* open society.

Closed Society (392) A social system in which there is little or no opportunity for an individual to move from one status level to another and the status groupings are castelike. *See also* caste system.

Coercion Power based upon the threat or use of force or violence. People feel compelled to follow the orders of leaders because they are afraid of what will happen if they do not conform.

Cohesion *See* social cohesion and solidarity.

Collectivity (392) A type of human group that is transient, temporary, spontaneous, and has little formal social structure. Some collectivities can develop into longer-lasting social movements.

Community (395) A geographical concentration of people who interact and develop a common social, economic, and political bond and activities. *See also Gemeinschaft and Gesellschaft.*

Competition (656) A basic social process whereby interacting individuals or groups agree to abide by certain rules in pursuit of commonly desired goals.

Compromise *See* bargaining and compromise.

Concentric Zone Theory Ernest Burgess' theory that ecological processes of cooperation and conflict, particularly over the use of land, cause communities to develop as a series of concentric circles. Each successive area contains different types of residents and activities. *See also* nuclei theory.

Conflict (655) A basic social process whereby interacting individuals or groups attempt to control, dominate, or conquer each other because they disagree on the means for attaining various goals.

Conflict Control (660) The assumption that conflict in any form is dysfunctional and, therefore, that it should be controlled by prohibiting or eliminating it from society. *See also* co-optation *and* repression.

Conflict Management (660) The assumption that conflict can be functional, as long as it is not violent or aggressive, and, therefore, it should be managed by redirecting it into planned and contained patterns of interaction. *See also* bargaining and compromise *and* nonviolent action.

Conflict Theory (77) Views society as a collection of self-interest groups, each one vying for power with all others. Therefore, conflict is seen as a natural and unavoidable result of human nature and the human quest for power over others.

Conformist Robert Merton's concept of an individual who accepts both the goals (ends) of society and the approved ways (means) of attaining them.

Conformity To act in accordance with socially approved norms while pursuing socially approved goals.

Conjugal Family A family unit where members are related by marriage. *See also* nuclear family.

Consanguine Family (505) A family unit where all members are related by descent from a common ancestor or by "blood." *See also* familism.

Contraculture Ruth Cavan's concept that extreme underconforming or extreme overconforming behavior represents detachment from and opposition to the prevailing culture. As a result, completely different norms, statuses, roles, and methods of social control arise in contracultures.

Control *See* social control.

Cooperation (655) A basic social process whereby interacting individuals or groups join together to achieve a common goal and share the rewards of their joint activity.

Co-optation (660) A method for controlling conflict or deviance by absorbing threatening individuals and groups into formal social organizations and institutions and getting them to pursue their goals in approved ways.

Craze (393) A form of collective behavior that appears and disappears suddenly and in which people feel threatened and entrapped and seek escape in highly individualistic and obsessive ways. Collective emotion leads to nonrational, often counterproductive, behavior.

Crime *See specific types* (traditional, victimless, *and* white-collar).

Crisis of Authority A weakening of traditional and bureaucratic bases of authority so that citizens are unwilling to grant unquestioned power to leaders. Leadership, therefore, tends to rely more upon coercion and repression. *See also* delegitimation.

Crowd (393) A loosely organized collectivity that forms around some mutually interesting object or event, is relatively short-lived, and within which people interact with one another in spontaneous and emotional ways.

Cultural Diffusion (657) The process by which elements of culture, usually norms and values, spread from one subgroup or society to another.

Cultural Drift Cultural changes which arise because innovators, usually spontaneous leaders, emerge to meet the special needs of a society at particular moments in history. Therefore, societies in the same region and at the same general level of social development may have markedly different norms and values.

Cultural Lag The situation in which the development or evolution of one cultural or social element of society (usually a role, relationship, norm, or value) lags behind the development of another cultural element (usually technology). Material inventions and social innovations often occur before other changes in the social system.

Culture (162) For sociologists, the mentifacts (norms, values, attitudes, beliefs) and the artifacts (material objects, tools, technology) of a society which take on symbolic importance as individuals and groups interact.

Culture of Civility An intellectual climate within a community that accepts deviant behavior for the rich mosaic it creates and rejects the popular stereotype of deviance as dysfunctional, evil, and dangerous.

Culture of Violence Norms and values that honor, reward, and glorify aggression and violence.

Cyclical Change (656) Change that follows repeating cycles through time, sometimes upward (advancement or better) and sometimes downward (decline or worse).

Data Collection (75) Part of the third basic step in the scientific method that includes the methods and techniques used to collect information related to the hypotheses and study design. *See also particular types of research methods (for example:* observation, public opinion polling, *and* questionnaire).

Death Rate (658) A measure of mortality calculated as the number of individuals who die in a given population per year per 1000 people.

Delegitimation (661) The process whereby the authority of leaders is weakened or erodes. People become unwilling to grant unquestioned power to leaders and refuse to obey orders. *See also* crisis of authority *and* nonviolent action.

Delinquency (656) Criminal acts committed by persons under a legal age limit and certain other deviant acts not considered criminal when committed by adults (e.g., being consistently late in the payment of debts).

Democracy (394) A political system in which power and authority are delegated by citizens to officials who are held accountable and may be removed from office. Sociologists also define a democracy as a social and political structure characterized by many competing associations that represent the members' special interests and mediate between governmental leaders and individual group members. *See also* mediating leader *and* pluralistic society.

Demographic Transition (658) A process of changes in population growth and size associated with modernization and industrialization. In early stages, the population grows rapidly because birth rates remain high while death rates fall rapidly. In later stages, the birth rate also declines and growth levels off.

Demography The scientific study of the size, distribution, and composition of populations and the factors that cause these characteristics to change over time.

Density The average number of people in a population for a specific area, usually one square mile. Louis Wirth theorized that low density encourages *Gemeinschaft* relationships, whereas high density encourages *Gesellschaft* relationships.

Desocialization A process whereby a person's learned skills, knowledge, and values are unconsciously (as in old age) or deliberately (as in military basic training) weakened, threatened, or questioned. *See also* resocialization *and* socialization.

Determinism: Social *and* Cultural The results of theories or paradigms which argue that certain social or cultural factors determine or explain most or all of human behavior.

Deviance (657) Individual or group behavior that varies from the accepted and approved norms (means) and goals (ends) of a society. *See also* means-ends relationship.

Deviance Theory (77) Views a certain amount of deviation from accepted norms and values as natural and unavoidable. Some social scientists using deviance theory also assume that deviation can be a desirable or functional adaptation to special problems or crises.

Deviant-case Analysis A research method that involves intensive analysis of one form of human group or behavior which differs from the theoretically hypothesized or traditionally assumed form for that group or behavior.

Differential Association (659) Edwin Sutherland's theory that deviant behavior, particularly delinquency, is the result of a normal socialization process, where individuals associate and relate in a context that encourages deviance rather than conformity.

Differential Rate of Socialization Occurs when the socialization process differs in intensity and speed from one social experience to another (when it is intense and fast for the young, but limited and slow for the aged).

Differential Socialization Occurs when socialization processes and experiences vary from one stage of an individual's life to another.

Diffusion *See* cultural diffusion.

Discretion (659) The tendency for authorities and officials to overlook, permit, or allow wide latitude for some forms of deviant behavior, because rigid and strict application of formal sanctions is unrealistic or impossible.

Discrimination Denying individuals or groups equal access to the goods, services, and privileges of a society, on the basis of grounds that are considered unfair or irrelevant to the social situation. *See also* minority group.

Disorganization: Social *and* Cultural A situation where prevailing social relationships, norms, or values weaken or break down, because people reject them.

Disorganization Theory (77) Views social problems as being the result of an undesirable or abnormal breakdown in the existing social order, which occurs when prevailing relationships, norms, and values are weakened.

Division of Labor The separation of individuals, roles, or groups on the basis of the functional work done in an organization or society, and the relationship of these separate entities to one another.

Domestic Family Carle Zimmerman's concept of how cyclical change causes extended trustee family forms to become tightly knit primary groups, focused around the daily life-sustaining activities of the household. *See also* atomistic family.

Downward Mobility Vertical movement by individuals or groups from a higher to a lower status.

Drift *See* cultural drift.

Dysfunction The results of a relationship or process that undermines or disrupts the stability, cohesion, or solidarity of a group, society, or culture. *See also* function *and* functionalism.

Educational Elitism (505) The tendency for schools to become less interested in meeting the different needs of many citizens and to focus upon meeting the special needs of only some citizens, usually the more privileged and higher status.

Ecological Areas (395) An area within which sociologists study how people and their activities and relationships naturally adapt to the land, to the natural and physical resources, and to one another.

Ecology In sociology, the study of the way in which humans distribute themselves in space and naturally relate to their physical environment and to one another.

Egoistic Suicide Emile Durkheim's concept of suicide which results when people feel lonely or isolated because of an absence of strong ties or bonds to others and, therefore, feel they have the right to take their own lives to escape a seemingly intractable problem.

Elitist Theories Political theories that assume there are ruling cliques or groups, in every community and society, which possess most power and make the key decisions.

Emotional Functions, Needs, *and* Tasks (504) All societies and groups possess two basic emotional needs: socialization and integration of members. Particular types of relationships, groups, norms, and leaders arise to meet these needs. *See also* morale-building institutions.

Empathy The ability to project oneself into another's place and role and imagine what the other person feels and experiences. The ability of humans to empathize makes the social and cultural order possible. *See also* game stage, role playing, *and* role taking.

Empirical Analysis and Investigation Scientific analysis and investigation based upon the accumulation of first-hand knowledge by personal or participant observation, experimentation, interviews and questionnaires, and so on.

Emergent-norm Theory A theory that humans have the capacity to reason, even in emotionally laden and irrational contexts. Their behavior is guided by norms, and as they interact new norms are produced in response to new needs. *See also* gaming approach.

Environmentalist View A theory of education that views the teacher as the central source of information and knowledge and believes that the classroom should be highly structured.

Estate System A system of stratification where status is allocated on the basis of one's role or position in terms of their relationship to the land. Some social mobility and interaction between estates is possible, though it is restricted.

Ethnic Group A group of people who see themselves or are seen by others as being related by ascribed criteria such as race, common language, common ancestry, and so on. *See also* ascribed position.

Ethnocentrism (164) The tendency to see the customs and values of one's own culture as superior to all others and the only right and correct way of doing things. *See also* in-group.

Evolutionary Change (656) Change that follows a straight line through time from simple to more complex social forms, from undeveloped to developed social structures, from worse to better social and cultural conditions, and so on.

Exceptionalistic View Sees social problems as occurring in particular categories of people as a result of special social and cultural characteristics they share. *See also* personal-troubles approach.

Ex Post Facto Assumption *or* Explanation An assumption or explanation which is made after an event takes place and is, therefore, usually a guess about the real causes of the event.

Expressive Associations *and* Leaders Associations or leaders that meet people's emotional needs, including the need to be related, the need to be creative and spontaneous, and so on.

Expressive Crowd (393) Crowds where interaction leads to collective behavior that revolves around emotional expression and release.

Exogamy Marrying outside of a specific community or group.

Extended Family (505) A family unit, generally large in size, consisting of two or more nuclear families, related by blood and living together.

Fad *and* Fashion (393) Forms of collective behavior that are less unusual, more widespread, less individualistic, and less subject to change than a craze. Fads tend to be more extreme and transitory than fashions.

Familism (505) Usually the characteristics of consanguine families, which include filial piety, the importance of having many sons, ancestor worship, and common family ownership of property.

Family (504) The morale-building institution primarily responsible for procreation, integration, and socialization.

Family of Orientation (504) The family into which one is born.

Family of Procreation (504) The family into which one moves and is created when marriage takes place.

Fashion *See* fad.

Feral Behavior Animal-like behavior that in young children was originally thought to be the result of their having been raised by animals, but is now understood to be the result of nonhuman behavior by parents toward their children. *See also* autistic children.

Fertility (657) The rate at which individuals are added to the population. *See also* birth rate.

Folkways (163) Informal norms governing behavior that is not considered vital to a society's survival, such as etiquette, fashion, and proper language usage. Violations of folkways carry less severe sanctions than violations of mores.

Force (507) Power in the form of involuntary coercion. *See also* authority.

Formal Social Controls (660) Formal methods and systems for controlling deviance, change, and conflict, including the use of force, laws, and so on.

Formal Voluntary Organizations (FVOs) Voluntary associations and organizations that possess formal (bureaucratic) characteristics. *See also* voluntary associations.

Function The work done by any part of a social system (relationship, group, norm, etc.) to maintain itself and to contribute to the stability, cohesion, and solidarity of the overall social system.

Functionalism (76) The view of society as an organic system which is composed of interrelated parts, each of which functions to maintain itself and to satisfy basic needs that are vital to the stability of the overall system.

Frustration Perspective The assumption that a high level of frustration can lead to individual or collective conflict and violence, depending upon the presence or absence of the following conditions: strong and legitimate authorities, rewards for loyalty and cooperation, success of previous uses of conflict or violence, and degree of organization and commitment among those who feel frustrated.

Gaming Approach A method of study that involves experimental laboratory situations, imitating real-life contexts (warfare, economic competition, racial conflict, etc.). This context allows the scientist to manipulate and control the variables that might influence the behavior of the subjects. Also a perspective of elementary collective behavior that views crowd interaction as following relatively normal decision-making processes. *See also* emergent-norm theory.

Game Stage George Mead's concept of the final stage in the development of a child's social self, when the child begins to empathize with others, to imagine what others feel, and to play at serious social roles. In the game stage, the child begins to act as a subjective "I". *See also* empathy, "I" and "me," *and* role taking.

Gemeinschaft (397) A community characterized by a high degree of stability and social cohesion, shared identity and commitment, broad consensus on norms and values, and primary-like interaction that extends beyond the family and peer group. *Gemeinschaft* is often associated with small, rural communities having relatively homogeneous populations.

Generalized Other (160) George Mead's concept of a person's general impression of what others, as larger groupings or communities, expect of him or her, developed by interacting with others and internalizing their attitudes and expectations.

Generalizing Perspective The orientation of the sociologist that seeks to explain human behavior as a result of variables which are universal and patterns of interaction which will occur again and again, rather than as a consequence of unique incidents and events.

Geographical Mobility Movement of individuals or groups from one region or area to another. *See also* internal versus international migration.

Gesellschaft (397) A community characterized by the rational pursuit of self-interest, little social cohesion, and impersonal secondary relationships. *Gesellschaft* is often associated with large, urban communities having relatively heterogeneous populations.

Ghetto (395) An ecological area where people of similar characteristics tend to concentrate, find a sense of belonging and *Gemeinschaft*, and provide their own public services and activities.

Grievance-tolerance Level (659) The concept of John Spiegel and Florence Kluckholn that people will tolerate frustrations until they reach a specific, measurable level, at which point conflict and violent behavior will result. *See also* frustration perspective.

Group (390) Two or more people who identify in some way and who take each other into account in their behavior. *See also* interaction.

Heterogeneity As applied to populations, having dissimilar and various kinds of groups, relationships, norms, and so on. Louis Wirth theorized that heterogeneity encourages *Gesellschaft* communities, whereas homogeneity encourages *Gemeinschaft* communities.

Homogeneous Having the same kind and nature of characteristics and attributes.

Horizontal Mobility Movement by individuals or groups from one position to another in the social system without a change in status.

Hypothesis (75) A proposition, or unproven statement, about how two or more variables are related to one another, usually in the form of an "if–then" statement. Hypotheses are educated guesses or hunches and their formulation constitutes the second basic step in the scientific method.

"I" and "me" (159) George Mead's concept of the two complementary and necessary aspects of the social self. The "I" represents the spontaneous, unrestrained, creative, and nonconformist aspect. The "me" represents the cautious, predictable, socially conforming aspect. *See also* game stage *and* play stage.

Idealistic Culture Pitirim Sorokin's concept of how cyclical change causes ideational cultures to become cultures where important ideas and values are related to mundane daily needs and problems. *See also* sensate culture.

Ideal Type A concept, developed by Max Weber, that exaggerates and oversimplifies observed characteristics in the real world in order to make comparative scientific analysis easier. The term "ideal" implies a perfect type, not a better or more desirable type.

Ideational Aspects of Culture — *See* mentifacts.

Ideational Culture — Pitirim Sorokin's concept of how cyclical change begins with cultures that stress ascetic and spiritual pursuits. *See also* idealistic culture.

Imitation Stage — George Mead's concept of the earliest stage in the development of a child's social self, when the child merely copies the isolated actions of others and does not have a concept of social roles. *See also* role playing *and* role taking.

Informal Social Controls — (660) Informal methods and systems for controlling deviance, change, and conflict, such as gestures of approval for desired behavior or disapproval for unacceptable behavior, usually within primary or peer group contexts.

In-group — Groups to which individuals feel they belong and within which they share an identity with others. In-group members develop a sense of "we." *See also* out-group.

Inner-directed Personality — David Riesman's concept of individuals who internalize norms and values and, therefore, act free from social pressures or constraints. *See also* other-directed personality, Protestant (Puritan) ethic, *and* tradition-directed personality.

Innovation *and* Invention — Creation of a technology, social form, or idea not previously a part of a culture, or the borrowing of a new trait from another culture. *See also* change agent *and* cultural diffusion.

Innovator — Robert Merton's concept of an individual who accepts the goals (ends) of society but uses disapproved ways (means) to attain them. *See also* means–ends relationship.

Instinct — A patterned behavioral response lodged within the neuromuscular structure of the organism and transmitted by heredity. Instincts explain the acts of animals, whereas social and cultural learning explain the acts of humans.

Institution — (396) A highly structured, long-lived, all-inclusive, and multipurposed human group.

Institutionalization — (396) The process whereby groups take on the characteristics of an institution.

Instrumental Associations *and* Leaders — Associations and leaders that meet people's task needs. *See also* task functions.

Integration — The social and cultural merger of individuals and groups so that they become interdependent, interrelated, and develop a sense of identity as a unified whole.

Interaction, Social — A relationship between two or more individuals who take one another into account and, therefore, become to some extent interdependent. *See also* group.

Interactionist View A theory of education that views the informal processes of interaction between students and teacher as most important and believes that the classroom should be informally structured to encourage creativity and flexibility.

Intergenerational Mobility Movement by members of a family from one generation to another into either higher or lower statuses.

Intermediary Associations Associations that mediate between the individual citizen and formal power centers in pluralist political systems. *See also* mediating group.

Internalization of Norms (659) The most effective method for controlling deviance or conflict whereby individuals accept the norms and values of society so completely that they become a part of their own self-perceptions.

Internal versus International Migration (658) Geographic movement of populations from one region within a country to another (usually from rural to urban areas) in contrast to movement from one country to another. One of the factors that influences demographic transition. *See also* rural–urban transition.

Interview Schedule A formal structured list of questions to be used in conducting interviews.

Invention *See* innovation.

Kurwille *See* rational will.

Labeling Theory (77) Views human behavior as being the result of social labels or names, usually applied to the less fortunate or to those considered to be deviant by the powerful and those who conform. Individuals internalize these externally applied labels into their own self-concepts and modify their behavior to fit the assigned status and role.

Lag *See* cultural lag.

Language of Threat One of the environmental factors that controls conflict in animal species. By aggressive actions, one animal communicates a position of dominance (territorial owner) to another; the other animal communicates a position of submission (territorial invader) by passive actions of compliance or surrender. Humans also use a language of threat, but cultural factors transform its nature in human societies. *See also* balance between aggression and fear *and* turf.

Latent versus Manifest Functions When the work done by any part of the social system is unintended or unanticipated, it is called latent. When the work done is deliberate or planned, it is called manifest. *See also* function.

Laws (163) Deliberately planned and formal norms enforced by specially authorized, secondary groups (courts, police, etc.). Misdemeanors represent violations of less important laws, whereas felonies represent violations of the important laws.

Legal-bureaucratic or Legal-rational Authority (507) Routine authority based upon rational rules and regulations. Legal-bureaucratic leaders possess power as a result of the formal roles they occupy and the laws that apply to those roles.

Legitimacy The power of ruling individuals and groups is valid in the eyes of both the rulers and the ruled and, therefore, people are willing to grant unquestioned power to leaders. *See also* authority.

Legitimation The process whereby power becomes legitimate, usually by being transformed into authority. *See also specific types of authority* (charismatic, legal-bureaucratic, *and* traditional).

Life Chances As a result of people's social status, the chances that they will have good or bad physical health, good or bad mental health, a short or long life, a happy or a broken marriage, and so on.

Life-styles As a result of people's social status, the kinds of goods and services they consume, how these are consumed, and the different kinds of esteem and honor they receive.

Line and Staff In formal organizations, line personnel occupy the jobs that contribute to the major production activities of the organization, whereas staff personnel serve in support positions.

Line-staff Conflict Conflict develops because workers in the line are oldtimers who have had to move up in the organization on the basis of experience, whereas staff are younger employees who have been hired for high-status positions because of formal training and expert knowledge.

Looking-glass Self (160) Charles Cooley's concept of the conscious self-image people form of themselves as a result of how they perceive others are reacting to them in social situations. Similar to the physical self-conception one develops by looking in a mirror.

Magic A system of beliefs and practices that serve the function of social control by allowing people to develop a relationship with mysterious, supernatural forces and beings, otherwise beyond understanding or control. *See also* religion *and* science.

Marginal Individuals *and* Groups Individuals and groups characterized by conflicting and different statuses (low income but high education, low education but high prestige, etc.).

Marginality Feelings of powerlessness and insecurity stemming from conflicting statuses and often the result of individuals who accept social goals but lack the means to attain them.

Mark of Sovereignty The use of the military to conduct civilian ceremonies for purposes of strengthening nationalistic feelings or popularizing specific rulers.

Mass Society Large, heterogeneous populations within which individuals experience feelings of anomie and anxiety.

Mass Theories Political theories that assume conditions of alienation, anomie, and apathy prevail in most modern communities and societies, and these conditions determine the nature of power and the quality of political life.

Maturationist View A theory of education that views the natural maturation processes of students as most important and believes that the classroom should be a heterogeneous environment containing opportunities for all kinds of individual and group experiences.

"me" *See* "I" and "me."

Means-ends Relationship Robert Merton's concept that different types of nonconforming behavior can be identified according to whether or not individuals accept or reject the goals (ends) of society and the ways (means) for attaining these goals. *See also* conformist, innovator, rebel, retreatist, *and* ritualist.

Mediating Leader *and* Group Leaders and groups which stand between individual citizens and the formal power centers in pluralist political systems. Mediating groups encourage democratic processes by becoming sources of new opinions, channels of communication, and contexts that develop the skills of leadership. Mediating leaders hold overlapping memberships in many associations and, therefore, encourage dialogue between competing interest groups. *See also* intermediary associations.

Medium of Personality Paul Bohannan's concept that at birth a child leaves a biophysical relationship for a social relationship within which a personality emerges as a result of the cultural context.

Mentifacts The nonmaterial, ideational aspects of culture, including ideas, beliefs, knowledge, sentiments, attitudes, and values.

Migration *See* internal versus international migration.

Military (508) The power institution that possesses a monopoly of force and violence in a society in order to provide a deterrence or defense from external aggression, to conduct offensive warfare, or to maintain civil law and order within the society.

Military, Civilian versus Traditional Civilian military forces resemble civilian groups in ideology and structure, whereas traditional military forces differ from civilian groups.

Military: Convergent, Divergent, and Mixed (508) Military forces can vary in ideology and organization. Convergent forces resemble civilian organizations and utilize authority based upon managerial philosophies stressing more democratic procedures and a command structure based upon bureaucratic principles. Divergent forces utilize authority based upon domination and obedience and a command structure that makes castelike distinctions between various levels. Mixed forces contain characteristics of both convergent and divergent forces.

Minority Group A group of people who have low status in the stratification system and who, as a result, are subject to unequal treatment in the form of segregation and discrimination.

Mixed Systems A stratification system that contains characteristics of both an open and a closed society.

Mob A type of expressive crowd that is difficult to control and may engage in destructive forms of collective behavior.

Mobility, Geographical *See* migration.

Mobility, Social (391) The manner in which individuals and groups can move within different types of status systems. *See also particular types of mobility* (career, horizontal, *and* vertical).

Modernization The process whereby traditional societies become urbanized through changes in technology, agriculture, industry, and population distribution and composition.

Morale-building Institutions Major institutions that essentially perform emotional functions by meeting socialization and integration needs in society.

Morale Leaders Those leaders who carry out the expressive purposes of an organization. *See also* expressive leaders.

Mores (163) Informal norms governing behavior that is considered a serious threat to a society's survival, such as incest or cannibalism. Violations of mores carry very severe sanctions, more severe than violations of folkways.

Mortality (658) The number of individuals in a given population who die every year. *See also* death rate.

Multinational Corporation (507) A large-scale, international power institution that develops an ideology and identity independent from the state, utilizes centralized authority, and derives power by monopolizing knowledge about the production, marketing, and financing of some product or service.

Myth A half-truth belief about some social phenomenon that becomes stereotyped and exaggerated and, therefore, contains only a partial relationship to reality. The "myth-breaking" role of sociology is one of the discipline's most important functions.

Nation-building Roles The use of the military to construct roads, operate factories, staff government agencies, run schools, dispense medical treatment, and perform other nonmilitary, essentially civilian tasks.

Nation-states *See* states.

Natural Systems Model A perspective that focuses upon the emotional, spontaneous, and informal patterns of interaction within formal organizations. This model assumes that the natural social system that evolves in response to the rational structure is most important. *See also* underlife.

Natural Will (*Wesenwille*) Ferdinand Tönnies' concept of the reason for the human ability to engage in emotional and impulsive behavior.

Neo-Malthusians Those who believe that there are limits to unrestricted and unlimited growth and change in the world, because the human potential for innovation and invention and the world's resources are limited.

Nonconforming Behavior Robert Merton's concept of behavior by a person who knows the norms of society but considers them unjust and violates them openly in order to bring about needed change. *See also* means–ends relationship.

Nonsymbolic Interaction Interaction involving instinctive or reflexive gestures that do not have cultural meanings to the initiator or to others. *See also* sign *and* symbol.

Nonviolent Action (661) A form of conflict management that is based upon the assumption that conflict is functional but violence is dysfunctional. Nonviolent action involves the peaceful withdrawal of obedience and legitimacy from authorities; that is, the refusal to obey. *See also* delegitimation.

Nonviolent Protest and Persuasion, Noncooperation, *and* Intervention The three basic tactics of nonviolent action. Acts of protest and persuasion attempt to convert an opponent to one's position; noncooperation, to compel an opponent to accommodate to one's demands; intervention, to coerce the desired responses from an opponent. *See also* nonviolent action.

Nonzero-sum Games The assumption that all players in a game will lose something and all players will win something and, therefore, it is to the interest and advantage of all players to cooperate and compromise so that everyone's winnings can be maximized and everyone's losses can be minimized. *See also* zero-sum games.

Normative Conflict A situation where the purpose and value associated with some norms compete with or contradict the purpose and value associated with other norms. The cause of much social deviance, change, and conflict.

Normlessness A situation in which people are not sure of what they can or should do and not do. *See also* anomie.

Norms (163) Agreed-upon and expected rules and regulations that govern behavior, usually associated with specific social roles. A blueprint prescribing proper role behavior in specific situations. *See also* folkways, laws, *and* mores.

Norms, Complimentary The purposes and values of different norms which compliment or support one another and come together to form a cultural constellation trait. *See also* normative conflict.

Nuclear Family (505) Conjugal family units, usually very small and consisting of the married couple and their children living together.

Nuclear Group of Leaders Walter Goldschmidt's concept of those leaders who have strong ties to the local community and consider themselves to be "insiders."

Nuclei Theory The theory that ecological processes of cooperation and conflict, particularly over the use of land, causes communities to develop as nucleated units of various sizes and shapes. Each unit contains different types of residents and activities. *See also* concentric zone theory.

Objective Control Morris Janowitz's concept of a military force that fights and follows civilian orders because soldiers feel it is their profession and they believe that political involvement is incompatible with the professional role. *See also* subjective control.

Observation *See* participant observation *and* personal observation.

Occupational Mobility Social mobility and movement from one status to another as a result of changes in one's occupation. *See also* career mobility.

Oligarchy (397) The tendency in formal organizations for power to concentrate into the hands of a few leaders.

Oligarchy, Iron Law of Robert Michels' concept that organizational oligarchy is the inevitable result of leaders who acquire specialized skills and knowledge connected with their office and develop a personal identification with that office, and of grass-roots members who loose touch with their leaders and become apathetic about political involvement.

Open Society (392) A social system in which it is possible for an individual to move from one status level to another and the status groupings are classlike. *See also* class system.

Organizational Revolution Kenneth Boulding's concept of the increasing number and influence of associations at all levels of contemporary society.

Organization Men and Women William Whyte's concept of members of organizations who identify so thoroughly with their organizations that they constantly sell their associations as aspects of themselves, and vice versa. *See also* other-directed personality.

Other-directed Personality David Riesman's concept of individuals who do not possess internalized norms and, therefore, are sensitive to the approval or disapproval of others in specific social situations. *See also* inner-directed personality *and* organization men and women.

Out-group Groups to which individuals do not belong and with whom they do not share a sense of identity. People develop a sense of "they" toward out-groups. *See also* ethnocentrism *and* in-group.

Panic (392) A form of collective behavior in which people feel threatened and entrapped and seek escape in highly individualistic ways.

Paradigm A major view or model of the world employed by scientists. A kind of intellectual roadmap that tells scientists what to look for, how to look, and what might be found.

Participant Observation (75) A data-collection technique by which the researcher actually becomes a participating part of the group life being studied in order to gain first-hand knowledge that might not otherwise be observed.

Particularistic View *See* exceptionalistic view.

Particularizing Perspective An orientation that seeks to explain human behavior and events as a result of unique incidents and occurrences which will not happen again. The opposite of the generalizing perspective of the sociologist.

Peer Group A group, often primary-like, of people of similar ages and common interests.

Personal Observation (76) A data-collection technique by which the researcher observes behavior as inconspicuously as possible in order to avoid involvement that might bias the results.

Personal-troubles Approach C. Wright Mills' concept that social problems can be viewed as a result of personal troubles that occur within individuals because of unique and limited experiences. Troubles are private matters influenced by the character of the individual. Mills rejected this view as inadequate for sociological analysis. *See also* public-issues approach.

Play Stage George Mead's concept of the second stage in the development of the child's social self, when the child begins to conceive of itself as an object of other people's actions toward it and plays at various social roles. In the play stage, the child acts as an objective "me". *See also* role playing.

Pluralistic Society A society characterized by many competing special-purpose interest groups which give power to many individuals and modify the power of formal political leaders and organizations. *See also* democracy *and* mediating leader.

Pluralist Theories Political theories that assume power in communities and societies is determined by the interplay of competing interest groups and decisions are made by a process of consensus and compromise. *See also* democracy *and* veto group.

Population Either the inhabitants of a given area or territory, or a larger group of people or phenomenon from which a sample is drawn for the purposes of scientific study.

Positive Checks According to Thomas Malthus, the natural and nonconscious events (famine, war, disease) that act as direct and immediate checks on population growth by suddenly increasing the death rate.

Power (506) The ability to influence the actions and attitudes of others.

Power, Personal versus Social Personal power is the ability to control crucial aspects of one's own life (life chances and life-styles); whereas social power is the ability to control aspects of the lives of others.

Power Institutions Major institutions that essentially perform task functions by meeting production and distribution needs in society.

Powerlessness, Sense of A feeling that one can no longer control crucial aspects of their own life or influence others to make decisions favorable to one's own interests. Often leads to anomie, anxiety, and conflict.

Prejudice Irrational, unfavorable, and stereotyped attitudes about the behavior and beliefs of individuals or groups, based upon prejudgments.

Preventive Checks According to Thomas Malthus, the conscious acts (abortion, moral restraints on sexual intercourse) which check population growth by decreasing the birth rate.

Priestly Role (506) Religious leadership roles that comfort people in times of personal and collective crisis. *See also* prophetic role.

Primary Controls Primary groups and relationships that control individual and collective behavior at the most personal and intimate level of interaction. *See also* informal social controls.

Primary Groups *and* Relationships (390) Groups and relationships where individuals interact on an intimate, spontaneous, and total basis and develop strong feelings of mutual identification and cooperation.

Process *See* social processes and dynamics.

Profession (396) An occupation that combines an altruistic motive with expertise based upon formal training and is often licensed by the state. *See also* calling, attenuation of.

Professionalization The process whereby an occupation takes on the characteristics of a profession.

Professionals, Free Professionals who have occupational autonomy, free from irresponsible or unknowledgable control by nonexperts and laypeople. As professionals increasingly work within organizational contexts, they tend to lose some of their autonomy and to become subject to the control of bureaucratic leaders.

Prophetic Role (506) Religious leadership roles that challenge people to live up to the highest cultural values and ideals. *See also* priestly role.

Protestant (Puritan) Ethic Calvinistic and Puritan beliefs and norms which stress hard work, frugal living, the rational use of time, and a benevolent but reserved manner toward friends and family. Max Weber theorized that the Protestant ethic played a crucial role in the development of capitalism in Western Europe.

Public A collectivity consisting of a geographically scattered group of people sharing common interests and concerns.

Public-issues Approach C. Wright Mills' concept that social problems can be viewed as a result of inadequate institutional arrangements which cause the development of major social issues. Public issues transcend the personal problems of individuals. Mills felt that this view was most appropriate for sociological analysis. *See also* personal-troubles approach.

Public Opinion The attitudes, opinions, and beliefs of a public.

Public Opinion Polling The scientific study of public opinion by the use of interviews and questionnaires.

Qualitative Methods Nonstatistical, nonnumerical methods of data collection and analysis in scientific research, including participant observation, personal observation, and so on.

Quality of Life The nature and character of relationships, roles, norms, and values in community life. *See also* well-being, social.

Quantitative Methods Statistical and numerical methods of data collection and analysis in scientific research.

Questionnaire: Open-ended *and* Self-administered A list of carefully designed and interrelated questions, often pretested for reliability and accuracy. Open-ended questions allow respondees to give broad and unstructured answers; self-administered questions are answered by the respondees without the aid of an interviewer.

Quest for Community According to Robert Nisbet, the breakdown of many traditional institutions in earlier *Gemeinschaft* societies creates feelings of anxiety and anomie in modern people and, as a result, they often seek new feelings of belonging and community by supporting the growth of superstates and totalitarian movements.

Rationality The ability of humans to plan deliberately a sequence of interrelated behaviors in order to reach some specific goal. The opposite of emotional and spontaneous behavior.

Rational Systems View A perspective that focuses upon the planned and formal patterns of interaction within organizations. This model assumes that the rational system is more important than the spontaneous, emotional responses of people within organizations. *See also* natural systems model.

Rational Will (*Kurwille*) Ferdinand Tönnies' concept of the reason for the human ability to engage in planned and deliberate behavior.

Reaction Formation According to Freudian psychologists, the tendency for individuals to reject the very things they most want or desire. This rejection often takes the form of extreme deviance as a way of "getting even" with a society that encourages impossible expectations.

Rebel Robert Merton's concept of an individual who rejects both the goals (ends) of society and the accepted ways (means) of attaining the goals and seeks to develop new goals and means. *See also* means–ends relationship.

Reification The tendency to oversimplify and, therefore, to overemphasize the importance of some social and cultural phenomenon.

Relative Deprivation (658) A concept or theory that deviance and conflict will arise when people perceive themselves to be unjustly deprived, not when they are actually deprived but unaware of it.

Religion A system of beliefs and practices, which serve the function of social control by allowing people to relate the experiences of the secular world to the supernatural forces and beings of the sacred world. In performing this function, religion plays a comforting, priestly role and a challenging, prophetic role. *See also* magic *and* science.

Repression A form of conflict control that assumes conflict is dysfunctional and seeks to discourage or eliminate it by the use of force. Also, the irrational suppression of minority groups.

Resocialization A process, following a period of desocialization, whereby new skills, norms, and values are transmitted to individuals to replace old skills, norms, and values.

Retreatist Robert Merton's concept of an individual who rejects both the goals (ends) of society and the accepted ways (means) of attaining them and, therefore, "drops out" of society. *See also* means–ends relationship.

Revolution (508) According to William Kornhauser, a form of internal conflict that involves any combination of the following features: substantial transformation of whole societies with the development of new institutions and forms of political legitimacy; polarization of forces which may or may not lead to violence; and mobilization of large numbers of people in support of a new ideology.

Riff-raff Theory A theory that assumes rioting is the result of violent behavior by the poor, unemployed, uneducated, unassimilated, deviant, and emotionally disturbed. *See also* blocked-opportunity theory *and* relative deprivation.

Riot An elementary form of collective behavior, involving feelings of emotional excitement and disturbance which can result in the formation of mobs that engage in destructive acts. Civil disturbances that are actually rebellions are frequently mistaken for riots.

Ritualist Robert Merton's concept of an individual who rejects the goals (ends) of society but unthinkingly follows the accepted ways (means) for attaining them. *See also* means–ends relationship.

Role, Social (161) The expected pattern of behavior and the network of rights, privileges, and responsibilities that accompany each position in the social structure.

Role Conflict (162) Situations where a person faces conflicting elements (rights, responsibilities, etc.) within a single role, or conflicting roles within a role set.

Role Playing Occurs when the young child begins to play at social roles but does not yet conceive of itself as the individualistic initiator of acts in the social context. Role playing is essentially imitative behavior in response to the actions of others. *See also* play stage.

Role Set (162) The many roles, some complementary and some conflicting, which cluster around a single social position or status.

Role Taking Occurs when the young child begins to imaginatively project itself into a number of social roles, taking on their aspects as part of its own self-conception. Role taking is creative, individualistic behavior. *See also* empathy *and* game stage.

Rural-urban Transition (658) The shift away from an agriculturally based society to an industrialized society, accompanied by the movement of people from rural to urban areas. Social scientists refer to two major historical shifts as two urban revolutions. One led to the development of ancient cities. The other started at the end of the Middle Ages and is continuing in contemporary society.

Sacred Social and cultural elements that are revered and respected for assumed suprahuman or transcendental qualities and character.

Sample A carefully selected and limited number of some phenomenon, taken from a larger population of the same phenomenon in order to be studied in detail. Something that resembles or typifies a larger population.

School (505) The morale-building institution that teaches the skills, knowledge, and values of one's culture, usually in a more formal manner than primary groups such as the family.

Science (73) A system of beliefs and practices that serve the function of social control by allowing people to develop the means for understanding and manipulating the secular world. Science is characterized by openness, cooperation, scepticism, objectivity, amorality, and the use of a precise procedure. *See also* magic, religion, *and* scientific method.

Scientific Method (73) A rational and systematic problem-solving method involving five basic steps, which allows other scientists to verify and replicate one's research. *See also* data collection, hypotheses, *and* study design.

Secondary Controls Voluntary associations that control individual and collective behavior and stand between the individual and larger organizations and society. *See also* mediating group.

Secondary Groups *and* Relationships (391) Groups and relationships where individuals interact on an impersonal, formal, and partial basis and actions become task-oriented and competitive.

Secondary Sources of Data Materials that are used by a scientist for a purpose different from their original purpose.

Sect An informal religious organization, often one that has broken away from an established church, which is characterized by spontaneous and emotional ritual and leadership and evangelical beliefs.

Secularization The process whereby social and cultural phenomena lose their sacred character.

Segregation: *De Facto* and *De Jure* Physical, social, or cultural separation of individuals and groups, usually because of discrimination. *De facto* segregation is separation by fact; that is, as a result of social patterns and behavior rather than official policy. *De jure* segregation is separation by law. *See also* minority group.

Self, Social (159) "Miniature societies" that humans possess in their views of themselves in relationship to others. *See also* "I" and "me" *and* socialization.

Sensate Culture Pitirim Sorokin's concept of how cyclical change causes idealistic cultures to become cultures where emphasis is placed upon physical pleasure and the satisfaction of the human senses. *See also* ideational culture.

Sentiments Leslie White's concept of one ideational aspect of culture that consists of attitudes and values.

Sign A gesture or sound that has an immediate and direct significance and a necessary connection with some object or idea. *See also* symbol.

Skidding *See* downward mobility.

Social Change *See* change.

Social Cohesion and Solidarity The degree to which individuals and groups in a society share common norms and values, become interrelated and interdependent, act as a unified whole, and develop a feeling of "oneness".

Social Control The informal and formal methods utilized by a society to get individuals and groups to conform and, therefore, the techniques for controlling or managing deviance, change, and conflict.

Social Integration *See* integration.

Social Interaction *See* interaction.

Social Mobility *See* mobility.

Social Movement (393) Long-lasting collective behavior, involving large numbers of people held together by shared beliefs, goals, and ideologies. Social movements can become structured and lead to the formation of associations and institutions.

Social Processes and Dynamics The aspect of human society which accounts for much deviance, change, and conflict. Continual changes in social phenomena through time.

Social Role *See* role, social.

Social Science (74) The applications of scientific perspectives and procedures to the study of human behavior in the social and cultural context. *See also* science.

Social Self *See* self.

Social Status *See* status.

Social Strain Individual and group feelings of ambivalence, anxiety, and frustration, often caused by status distinctions and mobility. Social strains can lead to deviance or conflict if not managed by strain-reducing mechanisms and institutions.

Social Structure (161) The stable patterns of interaction and role relationships that make social group behavior orderly and predictable.

Social System (391) Any social unit (group, community, society) consisting of interdependent parts that interact with each other in order to perform the basic functions needed to maintain the unit.

Socialization (160) The process whereby individuals develop a social self and are taught the necessary skills, norms, and values in order to become productive members of a society and to relate to one another.

Society The complexity of interrelated roles, relationships, subgroups, and culture which characterizes human populations. Both the human individual (the self) and society are dependent upon one another, and neither would be possible without the other.

Sociogram A diagrammatic way of portraying the personal choices and relationships among members of a group.

Sociology *and* Academic Sociology (74) The scientific study of human social life that focuses upon the social self, social roles, social interaction, culture, and forms of group behavior. Radical sociologists have accused the discipline of becoming an academic sociology, where the emphasis is placed upon a detached research analysis without regard for human problems or values. *See also* value-free science.

Solidarity *See* social cohesion and solidarity.

Spirit of Capitalism According to Max Weber, the spirit of capitalism is present when workers consider work important, are willing to accept hard work, and are able to adapt to new methods of work; and when entrepreneurs deal in goods of standardized quality, save their profits for investment in the business, and deal with workers and customers in a formal but benevolent manner. *See also* Protestant (Puritan) ethic.

Staff *See* line and staff.

States: Geographical *and* Functional (507) Power institutions that maintain the social order and unify citizens with a common culture. Some states meet task needs within specific geographical boundaries, while others perform specific types of functions (economic, religious) across geographical boundaries.

Status, Ascribed *and* Achieved (161–162) The position assigned to various roles within the social structure based on their estimated social value. Status can be either achieved through personal striving and accomplishment or assigned on the basis of inherited characteristics without reference to personal achievement. *See also* achieved position *and* ascribed position.

Strain *See* social strain.

Strata The positions assigned to various social groups on the basis of status distinctions related to prestige and privilege.

Stratification, Social A social system of differentiation within which various roles and groups are placed in a rank order and the distinctions carry with them characteristics that go beyond a simple division of labor.

Study Design (75) Part of the third basic step in the scientific method that consists of the researcher's plan for collecting and analyzing data in order to test hypotheses.

Subjective Control Morris Janowitz's concept of a military force that fights and follows civilian orders because soldiers feel that they are integrated into the civilian leadership structure and, therefore, they are really issuing the orders. *See also* objective control.

Super Industrialists Those who believe that there are no limits to growth and change in the world, because the more that is produced the more that can be produced.

Survey Research (76) A data collection technique in which the researcher administers a set of questions, usually pretested, to a sample of a group or population.

Symbol A gesture or sound which has a socially agreed-upon meaning that is not obvious but must be culturally learned. *See also* sign.

Symbolic Interaction Interaction between individuals or groups that involves the use of symbols for communication.

Symbolic Interactionism *or* Symbolic Interactionist Theory (78) A view of society as the product of interacting individuals who create a social and cultural context as they perceive, interpret, react to, and alter their immediate social situations by the meanings they give to those situations.

Symbolic Language Communication of knowledge which can be stored in the memory of a person, in a library, and in computers, because of the use of symbols. The special characteristic that makes human culture possible.

Task Functions, Needs, *and* Leaders (506) All societies and groups have two basic task needs: the production and distribution of goods and services necessary for growth and survival. Particular types of relationships, groups, norms, and leaders arise to meet these needs. Task leaders also carry out the instrumental purposes of an organization. *See also* instrumental leaders *and* power institutions.

Technology (508) Usually refers to the material aspects of a culture. Also can refer to the clustering of roles, relationships, groups, norms, and values that constitute and stimulate the knowledge and techniques necessary to meet task needs. Certain power institutions (multinational corporations, states) contain these clusterings.

Tertiary Controls The highest level of social control, far removed from individuals, consisting of elite leaders, groups, and organizations. *See also* formal social controls.

Theory A systematic and comprehensive explanation of relationships between various social phenomena or social processes.

Therapeutic Community Within bureaucratized organizations, a small self-governing group with primary-like interaction and within which authority relationships are subordinated to or parallel with therapeutic (healing and emotionally sustaining) relationships.

Traditional Authority (507) Permanent authority based upon custom and accepted practice. Traditional leaders possess power as a result of inherited status.

Traditional Crime (656) Deviant activities that involve forced violence to persons or property. The types of crimes for which official statistics are usually collected and which tend to be associated with lower-status persons and groups. *See also* victimless crime.

Tradition-directed Personality David Riesman's concept of individuals who conform to the traditional norms and expectations of society.

True Believer Eric Hoffer's concept of the militant and fanatical leader who feels frustrated, disaffected, and rejected. Tends to be the type of leadership in elementary and early forms of collective groupings (mobs, expressive crowds, sects, revolutions, etc.).

Trustee Family Carle Zimmerman's concept of how the earliest family form, before the impact of cyclical change, consists of an extended kinship group, religiously tied to both their ancestors and to the yet unborn members of the family system. *See also* atomistic family *and* domestic family.

Turf, Concept of One of the environmental factors that controls conflict in animal species. Animals stake out a personal territory and signal ownership to others by aggressive actions. Humans also utilize conceptions of personal and collective territory. *See also* balance between aggression and fear *and* language of threat.

Underlife Informal and unauthorized adjustments and responses by members of a bureaucratized organization to the formal rules and regulations. The underlife of an organization allows members to express themselves as unique human individuals despite formal constraints. *See also* natural systems model *and* rational systems view.

Universalistic View Sees social problems as resulting from imperfect or inequitable social relationships in the larger community and society. This orientation is the perspective employed by sociologists. *See also* public-issues approach.

Upward Mobility Vertical movement by individuals or groups from a lower to a higher status.

Urbanization The process of change from a rural to an urban society that includes population movement from rural to urban areas, the growth in the number and size of urban places, and the adoption of urban life-styles. *See also* rural–urban transition *and* urban way of life.

Urban Revolutions, First and Second *See* rural–urban transition.

Urban Way of Life Having the characteristics of a *Gesellschaft* society, including relationships that are superficial, anonymous, transitory, sophisticated, cosmopolitan, and rational. *See also* density *and* heterogeneity.

Value-added A concept from economics that sees each stage in the production process as adding some value to the final cost of the end product, and each successive stage as being dependent upon and related to the preceeding stage. This concept has been adapted by Neil Smelser to the study of the evolution of collective behavior.

Value-free Science The traditional and "ideal" notion that science should be free from personal judgment, prejudice, or bias. Younger and more radical scientists argue that this is unrealistic because all scientists bias their work by the selection of certain paradigms. They argue for a science that is deliberately value-oriented and socially concerned. *See also* sociology.

Values (163) Objects, ideas, or behavior that are perceived as intrinsically rewarding and, therefore, become goals of human pursuit.

Variables, Social (74) Measurable characteristics which describe shared and regularized patterns of social behavior. *See also* hypothesis.

Vertical Mobility Movement either upward or downward in status systems by individuals or groups.

Veto Group A group or association that represents the members' special interests, competes with other groups in a pluralist system for power, and has the ability to prevent undesired actions by others. *See also* pluralist theories.

Victimless Crime (656) Deviant criminal activities which dispense a service or product to a customer who voluntarily cooperates in the relationship. Those who supply the illicit product or service are usually considered to be low-status criminals, whereas those who use the illicit product or service are usually considered to be of higher status and noncriminal.

Violence Conflict in the form of extreme aggression aimed at the serious injury or destruction of persons, objects, or organizations, and involving explosive (spontaneous, sudden, massive) behavior.

Voluntary Associations Associations people join freely because they support the group's emotional or task-oriented functions and goals. *See also* formal voluntary organizations (FVOs).

War (508) International conflict involving the military forces of opposing societies and states.

Wars: Absolutist, Ideological, and Instrumental In absolutist wars, the enemy is seen as completely different, evil, and threatening, and the whole community is involved in war preparation and waging. In ideological wars, all the belligerents are characterized by a crusading spirit. In instrumental wars, the purpose is to obtain valuable political, economic, or religious resources by defeating or subjugating the enemy.

Wars: Primitive, Historic, and Modern Warfare in primitive society contributes to clan solidarity and reinforces prevailing norms. Historic warfare results in the disintegration and creation of many empires and civilizations. Modern warfare transforms wars from isolated battles between special states with small armies into conflicts involving the entire world and mass armies.

Well-being, Social The concept of a desirable quality of life in a community or society, as measured by per capita income, number of physicians available, percent of population with a formal education, and so on.

Wesenwille *See* natural will.

White-collar Crime (656) Criminal or semilegal activities committed by high-status individuals because they have access to the necessary knowledge and means for engaging in these acts. Abstract groups or organizations are usually considered to be the victims, rather than specific persons.

Worker Self-management A concept that transforms economic organizations into communities which are not committed to profit-making alone but also provide for social and political decision-making by workers and management alike on a number of noneconomic issues.

Zero Population Growth (ZPG) The condition in which a population is stable and is not increasing or decreasing in size, because the birth rate equals the death rate.

Zero-sum Games The assumption that, in a game, the winner's winnings will equal the loser's losses and, therefore, the game should be played in an aggressive and competitive manner so that the most capable player will win. *See also* nonzero-sum games.

Authors and Researchers Index

Note: This index contains the names of authors and researchers. For other name references see the *Subjects and Concepts Index.*

Subjects and Concepts Index

1 2 3 4 5 6 7 8 9 10